NEW ZEALAND
GOVERNMENT
& POLITICS

NEW ZEALAND
GOVERNMENT
& POLITICS

FOURTH EDITION

Raymond Miller

OXFORD

UNIVERSITY PRESS

OXFORD
UNIVERSITY PRESS

253 Normanby Road, South Melbourne, Victoria 3205, Australia

Oxford University Press is a department of the University of Oxford.
It furthers the University's objective of excellence in research, scholarship, and education by publishing worldwide in

Oxford New York

Auckland   Cape Town   Dar es Salaam   Hong Kong   Karachi
Kuala Lumpur   Madrid   Melbourne   Mexico City   Nairobi
New Delhi   Shanghai   Taipei Toronto

With offices in

Argentina   Austria   Brazil   Chile   Czech Republic   France   Greece
Guatemala   Hungary   Italy   Japan   Poland   Portugal   Singapore
South Korea   Switzerland   Thailand   Turkey   Ukraine   Vietnam

OXFORD is a trade mark of Oxford University Press
in the UK and in certain other countries

National Library of New Zealand
Cataloguing-in-Publication data

New Zealand government and politics/edited by Raymond Miller. 4th ed.
Previous ed.: 2003.
Includes index.

ISBN-13: 978-0-19-558492-9
ISBN-10: 0-19-558492-9

1. New Zealand—Politics and government—1972– l. Miller, Raymond, 1953–
320.993—dc 22

Typeset in India by diacriTech, Chennai.
Printed in Hong Kong by Sheck Wah Tong Printing Press Ltd.

Contents

List of Figures

List of Tables

Contributors

Peter Aimer was formerly a senior lecturer and honorary research fellow in the Department of Political Studies at the University of Auckland. He was co-author or co-editor of books on the 1990, 1993, 1996, 1999, and 2002 elections produced by the New Zealand Election Study programme. His history of the New Zealand National Airways Corporation, *Wings of the Nation*, was published in 2000.

Joe Atkinson is a Senior Lecturer and Director of Research in the Department of Political Studies at the University of Auckland. He teaches courses on tabloid news, the political content of television, and the political economy of information and supervises the Chapman Audio-Visual News Archive. A former metropolitan newspaper journalist (*Christchurch Star*), political columnist for *Metro* and *North & South* magazines, and media consultant and radio and television commentator, he has published research on television news, broadcasting policy, tabloid journalism, and election campaign coverage.

Tim Bale is Senior Lecturer in Politics at the University of Sussex in the UK, specialising in comparative politics. He previously taught at Victoria University of Wellington. His research on the New Zealand Green Party appears in book chapters and in journals like *Party Politics* and *Government and Opposition*. His latest book is *European Politics: a Comparative Introduction* (Palgrave, 2005).

Patrick Barrett is a lecturer in public policy in the Department of Political Science and Public Policy at the University of Waikato. His research interests include families and employment, population ageing and public policy.

Jonathan Boston is Professor of Public Policy and Deputy Director of the Institute of Policy Studies at Victoria University of Wellington. He has published many books and articles on a wide range of governmental and policy-related matters, including public management, the funding of tertiary education, and the provision of social assistance. As a member of the New Zealand Political Change Project (1995–2003) he had particular responsibility for conducting research on government formation and coalition management under MMP.

Ton Bührs is a Senior Lecturer at Lincoln University, where he teaches environmental policy. His research interests include New Zealand environmental policy, the institutional aspects of environmental policy development, strategic environmental policy, and comparative and international environmental policy. His publications include *Environmental Policy in New Zealand: The Politics of Clean and Green?* (Oxford University Press, Auckland, 1993; co-authored with Robert V. Bartlett), and many other articles and chapters on New Zealand environmental policy.

David Capie is a lecturer in the Political Science and International Relations programme at Victoria University of Wellington. He teaches courses on armed conflict and New Zealand's international relations, and has published widely on security issues in Asia and the Pacific. His recent books include *The Asia-Pacific Security Lexicon* (2002) and *Under the Gun: The Small Arms Challenge in the Pacific* (2003).

Helena Catt is the chief executive of the New Zealand Electoral Commission. She is on leave from the Politics Department at the University of Auckland. Her under- and post-graduate teaching has mainly been on democracy and comparative politics, with her research interests and published work covering democratic practice, representation, electoral systems, and comparative politics. At the Electoral Commission, she is heavily involved in education and information on electoral matters, including creating resources for citizenship education.

Christine Cheyne is a Senior Lecturer at Massey University where she teaches social policy and politics at undergraduate and postgraduate levels. Together with Mike O'Brien and Michael Belgrave, she is co-author of a major social policy text now in its third edition (*Social Policy in Aotearoa New Zealand: A Critical Introduction*, Oxford University Press, 2005). Her current research focuses on democratic governance, comparative urban policy, and public involvement in local authority planning and decision-making.

Alan Cocker is associate head of the School of Communication Studies at the Auckland University of Technology. His research interests include New Zealand media, international media policy, and a 'political economy' approach to the study of the information sector.

Noel Cox is associate professor and chair of the law discipline at the Auckland University of Technology. He has a PhD from the University of Auckland on the evolution of the New Zealand Crown. His publications include articles, book chapters, and monographs on the Crown and various aspects of public law, and also the book *Technology and Legal Systems* (2006). He is also active in public debate on constitutional matters in New Zealand.

Bruce Curtis is a senior lecturer in Sociology at the University of Auckland. He teaches courses in media, work, and organisations, and has an interest in research methods. His current research focuses on the impact of new managerialism on academic life and, more broadly, the role of digital/mobile technologies in reshaping work.

Cate Curtis has a PhD in psychology from Waikato University, where she currently teaches in the community psychology programme, including lectures on public policy, social determinants of health, and related areas. Her primary research interests lie in the field of self-harming behaviour, in particular the social factors implicated in risk, resiliency, and recovery. She is also employed as a senior consultant with Health Outcomes International, a private research agency that holds contracts with the Ministries of Education, Health and Social Development.

Paul Dalziel is Professor of Economics at Lincoln University. He has published numerous articles and ten books on New Zealand economic policy, including *The New Zealand Macroeconomy: Striving for Sustainable Growth with Equity, Redesigning the Welfare State in New Zealand,* and *Money, Credit and Price Stability.* His current research focuses on regional economic development.

Chris Eichbaum is a Senior Lecturer in Public Policy at the School of Government, Victoria University of Wellington. As well as periods working in the public service in both Wellington and Canberra, Chris has also worked as an advisor to Labour governments, most recently from 2000–03 as a Senior Ministerial Advisor to the Hon Steve Maharey, followed by a period as a Senior Policy Advisor in the Prime Minister's Office. His current research interests focus on the impact of political advisors on the institution of cabinet government, the political economy of central banking, and social-democratic politics.

Robin Gauld is Senior Lecturer in Health Policy, Department of Preventive and Social Medicine, University of Otago. He is the author of *Revolving Doors: New Zealand's Health Reforms* (2001), co-author with Derek Gould of *The Hong Kong Health Sector: Development and Change* (2002) and with Shaun Goldfinch of *Dangerous Enthusiasms, Amazing Disasters: E-Government, Computer Failures and Information System Development in the Public Sector* (2006), and editor of *Continuity amid Chaos: Health Care Management and Delivery in New Zealand* (2003) and Comparative Health Policy in the Asia Pacific (2005).

Grant Gillon was elected to Parliament in 1996 and served as an Alliance Member of Parliament for two terms. During his tenure in Parliament, Grant was appointed to the post of Whip, also serving on a number of Select Committees including the Cabinet Legislative Committee, Privileges Committee, and Business Committee. Grant Gillon is the President of the Progressive Party and was part of the campaign team for the 2002 and 2005 elections. Grant is currently undertaking a PhD on coalition arrangements under MMP and lectures part-time in social policy at Massey University.

Barry Gustafson is Director of the New Zealand Asia Institute at the University of Auckland. A Professor of Political Studies, he was formerly Head of the Department of Political Studies and for a time Acting Pro Vice-Chancellor (International) at that university. He has published books on the history of both the New Zealand Labour and the New Zealand National Parties and biographies of Prime Ministers Michael Joseph Savage and Robert Muldoon. He is currently completing a biography of Keith Holyoake.

Bruce V. Harris is a Professor of Law at The University of Auckland. His research and teaching interests are in the areas of constitutional and administrative law. His most recent published research has been concerned with the possible future design of the New Zealand constitution.

Bronwyn Hayward rejoins political science as a lecturer at University of Canterbury after 6 years full-time parenting and part-time consulting in public participation techniques and children's television production. Bronwyn previously taught at Lincoln University for 12 years and has served as a statutory appointment to the New Zealand Broadcasting Standards Authority 2001–02. Her published and current research focuses on the theory and practice of public participation and citizenship especially in environmental policy contexts.

Janine Hayward is a senior lecturer in Politics at the University of Otago. Much of her research and teaching focuses on Treaty politics. She recently co-edited a book on the Waitangi Tribunal with Nicola Wheen. She has previously worked at the Tribunal and has also written a commissioned report on Maori representation for the Crown Forestry Rental Trust.

Margaret Hayward teaches Politics and Government at Victoria University of Wellington. She was the first woman to be appointed a private secretary at parliament and that experience resulted in the *Diary of the Kirk Years*. She has worked in public relations, taught communication, and published on prime ministerial leadership, Muldoon and the media, and women and political leadership.

John Henderson is an associate professor in the Political Science Department at the University of Canterbury. He has published widely in the areas of New Zealand and Pacific politics, which he also teaches. He is a former director of the Prime Minister's Office (1985–89), and is the author of several studies on political leadership.

Wayne Hope is an associate professor in communication studies at the Auckland University of Technology. His principal research interests are critical theory, political economy, and media-sport relations. He writes for the *Political Review* and is a regular radio and television commentator on broadcasting issues.

Keith Jackson is Professor Emeritus of Political Science at the University of Canterbury. His current research centres on the operations of the New Zealand parliament and unicameralism in a comparative context. His publications include *New Zealand Adopts Proportional Representation* (co-authored).

Colin James is a political journalist of more than 30 years who writes a weekly column in the *New Zealand Herald* and a monthly column in *Management* magazine, with a special interest in party and electoral politics. He has written six books, including *New Territory* in 1992, and chapters in numerous books. He has contributed papers to seminars in five countries and held several university fellowships. Most of his writing is on www.colinjames.co.nz.

Geoff Kemp is lecturer in Political Studies at the University of Auckland, where his teaching includes politics and the media and the history of political thought. He was a newspaper journalist for twenty years before and while gaining BA, MPhil and PhD degrees at the University of Cambridge, where he was also research assistant on a project investigating public service broadcasting in the digital era. His current research centres on historical ideas of public expression and censorship.

Jennifer Lees-Marshment is senior lecturer in Comparative Politics in the Department of Political Studies at the University of Auckland. She is a leading academic in the field of political marketing: author of *Political Marketing and British Political Parties* and *The Political Marketing Revolution: Transforming the Government of the UK*, and co-editor of *Political Marketing in Comparative Perspective* and *Current Issues in Political Marketing*. She was founding chair of the UK Political Marketing Group.

Stephen Levine is a professor of political science at the Victoria University of Wellington. His teaching and research interests include voting behaviour and constitutional issues in the USA, Asia, New Zealand, and the Pacific, as well as Victoria's Parliamentary Internship Programme. He is co-author of *From Muldoon to Lange*, and was a contributing editor of books on the New Zealand elections of 1996,

1999, 2002, and 2005. He is co-editor of *Political Science* and of the Royal Society of New Zealand's Journal of Social Sciences, *Kotuitui*.

David Lindsey is studying towards a PhD in Political Studies at University of Auckland. He holds an MA in social and economic geography and a Postgraduate Diploma in politics. His work experience includes 13 years working in policy development roles in local government in Auckland. His publications include articles in the *New Zealand Planning Quarterly* and *New Zealand Geographer*, and an unpublished dissertation on conscience voting in New Zealand.

Elizabeth McLeay is an Associate Professor in the Political Science and International Relations Programme, Victoria University of Wellington. Apart from her publications on the New Zealand cabinet, she has written on the impact of electoral system reform, parliamentary committees, women and politics, and comparative public policy. At present she is working on a book on parliament and political representation in New Zealand.

Kate McMillan is a lecturer in the Political Science and International Relations Programme at Victoria University of Wellington. Her research and teaching interests focus on the politics of international migration, citizenship, and the media. In 2006, she edited a special issue of *Political Science* focusing on media and politics in New Zealand. She has also contributed chapters on New Zealand citizenship to *Tangata Tangata* (2004) and *New Zealand and International Migration* (2005).

Alan McRobie is currently a practising politician. He was elected to the Waimakariri District Council in 2001. Between 1969 and 1992, he lectured in New Zealand politics and history at both the Christchurch College of Education and the University of Canterbury. He has written extensively on New Zealand politics, particularly its electoral system, and was, for many years, a regular commentator on New Zealand's electoral politics. His most recent publication is the 2nd edition of the *Hazard New Zealand Historical Dictionary* (with Keith Jackson).

Raymond Miller is an associate professor and head of the Department of Political Studies at the University of Auckland, where he specialises in New Zealand politics, comparative parties, and political representation. He has collaborated on a number of election studies, including *Proportional Representation on Trial* (2002) and *Voters' Veto* (2004). His most recent publications include *Party Politics in New Zealand* (2005) and (co-edited with Michael Mintrom) *Political Leadership in New Zealand* (2006).

Michael Mintrom is an associate professor of Political Studies at the University of Auckland. He holds a PhD from the State University of New York at Stony Brook.

His research covers the politics of policy making, policy analysis, and educational administration. He is author of *Policy Entrepreneurs and School Choice* and *People Skills for Policy Analysts* (Georgetown University Press), and co-editor with Raymond Miller of *Political Leadership in New Zealand* (Auckland University Press).

Pat Moloney is senior lecturer in the Political Science and International Relations Programme at Victoria University of Wellington. He teaches and researches in the areas of political theory and sexuality studies. Recent publications included *On the Left: Essays on the History of Socialism in New Zealand*, edited with Kerry Taylor, and *Sexuality Down Under: Social and Historical Perspectives*, edited with Allison Kirkman.

John Parkinson is Lecturer in Politics at the University of York, United Kingdom, teaching democratic theory, comparative politics, and public policy. A New Zealander, he has published on CIR in New Zealand and Switzerland, deliberative democracy, representation, and restorative justice, and is presently researching the relationship between democracy and public space. His recent book, *Deliberating in the Real World: Problems of Legitimacy in Deliberative Democracy*, is published by Oxford University Press.

Robert Patman is an Associate Professor in the Department of Political Studies at the University of Otago. He is the Director of the Master of International Studies program there, has authored or edited six books and is one of the co-editors of the new Praeger Series on *The Ethics of American Foreign Policy*. He is also the author of *America's Biggest Strategic Failure: How the 'Somali Syndrome' Paved the Road to 9/11* (forthcoming).

Nigel Roberts is an associate professor of political science at the Victoria University of Wellington. His teaching and research interests include New Zealand and Scandinavian government and politics, comparative electoral systems, and voting behaviour. He co-authored *New Zealand Under MMP* and co-edited books on the last four New Zealand elections, and has won four Wallace Awards from the Electoral Commission for contributions to public understanding of electoral matters. He is a frequent media and TVNZ election-night commentator.

Chris Rudd is a senior lecturer in political studies at the University of Otago. He is co-author of *The Politics and Government of New Zealand* (2004), and co-editor of *Political Communications in New Zealand* (2004) and *Sovereignty under Siege? Globalization in New Zealand* (2005).

Claudia Scott is professor of Public Policy at Victoria University (VUW) and the Australia and New Zealand School of Government (ANZSOG). She was awarded an

ONZM for Services to Public Administration. Professor Scott's teaching and research interests include public policy analysis, local government, and strategic planning. She is Project Leader of a five year FRST research project on Strategic Policy and Planning for Local Governments.

Andrew Sharp is emeritus professor of Politics at the University of Auckland, and is professorial research associate in Politics at the School of Oriental and African Studies, London. He has published on the English history of ideas, Maori-Pakeha political ideas, and on the New Zealand constitution. He recently edited *Bruce Jesson: Collected Writings* and is currently working on the life of the missionary Samuel Marsden and a European history of thinking about the emotions of savages.

Richard Shaw is a senior lecturer in the School of Sociology, Social Policy and Social Work at Massey University, Palmerston North. He is co-author—with Chris Eichbaum—of *Public Policy In New Zealand*. With assistance from the Marsden Fund, he and Chris Eichbaum are currently researching the policy roles and influence of ministerial advisers in the New Zealand executive. In 2004, he was awarded a National Tertiary Teaching Excellence Award.

Kaapua Smith has a Bachelor of Arts (First Class Honours) in Māori Studies. She is currently undertaking her PhD in the Department of Political Studies at The University of Auckland. She has tutored in both the Māori Studies and Political Studies, and has worked as a researcher in the area's of Māori education and health. Her more recent work with Statistics New Zealand has been in the area of Māori youth working, and also as a political and youth commentator for Māori television

Katherine Smits is a lecturer in Political Studies at the University of Auckland. She is the author of *Reconstructing Post-nationalist Liberal Pluralism* (2005) and several articles on liberal political theory and cultural pluralism. She is currently working on a study of the effects of settler violence against indigenous people on Victorian liberal ideas.

Andrew Stockley is the Senior Tutor and a Fellow of Brasenose College, Oxford. He is a former Head of the Law School at the University of Canterbury and was Principal of College House, Christchurch from 1997 to 2006. He has published widely on constitutional law matters, including the role of the Crown and republicanism, Parliament and the electoral system, and the Treaty of Waitangi. He has a doctorate in history and is the author of *Britain and France at the Birth of America*.

Ann Sullivan is Nga Puhi. She is a political scientist and associate professor in Maori Studies at the University of Auckland. Her teaching and research covers a range of areas of Māori development with an emphasis on public policy.

Tim Tenbensel is a senior lecturer in health policy in the School of Population Health, University of Auckland. His teaching interests include health policy, public policy, and public management. He has published in a number of scholarly journals, including *Public Management Review* and *Policy Studies*.

Jacqui True is senior lecturer, Department of Political Studies, University of Auckland, New Zealand. Her research interests include international political economy, global civil society, feminist theory and methods, and gender policy analysis. She is the author of *Gender, Globalization, and Postsocialism: The Czech Republic after Communism* (Columbia University Press, 2003), co-author of *Theories of International Relations*, third edition (Palgrave, 2005), and co-editor of *Feminist Methodologies for International Relations* (Cambridge University Press, 2006).

Jane Verbitsky is a senior lecturer in the School of Social Sciences at the Auckland University of Technology. She teaches politics and conflict resolution, and researches in the fields of forced migration and peace education.

Jack Vowles is a professor of Political Studies at the University of Auckland. His main research interest is comparative political behaviour. He is principal researcher in the New Zealand Election Study (NZES). The most recent book published from this programme is *Voters' Veto* (Auckland University Press, 2004). Some of Professor Vowles' most recent journal publications can be found in the *British Journal of Political Science* and *Party Politics*. He teaches Political Participation and Research Design.

John Wilson is a visiting lecturer in politics at Victoria University of Wellington, where he has taught in the areas of environmental politics, political economy, and globalisation since 2001. He is the author of *New Zealand Career Master: a Complete Guide to Tertiary Studies in New Zealand*, and of forthcoming chapters on security and conflict issues in Tajikistan (ABC-CLIO), Iran, and Saudi Arabia (Praeger/ Greenwood).

Acknowledgments

This book is a product of the combined efforts of some fifty-two authors. While many are first-time contributors, there are some who have been involved in successive editions over the past decade. Their enthusiasm for the project, hard work, and responsiveness to requests, comments, and advice have made the editor's job a great deal more enjoyable than the size of this volume might suggest. I would like to thank the staff of Oxford University Press, Melbourne, for their continuing faith in this textbook, in particular Heather Fawcett, Katie Ridsdale, Tim Campbell, Michelle Green and Hannah Hind. Craig McKenzie handled the copy-editing job with speed and efficiency. I have also appreciated the support and help of my colleagues in the Department of Political Studies, University of Auckland, especially Jack Vowles, Edwin de Ronde, Jenny Long, Nick Christiansen, and Rosalind Henshaw.

Raymond Miller
The University of Auckland

Introduction

This new edition of *New Zealand Government and Politics* combines an up-to-date account of developments in New Zealand politics with essential background reading on the wider social, political, and international contexts within which change takes place. While international events are generally beyond our ability to influence, let alone control, they do have consequences for political decision-makers, as well as for the way we live. As experience has shown, there is nothing we can do about international migration, ageing first-world populations, rising oil prices, or the ever-present threat of terrorism. Developments of a purely domestic nature, on the other hand, are more responsive to public influence and control, as illustrated by the flow-on effects of the public's decision to adopt the Mixed Member Proportional electoral system, or MMP. Among the most significant outcomes of that decision were the reconfiguration of the two-party system into a multi-party one, the emergence of a more representative and assertive parliament, and the advent of coalition government. At the 2005 election, a total of two major and six minor parties were elected to the new parliament, including most controversially the new Māori party, a breakaway movement from Labour.

Much has been made of Labour's 2005 election victory, which gave Helen Clark the distinction of being the first Labour leader to win a third term. In a closely fought election contest, the results might just as easily have gone the other way. Following National's disastrous defeat three years earlier, when it received a mere 21 per cent share of the vote and twenty-seven out of 120 seats, the party embarked on the task of rebuilding its membership and electoral support. Most of the credit for its recovery was due to the efforts of its new leader and former Reserve Bank governor, Dr Don Brash. Despite a long association with right-wing economics, Brash proved to be a highly pragmatic politician, wooing mainstream voters with populist solutions to perceived problems in the areas of race relations, law and order, social welfare, and taxation. In a defining speech to the Orewa Rotary Club in January 2004, Brash blamed the government for creating a 'racially divided nation, with two sets of laws, and two standards of citizenship'.[1] He pledged an end to race-based laws and funding, as well as the removal of separate Māori seats. Within a month, the party's support jumped 17 percentage points, the most dramatic rise in the history of polling in New Zealand.

Elections provide incumbent governments with the chance to show-case their achievements. In 2005, Labour sought to exploit the economic and social benefits of low inflation, high employment, and strong economic growth. It could also boast some popular foreign policy decisions, including Clark's opposition to the US-led invasion of Iraq and stout defence of a continuing ban on the visit of nuclear-powered and -armed ships. A characteristic of successful leadership is the ability to reflect, and on occasions shape, the public mood. While New Zealand's independent foreign policy stance may have cost it a free trade agreement with the United States of America, there appeared to be broad public support for the view that it was a price worth paying. Among the compensating benefits that could be presented to voters were improved trade links with China, Singapore, Thailand, and Chile, and the reduced risk of a terrorist attack.

Balanced against Labour's achievements was a legislative record that threatened to loosen its hold on 'middle' New Zealand. In addition to its vulnerability to the claim that it supported 'special privileges' for Māori, Labour was responsible for a number of other potentially polarising decisions, including school amalgamations and closures in some highly marginal provincial seats, an end to the right of appeal to Britain's Privy Council (2003), with the allegation of 'creeping republicanism' entering into the debate, and the racially fraught foreshore and seabed ruling. Labour was further associated with support for three controversial conscience decisions, specifically the Prostitution Reform (2003), Civil Union (2004), and Relationships (2005) Acts. However, the legislation that posed the greatest electoral risk was the Foreshore and Seabed Act (2004). As well as providing the nascent Māori party with a compelling *raison d'etre*, the decision to place the foreshore and seabed in public ownership threatened a seven-decade partnership between Labour and its Māori voters.

Prior to the campaign, in an attempt to both lower public expectations and demonstrate a continuing commitment to tight fiscal restraint, the Finance minister, Michael Cullen refused to countenance tax cuts, the government's healthy surplus notwithstanding. The 2005 Budget, which critics derisively renamed the 'chewing gum' budget, made grudging provision for a small reduction in tax rates, but not until 2008. In contrast, National promised across-the-board tax cuts totalling $3.1 billion, at no apparent risk to existing levels of social spending. These promises provoked Labour into an unseemly bidding-war that included tax relief for low and middle-income families and the cancellation of interest on tertiary student loans. National's billboard campaign ruthlessly exposed Labour's selective generosity, as illustrated by the starkly contrasting images of Iwi-Kiwi and Tax-Cut.

Despite the proliferation of parties under MMP, the 2005 election quickly developed into a two-horse race, with the combined vote for the seventeen registered minor parties totalling a mere 19 per cent. Despite the challenge from a reinvigorated National party, Labour managed to retain its 2002 level of support, with 41 per cent and fifty seats, while National gained 39 per cent (up 18 percentage-points) and forty-eight seats. By pursuing a vote-maximization strategy without regard for the electoral consequences for its potential coalition partners, notably the small ACT party, National was left in a position of weakness relative to Labour. With virtually no realistic prospect of a centre-right government, Labour was able to form a minority Labour-Progressive government, with varying levels of legislative support from New Zealand First, United Future, and the Greens. Although they remained outside of government, the New Zealand First and United Future leaders negotiated ministerial appointments, with Winston Peters controversially accepting the senior position of Minister of Foreign Affairs, but outside of cabinet.

One of the hallmarks of Labour's three terms in government has been a stated commitment to cautious and pragmatic government. In 1999, the incoming Labour-Alliance government noted that 'New Zealanders have voted for a change but are weary of radical restructuring' (*New Zealand Parliamentary Debates*, 21 December 1999). Three years later, the Labour-Progressive government promised to be 'conservative and predictable' in its approach to fiscal management (*New Zealand Parliamentary Debates*, 27 August 2002). The 2005 Speech from the Throne struck a similar tone with its promise to be 'inclusive' and to look for 'a broad consensus about the way ahead'.[2] As Chris Eichbaum points out in his contribution to this volume, one of the lessons Labour learned from its near-loss to National in 2005 was the need to keep polarizing policy initiatives well and truly off the political agenda. Apart from the fact that this approach reflects Clark's personal style of leadership, according to Eichbaum this cautious and inclusive approach 'may also reflect an assessment that a more pragmatic, grounded, and less ideological orientation to matters of politics and policy was required as an antidote … to the neoliberalism of the 1980s and 1990s'. Apart from the families' tax package and interest-free student loans, there were few fresh ideas in Labour's modest programme of reform. From 2005, extra funding would be provided for early childhood and primary education, the government would continue to focus on primary health care, police numbers would be increased, and, as part of an agreement with New Zealand First, the government would enhance the range of entitlements for the elderly.

Plan of the book

Good textbooks help students make the necessary links between lectures, tutorials, and the formal requirements of their course. In this new edition, leading researchers in the field of New Zealand politics have provided a series of brief and topical chapters, the content of which is pitched primarily to an undergraduate student readership. In addition to the established readings, all of which have been updated, this edition includes some twenty-one new chapters. Each chapter provides an introduction to the topic and an analysis of relevant themes and issues, together with a commentary on any future threats and challenges facing New Zealand in such areas as national identity, social structure, and political values and institutions. The provocative and concise nature of the chapters makes them well suited for assigned tutorial reading. Each is self-contained, making it possible for it to be read without reference to other chapters in the volume. Chapters conclude with tutorial discussion questions, most of which have been pre-tested with small classes, as well as suggestions for further reading.

In the planning of this edited volume, no attempt has been made to impose a common viewpoint or analytical approach. Indeed, while most of the authors are engaged in research and teaching in the field of political studies, they have been joined by representatives from a wide range of disciplines, including constitutional law, economics, sociology, history, public policy, and media studies. Together, these contributors bring a breadth of perspective and approach not seen in less collaborative projects.

The content of this edition has been arranged thematically and divided into five sections. Teachers and students frequently complain of the difficulties involved in studying particular political developments in isolation. Part A is a new section that places the study of contemporary New Zealand politics within a range of contexts, from the historical and societal through to the regional and international. As well as introducing concepts such as biculturalism and multiculturalism, which are returned to in later chapters on the Treaty of Waitangi and race relations, this section explores some of the main demographic trends and their possible implications for the future of urban and regional development, as well as policy-making.

A second innovation concerns the expanded coverage of New Zealand's political institutions and actors. Parts B and C provide a comprehensive analysis of the legislative and executive processes, beginning with the debate surrounding the relevance and importance of Treaty and constitution, and progressing through the roles of the judiciary and head of state. Parliament's growing importance under MMP is reflected in the expansion of its treatment from a single chapter in the previous edition to three chapters, including discussions on the under-researched areas of conscience voting and the role of an MP. In Part C, the analysis turns to the formation and role of cabinet, together with two quite different studies of the personality and powers of the prime minister.

In an enlarged section on the representative process, Part D introduces the study of political behaviour, particularly with respect to voters, party members and activists, elected politicians, interest groups, and the role of the media. A current interest among researchers is to account for the decline in political participation, especially among particular sections of society, such as the young. A sub-section of five chapters is devoted to trends in civic engagement, the implications of declining engagement for the future of democracy and for our democratic system of government, together with some suggested plans for re-engagement.

Finally, Part E provides a varied collection of essays on policy-making and outcomes, with a particular emphasis on current political debates in the areas of health-care, Māori Treaty and social policy, immigration, and questions surrounding the issue of what level of humanitarian assistance should be offered to refugees. The book concludes with an examination of New Zealand's evolving security policy in the Pacific, particularly in light of the recent rise in regional instability and in the threat posed by terrorists and other criminal groups.

It is hoped that the range of topics covered and the diversity of views expressed will both inform and provoke, making this textbook a valuable tool in our classroom teaching and learning.

Raymond Miller
The University of Auckland

Notes

1   D. Brash, 'Nationhood', Rotary Club, Orewa, http://www.national.org.nz/Article. aspx?ArticleID=1614 (accessed 27 January 2006).

2   H. Clark, 'Speech from the Throne', 8 November 2005, Parliament Buildings, Wellington, http://www.beehive.govt.nz/ViewDocument.aspx?DocumentID=24330 (accessed 2 May 2006).

Context

Politics does not exist in a vacuum, but operates within many different contexts. To understand the politics of a particular country, we need to know something about its history, social setting, value structure, and place in a globalising world. Despite the time taken to shake off its colonial past, modern New Zealand is a politically independent and culturally diverse country, with an emerging consensus of opinion on the questions of national identity and what it is to be a New Zealander.

The broad themes covered in Part A can be summarised thus:

- **Historical Context.** The opening chapter explores the postwar themes of intimacy, continuity and change. New Zealand has an enviable reputation as an open and stable democracy, with a small population base of 4.1 million, a highly-developed sense of community, and a tradition of responsive and accountable government. During the early postwar years, the two main parties were in broad agreement over the need for high levels of government regulation and intervention. Beginning in the 1980s, the government embarked on a process of radical reform. The resulting changes discussed in chapter 1.1 include: significant market-led economic reform; adoption of a proportional electoral system; growth in the number and influence of small parties; and the advent of coalition (and generally minority) government.

- **Social Context.** Chapter 1.2 profiles the population and explores the implications of demographic change, focusing on such themes as increasing migration, urbanisation, an ageing population, and ethnic-based poverty. In chapter 1.3, the focus turns to the relationship between biculturalism and emerging multiculturalism, especially in relation to aspirations towards a shared 'Kiwi' identity. The chapter argues that, while there is no official policy of multiculturalism, it best reflects social reality.

- **Ideological Context.** Chapters 1.4 to 1.6 consider the influence of ideology on the political culture. After examining the relevance for New Zealand of more traditional ideologies, such as democracy, liberalism and socialism, the discussion turns to the recent impact of neo-liberalism and the politics of the Third Way.
- **Global Context.** In the final two chapters, the discussion returns to the issue of national identity, although within the broader contexts of economic globalisation, international security, and regional stability. As the authors of chapters 1.7 and 1.8 point out, while globalisation may help small countries like New Zealand forge a clearer sense of their own separate identity, it also acts as a brake on economic and political self-determination.

New Zealand since the War

Barry Gustafson

New Zealand political history since the end of the Second World War in 1945 can be divided roughly into three distinct periods. The first, from 1945–65, was marked by an emphasis on security, community and consensus; the second, from 1965–85, reflected growing insecurity, division and conflict; and the third, from 1985–2005, has seen the development of much greater independence, individualism and diversity.

During that time, and particularly over the past ten years, there has also been a proliferation of political parties, the result of a new Mixed Member Proportional (MMP) electoral system that was itself generated by the broader and radical political, economic and social changes and which, in turn, led to more cautious coalitions rather than decisive, and arrogant, one-party governments.

SECURITY, COMMUNITY, AND CONSENSUS, 1945–65

Some historians have suggested that there were two great watersheds in New Zealand history prior to 1965—the progressive achievements of the first Liberal government (1891–1912) and the first Labour government (1935–49).[1] Each of those governments restructured the economy; passed radical social welfare legislation; balanced embryonic nationalism with a clear commitment to collective security in alliance with a major protective great power (Britain before 1941 and the USA after); and facilitated considerable upward social mobility through educational opportunity and state-encouraged farm ownership schemes.

In fact, although there was change during this period, it was largely at the level of quantitative detail, not a fundamental qualitative change in values, perceptions, policies or outcomes. The first Labour government did not provide a dramatically

3

different direction, but consolidated and extended what the Liberals had started almost half a century before. That legacy of consensus was subsequently amended but not rejected. When National first came to power in 1949, it largely accepted what Labour had done to the economy and social security system. Instead it argued that it would be a better manager of the system.

Labour established the basis of the modern welfare state in New Zealand with its Social Security Act of 1938, which was intended to guarantee employment and to secure 'everybody from infants in their cots to old men and women … orphans, invalids and those unable to think or work for themselves' and to take away as far as possible fear caused by 'the ills of life and the inexorable advances of old age'.[2] One of that government's major achievements was to make secondary education available to all children. Subsequently, in 1958 Labour introduced 3 per cent housing loans and capitalisation of the child allowance to enable young couples on lower incomes to buy or build a home. National, which favoured a property-owning democracy, subsequently encouraged many state tenants to buy the homes they previously rented from the state.

On the issue of social security the consensus remained intact. There was no real challenge or alternative in health, education, or the care of the young, the sick, the aged, the unemployed. Politicians argued over the details and costs of delivery, but not over the structure of the system or the universal rights of all citizens to equal and adequate access. Deep divisions of opinion did not emerge until much later on the morality, desirability and sustainability of social security. Nor was it seriously questioned that there should be cooperative rather than individual provision of education, health and welfare, where each person as a responsibility of citizenship contributed through the tax system according to his or her ability and then as a right of citizenship received according to his or her need.

In 1945, after suffering decades of depression and war, the two main parties and most of the population were in broad agreement on a range of economic and other objectives, including the need to maintain full employment, fund adequately a public health system, and extend educational opportunity. There was a commitment to state planning, management and regulation, and an egalitarian redistribution of wealth from the relatively rich to the relatively poor through the taxation and social welfare systems. The economic orthodoxy at the time was 'Keynesianism', named after its most prominent proponent, the British economist John Maynard Keynes. Keynesians believe that markets cannot automatically maintain stable activity at full potential and that where the market is clearly failing to foster growth, or cope with a temporary economic crisis, or deal with social inequalities, then the government should intervene to achieve the desired result. Together with these economic and social welfare objectives, there was also agreement as to the country's security objectives, including strategic alliances with larger protectors such as Britain, the USA and Australia, and a commitment to forward defence.

New Zealand was seen for the first two-thirds of the century as a prosperous but fragile dependent economy with one major export, agriculture, and one dominant market and source of investment, Britain. Not until its terms of trade and balance of payments turned savagely and permanently against it in 1966–67 and Britain entered the European Community in 1972 did New Zealand finally grasp the fact that this relationship with Britain was ending and that New Zealand had to diversify rapidly both its exports and its markets.

INSECURITY, DIVISION, AND CONFLICT, 1965–85

During the second period, 1965–85, the earlier consensus was shattered as a result of a number of developments and events: a long-term deterioration in New Zealand's terms of trade; Britain's entry into the European Economic Community; the oil shocks of the 1970s; chronic inflation, high interest rates and rising unemployment; the divisive personality of prime minister Robert Muldoon, trying desperately and eventually unsuccessfully by traditional means to defend the old order; New Zealand's involvement in the Vietnam War; conflict over continued sporting contacts between New Zealand and apartheid South Africa; differing views on the significance of the Treaty of Waitangi and the position of the indigenous Māori; heated and irreconcilable division over abortion, especially in the late 1970s; and the escalating costs of expanding New Zealand's health, education and social services to meet demands far beyond those originally envisaged in the late 1930s by the founders of New Zealand's welfare state.

In the 1940s, 1950s and early 1960s, few questioned New Zealand's general alignment with the Western democracies against communism, and especially New Zealand's enthusiastic membership of ANZUS and antagonism towards the Soviet Union and the People's Republic of China. By the mid-1960s, however, a significant, vocal and active minority of New Zealand public opinion was opposing the US involvement in the Vietnam War and, more importantly, New Zealand's participation as a US ally.

In May 1965 the Holyoake National government, not without a great deal of reluctance and anguish, responded to US and Australian pressure and agreed to send combat troops to Vietnam. The contribution was seen as a premium on the ANZUS alliance insurance policy for New Zealand's defence, but payment was kept to a minimum. Only 3,500 New Zealand volunteers served in Vietnam between 1965 and 1972 and never more than 550 at a time. Casualties comprised 35 dead and 187 wounded. Limited though New Zealand's involvement was, however, it seriously divided New Zealand. Many younger people were particularly horrified by the brutality that was exposed each night on television. The widespread protests, which drew tens of thousands of New Zealanders onto the streets, were not confined to New Zealand's involvement, but attacked the USA and the war itself. Although National's victories at the 1966 and 1969 elections appeared to be endorsements of its policy of keeping troops in Vietnam, the troops were being brought home even before the election of the Kirk Labour government in 1972. The legacy of Vietnam, however, was an end to the bipartisan approach to foreign and defence policies, which had existed for the first twenty years after the war.

Other non-economic issues also divided New Zealanders. One was apartheid in South Africa, particularly with reference to All Black and Springbok rugby tours. From the late 1950s a growing number of New Zealanders became active opponents of apartheid. They were particularly offended by the periodic rugby games between the Springboks, who were a team drawn largely from racist Afrikaaner South Africans, and New Zealand All Black teams from which Māori were omitted solely on racial grounds. Some of New Zealand's greatest players were never selected if the opponents were South Africa. In 1960, thousands of New Zealanders at meetings and marches in the main streets of cities such as Auckland protested with the slogan 'No Maoris, no tour', but the tour of South Africa went ahead anyway. The issue continued to divide New Zealanders throughout the 1960s and 1970s even when, as in 1970, the South Africans offered to label Māori players 'honorary whites'. Finally, the Kirk Labour government in 1973 reversed an election promise of the previous year and forced the New Zealand Rugby Union to cancel a tour of New Zealand by a racially selected Springbok team. Muldoon allowed such a tour in 1981, which saw extraordinary street violence and battles between protesters and police and protesters and rugby fans. New Zealand was divided to an extent and to a degree of bitterness rarely seen before or since in its history. It was clear by the end of the tour that there would never be another one. The National government may well have won votes and seats in rural New Zealand, but it certainly lost them in the cities and suburbs at the election held a few months later.

During the period 1965–85 New Zealand also underwent significant societal change. By the 1980s the political culture had already started to become more individualistic; more heterogeneous both ethnically and ethically; less conformist and less egalitarian; more concerned with equality of opportunity than fair outcomes; and starting to accept that finite government income needed to be targeted according to need, not distributed universally according to citizenship. New Zealand society was increasingly more urbanised and industrialised and far less homogeneous than it had been in 1945. Demographically, there were more immigrants not only from Europe, Australia and North America, but also from the Pacific Islands, Asia and Latin America. Moreover, the electorate as a whole was better educated and more affluent. There were more white-collar workers, a diminishing proportion of manual workers, and many more people owned property than in previous generations. Social habits changed markedly with the increasing access of New Zealanders to automobiles, the growth of suburbia, and the advent of television. Television was to have an increasingly marked effect on political perceptions and outcomes as well as recreation and culture. All these trends were to increase after 1984, some quite exponentially.

The number and percentage of New Zealanders, especially younger New Zealanders, of Māori origin increased rapidly. Concurrently, the Māori became more urbanised, more visible, and more vocal. There was a growing awareness of the significance of the Treaty of Waitangi and of unresolved Māori grievances especially over the unjust loss of their land, their language and their culture.

The Māori demand for greater recognition from Pakeha society and especially Pakeha decision-makers and more effective participation in decision-making was matched by a concurrent challenge to the patriarchal nature of New Zealand society and politics. Māori women organised effectively through the Maori Women's Welfare League formed in 1951. One of its founding members, Whina Cooper, led a major land march in September 1975 to publicise the hope that not one more acre of Māori land would be alienated.

Women generally and increasingly asserted their rights to tertiary education, access to the professions and management, liberation from patriarchal dominance and domestic drudgery and fairer political representation. The birth control pill, which largely removed the fear of unwanted pregnancy, was a major factor in emancipating women, changing social attitudes and patterns and enabling them to pursue independent careers. The Women's Electoral Lobby (WEL), for example, was established in 1975, the same year as a United Women's Convention in Wellington attended by over 2,000 women. Among other things, WEL drew attention to the absence of women from the legislature. In the entire history of the New Zealand parliament prior to the 1984 election, a total of only twenty women had been elected, thirteen Labour and seven National MPs, and only two, Labour's Mabel Howard and National's Hilda Ross, had become cabinet ministers. Since the 1984 election, when twelve women were elected out of ninety-five MPs, the number of women MPs has risen to a record thirty-nine out of 121 in 2005, with the Prime Minister, Speaker of the House, Governor-General and Chief Justice all being women.

Both Labour and National governments prior to 1984 were happy to govern a pluralistic society in which the major corporate sectors of the economy were recognised and involved in decision-making at the national level. The politicians and civil servants constantly consulted the leaders of the farmers, manufacturers, employers and trade unions and legislation and regulation were used to intervene frequently in the economy and to resolve conflicts between or among the interest groups. The state was no mere referee but a major player, with its own vested interest and agenda, particularly in stabilising society and maximising production and export receipts. Some observers believed that New Zealand politics during this period was too consensual and that, in an attempt to maintain stability and security, hard decisions relating to the restructuring of the economy were delayed disastrously. Others felt that politicians lacked vision and/or courage and even if they recognised the imperatives for change feared voter backlash. Successive political leaders concentrated on short-term election-winning tactics rather than bold strategies designed to rescue a decaying economy and an increasingly obsolete, wasteful and counter-productive welfare state, which was locking some into an intergenerational dependency trap while failing to meet the needs of others.

Prior to 1984, the economy was subject to high levels of government intervention and regulation. Manufacturers and wage-earners were protected by import controls and farmers were encouraged to produce and were protected from fluctuations in overseas markets by subsidies, tax incentives, and producer boards. The banking system and value of the currency were tightly controlled. All came under increasing pressure to change and, in the face of the increasing difficulty of maintaining subsidies and regulation without distorting the economy further, it became obvious that there would need to be deregulation and greater automaticity, rationality and competition in the economy.

By 1984, New Zealand society was becoming much more diverse, the political culture was in a state of flux, and the two established parties were in search of new solutions to the country's growing economic problems. New Zealand's long period of political consensus had come to an end and deep divisions emerged not only between political parties but also within those parties and between reformist Members of Parliament and more conservative traditional supporters.

INDEPENDENCE, INDIVIDUALISM, AND DIVERSITY, 1985–2005

The election in 1984 of the fourth Labour government, led by David Lange and with Roger Douglas as Minister of Finance, ushered in the third period of radical economic reform, between 1985–93, which has largely remained unchanged ever since. The new government adopted similar policies to those advocated by American New Right economists and earlier implemented in the USA and Britain by Ronald Reagan and Margaret Thatcher. Underlying the reforms was a view that the state needed to be 'rolled back' because it had become too paternalistic, authoritarian and bureaucratic and a threat to individual freedom. Communal values and processes needed to be rejected and individual responsibility and accountability re-emphasised. State involvement in the economy and expenditure on the welfare state were questioned on the grounds of both efficiency and morality. It was wrong to force farmers, businessmen and workers to pay high taxes, which not only took away their incentives and rewards but also were used to subsidise uneconomic farmers and inefficient producers, distort the labour and finance markets, sustain a bloated bureaucracy that increasingly interfered in people's lives, and locked many poorer people into welfare dependency. A society was freer, more prosperous and more morally just when the managed economy and collectivised social action were both privatised.

The economic, and the resulting social, changes were accompanied by a clear move towards a more unilateral and independent foreign and defence policy, including nuclear-free legislation, which effectively ended the ANZUS Alliance with the USA and Australia that had been the cornerstone of New Zealand's foreign and defence policy for most of the postwar era.

After 1984, successive governments listened less to the traditional interest groups but proved much more receptive to the views of individual businessmen with vested interests, some of whom were active in a new Business Round Table, and to a new breed of professional consultants and lobbyists with close personal and political contacts to parliamentarians. The economic and social policies they pursued may well have been too radical for a majority of the population, although it could be argued that on economic, if not on social policy, the Labour-led governments since 1999 have tended to be more cautious and more concerned with public opinion than those that governed between 1984 and 1999.

Although started by Labour, the radical economic restructuring, deregulation, modernisation and globalisation of the New Zealand economy was carried on during the first term of the fourth National government, 1990–93, led by Jim Bolger as Prime Minister and Ruth Richardson as Minister of Finance. Motivated by both pragmatic necessity and free market ideology, New Zealand's economy, prior to 1984 arguably the most controlled in the Western world, was almost totally deregulated. Overseas investment in New Zealand was encouraged. State assets were largely privatised, many ending up owned overseas. Import and currency controls were removed and New Zealand became locked into the global economy. Subsidies to farmers and protection to manufacturers were removed, leading to bankruptcies, unemployment and, among farmers, a high number of suicides. The public service was totally restructured and for a time, under National in the early 1990s, the labour market was freed up. The political culture, including New Zealanders' shared values and perceptions, was transformed from the immediate postwar one based on consensus, conformity and collectivism to one based on competition, diversity and individualism.

The pace and extent of the reform was moderated after 1993, largely as a result of the adverse reaction of a majority of voters, but most of the major economic changes of the previous nine years were never reversed. Nor was the fourth Labour government's anti-nuclear legislation, which became both a cause and a symbol of New Zealand's independence from the USA, Britain and Australia in foreign and defence matters.

The period from 1985–2005 also saw dramatic social change in New Zealand. The country was opened up to massive immigration from Asia, especially during the late 1990s and the early years of the twenty-first century. In Auckland, for example, Asians, who comprised only 2 per cent of the population at the 1986 census, were 14 per cent by 2001, a greater percentage than those of Māori descent, who comprised 12 per cent at the same date.³ Many more women entered and rose to senior positions in politics, the public service, the professions and private sector management. All legal discrimination against homosexuals was removed. The banking, retail and hospitality sectors were transformed, not only by deregulation but also by rapid and dramatic technological developments and marked changes in New Zealanders' attitudes and habits. The widespread use of personal computers, Internet and email, and of mobile phones and text messaging, have also transformed business and social interaction.

There were ongoing attempts in the late 1980s and throughout the 1990s by both Labour and National governments to redress historic grievances arising from non-observance of the Treaty of Waitangi and subsequent illegal land confiscations. That consensus, however, appeared to end when fears that the government was encouraging racial division led to the National party, and particularly its leader Don Brash, stressing at the 2005 election the concept of one citizenship for all, while recognising that New Zealand had become a multiethnic and multicultural society.

This third period in New Zealand's recent political history was complicated further by the advent of a new system of electing the unicameral New Zealand parliament. Although no political party had won more than half the votes cast at any election after 1951, successive single party governments, elected under a first-past-the-post system in individual constituencies, had continued to act almost as elected dictatorships with a mandate to do whatever they pleased irrespective of the views of the voters represented by opposition politicians or a majority of the electorate. In 1993, a referendum introduced a mixed member proportional electoral system from the 1996 election, and since then no single party has been able to win a majority of the seats in parliament. As a result, governments have been made up of coalitions of two or more of the eight parties that are currently represented in the House of Representatives and which more fairly reflect the divisions that exist within the New Zealand population.

As a result of the revolutionary nature of Labour's economic and social policy reforms, there was considerable political confusion within the electorate that was compounded further by the actions of the National government after 1990 in accepting and carrying Labour's reforms further. Both major parties suffered severe defections of parliamentarians, party members and voters. Labour's membership dropped from about 60,000 to 6,000 and National's from 100,000 to about 20,000, though both subsequently recovered partially.⁴ Jim Anderton, a Labour MP and former party president, was expelled from the caucus in 1988 for opposing his government's privatisation agenda. He formed first the NewLabour party in 1989, the five-party Alliance two years later and the Progressives in 2002. In 1993, Winston Peters, a former Minister of Maori Affairs, was effectively expelled from the National party for also opposing its neo-liberal agenda. He formed the New Zealand First party. Both Anderton and Peters have remained in parliament ever since.

Other new parties also appeared out of the turmoil of the 1990s. The most successful, in that they also won seats in parliament, were ACT (the Association of Consumers and Taxpayers), formed by former Labour ministers Douglas, Richard Prebble, Ian Shirley and Michael Bassett, supported by former National ministers Derek Quigley and Ruth Richardson; United Future, a coalition of United, led by former Labour minister Peter Dunne, and the Christian Democrats, formed by the previously National minister Graeme Lee; the Greens, whose co-leaders Rod Donald and Jeanette Fitzsimons were first elected as Alliance MPs in 1996 before taking the Greens out of the Alliance in 1999; and the Māori party, formed after Tariana Turia left the Labour party in 2004. All four of these parties won seats, along with Labour, National, New Zealand First and Jim Anderton's Progressives at the 2005 election.

A single party, alternately Labour or National, governed New Zealand for fifty years after the end of the Second World War, and most New Zealanders accepted without question the two-party system. As long as successive governments reflected the values and policies of the consensus, most voters did not appear too worried by the lack of checks and balances which allowed those governments to exercise arbitrary power, subject only to limits self-imposed by the politicians' awareness of and respect for what was acceptable democratic behaviour. Certainly, without a written constitution, a constitutional court, or an upper house in the legislature, after the Holland National government abolished the Legislative Council in 1950, or the separation of executive and legislature, prime ministers could force legislation through parliament or rule by executive regulation without effective opposition between elections. Compared to the period between 1981 and 1993, however, arbitrary power was used between 1945 and 1981 with relative restraint, although one can find abuses from time to time throughout the postwar period. Since 1993, and especially since 1996, governments have again tended to be more cautious in not distancing themselves too much from public opinion.

The advent of MMP and the emergence of a number of smaller parties meant that since 1996 no single party has commanded a majority of the seats in parliament. Since 1996 there have been four coalition governments. The National–New Zealand First government lasted until 1998, when it was replaced by a minority National administration led by Jenny Shipley, supported by some breakaway former NZ First MPs and a renegade Alliance MP. A Labour–Alliance government led by Helen Clark won office in 1999, and that Labour-led administration was returned as a Labour–Progressive coalition, with some limited legislative support from the Greens, in 2002. In 2005, Clark became the first Labour leader in New Zealand history to win a third term as prime minister, leading a Labour–Progressive coalition with support from New Zealand First and United, whose leaders Peters and Dunne took ministerial posts outside cabinet. The National party, whose centre-right vote was seriously split and whose number of MPs was slashed at the 2002 election by voter defections to New Zealand First, ACT, and United, coalesced again at the 2005 election, winning only two seats less than Labour's fifty MPs and clearly reasserting itself as New Zealand's alternative government. As the various readings in this book will show, however, the country that both it and Labour wish to govern today is, as a result of radical changes since 1984, a markedly different one to the New Zealand that the first Labour government created in the 1930s and 1940s and which National managed for most of the sixty years after 1945.

DISCUSSION QUESTIONS

1   Discuss the merits of the argument that the postwar period to 1965 was marked by a fundamental continuity in the policies of the two major parties.
2   Why and to what extent did the postwar consensus begin to unravel in the 1970s and early 1980s?
3   What evidence is there for the view that the 1984 general election marked a watershed in the postwar history of New Zealand politics?
4   Is MMP responsible for today's multi-party system, or were there other causal factors?

NOTES

1   For example, Robert Chapman, 'From Labour to National', in Rice 1992, p. 351, says of the Labour Government's achievements in their first three years of office, 1935–38, 'The patterns and institutions thereby established long outlasted the party's own period in power. Like the Liberals after their victory in 1890, Labour after 1935 was able to set the terms of political debate and action for the next forty years ... The readiness to turn from one era to the next in 1935 came primarily from the breadth of feeling that it was no longer possible to go on in the old way'. See also Sinclair 1969, pp. 188 and 268–9.
2   Savage, *cit.* Gustafson 1986, pp. 226–7.
3   *NZ Herald*, 13 January 2006.
4   Statistics provided, but not for attribution, to the author by senior party officials.

REFERENCES

Chapman, R. 1992, 'From Labour to National', in G.W. Rice (ed.), *The Oxford History of New Zealand*, 2nd edn, Oxford University Press, Auckland, pp. 351–84.
Gustafson, B. 1986, *From the Cradle to the Grave. A Biography of Michael Joseph Savage*, Reed Methuen, Auckland.
Sinclair, K. 1969, *A History of New Zealand*, 2nd edn, Penguin, Middlesex.

FURTHER READING

Belich, J. 2001, *Paradise Reforged. A History of the New Zealanders from the 1880s to the Year 2000*, Penguin, Auckland, esp. pp. 270–549.

Gustafson, B. 1990, 'The National Governments and Social Change (1949–1972)', in K. Sinclair (ed.), *The Oxford Illustrated History of New Zealand*, Oxford University Press, Auckland. pp. 267–94.

Gustafson, B. 1992, 'Coming Home. The Labour Party in 1916 and 1991 Compared', in M. Clark (ed.), *The Labour Party After 75 Years*, Victoria University Press, Wellington.

Gustafson, B. 1993, 'Regeneration, Rejection or Realignment: New Zealand Political Parties in the 1990s' in G.R. Hawke (ed.), *Changing Politics? The Electoral Referendum 1993*, Centre for Policy Studies, Wellington.

James, C. 1997, 'The Policy Revolution 1984–93' in R. Miller (ed.), *New Zealand Politics in Transition*, Oxford University Press, Auckland, pp. 13–24.

Kelsey, J. 1993, *Rolling Back the State*, Bridget Williams Books, Wellington.

Miller, R. 2005, *Party Politics in New Zealand*, Oxford University Press, Melbourne, esp. pp. 25–64.

The Social Setting

Bruce Curtis & Cate Curtis

This chapter discusses the social setting of parliamentary politics in New Zealand by examining some of the building blocks of social statistics: the dynamics of fertility, mortality and migration in the population. These drivers of demographics are crucial in determining characteristics of the population such as age structure, ethnic composition and growth. The main source of this information is provided by Statistics New Zealand (formerly the Department of Statistics). The most important mechanism by which Statistics New Zealand collects material is, of course, the five-yearly census. Alongside this count of the resident population the ministry also conducts a variety of other surveys and makes many estimates and projections available through its publications and online materials.

Demographics—the profiling of the population—are themselves 'social facts' insofar as they are both a social setting for polity and are a product of that politics. Consider, for example, the rise of 'neo-liberalism' in New Zealand. Neo-liberalism can be defined as an approach that believes that markets, rather than state administration or bureaucracy, is the best way to allocate most resources in society. Kelsey (1995, 2002) and many other commentators have identified how the Labour government of 1984 to 1990 and successive administrations introduced and cemented a range of pro-business policies, including the sale of state-owned assets (e.g. Telecom, Bank of New Zealand, New Zealand Rail, state forests, power generation and supply, etc.) and the introduction of various forms of user-pays schemes (e.g. university fees, private health insurance, high interest rates). These policies undid much of New Zealand's previous 'experiment' (hence, the ironic sub-title of Kelsey's first book, *The New Zealand Experiment*) in social democracy and egalitarianism. They can also be understood in demographic terms. Thus the generation born in the Great Depression (in the 1930s) and who experienced the Second World War (1939–45) had a commitment to building up

Table 1.2.1: Percentage of enrolled voters who voted in general elections

Election	1972	1975	1978	1981	1984	1987	1990	1993	1996	1999	2002	2005
Voted	89.1	82.5	69.2	91.4	93.7	89.0	85.2	85.2	88.2	84.8	77.0	80.9%

Source: McVey 2005, p. 17

the 'welfare state'. By the 1980s this generation was aging/retiring/dying and their children—the baby boomers of the prosperous 1950s and 1960s—proved much less interested in the bureaucratic and subsidy arrangements of the welfare state. Arguably these baby boomers dismantled the politics of their parents' generation. In turn, their legacy is that around 30 per cent of the population—all those born since 1984—have no experience of anything other than neo-liberalism.

Nevertheless, there is little doubt that the demographics of New Zealand guarantee that a range of issues and stresses will be played out in the political realm in the coming decades: the role of migrants, the aging population and declining workforce, retirement and superannuation schemes, ethnic-based relative and absolute poverty, and so on. It is possible that these developments might even reverse the long-term decline in voter turnout in general elections (see table 1.2.1). Arguably this process, in particular the engagement of young Māori with parliamentary politics, is already underway.

SOCIAL STATISTICS

The estimated resident population in New Zealand for the year ended December 2004 was 4,061,400. Statistics New Zealand estimated that of the resident population 2,063,700 were female and 1,997,700 male. The median age—at which half of the population is younger, and half is older—was 35.2 years (Statistics New Zealand, 2005a, p. 1). About 79 per cent of the population were European, 15 per cent Māori, 7 per cent Pasifika and 7 per cent Asian (Statistics New Zealand 2005b).[1] About three-quarters of the population lived in the North Island (Statistics New Zealand 2005a, p. 127).

Precisely who the four-millionth resident is, of course, impossible to tell, but baby Sharnia—born in Levin, Thursday, 24 April 2003—was declared by Statistics New Zealand to be the most likely contender. Sharnia's birth was celebrated not only because four million is a nice round number but also because breaking this barrier has been a long time coming. Historically, projections of the growth of the New Zealand population have proven overly confident, as wars, economic depression, emigration (a guesstimate is that about half a million New Zealanders now live overseas) and declining fertility have slowed projected population growth. Indeed, some nineteenth century colonists and writers speculated that by now the population would exceed

Table 1.2.2: Ethnicity by age structure (%)

2001

Ethnicity	0–14	15–39	40–64	65+	Median
European	21	34	31	14	36.9
Māori	37	40	20	3	22.1
Asian	23	48	26	4	28.6
Pasifika	38	40	18	3	21.4
Total NZ	23	36	30	12	34.7

2021

Ethnicity	0–14	15–39	40–64	65+	Median
European	16	29	33	22	44.3
Māori	30	38	24	7	26.4
Asian	21	36	35	8	36.2
Pasifika	33	39	22	6	23.7
Total NZ	18	32	33	17	40.3

Source: Statistics New Zealand 2005b

six million. In other words, projections are notoriously inaccurate and the ones cited here from Statistics New Zealand (2005b) use up to nine combinations of mortality, fertility and migration to come up with their best estimate. Arguably, population projections are as much art as science. Regardless, the counts and estimates suggest that in 2004 baby Sharnia was part of the 51 per cent of the population that is female; 15 per cent that claimed Māori ancestry; 2 per cent of the population aged one; and 6 per cent living in the Manawatu–Wanganui Region. Sharnia will be eligible to vote in 2021. By then, the projections suggest, the population of New Zealand will be very different (see table 1.2.2).

1. Ethnicity and divergent birth rates: A diversifying population

Apart from the indigenous Māori, all New Zealand's resident population are recent migrants or have migrant ancestors. Around three-quarters of the resident population are European in origin, mainly because until the 1970s immigrants to New Zealand came overwhelmingly from Europe. More recent immigrants have come also from the Pacific Islands and Asia. Today these latter two communities each number about a quarter of a million of the resident population. Clearly, New Zealand is becoming less European in its ethnicity, largely because European birth rates are lower than those of other ethnic groups. Māori, Pasifika and Asian birth rates are higher than Europeans for two reasons: a younger age structure, and higher fertility. The younger age structure of these sub-populations creates a momentum for higher birth rates insofar as people in their early twenties are more likely to have children than those in their mid-thirties, for example.

Despite increases in New Zealand's population overall, over the last twenty years fertility (in terms of the number of children born to each woman) has been below the level required for the population to be replaced. The replacement level for the population—without migration—is calculated by Statistics New Zealand at 2.1 births per woman (that is, a child for each of the parents, plus a little extra to account for early deaths, etc.). The rate in 2003 was 1.95 births per woman (that is, sub-replacement). Fertility peaked in 1961 and in the last twenty years the replacement level has been reached only twice (in 1989 and 1990) (Statistics New Zealand, 2005a, p. 31). This downward trend is expected to continue through the twenty-first century. New Zealand's fertility rate is, however, higher than in any European country at present. In comparison, fifty years ago the average woman had at least three children. A number of reasons have been suggested for this change. Early in the twentieth century there was social and religious pressure for women to have children and women who did not were often stigmatised as selfish or unpatriotic. This pressure occurred within a different economic setting. Wages were relatively higher and families could afford to live on one income; indeed, it was expected that women would retire from the workforce soon after marriage, at least until their children reached school age. The advent of reliable contraception alongside the 'sexual revolution' of the 1960s gave women greater freedom of choice about when to have children and how many (if any).

The fertility rates differ between ethnicities; and, Māori and Pasifika fertility levels have remained well above replacement levels. For example, while it is trending down, the rate for Māori women is significantly higher than for the overall population. The rate in 2003 for Māori was 2.55 births per woman (significantly above replacement level of 2.1), while Pasifika women had, on average, 2.8 children and Asian women 1.88 children (Statistics New Zealand, 2005a, p. 31).

European, Māori, Pasifika and Asian populations are projected to grow between 2001 and 2021. As mentioned above, however, as a result of ethnic differences in birth rates the population of New Zealand is becoming more diverse, with the percentage of the population designated European declining. Europeans currently account for 79 per cent of the population; this is expected to fall to 70 per cent by 2021. The European population is projected to grow by 5 per cent. In contrast, the Māori and Pasifika populations will grow by 29 and 59 per cent, respectively. The Asian population is projected to grow by 145 per cent; however, much of Asian growth is expected from migration in the next decade. Thus, by 2021 the Māori population will constitute 17 per cent, Pasifika 9 per cent and Asian 15 per cent of the resident population (as noted, because of multiple ethnicities these percentages add to more than 100) (Statistics New Zealand 2005b).

Table 1.2.2 provides a breakdown of ethnicity by age for 2001 and a projection for 2021. In the 2001 section, 23 per cent of the total population were children, aged 0–14. However, the European population had less than this average (at 21 per cent) and the other ethnicities considerably more (Māori 37 per cent, Asian 23 per cent, Pasifika 38 per cent). Europeans had a smaller share of people aged 15–39 than other ethnicities, but a greater share of people aged 40–64 and 65+. The median age for each sub-population is shown in the final column; the age structure of Europeans is significantly older than for Māori, Asian and Pasifika. This difference in age structure provides an important component in population growth. By 2021 the age structure of all four ethnicities will be older but the younger dynamic of Māori and Pasifika will remain and ensure that an even greater share of the population will come from these ethnicities. In contrast, the age structure (and fertility) of the Asian population increasingly resembles that for Europeans and proportional increases stem from forecasted migration.

2. Declining fertility and longer life expectancy: An aging population

Table 1.2.2 demonstrates that over the next twenty years Māori and Pasifika will retain a significantly younger age structure than the European and Asian sub-populations. In 2001 the median age was 34.7 years. Europeans were the oldest ethnicity by far at 36.9 years, while Pasifika, Māori and Asians were far more youthful with median ages of 21.4 years, 22.1 years and 28.6 years respectively. Nevertheless, each of the ethnicities is aging (that is, the average age is greater). Indeed, the resident population has been aging since 1971. Measures of median age show the current population to be middle-aged and getting older. At 30 September 2005, half New Zealand's female population was over the age of 36.5 years and half the males were over the age of 34.7 years. The median age increased by 3.1 years for women and 2.8 years for men between 1995 and 2005 (Statistics New Zealand 2005d). By 2021 the median age is forecast to be 40.3 years. Europeans will still be the oldest ethnicity at 44.3 years, but all the others will have increased also with median ages of 23.7 years, 26.4 years and 36.2 years, for Pasifika, Māori and Asians.

The aging population has two drivers: declining fertility and longer life expectancy. In cases where declining fertility results in birth rates below that of replacement level (as is the case for Europeans) increasing average median age is relatively simple to grasp: the average increases because not enough babies are being born. However, populations can age where there are birth rates at above replacement levels (as is the case with Māori and Pasifika in particular). This dynamic is the result of people living longer—greater life expectancy. There is an extended trend in New Zealand for people living longer (sometimes referred to as reduced mortality). Thus, life expectancy at birth for women was 81.1 years in 2002, and 76.3 years for men. This is an increase from 78.3 years for women in 1992, and 72.5 years for men (Statistics New Zealand, 2005a, p. 80).

Declining fertility and longer life combine to produce an aging population. An increasing proportion of the population are aged over 65. The elderly comprised 12 per cent of the population in 2002, as compared with 11.5 per cent a decade earlier. Those aged 75 and over now make up 5.6 per cent of the total population, compared with 4.7 per cent ten years ago. However, the most significant factor to the aging population overall is found in older workers (aged 40–64). Aging 'baby boomers' accounted for 30.9 per cent of the population in 2004, up from 26.6 per cent in 1994. In contrast, the percentage of children aged 0–14 declined. Children now make up only 21.8 per cent of the population compared with 23.1 per cent in 1994 (Statistics New Zealand 2005a, p. 10). When ethnicity is included in our analysis of the population, the age structure for Europeans is startling. For example, the projections suggested by table 1.2.2 are that in 2021 there will be significantly more European people aged over 65, than children aged under 14. This is a reversal of the current ratio. For all ethnic groups, the proportion of children will decline. For example, children made up 37 per cent of the Māori population in 2001, but are expected to make up only 30 per cent in 2021.

3. Mortality and income: Disparity of Māori and non-Māori

The differences of age structure and fertility between Māori and non-Māori were touched upon above. Of even greater significance are differences in mortality. Table 1.2.3 shows some of the differences, measured as life expectancy.

Table 1.2.3 shows that while both the gender difference and the Māori/non-Māori difference in life expectancy at birth are narrowing, the latter remains far more significant. In the total population, women tend to outlive men by 4.8 years. This difference is replicated when the population is divided along Māori/non-Māori lines for the years shown. However, the difference in life expectancy between Māori and non-Māori is around twice that of the gender difference. This ethnic disparity was 8.2 years for both women and men in 2000–02. The significantly shorter life expectancy for Māori compared to non-Māori provides additional impetus in skewing the age structure of the latter towards the younger ages. In simple terms, it is by no means a foregone conclusion that a Māori man can expect to live to collect his superannuation at age 65.

Table 1.2.3: Life expectancy by ethnicity

Life expectancy	Māori—female	Māori—male	non-Māori—female	non-Māori—male
1995–97	71.3 years	66.0 years	80.5 years	75.3 years
2000–02	73.2 years	69.0 years	82.0 years	77.2 years

Source: Statistics New Zealand 2005a, pp. 79–83

This disparity in life expectancy is doubly problematic given the longstanding, lifetime economic disadvantage experienced by Māori in comparison to non-Māori. For example, Roper (2005, p. 56) notes the median income of Māori compared to non-Māori was '88.7 per cent in 1986; 75.5 per cent in 1991, 79.3 per cent in 1996, and 80 per cent in 2001'. If there is an equalisation of ethnic share of income, it seems likely to be a very long time coming.

4. Migration: Wide oscillations but of increasing significance?

New Zealand has a high migrant population when measured in terms of place of birth. At the time of the 2001 census, there were 698,628 residents of New Zealand who stated they had been born overseas. This group made up 19.5 per cent of the resident population count, up from 17.5 per cent in the 1996 census (Statistics New Zealand 2005c). Immigration seems to be on the increase, however, making projections about migration trends a decidedly fraught process. Whereas resident populations are subject to change from 'natural increases' (births minus deaths in the population), estimating the impact of net migration (the difference between the number of migrants arriving and leaving New Zealand) is far more problematic.

While natural increase in the resident population of New Zealand tracks a smooth downward curve since the 1960s, net migration demonstrates wide and unpredicted oscillations. Sometimes migration is positive and sometimes it is negative (e.g. more people left New Zealand than arrived in 1999–2001). Thus in 1979 net migration contributed a loss of 37,144 and was a factor in a decline in annual population of 10,051; in 2002 net migration contributed 32,800 of the annual population growth of 58,600 (Statistics New Zealand 2005a, p. 18).

What is more clear is that historically migration has been used as a means of importing skill, stimulating population growth, and, more recently, combating the aging population (an aging workforce, particularly those aged 40–64). Migration has also been the impetus for ethnic diversification, insofar as from the mid-1970s an increasing proportion of migrants have arrived from the Pacific and Asia. Nevertheless, the majority of migrants still arrive from 'traditional' (i.e. European) sources, while the birthplace region exhibiting the most significant growth was North-East Asia (such as China, Korea, and Hong Kong). The vast majority of the overseas-born population in the 2001 census came from the United Kingdom and Ireland, together with Australia and the Pacific Islands. The most significant countries of origin for overseas-born were England (178,203), Australia (56,259), Samoa (47,118), China (38,949), Scotland (28,683), South Africa (26,061) and Fiji (25,722) (Statistics New Zealand 2005c).

It seems likely that migrants will continue to be seen as contributing to positive population change and will be encouraged by government policies. What is less clear is the extent to which the number arriving in New Zealand will exceed those leaving—New Zealand may not necessarily remain an attractive destination for migrants. Nevertheless, historically net migration has been of growing importance to annual and longer-term changes in the population. For the years 2002–04, net migration contributed 97,300 to the population growth for the period of 180,800 (i.e., 54 per cent of population growth) (Statistics New Zealand 2005a, p. 18).

LOCATION, LOCATION: CONCENTRATION IN AUCKLAND

The New Zealand workforce is a highly mobile one and internal migration between regions of people seeking work has been a significant factor in population distribution. Much of this involves movement into big towns and cities (urbanisation). In the 2001 census, over 71 per cent of the resident population count lived in a main 'urban' area (defined as an area with a population of 30,000 or more). There is a long history of urbanisation and suburbanisation as the population has shifted away from rural settings. For much of the twentieth century this urbanisation involved the growth of five cities: Auckland, Hamilton, Wellington, Christchurch and Dunedin. However, since the 1960s Auckland has enjoyed an explosive growth, while from the 1990s the other four centres have levelled off (Dunedin has declined).

In 2004, 28.3 per cent of the population (1,145,700 people) were estimated to live in the Auckland metropolitan area (North Shore, Waitakere, Auckland and Manukau cities). In contrast, the population of the South Island was only 973,100 (24 per cent of the population), and 344,100 lived in Christchurch, with 121,900 in Dunedin. In other words, only about 12.5 per cent of the population lives in the South Island outside of Christchurch and Dunedin (Statistics New Zealand 2005a, pp. 127–34). North Island regions are also being denuded of people. The Gisborne, Taranaki and Manawatu–Wanganui regions joined with the West Coast and Southland in experiencing negative population growth in 2004 (Statistics New Zealand 2005a, p. 18).

Auckland is not only by far and away the largest centre of population and growth, it is also where the greatest changes in ethnic diversity and from migration have occurred. The 2001 census revealed that one in three people living in Auckland were born overseas. Two thirds of people of Asian and Pasifika ethnicities resident in New Zealand live in Auckland. Indeed, Asian (1 in 8 people in Auckland) and Pasifika (1 in 8) ethnicities now outnumber Māori (1 in 10) in Auckland. The concentration of numbers, diversity and related tensions in Auckland makes it extremely important to parliamentary politics and the broader socio-economic realm in New Zealand (Carter, Craig & Matthewman, 2004).

DISCUSSION

The simple social statistics used above—fertility, mortality and migration—suggest a number of dynamics in the next decades. These can be summarised as both diversification of the population and the increasing concentration of that diversification in Auckland. Differences in age structure and fertility coupled with immigration seem likely to result in greater ethnic variety. Decreased fertility and mortality seem likely to result in an aging population. Yet these overall results suggesting change can be somewhat misleading. For example, disparities between Māori and non-Māori life expectancy and income seem likely to remain. Other existing disparities are likely to be even more significant.

What is moot is the extent to which the dynamics of diversification, in terms of ethnicity, age structure and mortality, introduces likelihood for stress and disintegration in society. Clearly Māori, Pasifika and Asian peoples will form a greater proportion of those eligible to vote in future elections. They will form an even greater proportion of the working age population (particularly 15–39 years), while Europeans will be increasingly of retirement age. Among other things, it seems likely that the politics of retirement and superannuation will become of greater importance. But will relatively poor, working age Māori, in particular, be content to continue to pay taxes to support retired Europeans?

Similarly, Statistics New Zealand details very significant ethnic differences in terms of wealth, measured as net worth (assets minus liabilities). This is an important measure insofar as it captures home ownership and indebtedness. In 2001, European couples were on average worth about $210,000, Asian couples about $120,000, Māori couples about $30,000, and Pasifika couples around $10,000 (Statistics New Zealand 2003, p. 31). These are very significant differences and likely to be enduring insofar as they reflect a multitude of structural disadvantages faced by non-Europeans. Almost without doubt, such ethnic differences and grievances, and the relative poverty of Māori and Pasifika coupled with their young and dynamic populations, will be a source of conflict and possible change within New Zealand parliamentary politics. A betting man or woman would see the continuation of pressures which have brought the Māori party into parliament as an absolute certainty. Of greater uncertainty are the effects of increasing numbers of voting aged Pasifika and Asian peoples in general elections.

However, it is also possible—even likely—that these pressures will contribute to centrifugal or anomic forces in society. These pressures towards a loss of social connectivity—what some scholars call 'social capital' (Fine 2001)—can already be demonstrated across a number of dimensions. Roper identifies—from a variety of sources—the inequitable distribution of income. Thus, the top 20 per cent of income earners in 1982 secured 54 per cent of all income; in 1986 it was 32 per cent, in 1991, 1996 and 2001 it was about 59 per cent of all income. In contrast, the bottom 50

Table 1.2.4: Adults and children in family types

	Living Alone	Childless Couple	Solo Parent	Couple with Children	
Adults	511,300	818,300	167,900	865,130	2,362,630
Children	–	–	273,200	841,700	1,114,900
	511,300	818,300	441,100	1,706,830	3,477,530

Source: Statistics New Zealand 2005e

per cent of income earners in 1982 secured 8 per cent of all income. In 1986 it was 9 per cent, in 1991 5 per cent, and in 1996 and 2001 about 7 per cent. Little wonder then that the family—arguably the most important of all social institutions—is under pressure.

The displacement of the extended or intergenerational family by the nuclear family is commonly associated with the baby boom generation and the rise of suburbia. Figures from the 2001 census suggest that the nuclear family (one adult couple and children) is also under threat (see table 1.2.4).

Table 1.2.4 demonstrates that, of the 3,477,530 people surveyed, around half lived in the archetypal nuclear family (couple with children). Nearly half of all adults either lived alone or as part of a childless couple. Of course, a significant number of these childless families are made up of the elderly, who may well have had children previously, and a number of living alone will move into parenting relationships. However, the numbers of living alone and solo parent families suggests a splintering of the nuclear family. The links between solo parenting and child poverty are obvious. What is less clear are the ways in which the experiences of the 273,200 children with solo parenting will feed into parliamentary politics.

DISCUSSION QUESTIONS

1   What are the main demographic dynamics in the New Zealand population?
2   Do the disparities in life expectancy and income between Māori and non-Māori raise any serious issues for politicians?
3   What, if anything, is the relationship between an aging population and migration?
4   Is New Zealand likely to be more or less socially connected in 2021?

NOTES

1   The percentages of ethnic share of the resident population add to more than 100 per cent, because around 8 per cent of the population claim multiple ethnicities and are therefore counted twice by Statistics New Zealand.

REFERENCES

Carter, I., D. Craig & S. Matthewman 2004, *Almighty Auckland?* Dunmore Press, Palmerston North.

Fine, B. 2001, *Social Capital versus Social Theory: Political Economy and Social Science at the Turn of the Millennium*, Routledge, London.

Kelsey, J. 1995, *Economic Fundamentalism: The New Zealand Experiment*, Pluto Press, London.

Kelsey, J. 2002, *At the Crossroads: Three Essays*, Bridget Williams Books, Wellington.

McVey, A. 2005, 'Social Capital in New Zealand: Answer to the Turnout Puzzle or Interesting Cul-de-Sac', unpublished MA thesis, Department of Political Studies, The University of Auckland.

Roper, B. 2005, *Prosperity for All?: Economic, Social and Political Change in New Zealand since 1935*, Thomson, Southbank, Victoria.

Statistics New Zealand 2005a, *Demographic Trends 2004*, Statistics New Zealand, Wellington.

Statistics New Zealand 2005b, *Projections Overview*, www.stats.govt.nz/additional-information/default.htm, accessed 15 November.

Statistics New Zealand 2005c, *Reference Report—2001 Census: People Born Overseas*, www2.stats.govt.nz/domino/external/pasfull/pasfull.nsf, accessed 15 November.

Statistics New Zealand 2005d, 'National Population Estimates (September 2005 quarter)', Media Release, Statistics New Zealand, Wellington.

Statistics New Zealand 2005e, *Reference Report—Survey of Family, Income and Employment Dynamics*, www2.stats.govt.nz/domino/external/pasfull/pasfull.nsf, accessed 15 November.

Statistics New Zealand 2003, *The Net Worth of New Zealanders*, Statistics New Zealand: Wellington.

FURTHER READING

Carter, I., D. Craig & S. Matthewman 2004, *Almighty Auckland?* Dunmore Press, Palmerston North.

Cheyne, C., M. O'Brien & M. Belgrave 1997, *Social Policy in Aotearoa/New Zealand: A Critical Introduction*, Oxford University Press, Auckland.

Davis, P. & T. Ashton 2001, *Health and Public Policy in New Zealand*, Oxford University Press, Auckland.

Kelsey, J. 2002, *At the Crossroads: Three Essays*, Bridget Williams Books, Wellington.

Roper, B. 2005, *Prosperity for All?: Economic, Social and Political Change in New Zealand since 1935*, Thomson, Southbank Victoria.

Statistics New Zealand 2005, *Latest Statistics*, www.stats.govt.nz/default.htm, accessed 15 November.

Multicultural Identity in a Bicultural Context

Katherine Smits

By the beginning of the twenty-first century, three major and interrelated shifts in New Zealanders' thinking about their national identity, which had been developing over the previous two decades, burst into public debate. First, citizenship has become a hotly contested political term, invoked both to support civic education in schools and to attack 'special rights' for Māori.[1] But at a deeper level, the debate over citizenship reflects increased public interest in defining and describing New Zealand's national identity.[2] Second, biculturalism came to be widely (although not universally) accepted as the guiding policy for managing relations between Māori and Pakeha. And third, immigrant ethnic groups assumed a more public role as the ethnic composition of non-Māori in New Zealand, which had always been overwhelmingly British, began to shift significantly towards Asians and other non-Europeans. Just as writers and commentators struggled to define Pakeha identity as a response to Māori, the very composition of non-Māori New Zealand was beginning to change. Some critics called for the state to pursue a policy of multiculturalism instead of biculturalism—a move strongly resisted by some Māori activists.

Although the state-supported drive for citizenship education emphasised diversity, little attention was paid to the different and sometimes competing ways in which cultural diversity is understood in New Zealand. This chapter examines the relationship between biculturalism and emerging multiculturalism, both of which challenge the idea of a homogeneous 'Kiwi' identity, but which are often seen as conflicting, if not antithetical ways of thinking about social identity. I focus on public attitudes towards cultural diversity, and the impact of diversity on justice and individual rights in liberal democratic society.

THE TREND TOWARDS CULTURAL DIVERSITY

For most of New Zealand's history since European colonisation, the great majority of its immigrants have come from Great Britain.[3] While there was no official 'White New Zealand' policy, legislation from the late nineteenth century and well into the twentieth aimed to discourage Chinese immigration, and to encourage more British settlers (Marotta 2000, pp. 179–80). In the period after the Second World War, large numbers of immigrants came from Pacific islands, to supply labour market shortages created by the rural migration of Māori (Pearson 1991, p. 207). But with this exception, British domination of immigration continued essentially unchanged until 1987, when the Immigration Act was introduced by the Labour government as part of its social and economic reform programme. The new legislation aimed at a less discriminatory, and a more deliberately internationalist migration policy, targeting skills needed to fuel economic growth.[4]

The 2001 census revealed the impact of the legislative changes of the 1980s and the changing ethnic makeup of immigration to New Zealand (Statistics New Zealand 2001). Migration from Asia over the past decade had almost doubled. One in fifteen New Zealanders were of Asian origin (a proportion doubled from the previous census). The proportion of people of European descent declined from 83 per cent to 80 per cent. There were large increases in the number of New Zealanders born in Africa, the Middle East and Asia. Among first-generation immigrants, the proportion of the overseas-born population from Asia was 13 per cent, and from the Pacific Islands, 17 per cent. The majority of overseas-born New Zealanders are still from Britain, but recent trends indicate that Asian countries are close behind. In 2002–03, China and India accounted for 16 per cent each of all residence approvals, followed by Great Britain at 14 per cent, although Britain recorded the highest number of approvals again in 2003–04 (New Zealand Immigration Service 2004).

Cultural diversity expressed itself through greater linguistic and religious pluralism: while English remained the predominant language spoken, the number of multilingual people increased by 20 per cent from the 1996 census. Between 1996 and 2001, the relative numbers of Anglicans and Presbyterians declined, while the percentage of Hindus increased by 56 per cent from 1996, Buddhists increased by 48 per cent, and Muslims increased by 74 per cent.

In an empirical sense, New Zealand is without doubt a multicultural nation, its population drawn from all over the world. But in political terms, multiculturalism refers to state policy aimed at protecting and promoting cultural diversity through a range of programmes supporting minority cultural groups. These include teaching minority languages, multicultural curricula in schools and public accommodation of diverse cultural practices. Underlying the policy is the assumption that the host society is under an obligation to recognise and accommodate cultural difference, in order to enable minority groups to integrate on their own terms (Kymlicka 1995, pp. 10–11).

Unlike other countries with substantial polyethnic populations, such as Australia and Canada, New Zealand has never had an official policy of multiculturalism,[5] and there is considerable debate over whether government policy in New Zealand ought officially to recognise and promote the country as multicultural. For most of the country's history since European settlement, the official policy with respect to immigrants has been one of assimilation, with little state support for or recognition of minority cultural groups. Despite recent increases in the diversity of immigrants, little has changed with respect to either the recognition of cultural difference, or the promotion of cultural diversity.[6] Cultural pluralism in this country tends to be cast not as a social good, but as a constraining factor or a potential problem to be managed. There has been some movement: the Human Rights Commission lists as a key goal the promotion of harmonious relations between 'diverse groups', and part of the brief of the Race Relations Commissioner is to pursue this through projects like the Diversity Action Programme. But as Fleras and Spoonley conclude: 'The ground rules of society are inescapably rooted in Eurocentric values and structures; the game plan is unmistakably tilted towards perpetuating Pakeha power and culture' (Fleras & Spoonley 1999, p. 235).

CULTURAL RIGHTS IN LIBERAL DEMOCRACIES

The debate about multiculturalism in New Zealand must be viewed in the context of the increasing attention being paid to the impact of cultural diversity upon individual rights and civic community in Western democracies. In one sense cultural pluralism has been a central concern of liberal societies from their beginnings. The liberal tradition in Western political thought emerged out of religious diversity in the seventeenth century. Individual rights and liberties—civic and religious—were introduced to avoid the bloody conflict that followed the Protestant Reformation in Western Europe, and ever since, liberal democratic thinking has been uncomfortable with group rights and recognition. Only since the 1960s, with pressure from the new social movements, including many based on race and ethnicity, have political thinkers in Western democracies confronted the claims for such rights and recognition (Kymlicka 1995, pp. 62–9).

Multiculturalism is often defended in terms of the benefits that flow to society as a whole from the enrichment of cultural diversity: experience in dealing with people from different cultures prepares New Zealanders better for participating in the global economy. But from the perspective of minorities, multiculturalist policies also ensure that their members are treated fairly and equally. Several political philosophers have recently argued that pluralist democracies must afford some degree of official recognition to minority cultures in order to ensure individual self-respect or autonomy (Kymlicka 1989, 1995; Taylor, 1994). Will Kymlicka argues that state protection of minority cultures is essential because members of those groups require preservation of their cultural context in order for members to be able to exercise autonomy—the capacity to make free and self-determining life choices. Cultural groups are in this account worthy of preservation only as long as they are themselves liberal, in the sense that they too guarantee the freedom and autonomy of members. Other philosophers, like Bhikhu Parekh, defend the rights of cultural minorities whether or not they promote liberal values. Parekh argues that minority cultural group rights and claims should be assessed by balancing them with the rights of others, as part of the democratic political process (Parekh 2000, p. 263).

Kymlicka (though not Parekh) distinguishes national minorities from polyethnic groups on the basis of their role in ensuring individual autonomy. Polyethnic groups are the results of immigration, and do not comprise separate 'societal cultures' which shape and guide individual self-determination. Their members, Kymlicka argues, wish to integrate in the mainstream societal culture—but to be able to do so while retaining their cultural practices. Thus members of minority groups claim rights to maintain their forms of dress, or other cultural practices in public—whether at school, or while serving the state. By contrast, national minorities, such as indigenous groups, comprise separate societal cultures, whose protection and maintenance is essential for their members to make free and independent life choices. They aim not for integration, but for maintaining their separate existence, through a range of legal and constitutional protections (Kymlicka 1995, ch. 2).

Defences of multiculturalism from a liberal perspective must grapple with liberalism's traditional emphasis on individual rights. Kukathas, for example, argues that the state should not become involved in legitimising cultural minorities, but should only protect individuals' rights to join and leave cultural groups (Kukathas 1992). The problem of balancing recognition of minority cultures with protection of individual rights is particularly difficult in the case of illiberal cultures—those which discriminate against individual members or internal groups, such as women (Okin 1999). This issue has arisen recently in New Zealand, as I discuss below. Other critics have argued that recognition of cultural diversity detracts from the sense of common identity that holds a nation together. This last critique has been particularly influential in public debate in New Zealand, where it has been used against both biculturalism and multiculturalism (Brash 2004).

PUBLIC RESPONSES TO MULTICULTURALISM

In other polyethnic countries, debate about multiculturalism first emerged in response to non-Anglo European immigration. In the New Zealand case, however, cultural diversity became controversial in response to large increases in the numbers of Asian immigrants. As a result, the opposition to multiculturalism aired in public over the past two decades is difficult to disentangle from prejudicial attitudes towards Asian people. Changes in the ethnic composition of migrants have led to great cultural anxiety in New Zealand, and there has been often vociferous popular criticism of the 'Asian invasion'. Media treatment of the issue in the early to mid-1990s was dominated by crude, stereotypical images of Asian immigrants and warnings that cultural divisions would plague New Zealand society. Much of this was legitimised by the attacks of Winston Peters, leader of New Zealand First, who attacked the increase in Asian immigration. Anti-Asian feeling reached its height in the mid-1990s, after which the media commentary tended to be more critical of Peters and anti-Asian sentiment—in part due to concern about the economic effects of anti-Asian publicity (Spoonley & Trlin 2004, pp. 26–8).

The common charge that multiculturalism was socially divisive depended on the assumption that Asian immigrants wished to institutionalise alternative values and cultural practices into public life (rather than, as Kymlicka puts it, to redefine integration on their own terms). This was exacerbated by concern about the neo-liberal reforms of the 1980s, which were perceived as being socially fragmenting and destructive of community in New Zealand. The anti-Muslim feeling which emerged in the early twenty-first century, and to some extent displaced anti-Asian sentiment, was similarly tied in to other social concerns—in this case, over the increasingly secular nature of New Zealand society, which made it hospitable to other religious groups.[7] Anti-Muslim sentiment, which became widespread after the terrorist attacks of 11 September 2001 in the USA, reflected concern about both the threat of international terrorism and religious pluralism.

Opposition to multiculturalism increasingly took the form of attacks on the Muslim community for their alleged support for—or at least failure to criticise strongly enough—extremist Muslim radicalism. This became a focus for criticism by Peters, who emphasised the theme in the lead-up to the 2005 election, notably in a speech in which he linked increasing Muslim immigration into New Zealand with the threat of terrorism, suggesting that Muslim immigrants came from cultures with no respect for liberal values (Peters 2005).

The case of dress for Muslim women was a lightning rod for controversy about the relationship between cultural diversity and individual rights in many Western countries through the 1990s. Then in 2005, a witness in an Auckland criminal fraud case refused to give evidence unless she could appear in court wearing the *burqa*, a full-length garment that also covers the face.[8] The witness argued that she never appeared in public without the *burqa,* and, except for her husband and close male relatives, did not reveal her face to men. The defence argued that the witness's testimony would be diminished in value if her face could not be seen to assess its veracity, and as a result, the accused would not receive a fair trial. It further argued that granting such a request would amount to setting up a separate justice system for Muslims, and that in emigrating, the witness had agreed to adhere to New Zealand judicial customs and practices. Finally, defence argued that there was no requirement in the Qu'ran to wear a *burqa*, and that the witness was being forced to do so by a religious and cultural system which oppressed women. The court in the end decided on a compromise solution, in which the witness removed her *burqa* but testified behind a screen, where she was seen only by the judge and counsel.

This case brought to the surface several features of the controversies over multiculturalism highlighted above. Was the state obliged to take into account Muslim cultural practices here? According to Kymlicka's argument, it was—as long as those practices were not oppressive for women. In practice, as Okin would point out, the decision to wear concealing dress could well be the result of overweening social pressure. From Parekh's perspective, the relative rights of the Muslim witnesses and the defence need to be balanced, and if wearing the *burqa* is determined to impact substantially upon the rights of the defence, it should not be permitted.

THE BICULTURAL CONTEXT

The fact of increasing ethnic diversity in New Zealand has emerged in a context in which the discourse of ethnic and race relations has been dominated by the politics and ethics of the Treaty of Waitangi (Sharp 1991, p. 132). Treaty politics assume a bifurcated model of identity—Pakeha and Māori—with no formal place for non-European and non-Māori New Zealanders. Legislation and judicial interpretation from the mid-1980s has required policies to be interpreted and implemented subject to the principles of the Treaty, and 'bicultural' social and political policies have been inferred from its text and history. Several accommodations have been made by the majority culture: the adoption of Te Reo Māori as an official language and the increasing use of Māori language and protocol for ceremonial occasions, funding for Māori broadcasting and the arts, and changes to the school curriculum. But the extent of cultural change required under biculturalism remains unclear.[9]

Critics have argued that legalistic interpretations of the Treaty are inadequate to managing complex indigenous/Pakeha relations, and further, they ignore the polyethnic diversity of cultures that increasingly constitute New Zealand. Some have suggested that rather than seek historically accurate interpretations of the Treaty, race relations in New Zealand should be guided by broad principles of equality and justice (Sharp 1991; consistent with Kymlicka 1995, pp. 116–20). This would open the way for consideration of the claims of ethnic minorities as well as Māori, but the danger often cited is that it would relegate Māori to being just one group in a plurality of ethnicities. Because of their status as Tangata Whenua—first people—the Māori occupy a special role in New Zealand, and many argue that their language and culture have a right to public recognition which is more fundamental than the claims of immigrant groups.

It is with this in mind that some Māori commentators have fiercely opposed any recognition of New Zealand as multicultural. Ranginui Walker castigated the government in the late 1980s and 90s for failing to consult with Māori over the extension of immigration policy to cover non-Europeans. Immigrants from Asia were, he argued, driven by 'egocentric' motives, rather than 'a sense of altruism towards the host country' (Walker 1995, p. 293). They were insufficiently proficient in English, and their contribution to economic growth was low, as they 'usually employ their own people …' (Walker 1995, p. 295). In response, defenders of multiculturalism argue that non-European immigrants are being excluded from the debate on New Zealand's identity and future (Thakur 1995, p. 271). In a liberal argument similar to that of Kukathas, Ramesh Thakur argues that Māori, Pakeha and non-Europeans are all immigrants, and that the state should give no preferential recognition to the language and culture of any ethnic group, including Māori (Thakur 1995).

The emphasis on biculturalism that emerged in the 1980s has tended to homogenise and fix both Māori and Pakeha identity. Some critics have argued, for example, that biculturalism tends to favour pre-contact forms of Māori social organisation, rather than the more urban forms influential today (Levine 2001). In the case of Pakeha, the central question became one of distinguishing themselves from Māori, rather than examining their internal constitution as a group, and their relation to other immigrant New Zealanders. Not coincidentally, Pakeha became a much more important label and form of political identification in the 1980s (Spoonley 1991; King 1985; Schroeder 1986). Spoonley comments that a bifurcated model of identity persisted into the late 1980s, when tribal politics around the Waitangi Tribunal produced a new awareness of intra-Māori differences (Spoonley 1991, p. 158). This paradoxically may free up Pakeha to examine their own internal divisions and their relation to non-European and non-Māori New Zealanders.

What is the impact of multiculturalism on biculturalism? Some critics argue that the claims are fundamentally different: immigrant communities demand distributive justice in terms of greater access to positions of status and power within existing institutions and structures of governance—whereas Māori request special status within the constitution or recognition of Treaty-based claims (Pearson 1991, p. 210). But this is to dodge the issue of cultural assertion which emerged in the recent *burqa* case. A multiculturalist policy will not only allow polyethnic groups cultural expression in the public sphere, but will also support and protect minority cultures. As Kymlicka has argued, however, this is not the same as the more extensive claims of indigenous groups for cultural protection and self-determination (Kymlicka 1995, ch. 2).

A central problem here is the use of terms: biculturalism refers not only to the inclusion and celebration of Māori culture in the form of language and ceremonies, but is also used as shorthand for the legal and Treaty-based claims made for Māori rights. As Colin James argues, biculturalism in New Zealand is about power-sharing, not just tolerance of and support for minority culture (James 2004). For some critics, 'binationalism' is a more accurate and useful term, one which reflects the trend towards framing Māori political claims within the Treaty (Fleras & Spoonley 1999). Binationalism distinguishes indigenous from polyethnic groups, and more fully recognises 'nations within'—that there are separate nations in New Zealand with inherent collective rights to self-determination. Binationalism is agnostic on the composition and identity of non-Māori society, and thus is potentially more compatible with multiculturalism.

CONCLUSION

New Zealand is increasingly a polyethnic society, and although there is no official policy of multiculturalism, state institutions that deliver services are beginning to accommodate themselves to that reality (Fleras & Spoonley 2000). The Ministry of Education, for example, explicitly endorses recognition of multiculturalism in schools, in both curriculum and teaching strategy (see, for example, Gerritsen 2000). Political discourse has still not yet caught up with social reality, and the 2005 election campaign demonstrated that anti-multiculturalist discourse can be mobilised to attack particular ethnic and religious groups. It remains to be seen whether in his new post of Foreign Minister, Winston Peters moderates his attacks on non-European cultural minorities. Asian communities in New Zealand reacted to his appointment with concern, and expressions of hope that Peters would emphasise the more 'positive' aspects of 'Asian values' to which he has occasionally pointed.

If political discourse is to keep pace with the reality of polyethnicity, multiculturalism and biculturalism—or more properly, binationalism—can no longer be seen as mutually exclusive. As Kymlicka points out, both minority ethnic groups and national indigenous minorities make claims for cultural inclusion on the basis of equal respect for the individual rights of their members. Ethnic minorities aim not at cultural segregation, as critics like Peters assume, but at inclusion of their cultural practices in public life. For Māori, the inclusion of culture in the form of language, dress and custom is only one aspect of the political aims of the community. Under binationalism, Māori assert their status as a separate people within the nation, with legally guaranteed rights to self-government (tino rangatiratanga). A multicultural model of citizenship for New Zealand would recognise the different nature of these claims, and aim to accommodate both.

DISCUSSION QUESTIONS

1 Should the state recognise and protect cultural minorities, or is this incompatible with individual rights?
2 Does state support for cultural diversity have the effect of fragmenting the nation, preventing social cohesion?

3 Should immigrants in New Zealand have their cultural customs and practices recognised and protected in the same way as those of Māori? If not, what should the differences be?

4 Should the state in New Zealand protect minority cultural practices which may oppress groups such as women within minority cultural communities?

NOTES

1   See eg. 'Inquiry to Review New Zealand's Existing Constitutional Arrangements', Report of the Constitutional Arrangements Committee, presented to the New Zealand Parliament, August 2005; Brash 2004.

2   For a recent discussion of national identity in New Zealand, see Liu, McCreanor, McIntosh and Teaiwa 2005.

3   Small numbers of immigrants in the period before the Second World War came from Europe, particularly Germany and Croatia.

4   This legislative change was preceded by a review of immigration policy which declared that New Zealand was a country of immigrants—including the Māori. Several Māori activists declared their opposition to being characterised as immigrants in the same terms as later arrivals (Walker 1995, p. 286).

5   The USA also has no official policy of multiculturalism, but the meaning and value of cultural diversity has long been a key theme in US public discourse.

6   In 1999, the Fletcher report reflected concerns about lack of state resources and support for migrant settlement (Fletcher 1999).

7   These anxieties were revealed in public controversy in 2005 over whether or not Christian education classes should be held in state schools.

8   See *Police v Razamjoo* [2005] BCL 275.

9   Even this degree of biculturalism is not uncontroversial. In 2005, the new Māori party called for a public inquiry into the use of Māori customs through the state sector, arguing that such ceremonies were being coopted by the state for its own purposes, rather than being used for the good of Māori. See 'MP refuses to take back seat to Maori protocol', *New Zealand Herald* Thursday 3 Nov. 2005, A5.

REFERENCES

Brash, D. 2004, 'Nationhood', speech given to the Orewa Rotary Club, 27 January.

Fleras, A. & P. Spoonley 1999, *Recalling Aotearoa: Indigenous Politics and Ethnic Relations in New Zealand*, Oxford University Press, Oxford.

Fletcher, M. 1999, 'Migrant Settlement: A Review of the Literature and its Relevance to New Zealand', Report commissioned by the New Zealand Immigration Service, September.

Gerritsen, J. 2000, 'Diversity Rules', *Education Gazette*, 79/2, 7 February.

James, C. 2004, 'The Indigenisation of Aotearoa-New Zealand: the politics of the Treaty of Waitangi', paper for the Australian judges conference, 27 January.

King, M. 1985, *Being Pakeha*, Hodder and Stoughton, Auckland.

Kukathas, C. 1992, 'Are There Any Cultural Rights?' *Political Theory*, 20/1, pp. 105–39.

Kymlicka, W. 1989, *Liberalism, Community and Culture*, Clarendon Press, Oxford.

Kymlicka, W. 1995, *Multicultural Citizenship* Clarendon Press, Oxford.

Levine, H. 2001, 'Can a Voluntary Organization be a Treaty Partner? The Case of Whanau O Waipareira Trust', Report to the Ministry of Social Development, December.

Liu, J.H., T. McCreanor, T. McIntosh & T. Teaiwa (eds), 2005, *New Zealand Identities: Departures and Destinations*, Victoria University Press, Wellington.

Marotta, V. 2000, 'The Ambivalence of Borders: The Bicultural and the Multicultural', in P. Spoonley & G. Fischer (eds), *Race, Colour and Identity in Australia and New Zealand*, University of New South Wales Press, Sydney, pp. 177–89.

Mulgan, R. 1993, 'Multiculturalism: A New Zealand Perspective', in C. Kukathas (ed.), *Multicultural Citizens: The Philosophy and Politics of Identity,* The Centre for Independent Studies, St Leonards, NSW.

New Zealand Immigration Service, 2004, 'Trends in Residence Approvals, 2003/2004', Department of Labour, September.

Okin, S.M. 1999, 'Is Multiculturalism Bad for Women?' in J. Cohen, M. Howard & M.C. Nussbaum (eds), *Is Multiculturalism Bad for Women?* Princeton University Press, Princeton.

Parekh, B. 2000, *Rethinking Multiculturalism: Cultural Diversity and Political Theory*, Harvard University Press, Cambridge, MA.

Pearson, D. 1991, 'Biculturalism and Multiculturalism in Comparative Perspective', in P. Spoonley & D. Pearson (eds), *Nga Take: Ethnic Relations and Racism in Aotearoa/New Zealand*, Dunmore Press, Palmerston North, pp. 194–214.

Peters, W. 2005, 'The End of Tolerance', speech given by Rt Honourable Winston Peters to members of Far North Grey Power, 28 July.

Schroeder, J. 1986, 'Being Pakeha', *Canta*, 56/2.

Sharp, A. 1991, 'The Treaty of Waitangi: Reasoning and Social Justice in New Zealand?' in P. Spoonley & D. Pearson (eds), *Nga Take: Ethnic Relations and Racism in Aotearoa/New Zealand*, Dunmore Press, Palmerston North, pp. 131–47.

Spoonley, P. 1991, 'Pakeha Ethnicity: A Response to Maori Sovereignty', in P. Spoonley & D. Pearson (eds), *Nga Take: Ethnic Relations and Racism in Aotearoa/New Zealand*, Dunmore Press, Palmerston North, pp. 154–70.

Spoonley, P. & A. Trlin 2004, 'Immigration, Immigrants and the Media: Making Sense of Multicultural New Zealand', *New Settlers Programme*, Massey University, Palmerston North.

Statistics New Zealand, 2001, 'Census Snapshot 1' (Cultural Diversity)—Media Release.

Taylor, C. 1992, 'The Politics of Recognition', in A. Gutmann (ed.), *Multiculturalism and the 'Politics of Recognition'*, Princeton, Princeton University Press.

Thakur, R. 1995, 'In Defence of Multiculturalism', in S. Greif (ed.), *Immigration and National Identity in New Zealand: One People—Two Peoples—Many Peoples?* Dunmore Press, Palmerston North.

Walker, R. 1995, 'Immigration Policy and the Political Economy of New Zealand', in S. Greif (ed.), *Immigration and National Identity in New Zealand: One People—Two Peoples—Many Peoples?* Dunmore Press, Palmerston North.

FURTHER READING

Docker, J. & G. Fischer (eds) 2000, *Race, Colour and Identity in Australia and New Zealand*, University of New South Wales Press, Sydney.

Fleras, A. & P. Spoonley, 1999, *Recalling Aotearoa: Indigenous Politics and Ethnic Relations in New Zealand*, Oxford University Press, Oxford, 1999.

Greif, S.W. (ed.) 1995, *Immigration and National Identity in New Zealand: One People— Two Peoples—Many Peoples?* Dunmore Press, Palmerston North.

Kukathas, C. (ed.) 1993, *Multicultural Citizens: The Philosophy and Politics of Identity*, The Centre for Independent Studies, St Leonards, NSW.

Kymlicka, W. 1995, *Multicultural Citizenship: A Liberal Theory of Minority Rights*, Clarendon Press, Oxford.

New Zealand's Ideological Tradition

Pat Moloney

It remains a tenet of our nation's mythology that New Zealanders are pragmatic 'doers' rather than dogmatic 'theorisers'. Such a belief seems to downplay the influence of ideas upon New Zealand's political culture. However, the persistent representation of ourselves as a small, progressive democracy willing to experiment on a range of social, economic, and political issues is itself the product of a particular configuration of ideas. As this chapter will demonstrate, New Zealand's ideological traditions are diverse. If there is any truth to the myth of Kiwi pragmatism, perhaps it lies in our willingness and the institutional ability to trial novel ideas. Within the social laboratory of New Zealand a range of ideological strains have been cultured: colonisation, Māori sovereignty, democracy, liberalism and socialism. Some ideas, like liberalism and democratic socialism, have retained their prominence over great tracts of time; some, like revolutionary socialism, have made colourful but brief appearances; others, like Māori sovereignty, have been resilient occupiers of the margins always ready to challenge and re-invigorate the ideological field. What follows is a brief survey of the ideas that have informed and justified political practice in New Zealand for the last century and a half.

'BRITAIN OF THE SOUTH SEAS'

New Zealand became a colony of Britain in 1840. Behind this simple statement of historical fact lie a number of ideological imperatives that have determined the course of New Zealand's political history. The British Crown was led reluctantly to assume sovereignty over New Zealand by treaty and right of discovery in order to facilitate and control colonisation, as well as to 'protect' the indigenous population. By so doing it laid the foundations for the modern nation–state of New Zealand. References in the Treaty of Waitangi to the establishment of a 'settled form of Civil Government' and the 'Rights and Privileges of British Subjects' are historically specific in their meaning. By the middle of the nineteenth century the ideas and political agitation of radicals in England, of earnest evangelical missionaries at home and abroad, and of rebellious French and English settler communities in North America had significantly shifted the outlook of the British government with regard to colonial matters and had raised the political expectations of those living under colonial rule. Particular political institutions and their contemporary ideological justifications were weighty items of baggage brought by European settlers to New Zealand.

Edward Gibbon Wakefield was an influential colonial reformer and political economist of colonisation in the 1830s. The colony of New Zealand was, in his mind, to become the 'Britain of the South Seas', creating a new market for British manufactures and offering new fields for investment and employment. Avoiding the colonial mistakes of the past, he sought to transplant an entire society, with all its complex class and occupational divisions, and by so doing to preserve and invigorate 'civilisation' in the colonial wilderness. The modern colony was an experiment in 'the creation of happy human beings'. Prosperity and security for all social classes was achievable with managed immigration and concentrated settlement that would temper the natural ambition of individuals and coordinate their industry. Bound to the mother country culturally and economically, the extension of British dominion through colonisation came to be seen as compatible with local autonomy. Though details of his scheme of systematic colonisation unravelled under colonial conditions, his broader vision of New Zealand as a 'post-enlightenment experiment', as Erik Olssen puts it, certainly shaped our development (Olssen 1997, p. 198).

DEMOCRACY

Colonial conditions necessitated departures from Old World practices. For example, the democratic principle of political equality—everyone should have the same power to influence political decisions—was not universally applied in Europe until well into the twentieth century. Urban workers, agricultural peasants and women generally were not trusted with political rights because they were not considered to be permanent stake-holders, nor autonomous (their votes could be bought), nor informed (they lacked education). However, self-government was granted to settlers in New Zealand through the New Zealand Constitution Act of 1852. That Act established among other things a general legislature of elected representatives with most of the powers of domestic government. The franchise (those who had the right to vote) was liberal for its time: all men over twenty-one who had a small amount of landed property were eligible to vote. The ownership of property by individuals was seen as indicative of their settled interests and good character. It demonstrated a long-term stake in the colony, 'respectability' and industriousness. Wakefield's 'sufficient price' for land had sought to address the high cost and shortage of labour in colonies by obliging poorer immigrants to work for several years to acquire the means to purchase land. This was also a device certifying hard work, stability and prudence. At the end of the nineteenth century the new egalitarian image of the colony as a 'working-man's paradise' still held out to prospective immigrants the older ideal of 'independency' (Fairburn 1990, p. 46). The promise of self-advancement manifest in the private ownership of productive land—being one's own boss rather than working for others—was a moral and material goal realisable in the arcadia of New Zealand because of its natural abundance (fertile land), its classless, egalitarian society and the state's encouragement of small farming units. The rapid extension of political participation and democratic rights (even to the inclusion of women in 1893) went hand-in-hand with the aspirations and expectations of immigrants and the rhetoric of progressive development.

Although subordinate to London, the colony as a whole also enjoyed considerable autonomy. By 1854 the power of responsible government had been conceded; namely the presumption that ministers were responsible to the legislature (rather than to the Governor). The executive (the cabinet of ministers as it came to be called) had to enjoy the confidence of a majority of representatives in the legislature. The Governor was to act on the advice of ministers, except on those matters touching upon the Queen's prerogative and imperial interests. These were reserved to the Governor (who would consult Her Majesty's Secretary of State for War and the Colonies in London) and included Crown lands, Māori affairs and foreign policy. However, New Zealand's colonial parliament, like those in Canada and Australia, quietly, but relatively quickly, wrested control of all domestic affairs away from the Governor and London as they grew to become national parliaments within the empire.

New Zealand's political history has been experimental but, very importantly, not revolutionary. Civil government in New Zealand readily adopted the democratic principle of popular sovereignty—the people ruled. For older British settler colonies, like those of America, separation from the mother country had only been achieved by a war of independence. That break had in turn precipitated the establishment of republican institutions and in the USA the democratic principle was extended to include the direct election of political officials, from the county sheriff to, eventually, the federal president. By contrast, the Australasian colonies secured the right to manage their own affairs without a fight, without the abandonment of constitutional monarchy, the dissolution of imperial ties, nor major amendment to the Westminster parliamentary system. Given the timing of the founding of the settler colony, the concession of self-government was inevitable. Piecemeal modification of conventions by pragmatic colonial ministries, governors, and London marked the gradual transition to the full status of democratic nationhood. Given how bloody and fraught the transition to democracy is for many societies of the present day, New Zealand's heritage of democratic principles and practice is not something that should be taken for granted.

MĀORI SOVEREIGNTY

In 1866 John Stuart Mill, the liberal philosopher and reformer, was asked his opinion about affairs in New Zealand. Given the inhumane treatment of 'inferior races' by British colonists in the past, and given that self-government had been conceded to the settler parliament, Mill was pessimistic that the appetite of colonists for land could be reconciled with the just treatment of Māori (Mill 1972, pp. 1135–6, 1196). Although the third article of the Treaty of Waitangi guaranteed to Māori all the rights and privileges of British subjects, it failed to specify that, for Victorians, cultural identity defined who could be rights-bearing participants in civil society: one had to be or become British before those entitlements could be fully exercised. Wakefield, the Colonial Office, and the missionary societies (despite their differences over means) all assumed that indigenous societies were to be assimilated into European society. Wakefield described his New Zealand experiment as 'a deliberate and methodical scheme for leading a savage people to embrace the religion, language, laws and social habits of an advanced country' (Wakefield & Ward 1837, p. 42). Today's notions of cultural pluralism (recognition of the inherent value of the language and cultural practices of distinct groups) did not then exist. Colonial 'wastelands' (lands not utilised for intensive cultivation by the original occupiers) were looked upon as an imperial patrimony; with justice, Europeans thought, such land would be improved by the absorption of the redundant populations of the metropolis. Colonisation presumed the right (and the providential duty) of Europeans to extend their economic and cultural system over the entire globe. Even Mill distinguished between barbarous and civilised societies, justifying colonial rule in India on the paternalistic assumption that Indian society was not yet mature enough to exercise the individual freedoms he defended at home.

Colonisation alienated Māori from their land and resources and severely disrupted traditional social patterns. As settler numbers grew and the colonial government's sphere of influence expanded, Māori struggled to retain control over their own affairs. Although the largest landholders and having the most permanent interest in the country, the 1852 Constitution disenfranchised most Māori because they held property communally, not by individual title. Electoral districts coincided with European settlements and large numbers of Māori fell outside them. Assimilationist presumptions underpinned the decision of Earl Grey, the Colonial Secretary, not to institute a special Māori franchise, but 'to trust to their advance in civilisation and the acquisition of property, to enable them, by degrees, to take their share in elections along with the inhabitants of the European race' (cited in Dalziel 1989, p. 52). Questionable land purchases in Taranaki and Governor Grey's determination to crush the King movement in Waikato led inevitably to armed conflict. The New Zealand wars of the 1860s are properly described as 'a war of sovereignty' (Orange 1987, pp. 159–84).

The discourse of tino rangatiratanga, Māori sovereignty, is the indigenous counter-ideology to that of colonisation. In its contemporary forms it begins by foregrounding the Declaration of Independence of 1835 made by a confederation of Northern Māori chiefs as asserting and giving international recognition to Māori sovereignty. It reads the Māori version of the Treaty of Waitangi as a sacred compact between Māori and the British monarch in which the Māori chiefs 'confirmed their own sovereignty while ceding the right to establish a governor in New Zealand to the Crown ... [who] governed at the behest and on behalf of the chiefs' (Walker 2004, p. 93). Tino rangatiratanga, the authority entrusted to the tribal chief, was not, nor could have been surrendered. To the present day, Pakeha view the Treaty as adding legitimacy to the Crown's assumption of absolute sovereignty, while also guaranteeing certain limited rights to Māori. Reversing this entirely, Mike Smith sees the Crown's governance, kawanatanga, as a limited and delegated authority: '... we have subcontracted out some functions, some limited authority, to the kawanatanga to look after their own people and ensure that they lived peacefully within the realms of our society ... We have the authority, the predominant or primary say in what happens here' (Melbourne 1995, p. 103).

Denouncing the enduring legacy of colonisation and the 'integrationist' policies of the latter part of the twentieth century, younger Māori activists in the 1970s and 1980s challenged the very legitimacy of the Pakeha state: 'Maori sovereignty is the Maori ability to determine our own destiny and to do so from the basis of our land and fisheries. In essence, Māori sovereignty seeks nothing less than the acknowledgement that New Zealand is Māori land, and further seeks the return of that land' (Awatere, 1984, p. 10).

For many Māori the term 'tino rangatiratanga', nowadays proudly emblazoned on t-shirts, is best left untranslated. As Mason Durie explains, this avoids a head-on collision with the indivisibility of sovereignty asserted by the Crown. It can be understood to imply the idea of 'self-determination' and reference is often made to the United Nations Draft Declaration of the Rights of Indigenous Peoples 1993 where self-determination is defined as the right of indigenous peoples to 'freely determine their political status and freely pursue their economic, social and cultural development' (Durie 1998, p. 219–20). Mana motuhake (independence) is another aspect of the exercise of tino rangatiratanga and refers to the autonomy of distinct tribal groupings to assert their difference from each other and from Pakeha. It, in turn, is linked to mana whenua, tribal ownership of and governance over traditional tribal lands and resources. Some authors do speak of tino rangatiratanga as the sovereign power inherent in Māori collectively as a 'nation'. Kotahitanga, the movement for pan-tribal unity, has certainly been a longstanding response to colonisation (Cox 1993). However given valued and significant differences, conflicting interests and rivalries among the many iwi and hapu, a national Māori identity and a unified political voice has never solidified. Separatism has few proponents. As other chapters in this volume explain, debate around the Treaty today concerns the ongoing partnership between Māori, represented by iwi authorities, and the Crown, and negotiation over the institutional mechanisms necessary for biculturalism to be sustained. In the settlement of grievances against the Crown, the Waitangi Tribunal has sought to balance reparation for historical injuries suffered by particular iwi and hapu, existing property rights and political realities, restoration of mana and the building of capacity for sustainable futures (Sharp 1997, pp. 163–77). Articulating what Sharp has described as the 'jurisprudence of wairua, a peculiarly New Zealand/Aotearoan statement of (and an attempt at a solution of) the problem of justice between two peoples', the Tribunal, though acknowledging the state's sovereignty and speaking of moderation and compromise, acts as the nation's conscience by reminding the state of its obligations, both moral and legal, to honour the spirit or principles of the Treaty of Waitangi.

SOCIALISM AND LIBERALISM

Modern Pakeha and Māori identities have been forged, in part, in opposition to each other. By its very nature, this ongoing process of cultural formation involves misrepresentations and distortions. One frequent mistake, for example, is the identification of European ideas exclusively with individualism and competitive capitalism (in contrast with the communalism and subsistence production of traditional Māori society). Socialism is a major tradition of European thought that rejects the possessive individualism of classical liberalism and seeks to abolish the private ownership of land or capital that exploits the labour of the producers. It advocates instead the collective ownership of economic production and cooperative forms of organising society. Socialists of various hues have taken an interest in New Zealand, and New Zealand socialists have had a significant impact upon its political culture. They have differed though on the form a socialist society should take and the means by which it might be realised.

In the 1850s Robert Pemberton, influenced by the utopian socialist Robert Owen, devised a circular model town to be established in Taranaki and occupied by British workmen. On his elaborate town plan an educational academy, gardens, and recreational facilities are placed at its hub. Escaping the 'artificial' structures of the Old World where happiness was confused with the accumulation of wealth, he believed that human perfectibility was achievable if the labour of men was combined under conditions that elicited their creative potentials. New Zealand seemed the ideal setting for his experiment: The Happy Colony. As Lyman Tower Sargent has noted, New Zealand utopian writing is distinguished by the perception of a closer fit between present realities and utopian possibilities (Moloney & Taylor 2002, p. 170).

The British Fabians were democratic socialists who viewed utopian communes as part of a much broader historical tendency in the direction of cooperation. With its vastly expanded functions, the modern state now managed major industrial enterprises. They foresaw that when the numerically superior working-class was eventually given the vote, socialist political parties would govern and expand the sphere of collective production. Condemning the injustice and destructive inefficiency of competitive individualism, they sought, through their pamphlets, to encourage a gradual, peaceful and constitutional movement towards socialism. In the 1890s, the New Zealand Liberals under the premiership of John Ballance and then Richard Seddon were attacked by the opposition as 'reckless empirics and state socialists' (Reeves 1950, p. 274). American progressives and British socialists saw New Zealand as leading the world in the expansion of the state's commercial activities, in its interventions between labourers and employers; and in its social legislation. William Pember Reeves was an influential minister in that Liberal government and a Fabian socialist (Moloney & Taylor 2002, pp. 39–57).

Unlike his colleague, Sir Robert Stout, a classical liberal thinker wary that over-dependence on the state would sap initiative and undermine self-reliance, Reeves defended the predominance of the state in the life of the colony. His confidence in the beneficial effects of an active state stemmed from his conviction that the state was not the mere dispenser of largesse in the interest of one particular class, but had now assumed a universal character: 'I believe in the State because the State is now the people and the people the State, and because the people are orderly and well-educated'.[1] His famous labour legislation presumed that the state could impartially mediate disputes between worker and employer in the interests of the community as a whole.

A crucial plank in the Liberal programme was assisting closer settlement of the land (Sinclair 1991, pp. 172–88). Some, like Ballance and Reeves, favoured land nationalisation. Measures in that direction—changes in property taxes and the government purchase of private land aimed at breaking up the great estates of absentee landowners—were put in place. However, the goal of most Liberals was the encouragement of settlement by small farmers, either on freehold property secured with cheap loans offered by the government, or on long-term leasehold property with the state as a fair landlord. As Tom Brooking has demonstrated though, the bulk of the land purchased cheaply by the government and made available to small farmers was

Māori land (Brooking 1992). Despite protests from the Māori members of parliament, the Minister of Lands, John McKenzie and the Premier Richard Seddon, re-introduced Crown pre-emption (the Crown having exclusive right of purchase) and modified the Native Land Court legislation to expedite land sales. Māori land was looked upon as an unimproved wilderness and Māori depicted as 'lazy' landlords who were blocking more worthy and progressive European settlers from owning land. The Māori land policies of the 'enlightened' Liberals thwarted Māori economic development for a century. Such lessons have not been lost on Māori, and opposition to the recent foreshore and seabed legislation must be understood in light of such previous dealings with the state.

Until his death in 1906, the populist Seddon commanded a liberal–labour alliance wherein the appetite of farmers for loans, land, and an improved transportation infrastructure and the demand of workers for reasonable working conditions and remuneration could both be appeased. But many socialists saw the state not as an independent umpire, but as the agent of class oppression. Karl Marx and Friedrich Engels, publishing the *Communist Manifesto* in 1848, depicted the class antagonisms of the industrial era as leading to conflict between wage-labourers (the proletariat) and the employers of labour, those who owned productive resources (the capitalists or the bourgeoisie). As the exploitation of workers by capitalists (low wages and poor working conditions) worsened, revolution would be inevitable. In New Zealand the revolutionary strand of socialism had its highest profile between 1908 and 1913 when the 'Red Feds', the major trade union organisation, the Federation of Labour, was led by fiery radicals like Bob Semple, Paddy Webb and Pat Hickey (Olssen 1988). Influenced in particular by the American syndicalist group, the IWW, militant socialists in New Zealand sought the creation of a 'co-operative commonwealth' by organising the entire working class into one big union. Their revolutionary industrial unionism involved a repudiation of parliamentary politics and especially the state regulation of labour disputes introduced by Reeves. In the years preceding the First World War, the breakdown of capitalism and a workers' revolution seemed close at hand. With slogans like 'World's Wealth for World's Workers', rebellion in the form of general strikes and sabotage heralded the seizing of the means of production in New Zealand.

Lacking widespread support and in the face of a state determined to suppress working-class militancy, the strikes were broken and law-breakers imprisoned. But out of the seedbed of revolutionary socialism sprang the democratic socialism of the New Zealand Labour party founded in 1916. Although the party's manifesto for many years declared its objective to be 'the socialisation of the means of production, distribution and exchange', by the time it achieved election victory in 1935 and formed the first Labour government under Michael Joseph Savage, former militants quickly became loyal ministers of the Crown. The party expelled members of the Soviet-aligned Communist Party of New Zealand in 1926, and as Barry Gustafson makes clear, the socialism of men like Savage was not that of Marxist-Leninism (Gustafson 1986, pp. 143–53). They did not seek the destruction of capitalism, but the amelioration of its harmful excesses. 'Applied Christianity' was Savage's characterisation of the Labour party's programme to realise a just society. For democratic socialists, social justice for all members of society was to be achieved by the redistribution of wealth through progressive taxation and an expansive role for the state in the regulation of the capitalist economy. Given the misery of the Great Depression of the 1930s, Labour's social programme of 'cradle to grave' security, made possible by high prices for our primary produce that commenced with war-time demand, resonated with the country's aspirations.

CONCLUSION

In 1948 Leslie Lipson described New Zealand as an 'equalitarian democracy' in which the politics of democracy and the economics of socialism formed a unique blend (Lipson 1948, p. 482). Still then under the economic regulations and central planning of the war years, Lipson critically assessed that New Zealand had placed equality ahead of liberty, material security ahead of creative innovation. The homogeneity of the Pakeha population made political consensus easier to achieve, but also bred cultural intolerance and conformism. All this was to be challenged by new social movements in the 1970s and shattered by neo-liberalism in the 1980s (Mein Smith 2005, pp. 191–5, 208–13).

In the next chapter, Chris Eichbaum gives a full account of neo-liberalism. At that time Rogernomics (as the neo-liberal reforms instigated by Sir Roger Douglas, Minister of Finance in the fourth Labour government of David Lange, came to be known) was attacked as a 'foreign import' alien to New Zealand's ideological tradition. While the policies of the fourth Labour government certainly bore little resemblance to those pursued by the first Labour government, the impetus to experiment in the policy arena, as we have seen, was not new. New Zealand's ideological traditions are diverse; but few of the main ones have been covered here. Ideas matter in New Zealand (as elsewhere) because they inform, justify and modify political practice. Further ideological experimentation and rigorous debate would not be inconsistent with our traditions.

DISCUSSION QUESTIONS

1   Do New Zealanders place equality ahead of liberty, as Leslie Lipson thought we did in the mid-twentieth century?
2   Do New Zealanders still have a 'colonial mentality' as some Māori assert?
3   Can tino rangatiratanga be reconciled with the sovereignty of the New Zealand state?
4   What relevance, if any, does socialism have in New Zealand of the twenty-first century?

NOTE

1   William Pember Reeves, 21 July 1892, *New Zealand Parliamentary Debates*, Vol. 76, 1892, p. 38.

REFERENCES

Awatere, D. 1984, 'Maori Sovereignty', *Broadsheet*, Auckland.

Brooking, T. 1992, ' "Busting Up" The Greatest Estate of All: Liberal Maori Land Policy, 1891–1911', *New Zealand Journal of History*, vol. 26, pp. 78–98.

Cox, N. 1993, *Kotahitanga, The Search for Maori Political Unity*, Oxford University Press, Auckland.

Dalziel, R. 1989, 'Towards Representative Democracy: 100 Years of the Modern Electoral System', in A. Anderson et al. (eds) *Towards 1990*, Government Print, Wellington.

Durie, M. 1998, *Te Mana, Te Kawanatanga, The Politics of Maori Self-Determination*, Oxford University Press, Auckland.

Gustafson, B. 1986, *From the Cradle to the Grave: A Biography of Michael Joseph Savage*, Reed Methuen, Auckland.

Gustafson, B. 1992, 'The Labour Party', in H. Gold (ed.), *New Zealand Politics in Perspective*, 3rd edn, Longman Paul, Auckland, pp. 263–88.

Lipson, L. 1948, *The Politics of Equality: New Zealand's Adventures in Democracy*, University of Chicago Press, Chicago.

Melbourne, H. 1995, *Maori Sovereignty: The Maori Perspective*, Hodder Moa Beckett, Auckland.

Mill, J.S. 1972, *The Later Letters of John Stuart Mill 1849–1873*, F.E. Mineka & D.N. Lindley (eds), University of Toronto Press, Toronto.

Moloney, P. & K. Taylor 2002, *On the Left: Essays on Socialism in New Zealand*, University of Otago Press, Dunedin.

Mein Smith, P. 2005, *A Concise History of New Zealand*, Cambridge University Press, Melbourne.

Olssen, E. 1988, *The Red Feds Revolutionary Industrial Unionism and the New Zealand Federation of Labour 1908–1914*, Oxford University Press, Auckland.

Olssen, E. 1997, 'Mr Wakefield and New Zealand as an Experiment in Post-Enlightenment Experimental Practice', *New Zealand Journal of History*, 31/2, pp. 197–218.

Reeves, W.P. 1950, *The Long White Cloud Ao Tea Roa*, 4th edn, George Allen & Unwin, London.

Sharp, A. 1997, *Justice and the Māori: The Philosophy and Practice of Māori Claims in New Zealand since the 1970s*, 2nd edn, Oxford University Press, Auckland.

Sinclair, K. 1991, *A History of New Zealand*, Penguin, Auckland.

Vowles, J. 1987, 'Liberal Democracy: Pakeha Political Ideology', *New Zealand Journal of History*, vol. 21, pp. 215–27.

Wakefield, E.G. & J. Ward 1837, *The British Colonization of New Zealand*, London.

Walker, R. 2004, *Ka Whawhai Tonu Matou: Struggle without End*, Penguin, Auckland.

FURTHER READING

Durie, M. 1998, *Te Mana, Te Kawanatanga, The Politics of Maori Self-Determination*, Oxford University Press, Auckland.

Gustafson, B. 1992, 'The Labour Party', in H. Gold (ed.), *New Zealand Politics in Perspective*, 3rd edn, Longman Paul, Auckland, pp. 263–88.

Moloney, P. & K. Taylor 2002, *On the Left: Essays on Socialism in New Zealand*, University of Otago Press, Dunedin.

Vowles, J. 1987, 'Liberal Democracy: Pakeha Political Ideology', *New Zealand Journal of History*, vol. 21, pp. 215–27.

Walker, R. 2004, *Ka Whawhai Tonu Matou: Struggle Without End*, Penguin, Auckland.

The Third Way

Chris Eichbaum

As well as being New Zealand's oldest political party, since 1999 the Labour party has also been its largest and most influential. While political parties can be distinguished one from the other according to the emphasis placed on particular values and beliefs, and while Labour does exhibit some of the qualities of a modern 'catch-all' party, it remains in essence a social democratic movement. As such, it can be located on the centre-left of the political spectrum. Just what social democracy means both in principle and in policy practice has been the subject of much speculation and debate. This chapter focuses on the ideological dimensions of 'modern social democracy', and the 'third way' as a specific (if somewhat slippery and elusive) variant of a modern social democratic world view.

IDEAS AND IDEOLOGY

Our starting point in this chapter is with the notion of political ideology. In essence a political ideology is comprised of three elements. First, it enables us to make sense of the world as we find it in the here-and-now—in other words, it has an *analytical* or a *diagnostic* dimension to it. The assumption is that economic, political, and social systems and phenomena do not just happen by accident, and that we can make sense of the world by seeing things in terms of patterns of cause and effect. This aspect of political ideology provides answers, and, significantly, *conflicting* answers to questions about economic, political, and social life. Second, a political ideology provides a clear articulation of the way the world should be. In other words, it has a *normative* element to it. If the first element of an ideology is about making sense of the world as we find it, this second element is about clearly identifying the extent

47

to which there is a gap between that world, and the ways things *ought* to be. And third, how we bridge that gap between how things are and how things should be is by way of a political plan of action, otherwise known as a manifesto, a platform, or a political project.

Over the past twenty years, two political world views have dominated New Zealand politics and public policy—neo-liberalism, and a modern form of social democracy.[1] At their core these two competing ideologies posit a different balance respectively between the state and the market in economy and society. On a continuum which has a greater role for the state on the left, and a minimal role with greater resort to market forces on the right, the social democratic world view occupies the left of the spectrum, and the neo-liberal world view the right. According to the neo-liberal view, 'the market is ... morally and practically superior to government and any form of political control' (Heywood 2003, p. 55). As a political project, the aim of neo-liberalism is to reduce the size and the reach of government in economic and social life.

Social democracy, on the other hand, can be viewed as a parliamentary and reformist strategy—thereby clearly differentiating it from revolutionary socialist politics—designed not to abolish capitalism, but to humanise it, principally by regulating some aspects of economic activity and further developing the apparatus of the welfare state. As one study has observed, social democracy 'came to stand for a broad balance between the market economy, on the one hand, and state intervention on the other' (Heywood 2003, p. 140). The focus in this chapter is mainly on modern variants of social democracy.

Politics and public policy are always as much concerned with debating the past as positioning for the future. Neo-liberalism and its variants dominated politics and public policy in a number of countries during the 1980s and 1990s. Margaret Thatcher in Britain, Ronald Reagan in the USA, and Roger Douglas and Ruth Richardson in New Zealand all brought variants of a neo-liberal world view and political prescription to the fashioning of public policy, and the remaking of political, economic and social institutions. So dominant did it become that social democrats (in Britain, New Zealand, and elsewhere), and Democrats (in the USA) were all required to articulate an alternative to the neo-liberal ideology.

But parties in these countries were also required to engage with their own pasts, as well as with the particular orientations of their political adversaries. British Labour, for example, remade itself as *New* Labour and amended Clause IV of its constitution, which, with its commitment to public ownership, was far too evocative of a more dated socialist orientation. In the USA, President Clinton's New Democrats and the Democratic Leadership Council similarly attempted (with considerable short-term success) to remodel the Democratic party into a more centrist movement. The challenge facing the New Zealand Labour party was somewhat different. During the mid to late 1990s it was far less concerned with repudiating its socialist roots than distancing itself from the neo-liberal excesses of National, as well as of the previous (Labour) government. Thus, in a very real sense the search for a third way by the social democratic parties in each of these three countries was a product of two influences: the political and policy orientation of the principal political opponent (a *first* way), and the need to more clearly differentiate the modern variant of the party from the ideological and political 'baggage' of its past (a *second* way).

An awareness of the recent history of New Zealand politics, and of the Labour party in particular, is indispensable to an understanding of the political and policy orientation Labour brings to government and governance in the twenty-first century. Some of that story is given by the very large shadow that a former National prime minister, Sir Robert Muldoon, continues to cast over contemporary politics and public policy. In no small part Muldoonism did what it is often assumed left-wing governments do best—it made the case for the market. The fourth Labour government (1984–90) was in many respects most un-Labour like, and became more so the longer it was in office. If Muldoonism fuelled anti-statist resentment, the governments of a neo-liberal persuasion that followed it demonstrated the folly of abrogating too much policy influence to the market. Moreover, whether the bias was towards state or market, by the early 1990s the New Zealand electorate—in the face of governments that placed little value in an electoral mandate and the absence of checks and balances—had seen fit to constitutionally re-engineer politics by way of a change to the electoral system. On becoming the government in 1999, Labour needed to differentiate itself from its own past and from the market-liberal excesses of its immediate predecessors. Moreover it needed to rehabilitate the electoral mandate by doing in government what it had promised to do in the electoral contest for that opportunity—by keeping its word.

CLARIFYING THE SPECIFIC NATURE OF THE FIRST, SECOND, AND THE THIRD WAY

Over the past ten years the term 'third way' has been very much to the fore in debates about what a modern social democratic ideology and political and policy programme may entail. The term 'third way' is fundamentally imprecise and elusive. In short it means different things to different people and in different contexts. To label an aspect of politics or policy as 'third way' is simply to raise a set of further questions. There are multiple 'third ways' and the term has been used in a variety of ways over time. For example, social democracy itself has at times been described as a third way alternative to laissez-faire market liberalism on the one hand, and the various forms of the communist state on the other. In the context of American politics, Bill Clinton's New Democratic formula that he brought to the White House and the

US Presidency in 1992 has been characterised as a third way to the 'tax and spend' or 'big government' tendencies often associated with the Democratic party. Tony Blair's use of the term 'third way' helped to differentiate 'New Labour' from both Margaret Thatcher's laissez-faire style of economic management on the one hand, and the 'Old Labour' inclination to resort to higher (and arguably economically and politically unsustainable) rates of taxation and expenditure, and a more interventionist role for government in economic affairs.

This British version of the 'third way' was given added substance by the important contributions of Professor (now Lord) Anthony Giddens, formerly Director of the London School of Economics. In 1998, Giddens published *The Third Way: The Renewal of Social Democracy*, and this initial contribution has been built on in a number of subsequent publications (Giddens 2000, 2002, 2003). In essence, Giddens posits the need for a Third Way alternative to the 'new right' on the one hand (neo-liberalism) and the 'old left' on the other (traditional social democracy).[2] Giddens' ideal-type summary of the defining features of neo-liberalism, and of traditional social democracy is summarised below.

For Giddens, the third way provided an alternative to both neo-liberalism and the traditional form of social democracy. In essence, market liberalism was viewed as morally unattractive, and traditional social democracy as unsustainable. What was required was a new balance between individual responsibility (one of the hallmarks of a liberal world view) and collective responsibility (typically associated with a social democratic world view). Moreover, it was argued that many key policy issues transcended the 'old' distinction between left and right, leaving open the prospect of

Table 1.5.1: Main features of neo-liberalism and social democracy

The new right (elements of neo-liberalism and neo-conservatism)	Traditional/classical social democracy (the 'old left')
Minimal government	Pervasive state involvement in social and economic life
Autonomous civil society	State dominates over civil society
Market fundamentalism	Collectivism
Moral authoritarianism, plus strong economic individualism	Keynesian demand management, plus corporatism
Labour market clears like any other	Confined role for markets: the mixed or social economy Full employment
Acceptance of inequality	Strong egalitarianism
Welfare state as a safety net	Comprehensive welfare state, protecting citizens 'from cradle to grave'
Low ecological consciousness	Low ecological consciousness

Adapted from Giddens 1998

what was referred to as the 'radical centre'. In 1998 Giddens proposed a third way programme, informed by a set of third way values.

This articulation of the third way as an arguably coherent political and policy framework was not without its critics—indeed *The Third Way and its Critics* (Giddens 2000) attempts a summary and a rebuttal of the criticisms of third way politics. Those criticisms, as we note below, have distinct parallels in the New Zealand debate over the third way. Critics of the third way suggested that (adapted from 2000, pp. 22–6):

- It is an amorphous political project, difficult to pin down and lacking direction.
- It fails to sustain the proper outlook for the left and hence, whether deliberately or not, lapses into a form of conservatism.
- It accepts the basic framework of neo-liberalism, especially as concerns the global marketplace.
- It is essentially an Anglo-Saxon project, bearing the hallmarks of the societies in which it originated.
- It has no distinctive economic policy, other than allowing the market to rule the roost.
- In common with its two main rivals (neo-liberalism and traditional social democracy) it has no effective way of coping with ecological issues, save for giving token recognition to them.[3]

More recently, Giddens has acknowledged that the world has indeed moved on since the late 1980s and early 1990s and that political and social thinking needs to move with it. He acknowledged that there were some weaknesses in the initial third way ideas that needed to be remedied. Indeed, in 2003 Giddens offered the view that what was needed was a 'fourth way', and a revised version of the 'modernising' social democratic project. But he remains resolute in his view that 'the policy framework of

Table 1.5.2: Main elements of the third way

Third way values	The third way programme
Equality	The radical centre
Protection of the vulnerable	The new democratic state (the state without
Freedom as autonomy	enemies)
No rights without responsibilities	Active civil society
No authority without democracy	The democratic family
Cosmopolitan pluralism	The new mixed economy
Philosophic conservatism	Equality as inclusion
	Positive welfare
	The social investment state
	The cosmopolitan nation
	Cosmopolitan democracy

Source: Giddens 1998, pp. 66–70

the third way is coherent and intellectually powerful' (2003, p. 2). For Giddens, that framework involves the following (2003, p. 2):

- Government and the state need thorough-going reform, to make them faster moving, more effective and responsive, and to reflect the need for greater transparency and diversity in a society where consumer choice has been a prime force.
- The state should be more of an enabler than a direct provider or producer— command and control has visibly failed … [including] in the milder versions in Western societies where it took the shape of the nationalisation of the 'commanding heights' of the economy.
- Public investment has to be geared to what a society can afford—modernising social democrats place an emphasis on fiscal discipline, and upon improving the conditions of economic competitiveness.
- Economic and social justice can go hand in hand with a concentration on promoting high levels of job creation—having a job above the floor of a decent minimum wage is the best route out of poverty for anyone able to work.
- There is the need for a new citizenship contract based on responsibilities and rights—people who claim unemployment benefits, for example, should have an obligation to look for work.
- The right to live free from the fear of crime is a right of citizenship—the social democratic left should not abrogate this area of public policy, indeed, there should be no policy areas accepted as the inevitable terrain of the right.
- The third way framework is internationalist—it recognises that globalisation produces insecurities, tensions and conflicts alongside its benefits, but many of the benefits, including those generated by free trade, are real.

In answer to the question, 'what should progressives stand for?', Giddens' response was 'a strong public sphere, coupled to a thriving market economy; a pluralistic, but inclusive society; and a cosmopolitan world order, founded upon principles of international law' (Giddens 2003).

In the next section we seek some answers to the question, 'what do New Zealand progressives stand for?'

THE 'THIRD WAY' AND CENTRE-LEFT GOVERNMENTS IN NEW ZEALAND, 1999–2005

For the purposes of this discussion we can suggest two approaches to answering the questions: 'What variant of modern social democracy have Labour-led governments embraced since 1999?'; and 'To the extent that we can identify a model, to what extent does it approximate the "third way" (variously and imprecisely defined)?' The first approach is to look for explicit signals in Labour's own political and policy narrative that would give some indication of the ideological foundations of their programme in government. And the second is to examine the substance and mix of policy and to assess that against the kind of policy mix typically associated with various forms of a modern social democracy.

On the first measure, Labour in government has tended not to articulate a particularly clear or accessible ideological framework or coherent model for its policy programme. There are a number of possible reasons—there is a view within government that ideology in and of itself is a 'thought-economising' device, and that historically ideology has found its clearest expression in totalitarian excesses of the left or the right. In part, Labour's apparent aversion to 'big ideas' might be explained by the fact that in 1999 the incoming government, in the cause of rehabilitating the electoral mandate, was concerned to honour its pre-election manifesto commitments, and to the letter. The focus was less on ideas (which is something that parties 'do' in opposition) and more on policy implementation (which is what being in government is all about). In part, it may also reflect an assessment that a more pragmatic, grounded, and less ideological orientation to matters of politics and policy was required as an antidote to the more explicitly theoretical and ideological foundations of the neo-liberalism of the 1980s and 1990s.

There are, however, some markers in Labour's own narrative that suggested a coherent ideological framework. In the final days of the 1999 election campaign, the then leader of the opposition, Helen Clark, addressed a rally in Wellington and explicitly located Labour's programme in the context of a third way (cited in Kelsey 2002, p. 67; emphasis added):

> The heavy handed government of the Muldoon era drove New Zealand to the wall. But the no-handed government hasn't delivered the goods either. And that's why, like our friends in Western Europe and North America, *we have come to talk of a third way*
>
> - of smart, active, intelligent government
> - of government of vision and purpose
> - of government committed to leadership, to partnership, to facilitation, and to funding where the market fails and where investment in people is so critical.[4]

In February 2002, in a speech to a London audience, Prime Minister Helen Clark reflected on the circumstances facing the incoming government in 1999 (2002, emphasis added):

> So the challenges faced by our new government were not only to build a stronger economy and deliver more social justice, but also to keep our word to the electorate and make a minority coalition government elected under the MMP rules work ... Fortunately, and unlike 1984, there were *new social democratic models at hand* ... a social democratic revival had been in progress since Bill Clinton took his 'New Democrat' approach to the White House in 1992 ... .

In summary, *those of us who follow this path* have acknowledged the need for fresh thinking to cope with the changes in the world around us, not least of them being the fast pace of globalisation and the emergence of the knowledge economy. We have also determined to appeal to the broad mainstream of the population which abhors extremes and wants commonsense, practical solutions to everyday problems.

Today's social democrats operate in an environment where it is critical to maintain the confidence of business for the nation's economic health, and critical to carve out the nation's competitive niche in the international economy. That calls for sound macroeconomic policy, and for the state to take a leadership role in strategies for economic management, using the full ability it has to facilitate, co-ordinate, and broker, and using its funding powers to maximise investment and participation in education and skills training.

However, speeches to foreign audiences aside, there were few indications that Labour was willing to articulate to a domestic audience a coherent modern social democratic framework, whether of the third way or some other variant.

In the early part of the first full year of the new government, however, Social Development and Employment Minister Steve Maharey advanced a powerful case for constituting a coherent ideological foundation for Labour in government, arguing persuasively to a Labour party audience that:

It is important for us as a Party to make the connection between ideas and action, between principles and policy—to articulate a shared world view, and to articulate a well grounded vision of where we want to take our country (2000).

At the core of the challenge for Labour in government Maharey observed, was the need to rehabilitate the notion of 'government'. He went on to advance an argument that Labour in government was required, in effect, to find a third way alternative to the heavy-handed statism of Muldoonism and the free-market anti-statism of the new right, observing that the fourth Labour government had, 'failed to meet the challenge of finding a "third way" beyond these two extremes' (2000).

The following year, in a thoughtful presentation to an Auckland seminar hosted by the Foundation for Policy Alternatives and law firm Rudd, Watts and Stone, Maharey indicated a preference for using the expression, 'the new social democracy' over 'third way', observing that the discourse of the 'third way' was an imported one, and that the term was fundamentally imprecise. As a result, Maharey observed, in the New Zealand context use of the term 'third way' tended to demand that one, 'explain what it is not, before one can explain what it is.' Moreover Maharey commented that, '[t]here is a concern that it is a prescription that can simply be taken off the shelf and used in a variety of jurisdictions, a generic remedy for political indecision perhaps—take 5mls 3 times daily and move to the centre of the bed' (2001).

And in a particularly prescient comment given the central thesis of the Speech from the Throne that would be delivered in November 2005, Maharey noted that (2001, emphasis added):

> [T]here is a difference between taking someone else's package off the shelf on the one hand, and being open to the currents of progressive thinking within the international domain on the other. In short, we need to fashion *a New Zealand way*, but we need to mine the international seams of progressive thought and practice in doing it.[5]

In summary, these and only a limited number of other contributions aside, there are relatively few markers in Labour's own narrative while in government to suggest a programme or project consciously derived from a particular world view, or perhaps more importantly, any real attempt to locate particular policies and programmes within an overarching framework of ideas, and accessible by the wider electorate. This is a matter to which we return in our concluding comments.

The second test involves examining the substance and mix of policy and assessing that against the kind of policy mix typically associated with various forms of a modern social democracy (including variants of the third way). One would have to say that anyone looking for a policy mix that suggests a too-comfortable accommodation with neo-liberalism (as is claimed by a number of New Zealand critics of Labour's social democratic programme—see, for example, Kelsey 2002; Roper 2005), would be disappointed. Successive Labour-led governments have undertaken a number of initiatives, including:

- increased the rate of personal income tax (and been reluctant, as much for reasons of sound fiscal management, as for any other, to effect across-the-board personal and corporate tax reductions)
- repealed the Employment Contracts Act and replaced it with a statute that is more conducive to collective bargaining
- increased the minimum wage
- instituted income-related rents for state house tenants
- significantly increased income support through the Working for Families Package
- established a state-owned Kiwibank
- re-introduced a state monopoly for the provision of accident compensation insurance
- assumed (albeit out of economic and strategic necessity and not as a function of ideology) a significant public sector ownership interest in Air New Zealand and in the New Zealand rail system
- reoriented monetary policy to a flexible inflation-targeting regime that maximises the contribution of policy to economic growth and employment, while maintaining stable prices.

All of these, it might be argued, suggest a variant of a modern social democracy that comes without the policy appeasement that some suggest is characteristic of some variants of the third way.[6] However, this is not to suggest the absence of policy innovation to address the challenges of 'new times'. This is perhaps most clearly manifested in a much more developmental focus on welfare policy in general, and income support in particular.

The political contest for parties of the centre-left and the centre-right focuses on the centre of the political spectrum. But there is little new in that, indeed, as far back as 1957 Anthony Downs explained the logic of this in his seminal work *An Economic Theory of Democracy* (Downs 1957). Since the New Zealand state is increasingly a competition or market state, its role is to pursue strategies for national prosperity in conditions of global competition. Again, there is little new or indeed 'third way' in that. A further explanation is that Labour in government has been required to be sensitive to business interests. A basic understanding of the nature of unequal pluralism in the context of New Zealand's political economy suggests that this will always be the case. The issue is whether the extent of that inequality is such as to cause wholesale policy acquiescence to business demands. And on that score, the protestations of some on the left notwithstanding, there is little evidence to support the prosecution.

Indeed, as Kelsey herself notes, far from being accused of being too accommodating of neo-liberalism, some on the right have suggested that Labour's modern social democracy owes too great a debt to its more traditional ideological forebears.[7] There is an irony in the symmetry that has some on the left advancing the accusation that Labour in government has presided over a, 'more deeply embedded form of neo-liberalism' (Kelsey 2002, p. 50)[8] and some on the right claiming that Labour has been 'turning the policy clock back'.

Where the left critique—which in New Zealand has been selective and relatively shallow—may have some force is in the suggestion that Labour in government has failed to articulate a coherent philosophy or vision to underpin its policy programme (Kelsey 2002, p. 69). This is a matter we return to in the conclusion.

CONCLUSION

The third way as a concept is dated, perhaps as one commentator has suggested, even resting in the same way as Monty Python's 'Norwegian Blue parrot'.[9] Anthony Giddens has himself acknowledged that it may now be time for a fourth way. And while, as a concept, it had served to usefully illuminate some of the contextual challenges coming to bear on modern social democratic thinking, it is the iterative development of a *modern social democracy world view* within particular national, constitutional, and cultural contexts, and at particular historical junctures that is most deserving of attention. In essence the third way is simply one brand, and in New Zealand in 2006 it is one at that somewhat tired, dissipated, and uncertain.

We noted above that one of the more telling criticisms of the New Zealand variant of modern social democratic politics and policy-making has been the reluctance to advance the kind of ideological framework[10] that makes sense of the detail of policy in a coherent and accessible fashion. In some circles this is referred to as (the absence of) a *narrative framework*.

Given the comparative dimension to this chapter, it is perhaps fitting to note that this failure has been observed in other places as well. In July 2002 Britain's Chancellor of the Exchequer Gordon Brown (who has his admirers at very senior levels of the New Zealand government) handed down a budget that included significant increases in public expenditure in health, education, and welfare—Brown himself offered the observation that for him this was 'the social democratic moment'. But as *The Guardian*'s Polly Toynbee observed at the time, that moment was disguised in tones that were 'magisterially managerial, but verbally ideology free' (Toynbee 2002). To which the rejoinder might well be, 'but does that matter—surely it is the policy substance and detail that is more important?' Perhaps not. As Toynbee observed (2002):

> Political passion is the answer … A CEO announcing the dividend to shareholders is the wrong way to approach the public. The citizens are not customers passively waiting for public service delivery along with the milk … If people are not involved emotionally in the politics of making public services work, they will just demand more and more and the ballot box becomes the customer complaints desk … [Labour] might as well set about enthusing the voters: give them ideals, not pocket calculators.

The same accusation and advice could well have been levelled at Labour in government, particularly in its 2002–05 term. Major new initiatives such as Working for Families (in 2004) and KiwiSaver (in 2005) failed to fully resonate with the electorate, in large part because New Zealand Labour failed to appreciate the need to 'dish out ideology along with the cash'. And in the 2005 election campaign, Labour very nearly paid the ultimate electoral price. National party election bill-boards, while insulting to some, resonated with those looking for the kind of personal 'recipe knowledge' (ideology) to make sense of the world, and to inform the political choices they were being invited to make. As Toynbee notes, in this kind of situation the negative anecdote will have the power to defeat significant 'objective' improvements in economic and social circumstances (as New Zealand Labour discovered in the course of the 2005 election campaign).

That may well change over the term of the 2005–08 Labour-led government with an increasing acknowledgment that Labour needs to more assiduously articulate a narrative framework that allows citizens and the community to make sense of the government's vision and programmes as a whole, and to locate themselves, their families and their communities in the context of that vision and programme. In the Speech from the Throne following the 2005 election, there was perhaps a signal of a desire to provide some coherence, not just to the government's programme going forward, but also with the policy programme Labour-led governments have presided over since 1999. The speech notes that, '[t]he election result has given my government the opportunity to build on *the New Zealand way* of working that has <u>emerged over the last six years</u>' (Clark 2005).

Not a 'third way' but a 'New Zealand way'—and as the policy substance of that Speech from the Throne suggests, in many respects a modern social democratic way.

DISCUSSION QUESTIONS

1   Complete class exercise table 1.5.3 below.
2   What are the main elements of the Third Way? Does it represent a modern and progressive set of ideas, or one drawn largely from the past?
3   How persuaded are you by the view that the New Zealand Labour party has embraced the politics of the Third Way?

Table 1.5.3: Class exercise

Characteristic third way themes (Heywood 2003, p. 149)	Evidence for	Evidence against
A new politics and economics		
Socialism is dead		
Acceptance of globalisation		
Capitalism becomes an information society or knowledge economy		
Community and responsibility		
Rights and responsibilities bound together		
A consensus view of society (as contrasted to a conflict view)		
Inequality less a structural phenomenon than a reflection of the distribution of skills across society		

(Continued)

Characteristic third way themes (Heywood 2003, p. 149)	Evidence for	Evidence against
Concern with social inclusion substituted for commitment to equality		
Equality of opportunity rather than outcome Welfare targeted at the socially excluded—helping people to help themselves		
Idea of a competition or market state		
Principal role of the state is to pursue strategies for national prosperity in conditions of intensifying global competition		

NOTES

1   For a discussion on the salience of ideology for particular New Zealand parties, see Miller 2005, pp. 149–71.

2   As Giddens and others have noted (see, for example, Heywood 2003) the term 'new right' incorporates aspects of neo-liberalism or the liberal new right, and aspects of neo-conservatism or the conservative new right. For the purposes of the discussion in this chapter the term neo-liberalism will be used in preference to 'new right'.

3   Perhaps one of the more telling criticisms of the 'third way' as articulated by Giddens is the absence of a critique of capitalism (in effect a more searching and robust diagnostic and prescriptive component to the ideology of 'third wayism').

4   Others were also concerned at the need to fashion an alternative to the neo-liberal policy trajectory that had been a significant element of the fourth Labour Government's programme, and that had been intensified under successive National-led governments, particularly in the early 1990s. In a collection of essays published in the lead-up to the 1999 election and with the clear intention of encouraging a progressive shift in policy in the event of Labour being in a position to form a government, the argument was advanced that a new politics (a 'third way for New Zealand') was required in preference to the statist excesses associated with Muldoonism, and the neo-liberal thrust of politics and policy, particularly in the period from 1987 to 1996 (see Chatterjee et al. 1999). The case for change was predicated on the need for a new policy consensus to replace the 'Washington consensus' that had, as elsewhere, been so much in evidence in the New Zealand approach to economic and social policy reform in the mid to late 1980s and 1990s. In advancing a case, two of the authors argued that: 'a review of the Washington/Wellington consensus is now required ... Inquiry into the prevailing orthodoxy is also suggested by the emergence of a new brand in the

political marketplace—the Third Way ... At its most basic, the Third Way suggests an alternative to the polar options of laissez-faire capitalism on the one hand and statist regulation on the other. In the context of New Zealand's political history, the Keynesian mixed economy that was such a durable part of the New Zealand policy landscape is perhaps the "first" way and the liberal market monetarism of Douglas, Richardson et al., the interloping second' (Eichbaum & Harris 1999, p. 14).

5   Maharey proceeded to identify the principal challenges of a new social democracy: 'The challenge of economic management (fiscal discipline, stable prices, and a strategic and developmental role for the state) in which government seeks to both steer and coordinate through partnerships with business and with unions. The challenge of building state capacity, including the capacity and opportunity for meaningful citizen/ civil society engagement in governance, and the capacity for joined-up governance. The challenge of realigning economic and social policy through a developmental focus to social policy that advances social equity and economic growth and development objectives.'

6   Contrary to the predictions of some (and in particular neo-liberal critics) the policy mix has produced the lowest rate of unemployment in the OECD (3.4 per cent for the September quarter 2005), relatively stable prices, and a sound fiscal position.

7   Kelsey notes that early in the term of the 1999–2002 Labour-led government, 'Simon Upton claimed that business confidence was diving "because people are realising the Government is much less middle-of-the-road than they had expected" ... Upton condemned "the most Left-wing Government in the developed world since Francois Mitterrand came to power 20 years ago" for being "too ready to declare the death of neo-liberalism and discard many of the reforms of the past 15 years" ' (quoted in Kelsey, 2002, p. 77).

8   Part of the impetus for the 1999 publication of the collection of essays, 'The New Politics: A Third Way for New Zealand' (Chatterjee et al. 1999) was the concern that Labour in government would fail to initiate a real challenge and alternative to the Wellington variant of the Washington Consensus, and that some variants of the 'third way'—including aspects of Giddens' formulation—might be complicit in any such failure.

9   Writing in *The Guardian* on 14 July 2003 Larry Elliot observed that: 'The basic premise [of the Third Way] is that there is really not a lot wrong with the global economy that the good offices of the baby boomer progressives cannot put right. A surfeit of jargon will disguise the fact that the third wayers are free marketeers who have learned how to play the chords to Stairway to Heaven. Blair's political guru, Anthony Giddens, said last week that the third way is not a dead duck. Like Monty Python's parrot, presumably, it is just resting'.

10 To rehearse the essential nature of an ideology, it is a 'world view' that provides an analysis of the here and now, a sense of the alternative, and a road-map of ideas and policies to get from here to there.

REFERENCES

Chatterjee, S., P. Conway, P. Dalziel, C. Eichbaum, P. Harris, B. Philpott & R. Shaw 1999, *The New Politics: A Third Way for New Zealand*, Dunmore Press, Palmerston North.

Clark, H. 2002, 'Prime Minister's Address to the London School of Economics', Speech, 21 February (www.beehive.govt.nz).

Clark, H. 2005, 'Speech from the Throne', Speech, 8 November (www.beehive.govt.nz).

Downs, A. 1957, *An Economic Theory of Democracy*, Harper and Row, New York.

Eichbaum, C. & P. Harris 1999, 'Preface', in Chatterjee et al., *The New Politics: A Third Way for New Zealand*, Dunmore Press, Palmerston North.

Giddens, A. 1998, *The Third Way: The Renewal of Social Democracy*, Polity Press, Cambridge.

Giddens, A. 2000, *The Third Way and its Critics*, Polity Press, Cambridge.

Giddens, A. 2002, *Where Now for New Labour?*, Polity Press/Fabian Society and Policy Network, Cambridge.

Giddens, A. 2003, 'The Progressive Agenda', in *Progressive Futures*, Policy Network, London.

Heywood, A. 2003, *Political Ideologies: An Introduction*, Palgrave Macmillan, Basingstoke.

Hutton, W. 1996, *The State We're In*, Jonathan Cape, London.

Hutton, W. 1997, *The State to Come*, Vintage, London.

Hutton, W. & A. Giddens (eds) 2000, *On the Edge: Living with Global Capitalism*, Jonathan Cape, London.

Kelsey, J. 2002, *At the Crossroads: Three Essays*, Bridget Williams Books, Wellington.

Maharey, S. 2000, 'Partnership, Politics and the Social Democratic Project', Speech, 25 March (www.beehive.govt.nz).

Maharey, Steve, 2001, 'Values and Politics: Some Reflections on the New Social Democracy in a New Zealand Context', Speech to seminar hosted by the Foundation for Policy Initiatives and Rudd Watts and Stone, 26 March (www.beehive.govt.nz).

Miller, R. 2005, *Party Politics in New Zealand*, Oxford University Press, Melbourne.

Policy Network, 2003, *Progressive Futures*, Policy Network, London.

Roper, B.S. 2005, *Prosperity for All? Economic, Social and Political Change in New Zealand since 1935*, Dunmore Press, Palmerston North.

Toynbee, P. 2002, 'Labour Ought to Dish Out Ideology Along with the Cash', *The Guardian*, 17 July.

FURTHER READING

Giddens, A. 1998, *The Third Way: The Renewal of Social Democracy*, Cambridge, Polity Press.

Giddens, A. 2000, *The Third Way and its Critics*, Cambridge, Polity Press.

Heywood, A. 2003, *Political Ideologies: An Introduction*, Palgrave Macmillan, Basingstoke.

Kelsey, J. 2002, *At the Crossroads: Three Essays*, Bridget Williams Books, Wellington.

Maharey, Steve, 2001, 'Values and Politics: Some Reflections on the New Social Democracy in a New Zealand Context', Speech to seminar hosted by the Foundation for Policy Initiatives and Rudd Watts and Stone, 26 March (www.beehive.govt.nz).

Economic Setting

Paul Dalziel

The end of the twentieth century in New Zealand was notable for a remarkable programme of radical economic reforms carried out by the fourth Labour government of 1984 to 1990 and the fourth National government of 1990 to 1996. Almost all countries engaged in some market liberalisation during that period, but New Zealand went much further than any other Western country. David Henderson, who was head of the Economics and Statistics Department of the Organisation of Economic Cooperation and Development (OECD) at the time, observes (1996, p. 13): 'in no other OECD country has there been so systematic an attempt at the same time (1) to redefine and limit the role of government, and (2) to make public agencies and their operations more effective, more transparent, and more accountable'. Not only did the government privatise many of its trading departments (and corporatised the others), but innovative legislation such as the Reserve Bank of New Zealand Act 1989, the Employment Contracts Act 1991 and the Fiscal Responsibility Act 1994 severely restricted the previous ability of ministers to intervene in the economy in pursuit of short-term objectives. The motivation behind these statutory reforms was that general economic policy should be limited to promoting effective competition in domestic markets against a backdrop of balanced monetary and fiscal policies producing stable prices and tax rates.

The National–New Zealand First coalition government of 1996–98 and the minority National government after the dissolution on 26 August 1998 pursued policies in accordance with that vision, although some cracks in the consensus did emerge. The 1996 Coalition Agreement, for example, postponed by twelve months the second round of tax cuts scheduled for July 1997 in order to allow an increase in government spending of $5 billion over three years. The Policy Targets Agreement signed between the Minister of Finance and the Governor of the Reserve Bank on 10 December 1996 included for the first time references to economic growth, employment and development, while the ceiling of the inflation target range was raised from 2 to 3 per cent. And a keynote address to the National party by Bill English told delegates that it was time 'to write the next chapter of the New Zealand story', acknowledging that New Zealand's economic leadership had often come from government, partly as a result of its sheer size (English 1999). The 1999 general election produced a change of government that took this process a step further. The Labour–Alliance minority government raised the top income tax rate from 33 to 39 cents in the dollar, placed a moratorium on further sales of state assets, introduced new policies of direct government involvement in regional economic development, replaced the Employment Contracts Act 1991 with the Employment Relations Act 2000, and made a number of other policy changes that would have been unthinkable under the economic policy framework of the late 1980s and early 1990s. Helen Clark remained prime minister after the 2002 election, and the policies of her first term continued into the second.

The economic results were impressive. The economy expanded by 25 per cent in six years, inflation remained within the target band of 1–3 per cent per annum, and unemployment fell from 7 per cent in the middle of 1999 to below 4 per cent in 2005. Such a strong economic performance had consequences for the government's own budget, as tax revenue rose sharply. This set the scene for the main debate over economic policy in the 2005 general election. The Labour party argued that the surpluses generated by economic growth should be used to fund ongoing growth in public services such as social security, education, and health. The National party argued that the surpluses should be returned to citizens in the form of tax cuts, reducing the size of the public sector relative to the expanding economy over time.

These observations provide the structure of this chapter. Its first section briefly describes the economic rationale for the economic policy framework produced by the 1984–94 reforms. The second section discusses the direction adopted by the government after 1999, based on concepts that some authors have labelled as 'third way politics'. The third section describes the debate in the 2005 general election about New Zealand's future economic direction.

NEW ZEALAND'S COMPETITIVE MARKET FRAMEWORK

At the core of the major theoretical paradigm used by most professional economists lie two propositions known as the first and second theorems of welfare economics. The first theorem states that any equilibrium in a perfectly competitive economy is efficient, in the sense that no individual can be made better off without at least one other person being made worse off (a condition known as 'Pareto efficiency'). The second theorem states that any Pareto efficient outcome can be produced by an appropriate redistribution of initial endowments within perfectly competitive markets. These two theorems have been 'proved' within a sophisticated mathematical model known as general equilibrium theory, assuming that certain mathematical axioms hold (consumer preferences, for example, must be 'convex, continuous and strongly monotonic'). It should be noted that there is a debate within the economics profession about whether such formalist proofs are relevant for real world analysis (see, for example, the forum on this topic in the *Economic Journal*, no. 451, November 1998), as well as considerable work examining the consequences when the axioms of the model do not hold. Nevertheless, these two theorems provide the intellectual foundation for much economic policy advice, and it is easy to see why. Policy-makers want to avoid policies that are not efficient, and the theorems explain how perfect competition eliminates at least one form of inefficiency—Pareto inefficiency.

There are also dynamic reasons for creating markets that are *contestable* (that is, markets in which neither existing firms nor regulatory barriers can prevent new firms from entering the industry), if not perfectly competitive (that is, markets that have a large number of suppliers with absolutely no market power). The most important is the impact that contestability has on innovation and technological development. In an industry with one dominant producer (particularly if that producer is a government department not subject to normal commercial incentives), there is a strong temptation for the producer to rely on its market strength to earn an adequate rate of return on its capital rather than by being responsive to the demands of the market or to cost-saving opportunities. In a contestable market, such complacency would allow new entrants to undercut the dominant firm with innovative marketing or new technology, to the benefit of consumers.

In New Zealand, considerations such as these led to major policy reforms after 1984 to deregulate domestic markets, to reduce protection from imported goods, to open up public sector enterprises to greater competition, to privatise many of the government's former trading departments, and to focus the Commerce Commission on promoting contestability and prosecuting anti-competitive practices. Market-based reforms were also introduced into state-funded activities (symbolised in the renaming of hospitals as 'Crown Health Enterprises', before this name change was reversed in the 1997 Budget) and were also applied with less theoretical justification to network industries such as telecommunications and electricity supply. Perhaps most controversially, New Zealand's previous legislative framework for industrial relations going back nearly a hundred years was repealed in favour of the Employment Contracts Act 1991. The preamble of the new Act described its purpose as being 'to promote an efficient labour market', in keeping with the economic policy framework described above.

The main mechanism by which competition achieves efficiency is through changes in relative prices. In perfect competition, every market price performs two functions. It conveys to buyers the true marginal cost of supplying the good or service to the market, and it conveys to sellers the commodity's true marginal benefit to consumers. If a good becomes more expensive to produce, its price rises to send a signal to consumers to consider cheaper alternatives. If a good becomes more highly valued by purchasers, again its price rises, sending a signal to suppliers to reallocate resources to meet the increased demand. This mechanism is weakened, however, if such relative price signals are masked by general inflation or by fluctuations in the level of aggregate demand driven by erratic changes in government spending or taxation.

These considerations set the scene for reforms to the government's macroeconomic policy after 1984. First, the New Zealand dollar was floated in March 1985, so that market forces rather than the government now sets this most important price in a small open economy. Second, the Reserve Bank of New Zealand Act 1989 simplified the statutory objectives of monetary policy to provide a single focus on maintaining stability in the general level of prices. Third, the Fiscal Responsibility Act 1994 (more recently incorporated into the Public Finance Act 1989) set out generic principles for fiscal policy, including that government expenditure should not exceed its revenue on average over a reasonable period of time, and that the level and stability of tax rates should be reasonably predictable for future years. All of these initiatives sought to provide a stable macroeconomic environment, free of arbitrary short-term government intervention, to allow market prices to function efficiently in allocating resources within the economy.

At the microeconomic level (that is, considering individual firms and industries), the impact of these reforms on efficiency, innovation and the level of service was typically very positive, particularly in the privatised corporations that were previously government trading departments (Air New Zealand, the Forestry Service, the Railways Department and Telecom, for example). The reduction in import barriers increased the range of goods and services available for sale in New Zealand shops. Economic studies have shown substantial increases in productivity in key industries such as the finance sector and the transport sector. At the macroeconomic level (that is, considering the economy as a whole), the results of the economic reforms were not so positive, at least not immediately. Dalziel (2002), for example, showed that: (i) New Zealand sacrificed a large volume of real per capita gross domestic product after 1987 (especially compared to Australia); (ii) its average unemployment rate increased substantially after 1988; (iii) labour productivity growth declined after 1992; and (iv) the per capita real income of low-income households in 1996 was more than 3 per cent lower in absolute terms than it had been in 1984. In short, the programme of economic policy reforms did not turn out to be the panacea that many hoped it would be for New Zealand's poor economic performance.

THE 'THIRD WAY' FOR ECONOMIC POLICY

Thus the outcome of New Zealand's economic policy reforms contained an 'apparent paradox' (Brash 1998, p. 163). At the microeconomic level of individual markets, there were large improvements in labour productivity and consumer choice in many industries. At the macroeconomic level, per capita real income growth remained disappointing compared to other developed countries, and many New Zealanders found that their choices continued to be restricted by lengthy unemployment and persistent poverty. Faced with this evidence, some economists counselled patience, expressing cautious optimism that benefits from the reforms would emerge in time. Others argued that New Zealand's weak macroeconomic performance could be explained by the failure of the government to persevere with the process of reform, and urged market-based policies to be extended into areas such as primary and secondary education. The new government elected in 1999, however, argued instead that the reform programme's conception of the role of government in economic policy had not been adequate.

It was not hard in 1999 to produce a set of stylised facts to explain the reform paradox. It was generally agreed that there had been considerable disguised unemployment in New Zealand before the reforms, since government departments such as the Forestry Service and the Railways had been required to employ more workers than was necessary for their business. It was also generally agreed that many of the medium productivity jobs in the manufacturing sector could exist only because they had been protected by high tariffs on imported manufactured products. Thus when the economic reforms corporatised the government departments and removed the tariffs, this allowed managers to improve the profitability of their firms by making excess workers redundant and by purchasing cheaper imported goods at the expense of domestic producers. This contributed to the sharp improvements in productivity at the industry level.

At the national level, however, the macroeconomic impact depended on the fate of the workers made redundant during the restructuring. If many remained unemployed (the average unemployment rate in New Zealand appeared to have increased from around 3 or 4 per cent before 1984 to around 6 or 7 per cent after the reforms) and if the others were absorbed into new jobs with relatively low wages, then this would explain why there had been no improvement in the country's per capita real income growth and why poverty levels had increased. Low wages imply low productivity, while unemployed workers are not productive at all.

That stylised explanation was relatively uncontroversial in 1999; the real debate was whether economic policy could do anything about it. In particular, was it possible to design some set of policies that improved the economy's aggregate performance without creating self-defeating inefficiencies in individual markets? The importance of this question was not restricted to New Zealand, lying at the core of many political debates in countries such as the United Kingdom and the USA under the heading of 'third way politics' (see, for example, Giddens 2001). Within the 'third way' framework, it is argued that substantial direct state intervention in markets (the 'first way', introduced in New Zealand by the first Labour government in the 1930s) is no longer appropriate, and that the laissez-faire style of no state direction at all (the 'second way', introduced in New Zealand by the fourth Labour government in the 1980s) is also inadequate. Instead, there is a role for 'smart government' to improve on free market outcomes through the use of selective interventions in the economic system. This was the approach adopted by the New Zealand government after 1999.

Third way politics tends to mean different things to different people. Nevertheless, a common element is the claim that free markets on their own do not produce equal opportunities and social justice (and may widen wealth disparities over time), so that in a social democracy there is a role for the government to redress the balance between rich and poor in the marketplace. Compared to previous generations, there is less willingness to tax the rich (under Sir Robert Muldoon's government, for example, the top tax rate was 66 cents in the dollar; it is now 39 cents) in order to provide direct income support to the poor (consider, for example, the 1991 benefit cuts), but there remains a belief that the resources of the state can be used to make a difference for people who would otherwise have few opportunities in a totally free market system.

In particular, recall the second theorem of welfare economics that any Pareto efficient outcome can be produced by *an appropriate redistribution of initial endowments* within perfectly competitive markets. Third way economics can be interpreted as an application of the italicised part of this theorem. Instead of interfering with competitive markets, the objective is to design policies that provide extra resources (that is, extra endowments) to the most vulnerable members of society. These need not be simply a financial transfer to particular households in the form of generous social welfare income support, but might take the form of extra education and health resources in low income neighbourhoods. Or it might take the form of an integrated industry and regional development policy that aims to provide high productivity employment in areas of the country that otherwise have few economic opportunities. Or it might take the form of public sector investment in economic infrastructure in order to facilitate private sector initiatives that take advantage of new technologies and business opportunities. Or it might take the form of retraining allowances for workers affected by the closure of a large local employer as the result of economic restructuring or reduced import protection.

A good example of third way politics took place in the government's 2004 budget, which announced a new Working for Families programme expected to cost $1.1 billion per annum when fully implemented in 2007–08. This policy involved extra financial support for low-income families, particularly for low-income families with at least one parent in paid employment. The last time a government had sought to assist this group had been in 1996 when Bill Birch provided tax cuts targeted to low-income working families. Under that approach, only 7 per cent of the tax cuts were expected to go to the poorest 20 per cent of households, and the biggest winners were dual income households with no children. Michael Cullen's Working for Families package was much more effective at targeting resources to its target group.

The economic rationale for third way interventions is that the overall success of an economic system depends on all members of the system having the opportunity to participate in high productivity work, so that they are then in a position to exchange the fruits of their work in the marketplace. The system as a whole is weakened if significant numbers of people become trapped in unemployment or in low productivity jobs, particularly after a period of radical restructuring such as New Zealand experienced in the 1980s and 1990s. If the government is able to design economic policy that ensures productive work is widely available, then this has the potential to improve social welfare without reducing economic efficiency.

THE ECONOMIC POLICY DEBATE IN 2005

It must not be thought that third way politics is a simple solution to New Zealand's economic problems. It is just as possible for bad policy to be created within a third way framework as in other frameworks, and there remains scope for considerable debate about the details of an appropriate economic policy that is in accord with the principles just described. Nevertheless, the third way now seems to define the central position of New Zealand's political spectrum, so that there were few serious challenges in the 2005 general election campaign to the core elements of economic policy as they have been developed over the country's previous twenty years.

Instead, the main economic debate in 2005 focused on whether the policy framework should be adjusted towards a smaller public sector to allow for significant tax cuts. To set a context for that debate, consider the Statement of the Crown's Financial Performance, 2004–05, in table 1.6.1. The Crown's total revenue for the year ending 30 June 2005 was just over $67 billion. Most of that revenue came from taxation ($46.6 billion) amounting to 31.3 per cent of nominal gross domestic product for the same period. That revenue funded Crown expenses, of which the largest item was social security and welfare expenditure of $18.5 billion. This included New Zealand Superannuation grants of $6.1 billion, domestic purposes benefits of $1.5 billion and unemployment benefits of $0.8 billion. Education and health were the other large items of public expenditure, at around $8.5 billion each. Total expenses were less than total revenues by $6.2 billion, with about a third of that surplus ($2.1 billion) being used to build up the New Zealand Superannuation Fund.

Table 1.6.1: Statement of the Crown's financial performance, 2004/05

Revenues	$m	$m
Individual Tax	21,992	
Corporate Tax	8,420	
Goods and Services Tax (GST)	10,198	
Other Tax	6,014	
Levies, Fees, Fines and Penalties	3,115	
Sales of Goods and Services	11,331	
Other Revenue	5,995	
TOTAL REVENUE		67,065
Expenses	$m	$m
Social Security and Welfare	18,522	
Education	8,619	
Health	8,444	
Transport and Communications	5,948	
Economic and Industrial Services	4,859	
Law and Order	2,131	
Core Government Services	2,085	
Heritage, Culture and Recreation	2,032	
Defence	1,229	
Primary Services	1,128	
Other Expenditure	5,913	
TOTAL EXPENDITURE		60,910
Revenues Less Expenses		6,155

Source: Financial Statements of the New Zealand Government for the Year Ended 30 June 2005, Document B.11, downloaded from www.treasury.govt.nz

As the economy expands over time, tax revenue grows. In a typical year, the New Zealand economy might grow by 3 per cent in real terms, and inflation might be 2 per cent. That combination would generate about $2 billion in extra tax revenue, which is sometimes called the government's 'growth dividend'. The resulting increase in total revenue of $2 billion in the top half of table 1.6.1 could allow the government to spend an equal amount of extra expenditure on the items in the bottom half of the table without reducing the surplus. This approach was adopted in the 2005 budget, which explicitly allowed for $1.9 billion of extra spending each year to be funded by the growth dividend. This was to ensure that spending on public services such as social security, education, and health kept pace with expected growth in the economy.

The general election debate on economic policy started after the May 2005 budget, when Michael Cullen was criticised for failing to adequately address an anomaly in New Zealand's tax system. Taxpayers in 2005 faced three statutory tax rates: income up to $38,000 was taxed at 19.5 per cent, income between $38,001 and $60,000 was taxed at 33 per cent, and income above $60,000 was taxed at 39 per cent. Since inflation lay between 1 and 3 per cent, the threshold values of $38,000 and $60,000 were being reduced in real terms by about 2 per cent per annum. This pushed some taxpayers into higher tax brackets even when they had no increase in their real income. The 2005 budget promised to address this issue with small adjustments to the thresholds, but not until April 2008.

In contrast, the National Party's election campaign promised to raise the tax thresholds dramatically so that by April 2007 the $38,000 threshold would have been $50,000 and the $60,000 threshold would have been $100,000. National also promised to reduce the effective tax rate on lower-middle incomes, to remove the carbon tax scheduled for 2007 and to lower corporate taxes in 2008. The total annual cost of National's package by 2008–09 (including the elements it retained from the already existing Working for Families policy) was estimated at $4.6 billion. This was more than three times the value of Labour's package, which relied on Working for Families, modestly expanded from $1.1 to $1.5 billion per annum.

The sheer size of the National Party package produced some attractive features. First, it more or less matched Labour's aim of delivering additional resources to low- and middle-income families. Labour's targeted promises still tended to be more attractive for larger families, but National's tax-based promises tended to be particularly attractive for dual income families. Second, universal tax cuts would have allowed parents to keep more of their gross income, rather than facing a higher tax rate and filling out forms to claim tax credits for their children. This would have generated extra incentives for earning income in the first place. Third, National was able to offer higher disposable income to all taxpayers, including those who missed out under Labour's targeted policies. In particular, households with no children and high-income households would have benefited from their package.

A large part of the subsequent debate centred on whether the country could afford to spend an extra $3.1 billion on tax cuts. National's plan was to fund most of the cuts from future growth dividends. National Party Finance spokesperson, John Key, argued that the figure of $1.9 billion set aside in the 2005 budget for increased future spending each year was too much, and promised a target of $1.5 billion instead. This policy would have saved $0.4 billion in year 1, $0.8 billion in year 2, $1.2 billion in year 3, and so on. Eventually the savings would have been sufficient to cover the tax cuts, and any gaps in the interval could have been covered by increasing public debt. Thus it was clear that the tax cuts could have been implemented, but the price would have been a much smaller public sector relative to the size of the economy.

In the end, Labour won two more seats than National, but it is unlikely that the election result will have ended this particular debate. The trade-off between taxation and public services is one of the most sensitive issues that any government must face, and is often the main point of difference between a centre-left coalition and a centre-right coalition in modern politics.

DISCUSSION QUESTIONS

1 The criterion of 'Pareto efficiency' normally means that economists do not pay much attention to income redistribution, since this makes those who give up income worse off. What role, if any, do you think the state should have in interfering with the distribution of income produced by the marketplace?

2 Compared to other countries, New Zealand's economic reforms were more radical, more comprehensive and more quickly introduced. What sort of political mandate do you think a government should have before it introduces policy reform on that scale?

3 'The Third Way' is one of those slogans imported from overseas into New Zealand policy debates. Do you think that the concept has any relevance for current government policy? Explain your answer.

4 The preamble to the Employment Contracts Act 1991 described its purpose as being 'to promote an efficient labour market'. Section 3 of the Employment Relations Act 2000 describes its first purpose as being 'to build productive employment relationships through the promotion of mutual trust and confidence in all aspects of the employment environment and of the employment relationship'. To what extent do you think that labour should be treated as a market commodity like any other? What role, if any, do you think the government should play in regulating employment relationships?

5 The main economic policy debate in the 2005 general election focused on tax cuts versus maintaining the size of the public sector relative to the expanding economy. Do you think New Zealand taxpayers get value for money from the government's investment in public services such as social security, health and education?

REFERENCES

Brash, D. 1998, 'New Zealand's Economic Reforms: A Model for Change?', *Reserve Bank Bulletin*, 61/2, June.

Dalziel, P. 2002, 'New Zealand's Economic Reforms: An Assessment?', *Review of Political Economy*, 14/1, pp. 31–46.

English, B. 1999, 'Brilliant Back-Yarders', keynote address to the New Zealand National Party's 63rd Annual Conference, Wellington Town Hall, 11 July.

Giddens, A. (ed) 2001, *The Global Third Way Debate*, Polity Press, Cambridge.

Henderson, D. 1996, *Economic Reform: New Zealand in an International Perspective*, New Zealand Business Roundtable, Wellington.

FURTHER READING

Boston, J., Dalziel P. & S. St John (eds) 1999, *Redesigning the Welfare State in New Zealand*, Oxford University Press, Auckland.

Chatterjee, S., P. Conway, P. Dalziel, C. Eichbaum, P. Harris, B. Philpott & R. Shaw 1999, *The New Politics: A Third Way for New Zealand*, Dunmore Press, Palmerston North.

Dalziel, P. & R. Lattimore 2004, *The New Zealand Macroeconomy: Striving for Sustainable Growth with Equity*, Oxford University Press, Melbourne.

Easton, B. 1999, *The Whimpering of the State: Policy After MMP*, Auckland University Press, Auckland.

Giddens, A. 1999, *The Third Way: The Renewal of Social Democracy*, Polity Press, Cambridge.

Globalisation and Identity

Jacqui True

'Globalisation' refers to the multiple ways in which economies, cultures, and societies are increasingly integrating. Successive New Zealand governments have embraced globalisation and viewed global integration as an opportunity for New Zealand to improve its comparative economic position and to expand its international influence in global governance and multilateral forums. As Prime Minister Helen Clark has said:

> The New Zealand way is much more than the clichés of 'number eight wire' or 'punching above our weight'. It is based on the belief that as a confident, diverse, inclusive Pacific nation, we can work together to find new opportunities and market our best ideas profitably to the world (Clark 2005).

Critics however, often view globalisation as a threat to the nation–state and a force for the homogenisation of national identities. Those protesting against the actions of the World Trade Organization (WTO) during the Doha Round in Hong Kong, and against the World Bank, and the International Monetary Fund (IMF), claimed that global integration threatens local diversity. Yet claims of this sort run up against the emergence of stronger assertions of national identity and cultural distinctiveness by states and citizens. As states compete for global capital, for instance, we see intense efforts being made to play up the distinctiveness of local characteristics and competitive advantages. Louis Pauly (2000, p. 120) argues that the logic of markets embraces globalism while the logic of politics remains deeply marked by nationalism. Yet far from being contradictory, I contend that these logics can serve to reinforce one another (True 2004; Devetak & True 2006).

This chapter explores the interplay between economic globalisation and national identity in New Zealand through two examples. The first assesses the creation of

Brand New Zealand and efforts to play up New Zealand's national distinctiveness in the quest for global competitive advantage and economic development. The second example assesses the America's Cup yachting race as an example of a global spectacle. Like *The Lord of the Rings* movies or speculation about the 2011 Rugby World Cup, it put New Zealand on the world map while also having payoffs for the national economy. These examples suggest that both the economic and the political relations that come with globalisation are not only more complex but also often more subtle than has been portrayed by their most vocal critics. New Zealand's national identity has always been rooted in a narrative of economic progress, of the triumph of pioneering individuals against nature. In recent times, this national narrative has been reinvented to serve the ends of global economic success.

CHANGING IDENTITIES: FROM NATION–STATE TO BRAND–STATE

Economic nationalism and economic globalisation are not opposing forces, but integrally related, often mutually reinforcing ideologies and processes (see Helleiner 2002). In his article 'The Rise of the Brand State', Peter Van Hamm (2001) argues that states, cities, and regions, like firms, market themselves professionally through aggressive sales techniques to attract investment and business. In this quest to attract capital, the public relations expert Wally Olins (2000, p. 1) writes, 'nations increasingly emphasise nationality' even though global companies increasingly ignore it. Global interconnectedness facilitated by the revolution in information technology over the past two decades has made each state more aware of itself, its image, reputation, and attitude as seen in other parts of the world. This situation presents new opportunities for states to leverage their national stock.

In the global market, intense competition occurs over product differentiation as well as price. Consumer demand is increasingly complex and sophisticated. In her book, *No Logo*, Naomi Klein (1999) registers this change in the capitalist economy. Whereas once goods and services were distinguished by their material use value, now they are distinguished by their symbolic value. In contemporary capitalism, the product is the brand, and the brand is the product. Klein (1999, p. 17) gives the classic example of the *Absolut Vodka* marketing campaign: The actual 'product disappears and its brand [is] nothing but a blank-bottle-shaped space that [can] be filled with whatever content a particular audience most want[s] from its brand'. Apply that same formula to nation–states and you have 'nation–state', the 'brand–state'. Image and reputation are an essential part of the nation–state's competitive advantage in the global political economy: A nation–state's image—and the successful transference of this image to its exports—is just as important as what they actually produce and sell. Countries represent themselves to global employees, consumers, and investors as if in a beauty contest. In the case of New Zealand, a 'pure' clean, green image has been cultivated in the recent past, and a new brand identity is currently in the making (see Campbell-Hunt et al. 2001; Eagles 2002). In 2005 the global marketing organisation Anholt-GMI ranked New Zealand the tenth strongest national brand in the world.

New Zealand: Clean, green, and GE free?

New Zealand's clean, green image has been promoted for a number of years with a view to gaining a competitive edge for New Zealand exports and tourism business. The New Zealand Ministry of the Environment recently commissioned a report on New Zealand's brand and found that on an annual basis this image was worth about NZ$530 million to the tourism sector and NZ$938 million to the economy as a whole.[1] Linking New Zealand products to New Zealand's apparently clean and green environment has been found to have considerable payoffs for export revenues.

The producers of everything from food and wine, to fashion and film, to boats and biotechnology seek to distinguish their products on global markets by playing on New Zealand's environmental reputation, if not its actual environmental record. But this image is served up not only for foreign audiences; it also has the effect of bolstering New Zealand's own national identity, and commodifying the land for commercial gain while masking environmental problems (see Bell 2002; Bührs & Bartlett 1993; Hunt 1993). Most New Zealanders believe in the brand, as do tourists. They see New Zealand as a land 'little affected by industrial pollution, overpopulation, traffic congestion, noise, urban decay'; as a country associated with 'national parks, scenic beauty, wilderness areas, beautiful deserted beaches, green pastures and a friendly population' (Hunt 1993, p. 4). To continually reconfirm our own sense of identity and security in the nation, we need tourists to describe our country as 'beautiful'.

To avoid embarrassment in their quest for global distinction, New Zealand producers have been forced to live up to their 'environmental quality' branding at home (see Oram 2001; www.new-zealand.com/nzway.html). For example, a new sustainable winegrowing scheme has encouraged New Zealand winemakers to introduce environmentally sound practices so that they fulfil the logo 'New Zealand wine—riches of a clean, green land' when they market their product overseas. No other winegrowing region or country has developed as far-reaching an environmental scorecard on all aspects of its wine production, and there are reported to be European buyers that will reward this effort.

Likewise, the Sustainability Council, formed by five prominent New Zealanders, has sought to extend the moratorium on genetic engineering in order to make good on New Zealand's image overseas.[2] They believe that New Zealand butter, lamb, and fruit would lose its premium place in the market overnight if we adopted genetically engineered (GE, or genetically modified) agriculture. Moreover, they claim that New Zealand producers could obtain higher returns from food exports if they market themselves as clean, green, and 'GE-free' (Neill 2003). In this way, economic globalisation has provided the momentum for national self-consciousness about environmental sustainability, and indeed, a renewed sense of national identity based on environmental reputation. In turn, this local environmental awareness is expected to have payoffs on the global market.

One hundred per cent pure New Zealand

Since the early 1990s, New Zealand tourism has increased its revenues threefold from NZ$1.9 billion in 1990 to NZ$6.1 billion in 2005. Since 1999, visitor numbers have more than doubled to approximately 2.4 million per year (Chan 2005). The tourism sector is now second to the dairy industry in export earnings. This impressive growth can be attributed to the creation of a global marketing brand for New Zealand.

Tourism New Zealand, the government agency responsible for motivating international travellers to visit New Zealand, launched '100% Pure New Zealand' in 1999 (Morgan et al. 2002). It followed on the heels of re-branding efforts in other countries such as Great Britain ('from Rule Britannia to Cool Britannia') also seeking to re-energise their economic base with foreign capital. The '100% Pure' brand is the first New Zealand global marketing campaign that uses consistent messages and imagery in all markets, 'offering visitors a single, compelling reason to visit New Zealand'.[3] At a cost of $30 million per year, it seeks to capitalise on New Zealand's international reputation as an untouched paradise, and lately, as a safe haven from terrorism. Although the obvious question arises: How 'untouched' is New Zealand when more than two million tourists a year trample the same ground?

Anthropologist Jonathan Friedman (1995, pp. 201–2) distinguishes weak globalisation, where the local assimilates the global, from strong globalisation, which involves the homogenisation of local contexts. Tourist marketing campaigns like '100% Pure New Zealand' are akin to a weak form of globalisation. Such campaigns aim to capture market share by accentuating local novelty and representing it to the gaze of the global tourist. Strong globalisation is indicated by the creation of tourist venues in different local settings that reflect a standardised, predictable global product, such as Club Meds on Third World islands. Clearly, Tourism New Zealand would like to win tourist dollars on New Zealand's own terms, presenting a unique product to the global market. Indeed, Tourism New Zealand wants not more tourists but wealthier tourists who are prepared to pay a premium for authenticity and for the conservation of the locales they are visiting (Da Cruz 2005). Of course the authenticity of the New Zealand experience is questionable when it is deliberately crafted with an eye on the tourism dollar.

Selling the nation? Government branding

Since the '100% Pure' campaign was launched, the government has embarked on an overall branding effort to build an identity for New Zealand as a place of knowledge and prosperity that will earn it a more prominent competitive place in the global economy. In February 2002, Prime Minister Helen Clark (2002) outlined the government's 'framework for growing an innovative New Zealand'. She stated that 'government will work with the private sector to develop a consistent brand image of New Zealand across our industry sectors. As well as being seen as clean and green, we need to be more widely perceived as smart and innovative'. In short, while the 'clean and green' slogan captures the so-called 'untouched' physical beauty of New Zealand, it says nothing about the capabilities of New Zealanders in a globally competitive environment. In seeking to re-brand the New Zealand economy, 'the government is leveraging off both [the ongoing success] of *The Lord of the Rings* and the defence of the America's Cup. These two events help promote an image of New Zealand as technologically advanced, creative, and successful'.

The Labour-led coalition government has been very active in promoting a new brand identity to allow New Zealand to project itself externally. One of the major goals of the government's 'Growth and Innovation Framework' is to increase New Zealand's international connectedness. Implementing this goal involves attracting quality foreign investment; aggressive export promotion, deepening international networks, and improved branding of New Zealand offshore. In order to build Brand New Zealand, the government has poured considerable resources into non-traditional economic spheres such as sports, film, design, and tourism that represent New Zealand as an upmarket, innovative, and dynamic economy. This global marketing is intended to help New Zealand attract and retain international investment and talented people, including expatriate New Zealanders.

The designer fashion industry illustrates the government's support for a non-traditional economic sphere with growth potential. With its high profile the designer fashion industry could positively affect export performance across the whole New Zealand economy. Trade and Enterprise New Zealand considers it to be 'an industry that not only gives a very strong message about itself ... but it also sends a bigger message about New Zealand as a country, because through our creative skills in areas like fashion and film we have the ability to make really strong connections with global opinion makers in the lifestyle area' (Perrott 2005, p. 19).

Peter Van Hamm (2000, p. 3) argues that to do their jobs well in the future, politicians and public servants will have to train themselves in brand asset management. Their tasks, he says, will include 'finding a brand niche for their state, engaging in competitive marketing, assuring consumer satisfaction and most of all creating brand loyalty. Brand states will compete with super-brands, EU, CNN, Microsoft, the Catholic Church ... . In this crowded arena, states that lack relevant brand equity will not survive.' Indeed, small states like New Zealand will have to work extra hard to be seen and heard in such an arena, drawing on proportionately large government budgets for international marketing while utilising political leaders and prominent individuals as offshore ambassadors

LOYALTY TO NATION: THE AMERICA'S CUP CAMPAIGN

Economic globalisation does not herald the end of the nation–state or national identities. Scholte (2000, p. 163) makes the point that closer contact with 'foreigners' through global networks often heightens the sense of national distinctiveness. Indeed, 'global spectacles like the Olympics and the World Cup thrive on nationalist fervour'. The America's Cup yacht race is yet another spectacle where global competition ignites nationalism and national identity anew. More than a sporting event among nations, the America's Cup has always been a contest involving technology, design, and innovation. Since New Zealand won the Cup in 1995, New Zealanders have portrayed the challenge series as a contest between a small, relatively insignificant nation of modest means, on the one hand, and footloose corporate syndicates with twice the budget but none of the national passion, on the other. Thus, 'Kiwi' patriotism is pitted against the purchasing power of some of the world's wealthiest men.

The 1851 founding document of the America's Cup, 'The Deed of Gift', requires 'friendly competition among nations'. In the America's Cup Challenge of 2003, however, only the defender, Team New Zealand, represented a nation–state and was funded by public donations and a national set of corporate sponsors organised as a trust. The national myth has been that, with an abundance of coastal waters, all New Zealanders can partake in sailing from a young age, regardless of class upbringing. In contrast, the six teams that competed to challenge Team New Zealand in 2003 were each backed by billionaires who had derived their wealth from the profits of their multinational enterprises. They included Ernesto Bertarelli of Swiss-based Alinghi, Larry Ellison of San Francisco-based Oracle/BMW, and Craig McCaw and Paul Allen of Seattle's OneWorld.

The Alinghi challenger Bertarelli's private campaign, in particular, served as a counterpoint to the national campaign of Team New Zealand.[4] (Alinghi won the Louis Vuitton Cup in late 2002 and the right to challenge Team New Zealand in early 2003). Many of the foreign challengers hired the very New Zealand sailors, builders, and analysts who had worked together as part of Team New Zealand to successfully defend the Cup in 2000. But the mass Kiwi exodus was sparked when Bertarelli recruited the winning Team New Zealand skipper, Russell Coutts, as his skipper for the 2003 Challenge. Coutts, a New Zealander, was an Olympic yachting champion and the recipient of an imperial honour for his service to New Zealand.

He accepted a US$5 million offer to become the Alinghi skipper, taking with him Team New Zealand's strategist, Brad Butterworth. Thus, despite its history as a race among nations, one third of the sailors on the water in the semi-finals of the America's Cup Challenge were New Zealanders and former members of Team New Zealand.[5]

The Blackheart campaign

The spectacle of their former Cup-defending heroes selling out to the highest bidder provoked fellow New Zealanders into demonising the 'traitors' in a wave of overt nationalism. New Zealand's effort to support the home team was coined the 'loyal' campaign in an attempt to give Team New Zealand the hometown edge (ASB Bank 2003). The television advertisement showcasing the campaign featured a black and white line-up of prominent New Zealanders standing along the New Zealand coastline, arms-linked, hands across heart (as in the American pledge of allegiance). This visual was accompanied by the Team New Zealand theme song, 'Loyal', a popular hit from the 1980s composed and sung by local artist Dave Dobbyn. The subtext of the song was spoken softly, but no doubt was left about its intent. On the Team New Zealand advertisement, the nationalist message was stripped of all grace notes: 'They've come from all four corners to have a go at what's ours. It's their billions against our team of three point nine millions. Team New Zealand—we're with you all of the way.'[6]

Latching onto the darker side of the 'loyal' national campaign, a private campaign supporting Team New Zealand emerged in the run-up to the 2003 America's Cup Challenge. Coined the 'Blackheart' campaign, its slogan was 'country before money'. Founded by an advertising executive Dave Walden, and several prominent New Zealanders who described themselves as 'staunch and true' patriots, Blackheart took aim at Coutts and the other sailors who defected from Team New Zealand (Taylor 2002). They did not want to see the country lose the Cup to a foreign syndicate, nor did they want to lose the billions of dollars that every defence of the Cup was claimed to generate for the local economy:[7] 'When it comes to New Zealand I believe we have always seen this as a national team. That's why it's not called Team Steinlager or Team Lotto [the sponsors]. That's why it's got government money. There's a difference' (quoted in Chapple 2003).

Within a period of three months Blackheart became the fastest growing brand in New Zealand: 50 per cent of people had heard of it, and 30 per cent spontaneously recognised its logo (Chapple 2003). This is the classic stuff of banal nationalism: forging a national identity by mobilising the public against an enemy or traitor of the nation (Billig 1995).[8] Those behind the Blackheart campaign stood to lose more from New Zealand's loss of the America's Cup than the vast majority of New Zealanders. Many of its ringleaders had property investments in or near the Viaduct Harbour, a venue especially developed for the Cup race. The venue itself is a magnet for tourists to New Zealand and serves as a site for investors to gather their catch of foreign capital. In other words, the very foreigners who were the target of this nationalistic campaign were crucial to the ongoing wealth accumulation of the most vocal (millionaire) patriots.

Nationalism need not be at odds with globalisation. In New Zealand, the nationalist campaign is in fact made possible by financial liberalisation. The view of the Blackhearts and the 'loyal' patriots is that New Zealand can only have national economic development if it attracts foreign capital (Hendery 2003a, 2003b). The America's Cup yacht race is a perfect opportunity for New Zealand to showcase itself to global investors. It facilitates the branding of New Zealand in the global limelight. The notion is that benevolent capitalists in Auckland for the Cup defence can help fund New Zealand's move up the OECD score table.

At the deepest level, both the Loyal and the Blackheart campaigns were based on a fundamental contradiction. Team New Zealand winning the America's Cup in 1995 generated a huge boon for New Zealand for several obvious reasons (see Eagles 2003). It linked New Zealand's name with great sporting prowess and it underscored the country's technological edge, with potential spin-offs for the national 'knowledge economy'. At this level, New Zealanders loved to have foreigners come to visit and to admire their country. Of course, the nature of the event brought another dynamic to bear. That is, the foreigners were, in fact, most intensely interested in visiting New Zealand because they wanted to take away that asset that New Zealanders cherished and which many treated as the nation's ticket to future economic well-being. Many New Zealanders despised the power of the global capitalists that lured Kiwi sailors away and, in so doing, ended New Zealand's monopoly of the Cup. Yet the economic nationalism of the Blackheart and Loyal campaigns was vital because it stoked up the willingness of the average citizen and the government to keep pumping money into Team New Zealand. Without this financial and emotional outpouring, the local Team would have been high and dry long before the race started.

CONCLUSION

The processes of globalisation have opened new possibilities for states and new representations of national identity. Distinguishing the nation and promoting collective identity is an important goal of government in light of rapid economic globalisation. Efforts to reinvent New Zealand's national identity have emerged not as a form of resistance or opposition to the power of global capital, but instead as a way to capture the attention of powerful investors, talented people, foreign tourists and consumers. This is revealed by the international marketing campaigns of Tourism New Zealand and Trade and Enterprise New Zealand. Indeed, the processes of globalisation reward efforts to showcase the nation and positively differentiate it from others. In a competitive environment, political leaders must nurture the intangible and cultural assets of the nation, to attract and retain international investment and national (and expatriated) skills and talent. New Zealand's 2003 defence of the America's Cup yacht race was presented as a national struggle over a world sporting event. But loyalty to Team New Zealand was inextricable from loyalty to the economic nation, since staging the event and retaining the Cup was expected to produce major spin-offs for New Zealand's future economic well-being. Although New Zealand lost the America's Cup in 2003, the spin-off economic benefits have convinced the government to invest $35 million in Team New Zealand's challenge in the 2007 America's Cup race in Europe.

The government's support for the Rugby Union's pitch for the 2011 Rugby World Cup has also been unprecedented. In addition to offering to support New Zealand's hosting of the Cup with $2 of taxpayer money for every Rugby Union $1 without limits, Prime Minister Helen Clark flew to Dublin to personally lobby the International Rugby Board alongside All Blacks Captain Tana Umaga, rugby veteran Colin Meads, and Rugby Union officials. This financial backing along with the heartfelt slogan that New Zealand was a rugby 'stadium of four million' ensured New Zealand's bid was the credible winner of rights to host the Rugby World Cup (Tunnah & NZPA 2005). One economist predicts that the economic benefits of the 2011 Rugby World Cup for New Zealand will be huge, adding at least $408 million to New Zealand's GDP primarily by boosting investment. Clearly a keen rugby fan but with his eye on the economic spin-offs, Sport and Recreation Minister Trevor Mallard described the event as 'the biggest thing that's ever happened to New Zealand' (Bennett 2005).

Just as economic globalisation creates new opportunities for nationalism it also poses threats to national self-determination. Globalisation can undermine the cultural as well as the territorial and economic survival of the nation. Interesting contradictions can arise between the pursuit of global integration and the shaping of national identity. For example, the foreign capital generated by a branding campaign may undermine the very national identity that first attracted it. Increasing tourism and foreign investment pose problems for the sustainability of New Zealand's clean, green, and GE-free brand because they seek to exploit and profit from non-renewable natural resources. The actual payoffs and tradeoffs of government funding that some New Zealand citizens see as elitist or commercial initiatives, such as America's Cup yachting, the Rugby World Cup or Hollywood film productions like *The Lord of the Rings*, rather than local sporting events and films are not as transparent as they might be.

At the level of practical politics, it is in many ways troubling that those who protest globalisation have done little to point out these contradictions and politicise them. While critics of globalisation focus their activism on global institutions and multinational 'brand bullies', the politics of globalisation down at the national and local levels has very often been missed. In the context of globalisation, the nation–state still represents an important site for political action.

DISCUSSION QUESTIONS

1 What is nationalism and how has our conception of the nation changed in a globalising political economy?

2 What unites New Zealanders? Is it our clean, green image? Is it the global spectacle of our sporting events? What other things evoke Kiwi nationalism?

3 What is the difference between the 'nation–state' and the 'brand–state'? Who benefits most from the brand–state—foreign investors or national citizens?

4 At the time of the 2003 America's Cup challenge, wealthy businessmen from abroad were asked to comment on New Zealand's future economic prospects and strategy. Some suggested that the key to the future was for New Zealand to 'get its story of itself and what it stands for out in the world'. Is branding of this sort the passport to New Zealand's future economic growth?

5 What does it mean to put 'country before money'?

NOTES

1 Fonterra, New Zealand's largest company, estimates that the value of 'clean and green' to each dairy farmer is between $18,000 and $49,000 per annum (Elworthy 2002).

2 The founding members of the Sustainability Council are Sir Peter Elworthy, Annabel Langbein, Dame Susan Devoy, Sam Neill, and Professor Garth Cooper.

3 See the Official New Zealand Tourism website, www.100%pure.com.

4 As a representative of one of the family of five Team NZ corporate sponsors said, 'Team NZ is a national effort rather than a commercial syndicate'. Quoted in Eugene Bingham and James Gardiner, 'Heroes and villains', *New Zealand Herald*, 25–26 January, 2003, p. B3.

5 Ernesto Bertarelli, owner of the Alinghi syndicate, has made public his intention to simplify nationality rules for future teams competing for the America's Cup. This would turn the race from a competition among nations into a professional sport with an advantage to those syndicates with the most money ('Alinghi to make changes to America's Cup', *New Zealand Herald*, 21 January 2003, p. B6).

6 See the video-clip of the loyal campaign at www.xtra.co.msn.co.nz/teamnewzealand/ 0,9104,00.html.

7 Although difficult to calculate, the 2000 America's Cup defence is said to have created 8,000 full-time jobs, $640 million in additional spending, and to have boosted the national economy by almost 1 per cent (www.blackheart.com).

8 The nationalist crusade turned more sinister than banal in the month before the Cup challenge when the Alinghi syndicate said it had received anonymous letters threatening the children and family of team members (Julie Ash and Patrick Gower, 'Hate campaign threatens Alinghi's crew's children', *New Zealand Weekend Herald*, 4–5 January 2003, p. A1).

REFERENCES

ASB Bank 2003, 'Loyal Momentum Builds as Challenge Approaches', Press Release, 20 January.

Bell, C. 2002, 'Sustaining the Green Myth', paper presented at the University of Auckland Sustainability Lecture Series, August.

Bennett, A. 2005, 'Adding Up the Cash Conversion: Effect on Economic Growth Could Be Seen by 2008'. *New Zealand Herald*, 19 November: A3.

Billig, M. 1995, *Banal Nationalism*, Sage, New York.

Bührs, T. & R. Bartlett 1993, *Environmental Policy in New Zealand: The Politics of Clean and Green*, Oxford University Press, Auckland.

Campbell-Hunt, C., J. Brocklesby, S. Chetty, L. Corbett, S. Davenport, D. Jones & P. Walsh 2001, *World Famous in New Zealand: How New Zealand's Leading Firms Became World-Class Competitors*, Auckland University Press, Auckland.

Chan, K. 2005, 'Tourism New Zealand Signs New Advertising Deal', *New Zealand Herald*, 8 October, p. C3.

Chapple, I. 2003, 'Advertising Year in Review: Sails Pitch the Big News', *New Zealand Herald*, 3 January, pp. C1–2.

Clark, H. 2002, 'Growing an Innovative New Zealand', Prime Minister's Statement to Parliament, 12 February.

Clark, H. 2005, 'Prime Minister's Speech from the Throne', Delivered by Governor-General Sylvia Cartwright, New Zealand Parliament, November.

DaCruz, M. 2005, 'Tourism Writer Urges New Zealand to Charge More', *New Zealand Herald*, 8 October, p. C3.

Devetak, R. & J. True 2006. 'Diplomatic Divergence in the Antipodes: Globalisation, Foreign Policy and State Identity in Australia and New Zealand', *Australian Journal of Political Science*, 41, 2.

Eagles, J. 2002, 'Success Overseas Born of Doing It the NZ Way', *New Zealand Herald*, 28–29 September, p. C5.

Eagles, J. 2003, 'Cup a Showcase for Our Talents', *New Zealand Herald*, 15 January, p. C1.

Elworthy, P. 2002, 'Speech Launching the Sustainability Council of New Zealand', Sustainability Council Press Release, 3 July.

Friedman, J. 1995, 'Global System, Globalization and the Parameters of Modernity', in M. Featherstone, S. Lash & R. Robertson (eds), *Global Modernities*, Sage, London.

Hendery, S. 2003a, 'Wealthy Visitors Expected to Bring Their Wallets', *New Zealand Herald*, 24 January, p. C1.

Hendery, S. 2003b, 'Super-rich Visitors Sample New Zealand's Finest', *Weekend New Zealand Herald*, 15–16 February, p. C1.

Helleiner, E. 2002, 'Economic Nationalism as a Challenge to Economic Liberalism: Lessons from the Nineteenth Century', *International Studies Quarterly*, 46, 3, pp. 307–29.

Hughes, H.R. 1993, 'New Zealand's Clean Green Image—Fact or Fiction?', Thomas Cawthron Memorial Lecture No. 52, November.

Klein, N. 1999, *No Logo: Taking Aim at the Brand Bullies*, Picador, New York.

Matthews, P. 2002, 'I'm Helen, Fly Me', *The Listener*, 11 January, pp. 16–20.

Morgan, N., Pritchard, A. & Piggott, R. 2002. '100% Pure: The Creation of a Powerful Niche Destination Brand', *Journal of Brand Management*, 9, 4/5, pp. 335–54.

Neill, S. 2003, 'In the Field of GE Food We're Being Sold a Pup', *New Zealand Herald*, 3 January.

New Zealand Herald 2003, 'Clean, Green and from NZ', 21 January, p. A12.

Olins, W. 1999, *Trading Identities: Why Countries and Companies are Taking on Each Other's Roles*, The Foreign Policy Centre, London.

Oram, R. 2001, 'Brand New Zealand', *Unlimited Magazine*, 1 December, <www.sharechat.co.nz/features/unlimited/article.php/e348f217>.

Pauly, L. 2000, 'Capital Mobility and the New Global Order', in G. Underhill & R. Stubbs (eds), *Political Economy in a Changing Global Order*, 2nd edn, Oxford University Press, Oxford, pp. 119–28.

Perrott, A. 2005, 'Frocks and Suits—an Odd Couple', *Canvas Magazine, Weekend Herald*, 15 October, pp. 19–20.

Scholte, J.A. 2000, *Globalization: A Critical Introduction*, Palgrave, Basingstoke.

Taylor, P. 2002, 'Who Does Dave Walden Think He Is?', *Sunday Star Times*, 22 September, pp. C1–2.

True, J. 2004, 'Country before Money? Economic Globalization and National Identity in New Zealand', in E. Helleiner & A. Pickel (eds), *Economic Nationalism in a Globalizing World*, Cornell University Press, Ithaca NY.

Tunnah, H. 2005, 'Tana's Team of 4 Million', *New Zealand Herald*, 19 November: A1–2.

Van Hamm, P. 2001, 'The Rise of the Brand State: The Postmodern Politics of Image and Reputation', *Foreign Affairs 80*, September/October, pp. 2–6.

Watkin, T. 2003, 'Blackheart Sailed Off Course', *New Zealand Weekend Herald*, 18–19 January, p. B3.

Wise, M. with W. St John 2003, 'New Zealand Cries Betrayal', *New York Times*, 10 January.

FURTHER READING

Billig, M. 1995, *Banal Nationalism*, Sage, New York.

Burchill, S., A. Linklater, R. Devetak, J. Donnelly, M. Patterson & J. True 2005. *Theories of International Relations*, 3rd edn, Palgrave Macmillan, Basingstoke.

Devetak, R. & J. True 2006, 'Diplomatic Divergence in the Antipodes: Globalisation, Foreign Policy and State Identity in Australia and New Zealand', *Australian Journal of Political Science*, 41, 2.

O'Brien, R. & M. Williams 2003, *Global Political Economy: Evolution and Dynamics*. Palgrave Macmillan, Basingstoke.

New Zealand's Place in the World

Robert G. Patman

Foreign policy is the area of politics that seeks to bridge the boundary between the nation–state and its international environment. When we speak of New Zealand foreign policy, we are referring to decisions and actions that involve, to some appreciable extent, relations between New Zealand and other international actors.[1] In comparison to the domestic policy sphere, the makers of foreign policy in New Zealand are concerned with matters over which their control is distinctly limited and in which their knowledge is rarely better than imperfect. Yet, despite these constraints, New Zealand foreign policy has obtained a growing political significance. This trend was underlined by the 2005 general election campaign and the subsequent appointment of an outspoken nationalist, Winston Peters, as the Foreign Minister without cabinet rank in Helen Clark's new Labour-led government.

DOMESTIC ENVIRONMENT

The context for understanding New Zealand's foreign policy lies in its small size, democratic political system, and unique national attributes. The international relations literature suggests that two of the typical characteristics of small states are an internationalist orientation, consisting of keen participation in international and regional organisations, and a moral emphasis in external policy.[2] External organisations offer states with limited resources the opportunity to maximise their diplomatic efforts on the international stage. They also help to uphold international rules and norms that protect weak states from potential interference by more powerful ones.

New Zealand is a democratic society that is based on political and legal traditions derived from the Westminster parliamentary model of governance. The intimacy and transparency of the New Zealand political system means that public opinion is potentially a far more potent factor in the shaping of foreign policy than is normally the case in larger countries. Nevertheless, while public engagement in foreign policy has markedly grown since the 1960s, it remains subject to an important qualification: despite being elected members of parliament, cabinet ministers remain extraordinarily dependent on the advice of their bureaucratic advisers, in this case the Ministry of Foreign Affairs and Trade (MFAT).[3] Although organisations such as the New Zealand Institute of International Affairs (NZIIA), the Centre of Strategic Studies (CSS) in Wellington and the annual University of Otago Foreign Policy School have advanced the level of discussion on foreign policy, they are too small and few in number to seriously contest MFAT's dominance as the main source of advice for government on foreign affairs. MFAT officials provide ministers with institutional memory of prior policies adopted, modified, and supplanted. They interpret New Zealand's overseas obligations under treaties, international law, and precedents, and, through ministers, they research and present policy alternatives from which the cabinet may make its decisions. At the same time, polling evidence indicates that the New Zealand public remains much less focused on foreign than on domestic policy.[4]

New Zealand manifests some, though by no means all, of the characteristics commonly associated with a small state. Although it has a small GDP and only modest military capabilities, when viewed in the regional context of the South Pacific, New Zealand appears to be a relatively significant power.[5] As well as retaining the status of an administrative trustee power, and having constitutional responsibilities towards the Cook Islands, Niue and Tokelau, New Zealand is unique for its geographical isolation and absence of any direct security threat in the post-Cold War era. That situation is not typical for many states and has given Wellington some freedom of manoeuvre on a range of international issues.

PATTERNS IN THE EVOLUTION OF NEW ZEALAND FOREIGN POLICY

The emergence of a distinctive New Zealand foreign policy is a fairly recent development. From 1769, when Captain Cook first sighted the east coast of the North Island, until the end of the Second World War, New Zealand's status as a British colony meant that foreign policy was largely defined in London. While it had established its own diplomatic corps and military forces by the late 1930s, it still saw itself as one of Britain's staunchest allies. However, the pattern of New Zealand's external relations significantly changed after 1945. Australia gradually replaced Britain as New Zealand's major bilateral partner. Several factors played a part in this. First, there was a cumulative realisation in Wellington and Canberra that Britain was no longer in a position to defend them militarily. Doubts had begun with the British defeat at Singapore in February 1942.[6] In 1944, the two countries signed their first major bilateral agreement without Britain when they concluded a mutual defence pact in Canberra, often known as the ANZAC Treaty.[7] The Canberra Pact provided for cooperation in the South Pacific and was progressively expanded as the two allies fought together in wars in Korea, Malaysia, and Vietnam.

Second, the international pressures associated with the Cold War after 1947 propelled both New Zealand and Australia into a strategic alignment with the USA. In 1951, Australia, New Zealand, and the USA signed the ANZUS Treaty. This was basically a trilateral collective security agreement. Over the next thirty years, the US displaced Britain as the principal strategic partner of the ANZAC countries as the former colonial power retreated to Europe following the Suez Crisis of 1956 and the 1968 decision to withdraw the British navy from stations 'East of Suez'.[8] Australia and New Zealand subsequently participated in the UN-sanctioned but US-led intervention on behalf of South Korea against the attack from North Korea in 1950–53. Both supported the defence of Western interests under the leadership of the US through the ANZUS Treaty and SEATO. Both also assisted Britain in its defence of Malaysia against Indonesia (1963–65) and sent troops to fight alongside the US in its unsuccessful bid to save South Vietnam from communism in 1964–75.[9]

Third, New Zealand and Australia had to deal with the consequences of Britain joining the EU (then EEC) in January 1973. This development had been foreshadowed by Britain's unsuccessful EEC application in 1961. Forewarned of Britain's intentions, Australia and New Zealand started to coordinate economic policy. In 1966, they signed the New Zealand–Australia Free Trade Agreement and by the late 1970s the vast majority of trans-Tasman trade was already free of tariffs. Nevertheless, this period of economic transition, occasioned by Britain's move into Europe, was always going to be more difficult for New Zealand than Australia. By way of comparison, Wellington was more dependent on the British market, more reliant on staple agricultural exports and more closely identified with Britain than Canberra. While New Zealand pulled off a diplomatic coup by negotiating a special access agreement with the EEC for its farm produce until 1980 (Brown 1997, pp. 41–66),[10] it was clear that it had to diversify its export markets as a matter of urgency. In these new and challenging circumstances, New Zealand's economic relationship with Australia became pivotal to such efforts.

By the early 1980s, New Zealand foreign policy had matured and expanded. Wellington still had close links with Britain, but the nature of this linkage had changed significantly. Intellectually, New Zealand had moved from a world view that was rooted in London to one that was increasingly centred in Wellington.

NEW GLOBAL CONTEXT

Today, several decades on, there is a general recognition that New Zealand foreign policy is developing in a qualitatively new global context. Known as globalisation, this context is essentially characterised by increasing interconnectedness between societies, such that events in one part of the world have more and more effects on peoples and societies far away. It involves the 'straddling of social relations across space and time'[11] and contributes to the growing interdependence of nations, peoples, and economies in the world. This process has been underway for more than a century. But it gained greater prominence and added momentum from the early 1980s with technologically driven revolutions in communications and production and the subsequent end of the Cold War.

Forces such as expanding trade, the growth of foreign direct investment, and the internationalisation of the mass media seem to have made the world smaller and rendered national borders more porous. But globalisation by no means implies that local or national concerns are necessarily subordinate to global ones. On the contrary, enhanced connections across borders can fuel ethnic, national and religious consciousness and magnify economic divisions. At present, the world seems caught between the opposing trends of integration and divergence.

PROMOTING HUMAN VALUES AND HUMAN RIGHTS

This complex, multifaceted and contested globalisation process has significantly shaped New Zealand foreign policy in at least four areas. In terms of national identity, New Zealand is redefining itself and how it relates to the external world (see chapter 1.1). Extraordinary changes in New Zealand in the last two or three decades challenge the old view that it is a 'small corner of England out in the Pacific'.[12] Above all, there has been a recognition of the special constitutional and cultural position of Māori people (expressed in the Treaty of Waitangi in terms of *rangatiratanga* [dominion] and *kawanatanga* [government]), which, although still incomplete, has reflected and facilitated a weaving of things Māori into all parts of New Zealand's society and institutions.

New Zealand now has two official languages: English and Māori. Today many New Zealanders have become accustomed to the idea that their children will learn Māori in schools, though its use was strongly discouraged in the past. Māori concepts have also been extended into law, policy, and social institutions. And there has been a general acceptance of the idea of compensation for lands unjustly taken or purchased and for the recognition of rights conferred under the Treaty of Waitangi to the Māori people.[13] In 1995, there was even a formal apology from Queen Elizabeth II for the previous actions of the Crown.

It should be emphasised that globalisation is a key driver in the revival of indigenous rights and culture of New Zealand. While access to symbols of globalisation, such as the Internet, remains uneven, particularly in rural New Zealand, this technology has, in the words of one observer, provided 'unprecedented opportunities'[14] for Māori to project its language and culture, nationally and internationally. The fact that New Zealand has one of the highest rates of computer ownership in the world also lent momentum to this change.

A new sense of national identity has been further affected by the many new links New Zealand is building to other parts of the Pacific and the Asia–Pacific region. These ties have been forged for economic and diplomatic purposes. Languages for this region are now being taught in New Zealand schools. Many students from Asia–Pacific locales are studying in New Zealand universities.

In light of these changes, New Zealand governments, whether involving National or Labour, evidently believe they have a mandate to strengthen the country's international commitment to promote human rights. As one of the founding members of the UN, New Zealand strongly advocated the inclusion of human rights in the UN Charter. It was also closely involved in the drafting of the Universal Declaration of Human Rights in 1948.

With the proliferation of civil conflicts in the post-Cold War era, the promotion of human rights has gained a new strategic imperative. As Mary Robinson, the former UN High Commissioner for Human Rights, has noted: 'Today's human rights abuses are the cause of tomorrow's conflicts'.[15] And because New Zealand is engaged in a ground-breaking attempt to improve relations between Māori and Pakeha through the Treaty settlement process, it has become conscious that it has a distinctive contribution to make internationally in the field of indigenous rights and ethnic conflict. Certainly, New Zealand has been actively involved in the drafting of the UN's Rights of Indigenous Peoples treaty.

FOSTERING A LIBERAL INTERNATIONAL ECONOMIC ORDER

Despite its small size, New Zealand is a country with global economic interests. In the 1980s, New Zealand began to liberalise and reform its economy. As part of this process, New Zealand signed a series of agreements with Australia in 1983 known as Closer Economic Relations (CER). This is arguably the most comprehensive trade agreement in existence and spans a range of areas. These include free trade in most goods, market harmonisation in services and capital, mutual recognition of many standards and the creation of an open labour market.[16]

CER has substantially benefited both countries. Trade between Australian and New Zealand, for example, has increased by over 400 per cent since 1983.[17] Australia is now New Zealand's biggest export market, taking at least 21 per cent of its exports and New Zealand is currently the third largest market for Australian exports. Australia has also become New Zealand's primary source of investment capital, with Australian companies owning many of the key institutions in major sections of the New Zealand economy, such as banking and the mass media.

But globalisation has dramatically expanded the range of international opportunities for the New Zealand economy far beyond the CER market of around 20 million people. Today, New Zealand trades with more than 150 countries and is widely regarded as having one of the most open economies among the OECD countries. Moreover, New Zealand was one of the chief beneficiaries of the 1994 Uruguay GATT round which began to liberalise trade in agriculture. It also has a lot to gain from further liberalisation of trade in agriculture during the next World Trade Organization (WTO) round of negotiations.[18]

While the WTO is reviled by many opponents of globalisation for its weakening of the nation–state, it has actually had the opposite effect in many respects. Consider, for instance, the new rules that the WTO introduced for settling trade disputes between states. Far from weakening New Zealand's national sovereignty, these rules have in a sense actually enhanced it by levelling the playing field for small, less powerful trading nations. The WTO disputes resolution mechanism is binding and sets parameters for a country to pursue a trade dispute against another over a trade problem. That allows the dispute to be sealed off from the rest of the bilateral relationship. Since the mid-1990s, New Zealand has used the machinery of the WTO to resolve disputes with some large trade partners: the EU, Canada and, with Australia, the US over lamb. To date, New Zealand has had a 100 per cent success rate without apparently damaging the relations with any of the parties involved.[19]

Recently, both of the major political parties in New Zealand have identified trade liberalisation as a key foreign policy objective. The decision of the Labour–Alliance government to raise income tax in 1999 and its refusal to match Australia's reduction of the corporate tax rate to 30 per cent was criticised by some of the political opposition parties as undermining New Zealand's competitiveness as a location for foreign investment. On the other hand, since taking office in 1999, Labour has signed free trade agreements with Hong Kong and Singapore, and commenced trilateral Closer Economic Partnership (CEP) negotiations with Chile and Singapore in early 2003.[20] A CEP agreement was signed with Thailand in April 2005.

Australia moved outside of CER to secure a free trade agreement with the US— a measure which took effect on 1 January 2005. So far, New Zealand has been unsuccessful in its efforts to secure the same. Consolation of sorts came with the signing of an agreement with China which pledged to move rapidly towards the establishment of a free trade agreement between the two countries.

Along with growing government-level contacts, people-to-people contacts between New Zealand and the rest of the world are also rapidly expanding. The declining cost of international travel and startling advances in communications technology have made geography less of an obstacle than previously. In 2002, the number of tourists visiting New Zealand during a twelve-month period exceeded the two million mark for the first time. In 2004, there were 2.3 million visitors to New Zealand. This growth came barely a decade after New Zealand first recorded a million visitors in a year.[21]

SEEKING SECURITY

Even before the end of the Cold War, New Zealand demonstrated it was prepared to adopt a distinctive approach to security matters. Strains within the Western alliance began to appear in the mid-1980s when the non-nuclear Labour government led by David Lange refused to allow unrestricted access to New Zealand ports by US naval vessels with nuclear propulsion or arms. The US responded by excluding New Zealand from ANZUS and the exchange of strategic information and allied exercises with Wellington. Thereafter, the US described New Zealand as a friend, but not an ally.[22]

For the first decade of the post-Cold War era, the ANZUS rupture did not seem to affect the capacity of New Zealand and Australia to work closely together in the security realm. Both supported the US-led coalition against Saddam Hussein in the Persian Gulf War of 1990–91; the US–UN humanitarian intervention in Somalia, 1992–93; and worked closely together to achieve a peace settlement in Bougainville in 1998. Furthermore, New Zealand's forces served under Australian command in East Timor as part of INTERFET and close cooperation between both military forces has continued under UNTAET. According to the Deputy Secretary of the Australian Defence Department, New Zealand's very rapid and professional commitment to support INTERFET made 'a massive impression'[23] in Canberra. Both Australia and New Zealand also make up the International Peace Monitoring Group (IPMG) in the Solomon Islands.

Nevertheless, in the absence of the discipline of working together within the ANZUS framework, Australia and New Zealand began to emphasise different strategic outlooks. This was partly a function of geography. Australia focuses on Asia and tends to view its security in terms of a calculation of specific threats. New Zealand, on the other hand, believes its regional priority is in the South Pacific and tends to see security in a more comprehensive fashion, centred on collective security and the United Nations.

These differences of strategic perspective began to surface with the election of the Labour–Alliance coalition in 1999. From the beginning of her period in office, Clark made it clear that she did not regard New Zealand and Australia as a 'single strategic entity'.[24] In May 2000, the new Labour government abandoned the option negotiated by the previous National government to purchase 28 F-16 fighter planes from the US, on the grounds that the F-16s were too expensive for a country of New Zealand's size and military capability.

Twelve months later, the government completed its review of New Zealand's defence strategy. Citing 'an incredibly benign strategic environment', three major defence decisions were made: New Zealand's air combat and strike capability would be abandoned; the navy would be restricted to two frigates and some basic transport and coastal patrol vessels; and the army would receive the bulk of government expenditure, some NZ$700 million to provide it with high-tech communications equipment and military hardware.[25] In 2004, the New Zealand army took delivery of 135 LAV (Light Armoured Vehicles) built by General Motors Defense, Canada.

The government argued that these changes were intended to provide New Zealand with a modern defence force that could contribute more effectively to international peacekeeping operations. Few would dispute New Zealand's role in UN peacekeeping. In 2002, for example, it had over 800 military personnel serving in thirteen UN authorised peace support or humanitarian missions, including the Middle East, Sierra Leone, and Mozambique.[26] But while New Zealand peacekeepers certainly needed the new equipment earmarked for the army, it is questionable whether these extra resources necessitated the drastic downgrading of the country's air force and naval capabilities in the process. Considering that the 'new wars' of the post-Cold War era often demand a mix of military capabilities, including air power, to contain or prevent humanitarian tragedies, it could be argued that the government appeared to be projecting a vision of peacekeeping that no longer corresponded to the military realities on the ground.[27]

The recent New Zealand approach to defence has angered and alarmed its trans-Tasman neighbour. By presiding over what is seen as a serious degradation of New Zealand's military capabilities, the Clark government may have jeopardised Wellington's future ability to contribute to ANZAC alliance military operations.[28] With the recent decline in New Zealand military power projection capabilities, Australians could well perceive that New Zealand (the twentieth richest country in the world) is not prepared to assume a fair burden for common defence. New Zealand's decision to cancel its scheduled purchase of US F-16 combat aircraft is a case in point. Some Australian media commentators have described the government's defence policy as the 'bludger's option'. While the Howard government has been more publicly restrained in its comments, it did make it clear there would be 'domestic and international consequences'[29] flowing from New Zealand's new defence policy.

QUEST FOR MULTILATERAL DIPLOMACY

In the era of globalisation, New Zealand has continued to uphold the notion of a rules-based international order and to firmly support the UN as the embodiment of the multilateral process. Since 1945, New Zealand has signed up to all the major UN treaties and ratified virtually every key UN convention. That is something that some of the more powerful members of the UN cannot claim.

Successive New Zealand governments, particularly during the post-Cold War period, seem to believe that globalisation is reinforcing the multilateral process. According to this view, globalisation is challenging the traditional symbols of power in the international system, such as geography and size, and creating qualitatively new possibilities for small states like New Zealand to participate in global forums and forge new constituencies in support of its core objectives. This is a 'can do' approach to global diplomacy.[30] It rejects the view that international influence is totally dependent on power.

Certainly, New Zealand has shown a presence on the international stage that is out of all proportion to its size. Despite lacking economic, military, and political leverage, the country has secured a number of high-profile diplomatic positions over the last decade: it acceded to one of the non-permanent seats on the UN Security Council in 1992; Don McKinnon, former New Zealand Foreign Minister, was subsequently appointed to the position of Secretary General of the Commonwealth; and a former New Zealand prime minister, Mike Moore, won a three-year 'split term' as Director General of the WTO.[31]

On the other hand, New Zealand's old allies, Britain and Australia, have tended to behave as if globalisation is centred on the USA, the world's only superpower. On this view, enjoying the benefits of globalisation largely depends on achieving close relations with Washington. Unlike New Zealand, Britain and, to a lesser extent, Australia are middle range powers. And by presenting themselves as staunch allies of the USA, Tony Blair and John Howard anticipate political, military, and commercial favours coming their way, as well as increased clout in global institutions such as the United Nations and the WTO, and greater respect and recognition from regional major powers like China.[32]

These differences in perspective have placed New Zealand on the opposite side of Britain and Australia on two crucial international issues. The first concerns President George W. Bush's decision to proceed with a missile defence scheme.[33] The National Missile Defence (NMD) system is intended to protect the USA from ballistic missile attacks from 'rogue' states, such as North Korea, Iran and, until 2003, Iraq. At the time Washington announced a green light for the NMD project in 2001, former New Zealand Foreign Minister Phil Goff roundly condemned the concept. Citing concerns of China and Russia, Goff said a missile shield would not necessarily protect the US from terrorist acts and also 'risks undermining the current network of nuclear arms control and disarmament treaties'.[34] In contrast, Alexander Downer, the Australian Foreign Minister, has offered 'understanding' for the proposed American missile shield and believes China, an increasingly important partner to Australia, will eventually accept that the shield is not aimed at Beijing.[35] The British government has also made soothing noises about Bush's missile defence plan despite the opposition of many other EU countries.

The second, and more serious issue, has been the war in Iraq. Prime Minister Helen Clark had expressed her scepticism about the existence of weapons of mass destruction in Iraq prior to the invasion of that country in March 2003, and made it clear that New Zealand would not support any military operation carried out without authorisation from the UN Security Council.[36] By contrast, both Britain and Australia actively participated in the invasion with combat forces and have voiced agreement with the 'Bush doctrine'—namely, that the use of pre-emptive force is the necessary antidote to terrorism, and such measures cannot always wait for the formation of a multilateral consensus. After the invasion of Iraq was complete, New Zealand did eventually deploy a small unit of engineers to serve in a non-combat role alongside British occupation forces in Southern Iraq. However, Wellington continued to distance itself from the 'Coalition of the Willing' and withdrew all personnel from Iraq in September 2004.

During New Zealand's 2005 general election, Labour politicians campaigned on the basis that they had kept the country out of the war in Iraq. Conversely, opposition leader Don Brash was portrayed as someone who would return New Zealand to the 'bad old days' of great power subservience. His reported statement at a meeting in Washington that the anti-nuclear ban would be 'gone by lunchtime' was repeated throughout the Labour campaign. Similar electoral capital was made on his refusal to explicitly rule out the deployment of New Zealand combat forces to Iraq.

Although the Clark government has generally refrained from directly criticising the Iraq venture on the world stage, the Labour party has had no such reservations in the context of the election. Actor Sam Neill, who had been chosen to introduce Helen Clark at the launch of the party's campaign for re-election, described the war as 'a bloody fiasco' which was 'cruel, counter-productive, illegal and founded on lies'.[37]

Although the Clark government insists that New Zealand's support for the 'War on Terror' can exclude the invasion and ongoing occupation of Iraq, it is not clear that its traditional allies share this perception. The US government has signalled that any US–NZ free trade deal would be dependent on an appropriate level of support by New Zealand for the 'War on Terror'. It is worth examining New Zealand's participation in the 'War on Terror' in detail.

NEW ZEALAND AND THE 'WAR ON TERROR'

After the devastating attacks on the World Trade Center and the Pentagon on 11 September 2001, President George W. Bush declared war on what was called global terrorism. Two New Zealanders were among the 3,000 people killed on that fateful day. President Bush characterised the new conflict as a struggle between 'good and evil' and said 'either you are with us or you are with the terrorists'.[38]

The response of the New Zealand government was swift, but measured. New Zealand, according to the prime minister, pledged itself to making 'a solid contribution'[39] to the international effort against terrorism. This contribution included the deployment of a New Zealand SAS unit and an air force Hercules airplane to Afghanistan; the use of an ANZAC frigate, *Te Kaha*, an Orion surveillance aircraft and 242 navy and airforce personnel in a Canadian-led force patrolling the Arabian Sea and the Gulf of Oman;[40] the allocation of NZ$30 million over the next three years to boost New Zealand's domestic counter-terrorism measures in police, customs, immigration, intelligence, and defence areas;[41] and the passing of the Terrorism Suppression Bill to conform with UN Security Council resolutions to tighten legislative measures against funding, harbouring or otherwise assisting terrorist groups.

This anti-terrorist legislation had the support of all parties in parliament, except the Greens. Keith Locke, the foreign affairs spokesperson for the Green party, warned that the bill's provisions undermined individual liberty and threatened lawful protests. But while a democracy must be careful not to subvert itself in a struggle with terrorism, New Zealand seems less vulnerable than others in this regard. It is a small society in which anonymity is difficult. In the absence of a substantial terrorist threat to New Zealand, it is fairly safe to assume that there will be popular resistance to any abuse of government power.

Although the prospect of terrorism in New Zealand remains slight, the nation has not been immune from some of its effects. The Bali bombings of October 2002 killed three New Zealanders and around 190 Australians. Although no New Zealanders were among the casualties in the smaller 'anniversary' attack of October 2005, the sense of shock and outrage was nevertheless acute. The apparent discovery of terror cells during recent police raids in Australia have added to the sense that terrorism, and the battle to contain it, are moving closer to New Zealand's shores.

New Zealand has not been immune from the legal and moral struggles of the 'War on Terror' either. The case of the Algerian refugee Ahmed Zaoui has become an enduring legal dilemma for the New Zealand government. A former Associate Professor of Theology at the University of Algiers and candidate for the Islamic Salvation Front (FIS) in Algeria, Zaoui arrived in New Zealand bearing a false passport in December 2002 and applied for refugee status. Zaoui had been convicted in absentia by a French court in the aftermath of 9/11, because of his association with known terrorists. Acting on information received from a number of Western governments, including France, Belgium, and Switzerland, the New Zealand Intelligence Service ordered his immediate imprisonment at the maximum-security facility at Paremoremo. Initially he was held in solitary confinement. Since 2002, however, there has been a steady accumulation of public pressure for Zaoui's release, with many prominent New Zealanders weighing in to publicise the case. In December 2004, Zaoui was granted bail and currently resides in the Dominican Friary in central Auckland with a 10pm curfew. Legal activity is continuing to see whether he will be allowed to remain in New Zealand.

The case highlights the tension between democratic norms like the right to a fair trial, and the necessarily opaque operations of the intelligence services. It also puts

New Zealand into the company of many other countries currently wrestling with the moral ambiguities of the 'War on Terror'.

The imprisonment and then deportation of two suspected agents from Israel's Mossad intelligence agency in 2004 highlighted an entirely different, but no less real, threat to the safety of New Zealanders. The two men were attempting to acquire New Zealand passports, probably for use in international intelligence operations. Such activities could have seriously compromised the safety of New Zealanders travelling to foreign countries and met with a correspondingly stern response from Prime Minister Helen Clark: 'The New Zealand government views the act carried out by the Israeli intelligence agents as not only utterly unacceptable but also a breach of New Zealand sovereignty and international law.'[42] As well as cutting off all diplomatic relations with Israel, Clark also demanded an official apology. Although Jerusalem was initially reticent, the latter was eventually forthcoming in June 2005.

AFTERMATH OF THE 2005 ELECTION

As noted previously, international themes played a prominent, but not overarching, role in the New Zealand election of 2005. Nevertheless, its outcome will have a profound effect on the conduct of New Zealand foreign policy, at least in the short term. Winston Peters, an outspoken critic of New Zealand's immigration policies—particularly where they applied to the influx of Asians to the country— emerged as the new Minister of Foreign Affairs following intense inter-party negotiations after the election. His role is historically unusual because he will carry out his duties as Foreign Minister while at the same time remaining outside of cabinet.

Although it is still too early to assess Peters' competency in this position, his early forays in the role have tended to reinforce the view that he faces a steep learning curve in the months ahead. Crucially, his widely respected predecessor, Phil Goff, retains chairmanship of the external relations and defence committee, and is reported to have maintained many of the channels with foreign leaders that he developed during his tenure.[43]

CONCLUSION

In the last two and half decades, New Zealand foreign policy has faced a period of substantial readjustment. The advent of intensified globalisation coincided with profound changes in New Zealand's national identity and its role in the world. Sweeping deregulation of the economy and an ambitious attempt to improve relations between Māori and Pakeha through the Crown's recognition of indigenous rights has been linked to reinvigorated New Zealand support for international human rights, the expansion of free trade and multilateral institutions. At the same time, New Zealand has moved towards closer relations with the Asia–Pacific Rim and adopted a non-nuclear security policy.

By most standards, New Zealand's diplomacy over this period has been remarkably successful. Far from being sidelined by globalisation, the steady growth of a rules-based international order seems to have strengthened the sovereign independence of New Zealand. In a number of major international institutions, leadership positions have been occupied by New Zealanders. As a small and developed country, New Zealand seems to have been generally effective in exploiting the opportunities, and minimising the constraints, of a globalising world.

However, if this trend is to continue, the Clark government must recognise, especially after the events of 9/11, that it is not possible to compartmentalise or insulate New Zealand's foreign policy from broader domestic concerns relating to security and trade. The almost unilateralist stance, represented by the Clark government's 2001 defence restructuring programme, flies in the face of the close economic and political ties with Australia that the Labour-led government actively seeks to promote. If Wellington continues down this road, it will only do so at the price of losing influence with Australia on issues that matter to New Zealand. Similarly, while the appointment of Winston Peters as Foreign Minister may have a certain logic in domestic political terms for Prime Minister Helen Clark, the appointment could signal to other governments that New Zealand does not think foreign affairs has enough status to warrant a cabinet seat. For a country that gains so much from multilateralism and has a big interest in the expansion of free trade, especially in Asia, that could be a very damaging message.

DISCUSSION QUESTIONS

1   Examine the impact of Britain's entry into the EU (then EEC) in 1973 on the evolution of New Zealand's foreign policy.

2   How have changes in New Zealand's national identity affected its foreign relations?

3   Has globalisation enhanced or diminished the role of New Zealand's foreign policy?

4   Why have successive New Zealand governments in the postwar period staunchly supported the United Nations?

5   To what extent does the almost unilateralist approach of New Zealand's Labour-led government to security relations with Australia impede the prospect of close economic and political ties between the two countries?

6   Assess the claim that the refusal of the Clark government to back the US-led invasion of Iraq in March 2003 was a diplomatic and economic blunder.

NOTES

The author would like to thank Jeremy Hall for providing some valuable research assistance in preparing this chapter.

1   Frankel, J. 1963, *The Making of Foreign Policy: An Analysis of Decision-Making*, Oxford University Press, London, pp. 1–3.

2   Henderson, J. 1991, 'New Zealand and the Foreign Policy of Small States', In R. Kennaway & J. Henderson (eds), *Beyond New Zealand: Foreign Policy into the 1990s*, Longman Paul, Auckland, p. 6.

3   Upton, S. 2000. 'How New Zealand Sees Itself in the World', *New Zealand International Review*, 25/4, pp. 9–10.

4   Hoadley, S. 1997, 'Foreign Policy', In R. Miller (ed.) *New Zealand Politics in Transition*, Oxford University Press, Auckland, p. 299.

5   Jackson, R. 2001, 'Multilateralism: New Zealand and the United Nations', In R.G. Patman (ed.), *Sovereignty under Siege? New Zealand and Globalisation*, Ashgate, Aldershot.

6   Catley, B. 2001, *Waltzing with Matilda: Should New Zealand Join Australia?* Dark Horse Publishing, Wellington, pp. 51–2.

7   ibid. p. 52.

8   Patman, R.G. 1997, 'Introduction', In R.G. Patman (ed.), *New Zealand and Britain: A Special Relationship in Transition*, Dunmore Press, Palmerston North, p. 13.

9   Catley, B., *Waltzing with Matilda.*, p. 53.

10 ibid. p. 102; Brown, B. 1997, 'From Bulk Purchase to Butter Disputes', In R.G. Patman (ed.) *New Zealand and Britain: A Special Relationship in Transition*, pp. 41–66.

11 Anthony Giddens, cited in L. Murphy, 'Business and the City', Paper presented at UNESCO one day seminar on New Zealand and the World, Royal Society of New Zealand, Wellington, 22 June 2001.

12 Woods, N. 1997, 'Converging Challenges and Diverging Identities', in R.G. Patman (ed.) *New Zealand and Britain*, p. 27.

13 ibid. p. 38.

14 Zwimpfer, L. 2001, 'Digital Divide or Digital Opportunities—Two Sides of the Same Coin?', Paper presented at UNESCO one day seminar on New Zealand and the World, Royal Society of New Zealand, Wellington, 22 June 2001.

15 Mary Robinson, cited by I. Hill, former Director of Human Rights, Ministry of Foreign Affairs and Trade (MFAT) in 'New Zealand's International Human Rights Policy: A Small State Trying to Make a Difference', Paper presented at the University of Otago seminar, 17 May 2002.

16 Catley, B., *Waltzing with Matilda.*, pp. 86–9.

17 *Australian Financial Review*, 14 April 2000.

18 Banks, R. 2001, Deputy Secretary of Foreign Affairs and Trade, 'Globalisation and the Nation State, Challenges and Opportunities', *Record*, New Zealand Foreign Affairs and Trade, 10/1, p. 27.

19 ibid.

20 'Chile, NZ, Singapore—Closer Economic Partnership Talks', Press statement, Ministry of Foreign Affairs and Trade, Wellington, 14 November 2002.

21 *Sunday Star Times*, 22 December 2002.

22 Catley, B. *Waltzing with Matilda*, pp. 53–4.

23 White, H. 2000, 'An Australian Viewpoint on Strategic Issues', Paper presented to the 36th University of Otago Foreign Policy School, Dunedin, 29 June.

24 Catley, B., *Waltzing with Matilda*, p. 56.

25 *Otago Daily Times*, 12 April 2001.

26 Jackson, R., 'Multilateralism: New Zealand and the United Nations', In R.G. Patman (ed.) *Sovereignty under Siege? New Zealand and Globalisation.*

27 Patman, R.G. 2002, 'Globalisation and the "New Wars": Can New Zealand become an International Peacemaker?', *Future Times Journal*, Vol. 3, pp. 7–8.

28 Dickens, D. 2000, 'The ANZAC Connection: Does the Australian–New Zealand Strategic Relationship have a Future?', Paper presented at the 36th University of Otago Foreign Policy School, Dunedin, 29 June.

29 Australian Prime Minister, John Howard, cited by Jenny Shipley, Leader of the Opposition, National Party Release, Wellington, 31 July 2001.

30 Walter, N. 2000, 'New Zealand's Changing Place in the World', *Record*: New Zealand Foreign Affairs and Trade, 9/2.

31 *Japan Times*, 30 April 2000.

32 *Australian Financial Review*, 31 May 2000.

33 *The Canberra Times*, 2 April 2001.

34 Goff, P. 2001, 'New Challenges, New Approaches', Speech delivered at the Annual Dinner of the New Zealand Institute of International Affairs, Wellington, 14 May.

35 'US Missile Shield Puts Canberra in a Bind', *Muzi News*, at lateline.muzi.net/11/english/1068776.

36 *Otago Daily Times*, 13 November 2002.

37 *CNS News*, 22 August 2005: www.cnsnews.com/ViewForeignBureaus.asp?Page=%5C ForeignBureaus%5Carchive%5C200508%5CFOR20050822a.html

38 President George W. Bush's speech to both Houses of Congress cited in CNN.com on 20 September 2001; www.cnn.com/2001/us/09/20gen.america.under.attack/index.html

39 Prime Minister Helen Clark, Media Statement, 11 November 2002.

40 *Teletext National News*, Auckland, 11 November 2002: *Otago Daily Times*, 12 November, 2002; "New Zealand to Add Anti-Terror Forces", ABC news; abcnews. go.com/wire/World/ap20021111_18.html

41 Goff, P. 2002, 'Asia-Pacific Security Challenges', Speech delivered at the 37th University of Otago Foreign Policy School, Dunedin, 28 June.

42 *New Zealand Herald* online: www.nzherald.co.nz/search/story.cfm?storyid= EC4D796E-39E1–11DA-8E1B-A5B353C55561

43 *New Zealand Herald* online: www.nzherald.co.nz/search/story.cfm?storyid= 0004D44A-6633–137D-990483027AF1002A

FURTHER READING

Hoadley, S. 1992, *The New Zealand Foreign Affairs Handbook*, Oxford University Press, Auckland.

Kennaway, R. & J. Henderson (eds) 1991, *Beyond New Zealand II: Foreign Policy into the 1990s*, Longman Paul, Auckland.

McKinnon, M. 1993, *Independence and Foreign Policy: New Zealand in the World since 1935*, Auckland University Press, Auckland.

Patman, R.G. & C. Rudd (eds) 2005, *Sovereignty under Siege: Globalization and New Zealand*, Ashgate, Aldershot.

Pettman, R. (ed.) 2005, *New Zealand in a Globalising World*, Victoria University Press, Wellington.

Thakur, R. 1986, *In Defence of New Zealand: Foreign Policy Choices in the Nuclear Age*, Westview Press, Boulder, Colorado.

Trotter, A. (ed.) 1993, *Fifty Years of New Foreign Policy*, University of Otago Press, Dunedin.

Legislative Process

It is hardly surprising that colonial New Zealand adopted the 'Westminster' system of representative democracy. Among the distinguishing features of this model are an unwritten constitution, sovereign parliament, and two dominant parties, with legislative and executive power being concentrated in the hands of the same party. In more recent times there have been some significant deviations from this model, a trend that is a central theme of our discussion. Despite the absence of a 'written' constitution, the New Zealand parliament has passed a number of constitutionally significant acts, including the Constitution Act 1986 and Bill of Rights Act 1990. With the introduction of proportional representation in 1996, the era of two-party politics and single party majority government was brought to a close.

Part B covers the following topics:

- **Constitution**. Chapters 2.1 and 2.2 examine the main purposes and functions of the New Zealand constitution and consider the extent to which its 'flexibility' (unlike the constitutions of many other countries) provides the potential for further reform. Possible future changes include a 'written' constitution, entrenched Bill of Rights, incorporation of the Treaty of Waitangi within constitutional arrangements, and abolition of the constitutional monarchy.

- **Head of State**. The arguments for and against a republic, and the degree to which the monarchy continues to enjoy public support (both in New Zealand and Australia), are discussed in chapter 2.3. One of the chapter's main findings is that, unlike Australians, New Zealanders currently have little enthusiasm for the prospect of becoming a republic, with an elected or appointed president as head of state.

- **Judiciary**. Chapter 2.4 analyses a judicial and court structure that reflects the distinct characteristics of New Zealand's political history, including an independent judiciary and the absence of political appointments to the courts. As part of a review of the country's longstanding links with Britain, in 2003 the New Zealand government abolished the right of appeal to Britain's Privy Council and established a local Supreme Court as the ultimate appellate court. Chapter 2.4 explores this development.

- **Parliament**. Chapter 2.5 returns to the theme of recent deviations from the Westminster model in its discussion on the role of parliament. It notes that parliamentary sovereignty has begun to be questioned, especially with respect to the claims of advocates of Māori sovereignty and those who support a separate Māori parliament, as well as supporters of direct democracy. Chapter 2.6 addresses the question of what Members of Parliament actually do. Contrary to the widely held belief that politicians are over-paid and under-worked, this chapter argues that we are generally well served by our elected representatives. Part B concludes with a discussion in chapter 2.7 on the purpose and importance of parliament's 'conscience' or 'free' vote, especially in relation to the controversial Prostitution, Civil Unions and Relationships Bills.

Constitutionalism

Andrew Sharp

AN OUTLINE OF THE CONSTITUTION

The 'constitution' is that system of legal rules and politically-effective, if not legally-enforceable, conventions that govern the behaviour of the holders of public office in their relationships with each other and with the people they govern. But why should officials and the people they govern obey those laws and follow those conventions? It is most importantly because they share a commitment to the ideal of being governed under a constitution so as to enable a population (in our case New Zealanders) to live together. Minimally, this means that they are able to live at peace and not be continually distracted by arguments about property and authority: about who owns what, and who may control whom. At the very least, that is, there must be adherence to the ancient ideal of 'the rule of law'. Optimally though, modern constitutionalism also means that the state is both democratic (so that all people share in government or in controlling government), and liberal (so that all have their rights and liberties protected against the incursions not only of other people but of the governing powers themselves). This optimal set of ideals is 'constitutionalism' in its current New Zealand form.

In this view, New Zealand politics is to be seen and spoken of as played out within the confines of a liberal–democratic constitution. At the heart of the constitution seen this way are triennial elections to a House of Representatives, or, as it is usually called, 'parliament'. These elections produce about 120 members of parliament (MPs) of various political parties in numbers roughly proportional to the popular vote their parties have received. Such elections embody the ideal of representative democracy.

On the same representative principle, the leader of the largest party in parliament is then almost certainly asked by the Governor-General to form a government, which he or she then does in constructing a cabinet in which he or she is the prime minister. Cabinet, as evolving practice since the first Mixed Member Proportional (MMP) election in 1996 shows, is to be constructed out of members of the major party, together with members of other parties with whom the major party is in coalition or with which it has a favourable arrangement regarding voting in the house that is crucial to the survival of the government. The latest bout of cabinet-building after the 2005 election further shows that individual MPs, like Winston Peters, who do not formally bring any of their party support with them at all, may also be brought into the executive.

The members of cabinet meet regularly to discuss and decide on government policy. Each member (except when there is no party coalition or party agreement on legislative support as a condition of membership) is collectively responsible for the government policy on all matters. Each member heads a ministry or department for whose effectiveness and efficiency they are (without *any* exception) individually responsible on day-to-day matters as well as on more general policy issues. For their parts, public service officials answer to cabinet through their ministers. Besides controlling the public service in this way, cabinet under MMP remains, as it was under the old First-Past-the-Post electoral system (FPP), the leading force in preparing and shepherding legislation through the house. This is so despite the now greater complexity of party politics in the house and the greater power of a better-manned committee system more capable than in the past of attending to the details of legislation.

The cabinet in turn is, as under FPP, dominated but not controlled by the prime minister. National party prime ministers choose their cabinet members and allocate their portfolios, and Labour prime ministers have at least great influence on who of their MPs shall be in cabinet, and in any case, also allocate portfolios. Since the introduction of MMP, prime ministers have been pivotal figures in the construction and preservation of coalitions and agreements of legislative support. Though MMP has meant that they have a harder task controlling a cabinet some of whose members are not of their own party, it has nevertheless put them in a better position than anyone else within cabinet to organise the politics of office, influence and prestige. They have the greatest say in who shall be members of cabinet, what legislation cabinet and their own parties shall put to the House of Representatives, and the greatest knowledge of what coalition or other partners will and will not put up with. Whatever the balance of power in cabinets though, the cabinet (as in the British system of 'Westminster' government from which the constitution derives) dominates the executive and the legislative arms or 'powers' of government.

Distanced from such policy-making, executive, and legislative activities of government, is the judicial power. In the courts, it is said, only slightly mistakenly

(Harris 1995, pp. 265–85), that the law is not 'made' but only put into execution. It is administered in a non-partisan, non-political way by judges who are highly educated in the law and chosen by a process that puts great weight on their legal expertise and very little on their party political allegiances. And so, even though they are the creation of parliament-made law, the courts, led by the Supreme Court (founded in 2003) have their own independent spirit, expressed in the durable constitutional convention of the 'separation of powers'. While they are a part of the apparatus of government, courts and judges nevertheless restrain the activities of legislators, executives, and government advisers and administrators within the bounds laid down by law; and they protect the people from overzealous officials, guaranteeing their rights, for instance, to freedom of association, assembly, thought, expression and religion, and rights to due process of law where they are suspected of crimes. Whenever the executive or legislative powers attempt to interfere with the judicial functions of government, or seem to be making the task of independent adjudication more difficult, the public is sure to hear of it.

Such in general is the shape of government in New Zealand, largely a matter of convention (i.e. of recurring, approved practice) and known through normal political debate to a good proportion of New Zealanders. From a legal-constitutional point of view the system looks a little different though, and is known only to experts. The legal rules that constrain and the legal principles that guide governmental activity flow from a number of sources. They derive from the prerogative powers of the Queen of England (etc.) 'in right of New Zealand', and from certain parliamentary statutes and interpretive decisions of law courts. These are fleshed out and given weight by those local practices (sometimes moulded by international law and opinion) that have come by consensus to attain the status of 'constitutional conventions'.

None of the detail of all this is hard to find out, even for those who do not consult the leading New Zealand law journals. In 1993 Philip Joseph's *Constitutional and Administrative Law in New Zealand* first appeared. That large book covered the field as a whole from the perspective of a legal academic. The introduction of MMP in 1996, however, was to make a considerable difference to the law and working of the constitution, so that a second edition was necessary in 2001. From a more politically oriented perspective, the change to MMP also saw four Victoria University political scientists including Professors Jonathan Boston and Elizabeth McLeay produce a comprehensive set of documents recording and discussing the constitution: *Electoral and Constitutional Change in New Zealand: An MMP sourcebook* (Boston, Levine, McLeay & Roberts 1999). Perhaps the most accessible work, though, made public in 1996 and revised periodically since then, has been the concise and authoritative *Cabinet Office Manual*, a practical constitutional handbook for those in legislative and executive office.[1] And then there have been the ruminations on the constitution by the public lawyer with the greatest political experience of all, Sir Geoffrey Palmer, and his son, Matthew. Once a constitutional reformer, committed to a written constitution and a Bill of Rights on a North American rather than a Westminster model, Sir Geoffrey has more recently professed himself more sceptical about the possibility and desirability of great change in the current constitution (Palmer and Palmer 2004; Palmer and Hill 2002). Others have produced various mixtures of exposition and polemic that show constitutional thinking to be very much alive, at least among scholars.[2]

In these places the reader will discover how acts (or statutes) of parliament are made, and how the statutory basis of the constitution is to be found in certain of them, stretching from the English statute Magna Carta 1297 to the Electoral Act 1993 (and its amendments)—all made in New Zealand. These statutes—the English and UK ones once simply inherited but now sifted out and adopted where appropriate into New Zealand law by our Imperial Laws Application Act 1988—lay the basis for the 'rule of law' which authorises equally the powers of government and the rights of the people. For instance, Magna Carta—the 'great charter'—insists in the language of the reaffirmation of anciently existing rights that no one may be imprisoned or otherwise punished without due process of 'the law of the land', including trial by a jury of equals. The equally famous English Bill of Rights 1689 fleshes out the detail of what it claimed was then traditional English constitutional practice: the executive power cannot dispense with or suspend the operation of laws; MPs have freedom of speech and are immune from legal proceedings by any government or those outside its walls; property cannot be taken from people without their own consent—and hence there can be no taxation except with the consent of the representatives of the people in parliament. Prominent among the New Zealand Statutes, the Judicature Act 1908 sets out the powers of the judges and their independence from control by either the legislative or executive powers. The Constitution Act 1986 further distinguishes the three arms of government and speaks of parliament (i.e. the House of Representatives and the Governor-General) being the supreme legislative power in the land. The details of how governments and government-authorised bodies are to proceed are laid down in the State Sector Act 1988 and the Public Finance Act 1989. Other acts—the Ombudsmen Act 1976 and the New Zealand Bill of Rights Act 1990 in particular—protect the subject against wrongful administrative, judicial, and policing activity. Still others—notably the Official Information Act 1982 and the Electoral Act 1993—enable citizens to be informed of what their governments are doing even if they would cover their tracks, and to vote them in and out of office.

As for the rest of the constitution, it is too large and complex a subject to summarise here, and it is enough to say that:

1. The old royal prerogative, once an extensive English 'common-law' power allowing the monarch to act without parliamentary or legal control in emergencies for the good of the 'realm' is now, in regard to the Governor-General, almost completely controlled by statute and convention.

2. Court decisions and opinions tend to be subtle and detailed, and the relevant ones are not confined to the courts of New Zealand alone nor even to courts (UK, Canada, USA, Australia) practising English common law. They also include decisions of courts and tribunals operating under international law. Thus, for instance, a great number of Māori rights, besides being recognised by the courts under the common law doctrine of 'aboriginal title' and under judicial interpretations of the 'principles of the Treaty of Waitangi' as laid down by statute, are also coming to be claimed to be indigenous rights to self-government under international norms—if not international law.

3. There is, finally, the most puzzling constitutional conundrum of all, namely the question as to whether or not parliament is the legal 'sovereign': whether, that is, there is any limit to the scope of its law-making power. Is there nothing that it cannot make legal or illegal and thus required of or forbidden to its subjects without their being able to appeal to another authority? Or is it, or could it be made the case, that certain 'fundamental laws' should govern parliament's actions and themselves be immune from parliamentary legislation? Sir Edward Coke, a great legal scholar of early seventeenth century England, is famous for having embraced the latter view when he said: 'Magna Carta is such a fellow as he will have no sovereign'. He meant that the ancient common law of England (itself emerging from the customs of the people which existed 'time out of mind') was summed up and affirmed (not, notice, invented or authorised) in Magna Carta; and that the Great Charter of law clearly limited and controlled the king. Kings, though supreme lawmakers and governors, were themselves creatures of the law, and the law dictated things they could not do (McIlwain 1940). The question remains a live one, and difficult to answer. It is often stated in New Zealand as the question as to whether the highest court, the Supreme Court, has a power to 'judicially review' and nullify offending acts of parliament. The last Chief Justice, then Sir Robin Cooke and now Lord Cooke of Thorndon,[3] made Coke's claim amid much controversy among the legal profession. To the same government-controlling effect, but arising from alien (north American and European continental) traditions, Geoffrey Palmer, having failed to 'entrench' a Bill of Rights, continued for a time to advocate a written constitution, adopted and authorised in such a way as to put it beyond the power of a simple majority in parliament to override its requirements. Still others, calling on a native (but not mainstream constitutionalist) tradition, have claimed that the signing of the Treaty of Waitangi in 1840 was the act which, in federating Māori and the Crown, created the constitution, so that the terms of that confederation limit parliamentary sovereignty. The Westminster doctrine, best laid out by Alfred Venn Dicey (1897), is that parliament may legislate whatever it wishes, including changes to the constitution. It has not only the 'legislative' or law-making power, typically laid out in the written constitutions of other states, but the 'constitutive' power, often the subject of complex arrangements in written constitutions.

ON THE LACK OF INTEREST IN THE CONSTITUTION IN NEW ZEALAND

Since the 1770s all constitutionalists (except the English, who had settled with the restoration of kingship in 1660 for following and quietly adapting their customs rather than abridging them in One Great Document) have insisted on the very great importance of getting constitutions clear, and writing them down. Indeed they have shed blood to erect and preserve them, reserving the power of changing them (uselessly in fact) to complex procedures laid down in the 'written constitution'. Constitutions have been the progeny of rebellion against alien rule, political integration and disintegration, of great plans of enthusiastic reformation, and of efforts to make world practice conform to some ideal pattern set by leading states. Their construction and protection have called forth the most heroic endeavours of great men—and women. The most famous image of the birth of a revolutionary constitution is the painting by Delacroix in 1830. Liberty is at the barricades, statuesquely and chastely bare-breasted, the flag of the Republic in her upraised hand, rifle and bayonet in the other. The dead and dying are at her feet (Hawgood 1939).

New Zealanders, however, are not that much interested in their constitution. Our constitutional history since 1840 has in the main been characterised by the public's apathy and the politicians' sluggish reaction to overseas, especially British, initiatives. When, from 1984 on, Geoffrey Palmer, as a leading member of the Labour government, tried to introduce a Bill of Rights into the constitutional fabric, the measure excited neither the public nor politicians. When in 1986 an Officials Committee on Constitutional Reform drafted the constitution bill for updating and consolidating the statutory basis of the constitution, the select committee of parliament that considered the bill received a paltry eight submissions. When, from about 1987 the question arose as to whether a proportional system of election should replace first-past-the post, it was indeed clear enough to the experts that any change would have far-reaching and systematic constitutional implications; but in general the public debate confined itself to more specific questions. Which system would represent the population better? Which would provide more powerful government? Which would favour which political party or parties? There was a good deal of awareness of the political consequences of a change, that is, but much less sense that the nature of a whole system of rules and principles that governed politics was at stake, let alone a constitutional system (McRobie 1995 pp. 312–43). Contemplating these facts in 1993, Dr Joseph rightly remarked that 'seldom is politics *conceptualised* in constitutional terms' (Joseph 1993 p. 110). And things have not changed very much. When, in 1997, a collection of writings on New Zealand politics (*New Zealand Politics in Transition*) was published under the same editorship as this collection, its discussion of 'the constitution' was to be almost entirely found in only one chapter (out of forty): 'The head of state: the crown, the queen, and the governor-general' (Ladley

1997, pp. 51–61). The chapters on 'theories of state' were devoted to 'pluralism', 'feminism', 'neo-liberalism', and 'Marxism'. There was none on 'constitutionalism' until the 2001 edition. In October 1999, eighty-odd academics and others with claims to constitutional expertise endorsed and published arguments for the retention of 120 MPs in the face of the pending referendum wanting 100. Prominent among the signatories were Professors Boston and McLeay, whose book has been already mentioned. Their constitutional arguments were depicted in *The Dominion* and *The National Business Review* as 'political', 'partisan' and 'left-wing'—even though no party had espoused as policy any attitude to the question. In brief, in New Zealand political culture, when a question looks to be politically important, it ceases to be a constitutional one and takes on the colouring of political ephemera.

Like most interesting claims, this is an exaggeration. Since January 1995, to take a somewhat arbitrary date as a starting point for scanning newspapers and magazines, some questions *have* been conceptualised and debated as 'constitutional' matters. These have been questions as to whether New Zealand should become a republic, whether it should retain the Privy Council in England as its final court of appeal, whether the Bill of Rights should be 'entrenched', whether the constitution should be 'written', whether the judiciary might be better selected and disciplined, and whether Māori should have special rights that no other citizens have, including a separate constitutional status granting rights to self-government. Leaving aside the Māori questions, none of these issues has much roused the public's attention. Whereas businesses, public interest groups and political parties have their professional staffs and bands of enthusiastic amateurs operating in the public sphere, constitutional interests have been mainly represented by only a few lawyers and judges: the first hamstrung by their lack of popular profile, the second by their membership in a judiciary which by constitutional convention is supposed to stay out of politics.

Only three protagonists stand out as highly distinguished public figures advocating serious thinking about the constitution: the doomed National prime minister, Rt Hon. James Bolger (advocating the end of the Queen and a republic, from 1994–97); the prominent and charismatic but marginalised Labour ex-prime minister, Rt Hon. Mike Moore (advocating a constitutional convention to formulate reforms which would be put to test in a referendum, in 1998–99); and the retired ex-Labour prime minister turned professional lobbyist, Sir Geoffrey Palmer (for a reformed and written constitution along the lines of that of the USA). But the big constitutional issues they approached did not produce much traction. National's plans to scrap the Privy Council foundered in 1995 through lack of enthusiasm and opposition from Māori, and Labour's final abolition of appeal in 2003, though greeted with the (unconstitutional) claim that parliament could not carry out such an act and that a referendum was necessary, went through tolerably smoothly. Reform of the judiciary to make it more 'accountable' in the wake of the Judge Martin Beattie case was, though useful, hardly spectacular. Arguments between the prime minister and the chief justice in 2004–05 about the administration of the courts were interpreted by the media more as a personal matter between Helen Clark and Sean Elias than as a question of 'separation of powers'. There is no great enthusiasm among politicians (though there is rising public support) for a republic (to be discussed in chapter 2.3). The issues of a written constitution and an entrenched Bill of Rights are grist to the mill only to academic lawyers and fringe enthusiasts.

Why then, does constitutionalism—devotion to constitutional practice—matter?

THE SPIRIT OF CONSTITUTIONALISM

To picture public life as governed by the spirit of constitutionalism is to see it in a particular and distinct way. It is different, for instance, from seeing public life as purely political, or as a matter of management, or as the play of individuals and groupings pursuing their own, mainly economic, advantage.

Pictures of public life in the image of democratic politics, of management or of economics, are now dominant in New Zealand; but constitutionalism is older and wiser. The political and economic views see public life as a sphere of unsettled things, as a contest for advantage among equals, a clash of liberty against liberty. In the political view, parties, groups and individuals contest for mastery in the name of the public good. In the economic view, groups and individuals pursue their own economic advantage confident that their mutual contests are for the economic good of the whole. Constitutionalism, on the other hand, sees public life as working within rules and principles settled by tradition or agreement. It values continuity and stability more than change. A settled structure of expectations, it claims, is the basic prerequisite for the pursuit of change and opportunity; so that it values liberty indeed, but only that liberty settled by law. It may well be that the economic view of public life is coming to prevail over the political,[4] but from a constitutionalist perspective *both* those ways of seeing things and *both* sets of activities ought to be controlled by law. Freedom of contract for economic gain, no less than freedom in politics, should be limited in the name of a more permanent public good. Too much political freedom can strip individuals and groups of their legal rights, quite simply and easily, by legislation; too much economic freedom can lay waste the public estate and impoverish the people.

Constitutionalism also values equality, but again only within legal limits. The equality of all citizens must coexist with the inequalities of office prescribed by law and with the different and differentiated rights that individuals inherit from their families or gain through their own lawful exertions. For this reason, a constitutionalist will have no problem with 'special rights' that people have by virtue of entitlements that they inherit from the past, and will think that Dr Don Brash's famous Orewa speech of 2002, insisting on 'one law for all' and 'no special rights for Maori' was a political and not a constitutional claim.

Constitutionalism values legal authority. Those in authority must be obeyed and must be accorded due respect, even when they make mistakes and are wrong. Any recourse against them must be lawful. On the other hand, the legal rights of individuals and groups to property and political and economic freedoms must be respected by authority. This is why many constitutional experts were uneasy at the Labour-led government's abridgement of the rights of existing litigants by the 2005 Foreshore and Seabed legislation, and why for its part the government insisted that it was only the form and not the content of existing rights that was being changed. A single system of law must govern all: governors as well as people, and in this sense there is 'equality under the law' and 'one law for all'. Such is the spirit of constitutionalism. Law is sovereign: in the old republican adage, there should be 'the government of law and not of men'.

To see public life in the image of managerialism is also inimical to the spirit of constitutionalism. Managerialism thinks highly of the power to act efficiently in the light of clearly articulated goals, and distrust of subordinates is its hallmark (hence accountability regimes, contracts for specified outputs and distaste for stakeholders' sharing in governance). But suspicion of those in power is the hallmark of constitutionalism (hence the rule of law, the division of governmental functions, the balance of powers among officials). And constitutionalism is profoundly anti-revolutionary and sceptical. The trick, as one of the great English constitutionalists observed,[5] is more to keep the ship afloat than to steer confidently to any known destination. There are indeed experts on various matters, but there are no experts on the whole of public life. Managerialism, on the other hand, is somewhat Leninist. It might, like constitutionalism, stress adherence to settled procedures; but unlike it, it believes in governance by experts and in permanent revolution: politics, as the great Russian revolutionary once said, should become a matter only of 'accounting and control'. 'The authority of the government over persons will be replaced by the administration of things' (Lenin 1960, p. 161). There are no issues of equality, liberty and ideals of life to be contested, only a future of unbounded accumulation and welfare under the rule of an elite vanguard. Constitutionalism will have none of this.

This picture of constitutionalism is, I think, an attractive one, even though it is politically loaded. But its political bias (its tendency to favour particular interests) is not in any way a simple one. What does constitutionalism have to say, for instance, about the constitutional issues most pressing in public perception: those to do with special Māori rights, and in particular with special Māori rights to self-rule?

As to Māori rights in general, first: constitutionalism insists, in a detail expounded by the courts, that Māori have common law 'aboriginal title' to certain things (including in various aspects, traditional fisheries, and river and lake beds)—in just the same way that other citizens have their common law rights in whatever it is that they come to own by purchase, inheritance, gift or other lawful means. Second: constitutionalism insists in demonstrable detail that Māori have certain Treaty rights in so far as those rights are provided in statute and as defined and upheld in the courts—in just the same way that other individuals and groups have their statutory rights as defined and upheld in the courts. Third: the spirit of the laws insists that reparation is owed to everyone (including Māori) whose legal rights are violated and properties taken—and the detail of our laws sets out in many places procedures and rules under which reparation may occur, including the procedures and rules under which the Waitangi Tribunal, the Treaty Settlement Office, and the Crown operate. In brief, Māori claims and Māori politics in their intense insistence on their inherited rights and their litigation to enjoy those rights, are a model of constitutionalism. Those who would deny them those rights are supporters of arbitrary and unlawful government—in the name of democracy and equality perhaps, or on grounds of market freedom—but arbitrary and lawless nevertheless. How would they like a majority in parliament to legislate away what is legally theirs against their will?

On the other hand, certain other claims important to Māori are flatly unconstitutional: all claims to *tino rangatiratanga* unregulated by the law of the land; all claims to an independent Māori political nationhood originating with the Declaration of Independence 1835; many claims to 'autonomy' or self-government according to emerging international norms urged, for instance, by the Waitangi Tribunal. All these claims are denied not so much by the doctrine of the sovereignty of parliament but by the doctrine of the supremacy of the law of the constitution. The constitution leaves plenty of room for groups, freely assembled under the law, to deliver private and public services, to govern their internal workings, to act for their own ends, to be represented in parliament, and so on. It leaves room, too, for Māori to have a far greater constitutional presence than the present seven Māori seats in the house, were that presence to be legislated for. It does not, however, leave space for any entity not subjected to law: any arm of government *or* tribe. Iwi and hapu tend not to wish to see themselves as subject to any law but those they have consented to, and they tend to think that the current constitution is not well-designed to produce decisions or decision procedures that suit them. This is why, from a Māori and Crown's differing points of view, the constitution is at issue (Sharp 2002a, 2004). This is why—at least in this area of Māori–Crown politics—it is to be expected that the constitution will continue to be hotly debated.[6] The constitution and constitutionalism do really matter—both insofar as they are accepted and acted upon, and as they are challenged.

DISCUSSION QUESTIONS

1 What is constitutionalism?
2 What is the rule of law?
3 Is whether or not New Zealand has a written constitution an issue worth taking seriously?
4 Should Māori have special rights in a New Zealand constitution?

NOTES

1   See www.dpmc.govt.nz/cabinet/manual/index.html (last viewed 15 January 2006).
2   Places to start are A. Sharp 2002, 'Should Maori Group Rights be part of a New Zealand Constitution?' in G. Huscroft & P. Rishworth (eds), *Litigating Rights: Perspectives from Domestic and International Law*, Hart, Portland, Oregon, pp. 221–40, and other chapters in that collection; A. Sharp 2004, 'The Treaty in the Real Life of the Constitution', in M. Belgrave, M. Henare, M. Kawharu & D. Williams, *The Treaty of Waitangi: Maori and Pakeha Perspectives*, Oxford University Press, Auckland, pp. 196–206, and other chapters in that collection; A. Sharp 2002a, 'Blood, Custom and Consent: Three Kinds of Māori Groups in New Zealand and the Challenges they Present to Government and the Constitution', *University of Toronto Law Journal*, 51/1, pp. 9–37, and other articles in that number of the journal.
3   He became a British peer in December 1995.
4   For a refreshing series of reflections on this question in non-New Zealand contexts see John Dunn (ed.) 1990, *The Economic Limits to Modern Politics*, Cambridge University Press, Cambridge.
5   M. Oakeshott 1991, 'Political Education', in M. Oakeshott, *Rationalism in Politics and Other Essays*, expanded edition, Liberty Press, Indianapolis.
6   See Sir Douglas Graham against the other authors (Denise Henare most fully) in A. Quentin-Baxter (ed.) 1998, *Recognising the Rights of Indigenous Peoples*, Institute of Policy Studies, Victoria University of Wellington, Wellington. For more controversy (and suggested solutions), see K.S. Coates and P.G. McHugh 1998, *Living Relationships: Kokiri Ngatahi*, Victoria University Press, Wellington, B.Harris in chapter 2.2 of this volume, and the controversy in Colin James (ed.) 2000, *'Building the Constitution' Conference 1999*, Institute of Policy Studies, Wellington.

REFERENCES

Belgrave, M., M. Henare, M. Kawharu & D. Williams (eds) 2004, *The Treaty of Waitangi: Maori and Pakeha Perspectives*, Oxford University Press, Auckland.

Boston, J., S. Levine, E. McLeay & N. Roberts (eds) 1999, *Electoral and Constitutional Change in New Zealand: An MMP Sourcebook*, Victoria University Press, Wellington.

Cabinet, New Zealand 2006, *The Cabinet Manual*, www.dpmc.govt.nz/cabinet/manual/index.html

Coates, K.S. & P.G. McHugh 1998, *Living Relationships: Kokiri Ngatahi*, Victoria University Press, Wellington.

Dicey, A.V. 1807, *Introduction to the Study of the Law of the Constitution*, Macmillan, NY.

Dunn, J. (ed.) 1990, *The Economic Limits to Modern Politics*, Cambridge University Press, Cambridge.

Harris, B.V. 1995, 'The Law Making Power of the Judiciary', in P.A. Joseph (ed.), *Essays on the Constitution*, Brooker's, Wellington, pp. 265–85.

Hawgood, J.A. 1939, *Modern Constitutions since 1787*, Macmillan, London.

Huscroft, G. & P. Rishworth (eds) 2002, *Litigating Rights: Perspectives from Domestic and International Law*, Hart, Portland, Oregon.

James, C. (ed.) 2000, *'Building the Constitution' Conference*, Institute of Policy Studies, Victoria University of Wellington, Wellington.

Joseph, P. 1993, *Constitutional and Administrative Law in New Zealand*, Law Book Company, Sydney.

Joseph, P. (ed.) 1995, *Essays on the Constitution*, Brooker's, Wellington.

Joseph, P. 2001, *Constitutional and Administrative Law in New Zealand*, Brookers, Wellington.

Ladley, A. 1997, 'The Head of State: the Crown, the Queen and the Governor-General' in R. Miller (ed.) *New Zealand Politics in Transition*, Oxford University Press, Auckland, pp. 51–61.

Lenin, V.I. 1960, 'The State and Revolution (1917)' in *The Essential Left: Four Classic Texts on the Principles of Socialism/Marx, Engels [and] Lenin*, Unwin Books, London.

McIlwain, C.H. 1940, *Constitutionalism Ancient and Modern*, Cornell University Press, NY.

McRobie, A. 1995, 'The Electoral System' in Joseph, P. (ed.) *Essays*, 1995, pp. 312–43.

Miller, R. (ed.) 1997, *New Zealand Politics in Transition*, Oxford University Press, Auckland.

Oakeshott, M. 1991, 'Political Education', in M. Oakeshott, *Rationalism in Politics and Other Essays*, expanded edition, Liberty Press, Indianapolis.

Palmer, G.W.R. & K. Hill 2002, *Constitutional Conversations: Geoffrey Palmer Talks to Kim Hill on National Radio, 1994–2001*, Victoria University Press, Wellington.

Palmer, G.W.R. & M. Palmer 2004, *Bridled Power: New Zealand Government under MMP*, Oxford University Press, Melbourne and Auckland.

Quentin-Baxter, A. (ed.) 1998, *Recognising the Rights of Indigenous Peoples*, Institute of Policy Studies, Victoria University of Wellington, Wellington.

Sharp, A. 2002, 'Should Maori Group Rights be Part of a New Zealand Constitution?' in Huscroft & Rishworth (eds), *Litigating Rights*, pp. 221–40.

Sharp, A. 2002a, 'Blood, Custom and Consent: Three Kinds of Māori Groups in New Zealand and the Challenges they Present to Government and the Constitution', *University of Toronto Law Journal*, 51/1, pp. 9–37.

Sharp, A. 2004, 'The Treaty in the Real Life of the Constitution', in Belgrave, Henare et al. (eds) *The Treaty of Waitangi: Maori and Pakeha Perspectives*, pp. 196–206.

FURTHER READING

James, C. (ed.) 2000, *Building the Constitution*, Institute of Policy Studies, Victoria University of Wellington, Wellington.

Palmer, G.W.R. & M. Palmer. 2004, *Bridled Power: New Zealand Goverment under MMP*, Oxford University Press, Auckland.

Sharp, A. 2004, 'The Treaty in the Real Life of the Constitution' in Belgrave, Henare et al. (eds) *The Treaty of Waitangi: Māori and Pakeha Perspectives*, Oxford University Press Melbourne, pp. 196–206.

Tully, J. 1995, *Strange Multiplicity: Constitutionalism in an Age of Diversity*, Cambridge University Press, Cambridge.

Constitutional Change

Bruce V. Harris

Change is an inevitable constant feature of human life and therefore the organisation of human society. The law has to change in step with the community's changing expectations, or otherwise it will lose its credibility and related legitimacy. Without ongoing legitimacy the law and the mechanisms for its enforcement ultimately will collapse.

As discussed in the previous chapter, New Zealand, unlike most countries, does not have a comprehensive codified written constitution which constitutes and gives authority to the organs of government. New Zealand does have a constitution in that the system of government is established and empowered by law; however, that law is found in an eclectic collection of United Kingdom and New Zealand statutes and the common law developed by the courts. Constitutional conventions also play an important role in the operation of the constitution.

Constitutional conventions are not law and therefore will not be enforced by the courts. They are, rather, expectations of behaviour by public decision-makers, compliance with which is encouraged by political pressures. A leading example of a constitutional convention is the expectation that the Governor-General, in whom the law expressly vests considerable executive powers, only will exercise those powers on the advice of ministers who are themselves accountable to parliament for the action taken by the Governor-General upon their advice.

New Zealand constitutional law has often been changed as the country has evolved over the last 166 years from British colony to autonomous nation–state. There is a slowly growing current of discussion about the possible need for significant further changes to be made to New Zealand's constitutional law if it is to continue to provide an appropriate legal foundation for the type of society the community wants (see Harris 2004). In this chapter I propose to address: how constitutional change has been achieved in New Zealand in the past; the significant issues on the current New Zealand constitutional change agenda; and the processes which may be available for the community to decide and adopt any changes.

HOW CONSTITUTIONAL CHANGE HAS BEEN ACHIEVED IN THE PAST

The legislature, either that of the United Kingdom or that of New Zealand, has effected most of the changes to date to the New Zealand constitution. Since the Glorious Revolution (1688) the Westminster parliament has theoretically been unconstrained in its law-changing capacity. The New Zealand parliament has over time been regarded as acquiring a similar law-making sovereignty. The New Zealand constitution is described as 'flexible' because it has always been capable of easily being changed by the legislature in contrast to the difficulty of meeting the prescribed constitutional change procedures in many other countries.

The United Kingdom executive government and representatives of Māori entered into the Treaty of Waitangi in 1840. This led to the United Kingdom proclaiming sovereignty over New Zealand, and a decade on, the United Kingdom parliament enacting the New Zealand Constitution Act 1852. The 1852 statute established a bicameral legislature which was called the 'General Assembly'.[1] The General Assembly consisted of an elected House of Representatives, an executive appointed Legislative Council as a second legislative chamber and the Governor who gave the royal assent to proposed legislation. The General Assembly was given initially a limited law-making capacity in that it was expressly prohibited from making laws 'repugnant to the law of England'[2] and impliedly prohibited from making laws which purported to be effective beyond the territory of New Zealand.[3] In addition, the United Kingdom parliament retained the capacity to legislate for New Zealand until 1986.[4]

The United Kingdom and New Zealand legislatures were saved from the need to create a comprehensive set of laws for the new colony by the New Zealand parliament enacting a statute which provided that the common law, that is, court-made law, and the statute law of England, should apply in New Zealand so far as applicable to the local circumstances.[5] This meant that New Zealand inherited from the United Kingdom fundamental constitutional statutes such as Magna Carta (1297), the Bill of Rights (1688), and the Act of Settlement (1701).[6] New Zealand also was regarded by the participants in the system of government and the community as inheriting the more informal aspects of the United Kingdom constitution such as constitutional conventions (see chapter 2.1).

From this foundation in the 1840s and 1850s the New Zealand constitution has evolved incrementally through a series of constitutional changes of varying degrees of magnitude. Until 1947 constitutional change was primarily effected through enactments of the United Kingdom parliament. In the late 1940s the incumbent New Zealand government took an initiative to have the repugnancy and extra-territoriality restrictions on the law-making capacity of the New Zealand General Assembly removed. The United Kingdom parliament had created the opportunity for such change by enacting the Statute of Westminster 1931 which was available for adoption by the former colonies, by then known as 'British Dominions'. The New Zealand General Assembly passed the Statute of Westminster Adoption Act 1947, but this did not give the General Assembly plenary law-making powers since the central sections of the New Zealand Constitution Act 1852, such as those constituting and empowering the General Assembly, remained only alterable by the Westminster parliament.[7] Finally, the New Zealand parliament gained the freedom to change these sections after the United Kingdom parliament, upon the New Zealand parliament's request,[8] passed the New Constitution (Amendment) Act 1947. This new power of amendment allowed the New Zealand General Assembly in 1950 to abolish part of itself, the second chamber known as the Legislative Council.[9] The legislature changed from being bicameral to unicameral.

Each of the changes was taken upon the initiative of the incumbent New Zealand government and was effected through the law-making powers of either the United Kingdom or New Zealand legislatures. The pattern was not one of forceful groundswells of public opinion demanding particular changes, but rather the governing elite, supported by the respective legislatures, thinking that the changes were prudent at the time.

This has also been the pattern of the constitutional changes over the last fifty years. There have not been many and they have all been at the hand of the New Zealand parliament. The more major changes have been: the enactment of the Constitution Act 1986; the enactment of the New Zealand Bill of Rights Act 1990; the introduction of the Mixed Member Proportional (MMP) electoral system through the Electoral Act 1993; and the abolition through the Supreme Court Act 2003 of the right of appeal to the Privy Council with the institution of the new Supreme Court as New Zealand's final appellate court.

Of these changes, the introduction of the MMP electoral system was the only one where parliament determined referendum support was required.[10] All of the major changes have involved reports by government-appointed groups prior to the introduction to parliament of the change-enabling legislation. With each proposed change, opportunity has been provided for the public to make submissions to the select committee considering the bill during the parliamentary law-making process.

The Constitution Act 1986 was a tidying-up exercise, much of its content relating to the legislative, executive, and judicial branches of government being already provided in existing law. The Act repealed what was left of the New Zealand Constitution Act 1852 and terminated the right of the United Kingdom parliament to legislate for New Zealand.[11]

The New Zealand Bill of Rights Act 1990 has been a more significant and pervasive constitutional innovation than it was anticipated to be at the time of its enactment. Although it is not strictly binding on parliament,[12] it does have a strong influence on the content and interpretation of legislation, in addition to regulating the actions of the executive and the judiciary.[13] The Bill of Rights Act is an ordinary enactment of parliament which can be amended or repealed by simple majority.

The changes brought about by the Supreme Court Act 2003 were controversial, some critics arguing that the innovations needed to be supported by referendum approval.[14] Others considered the issues too complex for reliable formal approval assessment by the wider community (see Harris 2004, pp. 284–5).

Statutory enactment is not the only way by which constitutional change takes place in New Zealand. The courts can bring about constitutional change by developing the common law or by developing their interpretation of statutes. An example of constitutional change by developing the common law is the way the New Zealand courts have followed the lead of the English courts and departed from the old rule that they could not provide judicial review of government actions authorised by the common law rather than statute.[15] An example of constitutional change by developing the interpretation of statutes is the way the New Zealand Bill of Rights Act 1990 has been subject to a continuously evolving interpretation by the courts. This is illustrated by the courts' willingness to provide remedies not expressly provided for in the Bill of Rights. A remedy of damages is recognised as available for a breach by government of the Act,[16] and a court may issue a declaration that legislation is inconsistent with the Bill of Rights.[17] The latter declaration does not cause the inconsistent statute to be invalid because that statute is an enactment of parliament and parliament has sovereign law-making powers. The declaration of inconsistency does, however, draw to the attention of parliament and the community a statute which parliament may wish at its discretion to amend to comply with the Bill of Rights. The courts play a significant role in effecting constitutional change in New Zealand.

The processes by which constitutional change may take place have received comparatively little deliberate attention. With no comprehensive written constitution New Zealand does not have a specified legally mandated process for constitutional change. There is a small number of sections in the Constitution Act 1986 and the Electoral Act 1993 singularly entrenched, in the sense that their amendment is specified to require the support of either a 75 per cent majority in parliament, or the support of a majority of those voting in a national referendum.[18] The objective of the entrenchment is to ensure that appropriate consideration is given to proposed changes in relation to aspects of the electoral process and the term of parliament, and that there is cross-party and/or widespread support in the community for the proposed changes. However, although contrary to the spirit of the entrenchment and certainly constitutional convention, the sections imposing the entrenching procedural restrictions on future parliaments are not themselves entrenched and could legally be amended or repealed by a determined simple majority in the House of Representatives. As has already been appreciated, it remains true that parliament acting by simple majority can potentially change all of the present constitution.

It is generally accepted that if New Zealand wished to create an effectively entrenched written constitution, or other entrenched constitutional provisions, which were clearly beyond the reach of change by a simple parliamentary majority, the courts would look for evidence of widespread community support for the creation of what is called 'superior law', most likely provided by majority support in a national referendum (see Cooke 1984). Unlike the current 'single' entrenchment in the Electoral Act 1993 and the Constitution Act 1986, 'double' entrenchment would be employed whereby the statutory provisions providing for the entrenchment are themselves entrenched.

IS THERE A PRESENT NEED FOR CONSTITUTIONAL CHANGE?

Some would argue that New Zealand should be actively reassessing its present constitutional arrangements with a view to modifying their design so as to provide a better foundation for future New Zealand society (see Harris 2004). However, there is not a societal groundswell strongly pushing for particular changes, and neither is the constitutional elite pushing for change. Many of the constitutional elite, that is, the legal profession, judges, and academic commentators, do not support a greater formalisation of the constitution for fear of giving more law-making power to the non-elected judiciary. Their preference is that law-making responsibility should be conscientiously preserved for the democratically elected legislature.

The Constitutional Arrangements Select Committee, which was established in December 2004 to review aspects of New Zealand's existing constitutional arrangements, released its final report in August 2005 (see RCAC 2005). The Select Committee also did not agitate for significant constitutional change in the near future. The Committee acknowledged that New Zealand has potential constitutional change issues, but thought that it was unwise for the committee to engage with some of these issues in its report and 'unsettle the status quo' (see RCAC 2005, pp. 8, 17). Provoking division in the community was seen as possibly outweighing the benefits of the stimulated debate (see RCAC 2005, pp. 5, 50, 52). For those who are enthusiastic advocates of the importance of freedom of speech to the quality of political discourse and ultimately political decision-making, the Select Committee's reticence may be a little unsettling.

The recommendations of the Select Committee are modest. The Committee thought that: the House of Representatives should develop its select committee system to ensure that constitutional issues which arise in parliament's work are identified and specifically addressed; the community should have the opportunity to become better informed about constitutional matters; (by a majority) that there should be 'specific processes for facilitating discussion with Māori communities on constitutional issues'; civic and citizenship education should be improved in schools; and (again by majority) that the government should consider whether an independent institute could better facilitate constitutional understanding and debate in the community (see RCAC 2005, p. 5).

The unlikelihood of significant constitutional change in the near future is not a reason for not exploring the options for improving the design of the New Zealand constitution. The lack of codification and the flexibility of the present constitution are its distinguishing features. Only the United Kingdom and Israel have similarly uncodified constitutions. The main possibilities for redesign being discussed in New Zealand are all likely to involve a greater entrenched codification of the constitution and therefore a greater role for the courts in upholding the code against all three branches of government, that is, the legislature, the executive and the judiciary.

THE MAIN CURRENT CONSTITUTIONAL REDESIGN ISSUES

The main constitutional redesign issues which should be before the New Zealand community are: the need to settle better the legal position of the Treaty of Waitangi and other Māori interests; the likely need to facilitate the change from a constitutional monarchy to a republic; the possible need to give the Bill of Rights a status in superior law so that it is more effective to constrain the legislature; and the possible need to move towards a formal comprehensive written constitution as the source of, and limit on, all legislative, executive, and judicial power. Each of these issues needs to be considered in more detail.

1. The Treaty of Waitangi and other Māori interests

Māori are the indigenous people of New Zealand. Through representative chiefs they entered into the Treaty of Waitangi with the United Kingdom Crown in 1840. English language and Māori language versions of the Treaty were signed, there being significant differences between the two. Notwithstanding the pivotal role the Treaty played in facilitating the establishment of United Kingdom sovereignty over New Zealand, it remains by itself not part of New Zealand's domestic law and therefore will not be enforced by the courts.[19] Nevertheless, parliament has in recent years included 'the principles of the Treaty of Waitangi' as a relevant consideration in the decision-making of numerous public authorities.[20] Parliament has not gone on to define the principles of the Treaty of Waitangi so the courts and public authorities, particularly the Waitangi Tribunal,[21] have had to determine the principles from the wording of the two original versions of the Treaty.[22]

The Treaty can also have an influence on the law through its recognition as a principle of statutory interpretation. Where a statutory provision is ambiguous, the expectation is that the interpreting court will prefer the meaning which is more consistent with the Treaty.[23] The Treaty also has a pervasive influence on public decision-making independent of the law through the development of informal expectations that its requirements should be taken into account.[24]

There is considerable uncertainty in the community about what the Treaty requires in different situations. The Waitangi Tribunal through thirty years of hearing complaints about alleged government and legislative non-compliance with the principles of the Treaty of Waitangi has endeavoured to articulate what it considers the content should be in different contexts.[25]

The concept of rangatiratanga from Article 2 has been argued to support Māori claims to greater rights of self-determination (see Harris 2004, pp. 293–4). Such calls are common from indigenous peoples. The argument is that Māori should have better opportunities to govern themselves. This aspiration does not sit comfortably with those who believe that there should be one law for all in New Zealand and that New Zealand should not have a formal pluralism based on race in its legal system.[26]

Many Māori and some non-Māori would wish to have the Treaty made part of domestic law with the capacity to be enforced in the courts in its own right. Some wish to go further and have it included in any new entrenched written constitution which New Zealand may wish to adopt. The current mood of the wider New Zealand community does not support either formalisation of Treaty rights. In recent years the more conservative political parties have been calling for the removal from statute of the already existing references to the principles of the Treaty of Waitangi and other special statutory provision for Māori interests, such as that found in the Resource Management Act 1991.[27] The final report of the 2005 Constitutional Arrangements Select Committee would appear to include the future of Treaty and Māori interests among those issues considered too divisive for society to address deliberately at this time (see RCAC 2005, p. 8). For the foreseeable future, the compromise of the status quo is likely to continue with parliament determining selectively when the Treaty and other Māori interests are to be relevant to public decision-making (see Harris 2005, p. 215).

2. From constitutional monarchy to republic

The second area of possible major constitutional redesign on the horizon is facilitation of New Zealand's inevitable eventual move from being a constitutional monarchy to a republic. The 2005 Constitutional Arrangements Select Committee did not regard this as sufficiently imminent to demand their serious attention. The New Zealand head of state is the Queen of New Zealand,[28] who is currently a person determined by heredity and who resides in the United Kingdom, seldom visiting New Zealand. The head of state functions are performed on a daily basis by her representative, the

Governor-General, now but not always, a New Zealander appointed on the advice of the incumbent government.[29] Notwithstanding how strange the arrangement may appear to the outside observer, New Zealand has the design in common with other major Commonwealth countries such as Australia and Canada. It is not disputed that the arrangement continues to work remarkably well.

A change to a republic would not be likely to raise insurmountable issues. Three of the more major questions would be: how to select and appoint the new head of state; how to provide a replacement for the concept of the Crown, that is the legal manifestation of the executive in the current constitutional arrangement; and how to manage the reconceptualisation of the ongoing significance of the Treaty of Waitangi, given the Crown has been perceived as the government party to that arrangement? It is not likely that there will be difficulties determining the powers of the new head of state as there is likely to be a consensus that these should largely mirror the current powers of the Governor-General. (see chapter 2.3 for further discussion on this topic.)

3. Entrenching the Bill of Rights

The third issue is whether New Zealand should give a status in superior law to the Bill of Rights. Should the Bill of Rights be entrenched so that it cannot be amended by a simple majority in parliament? The entrenchment could take the form of requiring, as a prerequisite to amendment, a special majority in parliament or the support of a national referendum.

Such entrenching of the Bill of Rights would be likely to be accompanied by the courts holding invalid legislation found to be inconsistent with the Bill of Rights. The Bill of Rights would limit the law-making capacity of the legislature. Under the current understanding of the continuing sovereignty of parliament the courts do not have the jurisdiction to declare legislation inconsistent with the Bill of Rights to be invalid. An unambiguously worded statute can override the attempted protection for the individual provided in the Bill of Rights.[30] As mentioned above, the courts will declare statutes to be inconsistent with the Bill of Rights if need be, but this will not affect the validity of the inconsistent statute.[31]

The New Zealand Bill of Rights Act 1990 currently has an influence on the law-making of parliament through *The Cabinet Manual* expectation that ministers proposing legislation will 'draw attention to any aspects that have implications for, or may be affected by: ... the rights and freedoms contained in the New Zealand Bill of Rights Act 1990'.[32] Also the Attorney-General is obliged by s 7 of the Bill of Rights Act 1990 to draw the attention of the House of Representatives 'to any provision in [a] Bill that appears to be inconsistent with any of the rights and freedoms contained in [the] Bill of Rights'. Further, parliament when enacting legislation, is mindful that s 6 of the Bill of Rights has put in place a mandatory rule of statutory interpretation which requires that ambiguous statutes are to be construed consistently with the rights and freedoms contained in the Bill of Rights. This means that parliament should enact legislation with a clear mind as to whether it intends an enactment to be subject to, or to override, the rights and freedoms provided for in the Bill of Rights. The jurisdiction which the court has assumed to declare enactments inconsistent with the Bill of Rights also has the potential to influence parliament to amend such statutes to ensure that they are in line with the expectations the Bill of Rights has of all three branches of government.

Given the raft of ways by which the Bill of Rights currently may influence the law-making of parliament, there may be doubt as to whether a lot would be gained by entrenching the Bill of Rights and giving the courts jurisdiction to declare inconsistent legislation invalid. This doubt would have to be weighed in the constitutional change process.

4. Adopting a written constitution

A fourth major constitutional redesign issue on the horizon is whether New Zealand should move from its current flexible 'unwritten' and 'uncodified' constitution to a written or codified constitution. A written constitution could be the legal source of authority for all three branches of government. It could provide specific rules for the operation of the constitution and it could also include the Bill of Rights. Should the community wish to include the Treaty of Waitangi in domestic law, it too could be located in the written constitution.

Normally such comprehensive written constitutions are entrenched, the community seeing their content as the important law behind the law which should not be changed without much consideration and widespread support. It follows that the provisions of written constitutions are upheld by the courts against all three branches of government, including most dramatically constraining the law-making function of the democratically elected legislature.

The adoption of a written constitution would bring New Zealand closer to the constitutional design model employed in most other countries. It would also better facilitate community access to, and understanding of, New Zealand constitutional law, the sources of which are currently a disparate raft of statutes, common law, and constitutional conventions.

The increased formalisation of the New Zealand constitution may be argued against on two prominent grounds. The first is the difficulty that may be experienced in achieving justified amendments to an entrenched written constitution, given the degree of parliamentary and electoral support that the entrenchment may require for amendment to be possible. The fear would be that the codified constitution may ossify, get uncomfortably out of step with the expectations of the community and consequently lose its perceived legitimacy.

A second concern would be the power which may move from the legislature to the courts. An entrenched written constitution containing the Bill of Rights and the Treaty of Waitangi would charge the courts with the task of giving meaning and application to inherently indeterminate constitutional provisions. The executive-appointed courts' determinations would prevail over the decisions of the democratically elected legislature as to what the law is.

The critics would not only argue this to be undemocratic, but they would also argue that the courts' processes are unsuited to such ultimately determinant law-making. The courts are adversarial, rather than inquisitorial, so that the evidence and argument before the courts is largely determined by the parties to the litigation. The number of parties to the litigation is necessarily limited and there is not the same opportunity for community participation in the law-making as provided by the legislative process where proposals for new laws are often widely canvassed before being introduced into parliament. When in parliament, public participation is facilitated through the select committee hearings. The critics would further argue that the community perceived legitimacy of the courts to perform the judicial functions of government could be undermined should they be performing law-making considered to be in the nature of determination of policy for which political accountability would be the normal expectation.

THE CONSTITUTIONAL CHANGE PROCESS

The Constitutional Arrangements Select Committee, although aware of the above four constitutional redesign issues, chose not to engage with them. The committee considered that the present design of the constitution was not in crisis, and that there was not likely to be sufficient consensus in society for any of the major redesign possibilities to be profitably addressed at this stage.

Notwithstanding the report of the Constitutional Arrangements Select Committee, addressing the raised major constitutional redesign issues cannot be avoided indefinitely by the political process. For this reason the procedures by which decisions about these possible changes could be made should at least be explored.

Constitutional change takes place in different ways in different jurisdictions. Most often a written constitution will specify the procedure by which it may be changed. Often that procedure will facilitate entrenchment and be something different from the legislature acting by simple majority.

Where a comprehensive new legal order is being created in an autonomous country, the procedure employed authoritatively to put in place the new constitution will need to give it a legitimacy both from a technical legal point of view and also from the point of view of the community's willingness to own the constitution. Most new constitutional arrangements are 'autochthonous' in the sense that they gain their legitimacy from being put in place by the community in respect of which they are intended to operate. Such community approval may be evidenced by a referendum.

Unfortunately referenda are expensive, cumbersome, and clumsy societal approval mechanisms; the need to reduce complex constitutional proposals to questions capable of simple 'yes' or 'no' answers can cause majority referendum approval to be difficult to achieve.

A community may choose to put in place a constitutional assembly or convention with a composition different from that of the regular legislature and that assembly or convention may have the responsibility of creating recommended new constitutional arrangements. These arrangements may go subsequently to the regular legislature and a referendum for formal approval and consequent manifestation in superior law.

If New Zealand were to want to explore seriously major redesign of the constitution in terms of better settling the position of the Treaty and Māori interests in law, changing to a republic, entrenching the Bill of Rights and creating a written constitution, a constitutional change procedure or procedures suitable to these tasks in the New Zealand context would need to be designed. The procedure would have to take account of the bicultural context that exists in New Zealand and what the wider community would expect as a prerequisite to the new constitutional arrangements having legitimacy.

The process would need to have at least three distinct stages: first, appropriate education of the community in respect of the constitutional design issues being explored; second, widespread consultation followed by development of the proposal for the new constitutional design; and third, authoritative approval through an appropriate formal change mechanism. Each of these stages requires discussion.

The New Zealand community generally has only a superficial understanding of the current constitutional arrangements and how they operate. In order to facilitate effective participation by the community in constitutional redesign consultation, and for that community to participate wisely in the formal approval of any proposed new constitutional redesign, it has to have access to deliberate and appropriate government-funded education. The 2005 Constitutional Arrangements Select Committee has recognised this need (see RCAC 2005, p. 5).

The second stage, consultation followed by development of the proposals for a new constitutional design, requires consideration of the history and composition of the New Zealand community. The New Zealand constitutional law context currently recognises the Treaty of Waitangi in different ways, as discussed above, and the constitutional law in some respects makes different provision for Māori, an example being the Māori seats in the House of Representatives.[33] Over the last thirty years, the policy has been to recognise increasingly a bicultural rather than an assimilated community. It follows from this perspective that both the consultation stage and the formal approval stage should provide Māori with the opportunity to participate as a distinct group. Professor Mason Durie has suggested, against the background of the non-existence of a suitable existing national Māori organisation, that a Māori Constitutional Commission be created and charged with the responsibility of facilitating effective consultation with Māori (see Durie 2000, p. 423). I have written elsewhere that this commission could work together with a general constitutional commission, the latter body of persons of appropriate expertise having the overall responsibility for providing participation opportunities to the whole community (see Harris 2004, pp. 286–8). The two commissions could work together to bring forward recommended constitutional changes for approval by the formal constitutional change process.

Constitutional change has historically been incremental in New Zealand. There is a developing consensus that future constitutional change should also be incremental, rather than a comprehensive new constitutional design put in place at one time. Comprehensive change of a constitution at one time would be more likely to occur after a revolution or other constitutional crisis, not in circumstances when an existing constitution is functioning adequately, but is being updated to meet changing community expectations.

Incremental change also allows each significant constitutional issue to receive appropriate attention. The formal approval is focused on that issue rather than possibly it being lost in the need to approve or disapprove an eclectic group of constitutional changes as one package.

If the constitutional reform process were to be by way of incremental change, an order for considering the reform issues would have to be determined (see Harris 2004, p. 309). Obviously issues such as New Zealand becoming a republic would not be seriously addressed by the constitutional change process until a greater proportion of the community thought the time had arrived to consider seriously the issue. The better settling of the Treaty of Waitangi and Māori interests in New Zealand law, although arguably one of the more pressing of the country's constitutional reform issues, after being initially raised for consultation, may be better left to a more relaxed discourse over time. This would allow the participants in the conversation time for their understanding and thinking to evolve before being required to decide in a formal approval process (see Harris 2005, p. 214).

If the community accepts that Māori should have the opportunity to indicate as a group their approval or disapproval of proposed constitutional changes, a suitable formal approval process will have to be designed. I have suggested elsewhere (see Harris 2004, pp. 286–8), and above, that a possible model may be for the two constitutional commissions to facilitate the wide-ranging consultations and bring to parliament suggested constitutional changes. Parliament could bring its wisdom to bear upon the proposals, possibly amending them before resolving to give approval. The coming into effect of the changes could be conditional upon approval in a referendum. If it were thought that Māori support for the proposed changes were not sufficiently evidenced by the participation of the Māori constitutional commission in the proposal formation process, the referendum support could be required from separate Māori and general electorates (see Harris 2004, p. 285).

The structure providing for Māori involvement in the constitutional redesign and formal approval process inevitably will be controversial because the community, after increasingly recognising Treaty and Māori interests since the mid-1970s, has recently, led by the more conservative parliamentary political parties, swung back to policies based on the principle that there should be one law for all in the New Zealand community. Such policies may influence against Māori being specially provided for in the consultation and formal constitutional change approval process.

CONCLUSION

The major political parties are not energetically arguing for dramatic constitutional change; the Constitutional Arrangements Select Committee has not recommended that a constitutional change process be put in place, and the country continues to have a stable constitutional system that functions well when compared with many other countries. Nevertheless, there are constitutional change issues which the New Zealand constitutional elite and the wider community arguably should be discussing. The issues include: better settling the Treaty of Waitangi and Māori interests in the constitutional arrangements; deciding whether New Zealand should become a republic; deciding whether New Zealand should entrench the Bill of Rights and have it available to the courts to limit the law-making of the legislature; and deciding whether New Zealand should adopt a comprehensive entrenched written constitution. Conversations should also be taking place about the best possible design for a change process which not only will give any new constitutional arrangements a validity that the courts will recognise, but also will attract a widespread and ongoing confidence from the community.

DISCUSSION QUESTIONS

1   Discuss the characteristics of the process of constitutional change in New Zealand from 1840 to the present.

2   What scope do the New Zealand courts have to bring about constitutional change?

3   What aspects of the New Zealand constitution do you think will require change in the near future?

4   How should the Treaty of Waitangi and Māori interests be provided for in New Zealand's future constitutional arrangements?

5   What process should be employed to facilitate future constitutional change in New Zealand?

6   How would the role of the courts change should New Zealand adopt an entrenched written constitution which could limit the law-making powers of parliament?

NOTES

1   See s 32 of the New Zealand Constitution Act 1852 (UK).
2   See s 53 of the New Zealand Constitution Act 1852 (UK).
3   The extra-territorial limit on the law-making capability of the General Assembly was derived from the wording of s 53 of the New Zealand Constitution Act 1852 (UK) which provided that laws may be made 'for the peace, order and good government *of New Zealand*'.
4   See s 15(2) of the Constitution Act 1986 (NZ).
5   See s 1 of the English Laws Act 1858 (NZ) which was replaced by the English Laws Act 1908 (NZ). See now ss 3, 4 and 5 of the Imperial Laws Application Act 1988 (NZ).
6   For a list of the United Kingdom statutes which are part of current New Zealand law see the First Schedule of the Imperial Laws Application Act 1988 (NZ).
7   See ss 4 and 8 of the Statute of Westminster 1931 (UK).
8   See the New Zealand Constitution Amendment (Request and Consent) Act 1947 (NZ).
9   See the Legislative Council Abolition Act 1950 (NZ).
10   See s 2 of the Electoral Act 1993 (NZ) and the Electoral Referendum Act 1993 (NZ).
11   See ss 15(2) and 26(1) of the Constitution Act 1986 (NZ).
12   See s 4 of the New Zealand Bill of Rights Act 1990 (NZ).
13   See s 3 of the New Zealand Bill of Rights Act 1990 (NZ).
14   See, e.g., editorials in the *New Zealand Herald,* 14 May 2003 at A14 and 8 July 2003 at A12.
15   See *Burt v. Governor-General* [1992] 3 *New Zealand Law Reports* 672.
16   See *Simpson v. Attorney-General* [Baigent's case] [1994] 3 *New Zealand Law Reports* 667.
17   See *Moonen v. Film and Literature Board of Review* [2000] 2 *New Zealand Law Reports* 9 at 17 per Tipping J.
18   See s 268 of the Electoral Act 1993 (NZ) and s 17(2) of the Constitution Act 1986 (NZ).
19   See *New Zealand Maori Council v. Attorney-General* [1987] 1 *New Zealand Law Reports* 641 at 672 per Richardson J. and at 691 per Somers J.
20   See, e.g., s 9 of the State-Owned Enterprises Act 1986 (NZ) and s 8 of the Resource Management Act 1991 (NZ).
21   See the Treaty of Waitangi Act 1975 (NZ) as amended.
22   See generally *New Zealand Maori Council v. Attorney-General* [1987] 1 *New Zealand Law Reports* 641.
23   See J.F. Burrows, *Statute Law in New Zealand* (3rd edn, 2003) pp. 345–6, citing as examples *Huakina Development Trust v. Waikato Valley Authority* [1987] 2 *New Zealand Law Reports* 188 and *Barton-Prescott v. Director-General of Social Welfare* [1997] 3 *New Zealand Law Reports* 179.
24   See, e.g., the expectation (but not requirement of law) recorded in the *Cabinet Manual* (2001) paras 5.35–5.36 that ministers when seeking to have bills approved by the Cabinet Legislation Committee for introduction into parliament will confirm compliance with the principles of the Treaty of Waitangi.
25   See, e.g. *Report on the Crown's Foreshore and Seabed Policy* (WAI 1071, 2004) where the Waitangi Tribunal considered the content of the principles of the Treaty of

Waitangi which it thought should apply to the government's proposed legislation on the foreshore and seabed.

26   See, e.g., an extract from a speech delivered by the National Party Leader, Dr Don Brash, to the Orewa Rotary Club on 27 January 2004: *New Zealand Herald*, 28 January 2004, p. A18.

27   Ibid. See also the Principles of the Treaty of Waitangi Deletion Bill, which was introduced into Parliament by the Rt Hon Winston Peters on 10 February 2005, but negatived on its first reading on 8 June 2005.

28   See s 2 of the Constitution Act 1986 (NZ) and s 2 of the Royal Titles Act 1974 (NZ).

29   See s 2(2) of the Constitution Act 1986 (NZ) and clause 1 of the Letters Patent Constituting the Office of Governor-General 1983 (Statutory Regulations 1983/225, 1987/8).

30   See s 4 of the New Zealand Bill of Rights Act 1990 (NZ).

31   See note 17 above.

32   See *Cabinet Manual* (2001) para. 5.35.

33   See ss 45, 76, 77, 78 and 79 of the Electoral Act 1993 (NZ).

REFERENCES

Cooke, R. 1984, 'Practicalities of a Bill of Rights', F. S. Dethridge Memorial Address to the Maritime Law Association of Australia and New Zealand, reprinted in (1984) 112 Council Brief 4 and Hastings (ed.) *F. S. Dethridge Memorial Addresses 1977–1988* (1989) 71.

Durie, M. 2000, 'A Framework for Considering Constitutional Change and the Position of Māori in Aotearoa', in C. James (ed.), *Building the Constitution*, Wellington, pp. 414–24.

Harris, B.V. 2004, 'The Constitutional Future of New Zealand', *New Zealand Law Review*, pp. 269–312.

Harris, B.V. 2005, 'The Treaty of Waitangi and the Constitutional Future of New Zealand', *New Zealand Law Review*, pp. 189–216.

Report of the Constitutional Arrangements Committee, August 2005, www.constitutional. parliament.govt.nz/upload/Final_Report.pdf, noted in the text as 'RCAC 2005'.

FURTHER READING

Brookfield, F.M. 1999, *Waitangi and Indigenous Rights: Revolution, Law and Legitimation*, Auckland University Press, Auckland.

Durie, M. 1998, *Te Mana, Te Kawanatanga—The Politics of Maori Self-Determination*, Oxford University Press, Melbourne.

James, C. (ed.) 2000, *Building the Constitution*, Institute of Policy Studies, Victoria University of Wellington, Wellington.

Joseph, P.A. 2001, *Constitutional and Administrative Law in New Zealand*, 2nd edn, Brookers, Wellington.

Palmer, G. & Palmer, M. 2004, *Bridled Power*, 4th edn, Oxford University Press, Melbourne.

Head of State

Noel Cox & Raymond Miller

In this chapter we will discuss the nature of the monarchy in New Zealand, focusing on the changing role and influence of the Queen's representative, the Governor-General. There will also be an examination of some of the factors that might have an influence on New Zealand becoming a republic. The arguments for and against such a change in structure and symbolism will also be examined. Drawing on survey data,[1] we will measure the strength of republican sentiment among New Zealand voters, highlighting the social variables of age, gender, education, and ethnicity. It is frequently claimed that support for republicanism is strongest among the well-educated postwar generations (see, for example, Jesson 1996, p. 55). On the other hand, deep pro-monarchist feelings are said to be held by late middle-aged and elderly voters, as well as by Māori. A perception that public opinion among Māori is heavily in favour of the monarchy has divided the pro-republican movement, with some warning against advocating a hasty change of the status quo. They reason that, because the nation's founding document, the Treaty of Waitangi 1840, was a personal agreement between Māori chiefs and Queen Victoria, any attempt to remove the sovereign would be seen by most Māori as a threat to their rights under the Treaty (for example, Mulgan 1997, p. 66; Tunks 1996, p. 117). Finally, data will be presented showing what, if any, impact the 1999 republican referendum decision in Australia had on public opinion in New Zealand.

THE HEAD OF STATE

The term 'Head of State' frequently arises in discussions of political structures. Yet despite our familiarity with the term, it is hard to agree on a single definition. Indeed, prior to the late nineteenth or early twentieth century, 'Head of State' was virtually unheard of and rulers were generally referred to generically as 'princes'. In the absence of a clear definition of head of state (which is usually used in distinction to that of head of government), there is only a collection of common principles. There is some agreement on the powers and responsibilities possessed by many heads of state. These can generally be divided into four categories. The first category includes those powers which relate to the position of supreme government authority. The role of constitutional guarantor, and serving as the living symbol of the nation, fall into this category. The second category includes powers related to the creation of law. The promulgation of legislation and signing authority on international treaties demonstrate this power both within, and outside the country. The third category involves jurisdiction over the administrative and political agents of government. The appointment of officials is an example of this. Fourth, control of the state's monopoly on physical force is generally vested in the head of state. Formal command of military forces is an example of this fourth area of responsibility.

These four categories, and the responsibilities within them, are commonly described as within the purview of heads of state. They may, however, be exercised on the advice of a head of government, or by the head of government on delegated authority from the head of state. However, it is important to note that not all nations employ heads of state who exercise all of the powers addressed above. More importantly, from the perspective of New Zealand, in not all countries does a head of state personally exercise these powers and responsibilities.

Elizabeth II, commonly known as Queen of the United Kingdom, is currently the second longest-serving head of state in the world. She is presently the only person recognised as the head of more than one state (excepting the anomalous example of Andorra, of which the President of France is a co-Prince). This is primarily a product of the nature of the evolution of the British Empire into the Commonwealth. But as a direct consequence the head of state is represented in each of her realms by a Governor-General. For most practical purposes, except the appointment of a new Governor-General, this office is de facto head of state, and the next section will be concerned with the office of Governor-General.

EVOLVING MONARCHY

New Zealand's form of government, in common with other countries established predominantly by settlers from the British Isles—excepting only the United States of America—is that of a constitutional (or limited) monarchy. In 1840 the monarchy meant the 'British' monarchy. It was the Queen of the United Kingdom (not England as the Treaty styled her) who concluded the Treaty with Māori chiefs at Waitangi. With the growth of the newly settled colony, the British government entrusted more powers and responsibilities to the colonial parliament. This process was accelerated during the early part of the twentieth century when New Zealand, together with several other long-established British colonies, notably Canada and Australia, were granted the status of a 'dominion'.

Each dominion shared allegiance to the Crown. Although the personification of the Crown was the sovereign, it included the sovereign's advisers also. Initially these were primarily those based in the United Kingdom, but later came to include those located locally. Over time, each dominion began to develop its own concept of the Crown. Beginning in the 1930s the sovereign acted in relation to New Zealand only on the advice of New Zealand ministers. As the Queen came to be regarded more and more as the Queen of New Zealand, and only incidentally as the sovereign of these other countries, so a distinct New Zealand Crown evolved. Thus the once-single imperial Crown slowly evolved into a multiplicity of national Crowns. This meant that obligations once undertaken by the British Crown were now the responsibility of the New Zealand Crown. This can be illustrated with reference to the Crown's obligations under the Treaty of Waitangi. Although for all practical purposes such obligations were vested in the ministers of the New Zealand government, Māori continued to hold the sovereign responsible for upholding the terms of the Treaty. In 1984, for instance, Māori bypassed the New Zealand government by appealing to Queen Elizabeth to uphold the provisions of the Treaty.

This evolution of a distinct New Zealand Crown went hand in hand with the nationalising of the office of Governor-General. During the early part of the twentieth century the Governor-General was seen as the local agent of the British government. Despite being granted a measure of personal discretion, successive appointees were expected to refer contentious matters to British ministers or senior Whitehall officials. Although this link began to attenuate from the 1920s, the essentially British nature of the institution persisted for as long as appointments were limited to those who were not only born, but also domiciled, in Britain. As well as representing the Crown, the office of the Governor-General in New Zealand had come to represent, to some extent, the values and attitudes of a particular slice of British society transplanted into New Zealand, namely the aristocracy.

The first New Zealand-born Governor-General, Sir Arthur Porritt,[2] was appointed in 1967, and while this did not produce any significant immediate change in the functions of the office, it did mark the beginning of a transition in its character and style. Porritt was an eminent surgeon and former Olympic sprint medallist who, at the time of his appointment, was an (honorary) member of the Queen's Household. Like other prominent expatriate New Zealanders, such as the scientist Ernest Rutherford, he became well known only after leaving New Zealand. However, having forged a dual New Zealand-British identity, Porritt was seen subsequently as an important transitional figure in the nationalising of the office of Governor-General. When Porritt returned to Britain on the completion of his term, a former New Zealand high commissioner to London, Sir Dennis Blundell, became the first New Zealand-born Governor-General who was also a New Zealand resident. He held the post from 1972 until 1977. Because neither Porritt nor Blundell was a member of the British aristocracy,[3] there was no expectation among New Zealanders that they would conduct themselves as if they were. Moreover, while they represented the Queen, they did not in any sense represent Britain.

Thereafter every appointee has been a New Zealander, appointed (as indeed they had been formally since 1941 and informally since 1910) by the Queen on the advice of the New Zealand prime minister. While the powers of the office are limited, each modern incumbent has the potential to shape the character, and also the role, of the office of Governor-General in response to changing conditions and expectations. More recent appointments include the first Māori Governor-General (Sir Paul Reeves, 1985–90), followed by the first woman (Dame Catherine Tizard, 1990–96). Both were notable for stamping their distinctively New Zealand qualities and personalities on the office of Governor-General.[4] That the three most recent appointments (Sir Michael Hardie-Boys 1996–2001, Dame Silvia Cartwright 2001–06) and Anand Satyanand (2006–), were former Court of Appeal High Court and District Court judges respectively is a reflection of the potential for constitutional uncertainty surrounding the appointment and termination of coalition governments under the new electoral arrangements of MMP.

Although for most purposes the Governor-General is the head of state, the country is not a de facto republic, but rather a 'localised' monarchy (Ladley 1997). Appointees derive their status from both their constitutional position at the apex of the executive branch of government and from their role as representative of the sovereign. The office can be said to have three principal roles: community; ceremonial; and constitutional.[5] It is perhaps in their community leadership role, which includes both public engagements and commenting on social trends and issues, that governors-general are most conspicuous. According to Dame Catherine Tizard (1993, p. 4), it is the responsibility of the Governor-General to both acknowledge a sense of community spirit and affirm those civic virtues that give New Zealand a sense of identity and purpose. This aspect of the community role is not only demanding, but potentially dangerous, with incumbents being required to tread a fine line between the bland and the politically controversial. The ceremonial role, in contrast, is constrained by New Zealand's lack of any tradition of overt symbolism, pomp, and ceremony. Events such as the State Opening of Parliament have never played a major part in public life in New Zealand. The dangers inherent in the community leadership role were illustrated in 2002 when Dame Silvia Cartwright was criticised in some quarters for suggesting that the parental right to discipline children should be reassessed. She attracted further controversy by observing that imprisonment was not an effective way to reform criminals. In both cases she was drawing upon her prior experience as a High Court judge.

The third, constitutional role flows from the position of the Governor-General as representative of the sovereign. This said, most of the powers of the office derive from Acts and regulations rather than the royal prerogative. The Governor-General assents to bills and orders in council, opens and dissolves parliament, appoints ministers, and makes a range of other appointments. Once seen as an instrument of imperial will, the Governor-General is occasionally now seen as a constitutional safeguard against executive despotism.[6] However, arguments that the Governor-General can act as a guardian of the Constitution overstate the case. New Zealand's economic and social policies have been dramatically altered over the past two decades, without intervention from the Governor-General. This reflects the fact that the Governor-General can only intervene to preserve the constitutional order itself. Like the sovereign, the Governor-General will almost always act only on the advice of ministers responsible to parliament. However, as we have seen, the importance of the constitutional role was doubtless an important factor in the selection of Hardie-Boys, Cartwright and Satyanand following the introduction of MMP in 1996.

While the office of Governor-General has evolved over time, so too has that of the sovereign and of the monarchy as a whole. Just as the evolution of the executive government through the twentieth century often saw the diminution of the role of the Governor and then Governor-General, a process seen as strengthening the political independence of the country, so the Queen's role has also diminished at the expense of the Governor-General and other members of the executive, especially (in recent years) the prime minister.

ARGUMENTS FOR A REPUBLIC

A maturing sense of nationhood has caused some to question the continuing relevance of the monarchy in New Zealand. However, it was not until the then prime minister personally endorsed the idea of a republic in 1994 that the issue aroused any significant public interest or debate. Drawing on the campaign for a republic in Australia, Jim Bolger proposed a referendum in New Zealand and suggested that the turn of the century was an appropriate time symbolically for this country to break its remaining constitutional ties with Britain. Far from underestimating the difficulty of his task, he readily conceded that 'I have picked no sentiment in New Zealand that New Zealanders would want to declare themselves a republic'.[7] This view was reinforced by national survey and public opinion poll data, all of which showed strong public support for the monarchy. Nor has the restrained advocacy for a republic from Helen Clark, prime minister from 1999, done much to change this.

Public sentiment notwithstanding, a number of commentators have speculated that a New Zealand republic is inevitable and that any move in that direction by Australia would have a dramatic influence on public opinion in New Zealand. Australia's decision in a national referendum in 1999 to retain the monarchy raises the question of what effect, if any, that decision had on opinion on this side of the Tasman.

Apart from a few notable constitutional changes, such as abolition of the upper house and the introduction of a Bill of Rights, the present constitutional system very much reflects the country's colonial heritage. Writing in the 1950s, the historian Keith Sinclair argued that New Zealanders' claim to being 'more British than the British' had its roots in a deep-seated desire to be associated with the perceived moral and military superiority of the Britain of Queen Victoria (1959, pp. 297–9). The outpouring of loyalty and admiration with which the predominantly British immigrant population greeted royal visitors was a recurring reminder of New Zealand's close relationship with Britain. This link was retained while it suited New Zealand strategic interests. But the military and political realities of conditions in the South Pacific and Far East from the 1940s rendered the link with Britain—if not with the monarchy—less important than that with the USA. From the early 1950s, Britain's postwar military and economic decline began to nudge a reluctant New Zealand government away from dependency, both psychological and real. Landmark events in the country's journey towards full independence included the 1951 ANZUS defence agreement with Australia and the USA; the emergence of a stronger sense of regional identity under the third Labour government (1972–75) of Norman Kirk; and Britain's entry into the European Community (now the European Union) in 1974. The last decision effectively ended a trade relationship in which up to 90 per cent of New Zealand's farm produce had been destined for British consumption.

New Zealand's new post-colonial status was reflected in a number of largely domestic changes, including the relaxation of restrictions on non-United Kingdom immigrants, especially refugees and business migrants from Asia; the growing penetration of US culture and politics through the vehicle of mass communications, notably television; and the rise of individualistic, meritocratic and internationalist values as a result of globalisation and the economic and welfare reforms of successive neo-liberal governments. Reinforcing these trends was the decision of the voters in 1993 to replace the simple plurality electoral system, which had long been an integral part of the Westminster democratic model (Lijphart 1999, p. 21), with the German model of proportional representation. According to the prime minister of the time, the new electoral arrangement promised to be the catalyst for 'a clear break with the British system of government that we have followed thus far'.[8] It has been said that 'the tide of history is moving in one direction'.[9] Therefore, so the argument went, it was time for a republic. Although understanding of the operation of MMP has improved since its introduction, signs that it heralded more radical reforms have yet to emerge. It may even have resulted in greater caution.

But it is also possible to argue for a republic on the grounds of New Zealand's growing military and political isolation from Britain. The Thatcher government was conspicuously unwilling to become involved during the dispute with French government officials following the sinking of a Greenpeace vessel in Auckland harbour in 1985. The 'Rainbow Warrior Affair', as it came to be called, together with the fourth Labour government's anti-nuclear stance (which was strongly opposed by both London and Washington) were to become defining events in the development of a more assertive New Zealand identity (Alley 1987, p. 209). By the beginning of the twenty-first century the only remaining links with Britain of particular consequence were politico–cultural and historic. By this time, it could be argued, New Zealand had largely shed its British identity in favour of that of a South Pacific nation, with a trade, foreign and defence policy focus on the region of Asia–Pacific.[10] This was illustrated by the New Zealand Labour-led government's failure to support the 2003 decision of the British Labour Prime Minister, Tony Blair, to commit troops to President George W. Bush's invasion of Iraq. The monarchy has been indigenised—especially in its Treaty of Waitangi context—as its British aspects and attributes have withered (or been deliberately dismantled).

New Zealand republicans might consider it appropriate that their nation become a republic when Australia adopts that system of government, though that reason, on its own, implies a lack of independence of spirit—following Australia's lead where once we may have followed that of Britain, or more recently, the USA.[11] But there are also more substantial reasons. Perhaps the most persuasive is that the country's constitutional system ought to rest on firmer constitutional foundations than at present. Parliamentary sovereignty has arguably been inadequate when it comes to protecting individual rights and ensuring the accountability and integrity of governmental institutions. An entrenched constitution would help, though entrenchment is not contingent upon the country becoming a republic (see chapter 2.2). There are also some concerns about the adequacy of the present position of the Governor-General, particularly the prerogative (and unwritten) nature of many of the powers of that office (Winterton 1998). There is no certainty, however, that the powers of the head of state would be any more clearly defined in a republic.

In some respects the most important arguments which can be advanced for New Zealand becoming a republic are strictly symbolic. Most important among the symbolic aspects, and that upon which both Bolger and Clark have relied, is that it is 'inappropriate' for 'the Queen of England' to be head of state and to have power to appoint a Governor-General to 'exercise her royal powers on her behalf in New Zealand'.[12] This is so irrespective of the lack of use of those powers. It is this argument that has proven the strongest of those promoted by the republican movement in Australia, though ultimately it proved insufficient to persuade the majority to abandon a known system in favour of an untried one, however much it may have been preferred in principle.

PUBLIC OPINION

Having looked at some of the factors that might suggest a republic, we will now consider what people actually feel about the monarchy. In 2005, in response to the question, 'Do you think that New Zealand should become a republic with a New Zealand head of state, or should the Queen be retained as head of state?' some 48 per cent of voter respondents to the New Zealand Election Study (NZES) expressed support for the monarchy, compared with 34 per cent who preferred a republic (see table 2.3.1). While support for the monarchy in 2005 was somewhat weaker than three and six years earlier, as we will see, the 1999 survey coincided with the successful pro-monarchy referendum campaign in Australia. The attention given by the New Zealand media to the Australian debate may help explain the decline in the proportion of 'don't knows' among the 1999 respondents.

Gender and age are the two most crucial social indicators of voter opinion towards the monarchy. There is a popular though simplistic assumption that, because of their high exposure to an assortment of women's magazines many of which feature the monarchy and depict it as a largely matriarchal institution, women are significantly more likely to be monarchists than men. The relative merits of this assumption notwithstanding, in 2005 some 47 per cent of all women and 51 per cent of men are monarchists (NZES 2005).

Survey data over the past three elections shows that support for the monarchy tends to increase with age, with 66 per cent of all 2002 respondents of sixty years and over preferring the monarchy, compared with 25 per cent supporting a republic (see figure 2.3.1). It is hardly surprising that elderly women are the most devoted in their support for the monarchy. That said, opinion favours retention of the monarchy in every age group—even among the 18–24-year-olds, support for the monarchy ran at 46 per cent (up from 36 per cent in 1996), with 27 per cent favouring a republic (41 per cent) and a further 27 per cent failing to venture an opinion.

Table 2.3.1: Voter attitudes to monarchy/republicanism, 1996-2002

Attitude	1996	1999	2002	2005
Favour retaining Queen as head of state	51.1	62.2	51.2	48.7
Favour NZ becoming a republic	35.4	28.1	31.3	33.9
Don't know	13.7	9.7	17.5	17.1
	n = 4118	n = 1471	n = 4859	n = 2762

Source: New Zealand Election Study

Figure 2.3.1: Attitudes to monarchy by age

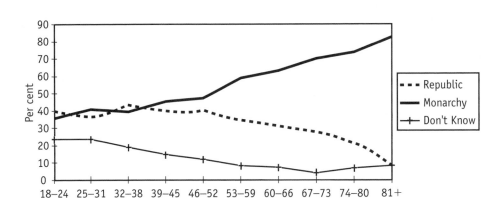

Table 2.3.2: Voter attitudes to monarchy/republicanism by ethnicity, 2005

Attitude	NZ European	Māori	Pasifika	Asian
Favour monarchy	50.7	41.4	60.7	32.5
Favour republic	33.2	36.2	21.4	37.5
Don't know	15.7	22.4	17.9	30.0

Source: New Zealand Election Study

On the basis of our survey data it is possible to reach the further generalisation that the higher the level of education, the stronger the support for a republic. Whereas 39 per cent of those with a university degree favour a republic, the level of support among those with no more than a primary school education is only 31 per cent. As for religious affiliation, Anglicans, Presbyterians, and Methodists proved to be strong supporters of the monarchy, whereas Catholics and those who did not profess a religious faith were not.

Completing the social profile of survey respondents are the views of Māori. Contrary to the perception of Māori as being strong monarchists, considerably fewer Māori than New Zealand European support the monarchy (see table 2.3.2). As with respondents generally, support for a republic is stronger among Māori men than women, and among young and young middle-aged voters rather than the sixty-year plus age group. Although the monarchy enjoys strong support among British-born respondents, ethnic Chinese show a preference for a republic.

Patterns of opinion by party vote confirm the importance of the generational factor in measuring the level and intensity of support for the monarchy (see table 2.3.3). With over half of all New Zealand First's 2005 voters being over the age of fifty, it is hardly surprising that the monarchy enjoys strong approval within that

Table 2.3.3: Voter attitudes to monarchy/republicanism by party, 2005

Party	Monarchy	Republic	Don't know
Labour	44.0	38.1	18.0
National	54.6	31.9	13.4
NZ First	59.4	28.7	11.9
ACT	55.9	23.5	20.6
Greens	35.8	44.7	19.5
United Future	63.5	27.0	9.5
Māori	47.0	33.3	19.7

Source: New Zealand Election Study n = 2685

party. Similarly, both National's (Vowles et al. 1995, pp. 22–3) and ACT's strong appeal to middle-aged and elderly Europeans, as well as to medium- to high-income earners, helps to account for the enthusiasm felt for the monarchy by those parties' supporters. In addition to appealing to a similarly conservative slice of the electorate, United Future (see chapter 3.5) draws strong support from Christians, with 62 per cent of its voter respondents being regular church attendees (NZES 2005).

As the results of table 2.3.3 show, the only party with more republicans than monarchists is the Green party. Clearly its more youthful voters reflect, if less intensely, the pro-republican sentiments expressed by the Green party's parliamentary candidates, most of whom endorse a republic. Unlike the Australian Labour party, which has long been identified with support for a republic (Warhurst 1993, p. 118), its New Zealand counterpart has played a much more low-key, even ambivalent, role. Although most of Labour's parliamentary candidates favour a New Zealand republic, the party's voters are somewhat less enthusiastic about the republican cause.

IMPACT OF AUSTRALIAN REFERENDUM DECISION ON OPINION IN NEW ZEALAND

Between 1996 and 1999, the most significant development in the republican debate concerned the Australian government's decision to conduct a republican referendum on 7 November 1999. Prior to the referendum, public opinion in Australia favoured reform. The Australian Election Study of 1998, for example, found that 65.8 per cent of respondents supported a republic, compared with only 34.2 per cent who wanted to retain the monarchy.[13] Since advocates of a New Zealand republic had long held the view that a 'Yes' vote in Australia would accelerate the trend towards a republic in New Zealand, the NZES pre-election 'rolling thunder' survey, which was conducted on a daily basis between mid-October and late November 1999, provided a unique opportunity to test any possible contagion effect of the referendum debate and outcome on public opinion in New Zealand.[14]

Figure 2.3.2: Trends in support, 17 October to 27 November 1999

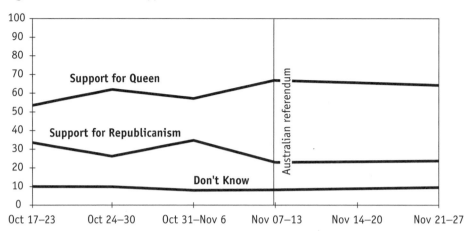

As we have seen, the figures in table 2.3.1 suggest that the Australian debate and outcome had the effect of consolidating public support for the monarchy within New Zealand. This is confirmed by the results in figure 2.3.2. Although support levels began at almost precisely the 1996 levels, during the three weeks leading up to the Australian referendum, support for the monarchy tracked upwards, reaching a high of 67 per cent immediately after the Australian referendum results became known.

Perhaps most disturbing for those who support a New Zealand republic was the sharp rise in the popularity of the monarchy among young voters (see figure 2.3.1). Whereas in 1996 only 36 per cent of 18–24-year-olds were monarchists, by the close of the 1999 Australian referendum campaign it had risen to 58 per cent. Over the same period, support for a republic had dropped from 41 per cent to 27 per cent. This trend among young voters has also been noticeable in Canada and Australia and was particularly evident during the Queen's golden jubilee celebrations in 2002. Support for the monarchy among these young people seems to be based upon a mixture of attachment to the person of the Queen (or of other members of the Royal Family, such as Prince William), or for the tradition of the monarchy, but (perhaps more so than for their parents and grandparents), appreciation of the political system which it represents.

CONCLUSION

Although the Australian referendum was lost by the advocates of a republic, support for change has been consistently stronger in Australia than in New Zealand, and especially so since the early 1990s. The significant variation in the popularity of republican sentiment between the two countries can be attributed to a number of factors, including New Zealand's more homogeneous and largely British immigrant population; its historical slowness in abandoning other relics of colonialism, including imperial honours and the right of judicial recourse to the Privy Council; the opposition to republicanism of some prominent Māori leaders; and the absence of a republican tradition either within the Labour and Alliance parties or through the survival of a republican association.[15] However, perhaps the most significant deterrent to the growth of republicanism in New Zealand, at least during the 1980s and 1990s, was the country's preoccupation with economic, political, and electoral change. With the level of public trust in the nation's politicians having reached an all-time low, the idea of replacing the monarchy with an elected or unelected president, in either case a vastly more expensive proposition for New Zealand taxpayers than retaining the monarchy, may have represented more change than many voters were prepared to countenance.

There is a further factor that militates against a too-ready assertion that it is only a matter of time before New Zealand becomes a republic. In some respects the very absence of the sovereign from New Zealand has done much to strengthen the institution of the monarchy. Largely entrusted to governors-general, who have limited terms of office, the Crown has gradually become entrenched as a useful synonym for the government.[16] But it has become more than that. Although the Crown's obligations under the Treaty of Waitangi are now exclusively the concern of the New Zealand government, the personal involvement of the sovereign as a party to the Treaty remains important to Māori.

While abolition of the monarchy might not be on the political agenda in New Zealand in the short term, reform may be. In recent years there has been some speculation regarding the possibility of changes to the laws governing succession to the Crown. These include either making Prince William the heir to Queen Elizabeth II, rather than his father, Charles, Prince of Wales, or repealing the Act of Settlement 1700 (12 & 13 Will III c. 2), which excludes Catholics from the Crown. A suggestion has also been made that the eldest child of the sovereign, irrespective of sex, should succeed.

While either the success of a republican referendum in Australia or an unpopular succession to the throne may advance the republican cause in New Zealand, this chapter has shown that the most convincing arguments for change are the influence on public opinion of events in Australia and New Zealand's changing demography. Should Australia become a republic as a result of a second referendum, perhaps following the death of the present monarch, it is not unreasonable to predict that New Zealand may make a similar move soon afterwards. This view is shared by the country's parliamentary candidates, almost one in two of whom believe that New Zealand will become a republic within the next five to ten years (only 10 per cent consider the monarchy to be here to stay) (NZES 2002). However, time has already proven these more optimistic—or pessimistic—views to be exaggerated.

Regardless of what happens on the other side of the Tasman, the inevitable attrition among the older groups of monarchist stalwarts may, within the next ten years or so, produce a majority vote for change—provided that the recent trend towards support for the monarchy among young people does not continue. A further demographic variable that could have an impact upon the popularity of republicanism is immigration. Support for the monarchy is strongest among British-born respondents and weakest among immigrants from outside the Commonwealth. The recent increase in immigrant numbers and the diversification of sources to include more immigrants from Asia (especially China, South Korea, and Taiwan), Western Europe and elsewhere will inevitably dilute the symbolism and mystique surrounding New Zealand's former status as a distant but loyal British colony, and may also loosen our attachment to the monarchy.

DISCUSSION QUESTIONS

1   What is the role of the Crown in modern government?

2   For what reasons might New Zealand become a republic?

3   Why do a majority of New Zealanders support the continuation of the monarchy?

4   To what extent does the Crown remain important as a Treaty of Waitangi partner?

5   In what ways has the Crown developed as a distinct New Zealand institution?

NOTES

1   The 1996, 1999, 2002 and 2005 New Zealand Election Studies were made possible by grants from the Foundation for Research, Science and Technology. The 1996, 2002 and 2005 surveys were conducted immediately after the general election. They questioned voters and parliamentary candidates. In 1999, a pre-election survey was conducted on a daily basis during the course of the campaign to track changes in voter attitudes on a range of issues.

2   Freyberg was born in London, and although largely brought up in New Zealand, had spent the greater part of his adult life abroad.

3   Though, after his retirement, Porritt was to become a de jure British aristocrat. It was customary, though not invariably the practice, for the Governor-General to receive a peerage, until Porritt's time.

4   Interview with Rt Hon. David Lange, 20 May 1998.

5   The Role of the Governor-General of New Zealand, 1997, p. 3.

6   Auckland District Law Society Public Issues Committee, The Holyoake Appointment, 1977, p. 7.

7   *New Zealand Herald*, 6 March 1995, p. 1.

8   This is not to suggest that the views of politicians and other opinion leaders are no longer reported. In March 1998, for example, the Secretary of Foreign Affairs, Richard

Nottage, reportedly told business leaders and policy-makers from the Asia–Pacific region that it was only a matter of time before New Zealand had its own indigenous head of state. He acknowledged that having a British monarch as New Zealand's head of state 'looks strange in Asian eyes'. *National Business Review*, 27 March 1998, p. 1.

9   *Dominion*, 16 December 1996, p. 12.

10   *Evening Post*, 9 May 1997, p. 2.

11   Noel Cox, 'Neo-liberal republicanism has no place in this country', *New Zealand Herald*, 5 November 1999 p A17.

12   *Daily News*, 8 May 1997, p. 6.

13   The Australian survey asked the question 'Do you think that Australia should become a republic with an Australian head of state, or should the Queen be retained as head of state?' It found that only 34.2 per cent wanted to retain the monarchy, with 9 per cent holding the view strongly. Two-thirds of all respondents (65.8 per cent) supported a republic. Australian Election Study 'User's Guide', 1998.

14   The data presented on attitudes to the monarchy in 1999 comes from an NZES pre-election telephone survey of 3500 New Zealanders, which began on 18 October and continued daily until election day on 27 November. The principal surveyor, Jack Vowles (Waikato University), using a rolling cross-section design, randomly sampled 80–90 eligible voters per day. Funding for the NZES was provided by the Foundation for Research, Science and Technology, as well as by the University of Waikato and University of Auckland research committees.

15   Of all the parliamentary parties, only the Green party of Aotearoa indicated a willingness to place republicanism on its agenda at the 1999 and 2002 elections. Of the newly elected Alliance members of Parliament after that election, Green Party MP Keith Locke in particular stated that he would promote republicanism, on the grounds that 'bowing before the British Queen reflects a colonial mentality'. The Republican Party of New Zealand was dissolved in 2000, but a new Republic of New Zealand Party was established in 2005. A short-lived New Zealand Republican Movement was formed in the late 1960s. The Republican Movement of Aotearoa/New Zealand was formed in 1994. Its patron is the author Keri Hulme.

16   In this respect the Governor-General is regarded by the Australians for Constitutional Monarchy as effectively the head of state of Australia (Abbott 1997).

REFERENCES

Abbott, T. 1997, *How to Win the Constitutional War*, ACM/Wakefield Press, Adelaide.

Alley, R. 1987, 'ANZUS and the Nuclear Issue', in J. Boston & M. Holland (eds), *The Fourth Labour Government: Radical Politics in New Zealand*, Oxford University Press, Auckland, pp. 198–213.

Jesson, B. 1996, 'Republicanism in New Zealand', in L. Trainor (ed.), *Republicanism in New Zealand*, Dunmore Press, Palmerston North, pp. 47–60.

Ladley, A. 1997, 'The Head of State: The Crown, the Queen and the Governor-General', in R. Miller (ed.), *New Zealand Politics in Transition*, Oxford University Press, Auckland, pp. 51, 61.

Lijphart, A. 1999, *Patterns of Democracy: Government Forms and Performance in Thirty-Six Countries*, Yale University Press, New Haven.

Mulgan, R. 1997, *Politics in New Zealand,* Auckland University Press, Auckland.

Perry, P. & A. Webster (eds) 1999, *New Zealand Politics at the Turn of the Millennium: Attitudes and Values about Politics and Government,* Alpha Publications, Auckland.

Sinclair, K. 1959, *A History of New Zealand,* Penguin, Harmondsworth, Middlesex.

Tizard, C. 1993, *Crown and Anchor. The Present Role of the Governor-General in New Zealand,* Government Printer, Wellington.

Tunks, A. 1996, 'Mana Tiriti', in L. Trainor (ed.), *Republicanism in New Zealand,* Dunmore Press, Palmerston North, pp. 113–32.

Vowles, J., P. Aimer, H. Catt, J. Lamare & R. Miller 1995, *Towards Consensus? The 1993 Election in New Zealand and the Transition to Proportional Representation,* Auckland University Press, Auckland.

Warhurst, J. 1993, 'Nationalism and Republicanism in Australia: The Evolution of Institutions, Citizenship and Symbols', *Australian Journal of Political Science,* vol. 28, pp. 100–20.

Winterton, G. 1998, 'The New Zealand Republic', in A. Simpson (ed.), *Constitutional Implications of MMP,* School of Political Science and International Relations, Victoria University of Wellington, Wellington, pp. 205–7.

FURTHER READING

Butler, D. & D.A. Low (eds) 1991, *Sovereigns and Surrogates: Constitutional Heads of State in the Commonwealth,* Macmillan, London.

Grainger, G. & K. Jones (eds) 1994, *The Australian Constitutional Monarchy,* ACM Publishing, Sydney.

Tizard, C. 1993, *Crown and Anchor: The Present Role of the Governor-General in New Zealand,* Government Printer, Wellington.

Trainor, L. (ed.) 1996, *Republicanism in New Zealand,* Dunmore Press, Palmerston North.

The Role of the Governor-General of New Zealand, Government House, Wellington, 1997.

Judiciary and Courts

Andrew P. Stockley

The courts adjudicate disputes involving legal rights and responsibilities, whether such disputes arise between individuals[1] or between individuals and government. The task of adjudication requires judges to interpret, apply, and develop the law. Often they enforce law made by other institutions (statutes enacted by parliament or regulations promulgated by the executive); on other occasions they must apply or develop their own case law (called common law) in order to resolve the dispute in question. While judges must defer to laws made by parliament, their ability to interpret those laws, to hold the executive to account if it acts outside the authority granted it by parliament, and to create law to deal with situations not otherwise covered, makes the judges important contributors to the substance of policy and the fabric of government and society as a whole.

THE COURTS

New Zealand has a hierarchy of courts, meaning that decisions can be appealed to higher courts, and judges are bound to follow the principles of law laid down by superior courts in similar cases. New Zealand's highest court is the Supreme Court, followed by the Court of Appeal, the High Court, and the District Court. Conflicting decisions of the lower courts must ultimately be settled by the Supreme Court or the Court of Appeal.

The Supreme Court Act 2003 ended the right of appeal to the Judicial Committee of the Privy Council. The Supreme Court held its first sitting in 2004 and comprises the Chief Justice and four to five other judges. Cases are heard by a bench of five judges, with the Chief Justice presiding.[2] The court must grant leave for an appeal to be heard, and will only do so if it involves a matter of general or public importance (including a significant issue relating to the Treaty of Waitangi) or if a substantial miscarriage of justice may otherwise occur.[3] The Supreme Court heard twelve appeals during its first year of operation.

In recent years the Court of Appeal has heard more than 500 appeals each year. Around three-quarters of these are criminal appeals. The Court of Appeal comprises seven judges, the most senior of whom is the president. Cases of sufficient importance are heard by a bench of five judges. The remaining cases are heard by three judges, sitting in two divisions (for civil and criminal appeals). High Court judges are appointed to assist, meaning, for example, that the Criminal Appeal Division can sit with one Court of Appeal and two High Court judges.

Figure 2.4.1: Hierarchy of the New Zealand court system

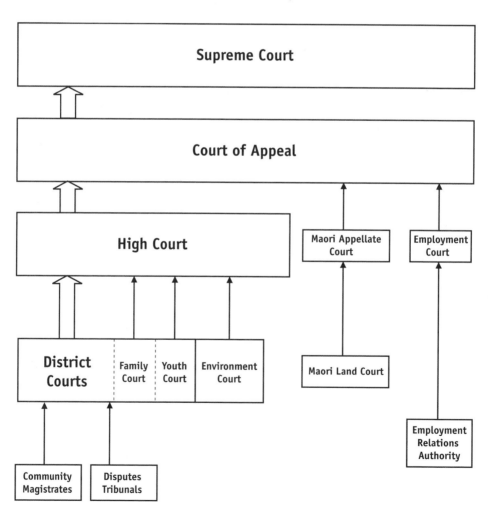

There are thirty judges of the High Court, headed by the Chief High Court Judge.[4] Cases are usually heard by a single judge, although on rare occasions they may sit in pairs (termed a 'full court') for matters of particular importance. Around 10 per cent of High Court judges' time is spent on appeals. Unlike the Supreme Court and Court of Appeal, which only act as appellate courts, the High Court is a court of first instance for the more serious criminal and civil cases. There are also six Associate Judges of the High Court, who hear a more limited range of cases.[5]

The vast majority of cases are dealt with at the level of the District Court. There is a statutory limit of 140 District Court judges, headed by the Chief District Court Judge. The trend of the last twenty-five years has been to enlarge the powers of the District Court. Judges holding appropriate warrants may now hold jury trials,[6] and the District Court has jurisdiction to hear civil cases involving up to $200,000 (or land valued to $500,000). Many matters once the preserve of the High Court are now dealt with by the District Court,[7] freeing the former to deal with increased serious offending, major commercial litigation, and administrative law cases. Sixty per cent of judges' sitting time in the District Court is spent on criminal matters and most of the cases arising at this level are more concerned with the proving of facts than with the complicated issues of law that confront the higher courts.

There are around 10,000 Justices of the Peace (JPs) who perform community functions such as taking oaths and declarations. Some 400 of these JPs, while not members of the judiciary, perform a limited range of judicial functions. Sitting in pairs, they are empowered to hear minor criminal and traffic cases, to conduct preliminary hearings for more serious offences, and to deal with bail applications and remand cases. Annually these JPs handle over 70,000 charges.

In 1998 the office of community magistrate was interposed between JPs and District Court judges. Community magistrates can adjudicate matters that would come before a JP, and, in addition, are empowered to direct fines enforcement and to deal with undefended cases that can result in up to three months' imprisonment or a fine of $7,500 (with the proviso that they can fine, or impose a periodic detention or community service sentence, but cannot imprison). It was intended that community magistrates deal with matters such as drink driving, driving without a licence, minor drug possession, and disorderly behaviour. Only the Chief Community Magistrate may hold a current practising certificate, the then minister suggesting that the position would suit retired lawyers, experienced JPs and Māori elders (kaumatua).[8] It is argued that community magistrates can free up District Court judges from routine and minor cases, and provide a means for testing community-based sentencing. Seven years on, community magistrates are still being trialled in the Waikato and Bay of Plenty and have not yet been introduced throughout the country.

Disputes Tribunals are also subordinate to the District Courts. Claims of up to $7,500 (or, by consent of both parties, $12,000) may be brought before a Dispute

Tribunal referee, who need not be legally qualified. Proceedings are informal and the parties involved cannot be represented by lawyers.

In addition to the courts of general jurisdiction, and subordinate institutions dealing with minor criminal and civil matters, there is a range of specialist courts and tribunals. The Youth Court and Family Court are constituted as divisions of the District Court, the former dealing with offenders under the age of seventeen, and the latter with matrimonial, child welfare, domestic violence, and mental health matters. Thirty-nine District Court judges hold warrants to hear Family Court cases. Seven others are appointed members of the Environment Court where, together with fifteen commissioners, they hear appeals from resource consent and planning decisions. The Employment Court and the Maori Land Court are separate from the District Court, and are currently constituted by four and eight judges respectively. Appeals from the Employment Court proceed directly to the Court of Appeal. Maori Land Court appeals are to the Court of Appeal by way of the Maori Appellate Court.[9] Last but not least is a raft of specialist government tribunals that exercise quasi-judicial functions. Judges sit on several (notably the Liquor Licensing Authority, and parole and district prison boards); many are constituted under statutes giving rights of appeal to either the District or High Court; while all are subject to the High Court's power of judicial review (ensuring they have exercised their powers legally, reasonably, and according to the requirements of natural justice).

1. The Supreme Court

The New Zealand court hierarchy is summarised in the diagram set out in figure 2.4.1. The establishment of the Supreme Court had been foreshadowed for some time. Labour and National administrations had announced their intent to abolish the Privy Council appeal (in 1986 and 1995 respectively) and the Clark government reiterated this in 2000. Canada had abolished the right of appeal in 1949 and Australia in 1986.[10] The only countries retaining the Privy Council appeal were small Caribbean and Pacific island states—and New Zealand.

While the calibre of the British law lords[11] is undoubted, and reflects the talent available in a much larger legal profession, New Zealand had long since developed its own statute law and a distinctive common law.[12] It was appropriate that the country's final appellate court should be a New Zealand court comprising New Zealand judges. The establishment of the Supreme Court means litigants will avoid the delay and expense of taking an appeal to London.[13]

Previous reform proposals[14] had been criticised for suggesting that the Court of Appeal become the highest court. Various lawyers argued the need for a second tier of appeal from the High Court to ensure full attention is given to the most complicated of cases. The establishment of the Supreme Court meets this concern. The Court of Appeal will remain the final arbiter of most appeals, focusing on correcting error and ensuring justice between the parties. The Supreme Court, by only accepting cases of broader importance, can look to clarify and develop the law.

The establishment of the Supreme Court will broaden the range and the volume of cases taken to our final appellate court. It has been predicted that the Supreme Court will hear forty to fifty appeals a year.[15] The Supreme Court will be able to make a better selection among civil cases and to hear more criminal appeals than the Privy Council. Comparatively few cases reached the Privy Council and it had no jurisdiction to hear appeals from the Family, Environment or Employment Courts. The Privy Council only ever heard six criminal appeals from New Zealand whereas the Supreme Court has heard three in its first year of operation.

Supreme Court judges will have a comparatively lighter workload than their colleagues on the Court of Appeal and correspondingly more time for collegial and individual reflection on the cases brought before them. Hearing a greater range and volume of appeals than the Privy Council, they should be better placed to perform the function of a final appellate court in developing and shaping the law.

The position of the Chief Justice has also been enhanced. The Chief Justice was previously a member of the Court of Appeal ex officio but usually sat in the High Court, which he or she headed. There was the potential for tension between the Chief Justice, as head of the judiciary, and the president of the Court of Appeal, who headed the country's most important court. The Chief Justice now combines both roles.

JUDICIAL APPOINTMENTS

Lord Cooke has suggested that New Zealand's system of government is built upon two fundamental principles: 'the operation of a democratic legislature and the operation of independent courts' (Cooke 1988). In this country, we expect a dispute between individuals to be heard and resolved by an impartial judge. And we expect that judge to be no less impartial should one of the parties before the court be a police prosecutor, a minister of the Crown, or some other agent of the state on whose behalf the judge dispenses justice.

Since 1935 successive governments have avoided making political appointments to the Bench. It would now be regarded as a breach of constitutional convention for a politician to be made a judge. To this extent, there is a clear separation of powers between the personnel who make up the judicial branch of government and the members of the legislature and executive.

Judicial appointments do, however, remain within the gift of the government of the day. The Governor-General appoints the Supreme Court, Court of Appeal, High Court, District Court, Environment Court, and Employment Court judges at the recommendation of the Attorney-General. The ministers of Justice and Labour previously recommended the appointment of District Court and Employment Court judges respectively, but the then Attorney-General, Sir Douglas Graham, successfully argued in 1998 that his office was better suited to do so, traditionally being required to act in a more non-political manner as a guardian of the public interest (for example, when approving prosecutions) and being the formal constitutional link between judiciary and government. The Attorney-General now recommends the appointment of all judges save the Chief Justice and Maori Land Court and Appellate Court judges. With respect to the former, Sir Douglas had proposed that the prime minister should continue to recommend the appointment, given that the Chief Justice heads the judiciary and acts as Administrator in the absence of the Governor-General. Political considerations have meant that the Minister of Maori Affairs continues to recommend the latter appointments.[16]

In 1999 the process of appointment was clarified in an effort to provide greater transparency and consistency. The Attorney-General's Judicial Appointments Unit advertises for expressions of interest from lawyers who wish to be considered. Nominations are sought from the heads of the different courts (who seek the input of the judges), the presidents of the Law Commission, Law Society, Bar Association, major district law societies, Maori Law Society, the convenor of the Women's Consultative Group of the Law Society, and the chairman of the Justice and Law Reform Select Committee. The Solicitor-General supervises the process of appointment to the Supreme Court, Court of Appeal, and High Court, while the Secretary for Justice oversees the process for appointments to the District and Employment Courts. Before making any appointments, the Attorney-General consults with ministers whose portfolios are considered relevant, in addition to the ministers of Maori Affairs and Women's Affairs.[17] Other consultation depends on the level of court involved, with the head of the relevant court and the president of the Law Society being involved as appropriate.

Such reforms notwithstanding, advocates of more radical change may feel that two criticisms remain unanswered. The power of appointment remains with the Attorney-General, leaving open the possibility that, despite convention and long-standing practice, an Attorney-General might one day feel tempted to make a political appointment. And although successive governments have committed to seeking greater diversity in the judiciary, some commentators have suggested more substantive reform is necessary to achieve a representative judiciary.[18]

There have been various proposals for a judicial appointments commission, comprising judges, the Solicitor-General, the Secretary for Justice, Law Society nominees, and perhaps several lay members.[19] In 1997, the then Chief Justice, Sir Thomas Eichelbaum, endorsed a judicial appointments commission with the power to nominate a shortlist for each vacancy from which the Attorney-General would normally make the appointment. If he or she appointed from outside the shortlist, this would be publicly notified. In 1998 the Labour opposition put forward a Judicial Appointments Board Bill. The Appointments Board would recommend a shortlist, from which the Attorney-General must appoint.

Recent Attorneys-General have been more suspicious. According to Sir Geoffrey Palmer (1995):

> A commission would be overly cautious. There would be a tendency towards safe appointments and blandness in my judgment … Furthermore in my experience Judges are anxious to exert influence on appointments. It is clearly right that they should be properly consulted. It is not appropriate that they should drive the process and I believe they would under most variations of the Judicial Commission proposal, even if it appeared they did not. If Judges are in the Commission they will exert great weight on the opinion of lay members. The tendency to turn the judiciary into a self-perpetuating oligarchy ought to be resisted.

Palmer also notes that if the government appoints commission members this could lead to political patronage positions. He is joined in his distrust by a former Attorney-General, Paul East, who argues that 'a judicial commission is more likely to continue to pick from the traditional pool rather than to strive to ensure the judiciary is representative of the whole cross section of society' (quoted in Palmer 1995, p. 81). Sir Douglas Graham has made similar comments: 'I do not favour going down that route. Nominating bodies or Judicial Commissions are fraught with problems and have not worked well in other jurisdictions'.[20]

In 2003 the appointment of the first judges of the new Supreme Court became contentious, with some politicians suggesting that the Attorney-General's ability to recommend the appointment of all the judges at the same time would enable her to influence the direction of the court. The criticism was contained when the Attorney-General (Margaret Wilson) recommended that the Chief Justice be joined on the Supreme Court by the four most senior judges of the Court of Appeal. In response to the debate, she issued a public consultation paper in 2004 on whether there should be a judicial appointments commission. The government has since decided not to proceed with this.

Supporters of the status quo argue that the principle of ministerial responsibility entitles parliament to question judicial appointments, and note that successive ministers have attempted to bring greater diversity to the Bench. In 1988 Dame Silvia Cartwright was the first woman to be appointed Chief District Court Judge, and in 1993 she became the first female High Court judge. More women have subsequently been appointed to the High Court Bench, one of whom (Dame Sian Elias) became the first woman to be appointed as Chief Justice, in May 1999. Several Māori have been appointed to the District Court, and in 1998 Eddie Durie became the first Māori High Court judge.[21] A number of recent appointees have not followed the usual path of being court lawyers prior to nomination to the Bench.[22]

Others suggest that more can be done. Women comprise a majority of new lawyers, but a small minority of the judiciary. Gill Gatfield (1996, pp. 405–23) notes that more than 50 per cent of Dispute Tribunal referees are women and suggests that lessons to be learnt include making direct approaches to women's organisations, including women in selection panels, and allowing part-time judges.[23] Most judges continue to be drawn from the ranks of highly successful lawyers, and have, as such, led reasonably competitive, wealthy, urban lifestyles. Jane Kelsey has contended that members of this 'legal and social elite ... cannot be expected to identify with, or even understand, the demands of Māori as tangata whenua, minority cultures, women or the poor' (Kelsey 1986).

JUDICIAL INDEPENDENCE

If the appointment process remains open for debate, the important point in terms of judicial independence is that the convention of non-political appointments endures. Once in office, there is a range of measures designed to protect judges. The Constitution Act 1986 prohibits reducing the salary of a High Court judge.[24] Parliament could always repeal this provision, but would break constitutional convention in doing so.

Until quite recently, the task of administering the court system, funding and building new courtrooms, and employing and controlling court staff was viewed as the responsibility of the executive, the judge's role being seen as one of adjudication not administration. But it could always be argued that the executive might exert improper influence through its control of court resources,[25] and in 1995 the government disbanded the old Justice Department, retaining a Ministry of Justice while establishing a Department of Corrections and a Department for Courts. The judiciary gained a stand-alone department focused solely on the needs of the courts, with a management committed to a high level of consultation with judges. But contrary to their wishes (Eichelbaum 1997, pp. 424–5), the department's chief executive was made responsible to a minister of the Crown, not the judiciary (as occurs at the federal level in Australia and the USA). Worse was to follow. In 2003 the Department for Courts was merged into the Ministry of Justice, a large policy department with competing priorities and a direct interest in matters litigated in the courts.[26] The Chief Justice expressed concern at the diminution in institutional independence: 'Our immediate judicial support does need to be under judicial control because it is inextricably bound up with judicial independence. It is not appropriate for our staff and systems to be part of the Executive' (Elias 2004, p. 220). In testimony to a select committee of the British parliament,[27] Dame Sian expressed her frustration at trying to have an annual report published on a website, a review undertaken into computer security, and her staff's wages reassessed, and commented 'We have no power at all'.

In addition to financial security and administrative autonomy, judicial independence is further manifested in the convention that the executive—both ministers and public servants—should refrain from criticising the judiciary. *The Cabinet Manual* enjoins ministers from expressing any views that 'could be regarded as reflecting adversely on the impartiality, personal views or ability of any judge'. Ministers are advised to 'avoid commenting on any sentences within the appeal period'. 'If a Minister feels he or she has grounds for concern over a sentencing decision, the Attorney-General should be informed' (*The Cabinet Manual* 2001, 115–17). The Standing Orders of the House of Representatives impose lesser—but nevertheless significant—restrictions on members of parliament, prohibiting 'offensive words' against members of the judiciary or referring to matters currently before the courts if this might prejudice judicial proceedings.[28]

Despite such sentiments, there have been occasional attacks on judges by ministers and members of parliament from both sides of the House. Politically motivated comments have included allegations that particular judges favoured old-boy networks, were 'second-rate lawyers', 'weak-kneed', and 'mollycoddling the thugs'.[29] There may, nevertheless, be some grounds for believing that the convention as presently enforced is too widely drawn. There is a distinction between abuse and legitimate criticism. Judgments are subject to appeal and to adverse comment from both academic and media opinion, and politicians should be able to comment on judicial decisions, like other members of society, provided that they do not malign the judge or his or her motivations.[30] In January 2000 there was public disquiet at a District Court judge discharging an American billionaire without conviction and suppressing his name after he brought a substantial amount of cannabis into the country. This warranted political comment in the light of inconsistent sentencing in other cases.[31]

Tensions between the judiciary and executive were evident in 2004 when the Chief Justice's comments on threats to the judiciary's institutional independence became public. The prime minister described Dame Sian's concerns as 'minor administrative matters' and commented: 'Unfortunately, once judges step into the political arena they will have to expect a response from politicians. That's why it is a very good principle for judges to stick to the bench, so that politicians can stick to politics'.[32] Dame Sian was later quoted as saying: 'I spoke out on the issue of institutional independence in New Zealand, and our Prime Minister said I should have gone to the Governor-General or Attorney-General. That indicates a profound lack of understanding about judicial independence and our constitutional arrangements and is, I suggest, quite a widespread view'.[33]

Conflicts over the siting of a new Supreme Court building and over salary and superannuation rates for the judiciary led to the Attorney-General describing Dame Sian as the judges' 'shop steward'.[34] The language used in the public airing of disagreements between executive and judiciary (that judges should 'stick to the bench', that the prime minister had showed a 'profound lack of understanding', and that the Chief Justice was a 'shop steward') benefited neither branch of government.[35]

JUDICIAL ACCOUNTABILITY

The underlying purpose of judicial independence is to protect against executive intimidation and consequent loss of public confidence. It does not exist to safeguard judges from criticism for incompetence or mistakes, nor to benefit judges personally. In 1987 the judges claimed immunity to changes announced to the method of taxing superannuation schemes, arguing that superannuation being deferred remuneration, the principle of judicial financial security would be infringed. The government concluded that a tax measure applicable to all citizens did not constitute a 'reduction' in salary (see Stockley 1997, pp. 162–3). Canadian authority goes further, holding that an equal reduction in salary for all persons paid by the government (judges and civil servants alike) is compatible with judicial independence, the important point being that the judiciary is not singled out.[36]

If the purpose of judicial independence is all-important, this was seemingly overlooked when the government declined to recommend the dismissal of Judge Martin Beattie in 1997. Sir Douglas Graham accepted the advice of the Solicitor-General that, having been acquitted of fraud charges, the judge could not be dismissed on the statutory ground of 'misbehaviour' for what amounted to the same allegations (the judge, being entitled to claim a $240 allowance for meals and accommodation for each day spent away from home, had claimed it on various occasions when he had not stayed away overnight).[37] While the judge's claim of honest mistake led the jury to find him not guilty of criminal conduct, society expects judges to meet a higher standard than 'non-criminal conduct'. The better view is that a judge who acts unethically but legally, or who fails to turn his or her mind to whether such conduct might be considered unethical, should be dismissed for 'misbehaviour'. The report by John Upton QC into Judge Beattie's travel claims found it 'difficult if not impossible, to follow [the judge's] … explanation for claiming in the way that he did' (quoted in Joseph 1998). Retaining Judge Beattie in office misused the concept of judicial independence and denied that of judicial accountability.[38]

The problematic nature of Judge Beattie's case led Sir Douglas to review the processes for dealing with complaints about judges and removing them from office. In 1999 he proposed amending the Constitution Act 1986, so that all judges would be liable to removal by the Governor-General on an address of the House of Representatives. This was not accepted and an address of the House is only necessary for the removal of Employment Court, High Court, Court of Appeal and Supreme Court judges.[39] All other judges are liable to dismissal by the executive without parliamentary involvement. Objections focused on the effects of significantly increasing the number of judges protected by the Constitution Act. The need to balance judicial independence with accountability suggests that the most elaborate safeguards against removal should be confined to the most important judges: lower court decisions can be appealed.

In 1999 a more formalised system was introduced to deal with complaints against judges (see Stockley 1999) and this has since been supplemented by the provisions of the Judicial Conduct Commissioner and Judicial Panel Act 2004. All complaints against judges must be made in writing to the Judicial Conduct Commissioner, who investigates the complaint and decides whether to dismiss it (if, for example, it is trivial or in effect an appeal against the decision), to refer it to the head of the relevant court (if the Commissioner considers there may have been inappropriate conduct but not sufficiently serious to remove the judge from office), or to recommend that the Attorney-General appoint a Judicial Conduct Panel (if the Commissioner considers there may have been serious misconduct which might warrant the judge's removal from office).

If a complaint is referred to the head of the relevant court,[40] he or she must decide whether it has substance.[41] If it does, the head of the court and the judge will discuss possible responses, which may include an apology, or counselling or training for the judge.

If the Attorney-General agrees with a recommendation to appoint a Judicial Conduct Panel, he or she must consult with the Chief Justice before appointing its members.[42] The panel has the powers of a commission of inquiry when investigating the judge's conduct. If the panel considers that there has been misbehaviour or incapacity (the statutory grounds for removing a judge), the Attorney-General must then decide whether to seek an address of the House (for the removal of a superior court judge) or whether, in the case of the inferior courts, to advise the Governor-General to remove the judge.

There is a necessary tension between judicial independence and accountability: too great a reliance on the former can abrogate the latter, yet if judges are too easily accountable to others, they lose their independence. The reforms of the last decade generally attempt to balance both values.

JUDICIAL RESPONSIBILITY

In return for their independence, judges are expected to exercise a measure of restraint. They must refrain from engaging in political debate or criticising government policy. Judges should give no cause to have their impartiality impugned. The doctrine of parliamentary sovereignty requires the courts to defer to acts of parliament, no matter what the judge's view may be of the merits of the legislation. Parliament, unlike the judiciary, is an elected institution. Whereas judges in the USA can strike down statutes as contrary to an entrenched, supreme law Constitution, the absence of any such New Zealand document means that parliament has the last word as to what is law.[43] A government with a strong majority in the House may use this fact to overturn court decisions it dislikes.[44]

The fact that the judiciary's ability to hold the executive to account can and has been vitiated through parliament need not be deplored. It means that, unlike the USA, the executive is not concerned to appoint a politically compatible judiciary. The power of the judiciary in the USA has resulted in a politicised appointment process. The comparative lack of power of New Zealand judges has helped maintain the convention of non-political appointments.

Political and public disapproval of a government interfering with the judicial process also exacts its own consequence. Together with limited parliamentary time, it means that a government is only likely to expend the political capital needed on high-profile cases that strike at the core of its policies.[45]

The importance of judicial independence—and accountability—is measured by the extent of judicial responsibility. Judges have significant power in interpreting the meaning of statutes and applying them to particular cases. Gaps in legislation require judges to develop appropriate law, and numerous examples can be given of their doing so in ways beneficial to consumers and citizens. Many civil liberties are derived from judges siding with the individual, whenever parliament left room to manoeuvre.[46] Judges have been unafraid to hold that the government cannot act outside the authority given it by parliament, and to require ministers, public servants, and government entities to act legally, reasonably, and fairly if they are to withstand judicial review. Parliament has entrusted the judges to give effect to the New Zealand Bill of Rights Act 1990, in the absence of clear legislative intent to the contrary. The Court of Appeal has given the Act an expansive, purposive interpretation, which, if on occasion creative,[47] has not been overturned, and clearly signals the importance of civil and human rights in today's society.

Some have alleged undue judicial activism in respect of the Treaty of Waitangi. While the courts have undoubtedly done more than parliament expected, statutory provisions such as 'Nothing in this Act shall permit the Crown to act in a manner that is inconsistent with the principles of the Treaty of Waitangi' (giving no definition of what those 'principles of the Treaty' might be) were clearly open to judicial interpretation. This provision imports Treaty principles into one area of law (the State-Owned Enterprises Act 1988), but to date the courts have declined to enforce the Treaty across other areas where there is no similar statutory incorporation.[48] At most, they have said they will presume that when parliament legislates, it is not intending to breach the Treaty. But, as always, the last word rests with parliament: it could in fact legislate contrary to that presumption, it could amend or repeal acts incorporating Treaty principles, and it could reverse Treaty jurisprudence if there existed sufficient political will. The Foreshore and Seabed Act 2004 is an example of this occurring.[49] Like the courts and successive governments, parliament recognises previous Treaty injustices, and is increasingly but still uncertainly searching for appropriate redress.

In many and varied areas the courts exercise great responsibility. The lower courts have been given wide discretion in imposing sentences; the appellate courts attempt to reconcile their decisions, to work within the confines of clear directions from parliament, and to find fair and just solutions in situations where parliament's intent is ambiguous or non-existent.

New Zealand's courts have met with a large degree of public confidence. New Zealand benefits from an independent, efficient, and responsible judiciary. The parameters of independence, diversity, responsibility, and accountability may not yet be fully certain, but they are being worked out.

DISCUSSION QUESTIONS

1　Outline the process by which New Zealand judges are appointed, and discuss whether this process could be improved.
2　Discuss whether a minister of the Crown or members of the judiciary should control the administration of the courts.
3　To what extent can politicians criticise judges, or judges criticise politicians? Discuss whether the conventions governing this area should be reformed.
4　If an individual judge acts improperly, what action can be taken against that judge? Does the protection accorded the judiciary need to be relaxed, or are there sufficient means of holding judges to account?
5　To what extent can the judiciary hold the executive to account? Should the judiciary be entitled to set aside Acts of Parliament that are immoral, or that breach the Treaty of Waitangi?

NOTES

1　Including corporate bodies.
2　Retired Supreme Court and Court of Appeal judges under the age of seventy-five may be appointed Acting Judges as needed.
3　Section 13, Supreme Court Act 2003.
4　The High Court was known as the Supreme Court until 1979. The Chief Justice headed the High Court bench until 2004.
5　Formerly called Masters of the High Court, they can deal with summary judgment applications, company liquidations, bankruptcy, and preliminary processes in most civil proceedings.
6　Eighty-six per cent of jury trials were held in the District Court in 2002/3.
7　For example, most criminal trials, sentencing for lesser offences, ordinary matrimonial property and estate litigation, bankruptcy, and liquidation lists.
8　'New Tier of Judges Planned', *Press*, Christchurch, 10 May 1997; 'Report on the Community Magistrates Bill', *Appendices to the Journals of the House of Representatives* (AJHR), 1998, 57–2. Thirty per cent of the first community magistrates appointed were Maori.

9   Comprising three or more Maori Land Court judges.

10 After severely restricting appeals in 1975.

11 Members of Britain's highest court, the House of Lords, who comprised most or all of the judges hearing appeals.

12 In 1999 the Court of Appeal reaching a result strikingly different from the House of Lords and the Australian High Court with respect to principles of defamation. See *Lange v Atkinson*, [2000] 1 *New Zealand Law Reports* 257.

13 It being estimated that it cost the Crown $100,000 to take a civil appeal to the Privy Council as opposed to $20,000 for a similar case in the Court of Appeal. Discussion Paper: *Reshaping New Zealand's Appeal Structure*, December 2000, Office of the Attorney-General, Wellington, p. 3.

14 *The Structure of the Courts*, March 1989, Law Commission, Wellington; New Zealand Courts Structure Bill 1996.

15 Report of the Advisory Group: *Replacing the Privy Council: A New Supreme Court*, 2002, Office of the Attorney-General, Wellington, paragraphs 73 and 77. It will be interesting to see how easily this target is met given New Zealand's lack of a written constitution and federal structure mean the Supreme Court will not deal with constitutional law challenges typical of many other jurisdictions.

16 'Judicial Appointments', Report to the Cabinet Strategy Committee, STR (98) 245, 12 October 1998; minutes of the Cabinet Strategy Committee and of Cabinet, STR (8) M 33/1 and CAB (98) M 40/10D(1), 14 and 19 October 1998.

17 The automatic inclusion of the ministers of Māori and Women's Affairs has been criticised by the *New Zealand Law Journal*, which has suggested that other ministers (e.g. Commerce) are of equal relevance. 'Amending the Constitution?', 1999 *New Zealand Law Journal*, p. 313.

18 For a contrary view, see Kerr (1998).

19 See for example *Report*, Royal Commission on the Courts, 1978, pp. 200–2; reaffirmed by the Law Society's Courts and Tribunals Committee, 'A Model Judicial Commission for New Zealand', 1997, 489 *Lawtalk*, p. 14.

20 'Judicial Appointments', note 16.

21 Durie was formerly chief judge of the Māori Land Court and chairperson of the Waitangi Tribunal. The Treaty of Waitangi Act 1975 was amended—not without controversy—to allow him to retain the latter position. *Report on the Treaty of Waitangi Amendment Bill*, *AJHR*, 1998, 175–1.

22 The only legal requirement is that a judge must have held a practising certificate as a barrister or solicitor for at least seven years.

23 Dispute Tribunal work is on a part-time basis. Cherie Blair, the British Prime Minister's wife, is the best-known example of a Recorder, effectively a part-time judge.

24 S.24. Supreme Court and Court of Appeal judges are ex officio members of the High Court.

25 Palmer (1995, p. 32) suggests that Sir Robert Muldoon deliberately deprived the courts of resources.

26 On the grounds of cost efficiency, following a review by the State Services Commission (although the Treasury disagreed with the need for a merger).

27 Considering replacing appeals to the House of Lords with a Supreme Court. House of Commons Select Committee on Constitutional Affairs, 25 May 2004.

28 SO 115 and 117. The Speaker ruled in 1951 that suggesting a sentence was inappropriate would be in breach of Standing Orders. (1951) 294 *New Zealand Parliamentary Debates* 329 (13 July 1951).

29 For these and other examples, refer Stockley (1997, pp. 167–8).

30 In 1996 there was considerable public criticism of Justice Morris for allegedly sexist comments made in the course of summing up for the jury in a rape case. The Chief Justice publicly reprimanded the judge, saying that his remarks had been 'inappropriate'. In the light of media and judicial criticism, ministerial comment would not have been out of place.

31 'US tycoon could have been jailed', *Press*, Christchurch, 11 January 2000. Several ministers did comment, albeit somewhat carefully. The judge's decision was overturned on appeal.

32 'Avoid the political fray, PM advises Dame Sian', *New Zealand Herald*, Auckland, 27 July 2004.

33 'Top judge takes a new swing at PM', *New Zealand Herald*, Auckland, 20 October 2004.

34 'Power struggle on judiciary role', *New Zealand Herald*, Auckland, 26 March 2005. The National party's justice spokesperson, Richard Worth, also attacked the Chief Justice for public comments she had made on sentencing.

35 Tension between the two branches had been exacerbated by the Court of Appeal's decision in *Attorney-General v Ngati Apa* [2003] 3 *New Zealand Law Reports* 643, which was overturned by the Foreshore and Seabed Act 2004, although at significant political cost.

36 *Reference re Public Sector Pay Reduction Act*, 1997, 150 *Dominion Law Reports* (4d) 577 (Supreme Court of Canada).

37 Judge Robert Hesketh, charged with the same offence, pleaded guilty and resigned from the bench. He was fined $8000 and struck off the roll of barristers and solicitors. He has since been readmitted to legal practice.

38 Beattie refused to resign from the bench and remained a District Court judge. He no longer sat in open court, the Chief District Court Judge having assigned him to hear accident compensation appeals.

39 Constitution Act 1986, s 23.

40 Or to the Chief Justice if concerning a head of Bench, or the Attorney-General if concerning the Chief Justice.

41 The Judicial Complaints Lay Observer, appointed by the Attorney-General, may review a complaint if the head of the court decides it has no substance and, if satisfied, may ask the head to reconsider the complaint.

42 To comprise a layperson, a judge or retired judge, and one other person (either a judge or a senior barrister or solicitor).

43 Lord Cooke has suggested that in extreme cases the courts might refuse to enforce an Act of Parliament (see 1988, p. 164, *Taylor v. New Zealand Poultry Board* [1984] 1 *New Zealand Law Reports* 398), but his view remains untested. Recently he has gained some support from Dame Sian Elias, 'Sovereignty in the Twenty-First Century: Another Spin on the Merry-go-round', 2003, 14 *Public Law Review*, pp. 148–63. Parliamentary sovereignty has been defended by the Deputy Prime Minister (and, for a time, Attorney-General) Michael Cullen, 'Parliament: Supremacy over Fundamental Norms?', 2005, 3 *New Zealand Journal of Public and International Law*, pp. 1–5, and 'Parliamentary Sovereignty and the Courts', 2004, *New Zealand Law Journal*, p. 243. Section 3(2) of the Supreme Court Act 2003 provides that 'nothing in this Act affects New Zealand's continuing commitment to the rule of law and the sovereignty of Parliament'.

44   Notable examples include the Clutha Development (Clyde Dam) Empowering Act 1982 and the Economic Stabilisation Amendment Act 1982. In both cases the government only had a one-seat majority. MMP of course renders single-party majority government less likely.

45   The two examples in n. 44 were central to Sir Robert Muldoon's 'think big' and wage- and price-freeze policies. The famous case of *Fitzgerald v. Muldoon* [1976] 2 *New Zealand Law Reports* 615, which was avoided by retrospective legislation, affected the National Party's superannuation policy, a key element of its 1975 election campaign.

46   A recent example is *Choudry v. Attorney-General* [1999] 2 *New Zealand Law Reports* 582.

47   In *Simpson v. Attorney-General* (Baigent's Case) [1994] 3 *New Zealand Law Reports* 647 the court allowed damages against the Crown for breach of the Act, despite the lack of a remedies section.

48   On the basis that, treaties being made by the executive and not Parliament, if treaties were enforceable by the courts, this would allow government to create law without parliamentary authority.

49   The Act avoided the effect of the Court of Appeal's decision in *Attorney-General v. Ngati Apa*, n. 35, where it departed from earlier precedent in allowing the possibility that the Maori Land Court could issue title over the foreshore and seabed.

REFERENCES

Cooke, Lord 1988, 'Fundamentals', *New Zealand Law Journal*, p. 164.

Eichelbaum, T. 1997, 'Judicial Independence Revisited', *Canterbury Law Review*, vol. 6, pp. 421, 424–5.

Elias, Dame S. 2004, '"The Next Revisit": Judicial Independence Seven Years On', *Canterbury Law Review*, vol. 10, pp. 219–22.

Gatfield, G. 1996, *Without Prejudice: Women in the Law*, Brookers, Wellington.

Joseph, P.A. 1998, 'Constitutional Law', *New Zealand Law Review*, p. 203.

Kelsey, J. 1986, 'Judges and the Bill of Rights', *Canterbury Law Review*, vol. 3, p. 163.

Kerr, R. 1998, 'Judging the Judiciary', *New Zealand Law Journal*, p. 331.

Palmer, G. 1995, 'Judicial Selection and Accountability: Can the New Zealand System Survive?' in B. Gray & R. McClintock (eds), *Courts and Policy: Checking the Balance*, Brookers, Wellington.

Stockley, A.P. 1999, 'Constitutional Law', *New Zealand Law Review*, pp. 185–6.

Stockley, A.P. 1997, 'Judicial Independence: The New Zealand Experience', *Australian Journal of Legal History*, vol. 3, pp. 145–69.

FURTHER READING

Annual Report 1 July 2004–30 June 2005, Ministry of Justice, Wellington, 2005.

Court of Appeal Report for 2002, Wellington, 2003.

Delivering Justice for All: A Vision for New Zealand Courts and Tribunals, Law Commission, Wellington, 2004.

Gray, B.D. & R.B. McClintock, R.B. (eds) 1995, *Courts and Policy: Checking the Balance*, Brookers, Wellington.

Parliament

Keith Jackson

Virtually every country has a representative legislature of some sort, even though they might vary in size, structure, composition, and influence. Today we take such institutions for granted, yet, restricting ourselves to parliaments, it comes as something of a surprise to discover that New Zealand has one of the world's oldest continuously functioning national parliaments (McGee 1985, p. 1). No more than eight other countries have continuing national parliaments that can claim to be older. Yet in polls that measure respect, politicians regularly rank among those for whom there is the least respect.[1] Given this and the longevity of parliament as an institution, how is it that it can be at once so central and so lacking in popular regard? Is the modern institution out of date, deficient, or merely misunderstood? Is it because it is, at the same time, the most open and the most opaque of our institutions? And has the introduction of the Mixed Member Proportional (MMP) electoral system led to any improvement?

MISUNDERSTANDINGS

Regardless of the strengths and weaknesses of today's parliament there is, without doubt, a great deal of popular misunderstanding. For example, New Zealand is still frequently described as 'unusual' because it is unicameral, yet a recent inventory of parliaments found that more than two-thirds were one-house legislatures (Patterson and Mughan 1999, p. 3). The Constitution Act 1986 s 14(i) defines parliament as 'the Sovereign in right of New Zealand'. Technically, parliament consists of the Governor-General and House of Representatives although in popular usage the term 'parliament' is frequently used loosely to describe the House alone. All members of a government must be, or become, members of the House of Representatives, although the House itself does not govern in the executive sense of that term. In another paradox, some of the practices of the House may appear arcane yet it is constantly updating its procedures and is hardly the antiquated institution that it may occasionally appear to be. The major function of a legislature is 'to represent the views of citizens, influence the policy-makers, and reserve for itself the formal, final say on policy as the ultimate means of assuring policy responsiveness' (Mezey 1979, p. 283).

Public misunderstanding of parliament results largely from two factors: a lack of public education and the effects of party dominance. Education about the workings of parliament is limited at best. We seem to expect that knowledge of it will occur almost by a process of osmosis. This situation has been exacerbated by the presence of a relatively recent coalition culture under MMP. This is but one of the important attitudinal adjustments that are the downstream consequences of the changed electoral system.

Parliament institutionalises conflict, and mainly features in the public eye as the site of constant struggles for party dominance. Ironically, one effect of MMP, which was intended to mitigate single party dominance, has been to strengthen and formalise the role of political parties in the chamber. There can be no question that parties have come to play a vital part in modern democratic government—but that does not mean that their role is not without its drawbacks. In the past, it was the development of highly cohesive political parties that led to executive dominance of the House of Representatives, producing a cabinet-dominated, as distinct from an assembly-dominated, political system. The result was to reduce the effective influence of the House drastically. Undoubtedly, the introduction of MMP in 1996 has meant that the potential for cabinet dominance by a single party has been reduced, but whether this is likely to be replaced in the long term by a nearly comparable level of cabinet dominance by major–minor party coalitions is still to be seen. Currently the trend appears to be toward minority coalition governments.

PARLIAMENTARY SOVEREIGNTY

Parliament's constitutional importance arises from its role as the sovereign body and representative vein in the decision-making process. It is a central tenet of the Westminster-type system that parliament has the unfettered right to make laws. It cannot be bound by laws made by previous parliaments and, in turn, cannot bind its successors. Judges cannot overturn its legislation provided it follows the manner and form as prescribed by statute. These rules continue to prevail both in New Zealand and elsewhere, but today the tradition concerning the indivisibility of parliamentary sovereignty is coming under increasing questioning. In Britain this has occurred in relation to the Treaty of Rome, and in New Zealand the issue has arisen in connection with the Treaty of Waitangi.

Demands for Māori sovereignty, autonomy, or separate Māori parliaments, are cases in point. The question was also implicit in a reported comment on the Tainui agreement by the then President of the Court of Appeal, Sir Robin Cooke, in October 1989, that 'In the end, no doubt, only the courts can finally rule on whether or not a solution accords with the Treaty principles'. Meanwhile, despite attempts to build the Treaty principles into a number of laws, there is an inherent irreconcilability between the role of the Treaty as viewed by many Māori and the doctrine of parliamentary sovereignty as interpreted by most non-Māori. At its extremes this is expressed by the Māori view that the minority tangata whenua are entitled to primacy while Pakeha support majority rule. In the 2005 general election campaign both the Labour and National leaders viewed the Treaty as an important historical document but were wary of its specific constitutional significance.

In a sense, unrelated to the Treaty, parliamentary sovereignty is also called into question in the distinction between binding and non-binding referenda. Both have been used in New Zealand and are examples of direct, as opposed to representative, democracy (for further discussion, see chapter 7.4). Technically, both forms need to be implemented by parliament, which raises the question as to whether, theoretically, parliament could refuse to implement a *binding* referendum if it so chose.

ROLES

There is no neat theory of parliament. Parliaments were not based on theory, certainly not on democratic theory: they evolved, and continue to evolve. Three functions traditionally associated with them are representation, legislation, and finance (or control) of the executive.

Some idea of what might be involved in such roles may be gained from the annual report of the Office of the Clerk of Parliament (I have selected a non-election year because it is more typical). During the period 1 April 2003 to 31 March 2004 the House sat for ninety-one calendar days or 433 hours six minutes plus 187 hours and fifty-three minutes in Committee of the whole House, in all a total of 620 hours and fifty-nine minutes. A total of fifty-eight government bills were introduced (plus forty-nine reinstated from the previous session), four members' bills (plus sixteen reinstated), two local bills (plus seven reinstated), and two private bills (both reinstated). In all, 140 bills received the Royal assent. There were 231 votes in the House and 813 in Committee of the whole House. Eighty-eight bills were referred to select committees, and select committees in turn presented 289 reports. Among other activities were 1094 questions for oral answer and 2771 for written reply; 116 Notices of Motion and fifty-eight Petitions (plus thirty-four reinstated from the previous session). All this activity was additional to twenty-six General Debates.

REPRESENTATION

As the name 'House of Representatives' indicates, representation is clearly a prime role of parliament, but representation of what? For much of its history, well-educated, white, middle-class males predominated. As Blondel (1966, p. 133) put it: '… politics is a middle-class job and the training appropriate for middle-class jobs is also a training for politics. The dice are loaded by the present structure of society as well as by the natural conditions which govern the job of politics in any society'. Today women play a much greater role than when Blondel wrote although even today they constitute less than one-third of the House (see table 2.5.1).

Under MMP, the introduction of list MPs in addition to the constituency MPs has helped to remedy some of the deficiencies of representation. Together with the increase in the size of the House of Representatives from ninety-nine to 120 MPs, and the retention of the Māori seats, representation of Māori, South Pacific, and Asian New Zealanders has been given a marked boost. Māori representation is now in line with their proportion of the population, and if the representation of women, at 32.2 per cent of the House, remains unfairly disproportionate, the Inter-Parliamentary Union nevertheless ranked New Zealand fifteenth out of 188 nations for female representation in March 2006.

But representation in New Zealand is mainly about the representation of political parties, a fact reflected in the MMP system. Representation, in the sense of keeping in close touch with voters through newsletters, and devices such as weekly 'clinics', remains a key part of an electorate MP's constituency role (for a full discussion on the role of an MP, see chapter 2.6). The role of the party list MPs, however, has been a matter of controversy. Not only is there no real job description, but the decision of eleven of them during 1996–99 to leave the party that appointed them, while remaining in parliament, raised an important issue of credibility, and resulted in the introduction of legislation to deal with this, the Electoral (Integrity) Amendment Act 2000. This Act expired in 2005 and (to date) has not been renewed.

The Royal Commission on the Electoral System believed that the party list system would enable the recruitment of candidates who might represent otherwise unrepresented groups (*AJHR* 1986, H.3 p. 64). So far, however, there appears to be a marked preference for the constituency role, with a consequent danger that for many MPs the list could become viewed as a stepping-stone to a constituency position. Sometimes this also works in reverse. At the 2005 general election there appeared to be a turnover of 37.5 per cent

Table 2.5.1: Female and Māori representation, 1990–2005

Per cent of all MPs	1990	1996	2002	2005
Women	16.5	29.0	28.0	32.2
Māori	5.2	14.2	15.8	17.4

Table 2.5.2: Party composition of the 48th Parliament, 2005–

Party	Party Vote	Electoral Seats	List Seats	Total Seats
Labour	41.10	31	19	50
National	39.10	31	17	48
NZ First	5.72	0	7	7
ACT	1.51	1	1	2
Greens	5.30	0	6	6
United Future	2.67	1	2	3
Māori	2.12	4	0	4
Progressive	1.60	1	0	1
Total		69	52	121

Source: www.electionresults.govt.nz

of MPs. A total of forty-five of 120 MPs resigned, retired, or were defeated in an electorate or on a party list. This, however, is deceptive for thirteen of the fourteen incumbents defeated in electorate seats promptly reappeared on the party lists—one even making it into cabinet and two others becoming ministers outside cabinet. Only one of the defeated incumbents had rejected the possibility of standing for the list.

It is difficult to see the justification for standing both for an electorate and as a party list MP, particularly if this results in defeated electorate MPs immediately returning to the House on the list. Despite the recommendation of the Royal Commission (1986 H.3, p. 69) there appears to be no good reason why candidates should not be restricted to either an elaborate contest or the party list. Otherwise it becomes very difficult to bring about meaningful change in the composition of the House within an existing party framework.

In its internal workings, the modern parliament is primarily about the representation of political parties, a fact long not recognised constitutionally, but now embedded in the MMP electoral system and represented in the House by the predominance of party bloc votes. The introduction of MMP has reduced the advantage that the two major parties enjoyed under the former First-Past-the-Post (FPP) electoral system. The effect has been to change the working of the House of Representatives, with minor parties now playing an integral part in proceedings. No longer is a single party likely to win a majority of seats, so coalition or minority governments are now the most likely outcomes. With cohesive, single-party dominance reduced, the influence of the House correspondingly increases.

LEGISLATION AND POLICY-MAKING

Legislation is the main activity in which parliament engages, raising the question of what is meant by modern law-making. Without question, parliament is the body with the authority to make law, and in this sense its key role is one of legitimation.

Figure 2.5.1: New Zealand Parliament 2005–08

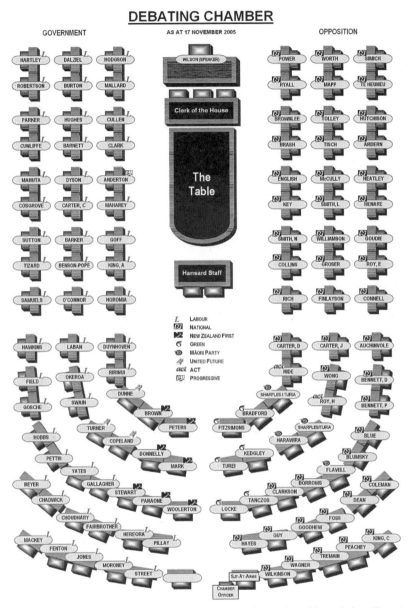

Source: http://www.clerk.parliament.govt.nz

Four types of bills are used in legislating: Government, Members', Local and Private. Government bills are those introduced by a minister, while any MP not holding ministerial office may introduce a Member's bill, provided the bill is drawn in one of the regular ballots. Local bills are confined to matters relating to a particular locality. Private bills (which incur a fee of $2000) usually relate to specific matters, such as private or community trusts, or amalgamation of banking corporations.

Beyond that the parliamentary process follows the usual pattern of three readings. The introduction of a bill is a formality authorising circulation. The first reading is a debate to decide whether the bill should be sent to a select committee. Virtually all bills, except those under urgency, are referred to select committees. At the second reading the House considers the principles of the bill as returned from the select committee. Following approval, bills go to the committee of the whole House to consider the details of drafting. The third reading debate is confined to the general appraisal of the bill as it has finally emerged. Following approval, it is then submitted to the Governor-General for the Royal Assent.

Most bills originate with the political executive and most of those are assented. In fact, the Clerk of the House has noted that, as far as he was aware, the defeat of the Local Government Amendment Bill (No. 5) (The Auckland Regional Services Trust Assets Bill) in 1998 was the first government bill to be defeated in toto in the twentieth century.[2] In 2003–4, 90.1 per cent of the bills enacted were government bills.

These bare figures disguise the fact that backbench pressures from within a party or, under MMP, across party lines can produce changes to government proposals or deter a government from acting altogether. With the increased size of the House and tendency to minority coalition government, there has also been a marked growth in the number of Members' bills introduced (but not assented). Since 1995, MPs have been able to propose legislation requiring expenditure, subject to a government veto if the legislation is deemed to have more than a minor impact upon the government's general fiscal policies.

The New Zealand parliament normally has between seventeen and twenty select committees. Thirteen are permanent 'subject' committees: Commerce; Education and Science; Finance and Expenditure; Foreign Affairs, Defence and Trade; Health; Government Administration; Local Government and Environment; Justice and Electoral Law; Law and Order; Maori Affairs; Primary Production; Social Services; and Transport and Industrial Relations (see table 2.5.3). There are three 'special purpose' permanent committees: Officers of Parliament; Privileges; and Regulations Review. The remainder is made up of ad hoc committees set up to conduct inquiries, examine specific topics or particular bills. Occasionally, an *ad hoc* committee may become semi-permanent. A current example is the Standing Orders Committee that reviews changes to standing orders, some of which have resulted, both directly and indirectly, from the introduction of MMP. Other ad hoc select committees current in the 2003–4 year were committees to inquire into hate speech, truck crashes and a committee to review New Zealand's existing constitutional arrangements.

A permanent parliamentary committee, the Business Committee, is a direct product of the introduction of the MMP system. Chaired by the Speaker, ex officio, and broadly representative of all parties in the House, it must act by consensus, determining the order of business, the times to be spent on it, and recommending to

Table 2.5.3: Parliament's subject select committees

Committee	Functions
Commerce	Business development, commerce, communications, consumer affairs, energy, information technology, insurance and superannuation
Education and Science	Education, education review, industry training, research, science and technology
Finance and Expenditure	Audit of the Crown's and departmental financial statements, Government finance, revenue and taxation
Foreign Affairs, Defence, Trade	Customs, defence, disarmament and arms control, foreign affairs, immigration and trade
Government Administration	Civil defence, cultural affairs, fitness, sport and leisure, internal affairs, Pacific Island affairs, Prime Minister and Cabinet, racing, services to Parliament, State services, statistics, tourism, women's affairs and youth affairs
Health	Health
Justice and Electoral	Crown legal and drafting services, electoral matters, human rights and justice
Law and Order	Corrections, courts, criminal law, police and serious fraud
Local Government/Environment	Conservation, environment and local government
Māori Affairs	Māori affairs
Primary Production	Agriculture, biosecurity, fisheries, forestry, lands and land information
Social Services	Housing, senior citizens, social welfare, veterans' affairs and work and income support
Transport/Industrial Relations	Accident compensation, industrial relations, labour, occupational health and safety, transport and transport safety.

Source: House of Representatives 2004, S.O. 188, pp. 55–7

the House a programme of sittings for the calendar year. It also acts as a committee of selection, deciding appointments to select committees. Theoretically, the committees choose their own chairpersons but this is largely dependent upon the amount of influence that the government of the day is able to bring to bear. Governments have always tried to manipulate committee chairs, and maintain a majority on each committee, so that they can influence outcomes.

Because of the relatively small size of the New Zealand legislature, most of the 'subject' committees are multi-purpose, multi-party bodies. For most of them, the bulk of their time is devoted to the scrutiny and amendment of bills and regulations (the 1995 Standing Orders Committee found that some of the committees spent up to 90 per cent of their time dealing with legislation). In addition, however, the same committees review the estimates and financial operations of government agencies, as well as undertaking investigations and hearing petitions. The busiest committees in 2003–4 were *Foreign Affairs, Defence and Trade*; Health; and Government Administration.

The advent of minority government has helped to tip the balance in favour of the committees acting with a greater degree of independence. New Zealand, therefore, runs a distinctive and generally successful system of parliamentary committees. The provision for public submissions on legislation, and the efforts made to facilitate these, form a particularly valuable part of the system. Many (but not all) committees are, however, overburdened and, by world standards, it can be argued that there are too many of them (cf. Inter-Parliamentary Union 1986, p. 626). As in other modern legislatures, most of the legislation enacted each year is not made by parliament directly. Instead, it takes the form of various types of regulations, such as orders in council, proclamations, or by-laws, made under powers delegated by parliament (McGee 1994, p. 406).

CONTROL OF THE EXECUTIVE AND LEGITIMACY

An important function of parliaments is the creation and support of governments. Under the former FPP electoral system, the decision about which of the two major parties was to form the government was effectively taken out of the hands of parliament and decided directly by the electorate. Under MMP the probability of minority or minority coalition governments largely has the effect of returning the initiative to the House for negotiations between political parties.

Under parliamentary systems, assemblies are usually of the 'arena' rather than the 'transformative' type (Greenstein and Polsby 1975, pp. 277–91).[3] They are thus more likely to influence rather than control the executive, even in times of minority government, for few governments are willing to risk defeat. The budget procedures are one of the key areas of influence and minority governments have proved keen to assure support for votes of supply and confidence, from the outset. Following the Budget policy statement, which is required by 31 March each year, the Finance and Expenditure Committee has six weeks to consider the statement before reporting back. Budgets (required to be introduced before 1 August) are now often introduced as early as May, and supplementary appropriations (authorising additional expenditure required) are passed before the end of the parliamentary financial year on 30 June.[4] The Estimates are considered by the various select committees within two months and the Appropriation Bill (authorising the Budget) passed by 31 October. These and other related measures have introduced much greater discipline, accountability, and transparency into the financial process enabling more effective criticism of governments.

The arena-type legislature, as its name suggests, is a show, but the significance of the various activities that take place there is easily underestimated, for the House of Representatives, perhaps above all else, provides the platform upon which government and opposition constantly struggle for psychological ascendancy. Over time, an opposition leader may begin to steal the initiative from a prime minister, ministers begin to falter at question time, mistakes are revealed, government backbenchers begin to squirm or a supremely confident government brushes off opposition attacks with ease. The psychological impact of these activities on the parties (both inside and outside the House) is difficult to overestimate. This is one reason why the daily question time, some of the key debates, and the work of the select committees (particularly in scrutinising the administration of government) are so important. Above all, however, it is the process that matters. The fact that the measures and activities of democratically elected governments are open to public scrutiny and criticism through clearly defined processes is the central issue in establishing the legitimacy of the political system.

TERM OF PARLIAMENT

New Zealand is unusual in the length of its term of parliament. Most countries favour four years, with approximately ten countries favouring the three-year term. Originally the five-year term was adopted in New Zealand, but this was reduced to three years in 1879, largely to make governments more accountable. Since then, a bill to establish a four-year term was passed in 1934 but was repealed by the first Labour government in 1936, and two further attempts to increase the term to four years by referendum (1967, 1990) have been defeated. Lacking a formal constitution, or an upper house, and with highly cohesive political parties for much of the last seventy years, it is arguable that the electoral system is the only strong democratic safeguard that the country possesses.

The main arguments against the three-year term are that it tends to encourage almost constant electioneering, and that there is insufficient time to judge the effects of policies, particularly economic policies, which may be introduced by a government. Accordingly, governments may be reluctant to introduce policies that they believe to be necessary but that are likely to prove electorally unpopular. Conversely, the four-year term is claimed to avoid these problems.

With the introduction of such safeguards as proportional representation and a Bill of Rights, the need for the triennial system has lessened, although New Zealand still lacks the formal Constitution that many would regard as a key safeguard. Moreover, what has not changed is the right of the prime minister of the day to recommend the date of the general election to the Governor-General. Extending the term of parliament to a permissible four years would merely give governments greater latitude in choosing the best time to call an election and, in all probability, would not greatly lengthen the average time that a government served. An alternative would be to combine the four-year term with a fixed or semi-fixed system, as in Sweden, where elections must be held every four years. If a government chooses to call an earlier election, the election scheduled at the end of four years must still be held. (Boston 1998, p. 116).

SIZE

Legislatures vary greatly in size. From 1902–69, the New Zealand House of Representatives had eighty members. Between 1969 and 1996 the total gradually increased to ninety-nine, and the introduction of MMP was linked to the decision to increase the size of the House to 120 MPs. In 2005 the House increased in size to 121 as a result of an 'overhang' in which the Māori party won more seats than it was entitled to by its party vote. Under MMP, the increase in the overall size of the House only lasts for the life of that parliament. A key factor in assessing parliamentary size is population, and empirical theory suggests that the number of seats in a national assembly tends to be close to the cube root of the population. Compared with most other nations of roughly comparable size, New Zealand still has an unduly small legislature. Israel, with 120 MPs for six million people, is one of the few democratic nations that are more parsimonious. The population criterion is not the only one, however.

The Royal Commission on the Electoral System, which favoured 140 MPs but recommended 120, cited five factors as important: representation of constituents; representation of the nation as a whole; provision of effective government; enactment of legislation; and scrutiny of the actions of the executive (*AJHR* 1986, p. 117). Of these, the representation of constituents in electorates poses the most intractable problem. Equality of numbers of voters can result in electorates very large in area. For example, even with a parliament of 120 MPs, large South Island electorates, such as Clutha-Southland, may be equivalent to as many as eighteen Auckland electorates. Most of the other criteria could be met by effective re-organisation, such as reduction in the size of cabinet, the recruitment of some of its members from outside parliament (rather than from parties not in formal coalition), the enactment of fewer laws, and the tighter organisation of the select committee system. Indeed, there is a strong argument that it is the size of cabinet in relation to the size of the House that is the key factor.

A Citizen's Initiated Referendum in 1999 that sought a reduction in the size of the House to ninety-nine members received overwhelming public support but has not been acted upon. Although the MMP electoral system might work with 100 MPs, it would become progressively more difficult to maintain effective proportionality under existing arrangements.

CONCLUSION

Frequently described as 'the single most important institution in the New Zealand political system', the modern New Zealand parliament rarely lives up to its ideal of constituting the great debate of the nation. It is perhaps best viewed as a platform for the continuing, frequently rhetorical, battle of political parties. It is an institution whose members consistently rank below everyone else in polls of public respect yet it remains a vital element in seeking to reconcile authority with freedom.

Despite the apparent lack of popularity, current New Zealand parliaments are superior to many parliaments in the past, or many overseas bodies. Parliaments are regularly regarded as 'being in decline', but many improvements have been made, and continue to be made, particularly in the workings of the New Zealand version. For better or worse, MMP has transformed representation in the House, as well as changing its party composition, while heavily reducing the possibilities of a single party gaining a majority of seats. It has demonstrated too that minority coalition government can work in New Zealand, albeit not to everyone's satisfaction. However, the changes to parliament resulting from MMP have demonstrated that while it is possible to bring about changes to institutions, attitudinal change follows more slowly.

DISCUSSION QUESTIONS

1   Is the concept of parliamentary sovereignty outdated?
2   Does parliament really represent the 'people'? If so, who and how?
3   Should there be a separate Māori parliament and what powers might such an institution have?
4   What is the ideal size and term for the New Zealand unicameral parliament?
5   New Zealand parliamentary select committees: workhorses or political pawns?
6   What should the role of party list members be?

NOTES

1   *National Business Review*, 21 May 2004.
2   *NBR*, 24 April 1998.
3   Greenstein and Polsby suggest that 'arena' and 'transformative' represent opposite ends of a continuum of legislative power. 'Arena' represents the 'formalized settings for the interplay of significant political forces in the life of a political system'. 'Transformative' describes 'legislatures that possess the independent capacity, frequently exercised, to mold and transform proposals from whatever source into laws'.
4   The financial business transacted by the House ensures that it meets at least annually and defines the last day in each year as 30 June, by which time that meeting must take place.

REFERENCES

AJHR. See *Appendices to the Journals of the House of Representatives.*

Appendices to the Journals of the House of Representatives 1986, H3, Report of the Royal Commission on the Electoral System, 'Towards a Better Democracy'.

Appendices to the Journals of the House of Representatives 2002, A8, Report of the Office of the Clerk of the House of Representatives.

Blondel, J. 1966, *Voters, Parties and Leaders,* Penguin, Harmondsworth.

Boston, J. 1998, *Governing under Proportional Representation: Lessons from Europe,* Institute of Policy Studies, Wellington.

Brennan, G. & A. Hamlin 1993, 'Rationalising Parliamentary Systems', *Australian Journal of Political Science,* vol. 28, pp. 443–57.

Copeland, G.W. & S.C. Patterson 1994, *Parliaments in the Modern World: Changing Institutions,* University of Michigan Press, Ann Arbor.

Greenstein, F.I. & N.W. Polsby 1995, *Handbook of Political Science,* vol. 5, Governmental Institutions and Processes, Addison-Wesley, Reading, Mass.

Inter-Parliamentary Union, Parliaments of the World 1986, 2nd edn, Gower, Aldershot.

Jackson, K. & A. McRobie 2005, *The Hazard Political and Historical Dictionary of New Zealand,* Scarecrow Press, Lanham, Md and Hazard Press, Christchurch.

McGee, D. 1985 & 1994, *Parliamentary Practice in New Zealand,* 1st & 2nd edns, Government Printer, Wellington.

McGee, D. 2005, *Parliamentary Practice in New Zealand,* 3rd edn, Dunmore Publishing, Wellington.

McGee, D. 1998, 'The Member of Parliament—Political Existentialist or Party Delegate'? *Table,* pp. 44–52.

Mezey, M. 1979, *Comparative Legislatures,* Duke University Press, Durham, NC.

Miller, R. 2005, *Party Politics in New Zealand,* Oxford University Press, Melbourne.

Olson, D.M. & M.L. Mezey (eds) 1991, *Legislatures in the Policy Process,* Cambridge University Press, Cambridge.

Palmer, G. *1979, Unbridled Power,* Oxford University Press, Auckland.

Patterson, S.C. & A. Mughan 1999, *Senates: Bicameralism in the Contemporary World,* Ohio State University Press, Columbus.

Taagpera, R. 1972, The Size of National Assemblies', *Social Research,* vol. 1, no. 4.

FURTHER READING

Boston, J. 1998, *Governing under Proportional Representation: Lessons from Europe,* Institute of Policy Studies, Wellington.

McGee, D. 2005, *Parliamentary Practice in New Zealand,* 3rd edn, Dunmore Publishing, Wellington.

McGee, D. 1998, 'The Member of Parliament—Political Existentialist or Party Delegate'? *Table,* pp. 44–52.

Mulgan, R. 1997, 'Parliament: Composition and Functions', in R. Miller (ed.), *New Zealand Politics in Transition,* Oxford University Press, Auckland, pp. 62–71.

Palmer, G. & M. Palmer 1997, *Bridled Power: New Zealand Government under MMP,* Oxford University Press, Auckland, pp. 116–82.

Role of an MP

Grant Gillon & Raymond Miller

Surprisingly, little is known about the role, functions and responsibilities of those we elect as our MPs. While voters directly choose their MP, too often the focus of attention is on the personal characteristics, perquisites, and pay packets of MPs, rather than on what they actually do. Unlike most other occupations, there is no formal job description for an MP. Since the Standing Orders were amended in 2003, MPs are not even required to turn up to parliament (Hunt 2003a, p. 81), and their allowances and entitlements are quite broadly defined. In the vaguely expressed words of the then Speaker, 'parliamentary business is the undertaking of any task or function that a member could reasonably be expected to carry out in his or her capacity as a Member of Parliament and that complements the business of the House of Representatives' (Hunt 2003b). In addition to this parliamentary role, attending to the needs of constituents and conducting party business are two important features of representation.

The actual role of an MP is steeped in constitutional and historical convention. Under MMP, there are two types of MP, the electorate and the list member. The introduction of list MPs in 1996 has meant a change of emphasis from a narrow geographical focus to representing wider regional and national interests, as well as distinct social and ethnic groups within the wider community. By virtue of their placement on party lists, list MPs are also more directly answerable to party officials and members than are the electorate MPs. This raises questions about how the two different categories of MP perform their role as the necessary link between electors, parliament, and the government. The Royal Commission on the Electoral System (1986, p. 53) anticipated that the work of electorate and list MPs would be similar, although they recognised that some list MPs might not perform as much constituency work as electorate MPs. The Electoral Act 1993, which was drafted in the event that there would be a majority vote in favour of MMP, failed to distinguish between the two categories of MP, apart from stipulating that each undergo a different method of election.

This chapter will focus on the role of MPs, especially any variations in the functions of electorate and list MPs. After considering the legislative, constituency, and party activities of an MP, the chapter will assess what parliamentary candidates and the public think the work of an MP involves, especially in relation to any criticism of the workload and accountability of list MPs.

LEGISLATIVE FUNCTION

The legislative function of an MP is carried out in a number of forums ranging from policy development in party committees and conferences to decisions by caucus, cabinet and their committees, and debating on the floor of the House. There are two main divisions within the House: government and opposition. Support parties that are not formal members of the governing coalition might give their approval to some pieces of legislation while opposing others. Ministers must be appointed from within parliament and they, along with backbench members from the governing parties, are responsible for the formulation of government legislation. Parliament elects MPs to the role of Speaker, Deputy-Speaker, and Assistant Speaker. They are responsible for the smooth running of the business of the House. Each party assumes responsibility for electing whips.

1. Whips

Party whips are entrusted with many of the oversight, administrative, and managerial roles around parliament. They are elected by party caucuses and are accountable to both the leader and the caucus. Some party whips actually do possess a symbolic leather whip that is passed on during a change of office, a tradition that stems from the association between the Westminster parliament and the recently abolished British sport of fox hunting (McGee 2005, p. 86). Historically, whips ensure that members are present in the House to both vote and serve on select committees. While the whip can cast a vote on behalf of an absent colleague, a minimum number of members must be on the premises to comply with the voting quota (House of Representatives 2006, cl. 140–56). The task of rounding up members is important, and can be extremely fraught. Whips attend the Business Committee and negotiate parliamentary business, administer party budgets, allocate speaking orders, cast party votes, and sign off members' expenses. Whips are the principal means of communication between parties, and sometimes act as mediators within their own caucus. They are best described as the oil that smoothes the machinery of parliament.[1]

2. Select committees

In the same way that MPs provide a vital link between the public and the government, select committees are the interface between the public, the government, and the House. Almost all MPs sit on select committees, of which there are thirteen 'subject' committees[2] and several special committees, such as Business, Officers of Parliament, Privileges, Regulations Review and Standing Orders. It is in these committees that much of the intensive legislative scrutiny and public hearings take place. (For a discussion on the nature and role of select committees, see chapter 2.5.)

The change to MMP was expected to improve the ability of MPs to carry out their collective parliamentary functions (Wallace 1986, p. 59). This was to be achieved by the increased numbers (from ninety-nine to 120 MPs) and enhanced representation, coupled with the ability of parties to use the lists to ensure the re-election of members with specialised knowledge. In some respects the desire for proportionality has provided mixed results. There are two benefits that are important to mention here. The first is that the government is not guaranteed a majority on each and every committee. This development necessitates a high level of cross-party negotiation and compromise in order for legislation to be passed. On occasion, bills have had to be 'parked' in select committees or permanently set aside because the government has not been able to reach agreement with its support parties. The other change attributed to the MMP is the opportunity available to most parties to chair at least one select committee. During the 2005–08 term of the Labour–Progressive government, for example, National MPs chaired the Primary Production (Hon. David Carter), Regulations Review (Richard Worth) and Government Administration (Shane Ardern) committees.

Most MPs agree that select committees have begun to play a more important role since the advent of MMP. As well as having greater influence over the policy-making process, committee members are more strongly committed to working consensually. Select committee resources have increased and there is a willingness to seek independent advice from sources other than government departments. These committees are increasingly becoming the forum both for MPs to express their independent views and for the public to present views to their representatives.

3. Parties

With the advent of MMP, parties were recognised in Standing Orders for the first time. The change in Standing Orders means that greater prominence is given to the role of parties, as opposed to individual members, than was the case in pre-1996 parliaments. Voice votes are called for and, if requested, as they often are, votes are taken in party blocs, with the Clerk calling out each party in order of size. The designated party whip (or other authorised member) stands and replies with the party's votes for, against, and any abstentions. Proxy voting has been allowed since 1995, replacing the old 'pairing' system. Members are now able to delegate another MP in writing, to cast his or her vote. The individual member is no longer required to attend the House in person in order to cast a vote. Furthermore, apart from conscience or personal votes, the voting is anonymous.

The second but related change occurred because of the introduction of list MPs. An increasing number of MPs (fifty-two in 2006) owe their position and re-election to the goodwill of the party, or, more particularly, the party leader. Since the development of the party system in the late nineteenth and early twentieth centuries, MPs have been subject to strict party discipline, although it was sometimes possible for dissident MPs to call on local support for re-selection against the wishes of the party leadership. Under MMP, list members are particularly vulnerable. This vulnerability was highlighted in two cases. The first occurred in 1997, when Alamein Kopu, an Alliance list MP, left the Alliance and offered her support to the National-New Zealand First government. The Alliance argued that Kopu should be evicted from parliament for breaching the proportionality of the House. Although the Alliance was unsuccessful, a bill was enacted that amended the Electoral Act ('Electoral (Integrity) Amendment Bill' 2001). This bill allowed a party leader to sign a statement advising the Speaker that an MP had acted in such a way as to distort the proportionality of parliament. In 2004–05, the ACT party took one of its MPs, Donna Awatere-Huata, to the new Supreme Court and successfully argued that the MP's actions had breached the relevant clauses in the act.

4. Caucus

MPs from the same party gather every Tuesday morning that the House sits (or more often if necessary) to attend a party caucus. The purpose of such meetings is to reach collective agreement on party policy, strategy and tactics. Caucus provides a forum for backbench members to hold their government ministers to account. The requirement to consult and negotiate with other parties to get legislation through the House means that caucus is not always able to direct or overrule its ministers. Non-government caucuses, on the other hand, have changed little with the introduction of MMP. Joint caucuses between government coalition partners were attempted between the National and New Zealand First parties (1996–98) and the Labour and Alliance parties (1999–2002), but they were little more than briefing sessions—in the case of the latter two parties, to hear a briefing paper on the Budget speeches and discuss the Kiwibank proposal.

In addition, cross-party groupings have occasionally been established. These ad hoc 'caucuses' tend to convene for a common purpose. Perhaps the most well known group is the inter-party 'Māori caucus', although there have also been attempts to establish a women's caucus, and there have even been joint meetings of South Island and Auckland MPs. An attempt to establish a regular Auckland caucus between 1996 and 1999 resulted in disagreement on a number of issues, with some members accusing the government-appointed chair of manipulating outcomes to give preference to government proposals. While they may start with the best of intentions, such groups tend to get bogged down in party politics, thereby reducing their chances of success. Traditionally, MPs have also gathered together on a non-party political basis with a view to facilitating communication with MPs from other countries or developing friendship groups. The MPs' branch of Amnesty International is an example of such a committee. It must be said, however, that only rarely do these groups provide a genuine opportunity for cross-party cooperation and agreement.

5. Debating chamber

The other main focal point for an MP's time is the debating chamber. Geoffrey Palmer once famously accused the New Zealand parliament of being the fastest lawmaker in the West (Palmer 1979, p. 77). The Royal Commission (Wallace 1986) subsequently promised that the introduction of MMP would bring a more measured approach to legislative change, with greater opportunity for inter-party consultation and policy consensus. The prediction of greater deliberation proved to be correct, certainly if the data accumulated by the Parliamentary Council Office (2004) is accurate. It found that more pages of legislation and volumes of statutes and statutory regulations were published in 2003–04 than in any previous year. The total normal sitting hours of the House in 2004 were 444, well up on the year ended 2000, when the House sat for 299 normal hours. Select committees increased their workload from 461 sittings in 2000 to 523 in 2004. If the volume of legislation passed and hours worked was an accurate guide to the workload of parliamentarians, then our MPs are working harder than ever before, but with less urgency.

The House normally sits between 2pm and 10pm on Tuesday and Wednesday, and between 2pm and 6pm on Thursday, although urgency can be taken by the government to sit outside of these times. Question time, which begins at 2pm, provides an opportunity for the opposition to scrutinise the actions of individual ministers. Twelve approved oral questions, which must be approved by the Office of the Clerk, are addressed to a variety of ministers. The questions are divided proportionately among the parties and are followed by a range of supplementary questions that have not been seen by the minister prior to being asked. Whereas the two major parties once had exclusive control of the question time, now the questions are divided up among the eight parliamentary parties. A former Speaker (Kidd 2005) has bemoaned the new format and argued that the distribution of questions among so many parties prevents the opposition from mounting a strong attack on government policy. Certainly the strategic use of question time by political parties severely limits their usefulness for individual MPs wanting to raise issues on behalf of the people they represent.

Probably the most well-known function of an MP is that of speaking in the House. Speaking times have been reduced as a result of the increased number of parties that wish to make their views known. Where previously some debates, such as the Second and Third Readings, were of an unlimited duration, now they have been set at a maximum of two hours. Most participating parties are limited to ten minutes, although members within a party may split the time between two members. The General Debate and Committee Stages speeches are for a maximum of five minutes each. A further phenomenon which has crept in is the practice of drafting bills in as few parts as possible, and then moving that the bill be voted upon 'part by part'. Instead of the previously unlimited debate on the committee stages, each part is often closed after only an hour of speeches. This has the potential effect of severely reducing the amount of scrutiny that the House gives each bill.

Standing Orders allows debate on matters deemed to be of urgent public importance. These 'urgent' debates are triggered by a letter from an MP to the Speaker, who decides whether the issue meets the criteria for setting aside the government's business. One such occasion occurred early in the 2005 session, when the National party education spokesperson received the Speaker's permission to debate the issue of the government's handling of the National Certificate of Educational Achievement (NCEA) examinations (New Zealand Parliament 2005c, p. 18,469). The debates are held straight after question time and even the requester is unaware of the Speaker's decision prior to its announcement. On matters of real importance, the most senior speakers from each party lead the debate. Urgent debates are for a set time and members speak on a proportional basis. These debates provide the opportunity for members to place the government under intense scrutiny, although often to no apparent effect. At the end of the allotted time the debate ceases without a motion arising, regardless of the points scored or views expressed.

CONSTITUENCY FUNCTION

While they are in parliament, MPs spend a great deal of time meeting lobbyists, community representatives, constituents, and an assortment of groups from their home electorates who happen to be visiting Wellington. Many volunteer and professional lobbyists seek appointments with MPs to discuss issues that are pertinent to their sector and to seek support for or against a particular measure. In most cases, it is easier for lobbyists to 'do the rounds' in Wellington than to visit MPs in their electorate offices. Constituents, on the other hand, generally find it easier to meet their MPs in their home areas.

Prior to the introduction of MMP, all MPs were electorate-based and held regular constituency clinics. This was regarded as being fundamental to our understanding of representative democracy (Palmer & Palmer 2004, p. 143). Today, each electorate MP is serviced with secretarial and other resources in parliament and is funded for an out-of-parliament office and staff. While most MPs prefer to hold an electorate seat, some senior MPs, such as Labour's Michael Cullen and National's Don Brash, have opted for the lighter constituency load of a list member. Despite the difference in constituency workload, there is no variation between electorate and list MPs either in pay scale or in the value of their parliamentary vote.

An electorate MP usually establishes at least one main office and, if the electorate is large, part-time branch offices in neighbouring towns. These offices provide the MP with vital two-way communication with constituents. MPs are often able to spend Mondays (except for ministers) and Fridays, together with weekends, in the home electorate. Their work includes holding regular clinics where constituents make appointments to discuss a matter of government action or policy, seek assistance over a personal issue, or even obtain witness to an official document. Engagements, such as attending community group meetings, school fairs, and sports days, take up the remainder of a member's electorate time. When MPs are in parliament or otherwise out of the office, salaried electorate secretaries become their eyes and ears.

It is in the electorate office that an MP usually grasps a local issue that forms the basis for official representation in parliament. These take a number of forms, including: petitioning parliament; sponsoring bills; or seeking information. Petitions received from constituents are presented to the House under the sponsorship of the local MP. But an MP may also be asked to approach a minister or department over a constituent's problems, such as an immigration or housing issue. As well as oral questions, MPs might choose to seek information on their constituents' behalf, using written questions to ministers. During 2004, the Clerk advised parliament that sixty-nine petitions were scrutinised and 21,090 written questions lodged. MPs use these activities to both provide information to the electorate and gain feedback and knowledge that is then used to guide parliamentary decision-making. In these ways, MPs can provide links between the people and the mechanisms of government.

Because the minor parties have few, if any, electorate MPs, they are under pressure to pool resources, share facilities, and operate out of the same office in the larger centres, thereby enabling the budget to be spread a bit further. Whereas electorate MPs represent a defined geographical area, list MPs tend to be directed by their caucus to assume a nationwide, sector, or geographic role. This might see list MPs viewing the whole country as their electorate. National's Pansy Wong, for example, has been given responsibility for liaising with the Asian community, and Labour's Ashraf Choudhary represents members of the Muslim community.

PARTY FUNCTION

The third main function of electorate and list MPs is to be a loyal and active member of their party. While it might be expected that, because they have fewer constituency obligations than electorate members, list MPs will be better placed to serve the interests of the party, this is not necessarily the case. At the local level, electorate MPs have a responsibility to nurture the grassroots party organisation by recruiting members and office-holders, organising branch and electorate activities, fundraising, and ensuring the smooth running of the local election campaign. As well as maintaining a local party organisation, MPs have a responsibility to attend and be active at the regional and national levels of the organisation, especially the annual conference, which provides an opportunity for the party to parade the talent it has on offer to the media and wider electorate.

Given the role, albeit limited, of party activists and delegates in nominating candidates for the party lists (see Miller 2004, p. 86), it is particularly important that aspiring list members maintain a high profile at both the local and regional levels of the party organisation. This may include membership of party committees, accepting public speaking engagements, and being involved in fundraising and electioneering. Indeed, a quick perusal of MPs' biographical sketches on party websites reveals a familiar pattern of party activism long before their election to parliament. In the case of the two major parties, this might include contesting a succession of unwinnable electorate seats prior to being selected in a marginal or safe electorate, as illustrated by the early political career of Helen Clark. In 1975 she was chosen as the candidate in the safe National seat of Piako.[3] Before winning the nomination for the safe Labour seat of Mt Albert in 1981,[4] she was president of the Labour Youth Council, executive member of the party's Auckland regional council, women's and policy councils, and national executive. The former leader of the National party, Bill English, served a similar political apprenticeship, including a term as chair of the Southland 'Young Nats' and executive positions on three different electorate executives before standing successfully for the seat of Clutha-Southland in the 1990 National landslide.

In contrast, progression through the ranks in the minor parties is likely to be much more swift and straightforward. As the careers of Doug Woolerton (New Zealand First), Rod Donald (Greens), Pita Sharples (Māori party) and other minor party politicians illustrate, however, minor party organisations cannot be sustained without ongoing involvement by elected politicians in a range of party activities.

ATTITUDES TO THE ROLE OF AN MP

The New Zealand Election Study surveyed voters and parliamentary candidates on the role of an MP (see, for example, Karp 2002 and Miller 2005). Survey data spanning every election since 1993 reveal that, for parliamentary candidates and MPs, the parliamentary function has increased in importance and the electorate function has correspondingly decreased since the advent of MMP. These changing views on the importance of parliament are consistent with the argument made earlier in the chapter about the increase in the power of parliament relative to that of cabinet. Of the various parliamentary activities, participating in debates (1993 22 per cent; 2002 33 per cent), serving on select committees (1993 52 per cent; 2002 81 per cent), and conducting media interviews (1993 19 per cent; 2002 46 per cent) have become significantly more important to candidates (Miller 2004, p. 101). In contrast, helping individuals sort out their problems (1993 67 per cent; 2002 44 per cent), conducting electorate clinics (1993 86 per cent; 2002 50 per cent), and representing the electorate (1993 62 per cent; 2002 46 per cent) have become less important than they were before the advent of MMP.

As might be expected, the parliamentary function is more highly valued and the electorate function less highly valued by list candidates, with the greatest variations being found in attitudes towards helping individuals, conducting electorate clinics, and holding other electorate functions. Overall, the data suggests that 'the role of the list MP has begun to crystallise around a number of parliamentary, party and regional responsibilities. As a result, there is now less need to replicate the constituency functions of electorate MPs, as illustrated by the decision of a growing number of list MPs not to maintain local electorate offices' (Miller 2004, pp. 101–02).

Finally, it is useful to consider whether there have been any changes in the attitudes of voters, as distinct from candidates, towards the role of list MPs. During and after every MMP election, list MPs have been criticised for a number of perceived shortcomings, mostly to do with the role of the party elite in determining the composition of the list, the ambiguous nature of the job description, and a lack of public scrutiny and accountability relative to that of an electorate MP. In the early years of MMP, list members were frequently accused of being party-hoppers who abandoned their party whenever the going got tough. More recently, the lists have been viewed as a safety net for defeated electorate MPs. These criticisms notwithstanding, there is evidence that public attitudes towards list MPs are improving. The NZES survey of voters found that public approval of the way list MPs handled their jobs rose from a mere 7 per cent in 1999 to 36 per cent in 2002 (Miller 2005, p. 208). While the bulk of respondents were either neutral or unwilling to express an opinion, disapproval of the role of list MPs had dropped from 29 per cent in 1999 to 10 per cent in 2002.

CONCLUSION

While the introduction of MMP resulted in the creation of a new category of MP, the list member, it also signalled other changes in the role and functions of MPs. The multi-party nature of the new, proportionally elected parliament, together with the growing incidence of minority government, have made parliament a more important institution than it was when Palmer coined the phrase 'unbridled power' in describing the pre-eminence of cabinet. This shift in the balance of power has had the effect of providing individual MPs with a more meaningful role as legislators and representatives of the people. It has not all been in the one direction, however. As this chapter has shown, the role of individual MPs has, to some extent, been constrained by the growing importance of party blocs. As we have shown, voting in the House is now taken as a party vote except in rare circumstances. MPs are no longer required to be in the House in order to cast their vote, nor are their names recorded on the voting tally. Unless they are especially vigilant, modern MPs may be inadequately informed both as to the nature of a particular piece of legislation and to the way in which the party whip is exercising their vote. This may have the added effect of increasing the anonymity of a member's voting history. With the vote being recorded against a party rather than an individual MP, it also reduces the member's personal responsibility for legislative outcomes.

The second effect of the increased party emphasis has been on the relationship between MPs and their electors. There is a growing concern that MPs, especially list members, are in danger of becoming too beholden to their party's parliamentary leaders. This danger was highlighted not only by the passage of the 'party-hopping' bill, but also the pressure placed on the three Māori Labour MPs who were threatened to vote against their government's Foreshore and Seabed legislation (Miller 2005).[5] As these examples show, the imposition of strict party discipline may come at great personal cost, especially where an MP's independent judgment or the interests of constituents are in conflict with those of the party leadership.

Despite these potentially disturbing trends, parliament continues to provide effective legislation while acting as a curb on the abuse of executive power. The Parliamentary Council Office provides sound empirical evidence confirming that a vast majority of MPs are effective legislators. In this role, and especially in relation to their work on select committees, MPs continue to provide an important link between government and the governed. Under MMP, MPs more fairly represent the many communities of interest and diverse views both in and to the government. While the evidence tends to suggest that there are times when MPs are more delegates of their parties than representatives of the wider electorate, the extent to which this concern affects the independence of our representatives will only be seen as the MMP system begins to mature.

DISCUSSION QUESTIONS

1   MPs do not have a formal job description. What would be the pros and cons of requiring MPs to work to a job description?

2   Should list MPs perform different duties to constituent MPs and, if so, how would the roles differ?

3   Delegate MPs act upon the will of their constituents whereas trustees exercise their own judgment. Should MPs operate as delegated or trustee representatives?

4 New Zealand's MPs are heavily influenced by their parties. How closely tied to party
   discipline should our MPs be?

NOTES

1 Although each party has a whip or equivalent position, some parties elect a deputy.
   The government has a senior whip and a junior whip. The whip of the senior coalition
   partner is usually also the senior government whip and the junior partner occupies the
   junior government whip position.
2 The subject select committees are: Commerce; Education and Science; Finance and
   Expenditure; Foreign Affairs, Defence and Trade; Government Administration;
   Health; Justice and Electoral; Law and Order; Māori Affairs; Primary Production;
   Social Services; and Transport and Industrial Relations.
3 At the 1975 general election, Piako's National candidate, J.F. Luxton, received 10,248
   votes, some 6,174 more than Labour's Helen Clark.
4 In Mt Albert in 1981, Clark received 12,231 votes, compared with 6,024 for the
   National candidate.
5 The MPs concerned were Tariana Turia (Te Tai Hauauru), Nanaia Mahuta (Tainui),
   and Georgina Beyer (Wairarapa). In the end, only Turia voted against the bill.

REFERENCES

Electoral (Integrity) Amendment Bill, New Zealand Parliament 2001, Electoral Act (1993).
House of Representatives. 2005, *Standing Orders of the House of Representatives.* Wellington:
   House of Representatives.
Karp, J. 2002, 'Members of Parliament and Representation', in J. Vowles, P. Aimer, J. Karp,
   S. Banducci, R. Miller and A. Sullivan, *Proportional Representation on Trial: The 1999
   New Zealand General Election and the Fate of MMP*, Auckland: Auckland University
   Press, pp. 130–45.
Kidd, D. 2000, Parliament under MMP. *Canterbury Law Review*, 7, pp. 507–15.
Kidd, D. 2000, 'Parliament under MMP', *Canterbury Law Review*, 7, pp. 507–15.
McGee, D. 2005, *Parliamentary Practice in New Zealand*, 3rd edn, Palmerston North:
   Dunmore Publishing.
McGee, D. 2005, personal interview with G. Gillon, 6 April, Parliament Buildings,
   Wellington.
Miller, R. 2004, 'Who Stood for Office and Why?' in J. Vowles, P. Aimer, S. Banducci, J. Karp
   and R. Miller (eds) *Voter's Veto: The 2002 Election in New Zealand and the Consolidation
   of Minority Governments*, Auckland: Auckland University Press, pp. 85–103.
New Zealand Parliament 1999a, *Parliamentary Debates (Hansard)* (Vol. 580).
New Zealand Parliament 1999b, *Parliamentary Debates (Hansard)* (Vol. 579). Wellington:
   House of Representatives.
New Zealand Parliament. 2005a, *Parliamentary Debates (Hansard).* Wellington: House of
   Representatives.

New Zealand Parliament 2005b, *Parliamentary Debates (Weekly Hansard) Book 33.* Wellington: House of Representatives.

New Zealand Parliament. 2005c, *Parliamentary Debates (Weekly Hansard) Book 79* (Vol. 623). Wellington: House of Representatives.

Office of the Clerk 2004, *Government Accountability to the House*, from www.google. co.nz/search?q=cache:5SYzoY1PaR8J:www.clerk.parliament.govt.nz/NR/rdonlyres/ 75FE8408–8C57–46D5–8E76–4C708AA9D893/0/GovernmentAccountabilitytothe House.pdf+mcgee+%22responsible+government%22+zealand&hl=en

Palmer, G. & M. Palmer 2004, *Bridled Power: New Zealand's Constitution and Government* (4th edn), Oxford & New York: Oxford University Press.

Palmer, G. 1979, *Unbridled Power?: An Interpretation of New Zealand's Constitution and Government.* Wellington: New York: Oxford University Press.

Wallace, J. (chair) 1986, Royal Commission on the Electoral System. (1986). *Report of The Royal Commission on the Electoral System—Towards a Better Democracy.* Wellington: Royal Commission on the Electoral System.

Wellington: House of Representatives.

FURTHER READING

Catt, H., P. Harris & N. Roberts 1992, *Voter's choice: Electoral Change in New Zealand?* Dunmore Press, Palmerston North.

Joseph, P. A. 2001, *Constitution and Administrative Law in New Zealand*, 2nd ed., Brookers, Wellington.

Levine, S. & F. Barker (eds) 2000, *The MP in MMP: The Changing Role of the New Zealand Member of Parliament.* Wellington: Research Committee of Legislative Specialists, International Political Science Association.

Martin, J. 2004, *The House: New Zealand's House of Representatives 1854–2004*, Dunmore Press, Palmerston North.

McGee, D. 2005, *Parliamentary Practice in New Zealand*, 3rd edn, Palmerston North: Dunmore Publishing.

Miller, R. 2005, *Party Politics in New Zealand*, Oxford University Press, Melbourne.

WEBSITES OF INTEREST

www.clerk.parliament.govt.nz/
www.elections.org.nz/
www.govt.nz/
www.parliament.govt.nz/
www.speaker.parliament.govt.nz/

Conscience Voting

David Lindsey

While MPs are generally subject to the collective decisions of their parties, on a range of moral or social legislation they are able to cast a 'conscience' vote, otherwise known as a 'personal' or 'free' vote. Issues that have been the subject of conscience votes include capital punishment, homosexual law reform, prostitution, gambling, abortion, pornography, smoking in public places, and the sale and consumption of alcohol. In recent years, some of the most controversial legislation has been decided by free or conscience votes, with the Prostitution 2003, Civil Union 2005 and Relationships 2004 Bills being among the most prominent examples.

Conscience voting is an indirect consequence of New Zealand's long tradition of government by party. While there have always been groups of politicians who form themselves into voting alliances, prior to the development of the party system these loyalties were usually informal and flexible. Following the development of the party system, it became increasingly difficult to get elected to parliament without first becoming a member of a political party. Decisions about how to vote in parliament were largely controlled by the party rather than the individual member. As a result MPs who had strong convictions on an issue, or who wished to represent the views of their constituents as opposed to those of their party, often found themselves at odds with their party's parliamentary leadership.

Conscience voting was first used in the 1870s to legislate the sale and consumption of alcohol. Although most MPs at the time agreed that alcohol was a disruptive influence on society, they disagreed on what to do about it. To a considerable extent, the debate reflected differing opinions about the role of the state, with some MPs arguing that government had no role in regulating what was considered a private matter, while others took the view that it must intervene for the protection of vulnerable citizens and the greater good of the whole community. As one might expect, given the controversy surrounding alcohol consumption in the late eighteenth and early nineteenth centuries, the lines of dispute were drawn between the prohibitionists, the moderates, and those opposed to any form of restriction. Conscience voting was restricted to issues surrounding the use of alcohol until the 1930s, when its scope began to widen slowly. Tensions were beginning to develop, however, between the policies of the two major parties and the personal moral values of some individual MPs. On the most controversial matters there was a need for a safety valve, and following the Second World War it increasingly took the form of the conscience vote. In addition, this period also witnessed a decline in the relative authority of institutional religion, allowing both social mores to shift and creating a moral vacuum that parliament was increasingly called upon to fill. These trends led to the use of more conscience votes across a wider range of issues such that between 1873 and 2005, 130 conscience votes were held—all but eight conducted since 1945.

Each party in the New Zealand parliament is free to determine how they will treat a particular vote. By default, parliamentary votes are conducted on a party basis, with each party declaring the number of their members and their collective voting intention to the Speaker of the House, and the Speaker declaring the result of the vote. When a party believes that it is in their best interests to not vote corporately however, they declare to the Speaker their intention to allow their members personal votes. Parties usually allow conscience voting because: 1) the issue at hand is not one the party has, or can be expected to have, a policy on; 2) an issue is so sensitive to the electorate that it is desirable that it be divorced from party politics; 3) the consciences of a proportion of MPs would be affronted if party whips were applied; and 4) it is an issue that is traditionally treated as a conscience matter. Parties may, however, also find its use convenient for political reasons. For example, a party may wish to avoid the appearance of disunity among their members, or they may see benefit in appearing to take the high moral ground on an issue by treating it as a conscience matter. A government may also perceive it as a way of garnering support from across the House over pieces of legislation it may not be sure it will win. The decision about whether to grant their MPs a free or conscience vote will vary from party to party and issue to issue. The Smoke-Free Environments Amendment Bill 2003, for example, was a conscience vote for some parties, notably New Zealand First and United Future, but not for others.

This chapter will discuss three of the most recent conscience votes, the Prostitution Reform, Civil Unions, and Relationships (Statutory References) Bills. But first, we will consider the four basic themes around which the merits of conscience voting tend to revolve: representation, accountability, decision-making, and personal conscience. These themes are not mutually exclusive, but examining them one by one is a useful way of considering the benefits that conscience voting brings to the process of creating legislation.

Table 2.7.1: The subjects of conscience voting by decade

Subject	1870s	1880s	1890s	1900s	1910s	1920s	1930s	1940s	1950s	1960s	1970s	1980s	1990s	2000s
Alcohol	1	1	2		2	1		2	8	11	13	9	3	2
Business/Employment							1	1		1		1	3	2
Gambling									4	9	2	3	6	1
Marriage/Family/Children									2	2	3	8	2	3
Crime and Punishment									1	1	1	1	1	
Administration										1		1	2	
Morality/Ethics										1				1
Health and Safety											3	3	1	
Homosexuality												2		
Life and Death														1
Grand Total	1	1	2	0	2	1	1	3	15	26	22	28	18	10

Note: the 2000s includes the period from 2000–2005.

Source: David Lindsey, 'Conscience Voting in New Zealand', unpublished dissertation, Department of Political Studies, University of Auckland, 2005

MERITS OF CONSCIENCE VOTING

1. Representation

Purist notions of democracy stress the direct link between the people and those who represent them. Representation is enhanced, it is argued, by MPs laying aside their own views and adopting positions that accord with those of their electors.[1] Because political decisions are sometimes made for the benefit of political parties rather than in the interests of individual MPs or their constituents, conscience voting is seen as an opportunity to free MPs from the mediating influence of political parties. In this context, conscience voting can be seen as a mechanism that allows individual MPs to consider the wishes of their voters ahead of, or as well as, the needs of their party.

Taking a contrary view, opponents of conscience voting charge that there is no guarantee that MPs will consult their electorate merely because party discipline has been removed, and casting MPs adrift from the supportive influence of parties and their policies may in fact provide less representation rather than more.[2] In addition, parties provide resources, policy positions, and coherence that MPs struggle to replicate on their own. Moreover, considerations of representation have been complicated since the adoption of MMP because list MPs do not represent the voters of one specific electorate. During conscience votes, list MPs therefore have the option of either voting according to their own opinions, the views of their party colleagues, 'adopting' an electorate to represent, or simply assessing the mood of the whole country and using that to inform the way they vote. Sometimes it is not clear what an MP should use to make his/her decision. On legislation like the Death with Dignity Bill (2003), for example, there was no social or legislative precedent, and few clearly defined positions within the community that the MP could confidently represent. Either way, arguments for conscience voting from the perspective of representation must account for the more complex relationship between voter and representation in the contemporary parliamentary system.

2. Accountability

Voting according to an MP's party loyalty inevitably transfers much of the responsibility for decision-making away from the individual representative. According to some commentators, this makes it harder for specific individuals to be held accountable for their decisions. Hiding behind the party decision can be seen as damaging the important democratic principle of accountability. In this context, conscience votes allow members' voting patterns to be identified, and voters who do not agree with the member's intended vote or justification for the vote then have an opportunity to lobby the member in advance of the vote. If all else fails, the MP concerned can be removed at the ballot box.

Conversely, holding a group of individuals accountable for parliamentary decisions is not necessarily in the voters' interests.[3] A party has a longevity that few individuals possess and it is only parties, not individuals, who have the ability to implement decisions. In addition, despite being able to identify those who voted for or against a bill, laying the blame (or praise) at an individual's feet fails to recognise the complexities of modern policy-making and the reality of politics. Numerous votes on multiple bills are often required for an integrated programme to be put in place—individuals would struggle to provide the continuity required to achieve this and with the inevitable shifting of allegiances it would be difficult to clearly ascertain who is responsible for what outcome. Legislation surrounding the sale and consumption of liquor regularly come before parliament and can be viewed as a continuing effort to regulate this issue appropriately. In addition, the Gambling Bill 2003 was a complex piece of legislation that took five years to pass and involved multiple conscience and party votes. As a result, conscience voting can effectively result in decisions that no one is accountable for. Furthermore, if every vote were to be potentially punishable by electoral defeat, individual members would be reluctant to see an unpopular though necessary programme through to completion, leading to inferior decision-making.

3. Decision-making

The freedom that members have during conscience votes forces them to think dialectically about their stance, consider alternative perspectives, and generally be clearer as to why they are casting their vote in the way intended. The quality of decision-making during conscience voting can therefore be an improvement over party voting. Because voting is done on an individual rather than a party basis it also allows for a wider range of opinions to be expressed during the parliamentary debate, potentially better matching the spread of opinion found in the public domain.

On the other hand, the complexity of modern government, together with the scale of the legislative agenda, may make it difficult for individual members to evaluate individual pieces of legislation, especially those of a highly technical nature. The issue of lowering (or raising) the drinking age, for example, is fraught with both moral and technical considerations that are difficult for individuals to sort through. In this situation, members 'who are unable to make up their minds, on the evidence before them, not unnaturally accept the advice of their leaders' (Berrington 1968, p. 369). Their leaders, in turn, are informed by their party's policy positions, which in turn are developed using a combination of ideology, pragmatism, and electoral acceptability. Thus, it can be asserted that political parties not only rescue the individual member from a practical and technical quagmire, but also provide the resources to develop policy that better matches the needs of the electorate.

Table 2.7.2: Parties and their members' votes on the final votes of selected conscience votes

	Prostitution Reform Bill (2003)			Civil Unions Bill (2005)		Relationships (Stat. Refs) Bill (2005)	
	Ayes	Abstain	Noes	Ayes	Noes	Ayes	Noes
Green party	9	–	–	9	–	9	–
Progressives	–	–	2	2	–	2	–
Labour party	41	1	10	45	6	50	1
Māori party	n/a	n/a	n/a	–	1	–	1
United Future	–	–	8	–	8	1	7
NZ First	–	–	13	1	12	2	11
National party	6	–	21	3	24	8	19
ACT NZ	4	–	5	5	4	4	5
Total	60	1	59	65	55	76	44

4. Conscience and personal integrity

Concern for the welfare and integrity of the MP is an additional consideration in the declaration of a conscience vote. It is fundamental to this view that moral decisions should be made by moral agents unmolested by political pressures. MPs are moral agents with their own views, convictions, and beliefs, and these bring valuable strength and diversity to a party. For the benefit of both the members of the party and the party itself, these convictions should be respected by allowing MPs to vote according to their personal beliefs on issues that touch their consciences. This was an important element for most parties in the decision to make the three bills considered in this chapter conscience votes. It is important to not exaggerate the cleavage between personal and party views however, as MPs normally would not join a party unless they agreed with a great majority of the policy positions for which it stood.

PROSTITUTION REFORM BILL

The Prostitution Reform Bill was first introduced into parliament in 2000 as a Members' bill. It was not passed into law until 2003 due to a protracted period of select committee hearings and public consultation. The bill essentially sought to decriminalise the selling of sex to make the selling of sex no more illegal than the purchasing of sex already was. The principal reason for this was to improve the health of sex workers by ensuring that the sex industry could be policed for occupational safety and health like any other industry. While no MP opposed the general aim of improving the health of sex workers, this was a very contentious piece of legislation due to it effectively legalising what many saw as an undesirable activity. Arguments were mounted against the bill on the basis of its legitimising of prostitution, whereby activities that are legalised by the state become, over time, legitimised. In the eyes of detractors, legalising prostitution was an unhelpful way of improving the health of participants. Supporters countered that sex workers should be treated in a similar manner to workers in any other industry, and deserved the protection of the law inherent in statutory recognition.

The Prostitution Reform Bill is a good example of the lobbying that occurs during conscience votes. Because MPs are not, in theory, constrained by their party's policies, opportunities exist for lobbyists to attempt to influence members' opinion in a way that is not possible during party votes. This bill attracted numerous lobbyists on both sides of the issue. Groups that would not normally agree with each other became allies for the purpose of promoting or stopping this bill, the result of which was to produce some unusual alliances. Those supporting the Prostitution Reform Bill included the NZ Prostitutes Collective, the Family Planning Association, the Wellington Independent Rape Crisis, the YWCA, the NZ Aids Foundation, the Maori Women's Welfare League, and the Council of Trade Unions. Those opposing the Bill included Maxim Institute, the Muslim community, a number of churches, and some feminist groups. The Prostitutes Collective, for example, had been working towards a law change for the sex industry since the late 1980s and the Prostitution Reform Bill was the culmination of that campaigning. Organisations involved in lobbying on both sides of the debate felt that their lobbying did make a difference to the debate, bringing the issues facing the sex industry into the open, raising awareness, and normalising the industry to an extent not previously experienced.

The Prostitution Reform Bill passed, on its final vote, by a margin of one, and then only because one MP abstained from voting. Both of the major parties were split in their voting patterns, although most Labour members voted for the bill and most National members voted against it. The closeness of the vote provided sufficient justification for opponents to attempt to consider the issue again, and they began a petition to try and force a referendum at the 2005 election. Despite opinion polls during the debate showing the general public relatively evenly split on the issue, this petition failed to gain the required number of votes, indicating that, for many people, once the decision was made they were prepared to accept it.

Conscience votes often present dilemmas for individual MPs. The desire to vote according to one's personal conscience needs to be balanced against the need to consider the wishes of those voters the electorate or list MP is elected to represent. Such a dilemma can be observed in the decision of the member, Labour's Dr Ashraf Choudhary, who abstained in the third and final vote. This MP felt a personal desire to vote against the bill but took his representative responsibilities seriously enough to note that the majority of his electorate favoured the bill. Further complicating his decision was his status as New Zealand's first Islamic MP. As such, he clearly felt a sense of responsibility to represent the Islamic viewpoint in parliament. Unable to reconcile these competing demands, and in order to preserve his personal conscience, he eventually abstained from voting, effectively allowing the bill to pass.

CIVIL UNIONS BILL

The Civil Unions Bill 2005 was a government bill designed to allow homosexual couples to legally formalise their relationship, enabling them to receive many of the benefits of married couples. Although not actually providing for homosexual marriage, civil unions were akin to marriage for many opponents of this bill who opposed the bill on moral grounds. A few also opposed it precisely because the bill did *not* provide for homosexual marriage, alleging that it thus continued to discriminate against homosexual people by not going far enough. Proponents of the bill maintained that there was no logical reason why couples in stable homosexual relationships should not receive the same civil and legal privileges as other couples, and that discrimination was not a value that should be promoted in New Zealand in the twenty-first century. Fierce lobbying was again conducted on both sides of the argument in an attempt to influence MPs' voting intentions. From relatively early in the bill's passage through parliament however, it was apparent that the Civil Unions Bill had a greater level of support than the Prostitution Reform Bill had received. In the third and final vote, the bill passed into law with a margin of sixty-five to fifty-five.

The Civil Unions Bill signalled a departure from historic patterns of conscience votes because it not only involved legislation pertaining to personal relationships but also explicitly rested upon liberal rather than historic Christian principles. That parliament was prepared to depart so radically from the historic use of conscience voting demonstrates that its application, while encased with expectations that have built up over years, can also be used to chart new territory in response to changing social attitudes.

Despite the final vote still being close, parties were less split on this bill than they were on the Prostitution Reform Bill. Members of parties on the left of the political spectrum tended to vote for the bill, while those on the right tended to vote against it (see table 2.7.2). While the permitting of civil unions, in common with most moral issues, is not an issue that maps directly on to the left–right political spectrum, voting patterns on conscience issues have historically tended to be dichotomised along this spectrum with a high degree of predictability. The ACT party however, provides an exception, for, on all three of the conscience bills considered in this chapter, the party was split five votes to four. This division reflects the fact that members within that party, while holding to libertarian views generally, interpret this stance in different ways. The neo-liberal group within the party believe in limited government for both economic and moral issues, while the neo-conservative group are prepared to adopt a more proactive role for the state on moral issues on the grounds that libertarianism is not inconsistent with providing moral boundaries.

RELATIONSHIPS (STATUTORY REFERENCES) BILL

Although the concept of pure morality does not exist in parliament, conscience legislation is not introduced into parliament in a vacuum but builds upon previously considered legislation. Bills, particularly those receiving conscience votes, are often part of a family of legislation, having either a common genesis or a similar subject matter. Legislation pertaining to alcohol, for example, has had a common thread running through it over the question of how much the state should be involved in regulating the drinking habits of private citizens. In a similar manner, the Relationships (Statutory References) Bill, an omnibus bill, built upon the Civil Unions Bill by altering a raft of legislation to ensure that the benefits of civil unions were reflected in all New Zealand legislation. As such, it logically followed the Civil Unions Bill, and, indeed, the pattern of voting on this bill reflected this fact.

The Relationships (Statutory References) Bill, introduced into parliament just five days after the Civil Unions Bill in 2004, though not passed into law until March 2005, received the greatest majority of the three conscience votes considered in this chapter. A sizeable portion of those MPs who voted for it had previously voted against the Civil Unions Bill. It is apparent that once the latter bill had passed into law, a number of MPs decided to support the Relationships Bill in order to ensure the law pertaining to homosexual relationships remained consistent. MPs who continued to oppose the bill tended to be the ones who had opposed the Civil Unions Bill on moral grounds, who still maintained that allowing homosexual unions to be recognised in law was morally irresponsible.

Both National and ACT were relatively divided on this bill, illustrating the morally conservative approach of a sizeable portion of National members and the dichotomous approach to moral issues found within the libertarian ACT party. The Labour party MPs, on the other hand, in concert with members of the other left-leaning parliamentary parties, were overwhelmingly supportive of the bill. This was consistent with their voting on the other two conscience bills discussed in this chapter.

CONCLUSION

Conscience voting is somewhat unique among parliamentary procedures in that it is maintained and shaped by expectations rather than regulations. While its basis is political, its operation is heavily influenced by the norms, debates, and standards prevalent within society at any given point in time. As such, it is subject to evolution and development as society itself evolves, and over the last half-century the subjects receiving conscience votes have gradually widened. It is therefore to be expected that over the next fifty years the subjects of conscience voting will change further.

Despite valid arguments on both sides of the debate over its benefits, an intangible benefit of conscience voting is that it heightens interest in parliament. The sense that the outcome of a legislative vote is not a foregone conclusion and an intuitive belief that the range of public opinion is somehow better represented during conscience votes ensures that citizens, organisations and lobbyists, not to mention the media, retain a heightened interest in proceedings when conscience votes are held. The unpredictability of the outcome also provides an incentive for parliamentarians to weigh up the importance of their own personal views compared to those of their constituents, however defined in this era of list and electorate MPs, and the members of the party they have been elected to serve.

DISCUSSION QUESTIONS

1   Discuss the arguments for and against the right to cast a conscience vote. Which set of arguments do you find the more convincing, and why?

2   Why has the incidence of conscience voting increased in recent years? Is this a healthy or unhealthy sign for the state of our democracy in New Zealand?

3   Account for the division in the ACT party vote on the Prostitution, Civil Unions and Relationships Bills. What should the libertarian's position be on each of these bills, and why?

4   If a party has an agreed policy on a 'conscience' issue, such as capital punishment or the drinking age, should its MPs be given a free vote or required to support party policy?

5   Imagine that you are an MP with a conscience vote on the reform of the prostitution industry. In forming your opinion as to how to vote, what factors would you consider authoritative? Why?

NOTES

1   See, for example, Right Honourable John Turner, former Canadian prime minister, 'Does Your Vote Really Count?' unpublished speech, Ottawa, 7 October 2003; and Office of the [Canadian] Prime Minister, 'Address by Prime Minister Paul Martin on the occasion of his visit to Winnipeg, Manitoba', 26 March 2004.

2   See, for example, D. Reevely, 'Free Votes Would Undermine Democracy, Critics Say', *Capital News Online*, 17 November 2000; and B. Cross, 'Members of Parliament, Voters, and Democracy in the Canadian House of Commons', *Parliamentary Perspectives*, Occasional Paper of the Canadian Study of Parliament Group, 2000.

3   See, for example, C. Franks, 'Free Votes in the House of Commons: A Problematic Reform', *Policy Options*, Institute for Research on Public Policy, November 1997, pp. 33–6; and P. Cowley, 'Unbridled Passions?' *Journal of Legislative Studies*, 4/2, Summer 1998, pp. 70–88.

REFERENCES

Berrington, H. 1968, 'Partisanship and Dissidence in the Nineteenth-Century House of Commons', *Parliamentary Affairs*, Vol. 21, Oxford University Press, London, pp. 338–74.

Cottrell, S.P. 1974, 'Parliament and Conscience', MA Thesis, University of Canterbury, Christchurch.

Cowley, P. 1998, 'Unbridled Passions? Free Votes, Issues of Conscience and the Accountability of British Members of Parliament', *Journal of Legislative Studies*, Vol. 4, No. 2, pp. 70–88.

Cross, B. 2000, 'Members of Parliament, Voters, and Democracy in the Canadian House of Commons', *Parliamentary Perspectives*, Occasional Paper of the Canadian Study of Parliament Group, Ottawa.

Franks, C. 1997, 'Free Votes in the House of Commons: a Problematic Reform', *Policy Options*, Institute for Research on Public Policy, pp. 33–6.

Hobby, M.G. 1987, 'The Crack of the Whip?: Party Cohesiveness and Institutional Consensus: The New Zealand House of Representatives 1936–85', MA Thesis, University of Canterbury, Christchurch.

Lindsey, D. 2005, 'Conscience Voting in New Zealand', Unpublished Dissertation, Department of Political Studies, University of Auckland.

Office of the [Canadian] Prime Minister 2004, 'Address by Prime Minister Paul Martin on the Occasion of his Visit to Winnipeg, Manitoba', 26 March.

Reevely, D. 2000, 'Free Votes Would Undermine Democracy, Critics Say', *Capital News Online*, 17 November.

Turner, J. (Right Honourable) 2003, 'Does Your Vote Really Count?', Former Canadian Prime Minister, Unpublished Speech, Ottawa, 7 October.

FURTHER READING

Cowley, P. 1998, 'Unbridled Passions? Free Votes, Issues of Conscience and the Accountability of British Members of Parliament', *Journal of Legislative Studies*, Vol. 4, No. 2, pp. 70–88.

Lindsey, D. 2005, 'Conscience Voting in New Zealand', Unpublished Dissertation, Department of Political Studies, University of Auckland.

Martin, J. 2004, *The House: New Zealand's House of Representatives 1854–2004*, Dunmore Press, Palmerston North.

McGee, D. 1994, *Parliamentary Practice in New Zealand*, 2nd edn, Wellington: Government Printer.

McKeown, D. & R. Lundie 2002, 'Current Issues Brief No. 1 2002–2003: Free Votes in Australian and Some Overseas Parliaments', Parliamentary Library, Parliament of Australia (available online).

Miller, R. 2005, *Party Politics in New Zealand*, Oxford University Press, Melbourne, pp. 195–210.

Executive

Process

During the latter part of the last century, the New Zealand political system, and the Westminster model more generally, were criticised for vesting too much authority in the hands of the executive branch of government. Cabinet was accused of exercising 'unbridled power' and being little more than an 'elective dictatorship'. While there are fewer grounds for criticism in an era of coalition government, the focus of attention has begun to shift from the power of cabinet to that of the prime minister. With assistance from the electronic media and sundry professional advisers and consultants, the modern prime minister has begun to adopt a number of the characteristics of a more 'presidential' style of leadership, especially in relation to the planning and execution of election campaigns.

Part C will discuss the following topics:

- **Cabinet.** Chapter 3.1 traces the transition from an all-powerful cabinet to one that must retain the confidence of parliament in order to remain in power. Merging the interests of several parties is a formidable challenge, particularly under the unusual circumstances surrounding Helen Clark's decision to appoint Winston Peters Minister of Foreign Affairs, but outside of the executive. Chapter 3.4 provides a comprehensive account of the complex circumstances behind this decision and compares the formation of the 2005 government with each of the three previous coalition cabinets under the Mixed Member Proportional (MMP) electoral system.

- **Prime Minister.** Chapters 3.2 and 3.3 focus on the personality, style and power of the modern prime minister. Drawing on the three styles of leadership developed by the American political psychologist, James David Barber, chapter 3.2 compares the leadership styles of New Zealand's recent and current leaders, including Helen Clark and Don Brash. While much has been made of the growth of prime ministerial power, chapter 3.3 argues that the need to negotiate agreements and make trade-offs with coalition partners has resulted in a significant reduction in the powers of the prime minister under MMP.

- **Advisers, Consultants and Bureaucrats.** Chapters 3.5 and 3.6 explore the numerous streams of advice given to government ministers. The image of an impartial and non-partisan public servant is commonly associated with the Westminster model. Chapter 3.5 argues that this image has been eroded in favour of the public-choice model, which starts from the proposition that human behaviour is motivated by self-interest. Chapter 3.6 assesses the impact of public sector reform, including the decline in the overall size of the public service.

- **Local Government.** The final chapter opens up a topic about which most people know relatively little, namely the role and influence of local government. As chapter 3.7 points out, much of what local government does, such as roading, public transport, environmental health, and cultural activities, has a major impact on our daily lives.

Cabinet

Elizabeth McLeay

The cabinet announced after the 2005 election comprised twenty Labour ministers, including Helen Clark as prime minister, plus the sole Progressive MP and leader, Jim Anderton. The prime minister had managed to arrange some dignified exits from the previous ministry, a tactic employed particularly effectively by one of her predecessors, National's Keith Holyoake. The new faces, combined with a substantial portfolio reshuffle, helped fulfil the ambitions of at least some MPs and suggested a renewed vigour within a government that was about to begin its third term. These were traditional moves in the reshaping of a ministry. Also familiar—at least to students of the recent past—was the requirement that the Labour and Progressive parties find support from outside their ranks if they were going to win votes of confidence, pass budgets, and implement their legislative plans. Political survival would depend on consultation and negotiation among leaders, within cabinet, and between ministers and the main supporting party or parties (McLeay 2006). But this time, unlike the previous MMP governments, two of those parties—New Zealand First and United Future—contributed a minister apiece to the ministry from outside of cabinet (see table 3.1.1).

Winston Peters, leader of New Zealand First, would hold the prestigious Foreign Affairs portfolio while Peter Dunne, leader of United Future, would be responsible for Revenue. Further, the Green party would provide government spokespersons on particular issues—a highly unusual situation even though, unlike New Zealand First and United Future, the Greens were not formally committed to support the government on confidence and supply votes in parliament but merely to abstain. These innovations led to speculation on the future of cabinet government as New Zealand had experienced it so far. The 2005 arrangements meant that five parties would be involved in policy development and implementation, with the New Zealand

First and United Future ministers responsible for major portfolios, despite being outside cabinet. These factors all had potential consequences for decision-making processes and collective cabinet responsibility.

Table 3.1.1: Labour–Progressive coalition ministry, 2005–

	Name	Principal portfolios
1	Helen Clark	Prime Minister; Arts, Culture and Heritage
2	Michael Cullen	Deputy Prime Minister; Finance; Tertiary Education
3	Jim Anderton	Agriculture; Biosecurity; Fisheries; Forestry
4	Steve Maharey	Education; Broadcasting; Research, Science and Technology; Crown Research Institutes
5	Phil Goff	Defence; Trade; Pacific Island Affairs; Disarmament and Arms Control
6	Annette King	State Services; Police; Food Safety
7	Trevor Mallard	Economic Development; Industry and Regional Development; State Owned Enterprises; Sport and Recreation
8	Pete Hodgson	Health; Land Information
9	Parekura Horomia	Maori Affairs
10	Mark Burton	Justice; Local Government; Treaty of Waitangi Negotiations
11	Ruth Dyson	Labour; ACC; Senior Citizens
12	Chris Carter	Conservation; Housing
13	Rick Barker	Internal Affairs; Civil Defence; Courts; Veterans' Affairs
14	David Benson-Pope	Social Development and Employment; Environment
15	Lianne Dalziel	Commerce; Women's Affairs
16	Damien O'Connor	Corrections; Tourism
17	David Cunliffe	Immigration; Communications; Information Technology
18	David Parker	Energy; Transport; Attorney–General
19	Nanaia Mahuta	Customs; Youth Affairs
20	Clayton Cosgrove	Building Issues; Statistics
21	Jim Sutton	Trade Negotiations

Ministers outside cabinet

	Name	Principal portfolios
22	Judith Tizard	Consumer Affairs
23	Dover Samuels	Minister of State
24	Harry Duynhoven	Transport Safety
25	Mita Ririnui	Minister of State
26	Winnie Laban	Community and Voluntary Sector
27	Mahara Okeroa	Minister of State

Ministers outside cabinet from other parties with confidence and supply agreements

Name	Principal portfolios
Winston Peters	Foreign Affairs; Racing
Peter Dunne	Revenue

Source: www.dpmc.govt.nz/

So what is 'Cabinet'? Undefined in constitutional statute, it is simply a committee of ministers that, in New Zealand, meets nearly every week to make public policy and many other decisions and to decide on political strategy. It is 'the central decision-making body of executive government' (Cabinet Office 2001a, p. 42).[1] Cabinet's significance lies in its composition. Chaired by the prime minister, it comprises the most influential members of the party (or parties) holding the confidence of the House of Representatives. Members of a ministry—that is, all ministers whether they sit in cabinet or not—hold constitutionally defined positions as ministers of the Crown and officially appointed by the Governor-General. Every minister is a member of the Executive Council (while under-secretaries are not).

Under the former two-party system, cabinet had dominated parliament. Cabinet formed a sizeable proportion of the governing caucus, which was tightly bound by party discipline. By dictating the direction of policy, cabinet ensured that there was little effective opposition to its collective will. Successive Labour and National governments between 1984 and 1993 showed how powerful cabinets could be under the two-party system. Since then, cabinets have had to moderate their policies in order to retain power. Parliament has become more assertive. The first years of the MMP parliament illustrated a primary rule about cabinet government. Government power over the legislative process depends on two intersecting factors: the number of votes that the cabinet can command in the parliament; and the extent of party cohesion.

The political executive is drawn from, and responsible to, the legislature. It has been argued (controversially) that this is an aspect of the constitution that diminishes accountability.[2] Although in some parliamentary systems (for example, Germany) MPs can be appointed from outside the legislature, in New Zealand, under the Constitution Act 1986, all ministers must be MPs. Moreover, when MPs become ministers they keep their parliamentary seats, whereas in some systems (in the Netherlands and Sweden, for example) ministers are required to resign from parliament on appointment, although remaining responsible to it for their actions.

Thus New Zealand's political executive is essentially government by amateurs, in the sense that the training of ministers is political rather than expert: ministers are drawn from the House rather than recruited as outside experts in particular policy areas. Ministers have not necessarily had any background or experience in their own portfolio areas, although lawyers hold the position of Attorney-General, and Agriculture tends to go to a farmer. In accordance with the practices of Westminster government, expertise in governing is supplied by the public service, while cabinet houses those versed in political skills, well honed by experience in the legislature, in the extra-parliamentary party, and perhaps even in local government and pressure groups. This type of background is in sharp contrast to that found in a political system that separates, rather than fuses, executive and legislative positions. In the USA, for example, cabinet appointees are much more likely to have specialised expertise in particular fields.

CABINET'S OPERATING RULES

It should be clear by now that the defining features of New Zealand cabinet government are rooted in the nature of the relationship between the political executive and the legislature. Four main principles can be identified. The first three are general characteristics of cabinet government, whereas the fourth is more characteristic of some systems than others.

1. Confidence of the legislature

As already outlined, the party or parties in government must retain the confidence of the legislature in order to remain in office. This constitutional convention is based on democratic principle because the people elect the parliament.

2. Collective cabinet responsibility

Ministers must follow this working rule (sometimes deemed a 'convention'). *The Cabinet Manual* states that:

> The principle of collective responsibility underpins the system of Cabinet government. It reflects democratic principle: the House expresses its confidence in the collective whole of government, rather than in individual Ministers. Similarly, the Governor-General, in acting on ministerial advice, needs to be confident that individual Ministers represent official government policy. In all areas of their work, therefore, Ministers represent and implement government policy. Acceptance of ministerial office requires acceptance of collective responsibility. Issues are often debated vigorously within the confidential setting of Cabinet meetings, although consensus is usually reached and votes are rarely taken. Once Cabinet makes a decision, then (except as provided in paragraph 3.23) Ministers must support it, regardless of their personal views and whether or not they were at the meeting concerned. (Cabinet Office 2001a, p. 44)

The exceptions to this rule are when coalition governments 'establish "agree to disagree" processes' allowing ministers of different parties to maintain different views in public where those parties hold differing policies (Cabinet Office 2001a, p. 45). This new development (compare Cabinet Office 1996a) was the fruit of government formation negotiations between Labour and the Alliance in 1999 (and see Gillon 2005).

The political ramifications of breaking collective cabinet responsibility are significant. A fragmented administration is vulnerable in parliament, especially where there is either a minority government, or a majority government with a narrow margin over its opponents. Intra-cabinet dissent threatens a government's public image, as was shown during 1987 and 1988 when the prime minister, David Lange, and his Minister of Finance, Roger Douglas, held publicly opposing views (Chapman 1992; Sheppard 1999). Moreover, public dissent exposes a prime minister's own vulnerability, in that it challenges his or her personal authority. Indeed, although there has been public disagreement within cabinet from time to time, when individuals challenge the prime minister's position, the dissenting minister risks dismissal. Hence Derek Quigley was asked to resign by Robert Muldoon in 1982 (see table 3.1.2 for lists of ministerial resignations). In 1988, Lange accepted Douglas's resignation when it was offered. Earlier that year, Richard Prebble had become the first minister in modern times to be actually dismissed when he was sacked by Lange.

In 1991, Jim Bolger dismissed Winston Peters (see McLeay 1995, pp. 186–204), who managed to be dismissed again in 1998, this time by Jenny Shipley. Peters vehemently criticised Shipley in parliament, ostensibly after a dispute over the sale

Table 3.1.2: Collective cabinet and individual ministerial responsibility: resignations and dismissals, 1960–2005*

Breaches of collective cabinet responsibility

D. Quigley (National) 1982, resigned

R. Douglas (Labour) 1988, resigned

R. Prebble (Labour) 1988, dismissed

W. Peters (National) 1991, dismissed

N. Kirton (New Zealand First) 1997, dismissed

W. Peters (National) 1998, dismissed

T. Turia (Labour) 2004, dismissed

Breaches of individual ministerial responsibility

D. Marshall (National) Conservation, 1996, resigned from portfolio but not from cabinet [vicarious ministerial responsibility]

M. McCully (National) Tourism, 1999, resigned from portfolio but not from cabinet [primary ministerial responsibility]

T. Delamere (Independent), Immigration, 1999, dismissed from portfolio but not from cabinet [primary ministerial responsibility]

D. Samuels (Labour) 2000, dismissed from cabinet [personal ministerial responsibility] and reappointed (as under-secretary, not minister) the following year

R. Dyson (Labour), 2000, resigned [personal ministerial responsibility] and reappointed the following year

P. Bunkle (Alliance), 2001, resigned [personal ministerial responsibility]

M. Hobbs (Labour), 2001, resigned [personal ministerial responsibility] and reappointed shortly after having been cleared of blame

L. Dalziel (Labour), 2004, resigned [primary ministerial responsibility] but was re-elected to cabinet after the 2005 general election

J. Tamihere (Labour), 2004, resigned [personal ministerial responsibility]

---

*The table does not include resignations for personal (e.g. family) reasons, policy differences that have not involved breaches of collective cabinet responsibility, or resignations where a minister's party has left a coalition.

of Wellington Airport, during which the New Zealand First ministers walked out of cabinet (McLeay 1999). Peters' prompt dismissal by the Governor-General on Shipley's recommendation showed that even deputy prime ministers who are leaders of other parties are subject to the patronage powers of the prime minister, primary adviser to the Governor-General. In 2004, a Labour minister was dismissed when she opposed the controversial Seabed and Foreshore Bill. Tariana Turia subsequently resigned from parliament and was then re-elected under the banner of a new party, the Māori party, which took four Māori electorates from Labour in 2005.

In coalition governments, ministers come to the cabinet table with differing philosophies, agendas, and personal allegiances. Nevertheless, the same pressures that underpinned the doctrine with single-party majority governments continue to play a role in coalition administrations. Indeed, under MMP there is perhaps added pressure for individual ministers to conform since there is a greater potential for government collapse and a new government being formed from among the other parliamentary parties, or for another general election to be called. It is not surprising, therefore, that cabinet government in both multi-party and two-party systems follows the practice of collective cabinet responsibility.[3]

The coalition agreement between New Zealand First and the New Zealand National party in 1996 (see chapters 3.5 and 5.3) reaffirmed collective cabinet responsibility and a mechanism was established to settle inter-party agreements. This did not prevent the dissolution of the coalition. Plainly, maintaining collective cabinet responsibility is difficult in coalitions containing differing political perspectives, parties fearful of losing identity and hence public support, and independent (even quarrelsome) individuals. In 1999, the incoming Labour–Alliance government adopted the different strategy for coping with differences with its modification of the collective responsibility rule. Despite being successfully tested over the Singapore free-trade issue, continuing policy differences within the Alliance, personality conflict, and frustration with the party's low opinion polling led to its split, although the ministers kept their portfolios until the mid-2002 early election. This was precipitated by, among other factors, the disarray of the minor coalition partner and the Green party's determination to oppose the government over aspects of its genetic engineering policy. The 'agree to disagree' clause was reaffirmed by the new government formed after the 2002 election between Labour and the two-MP Progressive party, and again found its way into the post-2005 coalition and support agreements. Prudently exercised, this innovative variation can be a means of surviving the stresses endemic to a coalition cabinet; frequent disagreements, on the other hand, are likely to harm the reputation of the government and allow its enemies to find useful chinks in its policy armour.

Ministers outside as well as inside cabinet have been constrained by the collective responsibility rule. In 2005, a further elaboration was developed when the two non-core coalition ministers, Winston Peters and Peter Dunne, were bound by the rule insofar as their own portfolios were concerned, but not for other issues. The Greens were similarly constrained concerning policies with which they would be involved. Furthermore, the post-election support agreements committed all the MPs within the three caucuses similarly to comply with collective responsibility on the issues with which they were involved. Freeing those parties from having to follow this rule on all other issues was designed to allow non-core parties involved in government to demarcate themselves from the policies emanating from the Labour–Progressive parties. In practice, however, given the absence of clear boundaries between different policy domains (foreign affairs and trade, and revenue and expenditure, for example), clarifying when and for what collective cabinet responsibility needs to be maintained will be interesting to say the least. Criticisms and pressure from the opposition benches can be potent pressures to expose differences or, alternatively, enforce the papering over between the policy cracks.

3. Individual ministerial responsibility

Ministers are individually responsible to the legislature for their own actions and for those of their public servants. The various aspects of this doctrine have been labelled 'personal ministerial responsibility' (actions relating to ministers' private lives rather than to their portfolios), 'primary ministerial responsibility' (relating to ministers' official responsibilities),[4] and 'vicarious ministerial responsibility' (the actions of public servants) (Martin 1991, 1994; Woodhouse 1994).

In June 2000 the Prime Minister, Helen Clark, dismissed the Minister of Maori Affairs, Dover Samuels, on the grounds that some of his past actions—undeclared to Clark at the time of his appointment—were inappropriate for his ministerial responsibilities. This was an unusual example of a penalty paid for non-compliance with the principle of personal ministerial responsibility. He reappeared in 2002 as an under-secretary and in 2005 as a minister outside cabinet. In October 2000 the Minister for Disability Issues, Ruth Dyson, resigned after failing a blood-alcohol test, to be subsequently reinstated by the prime minister. Two other ministers resigned when their accommodation allowances and entitlements were questioned. Marian Hobbs was subsequently returned to her former position. In 2004 John Tamihere, Labour, resigned from cabinet when aspects of his previous employment were investigated for fraud. He subsequently publicly criticised his colleagues, was not reinstated to the ministry, and lost his seat at the 2005 election. Near the end of the 2002–05 parliamentary term, an under-secretary, Taito Philip Field, was the subject of allegations concerning financial and personal relationships with constituents and was suspended from executive duties. He was not included in the 2005 ministry.

Just two ministers have resigned on the grounds of primary ministerial responsibility: Sir Apirana Ngata (1934), concerning the allocation of funds to iwi; and Lianne Dalziel (2004) who, as Minister of Immigration, was involved in a leaked letter on an immigration case and who subsequently misled parliament over the issue.

There have been instances when ministers have been criticised for not resigning, for example, Duncan McIntyre over the Marginal Lands Board loan affair in 1980 (Palmer 1987, p. 48). And there have been partial resignations when ministers have merely had particular portfolios removed but have remained in cabinet. For example, in 1999, Murray McCully resigned from just the Tourism portfolio after release of an Audit Office report on unlawful payments given to certain Tourism Board directors who had resigned. A few days before the 1999 election, Tuariki John Delamere had his Immigration responsibilities removed from him because he permitted entry to New Zealand to applicants who failed to meet the usual immigration requirements but who agreed to invest in Māori development.

Although New Zealand ministers answer for their actions and those of public servants, explaining what has happened, and taking responsibility for remedying what has gone wrong, there has been no tradition of ministers resigning in expiation (Palmer 1987, pp. 45–56). Ministers have offered to resign (Roger Douglas in 1986, and Koro Wetere in 1987) but no minister actually did so until Denis Marshall resigned from the Conservation portfolio (but not from cabinet) in 1996, one year after fourteen people were killed when a Department of Conservation viewing platform collapsed (Gregory 1998a, 1998b).

When considering this issue it is important to distinguish between, on the one hand, the acceptance of responsibility, by answering questions in the House and in public and remedying the situation, and, on the other hand, the sanctions for what has gone wrong. The debate in New Zealand, as elsewhere, has been muddled by the failure to make this distinction, and thus the extent to which individual ministerial responsibility has been practised as well as prescribed has been underestimated. The state sector reforms of the 1980s clarified the issues by holding ministers responsible for policies, while making the state services commissioner responsible for the behaviour of chief executives. In turn, chief executives are responsible for policy implementation and personnel issues and, hence, for imposing sanctions on incompetent employees. In another sense, however, the reforms allowed ministers to slide away from accepting that, ultimately, they must be publicly responsible for what their departments and ministries do, for they alone are accountable to parliament and the citizens of New Zealand.

When governments were sure of their parliamentary majorities, ministers who erred could be quietly shifted to another portfolio and/or equally quietly told that they might consider resigning their seats at the next general election. Under MMP, on the other hand, there have been signs that ministers may have to resign more frequently, especially for their own mistakes. For vulnerable minority governments it is preferable for individuals to resign and thus deflect blame from the government, thus avoiding endangering its stability of administration. And coalition partners might be decidedly reluctant to share responsibility for the mistakes of ministers in the other party or parties.

4. Collective decision-making

Major decisions are the product of collective cabinet decision-making, whether by the full cabinet or by one of its committees, very different from some countries where decision-making is more unilateral (ministers making decisions within their departments, as in Germany) or bilateral (one minister negotiating with another minister, as in the British budgetary process). A culture of consultation, made possible by the small size of the political system, has given cabinet government in New Zealand its distinctive character in this regard. Further, collective decision-making reinforces collective cabinet responsibility. I return to this theme later.

As can be seen, these four operating rules are the fruits of coincidence between political practice and tradition, political expectations, and political survival.

THE MINISTERS AND THEIR ROLES

When MPs enter parliament they might wish merely to serve their constituents and parties. Very soon, however, their ambitions focus upon promotion to cabinet. This has tended to reinforce the norms of cohesion and loyalty. The larger, 120-seat MMP parliament may provide more choice of ministers, although minority governments might have no more MPs (and perhaps even fewer) to choose from than was the case for single-party majority governments. Thus there is a strong case against shrinking the size of the parliament.

Before the advent of MMP, ministers were expected to have served at least one parliamentary term (although Wyatt Creech spent a mere two years there before entering cabinet in 1990). In 1996, however, five out of the nine New Zealand First ministers took their posts as brand-new MPs, one going straight into cabinet. The 1999 Labour–Alliance coalition showed a return to the former seniority criterion, with the exception of Margaret Wilson, an academic lawyer and former party president, who was voted straight into cabinet, and Parekura Horomia, who began his parliamentary career as a minister outside of cabinet.

It is up to the individual parties to decide how to select the members of cabinet (see McLeay 1987; 1995, pp. 51–77). In National, the prime minister selects the ministers and allocates the portfolios, although in practice the decisions are reached in consultation with senior colleagues. Leaders have even taken 'straw polls' of caucus. In comparison, although the Labour prime minister can allocate the portfolios and chooses the ministers and under-secretaries outside cabinet (not an insignificant power), the selection of cabinet ministers is by caucus vote, although leaders have not hesitated to make their own preferences known. (The leader and deputy are automatically in cabinet.) As for the minor parties, in 1996 Peters chose his team (and the portfolio allocations were agreed between the National and New Zealand

First leaders). In 1999, the Alliance leader, Jim Anderton, nominated his preferred candidates, who were then approved by both the Alliance Council (the governing body outside parliament) and the party caucus.

The different methods have had little effect on the calibre of cabinets, but they have contrasting impacts on the prime ministerial role itself. With the task of selecting goes power and hence authority. Although historically neither Labour nor National prime ministers have shown much willingness to dismiss incompetent and lazy cabinet colleagues, holding patronage powers has meant that National leaders have had more authority to persuade ministers to resign at the ends of parliamentary terms, so aiding cabinet rejuvenation. David Lange's lack of authority over cabinet, weakened by the friction with his Minister of Finance over social and economic policy, was demonstrated when caucus re-elected both Douglas and Prebble to cabinet during 1989. In contrast, Helen Clark exercised her power laid out in caucus rules to nominate mid-term vacancies. Elected ministers can also act more independently within cabinet, a flexibility that may deteriorate into unseemly squabbles. On the other hand, when a caucus elects a cabinet, then those ministers who make it into office can be sure that they have the support of at least a majority of their colleagues.

Since cabinet is drawn from the legislature, its composition reflects that of the larger body. For example, as parliament itself has become more youthful over the years, so too has cabinet. Certain criteria have also influenced the composition of cabinets: they have tended to be broadly representative geographically; contain members from rural and urban areas; and increasingly have included MPs from the various social groups represented in caucus.

Because Labour held all four Māori seats between 1943 and 1993, that party could include Māori in cabinet and, indeed, accepted the obligation to do so. Historically, Labour Māori MPs have agreed among themselves as to who would stand and be supported in the vote for cabinet places. The 1972–75 and 1984–90 Labour cabinets contained two Māori ministers, as did both the 1999–2002 and 2002–05 ministries. The cabinet announced after the 2005 election again included two Māori ministers. There were also Māori ministers outside cabinet in all three Labour-led administrations. The total 2005 ministry comprised 21 per cent Māori. Because it lacks Māori, National has had more difficulty in representing Māori in cabinet. There was a sole Māori in cabinet between 1978 and 1984 and also between 1990 and 1991 (when Peters was dismissed). There were no further Māori ministers until 1996, when the National–New Zealand First government was formed. Following New Zealand First's victory in all five Māori seats, three of that party's Māori MPs became cabinet ministers. After the collapse of the National–New Zealand First coalition, two Māori ministers sat in cabinet and one outside it.

As women have entered the House in larger numbers, they have taken up ministerial posts, although their number depends on the composition of the party from which they are drawn. There was one (Māori) woman minister between 1972 and 1975, and six women served in the Labour government 1984–90. The 1999 Labour–Alliance administration contained seven women inside cabinet (including the prime minister) and four outside cabinet, a record 44 per cent of the ministry. Three were from the Alliance. Women's representation declined to 31 per cent of the ministry in 2002; and the 2005 ministry included five women cabinet ministers and two women outside cabinet (see table 3.1.1). No woman served as a minister during the 1975–84 National administration. Three (one outside cabinet) served in the National and National–United governments between 1990 and 1996. In the 1996 coalition government, one National woman (Jenny Shipley) entered cabinet and another became a minister outside cabinet, along with two New Zealand First women.

Ministers have many roles. They are 'responsible for determining policy and exercising relevant statutory powers and functions within the ambit of their portfolios' (Cabinet Office 2001a, p. 16). They participate in parliamentary debate and answer questions on their portfolio responsibilities. Since 1985 cabinet ministers have not been members of parliament's select committees, but they are answerable to those committees for the legislation they propose and for their policies. Ministers have regular meetings with their senior public servants, deliver public speeches, and see delegations from pressure groups. Ministers are members of their party's caucus, where they might frequently have to explain and justify their policies. In the past they have kept close links with the chairpersons of caucus committees in their policy areas (important since the chairpersons were frequently also select committee chairs, a practice that happens less often under MMP). Ministers must look after their constituents if they are electorate MPs, and also take part in other community activities as required by their parties or through their own links and interests if they are elected through their party lists. Their primary focuses, however, are cabinet, cabinet committees, and their departments. They are supported in their tasks by their own ministerial offices, which increasingly have included political advisers (see chapter 3.6).

MEETINGS, COMMITTEES, AND ADVICE

One of the manifestations of collective decision-making discussed above is that the New Zealand cabinet meets regularly and sometimes at considerable length, although the latter depends on the personal style of the prime minister. In the year ended 30 June 2005, cabinet met forty-four times, considering an average number of fourteen items per meeting, 633 in total (Department of Prime Minister and Cabinet 2005, Appendix 2). Geoffrey Palmer has outlined the cabinet agenda thus: reports of cabinet committees; confirmation of bills; any ministerial submissions not covered in committee reports; and oral items, including management of parliament and appointments (2005, pp. 11–12). Votes have very seldom been taken in New Zealand cabinet meetings, leaving the prime minister in control of interpreting 'consensus'. Ministers outside cabinet scarcely ever attend the Monday cabinet meetings, although they are regular members of cabinet committees.

Commentators used to decry the extent to which cabinet meetings became embroiled in detailed decision-making, for the New Zealand cabinet made minor decisions as well as the major ones such as shaping the budget and signing international treaties.[5] Since the state sector changes of the 1980s, however, many of the former administrative decisions made by ministers have been devolved to public servants, thus reducing the potential amount of government business to be decided upon at the political level. And, ultimately, politics rule the content of the cabinet agenda: the survival and success of the government are of primary concern, along with matters relating to legislation and policy. Moreover, the agenda is subject to the concerns and eccentricities of the prime minister of the time.

Of course most decisions are not made in cabinet itself, but by individual ministers working with their senior public servants, through bilateral negotiation, and in cabinet committees. Most are uncontroversial. However, many policies will be decided upon in principle by full cabinet or cabinet committees. Furthermore, the doctrine of collective cabinet responsibility is recognised in the requirement that all cabinet committee decisions must be ratified in meetings of full cabinet (and this is not always a simple formality); and all controversial decisions also gravitate to full cabinet discussion. An extremely important development since 1982 has been the Official Information Act. This has opened up much of the decision-making process to the public. Indeed, many draft policy papers are placed on the government website, as well as being distributed for comment and feedback from key stakeholder groups.

It might have been the case that MMP and the requirements of coalition government had altered the character of cabinet meetings, which might have focused primarily on sorting out inter-party policy differences. That this has not occurred so far suggests the persistence and utility of traditional ways of decision-making and, perhaps, the recurrence of minority governments dominated by one party. The culture of collective cabinet decision-making might, however, be threatened by the 2005 innovation of including in the government, but placing outside cabinet, two party leaders whose support is needed for the survival of the administration. Undoubtedly, even if full and substantive cabinet meetings continue, there will be supplementary meetings of the party leaders and their heads of staff to sort out key decisions and strategies.

Designing the committee system (see table 3.1.3) is a significant exercise of prime ministerial patronage. In coalition governments, the shape of the committees is the product of inter-party bargaining. Through the pattern of committee allocation, especially the distribution of chairs, leaders can influence the interpretation of party manifestos, the pace of legislative change, and policy priorities in general. Coalition partners can ensure that their priorities are recognised by having their ministers on

Table 3.1.3: Cabinet committees in four ministries*

National–NZ First Government Prime Minister: Jim Bolger (February 1997)	National–NZ First Government Prime Minister: Jenny Shipley (February 1998)	Labour–Alliance Government Prime Minister: Helen Clark (February 2000)	Labour–Progressive Coalition Government Prime Minister: Helen Clark (February 2002)
Strategy and Priorities (14)	Strategy*** (16)	Policy (12)	Policy (12)
Industry and Environment (16)	Social Policy (16)	Economic Development (15)	Economic Development (18)
Health and Social Policy (17)	Economic (16)	Finance, Infra-structure and Environment (15)	Social Development (16)
Education and Employment Policy (14)	Legislation (15)**	Social Policy and Health (15)	Legislation (11)**
Treaty of Waitangi Issues (10)		Closing the Gaps (15)	Government Expenditure and Administration (9)
Expenditure Control and Revenue (14)		External Relations and Defence (8)	Appointments and Honours (12)
Government Administration (15)		Legislation (12)**	External Relations and Defence (8)
Legislation and House Business (11)**		Appointments and Honours (12)	Domestic and External Security Coordination (8)
Appointments and Honours (9)		Government Expenditure and Administration (10)	

Note: The 2005 cabinet committees were not available at the time of writing.

* Subcommittees and ad hoc committees are not included except for the Shipley ministry. The bracketed figures give the membership numbers.

** Including a party whip from each coalition partner.

*** In 1998 the Strategy Committee had three subcommittees: Expenditure Control, Government Administration, and Intelligence and Security (5).

the committees that are most germane to their policy priorities. The committees are the focal points for all central decision-making, from the budget through to new policy initiatives, and for the choice of policy mechanisms by which those initiatives will be implemented. Most of the important decisions are actually made in cabinet committees. Some are more important than others. In 1990, for example, Jim Bolger used the Cabinet Strategy Committee to lead the planned transformation of the welfare state. The committee's own list of terms of reference began: '(1) To consider, determine and bring together into a coherent framework, strategic policy directions and initiatives across the entire range of Government activity and to monitor progress' (Cabinet Office 1996b)

Whether they are inside or outside cabinet, all ministers serve on cabinet committees. Despite being a coalition cabinet, the cabinet system constructed by National's Jim

Bolger after the 1996 election was typical of the post-1984 structure. His successor, Jenny Shipley, attempted to streamline the policy process by reshaping the system quite dramatically, while Helen Clark returned to the earlier model, with her own imprint reflecting her government's policy priorities.

Underpinning the cabinet system is a support infrastructure. Along with Treasury and the State Services Commission, one of the core public service agencies is the Department of Prime Minister and Cabinet. Its function is to support the prime minister with both policy development and process. It provides a broad and coordinating overview and also pursues particular policy initiatives, depending on the goals of particular governments. Since 1990, examples have been the restructuring of the health sector and the Crime Prevention Unit. The provision of procedural and constitutional advice, together with servicing the cabinet and cabinet committees, is the task of the Cabinet Office, headed by the cabinet secretary (who wears another hat as clerk of the Executive Council, responsible directly to the Governor-General and the prime minister). An important undertaking is the production of the Cabinet Office circulars, which advise on processes, and *The Cabinet Manual* (and see also Cabinet Office 2001b). The latter is a key document for procedural guidance and constitutional interpretation, covering a whole range of matters from the pronouncement of principles on issues such as the conduct of caretaker governments to the bureaucratisation of the decision-making process. Much of the manual's authority is vested in the fact that successive prime ministers and cabinets have accepted it as the primary source of their working rules (McLeay 1999).

THE FUTURE OF CABINET GOVERNMENT

Despite the dramatic impact of MMP, New Zealand will continue to have cabinet government. As has been argued here, the core conventions of cabinet government remain, even if some of the practices vary somewhat from those of the past. New Zealand's particular form of cabinet government has, however, altered in character. Decision-making has become a more complex process, responding to the necessity for additional levels and directions of consultation, whether with coalition partners, supporting parties, or opposition parties. Parliament is particularly powerful when there are minority governments, but even majority coalition cabinets can find their powers somewhat shackled. Coalition partners must consult each other to ensure that their caucuses follow the lead of their colleagues in cabinet.

Thus this chapter has returned to one of its initial themes: the relationship between parliament and cabinet. This is appropriate, because it is the nature of this power relationship that determines the character of cabinet government in New Zealand. The interaction between stable and firm political leadership from cabinet on the one hand and consultative, flexible leadership on the other hand is a delicate one. The way in which cabinet leads the policy process has a decisive impact on the health of our political system and on the nature of our democratic culture. Because cabinet occupies central stage in the political system, the political actors who comprise it profoundly affect the perceived legitimacy of New Zealand parliamentary government. How cabinets behave, how accountable they are for their actions, and whether or not they keep their promises, affect how much trust there is in government.

DISCUSSION QUESTIONS

1 How can cabinet be consultative yet still provide stable and firm policy leadership?
2 Has the doctrine of collective cabinet responsibility become outdated under MMP?
3 Under what circumstances do ministers resign from their portfolio responsibilities? Should they resign—or be dismissed—more frequently?
4 The New Zealand state has been reformed, but the size of cabinet, and its composition, remains the same. Why has cabinet remained so large? Should ministers be chosen from outside the parliament?

NOTES

1 On the constitutional position of cabinet, see especially Joseph (1993) and Palmer and Palmer (2004). Excellent contemporary material about cabinet, including personnel, committees, and Cabinet Office circulars, can be found at www.executive.govt.nz. Insights can be gained from reading memoirs, especially: McQueen (1991), Richardson (1995) and Templeton (1991). For an international perspective see Laver & Shepsle (1994, pp. 285–389).
2 See Boston et al. (1998). Geoffrey Palmer (1992, pp. 171–4) favours an increased separation of powers. For a comparative perspective see Boston (1998).
3 The doctrine is characteristic of Australia, Canada, Ireland, Germany, the Netherlands, and the United Kingdom (State Services Commission 1995, p. 17).
4 The *Cabinet Manual* outlines principles to guide ministerial conflicts of interest (2001, pp. 19–25). The Cabinet Office administers the Register of Ministers' Interests, tabled in the House by the prime minister each year.
5 Treaties have been a function of executive government. Under revised standing orders, however, parliament now plays a greater role.

REFERENCES

Boston, J. 1990, 'The Cabinet and Policy Making under the Fourth Labour Government', in M. Holland & J. Boston (eds), *The Fourth Labour Government: Politics and Policy in New Zealand*, Oxford University Press, Auckland, pp. 62–83.
Boston, J. 1998, *Governing under Proportional Representation: Lessons from Europe*, Institute of Policy Studies, Victoria University of Wellington, Wellington, pp. 123–38.

Boston, J., S. Levine, E. McLeay & N.S. Roberts 1999, *Electoral and Constitutional Change in New Zealand: An MMP Source Book*, Dunmore Press, Palmerston North.

Boston, J., S. Levine, E. McLeay & N.S. Roberts 1998, 'The Political Executive', in A. Simpson (ed.), *The Constitutional Implications of MMP*, Occasional Paper no. 9, School of Political Science and International Relations, Victoria University of Wellington, Wellington, pp. 137–67.

Boston, J., S. Levine, E. McLeay & N.S. Roberts 1996, *New Zealand under MMP: A New Politics?* Auckland University Press with Bridget Williams Books, Auckland.

Boston, J., J. Martin, J. Pallot & P. Walsh 1996, *Public Management: The New Zealand Model*, Oxford University Press, Auckland.

Cabinet Office 1996a, *Cabinet Office Manual*, Wellington.

Cabinet Office 1996b, *Cabinet Office Circular CO* (96), 15 March.

Cabinet Office 2001a, *The Cabinet Manual*, Wellington.

Cabinet Office 2001b, *Step by Step Guide: Cabinet and Cabinet Committee Processes*, Wellington.

Chapman, R. 1992, 'A Political Culture under Pressure: The Struggle to Preserve a Progressive Tax Base for Welfare and the Positive State', *Political Science*, vol. 44, pp. 1–27.

Chen, M. 2000, 'Organising the Executive under a Changed Constitution: What Should be Included?' in C. James (ed.), *Building the Constitution*, Institute of Policy Studies, Victoria University of Wellington, pp. 289–97.

Department of the Prime Minister and Cabinet 1995, *Report of the Department of Prime Minister and Cabinet*, Wellington.

Department of the Prime Minister and Cabinet 2005, *Report of the Department of Prime Minister and Cabinet*, Wellington.

Eaddy, R. 1992, 'The Structure and Operations of the Executive', in H. Gold (ed.), *New Zealand Politics in Perspective*, 3rd edn, Longman Paul, Auckland, pp. 162–73.

Gillon, G. 2005, 'Collective Responsibility in New Zealand: How Relevant is the Doctrine under MMP?' Paper presented at the Annual Conference of the Australasian Political Studies Association, University of Otago, 28–30 September.

Gregory, R. 1998a, 'A New Zealand Tragedy: Problems of Political Responsibility', *Governance*, vol. 11, no. 2, 1998, pp. 231–40.

Gregory, R. 1998b, 'Political Responsibility for Bureaucratic Incompetence: Tragedy at Cave Creek', *Public Administration*, vol. 76, pp. 519–38.

Henderson, J. 1989, 'The Operations of the Executive', in H. Gold (ed.), *New Zealand Politics in Perspective*, 2nd edn, Longman Paul, Auckland, pp. 94–102.

Jackson, K. 1978, 'Cabinet and the Prime Minister', in S. Levine (ed.), *Politics in New Zealand*, Allen & Unwin, Sydney, pp. 63–77.

Joseph, P.A. 1993, *Constitutional and Administrative Law in New Zealand*, Law Book Company, Sydney.

Laver, M. & K.A. Shepsle 1994, 'Cabinet Government in Theoretical Perspective', in M. Laver & K.A. Shepsle (eds), *Cabinet Ministers and Parliamentary Government*, Cambridge University Press, Cambridge.

McLeay, E. 1987, 'Selection Versus Election: Choosing Cabinets in New Zealand', in H.D. Clarke & M.M. Czudnowski (eds), *Political Elites in Anglo-American Democracies*, Northern Illinois University Press, Dekalb, Illinois, pp. 280–306.

McLeay, E. 1995, *The Cabinet and Political Power in New Zealand*, Oxford University Press, Auckland.

McLeay, E. 1999, 'What Is the Constitutional Status of the New Zealand Cabinet Office Manual?' *Public Law Review*, vol. 10, no. 1, pp. 11–16.

McLeay, E. 2000, 'Organising the Executive under a Changed Constitution: The Cabinet', in C. James (ed.), *Building the Constitution*, Institute of Policy Studies, Victoria University of Wellington, pp. 298–307.

McLeay, E. 2006, 'Leadership in Cabinet under MMP', in R. Miller & M. Mintrom (eds), *Political Leadership in New Zealand*, Auckland University Press, Auckland, pp. 92–112.

McQueen, H. 1991, *The Ninth Floor: Inside the Prime Minister's Office—A Political Experience*, Penguin, Auckland.

Martin, J. 1994, 'The Role of the State in Administration', in A. Sharp (ed.), *Leap into the Dark: The Changing Role of the State in New Zealand since 1984*, Auckland University Press, Auckland, pp. 41–67.

Martin, J. 1991, *Public Service and the Public Servant*, State Services Commission, Wellington.

Mulgan, R. 1997, *Politics in New Zealand*, 2nd edn, Auckland University Press, Auckland.

New Zealand First and New Zealand National Party, 1996, 'Agreement between New Zealand First and the New Zealand National Party', 7.3.

New Zealand House of Representatives 1995, *Report of the Standing Orders Committee on the Review of Standing Orders*, Wellington.

Palmer, G. 1987, *Unbridled Power: An Interpretation of New Zealand's Constitution and Government*, 2nd edn, Oxford University Press, Auckland.

Palmer, G. 1992, *New Zealand's Constitution in Crisis: Reforming our Political System*, John McIndoe, Dunedin.

Palmer, G. 2005, 'The Cabinet, the Prime Minister and the Constitution', paper for the Third Annual New Zealand Centre for Public Law Conference on the Primary Functions of Government: The Executive, 24–24 November.

Palmer, G. & M. Palmer 2004, *Bridled Power: New Zealand's Constitution and Government*, 4th edn, Oxford University Press, Auckland.

Richardson, R. 1995, *Making a Difference*, Shoal Bay Press, Christchurch.

Roberts, J. 1987, *Politicians, Public Servants and Public Enterprise: Restructuring the New Zealand Government Executive*, Victoria University for the Institute of Policy Studies, Wellington.

Sheppard, S. 1999, *Broken Circle: The Decline and Fall of the Fourth Labour Government*, PSL Press, Wellington.

State Services Commission 1995, *Working under Proportional Representation: A Reference for the Public Service*, Wellington.

Templeton, H. 1991, *All Honourable Men: Inside the Muldoon Cabinet 1975–1984*, Auckland University Press, Auckland.

Weller, P.P. 1985, 'Cabinet Committees in Australia and New Zealand', in T.T. Mackie & B.W. Hogwood (eds), *Unlocking the Cabinet: Cabinet Structures in Comparative Perspective*, Sage, London, pp. 86–113.

Wood, G.A. 1988, *Governing New Zealand*, Longman Paul, Auckland, pp. 12–24.

Wood, G.A. (ed.) 1996, *Ministers and Members in the New Zealand Parliament*, 2nd edn, University of Otago Press, Dunedin.

Woodhouse, D. 1994, *Ministers and Parliamentary Accountability in Theory and Practice*, Clarendon Press, Oxford.

FURTHER READING

Boston, J. 1998, *Governing under Proportional Representation: Lessons from Europe*, Institute of Policy Studies, Victoria University of Wellington, Wellington, pp. 123–38.

McLeay, E. 1995, *The Cabinet and Political Power in New Zealand*, Oxford University Press, Auckland.

Mulgan, R. 1992, 'The Elective Dictatorship in New Zealand', in H. Gold (ed.), *New Zealand Politics in Perspective*, 3rd edn, Longman Paul, Auckland, pp. 513–32.

Palmer, G. & M. Palmer 2004, *Bridled Power: New Zealand's Constitution and Government*, 4th edn, Oxford University Press, Auckland.

Prime Minister: Personality and Style

John Henderson

In the 2005 election Prime Minister Helen Clark won an historic third term in office, the first post Second World War Labour leader to achieve this political landmark. But she still has a long way to go to match National party leader Keith Holyoake's nearly twelve years (1960–72) in office. Another long-serving National leader was Sir Robert Muldoon, who was prime minister from 1975 to 1984. But Clark's achievement is greatly enhanced by the fact that she has remained in office during New Zealand's introduction to multi-party politics under the proportional MMP electoral system, which critics feared would bring unstable short-lived administrations. Furthermore, Clark's assertive dominance over her government is as complete as any post Second World War leader, including National Prime Ministers Holyoake and Muldoon. She has continued along the path of asserting a more presidential style of government.

This chapter focuses on the impact of the prime minister's style and personality on the way the political leadership role is performed. The analysis draws on both academic[1] and journalistic assessments,[2] and the author's experience in the 1980s of heading the staff of Prime Minister David Lange.[3]

BACKGROUND REQUIREMENTS

The journey to the office of prime minister begins a long way back from the visit to Government House for the swearing-in ceremony. For those holding ambitions to the highest office in the land an essential first step is to be elected a member of parliament. In contrast to presidential systems of government, parliament is the essential training ground for aspiring political leaders. During what is, in effect, a period of apprenticeship, usually of several years, future prime ministers need to demonstrate their leadership talents to their colleagues, and through the media to the public. The length of parliamentary experience varies widely. Clark served eighteen years in parliament before becoming prime minister, and Shipley ten years. On the other hand, National party leader Don Brash had just two years' parliamentary experience prior to his unsuccessful bid to become prime minister in the 2005 election. His political inexperience was exploited by political opponents both before and during the 2005 campaign.

Because National and Labour caucuses determine when their party leadership should be changed, chairing caucus and performing well on the floor of parliament are key tasks for the party leaders, including the prime minister of the day. One of the main reassurances that caucus will be seeking is that the leader will be able to deliver victory at the next election. The leader's ability to promote his or her party to the voters is, therefore, a vital attribute. It is assessed mainly through public opinion, as measured by party and media opinion polls. In 1997, Shipley convinced her caucus that she should replace Bolger as leader by arguing that she would be able to turn around National's low polling and provide a better chance of winning the 1999 election. Her failure to achieve this objective led to her replacement as leader by Bill English. National's poor performance in the 2002 election—the worst in the post Second World War period—inevitably led to media speculation that its leader, Bill English, would face a challenge to his leadership. In 2003, he was replaced by Brash. But although Brash held Labour to a narrow win in the 2005 election, his failure to deliver victory almost immediately led to speculation that he would be replaced. A particular factor counting against Brash is his age—he will be 68 at the time of the next scheduled election in 2008—it should, however be noted that Labour's Walter Nash was 75 when he became prime minister in 1957. Possible replacements for Brash include National's Finance spokesman, John Key. He is an effective television performer, but (like Brash) has limited parliamentary experience, having been elected in 2002. Former leader Bill English is a further likely contender (who can point to Australian Prime Minister John Howard as evidence that successful comebacks are possible). National's deputy leader, Gerry Brownlie, cannot be ruled out.

Similar considerations of political marketing have determined Labour's leadership. In 1990 the Labour prime minister, Geoffrey Palmer, was replaced by Mike Moore just weeks before the general election in a desperate and unsuccessful effort by Labour MPs to enhance their party's electoral fortunes. When Moore failed to lead his party to victory in the 1993 election he was replaced by Clark. Clark was the first woman to lead a major New Zealand political party. Her success as prime minister has left her the unchallenged leader. This has not always been the case. In June 1996 (when Labour was in opposition), in response to low polling she faced, and narrowly survived, a leadership challenge from her deputy, Michael Cullen (see also chapter 3.4). Although Labour failed to win the general election later the same year, her credible performance, and the closeness of the result, effectively ensured she would continue as leader, and put to rest speculation that women leaders were an electoral liability. Indeed, Clark could take as a compliment National's decision to appoint Jenny Shipley as their leader. Clark entrenched her position as leader at the 1999 general election, and was reaffirmed as New Zealand's leader in the 2002 and 2005 elections.

STYLE AND PERSONALITY

While prime ministers and party leaders face broadly similar tasks, the way they perform these roles will vary according to the style and personality of the individual leader. An American political psychologist, James David Barber,[4] identified three core 'role demands' (Barber 1988, pp. 55), which, although devised to interpret the behaviour of US presidents, can be usefully applied to leaders in all democratic systems, including New Zealand. The first of these requirements is the need to speak to groups and audiences both directly and through television (the rhetorical function); the second is the need to deal with political colleagues, staff, and other people (interpersonal relations); and the third is the requirement to cope with the massive flow of people and paper the job generates (the management function). Barber demonstrates how leaders adopt the style that works best for them, and that this tends to be the approach they adopted to gain their first political success. Not surprisingly, politicians tend to latch on to what seems to be a winning formula, and identifying this provides a means to predict the future style of a leader.

Recent New Zealand prime ministers and party leaders have been characterised by one of these three styles. Former Prime Ministers Muldoon and Lange, and New Zealand First leader, Winston Peters, all owed much of their political success to their ability to perform on television and before a crowd. In contrast, Prime Minister Helen Clark's dominance and Jim Bolger's long eleven-year period as party leader are proof that political success is not dependent on stage performance. Bolger's success, like that of the former Labour leader Mike Moore, was due much more to his behind-the-scenes abilities in 'interpersonal' relations. Clark has excelled at political management. Shipley and Palmer, like Clark, are examples of leaders who have concentrated their efforts on the management role. National party leaders Bill English and Don Brash also sought to follow this management style, but with less success.

The inability to perform some of these core demands also helps explain the difficulties some prime ministers experienced. Lange, for instance, was handicapped by his limited skills in the management and interpersonal relations roles—in the latter case the ability to lobby on his own behalf. Palmer, Bolger, Shipley, Clark, English, and Brash on the other hand, all experienced difficulty with the 'rhetorical' role—and particularly the ability to perform well on television. With coaching, Clark has greatly improved her television style.

To assess the impact of the personality of leaders on the performance of their leadership roles it is important to ascertain their motivations for choosing a political career. Barber surveyed the biographies of US Presidents to identify four basic personality types—which he determines by analysing the amount of activity leaders put into their political roles (active or passive types) and the degree of satisfaction they gain from this political activity (positive or negative types). While leaders are unlikely to fit perfectly into any one type, Barber demonstrates the distinctive character of each of the four resulting leadership types: active positive, active negative, passive positive, and passive negative (Barber, 1997, pp. 4–5).

The 'active positive' type throws considerable energy into the job of leader, and enjoys it. These leaders are motivated particularly by a desire to achieve certain goals and policies. They take an essentially rational view of politics, and what can and cannot be achieved. They are prepared to move on from politics when they feel they have contributed all they can. Palmer, Bolger, Shipley, Brash, and Clark are examples of this type.[5] Brash, for instance, is a self-confessed workaholic, who believes problems can be resolved through rational analysis.

The 'active negative' leaders, on the other hand, put considerable energy into the job, but gain little personal satisfaction from politics. They strive for leadership because they are driven. Politics can, as Moore has reflected about his political career, be an addictive 'drug' (Moore, 1987, p. 57). This appears to have been the case for both Moore, who was unable to accept his replacement as Labour leader by Clark, and Anderton, who made an unsuccessful attempt to relinquish the leadership of his former party, the Alliance, and take a break from politics. Power is the principal motivating force for this type. They seek to dominate their parties and administrations (as, for instance, occurred in the cases of Kirk and Muldoon) and, having achieved high office, are most reluctant to relinquish it.

As might be expected, there are fewer examples of the passive types. Politics is a demanding profession. The 'passive negative' types are in politics because they think they ought to be. While reluctant to serve as leaders, they will, if called upon, out of a sense of duty to their party and country. Labour's Bill Rowling, who took over as prime minister in 1974 following Kirk's death, is an example of a leader who did not push himself forward, but was prepared to be drafted for the job by his colleagues. Bill English also demonstrated 'passive' tendencies, and his political style is somewhat similar to that of Rowling.

The 'passive positive' types are attracted to the group and social context of politics, which is a people-oriented profession. They seek to feed on the affection of their followers, but avoid the conflict that is also an inevitable part of politics. David Lange is an example of a leader who was essentially a skilled performer on the political stage.

When his 'performances' were no longer appreciated, and his administration became consumed by the conflict over economic policy, he resigned from office.

The onset of MMP raises the fascinating question of what type of leader is most likely to be successful under a proportional electoral system. In terms of style, while rhetorical abilities will always be a valuable political asset, skills in management and interpersonal relations are particularly important for negotiating and maintaining the agreements between coalition parties. In terms of philosophy (or world view), it is the strongly ideologically motivated and idealistic leaders who are likely to have most difficulties with MMP politics. To succeed in gaining or sharing power, compromise with other party leaders is essential. For ideologues such compromise is obviously difficult—it is likely to be seen by either leaders or followers, or both, as a betrayal of their party's principles. On the other hand, the more flexible attitude of the pragmatic type of leader seems to be an advantage under MMP. Clark's success as prime minister has resulted from a combination of strong leadership and political pragmatism.

For similar reasons, the dominating power-seeking type of personality is unlikely to succeed in MMP coalition politics. The predominantly passive types of leaders may be more accommodating in the coalition building process, although they may lack the commitment to drive negotiations, which will inevitably involve conflict, to a conclusion. As is the case in democratic systems generally, Barber's 'active positive' types are the most desirable leaders, as they can separate their political goals and personal ego needs. This type of leader is best able to both provide the necessary drive to achieve policy goals, while at the same time recognising that achievement and stable government requires careful management and compromise.

CONCLUSION

An earlier assessment by this author (Henderson, 2001(c)) concluded that conciliatory rather than dominating leadership style was likely to succeed in the MMP era. But this does not seem to be the case with the current party leaders. National leader Don Brash, like his predecessor, Bill English, is an intelligent, conciliatory, and pragmatic politician, apparently well suited to MMP politics. But the 'passive' tendencies inherent in their style of leadership have prevented them from establishing their leadership credentials with the wider New Zealand public. Prime Minister Helen Clark's assertive style dominates the New Zealand political landscape. Her emphasis on policy goals and 'hands-on' approach puts her in Barber's category of 'active positive'. To some extent, this reflects Clark's mental agility, grasp of detail, and confidence of being able to communicate effectively with the media and wider public. On becoming prime minister, for example,

Clark resumed the practice of the prime minister holding televised post-cabinet press conferences, which had been abandoned by Bolger and Shipley, both leaders who preferred a more controlled relationship with the news media. The practice of regular open press conferences by the prime minister is to be welcomed as a means for the media to hold the government publicly accountable for government actions.

Barber saw 'active positive' as the most desirable leaders as, in contrast to the 'active negative' type, they are able to separate their political goals from personal ego needs. Clark has yet to be challenged in such a way as to put this separation to the test. Meanwhile the support for her dominating leadership style among the public is further evidence that New Zealanders like strong and tough leaders. MMP has not changed this—at least not yet.

DISCUSSION QUESTIONS

1　How helpful is the Barber model as a tool for assessing the personalities, styles, and effectiveness of recent New Zealand prime ministers?

2　Account for Helen Clark's success as a political leader. Do you agree with Henderson's judgment that she is an 'active positive' leader?

3　Assess the impact of personality on the performance of the modern prime minister. Illustrate with reference to the leadership of at least one of the following prime ministers: Robert Muldoon, David Lange, Geoffrey Palmer, Mike Moore, Jim Bolger, or Jenny Shipley.

4　In what ways has the advent of coalition government changed the qualities and skills required of a successful leader.

5　Compare and contrast the leadership styles of National's Don Brash, John Key, and Bill English. Which politician, in your view, is best equipped to lead the party into the next general election?

NOTES

1　See especially Weller 1985; Alley 1992; and McLeay 1995.

2　For instance, see McMillan 1993.

3　The author worked as Director of the Prime Minister's Office during David Lange's term as Prime Minister. For another 'insider' account see McQueen 1991.

4　See especially Barber 1977.

5　For the author's application of Barber to New Zealand Prime Ministers, see Henderson 2001(a), 2001(b), 1992, 1980, 1978. New Zealand biographical and autobiographical accounts of Prime Ministers providing the raw material for a New Zealand application include: Bolger 1998; Clark 2005; Edwards 2001; Grant 2003; Gustafson 2000; Hayward 1981; Henderson 2005: Lange 2005; Moore 1987; Wolfe 2005.

REFERENCES

Alley, R. 1992, 'The Power of the Prime Minister', in H. Gold (ed.), *New Zealand Politics in Perspective*, Longman Paul, Auckland, pp. 174–94.

Barber, J.D. 1988, *Politics by Humans*, Prentice Hall, New Jersey.

Barber, J.D. 1977, *The Presidential Character*, Prentice Hall, New Jersey.

Boston, J. 1988, 'Advising the Prime Minister in New Zealand', *Politics*, vol. 23, pp. 8–20.

Bolger, J. 1998, *Bolger: A View from the Top*, Penguin Books, Auckland.

Clark, M. 2005, *For the Record: Lange and the Fourth Labour Government*, Dunmore, Palmerston North.

Edwards, B. 2001, *Helen: Portrait of a Prime Minister*, Exisle, Auckland.

Grant, I.F. 2003, *Public Lives: New Zealand's Premiers and Prime Ministers, 1856–2003*, New Zealand Cartoon Archive, Wellington.

Gustafson, B. 2000, *His Way: A Biography of Robert Muldoon*, Auckland University Press, Auckland.

Hayward, M. 1981, *Diary of the Kirk Years*, Reed, Wellington.

Henderson, J. 2005, 'The Warrior Peacenik', in M. Clark (ed.), *For the Record*, Dunmore, Palmerston North, pp. 136–44.

Henderson, J. 2001(a), 'Predicting the Performance of Leaders in Parliamentary Systems. New Zealand Prime Minister, David Lange', in O. Feldman & L. Valenty (eds), *Profiling Political Leaders*, Praeger, Westport CT, pp. 203–16.

Henderson, J. 2001(b), 'Muldoon: The Inner Man', *Political Science*, 53/1, pp. 45–8.

Henderson, J. 2001(c), 'Prime Minister', in R. Miller (ed.), *New Zealand: Government and Politics*, Oxford, Melbourne, pp. 106–16.

Henderson, J. 1992, 'Labour's Prime Ministers and the Party: A Study of Contrasting Political Styles', in M. Clark (ed.), *Labour After 75 Years*, Victoria University, Wellington.

Henderson, J. 1980, 'Muldoon and Rowling: A Preliminary Analysis of Contrasting Personalities', *Political Science*, vol. 32, pp. 47–54.

Henderson, J. 1978, 'Muldoon and Kirk: Active-Negative Prime Ministers', *Political Science*, vol. 30, pp. 111–14.

Lange, D. 2005, *My Life*, Penguin, Auckland.

Hunn, D. & H. Lang 1989, *Review of the Prime Minister's Office and Cabinet Office*, State Services Commission, Wellington.

McLeay, E. 1995, *The Cabinet and Political Power in New Zealand*, Oxford University Press, Auckland.

McLoughlin, D. 1999, 'The Collected Thoughts of Helen Clark', *North and South*, April.

McMillan, N. 1993, *Top of the Greasy Pole: New Zealand Prime Ministers of Present Times*, John McIndoe, Dunedin.

McQueen, H. 1987, *The Ninth Floor: Inside the Prime Minister's Office*, Penguin Books, Auckland.

Moore, M. 1987, *Hard Labour*, Penguin, Auckland.

Weller, P. 1985, *First Amongst Equals: The Prime Minister in the Westminster System*, Allen & Unwin, Sydney.

Wilson, M. 1994, 'Relations Between the Executive and the Legislature', in G. Hassall & C. Saunders (eds), *The Power and Functions of Executive Government*, University of Melbourne, Melbourne.

Woolfe, R. 2005, *Battlers, Buffers and Bully Boys. How New Zealand Prime Ministers have Shaped the Nation*, Random House, Auckland.

FURTHER READING

Clark, M. 2005, *For the Record: Lange and the Fourth Labour Government*, Dunmore, Palmerston North.

Edwards, B. 2001, *Helen: Portrait of a Prime Minister*, Exisle, Auckland.

Henderson, J. 2001, 'Predicting the Performance of Leaders in Parliamentary Systems. New Zealand Prime Minister, David Lange', in O. Feldman & L. Valenty (eds), *Profiling Political Leaders*, Praeger, Westport CT, pp. 203–16.

Miller, R. 2005, *Party Politics in New Zealand*, Oxford University Press, Melbourne (chapter 7).

Miller, R. & M. Mintrom (eds) 2006, *Political Leadership in New Zealand*, Auckland University Press, Auckland.

Weller, P. 1985, *First Amongst Equals: The Prime Minister in the Westminster System*, Allen & Unwin, Sydney.

Prime Minister: Power

Margaret Hayward

This chapter considers how prime ministers have been empowered or constrained by New Zealand's changing electoral and political environments. As one study on political leadership has noted, 'prime ministers' substantial powers can never be exercised without an appreciation of the environment' (Weller 1989, p. 3). Under the former First-Past-the-Post (FPP) electoral system two parties dominated and, with a unicameral parliament, the powers of the prime minister were relatively unfettered. In contrast, under the Mixed Member Proportional (MMP) electoral system the role of the prime minister is much more complex. Among the constraints now imposed on a prime minister's power is the need to negotiate coalitions and support agreements with oft-times disparate political parties and independent MPs.

IMPACT OF CHANGING POLITICAL AND ELECTORAL ENVIRONMENTS

For much of the past century, prime ministers had considerable power. The variables that contributed to their dominant position were wide-ranging and included the unitary nature of the political system, single party majority government, and the dominance of the state within a mixed economy. These powers of the prime minister were further enhanced during times of economic depression or international conflict. In comparing the role of the Westminster-style prime minister with that of the president of the USA, Patrick Weller has observed that: 'Presidents have some capacities that prime ministers might covet: personal mandates and the certainty of fixed terms. In other instances prime ministers have the ability to push their wishes through cabinet and parliament with an ease and rapidity that presidents would dearly like to emulate' (1992, pp. 202–3).

The New Zealand prime minister heads the executive, approves the legislative programme, decides how many ministers will be inside and outside cabinet, allocates portfolios to those ministers, sets the agenda for cabinet, and, as the chair of both cabinet and caucus, is the final arbiter on all decisions. The prime minister decides who will chair cabinet committees, and usually personally chairs the important Policy and Strategy cabinet committees and the Honours and Appointments Committee, the latter of which provides for considerable patronage powers. As well, prime ministers are ex-officio members of all cabinet committees. At the weekly meeting of the Executive Council, which is presided over by the Governor-General and includes all ministers, whether inside or outside cabinet, the prime minister briefs the Governor-General on any significant political constitutional issues that may have arisen.[1]

Beginning in the 1980s, the introduction of a deregulated market economy and the devolution of the state sector resulted in a reduction in the formal powers of the prime minister. As a result, greater attention began to be paid to informal powers, sometimes referred to as a leader's expert and referent powers.[2] As Foley has observed in relation to the reforming leadership of a former British prime minister, Margaret Thatcher, 'personality can be the single most potent contribution to the pattern of events' (1993, p. 269). In a similar vein, successive New Zealand prime ministers have needed to exploit their personal attributes to both control the flow of information, especially through the electronic and print media, and manage the day-to-day operations of their cabinet and caucus.

For most of the ten-year period since the introduction of MMP, New Zealand has been governed by minority coalitions—in 2005 the government had a majority only on votes of confidence and supply (to be discussed more fully in chapter 3.5). In 1996, the incumbent Governor-General, Sir Michael Hardie-Boys, who had been a Judge of the Court of Appeal, announced how he would exercise the powers of his office where the outcome of an election was unclear.[3] Parliamentary parties could be relied upon to resolve any coalition formation difficulties as might occur and the parties would make it clear by 'appropriate public announcements of their intentions'. He envisaged no situation that was likely to arise where the Governor-General would be required to exercise independent judgment, thereby risking the political neutrality of the Office (Hardie-Boys 1997, p. 3).

Before a government is formed, the relevant parties make coalition agreements and support agreements with each other. These agreements may cover policy issues that cut across the beliefs of the major party. However, unlike the detailed agreement between the National and New Zealand First parties between 1996 and the coalition's collapse in 1998, agreements now usually have 'good faith and no surprises', and 'agree to disagree' clauses to prevent the junior coalition partner(s) from appearing to be a pale reflection of the major party. Under a coalition, the cabinet table is shared with ministers appointed by the coalition party or parties, and absent prime ministers often have to rely on an acting prime minister drawn from one of the minor coalition parties.

Much of a prime minister's time is now taken up with negotiating agreements and regular meetings with the leaders of the coalition party and support parties. For example, the four agreements drawn up with the Progressive Party, New Zealand First, United Future, and the Greens in November 2005 all stated that there would be a regular meeting between the prime minister and their respective leaders. If prime ministers are to fulfil their obligations throughout the country and overseas they must delegate far more than in the past, and they must rely on an experienced and trusted negotiating team to work though cabinet agendas, party and policy issues, and shared patronage of the thousands of boards and quangos that contain government appointees.

Despite a gradual reduction in the powers of the prime minister since the advent of economic and electoral reform, this should not be over-stated. As a former National prime minister, Jim Bolger, has acknowledged, in the absence of a majority of ministers agreeing with the prime minister's position, it is always possible for the prime minister to impose his or her will on cabinet.[4] Furthermore, prime ministers are able to use post-cabinet and post-caucus media conferences to present their understanding of any decisions. Recent constraints on the power of the prime minister notwithstanding, asserts that of Helen Clark prime ministers still 'have enormous power to influence outcomes' (Edwards 2001, p. 328).

Prior to 1996, there were no formal statements describing the powers of the prime minister. In the view of a former prime minister, Geoffrey Palmer, this was hardly surprising, given New Zealand's direct transplant of Westminster constitutional principles and practices. Although the most humble clerk in the New Zealand public service had a list of defined duties, none existed for the most powerful post in the land (Palmer 1992, p. 150). A few statutes did, however, spell out some of the powers of the prime minister. These included the State Services Act 1962 authorising the prime minister to direct an investigation or inquiry on any matter (other than that involving judicial proceedings) and to have the Ombudsman report on it to the prime minister. The Official Information Act 1982 gave the prime minister the authority to curb the release of information deemed prejudicial to the security, defence, and international relations of NZ. Under the New Zealand Nuclear Free Zone, Disarmament and Arms Control Act 1987 the prime ministers were designated as having the power to grant approval for the entry of visiting military platforms, but only if they were satisfied that they were not carrying nuclear explosive devices. Prime ministers are also in charge of the Security Intelligence Bureau and, prior to 1975, most also chose to be the Minister of Foreign Affairs and represent New Zealand at international forums.

The Cabinet Manual, revised in 1996 to allow for any changes resulting from the introduction of MMP, defines the office and role of the prime minister more fully. However, as Helen Clark stated following her decision to appoint two leaders of support parties as ministers outside cabinet, who would be bound by cabinet collectivity only on their portfolio responsibilities, '*The Cabinet Manual* continues to evolve'.

GAINING AND LOSING THE PRIME MINISTERSHIP

While cabinet is the focal point for government decision-making, caucus is the centre of prime ministerial power, for without the confidence of their caucus they are no longer the prime minister or the party leader. Unlike Canada and the United Kingdom where leaders are chosen by electoral colleges or a vote of the membership, in New Zealand the choice of leader in the two major parties is firmly under the control of the caucus.

In the New Zealand National party, the leader must gain and retain the confidence of a majority of caucus members although the party's Board of Directors must endorse caucus's decision (1999: Rule 87c). There are no rules about the length of tenure, nor timetabled re-selection caucuses where a leader may be further endorsed or face a challenge. Not until Jenny Shipley became leader in 1997 did the leadership go to someone other than the deputy leader, but even then the change of leadership was carried out discreetly. When prime minister Bolger, upon returning from overseas on 1 November 1997 was told he had lost the support of caucus, he was able to negotiate a departure date that enabled him to undertake a planned state visit to China and attend an APEC conference. Not so discreet was the leadership bid in 2003, when Bill English, confident that he had the numbers to survive a leadership challenge, agreed to a vote, which was subsequently won by a new list MP and former Governor of the Reserve Bank, Don Brash.

In the New Zealand Labour party, selection of the party leader has been the right of caucus members since the first leader, Harry Holland, was elected in 1919. The parliamentary Labour party caucus rules stipulate that selection is by exhaustive ballot. Since 1939, leaders have been required to have their support tested at a leadership caucus once in every parliamentary term (every three years). On only one occasion has there been a change of leader at the three-yearly leadership caucus: in 1965 when Norman Kirk deposed Arnold Nordmeyer.

Since the 1980s, remaining leader of a major party has been conditional on an ability to win elections (between the 1960s and the 1980s the Labour party was more forgiving, with Walter Nash, Norman Kirk, and Bill Rowling each losing more than one election before either being replaced or leading their party to victory). Today, they must also remain high in the 'preferred prime minister' polls or face an inevitable challenge from ambitious colleagues. The Labour party experienced a loss of popularity from 1989 to 2003 resulting in four leaders in five years. Similarly, in the six years from 1997 to 2003 the National party had four leaders, reflecting their poor showing in the polls.

An example of a leader who has survived despite being desperately low in the polls is Helen Clark, largely due to her ability to use her formal and informal powers to dominate her party, parliamentary caucus and, since 1999, cabinet. In 1993, Clark had inherited a divided and angry caucus with MPs whose philosophies ranged from the centre-right to the far left. Clark had long been aware that caucus was the equivalent of the leader's electorate and that MPs must be nurtured, listened to, and heeded.

She immediately organised a three-day retreat where she asked her MPs to explain to each other why they were in the Labour party. It was a breakthrough, as most found they had more similarities than differences. Clark also made it clear she was going to 'put an end to factional rewards for support'. She appointed the front bench on ability, resulting in half the front bench being people who hadn't voted for her in the leadership election. Then she worked to make committees inclusive. 'Helen would say, "Oh that's got three right-wingers on it, we need a couple from the left"'.[5]

Even so, when her preferred prime minister polling dropped to an unprecedented low of 4 per cent in May 1996 (Bolger was at 22 per cent and Peters 29 per cent), she was challenged by a group of senior caucus colleagues. Clark refused to step aside, telling them to take a vote in caucus. Her power base had been the extra parliamentary party and party members swung into action, making it clear they preferred her to any contender. As a result, no caucus vote was taken. Shortly afterwards the deputy leader, David Caygill, resigned and a member of the challenging group, Michael Cullen, became deputy leader.

Prime ministers have used their formal and informal powers in different ways to retain support and control. Rob Muldoon humiliated those who argued with him to the point of 'tears running down their faces'.[6] In contrast, Bolger was prepared to let everyone express an opinion and didn't ridicule, although he was accused of being able to talk any problem into the ground.[7] Shipley was regarded as efficient and fair. However, she often found managing her caucus more complex than managing a coalition with minor parties. 'They occupied as much, if not more, of my time and created far more frustration …'[8] Lange had a light, humorous touch but would try to avoid certain items on the agenda and often lose interest and leave caucus or cabinet. Moore had a reputation for switching between topics somewhat disconcertingly, and if he disagreed with the person speaking, 'he would turn his back to them and look out the window'.[9] Clark's management style, on the other hand, is to run caucus and cabinet efficiently and fairly. 'People have their say but then it's "thanks for your contribution and let's move on": so it's a combination of both her personality and the formal structure to get the outcome that she wants …'[10]

PRIME MINISTERS AND CABINET

Cabinet is the central decision-making body of executive government and usually meets weekly, on a Monday (see chapter 3.1). The prime minister is the ultimate arbiter of cabinet procedure. In response to the time-consuming Bolger style of chairing cabinet, for example, Shipley allocated only one half-day every two weeks to cabinet meetings. Discussion was brief, as ministers were asked to report on decisions already made in the cabinet committees, which Shipley had formed into teams, such as the Economic Team and the Social Responsibility and Strengthening Families Team. This committee structure reflected her desire that 'coalition cabinet decision-making [be] even better prepared for than it had been under Mr Bolger'.[11] Under Clark, however, cabinet has reverted to meeting weekly.

Whereas the Labour caucus chooses its cabinet through an exhaustive ballot, National prime ministers have the power to appoint their own cabinets. This gives them considerable powers of patronage. Both Keith Holyoake and Muldoon required prospective ministers to sign undated resignations before they took the oath of office. Bolger, who was determined not to repeat Muldoon's dominating style, discontinued the practice. Until the introduction of MMP, both Labour and National prime ministers could decide the number of ministers in their cabinet and allocate the portfolios. Now the number of cabinet ministers and the portfolios they hold are negotiated with the coalition partner.

Since 1940, when Peter Fraser became prime minister and instructed that caucus elect his replacement to cabinet, the Labour caucus has jealously guarded its right to elect the members of cabinet. Lange was happy with the system: 'I absolutely was driven crazy and probably would have left the country if I had to make the choice of who to put in cabinet'.[12] Clark, on the other hand, was less enthusiastic, saying it was 'one of the great limitations of the Labour party's rules'.[13] Lange may have been happy with caucus choosing his cabinet, but by 1987 he was unhappy with caucus holding out against the economic changes proposed by the Minister of Finance, Roger Douglas, and used his prime ministerial powers to introduce a new category of 'minister outside cabinet'. Ministers outside cabinet were deemed to be part of the executive, and thus subject to the doctrine of collective responsibility for cabinet decisions. This said, they take no part in cabinet decisions unless they are related to their particular portfolio. As Lange observed, 'I had to give the collective responsibility of standing beyond cabinet to other people who were non-cabinet so that we were always able to dominate caucus'.[14] The second Lange cabinet comprised 20 ministers plus four ministers outside cabinet (chosen by Lange) and four under-secretaries (also chosen by Lange) increasing the executive to twenty-eight. With the addition of office-holders, such as the party whips, cabinet had a majority in a caucus of fifty-seven. Lange had predicted that a cabinet majority in caucus would not occur under MMP: 'If you've got 120 MPs in parliament, you can't possibly buy your way out of it that way'.[15] He was wrong. Clark's 2005 executive, which included twenty-six Labour ministers (twenty cabinet and six ministers outside cabinet), was in a majority in the Labour caucus of fifty, even without the support of other office-holders.

Since Clark is the first prime minister to successfully navigate through two terms (and into a third) under MMP, I will concentrate on her handling of cabinet. From the outset of her first term she made her expectations clear. At the time cabinet was elected, she said that as Labour hadn't had the opportunity to be in office very often she wanted ministers performing well; that 'everyone was there on performance and there were plenty of others waiting to take their jobs' (Laugeson 2000, p. A4). Over the next three years the prime minister was true to her word. If ministers' actions were under a cloud they were stood down till an inquiry was held. In her first year as prime minister four ministers either resigned or were stood down pending inquiries. Three of the four eventually were reinstated with some changes in portfolios.

Clark was also the first Labour prime minister to use Caucus Rule 31, passed by caucus in 1974, to allow a prime minister to nominate a replacement when a minister had resigned or had been dismissed. In July 2000 she nominated Parekura Horomia as the replacement Minister of Maori Affairs after Dover Samuels had been dismissed. Clark took the opportunity to reiterate her dissatisfaction with the sixty-year-old tradition of caucus electing ministers, saying it was not 'the best practice for leaders to be accountable for teams they don't pick'. She would not force the issue but would try to bring it about at some 'dim distant time when I cease to be leader of the Labour party'.[16]

Unlike previous prime ministers she gave Tariana Turia, Minister for the Community and Voluntary Sector and Associate Minister of Maori Affairs outside of cabinet, permission to abstain from voting on the Seabed and Foreshore Bill in 2004, although *The Cabinet Manual* made no exception for ministers outside of cabinet to abstain. Turia later resigned from Labour and formed the Māori party.

Coalition cabinets call for leaders to be pragmatic and inclusive. Prime ministers have had to overcome personal slights and share their bench in parliament with minor party leaders they may have distrusted over many years. Bolger had to mend an acrimonious relationship with Peters—he had once dismissed Peters from the National cabinet and, when Peters' behaviour failed to improve, his National colleagues expelled him from caucus. Similarly, Shipley and Peters were never on good terms—rather than go into coalition with her when she became National party leader in 1997, he had contacted Clark to try and form a Labour–New Zealand First government, but was rejected. A coalition between Labour and the Alliance also seemed unlikely because a close working relationship between Clark and Anderton had turned sour ten years previously, when he was on the point of defecting from the Labour party. In 1998, when it was obvious that Labour would need a coalition partner, the two leaders mended their relationship. Dunne, too, had resigned from the Labour party and provided vital support for the National party in 1996, serving in Bolger's cabinet. In an MMP environment, prime ministers must ignore personal feeling of antipathy or betrayal and take the long view.

DEPARTMENT OF THE PRIME MINISTER AND CABINET

Policy advice adds greatly to the power of the prime minister for, as Bolger contended, knowledge is power. Until 1975, what was termed the Prime Minister's Department had been administered by the Department of External (Foreign) Affairs, headed by the Secretary of External Affairs. Muldoon, as Minister of Finance rather than Foreign Affairs, established his own department, which was led by Bernard Galvin from the Treasury. Importantly, he also established an advisory group of experts, seconded from both the private and public sectors. This advisory group concept was adopted by Lange when he became prime minister in 1984.

Palmer initiated a review that recommended a single department be established to combine the Cabinet Office with the advisory side of the Prime Minister's Office, with the number of policy advisers to be increased from eight to twenty. A separate Prime Minister's Office would carry out the political advice function and liaison with political parties. Both Bolger and Shipley had a similar structure but, as Shipley's popularity declined, she increased the number in the press office from three to seven and consulted with public relations specialists. She also changed the culture in the prime minister's office. Shipley ran a very professional office consisting largely of people who had no political affiliations, as she had issues of trust both with the party and with some of her cabinet colleagues.[17] In Clark's office Heather Simpson, who has worked with Clark since the 1980s, is chief of staff. She has played an important advisory role, coordinating policy advice and maintaining relations with coalition and support parties. Clark has added a communication unit to the Prime Minister's Office that has been active in improving relationships with the media. Headed by a former journalist, Mike Munro, it has also assisted the prime minister with advice about her public image and presentation.

The public platform is vital in retaining prime ministerial power as David Lange clearly demonstrated. But no longer do election campaigns consist of leaders declaiming for two hours in draughty town halls; they now have to win support in nationwide televised political debates with other leaders and appear poised and in control. One bad performance can undo a whole election campaign. Geoffrey Palmer, for example, was adamant that:

> Television has changed the complete character of political leadership. People have to be attractive, they have to be telegenic, they have to be friendly, they have to have celebrity qualities. Their political qualities are secondary, their ideological beliefs are secondary, or thirdly. Their entire approach must be that of a salesperson.[18]

While most would agree that prime ministers and leaders of political parties are much more than salespeople, when policies have been decided it is the prime ministers or party leaders who have to 'sell' them.

CONCLUSION

The public is able to exercise two important restraints on the power of the prime minister. First, voters have retained the right to choose their government every three years despite two referendum attempts to increase the length of the parliamentary term to four years. Second, the existence of the MMP electoral system serves as a reminder that much of our recent political history was characterised by a lack of public trust in political leaders, from Muldoon, who presided over a divisive Springbok rugby tour, to Lange, whose promise of gain following several years of economic pain proved largely illusory. Similarly, Bolger's promise of a 'Decent Society' was followed by cuts to pensions and the introduction of the Employment Contracts Act, which disempowered many in the workplace. Trust in politicians plummeted from 33 per cent in 1975 to 4 per cent in 1992, leading to growing public demand for a new, proportional system of representation. In 1999, Clark turned the lack of trust to advantage, issuing a 'credit card' (based on that used by New Labour in the United Kingdom) of seven promises and honouring most of them within the first twelve months. One of the four objectives of her brief coalition agreement with the Alliance was 'to restore public confidence in the political integrity of parliament and the electoral process'.[19]

In the past, New Zealanders admired strong uncompromising leaders who exploited to the full the formal and informal powers at their disposal. In the new political environment of MMP, the authoritarian style of leadership is much less likely to succeed, with the result that leaders in the mould of Sidney Holland or Rob Muldoon might find it difficult, if not impossible, to construct and lead a successful coalition government. In short, the MMP environment has changed the power structure of the prime minister. New Zealanders still want strong decisive leaders who can present a clear vision for the future, but they must also be skilled at managing a diverse caucus and a multi-party parliament. A prime minister's power now lies in the art of compromise and persuasion, while still delivering on the promises made to voters.

DISCUSSION QUESTIONS

1 Compare the powers of prime ministers elected under the FFP electoral system with the powers of prime ministers in an MMP environment.

2 Should prime ministers be able to select their own cabinet ministers? What are the advantages and disadvantages?

3 Should the caucus of the two major parties select their leaders as at present, or should party members or a broad-based electoral college have that responsibility?

4 What qualities does a prime minister need to lead a coalition government which has a number of support parties?

5 The prime minister in cabinet is 'first among equals'. How equal is the prime minister?

NOTES

1 See www.dpmc.govt.NZ/cabinet/manual.1 for the current version of *The Cabinet Manual*.
2 French and Raven identified five types of power: reward power, coercive power, legitimate power, expert power, and referent power. Expert and referent power are gained because of the leader's qualities. Subordinates follow them because they are revered for their knowledge and expertise or because they have earned their respect and admiration.
3 The Governor-General, the Rt Hon Sir Michael Hardie-Boys, Speech to the Annual Dinner of the Institute of International Affairs, Wellington, 24 May 1996, p. 10.
4 Bolger wrote that when the decision was made to build the Museum of New Zealand—Te Papa—he thought five of the twenty Cabinet Ministers were in favour and the rest uncertain or strongly against.
5 Interviews, Ruth Dyson 12/12/00, Judy Keall 1/12/02 and Judith Tizard, 15/11/00.
6 Don McKinnon interview, *The Grim Face of Power*, Communicado, 1995.
7 Interview Joy McLaughlan, 16/3/00.
8 Interview Jenny Shipley, 29/2/02.
9 Interviews Judith Tizard 15/11/00 and Annette King 25/8/94.
10 Interview Ross Vintiner, former Chief Press Secretary to David Lange, 30/9/01.
11 Interview Simon Murdoch, former Chief Executive of the Department of the Prime Minister and Cabinet, 1991–98, 5/12/98.
12 Interview David Lange, 10/12/97.
13 Kim Hill interview, 'Nine to Noon', *Radio New Zealand*, 28/6/00.
14 Interview David Lange, 10/12/97.
15 Interview David Lange, 10/12/97.
16 'Clark expects little support from MPs for change', *The Dominion*, 4/7/00, p. 2.
17 Interview Doug Martin, formerly Shipley's Chief of Staff, 7/2/04.
18 Interview Geoffrey Palmer, 16/6/00.
19 Coalition Agreement between the Labour and Alliance parties, 6 December 1999.

REFERENCES

Bain, H. 2005, 'PM Gives Beyer's Bill the Chop', *Sunday Star Times*, 30 October, p. A2.
Bolger, J. 1999, *View from the Top: My Seven Years as Prime Minister*, Viking, Auckland.
Coalition Agreement between the Labour and Alliance parties, 6 December 1999.
Edwards, B. 2001, *Helen: Portrait of a Prime Minister*, Exisle, Auckland.
Foley, M. 1993, *The Rise of the British Presidency*, Manchester University Press, Manchester.
French J. & B.H. Raven 1959, 'The Bases of Social Power', in D. Cartwright (ed.) *Studies of Social Power*, Institution for Social Research, Ann Arbour, MI.
Hardie Boys, M. 1997, 'Harkness Henry Lecture to the University of Waikato', *Waikato Law Review*, Vol. 5.
Laugeson R. 2000, 'Accountability also Applies to Ministers, says Clark', *Sunday Star-Times*, 20 February, p. A4.

Palmer, G. & M. Palmer 2004, *Bridled Power: New Zealand's Constitution and Government,* 4th edn, Oxford University Press, Melbourne.

Palmer, G. 1992, *New Zealand's Constitution in Crisis: Reforming our Political System,* John McIndoe, Dunedin.

Rhodes, R.A.W. 1997, 'Coherence, Capacity and the Hollow Crown', in P. Weller, H. Bakvis & R.A.W. Rhodes (eds), *The Hollow Crown: Countervailing Trends in Core Executives,* Macmillan, London.

Weller, P. 1992, 'The Development of the Australian Prime Minister', *From Menzies to Keating: the Development of the Australian Prime Minister,* Melbourne University Press, Melbourne.

Weller, P. 1990, 'The Cabinet', in C. Jennett & R.G. Stewart (eds) *Hawke and Australian Public Policy: Consensus and Restructuring,* Macmillan Education, South Melbourne.

Weller, P. 1989, *Malcolm Fraser PM: A Study in Prime Ministerial Power in Australia,* Penguin, Ringwood, Vic.

FURTHER READING

Boston, J., S. Levine, E. McLeay & N.S. Roberts (eds) 1997, *From Campaign to Coalition: The 1996 MMP Election,* Dunmore Press, Palmerston North.

Boston, J., S. Church, S. Levine, E. McLeay & N.S. Roberts (eds) 2000, *Left Turn: The New Zealand General Election of 1999,* Victoria University Press, Wellington.

Boston, J., S. Church, S. Levine, E. McLeay & N.S. Roberts (eds) 2003, *New Zealand Votes: The General Election of 2002,* Victoria University Press, Wellington.

Gustafson, B. 2000, *His Way: A Biography of Robert Muldoon,* Auckland University Press, Auckland.

Lange, D. 2005, *My Life,* Viking, Auckland.

Miller, R. 2005, *Party Politics in New Zealand,* Oxford University Press, Melbourne (chapter 7).

Forming a Government

Jonathan Boston

Prior to the introduction of the Mixed Member Proportional (MMP) system of representation in 1996, it was usual for the process of government formation in New Zealand to be remarkably straightforward. In most instances, certainly between the mid 1930s and the early 1990s, it was evident within a few hours of the polls closing which of the two major parties—Labour or National—had won a majority of the seats in parliament. Thus there was little, if any, doubt over which party leader should be called upon by the Governor-General to form the next government. Given the absence of any need for inter-party negotiations, a new government could be sworn in as soon as special votes had been counted, usually within ten to twelve days of the election.

As widely expected, the introduction of MMP has brought an end to the days of single-party majority governments. With no one party able to secure an overall parliamentary majority, negotiations between two or more parties must now be undertaken before a new government can be formed. As well as complicating the process, this can give rise to significant delays, as graphically illustrated by the events following the 1996 general election. Having said this, the complexity and duration of post-election negotiations depends on whether a bloc of ideologically connected parties secures an overall majority, as in 1999 and 2002, or whether a non-aligned party (or parties) close to the middle of the political spectrum holds the balance of power, as in 1996 (and to a lesser extent in 2005). Under the former scenario, it is perfectly possible for a new government to be formed as quickly as it was under the plurality system—as demonstrated by the events of late 1999 and August 2002.

This chapter briefly explores the process of forming a government in New Zealand, against the backdrop of the introduction of MMP. First, it considers the incentives and constraints that shape the kinds of governments formed (majority versus minority, and single-party versus multi-party).[1] Attention is given to both the institutional context within which government formation occurs, and the political context, including the character of the party system and the configuration of the parties in parliament. Second, the chapter compares and contrasts the events immediately following the MMP elections in 1996, 1999, 2002, and 2005.[2] Finally, some suggestions are offered on how the rules governing the process of government formation could be modified, assuming the retention of a system of proportional representation.

GOVERNMENT FORMATION

Numerous incentives and constraints shape the process of government formation under proportional representation. These include:

- the constitutional rules and conventions that govern the process
- the number, configuration, and relative strength of the parliamentary parties, and, in particular, which combination of parties can command a legislative majority
- the nature of the policy and ideological issues that divide the parties
- the experience, expertise, and vulnerability of the respective party leaders
- the nature of any pre-electoral pacts or implicit understandings
- the prevailing political culture, most notably the attitudes of political elites concerning the preferred kind of government (Boston et al. 1996, pp. 98–104).[3]

Given the very wide range of variables, it is not surprising that every situation under which a government is formed is different. At the same time, important patterns and regularities can be discerned. Of critical importance are the rules, both formal and informal, under which government formation occurs.

RULES OF GOVERNMENT FORMATION AND TERMINATION

Such rules create identifiable incentives, constraints, and opportunities, thereby influencing the pattern of inter-party bargaining and the probability of certain kinds of outcomes (for example, whether minority governments are likely or unlikely). Parliamentary democracies differ, for example, with respect to the role played by the head of state, the rules governing the investiture of new governments, whether 'formateurs' or 'informateurs' are appointed to lead or oversee the formation process,[4] and the circumstances under which a government is expected to resign.

Of these, the most important distinction concerns the rules of investiture. Bergman (1995, pp. 40–52) distinguishes between 'positive parliamentarism', under which a party or a coalition is required to win a vote of investiture in the legislature before it can form a government, and 'negative parliamentarism', under which there is no such vote of investiture but any new government must be able to win a subsequent vote of confidence or else resign. As a general rule, countries with 'negative' formation rules have more minority governments, smaller minority governments, and shorter formation processes than countries with 'positive' rules. For instance, De Winter (1995, p. 136) found that government formation in countries with negative rules took eight days less, on average, than in countries with positive rules.

While Bergman's analysis is useful, it is important to distinguish not only between negative and positive formation rules, but also between the different legislative thresholds that a party or parties must pass in order to attain (or retain) office (De Winter 1995, pp. 135–6). More specifically, the following categories of country can be identified as, those where:

- a party or parties must win a positive investiture vote by an absolute majority (e.g. Germany and Spain)
- a party or parties must win a positive investiture vote by a relative majority (e.g. Ireland, Italy, and Greece)
- a party or parties can survive an investiture vote unless there is an absolute majority of all MPs against it (e.g. Portugal and Sweden)
- an investiture vote is not required (e.g. Austria, Britain, Denmark, Finland, and Norway).

From this standpoint, as De Winter (1995, p. 136) argues, 'the negative rule implies that the government should be tolerated by an absolute majority, while the positive rules require that governments are explicitly endorsed by at least a relative majority'.

Just as there are positive and negative rules relating to government formation, a similar distinction can also be made regarding the rules affecting government resignations. Thus, under a negative resignation rule a parliamentary censure motion (or vote of no confidence) is deemed successful if it secures at least a relative majority. This is the situation in Britain, Denmark, Ireland, and Norway, among others. By contrast, under a positive resignation rule a government can survive unless an absolute majority of all MPs vote against it on a specific motion of censure (as in Greece, Portugal, and Sweden) or it loses a 'constructive' vote of no confidence (as in Germany and Spain). Under a constructive censure motion an alternative government or prime minister must be proposed as part of the motion. Positive rules obviously make it more difficult for the legislature to force a government's resignation, thereby enhancing political stability. In fact, according to De Winter (1995, p. 140), governments in countries with negative resignation rules are more than twice as likely to be defeated due to a lack of parliamentary support on a censure motion as governments in countries with positive resignation rules.[5]

The critical importance of these different rules was illustrated in Italy in October 1998 when Romano Prodi's centre-left government lost a confidence vote in the lower House by a single vote—313 to 312. He was thus forced to resign. Since there are 630 MPs, if an absolute (rather than a relative) majority had been required to defeat the government, Prodi would not have lost the vote.

In Bergman's terms, New Zealand's constitutional arrangements place it unequivocally within the category of negative parliamentarism (Boston et al. 1996, pp. 99–100). Indeed, by international standards it has a remarkably open-ended and permissive process of government formation—what is referred to in the relevant literature as 'free-style bargaining' (Laver and Schofield 1990; Muller and Strom 1997). For instance, a government is not required to hold a majority of seats, nor does it need an absolute parliamentary majority to win a vote of confidence—it merely requires a simple majority. Equally, there is no requirement for a new government to receive a confirming vote in parliament before it can assume power. Against this, no Governor-General is likely to swear in a new prime minister without a public, authoritative, and unequivocal assurance that the person in question is able to win a vote of confidence (at least in the short term) when such a vote occurs.[6] Moreover, although there is no provision for an investiture vote, it is highly likely that a new government's support will be tested in the House soon after it has been sworn in—most probably at the conclusion of the Address-in-Reply debate. If the government loses a vote of confidence, it must resign.

Further, there are no explicit rules regarding the manner in which inter-party negotiations are conducted. Hence, unlike the situation in many other jurisdictions, there is no provision for the appointment of formateurs or informateurs. Instead, the party leaders have an entirely free hand in managing the process, and are at liberty to adopt whatever bargaining strategies are deemed appropriate in the interests of forming a viable government.

Nor are there any constitutional constraints on the duration of the government formation process. To be sure, the Constitution Act 1986 requires parliament to meet within six weeks of the return of the writs from a general election,[7] but while this provides a political incentive to complete the process within the designated time frame, there is no legal requirement for a government to be sworn in by the time the House resumes. Lastly, it is relatively easy for parliament to force a government's resignation since a vote of no confidence requires only a relative majority to succeed. Against this, the occasions upon which a confidence motion can be moved are very limited under the House's existing standing orders.

All in all, New Zealand's rules regarding government formation and termination are very flexible by international standards, thereby facilitating a wide range of practices and procedures. Although the 'negative' nature of the formation rules facilitates a swift process, in the absence of any constitutional limitation on the timetable for inter-party negotiations there is little (other than political pressure) to prevent protracted negotiations of the kind witnessed in 1996. Equally, while the current rules facilitate the formation of minority governments, they do not encourage their survival. There remains a strong incentive, therefore, for parties to seek majority coalitions, or at least medium-term support arrangements with ideologically compatible parties.

THE PARTY SYSTEM

Whatever the constitutional rules and conventions, another factor that has a decisive bearing on the process of government formation is the character, and in particular the 'dimensionality', of the party system. As a general rule, government formation is less complex and uncertain where the party system is unidimensional rather than multidimensional. In the former case, there is a single, dominant issue dimension (or ideological continuum) and all the parliamentary parties are positioned somewhere along it. Typically, the most important issue dimension in democratic countries is the socio-economic (or left–right) dimension. This is undoubtedly the case in New Zealand (Brechtel and Kaiser 1999).[8] Where there are two or more politically salient issue dimensions, parties that are close to each other on one dimension may be deeply divided on another, thus making it difficult to construct cohesive and durable coalitions. For instance, Norway's Conservative party holds strongly divergent views from its potential centrist allies (the Centre party, the Christian People's party, and the Liberals) on whether the country should join the European Union. For some years, this more or less ruled out the possibility of a coalition government of the centre-right, even when the relevant parties held an overall majority in the Storting (Shaffer 1998, pp. 128–30).

Another factor related to the question of dimensionality is whether the party system is characterised by a 'two bloc' or a 'balancing centre' pattern. Where all the parliamentary parties are grouped into two relatively cohesive and stable blocs, the government will invariably be formed by the bloc that has the majority of the seats. In such circumstances, the process of government formation can be relatively swift and straightforward—as demonstrated by the negotiations between Labour and the Alliance following the 1999 general election in New Zealand. Against this, where there is a party (or parties) in the middle of the political spectrum that is prepared to switch sides depending on the political context, forming a government is likely to be more difficult, complex, and protracted. This will be all the more so if the party in question holds the balance of power and seeks to use its strategic position to maximum advantage. This, of course, is precisely what happened with New Zealand First in 1996.

Similar problems can also arise under a bloc system where there are more than two blocs or where the blocs are unstable (for example, because of a degree of multidimensionality). The latter issue was relevant in 2005 when the Māori party, although ostensibly part of the centre-left block, chose to offer conditional support for a possible National-led government because of fundamental disagreements with the Labour party over the Foreshore and Seabed Act.

Where no single party enjoys an overall parliamentary majority, the bargaining power of any particular party depends not so much on its relative size but rather on its position along the relevant issue dimension (or dimensions). Hence, a party located at the median point on the dominant dimension in a largely unidimensional party system will be in a pivotal position and thus able to exert an influence out of all proportion to its size. Although there are a number of different techniques for measuring the bargaining power of parties in the government formation process, it is generally agreed that a party's influence 'is proportional to the number of coalitions to which its membership is crucial for victory' (Nagel 1999b).[9] Hence, the party in the strongest position is the one that is a necessary component of all the politically feasible (or 'connected') minimum winning coalitions (MWCs). Conversely, the party in the weakest position is the one that is not part of any of the politically feasible MWCs. Of course, the position of 'weakest' or 'strongest' can be shared by more than one party at a time.

Note that an MWC is a coalition that has the minimum number of parties necessary to secure a parliamentary majority, while a connected coalition is one where the parties are relatively close to each other on the relevant issue dimension(s). According to the theoretical literature on government formation, the most likely coalition is a minimum connected winning coalition (MCW). This is because such coalitions have a greater chance than disconnected coalitions of satisfying the policy preferences of their members and supporters, while at the same time minimising the number of people with whom power—and thus all the benefits of office—must be shared.

Let us take a specific example. Following the 1996 general election in New Zealand, there were four possible MWCs:

1 National and Labour
2 National and New Zealand First
3 ACT, National, and the Alliance
4 New Zealand First, Labour, and the Alliance.

Of these options, only the second and fourth were MCWs. The first option, while conceivable, had been categorically ruled out by Labour; the third would have involved parties at opposite ends of the political spectrum cooperating in office, a virtually unthinkable scenario. Significantly, the connected coalitions both included New Zealand First. Therefore, the party was guaranteed a major role in the policy process (whether or not it entered office). Moreover, the fact that New Zealand First was crucial to both MCWs gave it—at least on one measure—double the bargaining strength of the two largest parties, Labour and National. It is perhaps not surprising, in these circumstances, that it managed to secure so many of its policy goals during the coalition negotiations with Labour and National.

While MCWs are relatively common internationally, not all governments in countries with proportional representation are coalitions, and not all enjoy a formal parliamentary majority. Indeed, roughly a third of democratic governments hold only a minority of seats in their legislatures. There have also been many instances, especially in Belgium and the Netherlands, of 'oversized' coalitions (where there are more parties than necessary to guarantee a majority). Quite apart from this, not all governments that are MWCs are connected coalitions. But if MCWs are the most rational outcome of inter-party bargaining, why are so many governments not of this type?

Such questions have attracted vigorous debate among coalition theorists (Strom 1990). While no definitive theoretical explanation has so far been provided, the reasons for the formation of non-MCWs are not difficult to identify. For instance, oversized coalitions are sometimes the direct result of constitutional provisions (as in Belgium) that require particular cultural or ethnic groups to be included in the executive. Likewise, there are at least two reasons why minority governments are relatively common. First, large parties in multi-party systems sometimes take a strategic decision not to enter into coalition arrangements in the hope that this will strengthen their overall electoral support. Such a strategy was pursued for many decades by the Norwegian Labour Party, and was also the policy of Fianna Fail in Ireland until the late 1980s. Second, smaller parties often prefer not to join a coalition because they believe that the advantages (such as the perks of office and greater policy influence) are outweighed by the disadvantages (such as the likely loss of voter support at the next election). Moreover, where a party holds a pivotal parliamentary position, its policy influence may be little affected by whether it enters office or not. Becoming a support party can thus be an attractive option: it avoids most of the risk associated with incumbency, and it frees the party from the constraints of collective responsibility. Against this, it means that the senior members of the party must forgo the perks of office (for example, higher salaries, chauffeur-driven cars, and a ministerial house). But this only matters if such 'rewards' are appealing to those concerned (and in some jurisdictions, Norway for example, ministers earn very little more than backbench MPs).

GOVERNMENT FORMATION UNDER MMP

Thus far, New Zealand has had four MMP elections—October 1996, November 1999, July 2002, and September 2005. These elections each generated different results in terms of the size and configuration of the parties in parliament (see table 3.4.1). This in turn contributed to different processes of government formation.

Table 3.4.1: The state of the parties after the 1996, 1999, 2002, and 2005
general elections

Party	*1996*	*1999*	*1999*	*2002*	*2005*
	Final results	*Election night*	*Final results*	*Final results*	*Final results*
ACT	8	9	9	9	2
National	44	41	39	27	48
United (1996, 1999)	1	1	1		
United Future (2002, 2005)				8	3
New Zealand First	17	6	5	13	7
Labour	37	52	49	52	50
Alliance	13	11	10	–	–
Progressive Coalition/ Progressives	–	–	–	2	1
Greens	–	–	7	9	6
Māori party	–	–	–	–	4
Centre-right majority, including New Zealand First (1996)	20				
Centre-left majority (1999, 2002)		6	12	6	
Centre-left majority, including Māori party (2005)					1
Total number of seats	120	120	120	120	121

THE 1996 ELECTION

As already noted, the 1996 election left New Zealand First (with seventeen of 120 seats) holding the balance of power. This enabled the party to determine not only which of the two major parties would hold office, but also whether there would be a coalition or a single-party government. Additionally, it gave New Zealand First—and, in particular, its leader, Winston Peters—substantial influence over the conduct and duration of the inter-party negotiations to form a new government, the nature of the resultant coalition agreement, and the manner of the new government's announcement.

By international standards, the events surrounding the formation of the first MMP government were unusual in a number of respects. To start with, the process was very protracted. The inter-party negotiations commenced on 21 October, nine days after the election, and continued for seven weeks. It was thus two months before the new government was formed. The period of caretaker government (by National and United) was undoubtedly the longest for more than half a century. In other countries with proportional representation it takes an average of three to four weeks to form a government; only rarely does the process extend for as long as two months (Bergman 1993, p. 288). No doubt the novelty of MMP contributed to the lengthy nature of the negotiations, as did the provisions of the Constitution Act. Had the House been required to meet within a month of the election (rather than two months) there would have been strong political pressure for a speedier process.

Second, New Zealand First decided to conduct simultaneous, parallel negotiations with Labour and National, to prepare two separate comprehensive coalition agreements, and to give absolutely no indication of its coalition preferences until the completion of the talks. In effect, the major parties were invited by New Zealand First to enter a tendering process for the right to govern. Obviously, by proceeding in this way New Zealand First hoped to place maximum pressure on both major parties to make policy concessions. Elsewhere in the world a party holding the balance of power will often attempt to play one side off against the other. But it is unusual for two major parties to enter a protracted bidding round during which detailed coalition agreements are drafted and finalised before a particular outcome is reasonably assured.

Third, the provision of assistance to the coalition negotiators from the public service was managed through a highly regulated and restrictive regime, closely supervised by the State Services Commission (SSC) and the other central agencies. Under this regime the resources of government departments were made available, on request and with the approval of the prime minister, to each of the parties involved in the coalition talks (SSC 1996). The caretaker government, therefore, did not enjoy significant advantages over its rivals. However, under the SSC's guidelines, departments were only permitted to provide information and analysis; they were prohibited from tendering advice. Accordingly, while officials could estimate the costs and outline the potential implications of a particular policy proposal, they were supposed to avoid any explicit comment on its merits. Equally importantly, there was no provision for departments to provide detailed oral briefings, and this made the process even more cumbersome and time-consuming.[10] During the coalition talks, the negotiating teams—especially National's team—drew heavily on departmental officials, and numerous costings were undertaken, particularly in areas like education and health (SSC 1997). A significant proportion of this work was performed, as expected, by the Treasury. Additional financial resources were made available by the caretaker government to enable the negotiating parties to employ external (i.e. non-departmental) advisers. Only New Zealand First, however, made use of such funds.

Fourth, by international standards the coalition agreement signed by National and New Zealand First was a lengthy, detailed, legalistic, and inelegant document, combining features of a party manifesto and a budget.[11] An unusual feature was its specification of a medium-term fiscal strategy that included provision for extra public expenditure of $5 billion during the period 1997–2000. Very few coalition agreements elsewhere contain such explicit fiscal commitments.

Finally, National agreed to provide its smaller coalition partner with nine of the twenty-six ministerial positions, together with the most senior economic position in the government (the Treasurer). Further, the coalition agreement stated that New Zealand First's share of ministerial positions would rise to eleven in October 1998, with eight of these being within the cabinet. This would have given a party with only 28 per cent of the MPs in the coalition around 42 per cent of the positions within the executive—a highly disproportionate outcome by international standards. As matters transpired, the coalition collapsed before this arrangement was due to take effect (see Boston, Church & Pearse 2004).

THE 1999 ELECTION

The events immediately following the second MMP election were in marked contrast to those three years earlier. Whereas the first MMP election left neither the centre-right nor the centre-left in command of a parliamentary majority, in 1999 there was an unequivocal centre-left majority. On election night, Labour and the Alliance held 63 seats, thereby giving the centre-left six more seats than New Zealand First and the centre-right bloc (see table 3.4.1). The Greens, having fallen just short of the 5 per cent threshold and having failed to win a constituency seat, appeared unlikely to retain parliamentary representation. However, once special votes had been counted ten days later, the composition of the House was substantially different, with the Greens securing seven seats. While this increased the overall majority enjoyed by the centre-left parties to twelve, it also reduced the number of seats held by Labour and the Alliance from sixty-three to fifty-nine. Hence, Labour and the Alliance moved from having an overall majority on election night to a situation where they needed support from the Greens in order to govern.

But even before the fate of the Greens had been clarified, a new Labour–Alliance coalition had been formed. The remarkable speed with which this occurred took many by surprise. However, there were very good reasons for the rapid pace adopted. First, the two parties had established a good working relationship during the preceding sixteen months and had already given careful consideration to how such a Labour–Alliance government would be constructed (see Bale, Boston & Church 2005). Second, both parties were determined to avoid any repetition of the protracted events surrounding the formation of the National–New Zealand First government. Third, with the close proximity of Christmas, a quick government formation process was essential if the new parliament was to meet before the Christmas–New Year break.

Importantly, the two parties had agreed long before the election that their coalition agreement would be short and procedurally oriented, and would eschew the specificity that had characterised the National–New Zealand First approach. In the event, a coalition deal was negotiated within five days, ratified by the relevant party organisations within a week, and signed barely nine days after the election. The new cabinet was subsequently sworn in on 10 December, within two weeks of the election, and held its first meeting three days later. Meanwhile, parliament was convened on 20 December for the election of the Speaker, with the Speech from the Throne (setting out the government's policy agenda) the following day.

Two features of the 1999 agreement are especially striking, certainly from an international standpoint. The first is its brevity. At less than 500 words, the document ranks as one of the shortest coalition agreements to have been prepared in recent decades (Boston et al. 1999, p. 19). Indeed, it is even shorter than the coalition agreement between National and United in February 1996 (Boston et al. 1999, pp. 315–16).

The second interesting feature is the inclusion of a provision for the parties to differ publicly from time to time on important policy issues:

> Where either party leader considers that a distinctive policy matter raises an issue of importance to the party's political identity, the leader will raise this with the coalition management committee which will resolve an appropriate course of action, including possibly identifying the matter as one of 'party distinction'. In this event there may be public differentiation between the parties in speech and vote which will not be regarded as being in breach of the convention (of collective cabinet responsibility). Such issues are expected to be infrequent and the parties recognise that dealing with them openly and responsibly is critical to the credibility of the coalition. Differentiation on such issues will not detract from the overall acceptance that the two parties are taking joint responsibility for the actions of the government (Coalition Agreement between the Labour and Alliance parties, p. 1).

Of course, it is not uncommon for coalition partners to 'agree to disagree' from time to time. On occasions coalition agreements in other democracies make provision for the parties to dissent publicly on one or two specific issues that are known to be controversial. It is unusual, however, for a coalition agreement to include an explicit provision enabling the parties to differ on matters that have yet to be specified.

It was widely recognised that any decision by the government to invoke this 'agree-to-disagree' provision would carry significant political risks and that these would need to be carefully managed. Moreover, it was readily apparent that Labour would not tolerate a situation in which its coalition partner was constantly seeking to dissociate itself from unpopular government policies. As expected, the agree-to-disagree provision was only employed on a few occasions, the most notable being over the Free Trade Agreement with Singapore, which the Alliance strongly opposed. Nevertheless, the decision to facilitate occasional disagreements through a transparent, orderly, and managed process undoubtedly helped to reduce the amount of public feuding between the parties, and ensured that when conflicts did occur the political damage was less than might otherwise have been the case. Furthermore, the explicit commitment to the convention of collective responsibility meant that when the agree-to-disagree provision was invoked the losing party (i.e. the Alliance) was still bound to uphold the policies of the government and accept responsibility for its performance.

In keeping with coalition arrangements elsewhere, ministerial positions in the new Labour–Alliance government were allocated on a broadly proportional basis, but with the Alliance receiving a slightly greater share than that dictated by its parliamentary representation. Of the twenty positions in the cabinet, sixteen went to Labour and four to the Alliance; and of the six positions in the executive outside the cabinet, Labour received four and the Alliance two (one of these being a parliamentary under-secretaryship). With few exceptions, the key portfolios (including Finance, Education, Health, and Social Services) went to Labour ministers. Against this, the leader of the Alliance, Jim Anderton, became deputy prime minister and was given broad coordinating responsibilities in relation to the government's programme of economic development.

As noted, the Greens were largely excluded from the government formation process (Bale & Dann 2002). This was partly because of the widespread expectation in the days following the election that the party would not secure parliamentary representation, and partly because of the ambivalence that the Greens had expressed during the election campaign about seeking ministerial positions. Additionally, the Alliance, having formed a privileged relationship with Labour, was not keen to involve the Greens in the new government unless absolutely essential. However, once it became evident that the Greens had secured seven seats and thus held the balance of power in the new parliament, it was obvious that some rethinking would be required.

As matters transpired, the Greens chose not to seek places in the new ministry. Instead, the party negotiated a formal support agreement with Labour and the Alliance, though this was never ratified. In accordance with this protocol, the Greens agreed to support the new government on matters of confidence and supply, and to cooperate with the Labour and Alliance parties in good faith to ensure stable and effective government. In return, the coalition partners agreed to consult the Greens on the government's policy intentions and priorities, to provide the party with the opportunity to contribute to policy development, and to give serious consideration to policy proposals advanced by the Greens. In many respects the protocol negotiated between the government and the Greens was similar in substance, if not in form, to the arrangements between support parties and minority administrations in other jurisdictions, such as the agreement between the Social Democratic government and the Centre party in Sweden between mid 1995 and mid 1998 (Boston 1998, pp. 81–4).

THE 2002 ELECTION

The results of the early election, on 27 July 2002, bore a close resemblance to those of late 1999. For one thing, it was evident on election night that the parties of the centre-left—i.e. Labour, the Greens, and the Progressive Coalition (formed by Jim

Anderton just prior to election following deep divisions within the Alliance)—would continue to enjoy a solid majority in parliament (albeit reduced from twelve to six seats). Accordingly, there was no question of a change of government. For another, Labour again achieved the status of being the largest party, increasing its share of the party vote and obtaining close to double the number of seats of National (the biggest centre-right party). More significantly, the election results gave Labour, as in 1999, a very strong bargaining position: not merely was it strategically placed as the party representing the 'median voter' on the dominant socio-economic dimension, but it was also the 'pivotal' party in the legislature, in the sense that it was a necessary member of all the potential ideologically connected minimum winning coalitions. It was inevitable, therefore, that Labour would lead and dominate the next government.

At the same time, there were at least three significant differences from the election results in 1999. First, the new Progressive Coalition party, with just two seats, was in a much weaker bargaining position than the Alliance had been in almost three years earlier. Second, Labour and its former support party, the Greens, were deeply divided over the controversial issue of genetic modification. In May 2002, the Greens had declared that they would not give support on confidence and supply to any government, whether of the centre-left or centre-right, that lifted the moratorium on the commercial release of genetically modified organisms. Labour, by contrast, was committed to lifting the moratorium, and was not prepared to revise its policy stance. Third, partly as a result of the dispute between the two former allies, there was a substantial surge in support for the fledgling centrist-cum-Christian party, United Future, during the final weeks of the election campaign. Having had only one MP, Peter Dunne, for nearly six years, United Future secured almost as many votes as the Greens, and won eight seats. In strategic terms, this proved to be highly significant since it gave Labour the option of building a legislative coalition across the middle of the political spectrum and meant that it would no longer be largely dependent upon the Greens.

Formal inter-party negotiations to form a new government commenced within days of the election and were completed within a month. The Labour leader, Helen Clark, had stated repeatedly during the election campaign that her preference was to form a coalition with Jim Anderton's new party, assuming that it secured parliamentary representation. She had also made it plain that, if Labour and the Progressive Coalition lacked an overall majority, she would prefer to establish a minority government (as in 1999) rather than attempt to form a three-party majority government. The leaders of the other parties involved in the negotiations largely shared her preferences. Anderton, for his part, was keen to remain in the cabinet, but had little desire to have another small party represented within the government. Mindful of the costs of incumbency and aware of the inexperience of his new team, Dunne believed that United Future would be better to seek a legislative, rather than an executive, coalition with Labour. Meanwhile, the Greens were disappointed by their failure to secure a large increase in their share of the party vote and were unwilling to compromise on the issue of genetic modification.

Accordingly, there was little prospect of them agreeing to another support arrangement with Labour. Against this, the Greens doubted the long-term wisdom of adopting a largely oppositional stance. It was thus decided that the party should seek an arrangement with the government under which there would be cooperation on areas of mutual interest. This was welcomed by Labour—which had no desire to be too heavily dependent on the conservative-oriented MPs of United Future.

In the event, three separate agreements—a coalition agreement, a support agreement, and a cooperation agreement—were signed during August 2002. The coalition agreement between Labour and the Progressives was ratified on 8 August. Modelled on the agreement in December 1999, it was succinct (barely 430 words) and largely process-oriented. As in 1999, there was provision for the two parties to take different positions in public and in parliament. A separate support agreement was signed shortly afterwards. Under this deal, which had many parallels with the previous unsigned agreement with the Greens, United Future offered to support the government on issues of confidence and supply. In return, the government agreed to give priority to a number of policies to which United Future was strongly committed, including the establishment of a Commission for the Family. The agreement also provided for detailed consultations with United Future over the government's legislative programme and priorities, major policy initiatives, and budgetary parameters. Less than two weeks later, on 26 August (the day before the formal state opening of parliament), the government signed a cooperation agreement with the co-leaders of the Green party, Jeanette Fitzsimons and Rod Donald. This had much in common with the support agreement, except that it included no commitment from the Greens to vote with the government on issues of confidence and supply.

THE 2005 ELECTION

The fourth MMP election, held on 17 September 2005, generated a complicated political environment for government formation. Once special votes had been counted Labour enjoyed a two-seat lead over National (fifty to forty-eight). With the Greens having won six seats (a loss of three) and the Progressives only one (half their previous number), the centre-left could confidently rely on fifty-seven votes in the 121-seat parliament, four short of an absolute majority. (There was an 'overhang' of one seat as a result of the Māori party winning four electorate seats yet being entitled to only three on the basis of its 2.1 per cent share of the party vote.)

On the other side of the House, the two unequivocally centre-right parties—National and ACT—had fifty seats. Of the two broadly centrist parties, New Zealand First won seven seats (a loss of six) and United Future three (a loss of five). Potentially, therefore, the parties of the centre-right commanded sixty seats.

Complicating matters were the following considerations. First, the position of the Māori party was uncertain. During the election campaign the party leadership had more-or-less promised not to support a National-led government, partly because of fundamental policy disagreements over the status of the Treaty of Waitangi and the future of the separate Māori seats (which National had promised to abolish, but which the Māori party had pledged to entrench). Equally, it was plain that the overwhelming majority of those voting for the Māori party wanted a Labour-led government. Against this, there was considerable bad blood between Tariana Turia, the co-leader of the Māori party, and the Labour leader, Helen Clark. To compound matters, Labour was unwilling to contemplate any significant changes to the controversial Foreshore and Seabed Act 2004—which had prompted Turia's departure from Labour—and preferred not to rely on the Māori party for support on votes of confidence and supply. In these circumstances, Clark and her colleagues had little choice but to seek support from New Zealand First and United Future.

Second, Winston Peters had pledged during the election campaign that New Zealand First would support, at least in the first instance, the party that gained the most seats. This meant, in effect, that the party was morally obliged to assist Labour to form a government, if this were at all possible. Additionally, the party had committed itself to remaining on the cross-benches rather than being part of an executive coalition. On the other hand, the leadership of the party was closer in ideological terms to the moderate wing of National than to the parties of the centre-left.

Labour, for its part, was mindful of its experience of negotiating with Winston Peters in 1996, not to mention the subsequent collapse of the National–New Zealand First coalition. Accordingly, it had little desire to rely solely on New Zealand First for support. But its options were very limited. United Future, with only three seats, could not give the centre-left an absolute parliamentary majority, but only a relative majority (which, to achieve, required either the Māori party or New Zealand First to abstain on votes of confidence and supply). Further, United Future seemed predisposed to a deal with National and had declared that it would not support a government that included the Greens. Yet the potential for a stable National-led government was limited given the fundamental policy differences between the five parties whose support, active or tacit, would be required.

In the event, on 17 October, some four weeks after the election, Helen Clark announced the formation of a four-party centre-left government, embracing Labour, the Progressives, New Zealand First, and United Future. For the first time since 1998 the new government had an absolute parliamentary majority, with sixty-one votes against a potential (but highly unlikely) combined opposition of sixty. There were four unusual features of the new governing arrangements.

First, the new coalition initially presented itself as a two-party government, with a coalition agreement between Labour and the Progressives, support agreements with New

Zealand First and United Future, and a cooperation agreement with the Greens (under which it agreed, in return for policy concessions, not to vote against the government on confidence and supply). Yet both New Zealand First and United Future secured places within the executive (although outside the cabinet)—with Winston Peters as Foreign Minister and Peter Dunne as Revenue Minister. The suggestion that these two parties were not part of the 'coalition government' was designed to circumvent Peters' pre-election commitment not to enter a 'coalition'. But such a proposition is difficult to reconcile with the international literature on coalitions. A potentially better way of interpreting the new governing arrangements is to regard them as a two-tier coalition, with an inner coalition (comprising Labour and Progressive) and an outer coalition (comprising New Zealand First and United Future).

Second, under normal coalition arrangements New Zealand First, with more than twice the seats of United Future, would have received at least two places in the executive. No less surprising was the fact that the prestigious portfolio of Foreign Affairs should have been given to a minister outside the cabinet. It is rather doubtful that Peters will claim that he is not part of the 'coalition government' when dealing with his overseas counterparts!

Third, the support agreements with New Zealand First and United Future appear to extend the application of the 'agree-to-disagree' provisions, thereby altering the application of the doctrine of collective responsibility. It is unclear at this juncture how the new provisions will be applied in practice. Fundamentally, however, the capacity to facilitate party distinctions within coalitions is limited by a range of political pressures and considerations. For such reasons, 'loose' coalition discipline is relatively rare in other multi-party systems.

Finally, the cooperation agreement between the government and the Greens (which was in some respects the most comprehensive of the four agreements) included a provision under which Green MPs will be designated spokespersons for the government in specific policy areas. In these areas the MPs in question will have direct access to government officials, be able to request reports from officials and be able to attend the relevant cabinet committee dealing with the designated policy areas.

Collectively, these developments represent an undoubted evolution in the application of New Zealand's constitutional conventions and governing arrangements (White 2005). It will be interesting, to say the least, to observe how they work in practice.

CONCLUSION

Government formation is influenced by two major considerations: the institutional context and the political context. The introduction of MMP in New Zealand has left the rules and conventions surrounding the process of forming a government largely unchanged, but it has significantly altered the political environment. Most importantly, it has brought an end to the long era of single-party majority government. This means that the formation of new governments (whether after an election or between elections) requires negotiations between two or more parties.

As outlined in this chapter, the rules within which these negotiations occur in New Zealand are flexible and permissive, certainly by international standards. This relative lack of constraints poses no major difficulties when there is a largely unidimensional, two-bloc party system (as in 1999), or when a responsible centrist party is willing to act as a support party in a context where the ideological bloc that holds the majority of the seats is deeply divided on a matter of high political salience (as in 2002). But when the parliamentary position is more ambiguous, as in 1996 and 2005, the flexibility provided by current constitutional provisions may exacerbate the degree of political uncertainty, making the process of government formation more protracted.

Accordingly, there may be merit in reviewing the existing constitutional framework and considering a number of possible modifications, including:[12]

- a change to the Constitution Act requiring parliament to meet within thirty days of an election
- a requirement for parliament to endorse a candidate for prime minister before a new government can be sworn in
- changes to the rules surrounding votes of confidence (such as the introduction of 'constructive' votes of confidence)
- provision for the appointment of an informateur under certain circumstances to oversee the process of inter-party bargaining.

Changes of this nature will not, of course, prevent small parties like New Zealand First from exploiting their bargaining power, when and if they enjoy a pivotal position within the legislature. But these changes could serve to strengthen the role of parliament in the government formation process, and to enhance governmental durability.

DISCUSSION QUESTIONS

1. What lessons can be learnt from New Zealand's first four experiences of coalition negotiations under MMP?
2. Why did New Zealand First choose to form a government with National in 1996 rather than with Labour, and why did it choose to support Labour in 2005?
3. Why did the National–New Zealand First coalition collapse?
4. Assess the risks, benefits, and costs for Labour of deciding to go into government with the Alliance in 1999.
5. Assess the risks, benefits, and costs for the Alliance of deciding to go into government with Labour.

6 What is the difference between a coalition agreement and a support agreement?

7 What are the differences in policy influence between a small party that enters office as part of a minority coalition government, and a small party that acts as a support party for a minority coalition government?

8 Do small centre parties enjoy a disproportionate amount of political power under MMP?

NOTES

1 There is an extensive theoretical and empirical literature on government formation, particularly the formation of coalition governments. See, for instance, Bogdanor (1983); Boston (1998, pp. 20–61); Budge & Keman (1990); Laver & Schofield (1990); Laver & Shepsle (1994; 1996); Muller & Strom (1997); and Strom (1990).

2 For varying accounts of political, constitutional, and policy context surrounding the process of government formation in 1996, 1999, 2002, and 2005, see Bale, Boston & Church (2005); Boston (2000, pp. 239–75); Boston (2005); Boston & Church (2003); Boston & McLeay (1997, pp. 207–46); Brechtel & Kaiser (1999, pp. 3–26); McLeay (1997, pp. 23–34); Miller (1998, pp. 120–34); and Miller (2002, pp. 114–29).

3 For analyses of the influence of constitutional rules and conventions on the government formation process see Bergman (1993, 1995); Strom et al. (1994, pp. 303–35); and De Winter (1995).

4 A 'formateur' is usually a party leader who is called upon by the head of state to attempt to form a government. An 'informateur', by contrast, is typically a senior politician (such as the Speaker of Parliament) who is given the task (by the head of state or under the constitution) to consult with the party leaders and identify the person who is most likely to command the support of the legislature (i.e. the formateur).

5 In countries with positive resignation rules (e.g. France, Germany, Greece, Portugal, Spain, and Sweden) some 8.4 per cent of governments between 1945 and 1990 were defeated due to a lack of parliamentary support, whereas in countries with negative resignation rules (e.g. Austria, Britain, Denmark, Finland, Ireland, Italy, and Norway) the figure was 18.2 per cent.

6 For an analysis of the constitutional principles relating to the role of the Governor-General in government formation and termination, see Boston et al. (1996, pp. 105–10); Ladley (1997, pp. 51–61); Hardie Boys (1998a, 1998b, 1999); Joseph (2001, pp. 666–78); and State Services Commission (1995, pp. 87–99).

7 This meant that following the 1996 election Parliament was required to meet by 1 December; after the 1999 election it was required to meet by 28 January 2000.

8 For a somewhat different view see Nagel (1999a, pp. 27–31).

9 See also Laver & Shepsle (1996).

10 The rules were reviewed prior to the 1999 election, with provision being made for departments to provide oral briefings during the 'preferred partner' stage of the negotiations.

11 See Boston et al. (1999, pp. 316–37). For a review of the nature of coalition agreements in other countries see Strom & Muller (1998).

12 For a fuller exploration of this matter see Boston (1998, pp. 94–122).

REFERENCES

Bale, T, J. Boston, & S. Church 2005, 'Natural Because it Had Become Just That'. Path Dependence in Pre-electoral Pacts and Government Formation: A New Zealand Case Study', *Australian Journal of Political Science*, vol. 40, no. 4.

Bale, T. & C. Dann 2002, 'Is the Grass Really Greener? The Rational and Reality of Support Party Status: A New Zealand Case Study', *Party Politics*, no. 8, pp. 349–65.

Bergman, T. 1995, *Constitutional Rules and Party Goals in Coalition Formation: An Analysis of Winning Minority Governments in Sweden*, Umea University, Umea.

Bergman, T. 1993, 'Constitutional Design and Government Formation: the Expected Consequences of Negative Parliamentarism', *Scandinavian Political Studies*, vol. 16, no. 4, pp. 285–304.

Bogdanor, V. (ed.) 1983, *Coalition Government in Western Europe*, Heinemann, London.

Boston, J. 2005, 'Hard Sums', *The Dominion Post*, 20 September, B5.

Boston, J. 2000, 'Forming the Coalition between Labour and the Alliance', in J. Boston, S. Church, S. Levine, E. McLeay & N.S. Roberts (eds), *Left Turn: The New Zealand Election of 1999*, Victoria University Press, Wellington.

Boston, J. 1998, *Governing Under Proportional Representation: Lessons from Europe*, Institute of Policy Studies, Wellington.

Boston, J., S. Church & H. Pearse 2004, 'Explaining the Demise of the National-New Zealand First Coalition', *Australian Journal of Political Science*, vol. 39, no. 3, pp. 585–603.

Boston, J. & S. Church 2003, 'Government Formation after the 2002 General Election', in J. Boston, S. Church, S. Levine, E. McLeay & N.S. Roberts (eds), *The New Zealand General Election of 2002*, Victoria University Press, Wellington.

Boston, J., S. Levine, E. McLeay & N.S. Roberts (eds) *1999, Electoral and Constitutional Change in New Zealand: A Source Book*, Dunmore Press, Palmerston North.

Boston, J., S. Levine, E. McLeay & N.S. Roberts 1996, *New Zealand Under MMP: A New Politics?*, Auckland University Press with Bridget Williams Books, Auckland.

Boston, J. & E. McLeay 1997, 'Forming the First MMP Government: Theory, Practice and Prospects', in J. Boston, S. Levine, E. McLeay & N. Roberts (eds), *From Campaign to Coalition: The 1996 MMP Election*, Dunmore Press, Palmerston North, pp. 207–46.

Brechtel, T. & A. Kaiser 1999, 'Party System and Government Formation in Post-reform New Zealand', *Political Science*, no. 51, pp. 3–26.

Budge, I. & H. Keman 1990, *Parties and Democracy: Coalition Formation and Government Functioning in Twenty States*, Oxford University Press, Oxford.

De Winter, L. 1995, 'The Role of Parliament in Government Formation and Resignation', in H. Doring (ed.), *Parliament and Majority Rule in Western Europe*, St Martin's Press, New York.

Hardie Boys, Sir M. 1999, 'The Constitutional Challenges of MMP: A Magical Demystification Tour', in *Governing Under MMP: The Constitutional and Policy Challenges*, Institute of Policy Studies, Victoria University of Wellington, IPS Policy Paper, no. 1, pp. 27–31.

Hardie Boys, Sir Michael 1998a, 'The Role of the Governor-General under MMP', in A. Simpson (ed.), *The Constitutional Implications of MMP*, School of Political Science and International Relations, Victoria University of Wellington, Occasional Publication No. 9, pp. 63–77.

Hardie Boys, Sir M. 1998b, 'Continuity and Change: The 1996 General Election and the Role of the Governor-General', in A. Simpson (ed.), *The Constitutional Implications of MMP*, School of Political Science and International Relations, Victoria University of Wellington, Occasional Publication No. 9, pp. 78–95.

Joseph, P. 2001, *Constitutional and Administrative Law in New Zealand*, 2nd edn, Brookers, Wellington.

Ladley, A. 1997, 'The Head of State: The Crown, the Queen and the Governor-General', in R. Miller (edn), *New Zealand Politics in Transition*, Oxford University Press, Auckland, pp. 51–61.

Laver, M. & N. Schofield 1990, *Multiparty Government: The Politics of Coalition in Europe*, Oxford University Press, Oxford.

Laver, M. & K. Shepsle 1996, *Making and Breaking Governments: Cabinets and Legislatures in Parliamentary Democracies*, Cambridge University Press, New York.

McLeay, E. 1997, 'Forming a Government', *Legislative Studies*, no. 11, pp. 23–34.

Miller, R. 2002, 'Coalition Government: The Labour–Alliance Pact', in J. Vowles, P. Aimer, J. Karp, S. Banducci, R. Miller & A. Sullivan, *Proportional Representation on Trial: The 1999 New Zealand General Election and the Fate of MMP*, Auckland University Press, Auckland.

Miller, R. 1998, 'Coalition Government: The People's Choice', in J. Vowles, P. Aimer, S. Banducci & J. Karp (eds), *Voters' Victory? New Zealand's First Election Under Proportional Representation*, Auckland University Press, Auckland, pp. 120–34.

Muller, W. & K. Strom (eds) 1997, *Koalitionsreierungen in Westeuropa: Bildung, Arbeitweise und Beendigung*, Signum Verlag, Wien.

Nagel, J. 1999a, 'Assessing the Dimensionality of Politics: A Comment on Brechtel and Kaiser', *Political Science*, no. 51, pp. 27–31.

Nagel, J. 1999b, 'The Defects of Its Virtues: New Zealand's Experience with MMP', in H. Milner (ed.), *Is it Time to Change Canada's Electoral System?*, Broadview Press, Peterborough, Ontario.

Shaffer, W. 1998, *Politics, Parties and Parliament: Political Change in Norway*, Ohio State University Press, Columbus.

SSC. See State Services Commission.

State Services Commission 1995, *Working under Proportional Representation: A Reference for the Public Service*, Wellington.

State Services Commission 1996, *Negotiations between Political Parties to Form a Government: Guidelines on Support from the Public Service*, Wellington, 21 October.

State Services Commission 1997, *Information Supplied by the Public Service in Response to Requests Made by Political Parties Taking Part in Coalition Formation Talks*, Wellington, 5 February.

Strom, K. 1990, *Minority Government and Majority Rule*, Cambridge University Press, Cambridge.

Strom, K., I. Budge & M. Laver 1994, 'Constraints on Cabinet Formation in Parliamentary Democracies', *American Journal of Political Science*, no. 38, pp. 303–35.

Strom, K. & W. Muller 1998, 'Coalition Government in Parliamentary Democracies', paper prepared for the International Conference on Opportunities and Dilemmas of Parliamentary Leadership, Ljubljana, Slovenia, 6–9 July.

White, N. 2005, 'Deconstructing Cabinet Collective Responsibility', *Policy Quarterly*, vol. 1, no. 4, pp. 4–11.

FURTHER READING

Boston, J. 1998, *Governing under Proportional Representation: Lessons from Europe*, Institute of Policy Studies, Wellington.

Laver, M. & K. Shepsle (eds) 1994, *Cabinet Ministers and Parliamentary Government*, Cambridge University Press, New York.

Laver, M. & K. Shepsle 1996, *Making and Breaking Governments: Cabinets and Legislatures in Parliamentary Democracies*, Cambridge University Press, New York.

Consultants and Advisers

Richard Shaw

Abraham Lincoln once commented, 'My policy is to have no policy' (Heywood 2002, p. 399). Perhaps the American president was simply keeping his options open, but it is difficult to imagine any politician openly admitting to that stance today, given the critical contribution made by the political executive to the design and implementation of public policy. This chapter explores some of the different sources from which government ministers obtain policy advice. It focuses on the provision of advice by officials in the public service, by private consultants, and by political advisers in ministers' offices. The chapter begins with a brief discussion on the nature and importance of policy advice. There follows an exploration of two different ways of explaining the relationship between ministers and their advisers, and an assessment of the manner in which one of those frameworks has influenced the direction of public sector reform. Finally, some of the ramifications of the public sector and electoral reform processes for the provision of advice to ministers are teased out, particularly in relation to the use of contracts, consultants, and political appointments in ministers' offices.

POLICY AND POLICY ADVICE

In its simplest form, 'policy' is what governments do (and, sometimes, what they do not do): the decisions they take, the money they spend, and the services they fund and/or provide. For most people, the delivery of goods and services is the most visible manifestation of the policy process. However, the study of public policy is as much concerned with the 'how' of policy-making, as it is with the 'what' of policy delivery. In this respect, policy is often thought of as a process comprising of a series of interrelated stages. Typically, the policy cycle includes:

- identification of policy issues that require government attention
- consideration of a range of policy options
- decisions about the course of action to be followed (if any)
- design of a policy programme
- implementation of that programme
- evaluation of the impact of policy delivery.

While thinking about policy in this way helps us make sense of what is, in reality, a messy, bustling policy environment, there are a few pitfalls to be avoided when using the policy cycle. For one thing, although the model implies that policy is something that develops in a neat, linear manner from inception to implementation, in fact, the material world is not like that. The policy process is an inherently untidy, unpredictable business: people and ideas come and go, and stages in the cycle are reversed, rushed through or missed completely. In short, at heart policy-making is an intensely political (rather than purely rational) process.

That said, one of the advantages of approaching policy as a process is that it alerts us to the importance of thinking through what is to be done. The term 'policy advice' describes the information and knowledge that the political executive requires to inform the decisions it takes at each stage of this cycle. Policy advice is, in a sense, the oil that lubricates the wheels of the machinery of government, as public policy is developed, implemented, and evaluated. Good advice can be vital to the success of public policy. As one commentator has suggested, ministers may only be 'as good as the advice [they] get' (Hawke 1993, p. 1).

Ministers get that policy advice from a variety of sources: officials from government departments; consultants; political advisers; interest groups; independent think tanks; and individual experts. The matter of precisely where, and from whom, cabinet obtains its advice is an important one. Policy advice is not value-free. It tends to say something about 'which values matter [to the adviser] and how they should be ranked' (Boston et al. 1998, p. 71), and may also reflect the priorities of the institutions within which those advisers work. Moreover, policy problems are invariably complex, and so advisers need intellectual 'maps' to assist them to sift, organise, and interpret the myriad data required to act upon a given policy issue (Shaw 1999a, p. 47). These 'policy frames' need not favour the position of one particular political party over another, but they will inevitably accommodate certain policy options and exclude others.

MODELS OF BUREAUCRACY

The public policy literature contains a number of different models that explain the relationships between government ministers and their officials. One of the most influential of these is the 'Westminster model', which regards public servants as value-free technicians, appointed on merit, and who are responsible for advising on and implementing the policies of the government of the day. The 'public choice' model, on the other hand, is rather suspicious of the motives of officials, and argues that their engagement with the policy process is largely motivated by self-interest.

1. The Westminster model

In political systems that derive from Westminster, as the New Zealand system does, ministers have traditionally sourced the bulk of their policy advice from bureaucrats working in the professional public service. In classical economic terms, government officials have exercised a near-monopoly over the provision of advice. The Westminster model imposes certain obligations and responsibilities on officials. The essence of these is that '[p]ublic servants serve the government of the day in the formulation and implementation of its policies; but they do not serve the interests of the political parties that comprise that government. The non-partisan nature of the public service is important because it reinforces continuity between governments, aversion to patronage, and the provision of free, frank and fearless advice' (SSC 1995, p. vii).

In the traditional model a public servant's principal constitutional obligation is to the Crown, rather than to the members of the political party or parties that hold office. It therefore anticipates that government officials will take a dispassionate stance when providing advice to their ministers. Advice should be 'comprehensive and balanced, should reflect the adviser's best judgement of the data, and should be independent of (but not ignorant of) the minister's known preferences' (SSC 1995, p. 26). This suggests that public servants must speak truth to power: that is, they have a duty to tell ministers what they need to hear, rather than what they would like to hear. That distinction is a vital one. In practical terms, the duty of officials to tender 'free, frank, and fearless' advice provides some assurance that governments will be given advice that reflects the best professional assessment of an impartial public service, rather than that which simply reflects political expediencies. From time to time this may require officials to advise a minister against proceeding with a particular policy, should their professional assessment be that the implementation of that initiative would have negative policy consequences.

2. The public-choice model

In the Westminster tradition officials are presumed to be non-partisan servants of the Crown. In recent years, however, an altogether different model has come to dominate thinking about the role and motivations of the public service (and, for that matter, of politicians and voters more generally). The public-choice (or rational-choice) model has its roots in economic analyses of decision-making in representative democracies. It applies economic methodology to the study of politics, and is built upon the neoclassical notion that self-interest drives all human behaviour.

When applied to the bureaucracy, public choice predicts that officials will tender advice to ministers that is designed to maximise their personal pecuniary interests, and to advance those of the agencies in which they are employed. Public servants are thought to be particularly motivated to maximise departmental budgets. Because the utility of officials is assumed to be related to the overall level of their agencies' budgets, public-choice theorists contend that rational, opportunistic bureaucrats will provide advice that supports increases in departmental budgets: the greater a department's budget, the greater the benefit that flows down to individual officials (in the form of salary increases, improved conditions of employment, opportunities for promotion, and so on).

To this end, it is assumed that bureaucrats will try to 'capture' the policy process by furnishing advice that is tailored to their particular department's interests. Policy capture is considered a particular risk in agencies in which officials are 'responsible [both] for policy advice concerning their sectoral responsibilities [and] for the implementation of policy decisions' (Treasury 1987, p. 75). Public choice also presumes that officials will promote advice that favours the public provision of goods and services rather than the delivery of services through private or voluntary sector agencies. Greater service provision through public agencies is likely to require larger operational budgets for departments. In turn, those budget increments will generate more employment and promotion opportunities for officials, and increase the influence wielded by departmental officials over both the development and implementation of public policy.

POLICY ADVICE IN A REFORMED ENVIRONMENT

Notwithstanding its various empirical and theoretical shortcomings, public choice has been immensely influential in shaping the direction of public sector reform in New Zealand.[1] Those reforms, which are dealt with in detail elsewhere in this volume, have fundamentally altered the institutional environment in which the political executive seeks policy advice.[2]

1. Westminster meets contractualism

One of the features of the reformed relationship between ministers and officials is the extent to which it is regulated by contracts, or contract-like documents. This reflects the public-choice suspicion that officials have a tendency to substitute their own interests for those of ministers. Typically, the purpose of the various contracts within the executive branch is to ensure that officials' actions are closely aligned with ministers' preferences.

For instance, ministers formally purchase policy advice (and other outputs) from departments. Ministers' purchase requirements are contained in an annual output plan entered into with one department or more, and responsibility for delivering the outputs specified in that quasi-contract rests with the relevant department's chief executive. Since 2003, each department has also produced a Statement of Intent (SOI). The SOI, which is negotiated as part of the Budget process, sets out what a department is trying to achieve over the medium term, how it will go about doing so, and the policy logic behind its proposed actions. Ministers play a role in the framing of SOIs, so that departments' activities reflect ministers' priorities and are linked with the government's policy objectives.

These arrangements have been beneficial in several respects. Ministers are able to specify more clearly the policy requirements they have of officials (although it is still considered improper for a minister to direct officials to provide advice that is tailored to the minister's personal preferences), and to quantify the public resource that departments will receive for generating that advice. The framework has also facilitated ministers' ability to seek policy advice from outside the public service. Governments have never been formally constrained to source advice from officials, but the reforms have arguably increased the contestability of the policy process by granting ministers greater latitude to purchase advice from non-departmental sources, or, indeed, from departments other than those for which they have primary political responsibility.

However, the model also possesses certain flaws. For instance, it has proved remarkably difficult to estimate accurate prices for policy advice. The risk for departments is that ministers purchase advice from them at prices that are lower than the costs incurred in producing that advice. Over the long term, such under-funding can have serious consequences for the ability of departments to provide advice to the standards demanded by government.

The advent of time-limited employment contracts for senior public servants has also rattled the Westminster cage. The chief executives of the departments are formally employed by the State Services Commissioner, rather than by ministers, but critics of the reforms have argued that the demise of the permanent departmental head has amplified the risk that officials will curry favour with politicians by tailoring advice to ministers' partisan preferences. There is little evidence to suggest that the convention of public service impartiality has been seriously eroded in the new environment, but the concern that short-term contracts constrain the advice tendered to ministers remains. As one former senior public servant has noted: '[H]uman nature suggests that the freedom and frankness of advice from someone at the outset of a 5-year term may be greater than that from someone who hopes to renew an expiring contract' (Hensley 1995, p. 22).

2. Policy coherency and coordination

The large-scale restructuring of government departments during the late 1980s and throughout the 1990s, and in particular the preference for separate policy and delivery organisations, had its roots in advice provided to the fourth Labour government by Treasury officials, who argued in their 1987 post-election briefing papers, 'Government Management' (Treasury 1987), that '[i]t is hard to escape the conclusion that advice on [government intervention] from an agency which is involved in public provision is likely to be biased in favour of that existing provision. More generally, it would appear that an agency whose existence is inextricably linked to the continuation of existing policy is likely to be biased in favour of existing policy' (Treasury 1987, p. 75).

There is a clear link between these public-choice sentiments and the solution proposed by Treasury to the alleged incidence of capture. In essence, the decoupling of policy and implementation was intended to increase organisational focus, and, importantly, to minimise the risk of provider capture. Advisers based in a policy agency that has few or no implementation responsibilities are less inclined, the analysis suggests, to generate policy that uncritically endorses the delivery activities of another department, and much more likely to consider the merits of provision by non-departmental providers.

On that basis, successive administrations between 1987–99 set about pulling apart departments which combined policy and operations, and setting up (often smaller) organisations with fewer responsibilities to attend to. As with output plans and SOIs, there are some advantages to organising the machinery of government in this way. Single- or dual-function departments often have a sharper focus; they can be held to account for a more clearly defined range of services; and there may be greater incentives (particularly in policy 'shops') to consider the merits of a wider range of service providers.

Equally, however, the wholesale restructuring of the sector created problems. For instance, in some areas it became more difficult to coordinate policy and operational activities, and in particular to ensure that policy advice accurately reflected the realities of service delivery on the ground.

The fragmentation of the public service has also made it harder to ensure that the advice received by ministers is coordinated across different policy domains. The business of coordinating policy is, by its very nature, a testing one, given that 'there are few, if any, major policy issues that do not overlap several sets of Ministerial and departmental interests. This, together with the fact that modern governments tend to set very extensive and ambitious reform agendas, generates a mass of concurrent policy development activity that can be extraordinarily difficult to sequence, prioritise, and co-ordinate' (SSC 1999, p. 15).

Those challenges have been magnified by the creation of a great many new government agencies in the post-reform period. This has contributed to difficulties in ensuring that the advice governments receive (and the policies implemented on the basis of that advice) is consistent and coherent across policy portfolios (Boston et al. 1996). For instance, the current Minister of Social Development and Employment is responsible for the Ministry of Social Development MSD. Among other services

MSD administers welfare benefits and delivers employment-related programmes, both of which used to be the responsibility of the former Department of Work and Income (which merged with the Ministry of Social Policy in October 2001 to form MSD). It also provides the minister with policy advice on those activities, and on social policy more generally. But the minister also obtains advice on employment matters from the Department of Labour. The potential for cross-cutting and potentially contradictory advice is clear.

Part of the problem is that the reforms have contributed to a preoccupation within the various departments with their own concerns, sometimes to the exclusion of a sense of common purpose across the public service. John Martin (1991) has described the process as 'departmentalism', which he compares unfavourably with the greater unity of purpose and interdepartmental cooperation that arguably characterised the pre-reform public service.

Labour-led governments formed since the 1999 election have begun to address these and other issues. First, the Capability, Accountability and Performance project has encouraged collaboration across public agencies, so as to ensure that the activities of government departments are consistent with the government's policy objectives, and to improve the quality and usefulness of the information that departments produce. Second, as discussed in the chapter on the public service, in 2001 there was a comprehensive review of the public sector, conducted by the State Services Commission. The report of the Review of the Centre (see www.ssc.govt.nz) identified several issues requiring attention, including fragmentation within, and variable standards of service delivery across, the sector. Among the solutions proposed by the Review, and which have since been implemented, were greater networking between departments, and the use of inter-departmental teams of officials to address entrenched (or 'wicked') policy problems.

ELECTORAL REFORM AND THE POLICY ENVIRONMENT

Along with those made in the public sector, the reforms of the electoral system implemented in the early 1990s have also had a marked impact on the policy process. One of the characteristics of multi-party and/or minority governments is their tendency to look to a wider range of sources of policy advice than was typical under the old electoral arrangements. Thus, a government comprising two (or possibly more) parties will bring multiple points of view to the policy process: not only the respective parties in government, but also the constellation of interest groups and stakeholders which hover around those parties will seek to contribute their particular views on the ways things should be done. As a consequence, the policy process becomes more open, and it is that much harder for one party, and an associated set of interests, to drive the policy agenda.

Coalition and minority governments pose particular challenges to the permanent public service. Most obviously, public servants have had to master the art of advising governments made up of more than one political party. In practice, this has meant ensuring that official advice to the ministers of one party is also made available to members of that party's coalition partner.

The demands associated with that new dynamic are increased when governments give their support parties regular access to officials (as the Labour–Alliance coalition did for the Greens, and the Labour–Progressive coalition did for United Future). That requires more extensive communication between coalition partners, between governing and non-governing parties, and among officials. Much of the responsibility for the coordination of this activity has fallen to the central agencies, and in particular to the Department of the Prime Minister and Cabinet. In the view of a former senior official of that department, officials have been relatively successful at keeping the lines of advice and communication within multi-party governments open, largely through the establishment of 'good processes, and good relationships, and [by] maintaining access to each other'.[3]

Prior to the adoption of MMP there were particular concerns that the neutrality of officials might be compromised during the process of coalition formation. Constitutional convention stipulates that officials continue to serve the government of the day during periods of caretaker government. However, the public service must also safeguard its ability to work with future governments. When more than one party is involved in the formation of a government, this ability could be put at risk should caretaker ministers request advice from officials that is subsequently used for partisan purposes during coalition negotiations. During the protracted coalition discussions in 1996, an elaborate series of arrangements administered by the State Services Commissioner insulated officials from this threat. A central committee of very senior public servants was inserted between the negotiating parties and the officials, and the manner in which that committee managed politicians' requests for information, and officials' responses to those requests, was generally felt to have successfully protected the public service against claims of impropriety (Shaw 1999a, p. 42).[4] As a result, the arrangements have applied after each subsequent election (although, given that in each instance the process has been more straightforward than in 1996, they have not been much used).

CONTESTABILITY IN THE 'MARKET' FOR POLICY

Along with other developments, the combined effect of the processes of state sector and electoral reform has been to open up the policy 'market'. Where once public servants provided virtually all of the advice put before ministers, these days they compete for the minister's ear with a scrum of other policy actors. Two of these, in particular, merit closer attention, not least because their activities raise fundamental questions regarding the continued application of core Westminster conventions in Wellington.

1. Consultants

In the post-reform era there has been an increasing tendency for ministers to source policy advice from private sector consultants. Departments, too, have made liberal use of consultants, usually on the grounds that they undertake one-off projects for which there is no need to retain permanent staff, or because the agency lacks personnel with the skills required to execute particular tasks efficiently. Consultants are used for a wide range of purposes, including the recruitment of staff, public relations, the preparation of departmental submissions to select committees, and reviews of internal operations.

At different times over the last fifteen or so years, the practice of going beyond the departments and using external consultants has been a contentious one. This has not necessarily been because the quality of consultants' advice has been found wanting; indeed, a large part of the case for using consultants is that they contribute an alternative point of view to that which departments can furnish. Rather, it has been the cost to taxpayers that has been, at various times, a matter of considerable public interest. Precise data are difficult to come by, not least because such information is frequently withheld by agencies on the grounds of 'commercial sensitivity'. As far back as 1992–93, it was estimated that departments spent in the vicinity of $48.5 million on external advice (Morris 1994, p. 5, cited in Boston et al. 1996, p. 126). Only three years later, however, research undertaken for the Treasury (by consultants Deloitte Touche Tohmatsu!) calculated that approximately $700 million had been spent on both policy advice and services across departments between July 1995 and December 1996 (SSC 1998, p. 22).

The use of consultants varies from department to department. Some spend very little on external advice, while others make extensive use of the private sector. For example, the Ministry of Culture and Heritage spent only $350,000 on consultants, public relations, and external advice between late 1999 and March 2002 (NZPD 2002, p. 699). In contrast, since its inception on 1 January 2003, the Tertiary Education Commission has spent some $3,981,423 on consultants. That money has purchased support for the Commission in designing assessment methodologies, advice on communications, and assistance in carrying out the Commission's workload.[5]

The raw data on consultancy fees should be treated with considerable caution—for example, the information can be relatively meaningless without some comparison with the costs a department would incur if services it purchases externally were generated internally. Moreover, it should not be assumed that money spent on engaging outside assistance is necessarily wasted. The Tertiary Education Commission, for instance, has a policy of only employing consultants if the expertise required is not available within the organisation, if time precludes the use of its own employees, or if it is clearly inappropriate for its own staff to undertake the task(s) in question.

Nevertheless, the use of consultants does raise crucial questions about the ability of departments to undertake tasks that are often considered to be 'core business'. The broader point, perhaps, is that some public service organisations purchase external assistance because they lack the policy expertise that they might reasonably be expected to possess. That may have to do with the fact that, while the numbers employed in the core public service have rebounded somewhat since 1999 (at which point they had slumped to just over 31,000, the lowest total since the First World War), at a little over 40,000, there are still many fewer public servants these days than used to be the case.

Departments cannot shed staff without also losing a certain amount of policy wisdom and capability. The irony is that many of the consultants used these days by departments are former 'middle-level and senior public servants [who] resigned to take up positions in consultancy firms, and [who] in some cases have been almost immediately re-hired on contract by their former employer' (Boston et al. 1996, p. 126).

2. Political appointments

While the consultant question was a highly controversial one in the mid-1990s, it has attracted rather less attention since Labour-led governments began increasing the number of core public servants in the late 1990s. To some extent it has been supplanted by concerns over the increasing use of political advisers in ministers' offices. All governments draw on the services of officials who are seconded from departments to work in ministers' offices for short periods of time (generally between three months to a year or so). These public servants, often referred to as Private Secretaries act as a point of liaison between a minister and his or her department, and are bound by the public service convention of impartiality.

In addition, however, ministers take on political staff for the purpose of providing explicitly partisan advice. (Such staff may also be responsible for what is sometimes referred to as 'political risk management' (or 'spinning'), something that is certainly not a core public service function.) These ministerial advisers (who are also described as 'political staff' or as 'personal appointees') are formally employed on short-term contracts by Ministerial Services, which is a unit within the Department of Internal Affairs. However, although they are technically public servants, ministerial advisers are not expected to adhere to public service standards of impartiality. Quite the reverse: their job is to provide ministers with an expressly *political* assessment of the merits or otherwise of a particular course of action. Objectivity is left to permanent officials.

Table 3.5.1: Numbers of ministerial advisers (1998–2003)[6]

Designation	1998	1999	2000	2001	2002	2003
Ministerial Adviser/Senior Adviser	0	3	11	14	19	22
Executive Assistant	15	23	16	13	10	8
Press Secretaries/Media Assistant	24	24	21	24	20	21
Total	39	50	48	51	49	51

The indications are that the number of ministerial advisers deployed in ministers' offices has climbed in recent years (see table 3.5.1).

There are several likely reasons behind this trend. One is that MMP has created a series of political relationships that call for precisely the sort of support provided by ministerial advisers. Within both coalition and minority governments there are various tasks that can be performed by political advisers but which are well beyond the pale for public servants. For instance, advisers can get involved in the political dimensions of post-election coalition negotiations. They also have key roles to play in the management of relationships between coalition partners, and between minority governments and the parliamentary parties on which those administrations rely for support. It would be highly inappropriate for public servants to have anything to do with these sorts of activities.

But there are other factors behind ministers' increasing recourse to political advisers. Recent research on the issue (see Eichbaum & Shaw 2005) suggests that, quite apart from the influence of MMP, the policy-making world has simply become a much more complicated place than it used to be. People are more demanding of governments, ministers are subject to much more scrutiny than was once common—particularly from the media—and policy issues seem to become more, rather than less, difficult to resolve. In this environment, the argument goes, ministers need all the assistance they can get, including that which they gain from their political advisers.

MORE WASHMINSTER THAN WESTMINSTER?

The more critical issue, perhaps, concerns the effect ministerial advisers might be having on relationships within the executive branch. In particular, it is important to understand the various challenges they present to the traditional relationship between ministers and departmental officials. One such issue was raised by a former State Services Commissioner in his 2002 Annual Report to Parliament, in which he expressed concern that ministerial advisers might pose a risk to the political neutrality of the public service (SSC 2002). The argument goes that ministerial advisers might pressure officials to produce advice consistent with ministers' political aims and objectives, rather than reflecting their best professional judgment.

A second possible problem is that if (a) ministers become overly reliant on their ministerial advisers, and (b) those advisers consistently impede officials' access to ministers, then professional public servants may find themselves excluded from the policy process. This particular challenge is really about the respective roles of ministerial advisers and officials: are they in competition, or is there room for cooperation?

On the matter of politicisation, officials appear to be split on the extent to which ministerial advisers have compromised the neutrality of the public service. A third (35.1 per cent) of respondents in a survey of senior public servants felt that advisers threaten the impartiality of the public service.[7] But slightly more than a third (37.8 per cent) did not perceive any such risk, while 23.9 per cent were undecided on the matter. Indeed, a good many officials seem inclined to the view that ministerial advisers can actually be of assistance to them. A number pointed out that precisely because they can take care of the overtly political dimensions of policy advice, ministerial advisers can free public servants up to get on with the business of crafting free and frank advice for ministers. In short, political staff can absorb pressures from ministers that might under other circumstances expose public servants to the threat of politicisation.

As for the possible marginalisation of the public service, again, the indications are that most senior officials do not believe they are being cut out of the policy-making 'loop'. Although 22.4 per cent of survey respondents believe that ministerial advisers try to block officials' access to ministers, and 15.4 per cent that they tamper with departments' advice, many more are of the opinion that advisers neither deliberately obstruct officials (58.4 per cent) nor interfere with the advice officials put before ministers (48.9 per cent). Notwithstanding that 72.7 per cent of those surveyed concluded that relations between advisers and permanent officials are generally positive, it is worth reflecting on the degree to which the central tenets of the Westminster model (described above) have been modified by the arrival of ministerial advisers *en masse*.

In one sense, the Westminster 'ideal' assumes that the public service exercises a monopoly over providing advice to ministers. In this respect, the demise of that monopoly—which is what has occurred with the advent of ministerial advisers—could be interpreted as a departure from the ideal. But, on the other hand, as Shergold explains:

> There is nothing in the Westminster tradition that suggests that public servants should have a monopoly in the advice going to government: indeed, from a democratic perspective there is everything to be gained by a contestable environment, in which the well-honed policy skills and experience of public servants are challenged by alternative perspectives from within and outside government (2005, p. 6).

Shergold's assessment is that it is perfectly possible to have both ministerial advisers *and* Westminster. In other words, the fact that ministers in Wellington have regular recourse to ministerial advisers does not mean that our system now resembles the overtly politicised Washington model. New Zealand still possesses a professional, impartial public service, although admittedly it has been joined in the policy marketplace by some partisan colleagues.

CONCLUSION

Both of the major processes of reform experienced in New Zealand in the closing years of the twentieth century had an impact on the arrangements through which policy advice is fed into the executive. On the future implications of electoral law reform for policy advice there is an emerging consensus that New Zealand's flexible constitutional arrangements will continue to allow the policy apparatus to adjust to the exigencies of the new electoral system. Many commentators and policy practitioners would probably concur with Boston's conclusion (1998, p. 41) that, the increased deployment of ministerial advisers aside, the consequences of MMP for the policy functions of public servants have been relatively modest. Policy networks may have become more complex, particularly as coalition minority governments are now the norm, but the institutions that guide the formulation and provision of advice appear unlikely to undergo any fundamental change beyond that already experienced.

There is rather more debate about the ramifications of the public service reforms for the provision of advice. Enthusiasts contend that the changes have made the policy process more 'porous', and that they have minimised the risk of policy capture by public servants. (Equally, ministerial advisers have played a role in this.) Critics, however, counter with the argument that the new arrangements simply encourage governments to bypass (or, worse still, to run down) the institutional wisdom and policy expertise that resides within the public service. They also claim that the changes permit ministers to procure policy advice that tells them what they wish to hear, rather than what they may need to be told. There is less truth, they might contend, being spoken to power.

Two things remain beyond dispute. The first is that the reforms have had an enduring impact on the architecture of the public service, and therefore on the institutional context within which policy advice is generated. It has become altogether more open, contestable and—arguably—rigorous. The second is that many important policy issues remain unresolved. The challenge, as ever, facing ministers, officials, advisers, and consultants is to devise and implement public policies that make a positive difference for the peoples of New Zealand.

DISCUSSION QUESTIONS

1 Why is good policy advice so important to successful policy implementation?
2 In your view, does the source of policy advice (from departmental officials, ministerial advisers, or from consultants) have any bearing on the quality of that advice?

3 What are some of the arguments for and against ministers accessing advice from consultants?

4 How might the use of consultants compromise the ability of a government to design and implement policy in a coordinated way?

5 In your view, and from the point of view of the quality of policy advice, is the greater use of political advisers within ministers' offices a positive or negative development?

NOTES

1 The public-choice model has been particularly criticised for its limited predictive capacity. For example, the budget-maximising hypothesis would suggest that, over time, it would be reasonable to expect an increase in the size of the public service workforce, a greater role for departments in the provision of goods and services, and an increase in the proportion of gross domestic product (GDP) comprising public expenditure. In the case of New Zealand the reverse of each of these predictions has applied. First, the size of the public service workforce has fallen from 88,000 in 1984 to just over 40,000 in 2005 (SSC 2005). Second, there has been a clear trend away from the purchase by government of outputs from its own agencies. Between 1990 and 2004, public spending on goods and services delivered by departments fell from approximately 20 per cent of overall public expenditure to just under 14 per cent (Statistics NZ 2004). Third, total government spending as a proportion of GDP fell from 41.8 per cent in 1992–93 to 29.7 per cent in 2004, and is expected to rise to 32.4 per cent by 2009 (Treasury 2004). Third, total government spending as a proportion of GDP fell from 41.8 per cent in 1992–93 to 32.5 per cent in 2001–02 (Treasury 2002), at which level it is expected to remain for some years.

2 Some features of the new environment are found in legislation (particularly in the State Owned Enterprises Act 1986, the State Sector Act 1988, the Public Finance Act 1989, and the Fiscal Responsibility Act 1994 (which was incorporated into the Public Finance Act in 2004)). Others are associated with the restructuring of government departments, for which legislation has generally not been required. For the purposes of this chapter, the critical aspect of that particular process has been the breaking up of large, multifunction bureaucracies into discrete policy ministries and operational departments.

3 Interview with author, 1998.

4 Members of the committee were the State Services Commissioner (Don Hunn), the chief executive of the Department of the Prime Minister and Cabinet (Simon Murdoch), the Secretary to the Treasury (Murray Horn), and the Secretary of the Cabinet (Marie Shroff).

5 These data were obtained from the online version of Answers to Written Questions (see www.clerk.parliament.govt.nz). The question was no. 5341, asked of the Minister responsible for the Tertiary Education Commission, Hon. Steve Maharey, by Hon. Bill English on 16 April 2004. A request for more recent information is pending a response.

6 Data obtained under the Official Information Act 1982. Prior to 1998, the relevant data were not kept. The key trend is the increase in the number of Ministerial Advisers and Senior Advisers.

7   The research was supported by the Marsden Fund and administered by the Royal
     Society of New Zealand. It surveyed 548 officials in twenty-one government
     departments (response rate = 34.4%). For details, see Eichbaum & Shaw (2005).

REFERENCES

Boston, J. 1998, 'Public Sector Management, Electoral Reform and the Future of the
    Contract State in New Zealand', *Australian Journal of Public Administration*, vol. 57,
    no. 4, pp. 32–43.
Boston, J., S. Levine, E. McLeay, N. Roberts & H. Schmidt 1998, 'The Impact of Electoral
    Law Reform on the Public Service: The New Zealand Case', *Australian Journal of
    Public Administration*, vol. 57, no. 3, pp. 64–78.
Boston, J., J. Martin, J. Pallot & P. Walsh (eds) 1996, *Public Management: The New Zealand
    Model*, Oxford University Press, Auckland.
Eichbaum, C. & R. Shaw 2006, 'Ministerial Advisers, Politicization and the Retreat from
    Westminster', *Public Administration*, forthcoming.
Hawke, G. 1993, *Improving Policy Advice*, Institute of Policy Studies, Wellington.
Hensley, G. 1995, 'Free and Frank Advice to Ministers—Reappraising Ethical Fundamentals',
    Public Sector, vol. 18, no. 3, pp. 21–6.
Heywood, A. 2002, *Politics*, 2nd edn, Macmillan, London.
Martin, J. 1991, *Public Service and the Public Servant: Essays by John Martin*, State Services
    Commission, Wellington.
Morris, R. 1994, 'The Pricing of Policy Advice: The Proposed Cabinet Benchmark'. Paper
    presented to the Public Sector Financial Accounting and Management Conference (IIR),
    Wellington.
New Zealand Parliamentary Debates 2002, Supp. 2, 11/3, 24 March, pp. 699, 701.
NZPD. See *New Zealand Parliamentary Debates*.
Shaw, R. 1999a, 'Rules or Discretion? Officials and Government Formation under MMP',
    Political Science, vol. 51, no. 1, pp. 32–58.
Shergold, P. 2005, 'The Need to Wield a Crowbar: Political Will and Public Service',
    Dunstan Oration, Adelaide, 7 April.
SSC. See State Services Commission.
State Services Commission 2005. *Quarterly Employment Survey*. Wellington: State Services
    Commission.
State Services Commission 2004. *Human Resource Capability Survey of Public Service
    Departments as at June 2004*, Wellington.
State Services Commission 2002, *Annual Report of the State Services Commissioner*, Wellington.
State Services Commission 1999, *Yearly Employment Survey of Public Service Departments
    and Selected State Sector Organisations*, Wellington.
State Services Commission 1998, *Assessment of the State of the New Zealand Public Service*,
    Occasional Paper no. 1, Wellington.
State Services Commission 1995, *Working Under Proportional Representation: a reference for
    the public service*, Wellington.
Statistics New Zealand 2004, *Crown Accounts Analysis: Year Ended 30 June 2004*,
    Wellington.

Treasury 2004, *Pre-election Economic and Fiscal Update 2004*, Wellington.
Treasury 1987, *Government Management*, Wellington.

FURTHER READING

Boston, J. 1998, 'Public Sector Management, Electoral Reform and the Future of the Contract State in New Zealand', *Australian Journal of Public Administration*, vol. 57, no. 4, pp. 32–43.

Boston, J., S. Levine, E. McLeay, N. Roberts & H. Schmidt 1998, 'The Impact of Electoral Law Reform on the Public Service: The New Zealand Case', *Australian Journal of Public Administration*, vol. 57, no. 3, pp. 64–78.

Boston, J., J. Martin, J. Pallot, J. & P. Walsh (eds) 1996, *Public Management: The New Zealand Model*, Oxford University Press, Auckland.

Martin, J. 1991, *Public Service and the Public Servant: Essays by John Martin*, State Services Commission, Wellington.

Schick, A. 1996, *The Spirit of Reform: Managing the New Zealand State Sector in a Time of Change*, State Services Commission & Treasury, Wellington.

Shaw, R. 1999b, 'Rehabilitating the Public Service—Alternatives to the Wellington Model', in S. Chatterjee, P. Conway, P. Dalziel, C. Eichbaum, P. Harris, B. Philpott & R. Shaw, *The New Politics: A Third Way for New Zealand?*, Dunmore Press, Palmerston North.

Shaw, R. & C. Eichbaum 2005, *Public Policy in New Zealand: Institutions, Processes and Outcomes*, Auckland, Pearson/Prentice Hall.

The Public Service

Richard Shaw

In the television series *Yes Minister*, Nigel Hawthorne plays the *uber* bureaucrat Sir Humphrey Appleby, who is the real power behind the ministerial throne. When asked whether a certain investigation has been completed, Sir Humphrey harrumphs that:

> If there had been investigations, which there haven't, or not necessarily, or I'm not at liberty to say whether there have, there would have been a project team which, had it existed, on which I cannot comment, would now have been disbanded, if it had existed, and the members returned to their original departments, if indeed there had been any such members.

At one level *Yes Minister* and its sequel, *Yes Prime Minister*, make for witty, well-crafted viewing. But at another they promote a jaundiced view of public servants that is not, and perhaps never has been, a fair or accurate depiction of the role of public servants.

This chapter sets out to provide a more realistic (if less entertaining) account of the New Zealand public service. It begins by defining the public service, describing the things it does, and discussing the principles that guide its actions. The bulk of the chapter, however, is given over to an assessment of the reforms which have so dramatically altered the face of the public service over the last two decades, and of the challenges it confronts in the first decade of the twenty-first century.

WHAT IS THE PUBLIC SERVICE?

The public service comprises the government departments listed in the First Schedule to the State Sector Act 1988. There are currently thirty-five departments, although the precise number dips and rises as departments are created, reshuffled or abolished.

Collectively, they comprise the administrative arm of the executive branch of government, whose core functions are to serve 'the Government of the day, within the framework of the law, by providing it with advice and delivering services to the public' (SSC 1995: vii).

The size of the departments varies enormously. As at June 2005 there were 40,325 full-time equivalent positions (FTEs) in the public service (SSC 2005a). A handful of large departments accounted for the bulk of this employment: twelve departments had more than a thousand FTEs, and three—the Ministry of Social Development, the Department of Corrections and the Inland Revenue Department—had more than three thousand FTEs positions each. The Ministry of Social Development (which among other things is responsible for social policy and the administration of the benefit system) is the largest department: with some 9,075 FTEs, it accounts for around 22 per cent of all public service jobs. At the other end of the scale, some departments employ very few staff. Women's Affairs, for example, has only 25 FTEs.

Although this chapter concentrates on the public service, it is important to note that in addition to the departments, 'the government' includes a host of other agencies. For example, there are close to three thousand Crown entities (most of which are school Boards of Trustees) which operate at arm's length from the political executive, and which are subject to the provisions of the Public Finance Act 1989 and the new Crown entities legislation (discussed below). Beyond that, there are organisations such as tertiary education institutions and state-owned enterprises (SOEs), which are part of the wider state sector. Still further out, there are some eighty-six city, district, and regional councils. Collectively, these councils make up the local government sector.

WHAT DEPARTMENTS DO

As well as varying in size, government departments engage in many diverse activities. One way of distinguishing departments one from the other is by identifying their major function(s). Bear in mind, however, that while this functional approach helps tease out the things the public service does, in reality few departments have a single function. Most carry several responsibilities, although one or two of these may dominate operations.

One of the core functions of departments is the provision of policy advice. Ministers are collectively responsible for deciding on government policy. Typically, ministers ask their departmental officials for advice as part of the decision-making process. The sorts of things they may wish to receive advice on include the likely costs and benefits of particular interventions. Policy decisions often entail an understanding of the nature and extent of a given problem and the commitment of financial resources. The days when departments had a near-monopoly on delivering services are long gone, with the lion's share of policy implementation now being undertaken by Crown entities and community and voluntary sector agencies. Many departments, however, retain some operational responsibilities. The Identity Services Group of the Department of Internal Affairs, for instance, issues passports and manages applications for New Zealand citizenship; the Tenancy Services division of the Department of Building and Housing provides tenancy advice, education, and mediation services for tenants and landlords.

In addition to delivering their own programmes, some departments also purchase services from others. Thus, Child, Youth and Family Services, which is part of the Ministry of Social Development, delivers statutory care and protection and youth justice services to children and young people, and their families and whanau. But it also enters into contracts with community and voluntary (or 'third sector') agencies that provide a range of complementary services.

The negotiation of a contract between a government department and another organisation is a complex business. Departments must decide which services they need to obtain, a contract may be put out to tender, bids from competing agencies are received and processed, and in due course a contract is negotiated and signed. But the department's interest in matters is far from finished at this point. Departments (and other funding agencies) regularly monitor contracts to ensure that they are being fulfilled. In general terms, the purpose of this monitoring function is to ensure that the contracted agency is actually delivering what it undertook to provide.

CENTRAL PRINCIPLES

There are three fundamental principles guiding the government departments as they set about the activities described above. First, they are governed by the rule of law and can be held accountable in the courts for any breaches of the law. Secondly, the principle of ministerial responsibility wraps around the relationship between (a) the executive branch and parliament, and (b) ministers and their departments. There are two dimensions to ministerial responsibility. The first—collective ministerial responsibility—means that ministers are collectively responsible to the legislature, and thence to the public, for the outcomes of government policies. The conventional view has long been that this requires all ministers to publicly support decisions taken by cabinet (although whether or not this remains the case given the arrangements negotiated by the Labour-led government with New Zealand First and United Future after the 2005 election is a moot point).

Second, as well as being collectively responsible, ministers are individually accountable for the performance of their departments. It is the prerogative of ministers to take policy decisions, and the duty of officials to carry out ministers' policies and instructions. While public servants may explain government policies, they should not express personal views on them, or respond publicly to criticism of them. Rather, it is the ministers who must stand up in the House and account to the public for the success or failure of their policies.

Third, the public service is bound to act in a politically impartial manner. This means that the public service must be free of political interference or patronage and serve the government in a professional and impartial manner (SSC 2002, p. 2). Officials serve the government of the day, *not* the political parties making up the government, and thus are expected to offer ministers free, frank, and fearless advice. If that means tendering advice which ministers find politically unpalatable, so be it: public servants' advice must reflect their best assessment of the issues and options, rather than some sense of what they think ministers might want to hear.

While public service impartiality is a cornerstone of Westminster constitutions (see Rhodes & Weller 2005), things have not always been that way. In fact, prior to the passage of the Public Service Act in 1912 New Zealand ministers personally approved the appointment of public servants, took decisions regarding remuneration and conditions of employment, and oversaw the routine operations of their departments. In effect, the public service operated largely on the basis of political patronage.[1]

There were various problems associated with running a public service according to the personal whims of ministers. For one thing, appointments were not necessarily made on the basis of the expertise or merits of competing candidates, but on the nature and closeness of the relationship a candidate might have had with a minister (or with someone close to the minister). Moreover, public servants had every reason to ensure that their minister was happy with their advice, even if that meant it was inconsistent with either the collective interest of the wider administration, or the adviser's professional assessment of the best way forward.

The 1912 Act put an end to much of this, ushering in what a former State Services Commissioner described as a 'long and proud tradition of political neutrality' (SSC 2002, p. 2). Political patronage was ended by removing responsibility for the hiring and firing of public servants from ministers and vesting it in an independent body, the Public Service Commission. In this way, departments that had previously functioned as independent fiefdoms—each in thrall to its minister—were gathered together in a unified public service. The legislation also established a career, or professional public service. No longer was employment in the service dependent on the vagaries— or political survival—of a particular minister; instead, public servants were to be appointed on the basis of merit. With one or two exceptions, such as the establishment of the State Services Commission in 1962, the 1912 arrangements endured for the better part of the twentieth century.

PUBLIC SECTOR REFORMS

Beginning in the mid-1980s, New Zealand embarked on a programme of public sector reforms that was arguably the most radical attempted anywhere in the world. The changes were comprehensive: the public financial management system was overhauled, the statutory basis of relations between ministers and senior officials was revised, and responsibility for employment matters was decentralised from the State Services Commission to the heads of government departments.

The story of the reforms is altogether too long and intricate to be recounted in full here (see Boston & Eichbaum 2005; Boston et al. 1996; Chatterjee et al. 1999; Kelsey 1997; Schick 1996; Scott 2001). The abbreviated version begins with the motives of the political and bureaucratic elites who drove the first spate of changes and who, among other objectives, wanted to cut back on public spending, improve the quality of service delivery, and tighten bureaucratic accountability. Some of the most significant reforms were:

- *Separation of the government's trading interests from its non-commercial activities* (in health, welfare, education, etc.). Departments which for decades had provided services in the postal, banking, rail, insurance, shipping and telecommunications sectors were set up as SOEs and required to return a dividend to the government. Many, but not all of these SOEs, were later privatised.
- *Restructuring of all remaining departments.* New Zealand's reformers enthusiastically embraced economic theories that portrayed public servants as self-serving, putting their own personal interests ahead of the interests of others. To curb their influence, the reformers set about systematically dismantling the government's own departments. Often, this entailed splitting roles—policy and operations; funder, purchaser, and provider—and locating them in different organisations (or in autonomous units within a department). Quasi-markets were created across the public sector in which departments competed not only with each other, but also with other providers in both the public and private sectors.
- *Introduction of output budgeting.* Departments were traditionally funded according to the annual cash cost of their inputs (overheads, salaries, rents, etc.). The Public Finance Act 1989 introduced a new public financial management regime under which departments' appropriations reflected the cost of their outputs. In other words, funding levels were determined according to what the various departments produced. In principle this makes it easier for ministers to specify what they want departments to deliver, and to keep a tighter rein on public spending.
- *Reallocation of responsibility for employment decisions.* In 1912, responsibility for employing, promoting, and dismissing public servants had been handed to the Public Service Commission. The State Sector Act 1988 took the employment relationship a few steps further. The heads of departments, who had previously been employed on a permanent basis, were reclassified as Chief Executive Officers (CEs) and placed on short-term contracts. CEs themselves are employed by the State Services Commissioner, but employ all staff in their departments.

REFORMS ASSESSED

Most commentators now accept that the public service is more efficient and performance-oriented, that there is greater transparency in the use of scarce public resources (at least in some sectors), and that there have been improvements in the standard of the services delivered to citizens. But those gains have come at a cost. Many public servants lost their jobs during the early stages of corporatisation and privatisation, and throughout the 1990s those who remained in the public service were subject to constant agency restructurings, more stressful work environments, and reduced job security. Departments were required to achieve more with fewer resources, and incessant structural change contributed to low morale in many organisations, and the end result was an increasingly fragmented sector.

Towards the end of the last decade it became clear that the public service was struggling with capacity and capability issues. In essence, some departments lacked the intellectual, physical and other resources they needed to do what governments demanded of them. To understand how this came about, it is helpful to distinguish between the government's ownership and purchase roles. Governments wear two departmental hats: a 'purchase' and an 'ownership' hat. The difference is reflected in the distinction between the roles of 'vote' ministers and 'responsible' ministers. The former are responsible for purchasing outputs (policy advice, services, etc.) from departments on behalf of the government. They represent the purchase interest. Responsible ministers, on the other hand, represent the government's interest as the owner of the departments. In this capacity, ministers must ensure that departments are able to do what is asked of them over the short, medium, and long term. A minister is, in a sense, his or her department's 'champion', responsible for making sure they receive the right mix and quantum of resources required for doing the job.

These two roles can pull in quite different directions. A vote minister wants value for money (that is, more for less), while a responsible minister opposes having the department's budget squeezed so tightly that its institutional capacity is compromised. Throughout the 1990s this tension was routinely resolved in favour of the purchase role, as successive governments kept the departments on tight funding leashes. While this may well have been fiscally desirable, departments found it harder and harder to fulfil their required role.

One manifestation of this was a gradual reduction in the departments' workforce. Table 3.6.1 depicts recent trends in employment across the public service. Between 1991–99 the numbers fell steadily. To a degree this simply reflected a reshuffling of the institutional boundaries—as departments were reconstituted as SOEs or Crown entities, their employees were no longer considered to be public servants. There is no escaping the fact, however, that during the 1990s there was a steep fall in the overall numbers working in government departments. Staffing reductions can produce problems for departments on several fronts. For one thing, they place severe strain on

Table 3.6.1: Employment in the public service (1991–2005)

1991	1993	1995	1997	1999	2001	2003	2005
49,805	40,261	34,656	32,925	30,702	31,440	34,460	40,325

Source: SSC 2005a

an agency's resources and its ability to get things done—especially if they occur at the same time as public demand for a department's services increases.

Staffing cuts also contribute to the loss of institutional wisdom. If this process occurs incrementally, then to some extent the negative consequences may be mitigated. But when a department haemorrhages experienced staff, who take with them a deep knowledge and understanding of how the organisation works, the effects on its ability to carry out its core functions can be seriously compromised.

Since 1999, successive Labour-led governments have set about tackling these issues. Perhaps most significantly, as table 3.6.1 demonstrates, they have overseen a 'bounce' in the public service workforce. Overall, staffing numbers have risen by some 34 per cent since 2000 (SSC 2005a). While the total number of public servants is still well short of pre-reform levels (and is unlikely ever to return to the 90,000 or so who worked in the public service when the reforms began in earnest), conditions have certainly improved from the low point of 1998/1999, when there were fewer officials than at any time since the First World War (note that the public service accounts for just 2.4 per cent of all employment in New Zealand.)

Another initiative was the creation in 2000 of the State Sector Standards Board. The Board canvassed ways whereby public trust in the sector could be improved, as well as setting expectations for the various state sector agencies. As much as anything else, the creation of the Board signalled a willingness to address the prevailing climate of public mistrust and to express a commitment to the future of the public service. It had become increasingly apparent, for example, that restructuring was not the panacea that some reformers had imagined. While restructuring can produce neater institutional arrangements and clarify lines of accountability, both highly desirable objectives, it proved less successful in providing solutions to entrenched policy issues, a point made by the State Services Commissioner in his 1998 Annual Report to Parliament: 'In New Zealand we may have slipped into what could be termed a 'restructuring culture'—a culture in which we reach for the restructuring option instinctively, regardless of the nature of the problem we are trying to solve' (SSC 1998, p. 8).

Structural change can be costly. It is hard enough to accurately quantify the financial costs (and benefits) of restructuring, but even more difficult to calculate its non-financial costs, such as the corrosive impact on staff morale, and the effects on citizens who depend on the smooth and continuous provision of services. One of the unforeseen by-products of an increasingly fragmented sector was the lack of incentive for employees of one department to work closely alongside those in another. The proliferation of agencies also threw up its own set of coordination problems. All other things being equal, the challenges associated with coordinating the activities of the machinery of government multiply as the number of agencies involved in the design and implementation of policy grows. That is not solely an issue for relations between departments. Rather, as government departments have increasingly shed responsibility for delivering services to the third sector, it has become more difficult to ensure that everyone concerned is pulling in the same policy direction.

The public service/third sector nexus presents yet another significant conundrum. Typically, a large portion of the funding received by community and voluntary agencies is public money. That creates a contractual relationship between an agency (as provider) and a department (as the funder or purchaser). This raises some pertinent concerns. For instance, the negotiation and monitoring of contracts is an imprecise and costly business. Third sector agencies can find the whole process an onerous and unsettling one, in part because it is difficult to lock in stable, predictable funding relationships. Sometimes, too, contracts encourage a compliance mentality. This may stifle innovation (because agencies have incentives to do only those things they have received funding for), and constrain an agency's ability to respond to a new or sudden issue that lies outside the terms of the contract.

The response to these and other difficulties stemming from fragmentation has taken the form of a search for 'joined up' government. This included the announcement of a stocktake of the public sector by the Minister of State Services in July 2001.[2] The Advisory Group responsible for the Review of the Centre was tasked with identifying ways of addressing some of the flaws in the new model of public management. In its report, the Group recommended a raft of initiatives aimed at:

- integrating the delivery of services to citizens
- improving coordination across public agencies
- encouraging a focus on the achievement of outcomes
- strengthening the culture and values of the state sector.

Implementing its recommendations has since been a priority for the public service. Interesting things have been done: for instance, 'circuit breaker teams' drawing from different departments have been established to deal with problems in which multiple agencies are involved.

Other recommendations were implemented with the passage of the Public Finance (State Sector Management) Bill.[3] One or two aspects of the legislation deserve particular attention. The first are the subtle changes made to the structure of the public financial management system. Since 1989, appropriations have attached to one class (or bundle) of outputs. Now, however, a single appropriation may comprise more than one output class. That innovation, along with others such as the provision for more than one minister to have responsibilities in relation to a single vote, has built a good deal more flexibility into the Budget process, and will make it easier for agencies to cooperate on policy issues which require a cross-agency approach.

The new Crown Entities legislation is also, at root, an attempt to reduce the effects of fragmentation. To tidy up arrangements within the Crown entity sector the Act creates several distinct categories and types of Crown entity. The purpose of this is to enable ministers to determine with greater precision the degree to which Crown entities are required to work closely with government. Crown Agents, for instance, have a close working relationship with the government of the day (e.g. District Health Boards). On the other hand, Independent Crown Entities are able to operate at arm's length from the government. The Electoral Commission, for example, is classified as an Independent Crown Entity because it must operate—and must be *seen* to operate—independently of the government of the day.[4]

FROM OUTPUTS TO OUTCOME

The developments outlined above add up to what is perhaps the most significant development in the public service since 1999, that is, the shift away from an almost exclusive concern with the efficient production of outputs to an emphasis on the achievement of positive outcomes for citizens. While governments invested heavily in specifying, pricing, and delivering outputs, they paid much less attention to thinking about—and assessing—the differences these outputs made to the material lives of citizens. These priorities are now changing. The implementation of the recommendations of the Review of the Centre, for instance, is having the result of improving the capacity of the public sector to deliver results for people. Similarly, the new public finance innovations are intended to give government greater flexibility in using public resources to tackle policy problems.

The rediscovery of outcomes has also driven the development of the 'Managing for Outcomes' approach, which encourages the management of departments in ways that contribute to the achievement of results. The logic behind the approach has been described thus:

> Outcomes are influenced by many factors. Some are in our control: others are not. Because of this, chief executives are not accountable for achieving outcomes but are held accountable for 'managing for outcomes'. In other words they continue to be accountable for the delivery of outputs and for altering the mix of outputs as circumstances dictate. Good information on results, on what is working and what is not helps in decisions about what to start, what to stop and what to continue or expand (SSC 2005b, p. 1).

Focusing on results has had important ramifications for the style of contracting the public service engages in, both within and between departments, and between departments and other providers. Rather than trying to pin down to the nth degree what outputs are to be provided, in which quantities and over which timeframes, there has been a conscious shift towards contracts which 'bridge the gap between the Government's high-level and broadly-framed goals and the outputs of the contracted organisation by stating "intermediate outcomes"' (SSC 2001, p. 11). As a result, tightly specified purchase agreements have made way for departmental output plans, and Chief Executive performance agreements have been put aside in favour of Statements of Intent. A Statement of Intent sets out what a department is trying to achieve, how it will go about doing so, and the policy rationale behind its choice of interventions. Output plans, which ministers and CEs negotiate, are more specific documents. They identify the goods and services a department will deliver, and spell out the ways in which these link with the broader outcomes set out in the Statement of Intent.[5] The point is that both are part of the attempt within the public service to 'avoid the "compliance culture" that so easily emerges [when we] focus on specification, monitoring and reporting almost for their own sake rather than for the sake of improving the lot of New Zealanders' (SSC 2001, p. 12).

CONCLUSION

There is a tendency to think that the reform process ended with the last century. As our discussion has shown, that is not the case. While the most radical reforms were implemented during the 1980s and 1990s, the public service continues to evolve. Recent developments, however, have been altogether less wrenching for the public service and its inhabitants. Characterised as a process of 'consolidation, development and renewal' (Boston & Eichbaum 2005, p. 2), it has been notable for a more measured, less dogmatic approach to reform, and by a willingness to accept the virtues and merits of public service which was largely absent from much of the first phase of the reform process. If the 1990s can be described as a pulling apart of policy (from operations), ownership (from purchase), and outputs (from outcomes), then the present decade marks a reunification. There is a new emphasis on working across departmental boundaries; and the false dichotomy between ownership and purchase is being gradually replaced by an emphasis on achieving substantive results for citizens.

In the process, the public service has shifted its gaze. No longer is it exclusively concerned with the efficiency of its internal processes. Instead, it is increasingly outward looking, harnessing its collective efforts to the achievement of better policy results for those who most matter: New Zealand's citizens. Sir Humphrey would barely recognise the place.

DISCUSSION QUESTIONS

1 Debate the advantages and disadvantages of having a politically impartial public service.
2 List and discuss the strengths and weaknesses of the reforms made between 1986–99.
3 In recent times agencies in the community and voluntary sector have assumed a larger role in providing services to citizens than they once had. What is the appeal of this? Conversely, what are the risks?
4 Do we even need a public service? Why not simply contract everything out for private sector delivery?

NOTES

1   Much of the material in this section comes from documents on the website of the State Services Commission (www.ssc.govt.nz).
2   The documents associated with the Review of the Centre, and its implementation, are available on the State Services Commission's website.
3   The Bill was passed on 16 December 2004 having been split into four separate Acts: Public Finance Amendment Act 2004; State Sector Amendment Act (No. 2) 2004; Crown Entities Act 2004; and State-Owned Enterprises Amendment Act 2004.
4   In addition, and also in response to the recommendations which came from the Review of the Centre, the legislative changes beefed up the State Services Commissioner's leadership role in the wider state sector. The Commissioner may now provide advice and guidance on (a) standards of integrity and conduct, (b) management systems, structures and organisations, and (c) the development of senior leadership and management capabilities right across the sector.
5   These documents not only guide departments' activities, they are used to hold CEs to account for what they do and how they do it. Ministers assess departments' delivery performance against their output plans. So does the State Services Commissioner when reviewing the performance of a CE on behalf of the responsible minister.

REFERENCES

Boston, J. & C. Eichbaum 2005, 'State Sector Reform and Renewal in New Zealand: Lessons for Governance'. Paper for the conference on Repositioning of Public Governance: Global Experiences and Challenges, Taipei, 18–19 November.

Boston, J., J. Martin, J. Pallot & P. Walsh (eds) 1996, *Public Management: The New Zealand Model*, Oxford University Press, Auckland.

Chatterjee, S., P. Conway, P. Dalziel, C. Eichbaum, P. Harris, B. Philpott & R. Shaw 1999, *The New Politics: A Third Way for New Zealand*, Dunmore Press, Palmerston North.

Kelsey, J. 1997, *The New Zealand experiment: A World Model for Structural Adjustment?* 2nd edn, Auckland University Press (with Bridget Williams), Auckland.

Rhodes, R. A. W. & P. Weller 2005, 'Westminster Transplanted and Westminster Implanted: Explanations for Political Change', in H. Patapan, J. Wanna & P. Weller, (eds), *Westminster Legacies: Democracy and Responsible Government in Asia, Australasia and the Pacific*, University of New South Wales Press, Sydney.

Schick, A. 1996, *The Spirit of Reform: Managing the New Zealand State Sector in a Time of Change*, State Services Commission, Wellington.

Scott, G. 2001, *Public Management in New Zealand: Lessons and Challenges*, Business Roundtable, Wellington.

SSC. See State Services Commission.

State Services Commission 2005a, *Quarterly Employment Survey*, Wellington.

State Services Commission 2005b, *Getting Better at Managing for Outcomes: A Tool to Help Organisations Consider their Progress in Results-Based Management and Identify Development Objectives*, Wellington.

State Services Commission 2001, *Annual Report of the State Services Commission*, Wellington.

State Services Commission 1998, *Annual Report of the State Services Commission*, Wellington.

State Services Commission 1995, *Working under Proportional Representation. A Guide for the Public Service*, Wellington.

FURTHER READING

Boston, J. 2001, 'New Zealand? "Cautionary Tale or Shining Example?"' in R. Rhodes & P. Weller (eds) *The Changing World of Top Officials: Mandarins or Valets?* Open University Press, Buckingham.

Cheyne, C., M. O'Brien & M. Belgrave 2005, *Social Policy in Aotearoa New Zealand: A Critical Introduction*, 3rd edn, Oxford University Press, Melbourne.

Gregory, B. 1998, 'A New Zealand Tragedy. Problems of Political Responsibility', *Governance*, 11/2, pp. 231–40.

Norman, R. 2003, *Obedient Servants? Management Freedoms and Accountabilities in the New Zealand Public Sector*, Victoria University Press, Wellington.

Palmer, G. & M. Palmer 2004, *Bridled Power. New Zealand's Constitution and Government*, 4th edn, Oxford University Press, Melbourne.

Shaw, R. & C. Eichbaum 2005, *Public Policy in New Zealand: Institutions, Processes and Outcomes*, Pearson/Prentice Hall, Auckland.

Local Government

Christine Cheyne

Local government's place in our political system and, in particular, the executive process, is often overlooked and poorly understood by citizens. Moreover, local government is frequently the butt of jokes and sceptical media comment. However, by getting to know something of its potential influence on our day-to-day lives, it is possible to see local government in quite a different light. Since 2002, local government has gained a new prominence in our system of government. This is the result of changing views about the role of central government in providing goods and services, and about the role of citizens and communities in efforts to generate what is known as the 'four well-beings': social, economic, environmental, and cultural well-being.

This chapter begins with an overview of local government, defining the term and clarifying its use in this chapter. The structure and purpose, functions and funding of local government in New Zealand are discussed. Two key dimensions of our system of local government, namely representation and participation, are then examined. Finally, the chapter considers the impact of current trends in public management and the ramifications of these for local government in New Zealand in the future.

OVERVIEW OF LOCAL GOVERNMENT

At the outset it is important to clarify what the term 'local government' means. Local government can be described simply as that level of government that exists below parliament and central government. It encompasses not only what is traditionally understood as local government (city, district, and regional councils), but also district health boards and a number of other bodies that are elected by citizens in particular communities. For this reason, at the time of local elections, voters will find that they have voting papers for several bodies, not just their city/district council.

The focus of this chapter is the core local government bodies of city/district councils and regional councils. The current structure has been largely unaltered since 1989, at which time there was a wide-reaching reform of local government through amendments to the Local Government Act 1974. However, reform of local government legislation was a policy priority of the Labour–Alliance government. Both parties had signalled in their 1999 election manifestos that they sought to strengthen local government. As parties with social democratic roots, they regarded a strong local government sector providing opportunities for grassroots citizen participation to be a key feature of a democratic society. In November 2000 a major review of local government law was announced. This included a review of the Local Government Act 1974 which aimed to strengthen its planning, reporting, and accountability requirements. The legislative review resulted in the passage of two key statutes: the Local Electoral Act 2001 and the Local Government Act 2002.[1]

STRUCTURE AND PURPOSE

Local government has been a feature of executive government in New Zealand since 1842, when the Municipal Corporations Ordinance provided for locally elected bodies to be created to administer the newly established Pakeha settlements. From the mid-nineteenth century the structure of local government reflected its purpose, namely to allow citizens to be involved in decision-making in the locality in which they lived. During the nineteenth and early twentieth centuries the structure of local government evolved into a complex myriad of overlapping units of local government, some of which were multi-purpose (for example, cities and boroughs), but many of which were single purpose (for example, pest destruction and roading boards).

In 1989, a series of reforms created a system of local government that comprises two main types of authority: regional councils (the boundaries of which are based on river catchments), and territorial authorities (city/district councils). There are twelve regional councils, sixteen city councils and fifty-eight district councils. Both regional and territorial councils are divided into sub-local areas, known as wards, for the purpose of elections.

Both regional and territorial councils are multi-purpose authorities and replace a multitude of single purpose authorities that existed prior to 1989. Local authorities are known as 'creatures of statute', meaning that they were created by law. Their purpose (or role) is set out in s 10 of the Local Government Act 2002. It states:

The purpose of local government is—

(a) to enable democratic local decision-making and action by, and on behalf of, communities; and

(b) to promote the social, economic, environmental, and cultural well-being of communities, in the present and for the future.

This new purpose can be described as the 'sustainable development purpose', highlighting as it does the need for an integrated and long-term perspective when promoting community well-being. Sustainable development is a concept that has been of increasing significance since the United Nations Conference on Environment and Development (also known as the Earth Summit) at Rio in 1992 (Parliamentary Commissioner for the Environment 2002). Countries around the world agreed at that time to pursue development in a more balanced way, recognising the linkages between social, economic, and environmental factors. In addition, they acknowledged that the well-being of current and future generations was a key consideration. Local government's role in enabling local decision-making will be discussed in more detail later in the chapter. For now, it is sufficient to note that the existence of local government reflects the acceptance that within a nation–state there are diverse communities. These local communities are often better placed to make decisions about their resources and needs than the more lofty and remote central government.

FUNCTIONS

When the current structure of multi-purpose regional and territorial councils was established in 1989, regional council and territorial authorities took on particular functions. The key functions of regional councils (such as the Auckland Regional Council) include: resource management; regional land transport planning; biosecurity; harbour administration; and regional emergency management (civil defence). The functions of the seventy-four territorial authorities (that is, city and district councils) are broader than those of regional councils and include: community well-being and development; public health and safety (for example, building control, dog control, and environmental health); physical infrastructure (such as roads, sewerage, water supply, and stormwater management); recreation and cultural activities; and resource management (land use planning and development control).

Numerous statutory provisions require local authorities to perform these and other functions. However, the extent to which some functions are carried out is influenced by political will, together with staffing and financial resources. Many small territorial authorities spend a significant proportion of their budget on a few functions (e.g. roading), with the result that their capacity to undertake other functions is severely curtailed.

Four district councils (Gisborne, Marlborough, Nelson, and Tasman) are in fact known as 'unitary authorities', in that they carry out the functions of regional councils in addition to territorial authority functions. Unitary authorities have generally been created in places where there is a very large geographical spread with a very small population and significant resource management issues.

There is also a sub-local tier of local government below the level of city/district councils. Community boards were introduced in 1989 at the time of some controversial amalgamations in which a plethora of small authorities were turned into a much smaller number of city and district councils. In places where these new units of local government encompassed what had been very distinct communities, community boards were created to recognise the existing identifiable communities.

In 2004, forty-eight of the seventy-four territorial local authorities had one or more community boards. The total number of boards is 144 (Department of Internal Affairs 2005). Essentially, these are sub-local advisory bodies, which are intended to be advocates for their communities and a means whereby the territorial authority can consult with the community. Typically, community boards are responsible for local decision-making at the ward level, assessing and responding to local needs, providing input to the local authority's annual and long-term plans, and enhancing communication with community associations and special interest groups. They are likely to focus on issues relating to development and maintenance of road works in their area, as well as water supply, sewerage, stormwater, drainage, parks, recreational facilities, community activities, community advisory services, libraries, community centres, and traffic management.

In city and district councils where there are no community boards, there are a variety of sub-local units of territorial government including formal ward committees (which are standing committees of the territorial authority or which report to a standing committee) and informal committees.

FUNDING

The significance of local government becomes evident when considering its annual operating expenditure, which totals over $4 billion. The local government sector contributes approximately 3.5 per cent of the country's Gross Domestic Product. As noted above, the capacity of local government to perform certain functions may be determined by the level of its financial resources. The issue of local government funding has for a long time been highlighted by the local government sector, which contends that it carries out many functions on behalf of central government without any compensating transfer of resources from central government (Joint Central Government/Local Authority Funding Project Team 2005).

Indeed, New Zealand's local government sector is relatively independent of central government, obtaining approximately 60 per cent of its revenue from rates (a property tax) with more being raised locally through charges for services and fines. Around 12 per cent of its revenue comes from central government, mainly in the form of targeting funding (primarily for roads and public transport). Some revenue comes from investments and other sources. The small proportion of funding from central government ensures that local government remains independent. However, there are also concerns that local government's costs have been increased by government policies that have imposed new responsibilities on local government and transferred functions from central government to local government.

Having outlined some of the key structural characteristics of local government in New Zealand, we can now focus on the features of local government that shape its contribution to executive government. In the next section we look at how decision-making happens, by considering, first, the role of elected representatives, including their interface with management and, second, the role that citizens can play in local authority decision-making.

Representation and participation are arguably the hallmarks of liberal democratic institutions. Liberal democracies are characterised by the election of representatives who form a governing body. Voting in elections is one form of political participation, sometimes referred to as electoral participation. As noted earlier, the purpose of local government as set out in the Local Government Act 2002 is 'to enable democratic local decision-making and action by, and on behalf of, communities'. This signals both that we have a system of representative local government whereby elected representatives form governing bodies, and that people in their communities participate in decision-making. In the next section we explore some of the key features of our system of local representative democracy, including the interface between elected members and appointed local authority staff, before turning to the issue of local political participation.

REPRESENTATION

Local elections are held once every three years, on the second Saturday in October. The most recent elections were in October 2004. The Department of Internal Affairs, as the central government agency responsible for local government policy and legislation, collates statistics following the triennial elections. In 1989, postal voting was made mandatory, but this subsequently became optional from 1992. Table 3.7.1 shows the average turnout in local elections and compares this with turnout in parliamentary elections. The turnout data for local elections is based on the average turnout for council elections in city/district councils and regional councils.

Average turnout data conceals what are likely to be quite different turnout rates among different groups in the population. Smaller surveys that have been conducted

Table 3.7.1: Voter turnout in local and general elections, 1989–2005

	Local Elections %	General Elections %
1989–90	58.3	85.2
1992–93	53.6	85.2
1995–96	52	88.3
1998–99	55	84.8
2001–02	50.3	77.0
2004–05	46.3	81.0

Source: Department of Internal Affairs (2005); Electoral Commission (2005)

indicate that young people and Māori are likely to have disproportionately low turnout rates (see, for example, Local Government New Zealand 2002).

Within the boundaries established by the Local Government Official Information and Meetings Act 1987 and the Local Government Act 2002, local authorities are able to determine their meeting schedules and governance structures. Meetings are usually held on monthly or six-weekly cycles, and councils generally establish a number of standing committees, sub-committees, and advisory groups to deal with issues in particular areas (for example, Finance Committee, Transport Committee, Leisure Committee) and make recommendations to the full council. Non-elected members may be appointed to sub-committees and advisory groups.

Community boards, which were mentioned earlier, are delegated certain powers by the territorial authority. Among the powers they are not permitted to exercise are the levying of rates, appointing staff, or owning property. Community boards may be partly elected by the community and may include elected members appointed by the territorial authority, or they may be entirely elected.

The New Zealand system of local government has been identified as reflecting the council-manager model. This is where the council appoints a manager to implement decisions. The Local Government Act 2002 requires elected councils to appoint a Chief Executive Officer. This reflects the provisions in the State Sector Act 1988 whereby ministers appoint chief executives of government departments. In both the State Sector Act and the Local Government Act the chief executive has full responsibility for the employment and implementation of staff. According to Svara (1990, p. 51) in the council-manager system:

> the mayor and the council occupy the overtly political roles in government, and the manager directs the administrative apparatus, an activity which provides ample room for influencing and shaping policy without the burdens (or opportunities) attendant to elected leadership status.

This system of directly elected mayors is not found in all countries, although there does appear to be a trend towards directly elected mayors in Western and Central Europe. In New Zealand, directly elected mayors are found only in territorial authorities. In regional councils, the presiding member of the council (the chairperson) is not elected by the electors at large but rather by the membership of the council.

The mayor and councillors in city and district councils have the following roles:

- setting the policy direction of the council
- monitoring the performance of the council
- representing the interests of the city (on election all members must make a declaration that they will perform their duties in the best interests of the whole city/district)
- employing the chief executive (under the Local Government Act the local authority employs the chief executive who, in turn, employs all other staff on its behalf).

In addition, the mayor has the following roles:

- presiding member at council meetings. The mayor is responsible for ensuring the orderly conduct of business during meetings (as determined in standing orders)
- advocating on behalf of the community. This role may involve promoting the community and representing its interests. Such advocacy will be most effective where it is carried out with the knowledge and support of the council
- acting as ceremonial head of the council
- providing leadership and feedback to other elected members on teamwork and chairing committees.

From the above it should be clear that, although mayors are directly elected by voters, the model of political leadership discussed here gives them no greater formal power than other elected members. What they may enjoy is a more 'symbolic' form of power derived from their figurehead role.

Local government legislation in New Zealand has been relatively silent on the matter of the responsibilities of the mayor and elected members, other than addressing some obvious areas of conflict of interest and legal and financial probity, and requiring councils to adopt a Code of Conduct that governs the behaviour of elected members. By contrast, the responsibilities of chief executives are prescribed in some detail in s 42 of the Local Government Act 2002. Whether there should be more explicit legislative provisions relating to elected members is a matter that may be considered in future legislative reviews and evaluations.

The Local Government Act 2002, as with similar legislation in other countries, signals a governance role for local political leaders that requires new skills and attributes. In particular, the new purpose given to local government, the new power to promote well-being, and the new long-term planning processes require elected members, and the mayor in particular, to provide leadership. Such leadership requires certain skills, including an ability to consult and cooperate with other public sector agencies in the area (central government and neighbouring local authorities) and other stakeholders (in particular, businesses and the community and voluntary sector). We return to this later in the chapter in our discussion on contemporary governance trends.

PARTICIPATION

As noted in our discussion on representation, electoral participation (voting) is one important form of local political participation. Of course, this is not restricted to the triennial elections of elected representatives, but includes a number of other polls (for example, by-elections, and referenda on particular topics such as fluoridation) that occur from time to time in particular local authorities.

However, voting is not the be-all and end-all of participation. Over recent decades, increasing attention has been given to the need to encourage political participation between elections. It is widely recognised that ongoing public participation can enhance the accountability of elected members to the citizenry, thereby improving the quality and successful implementation of decisions. Devices intended to advance the cause of democratic participation that have been recognised in recent local government reform (Cheyne 2002) include public submissions on draft annual plans and the introduction of a designated 'Special Consultative Procedure' to enhance annual plan consultation and other decision-making processes. The intention behind these reforms was to promote greater openness, transparency, and responsiveness in the way local government conducts its activities. Many important insights were gained as local authorities implemented the statutory consultative procedure and sought to respond to public aspirations for greater influence over local authority decision-making.

The issue of Māori representation and participation in local government has been a focus of legislative reviews since the late 1980s (Hayward 2003). The local government legislative review in the early 2000s attempted to respond to the issue in two key ways: first, by making requirements of local authorities to encourage contributions by Māori to decision-making processes; and, second, by allowing local authorities to establish a Māori ward or wards for electoral purposes. There is still considerable disenchantment among Māori with local authority decision-making processes and there is serious under-representation of Māori elected members. The provisions of the Local Electoral Act 2001 appear to be inadequate and those in the Local Government Act 2002 are far from being fulfilled.

CHANGING GOVERNANCE TRENDS

While the structure of representative local government has remained largely unchanged, the Labour-led coalition government is committed to the development of a stronger relationship between central and local government. This was given concrete expression in the establishment of a regular Central/Local Government Forum meeting attended by senior political leaders in each sector. The Forum resulted in a number of initiatives, including a major study of local government funding (Joint Central Government/Local Authority Funding Project Team 2005). In addition, the Department of Internal Affairs received a directive from cabinet to foster central government engagement in local authority community outcomes (Carter 2004). Key central government agencies, notably the Ministry of Culture and Heritage, Ministry of Economic Development, Ministry for the Environment, and Ministry of Social Development, are becoming more involved in local authority planning processes.

The linkages between central and local government reflect the contemporary interest in the concept of 'governance', which acknowledges that 'government' is one of many actors in the pursuit of desired political outcomes (including an increased consciousness of community well-being). What is needed is better coordination of the various actors, both government and non-government. In addition, in the wake of the Review of the Centre (State Services Commission, 2001) central government agencies are seeking better linkages between their head offices departments and regions and the key community leaders at the local and regional level. Linkages with local authorities, as the recognised democratically elected bodies playing a community leadership role, are of increasing significance.

Can the new long-term planning process (the Community Outcomes Process and Long-Term Council Community Plan) achieve its objectives? Blyth (1999), who carried out research on Wellington City Council's strategic planning in the early 1990s, found that there was limited implementation of the strategic plan. Buhrs (2002) notes that green planning has failed to reach its potential due to a lack of institutional capacity. In New Zealand, and internationally, there is evidence of citizen fatigue and cynicism about poorly designed and conducted public participation.

CONCLUSION

Local government has performed an executive role since the earliest days of settler government in New Zealand in the mid-nineteenth century. Although local government's constitutional status has always been, and remains, relatively weak in formal terms because it does not have the protection of entrenched legislation, nevertheless, the role of local government has been enhanced in a number of ways at the start of the twenty-first century. In particular, the commitment to building a closer relationship between central and local government and the strengthened provisions for public participation signal that local government has a unique and vital role to play in New Zealand's political system.

DISCUSSION QUESTIONS

1 What is meant by the 'sustainable development' purpose of local government?
2 In what ways does recent local government legislation seek to strengthen Māori representation and participation in local government? Discuss the arguments for and against these initiatives.
3 What are the key opportunities for citizens to influence local authority decision-making? What more could be done to increase levels of public participation in decision-making?
4 Should the powers and resources of local government vis-à-vis those of central government be increased? Discuss in relation to such issues as housing, the environment, and transport.
5 What can be done to increase turnout in local body elections, especially among the young?

NOTE

1   These, however, are not the only local government legislation of the last six years, and indeed there is a raft of other statutes that define the parameters and characteristics of local government.

REFERENCES

Blyth, S. 1999, 'Shifting to a Sustainable City? Citizen Participation in Wellington's Our City—Our Future Strategy', unpublished MA (Social Policy) thesis, Massey University, Palmerston North.

Buhrs, T. 2002, 'New Zealand's Capacity for Green Planning: A Political-Institutional Assessment and Analysis', *Political Science*, 54/1, pp. 27–46.

Carter, C. 2004, 'Central Government Engagement in Community Outcomes Processes' (POL (04) 114). Cabinet Paper released under the Official Information Act 1982.

Cheyne, C. 2002, 'Public Participation in New Zealand Local Government: A Historical Account', in J. Drage (ed.), *Empowering Communities? Representation and Participation in New Zealand's Local Government*, Victoria University Press, Wellington.

Department of Internal Affairs 2005, Local Authority Election Statistics 2004—Draft, www.dia.govt.nz/diawebsite.nsf/wpg_URL/Services-Local-Government-Services-Local-Authority-Election-Statistics-2004?OpenDocument.

Drage, J. (ed.) 2002, *Empowering Communities? Representation and Participation in New Zealand's Local Government*, Victoria University Press, Wellington.

Electoral Commission, 2005, 2005 General Election—Official Result, www.electionresults.govt.nz/

Justice and Electoral Committee 2005, 'Inquiry into the 2004 Local Elections, New Zealand Government', Wellington.

Joint Central Government/Local Authority Funding Project Team 2005, *Local Authority Funding Issues, Local Government New Zealand*, Wellington.

Parliamentary Commissioner for the Environment 2002, 'Creating our Future. Sustainable Development for New Zealand', Parliamentary Commissioner for the Environment, Wellington.

State Services Commission, 2002, 'Report of the Advisory Group on the Review of the Centre', www.ssc.govt.nz/display/document.asp?NavID=105&DocID=2429.

Svara, J. 1990, *Official Leadership in the City: Patterns of Conflict and Cooperation*, Oxford University Press, New York.

FURTHER READING

Bush, G. 1995, *Local Government and Politics in New Zealand*, 2nd edn, Auckland University Press, Auckland.

Bush, G. 2003, 'Local Government' in R. Miller (ed), *New Zealand Government and Politics*, 3rd edn, Oxford University Press, Melbourne.

Cheyne, C. 2002, 'Public Participation in New Zealand Local Government: A Historical Account', in J. Drage (ed.), *Empowering Communities? Representation and Participation in New Zealand's Local Government*, Victoria University Press, Wellington.

Hayward, J. (ed.) 2003, *Local Government and the Treaty of Waitangi*, Oxford University Press, Melbourne.

Local Government New Zealand 2002, *To Vote or Not to Vote. A Snapshot of the 2001 Local Government Elections*, Local Government New Zealand, Wellington.

New Zealand Society of Local Government Managers, Local Government New Zealand, and Department of Internal Affairs 2003, *The KNOWHOW Guide to Decision Making under the Local Government Act 2002*, Local Government New Zealand, Wellington.

Representative

Process

Despite New Zealand's substantial experience of representative democracy, with an electoral system that spans over 150 years, rates of participation in elections and political parties are in decline. The case for public engagement is built on at least two arguments: it allows us to exert a measure of influence over the 'public' sphere of our lives; and it provides some protection against the possibility that the political elite will gradually transform the political system into an 'elective dictatorship'. Given that participation rates are particularly low among the younger generations, there have been calls for citizenship education geared towards increasing the levels of political literacy and involvement.

Part D is structured around the following general interests:

- **Elections**. Chapters 4.1 to 4.4 explore the linkages between elections, campaigns and voters, with the last chapter combining these three elements in its analysis of the 2005 campaign. Chapter 4.1 raises the conundrum of why, despite greatly increased competition for the party vote under proportional representation, voter turnout has fallen to historic lows. In focusing on why the young are less likely to vote, chapter 4.2 weighs up the relative merits of the life-cycle and generational theories of voter participation. On a similar theme, chapter 4.3 describes the ways in which campaigning has changed over time and concludes that campaigns have become more centrally planned and professional, and that public participation has declined as a result.

- **Parties.** With over 20 parties contesting the 2005 campaign, and with eight of these parties going on to win seats in the new parliament, the scope of our analysis has been limited to the major parties, the two most popular minor parties (New Zealand First and the Greens), the new Maori party, and the political future of the religious right. In winning a total of four seats in its first general election, the Maori party has revived interest in the potential viability of an indigenous party in New Zealand's crowded multi-party system.
- **Media.** Chapter 6.1 poses the question of why public deliberation is important in a democracy. It argues for greater public involvement, 'even if time and attention span are just two of the enemies of a fuller role for direct participation'. Among the barriers to greater public deliberation are: the growing concentration of media ownership and control the hands of transnational media empires (chapters 6.2 and 6.6); the blurring effects of the politics of spin (chapter 6.3); and the controlled release of information by the politico-communications elite (chapters 6.4 and 6.5).
- **Participation**. The final chapters in Part D consider methods of participation and ways by which it can be encouraged. Suggestions include becoming a member of a community organisation (chapter 7.1) or interest group (chapters 7.2 and 7.3), or through the increased use of petitions and referenda (chapter 7.4). The final chapter discusses various attempts to encourage active citizenship, including introducing citizenship education as a compulsory part of the school curriculum.

4.0   Elections

Elections and the Electoral System

Alan McRobie

Voting is one of the commonest and simplest of political acts in today's world. Yet elections in which virtually all adult citizens are entitled to vote are a relatively recent phenomenon. It is only in the period since the end of the Second World War that by far the great majority of the world's states have adopted elections as a means of choosing the members of their legislatures. Yet many of the 213 nations that were, in 2004, identified as having an electoral system (IDEA 2005, pp. 166–73) do not meet the criteria for 'democratic elections' as defined by scholars and others.

How do we define a 'democracy'? According to Schumpeter (1976, p. 269) democracy is 'an institutional arrangement for arriving at political decisions in which individuals acquire the power to decide by means of a competitive struggle for the people's vote'. By this definition democracy is a process of establishing and maintaining the rule of law in which a nation's leaders are chosen in regular, free, fair, and competitive elections; where a government defeated in an election peacefully surrenders power and authority to the victor; and where the victor exercises that power during its tenure in office to make and implement policies for which it is subsequently accountable to voters at the next election (Butler & Ranney 1994, pp. 11–12; Weiner & Özbudun 1987, pp. 4–5).

Butler, Penniman and Ranney (1981, p. 3) have identified a number of conditions that characterise democratic elections:

- All adults have the right to vote.
- Elections are held at regular, prescribed intervals.
- All groups in the society have the opportunity to form political parties and nominate candidates.

- All seats in the legislature are subject to election and are usually contested.
- Election campaigns are conducted 'fairly' in the sense that all candidates are able to promote their views, and electors are able to discuss and evaluate them.
- The act of voting is free and without intimidation, and the ballot is secret.
- The outcome of the election is reported honestly.
- The winning candidates are duly installed in office for the duration of the prescribed term.

Elections are, therefore, about citizens' right to decide, periodically, who will govern them. But the connection between choosing between candidates and parties, and deciding between policies promoted by them is, at best, indirect (Butler et al. 1981, p. 300; Harrop & Miller 1987, p. 199). While voters are not asked explicitly or directly during an election to determine the current issues of public policy, they are being asked to nominate which candidate, or which political party, they wish to see represented in the country's legislature and forming the next executive. Elections in modern liberal democratic societies thus provide the means whereby the mass population can be encouraged to form a sense of political community through being able, at least ostensibly, to bring a measure of influence to bear on those who govern them. They also provide an essential mechanism linking governors and governed, although the predominant direction of this linkage is downwards.

ELECTIONS IN NEW ZEALAND

New Zealand was one of the first countries to begin developing an electoral system embracing the criteria now generally accepted as the hallmarks of democratic government. It is one of the few countries whose democratic electoral system extends over one-and-a-half centuries. This does not mean, however, that each step along this path was carefully and meticulously planned; rather, New Zealand's electoral system has evolved over time in an incremental and somewhat piecemeal fashion.

The basis for New Zealand's electoral system is to be found in the Constitution Act 1852, which granted representative government and authorised the establishment of electoral districts. The first competitive elections were held between July and October 1853 five-yearly until 1876, and thereafter, with a small number of exceptions, triennially.

The right to vote is a central element of any democratic system. From the outset New Zealand's franchise provisions (which, at first, were restricted to males) were grounded on a very liberal property qualification (McRobie 1989, p. 29; Atkinson 2003, pp. 23–4). Universal manhood suffrage, from age twenty-one and based on residence, was introduced in 1879. Women won the right to vote on the same basis as men in 1893—a world first at a national level—and in 1919 they won the right to be elected to parliament. The minimum voting age was lowered to twenty in 1969 and eighteen in 1974.

Although electoral rolls were established and maintained on an annual basis from the time of the first elections in 1853, compulsory registration was not introduced until 1924 for general electors.[1] Multiple voting characterised the country's earliest elections, but the idea that all votes should be of equal value was strongly held, and in 1889 multiple voting on the basis of property ownership was abolished. Seven years later the sole qualification for registration as an elector was restricted to one's place of residence. Even so, it was not until the abolition of the country quota[2] in 1945 that New Zealand achieved something approximating 'one person–one vote–one value'.

An important development in the direction of free and fair elections was the adoption, in 1870, of an Australian innovation, the secret ballot, designed to prevent intimidation of voters. Other advances were the early adoption of laws against illegal and corrupt practices such as personation (voting in the name of another registered elector), bribery, treating,[3] or seeking to exert undue influence on voters; and providing for the orderly resolution of elections where the result is disputed. The 1852 Constitution Act provided that the House of Representatives would adjudicate on disputed elections; in 1880 parliament surrendered this power to the Supreme Court.

Another contentious issue in polities where representation is based on single-member districts is the manner in which electoral districts are defined. In many states this is seen as a political question to be resolved ultimately by politicians themselves. Where politicians are directly involved, the potential for gerrymandering is a distinct possibility. New Zealand's approach to electoral redistribution has long differed from that of other countries. As early as 1887, redistributions were removed from political influence with the establishment of an independent, non-partisan Representation Commission.[4] Since then, the political impact of electoral redistributions has been the result of chance factors, not deliberate manipulation.

Today, New Zealand's electoral law treats Māori and non-Māori more or less equally, but this has not always been the case. Although Māori were granted universal manhood suffrage 12 years before non-Māori (Levine 1978, p. 272), this was very much an exception. The secret ballot did not apply to Māori elections until 1937; the registration of Māori electors, first legislated for in 1914, did not apply until 1949; and the compulsory registration of Māori electors did not take place until 1956. Despite substantial changes to both the number and distribution of the Māori population, the Representation Commission was expressly prohibited from redrawing the boundaries of the four separate Māori electorates until 1983, and the rules governing Māori and non-Māori representation were not placed on a broadly equal footing until 1993, although while the provisions governing the regular revision of the boundaries of general electorates are entrenched, the same protection is not accorded the revision of Māori electorate boundaries.[5]

Competitive elections have long been a feature of the New Zealand political scene. Although some seats in the country's earliest elections were not contested, uncontested elections have been rare since the emergence of organised political parties at the end of the nineteenth century. However, until the Mixed Member Proportional

(MMP) electoral system was introduced in 1996, electoral contests were essentially ones between candidates seeking to represent a specific electoral district. Thus, during the First-Past-the-Post (FPP) era, political parties were very much at the periphery of the electoral system. In its original form, the Electoral Act 1956 made no reference to political parties, and later amendments incorporating provisions relating to parties were confined to the right of parties not directly represented on the Representation Commission to make submissions to that body before it commenced its deliberations, and parties' right to display logos, rosettes, ribbons, and streamers on election day. The adoption of MMP has shifted political parties from the periphery to the very centre of the electoral system.

NEW ZEALAND'S ELECTORAL SYSTEM

An electoral system is a body of laws that authoritatively establishes the procedure through which a community's political preferences are expressed (Quintel 1970, p. 752). These rules are of primary importance because their content and administration largely determine who will write all the other laws governing the community's behaviour (Rae 1971, pp. 3, 14). While the content may differ in detail across different democratic states, a number of basic considerations—the structure of the system, eligibility to vote, conduct of elections, the way in which votes cast are turned into seats in the legislature, the manner in which disputes are resolved, and the administrative structure overseeing the electoral process—are common to all.

New Zealand's electoral law is enshrined in two key pieces of legislation—the Constitution Act 1986 and the Electoral Act 1993—and also, to a slightly lesser degree, in the Broadcasting Act 1989. Together they provide the framework governing the conduct of the country's elections. The first two are unusual in the New Zealand context because they are the only pieces of legislation where nominated sections cannot be amended or repealed by a simple parliamentary majority. Section 17 of the Constitution Act 1986 (a provision entrenched by s 268 of the Electoral Act 1993) sets the maximum life of each parliament at 'three years … and no longer'. It is common, however, for a parliament to be dissolved shortly before its expiry date by the prime minister recommending a dissolution, which is then accepted by the Governor-General.

ELECTORAL BOUNDARIES

Electoral redistributions are carried out following each five-yearly census and are designed to maintain electoral equality. The rules governing redistributions seek to achieve a balance between maintaining independence from political interference and taking account of the political interests of those directly affected by the redistribution process.

The Representation Commission is required to redraw boundaries in accordance with a number of specified criteria. Equal population numbers, based on total population subject to a permitted variation from the established quota of plus or minus 5 per cent, is mandatory. In addition, a number of discretionary criteria—existing boundaries, community of interest, communications, topographical features, and projected changes in population during the life of the districts created—may be applied to produce coherent districts.

The commission has a maximum of six months to complete its work, which includes the preparation of proposed boundaries following submission from political parties represented in parliament and independent MPs, the receipt and consideration of objections and counter objections to its proposals, and the announcement of its final decisions—which have the force of law. All significant political parties (in practice, those with parliamentary representation) are entitled to make a submission to the commission before it commences its deliberations, but public participation is confined to the objection and counter objection segment of the process.

The commission has been responsible for determining the boundaries of the separate Māori electorates only since 1983. Māori have been able to choose whether to be registered on the general electoral roll or on the Māori roll since 1976, although this had no practical effect until 1995, when the number opting for the Māori roll was used to determine the number of Māori electorates for the first time.

FUNDING

Since 1896 the electoral legislation has prescribed limits on the amount of money individual candidates can spend on their election campaigns in the three months prior to each election. The present (2005) limit is $20,000.[6] Since the adoption of MMP, limits have also been placed on the amount that registered parties are able to spend—a maximum of $1 million plus $20,000 for each electorate contested. Parties that are not registered (and, therefore, are not able to contest the party vote) may spend up to $20,000 for each seat contested. Despite the emphasis on equal opportunity, the greater ability of more-established parties to raise finance is likely to give them a distinct advantage.

Since 1990, registered parties have been eligible to share in an allocation of public funding and election broadcasting time. Eligibility is based on a number of factors including the electoral support in the previous general election and any subsequent by-election, the number of MPs a party currently has, and other evidence of public support such as party membership and the results of public opinion polls. In 2005 the total amount available for public funding was increased from $2.081 million to $3.212 million—the first such increase since 1990. Nevertheless, the larger parties continued to be granted the lion's share of the total: Labour, the largest parliamentary party, was allocated 34.2 per cent of the total amount available, National received 28 per cent, while ACT, Green, New Zealand

First, and United Future were each allocated 6.2 per cent. Fourteen other parties shared the remaining 13.0 per cent.[7] Parties are not permitted to use their own resources to buy additional broadcasting time. Although this restriction is intended to prevent parties from 'buying' their way into office, the advantage clearly lies with the larger parties. Because television is now the dominant mode of election campaigning, the differential allocations of state funding and broadcasting time appear to run counter to the long-standing objective of providing all who seek elective office with equality of opportunity.

ELECTORAL REGISTRATION

Before a valid vote can be cast electors must first be registered. A qualified elector is one who is aged eighteen years or older on polling day; is a New Zealand citizen, or has been granted permanent residence; and who, at some stage, has lived in New Zealand continuously for at least one year and in an electoral district for at least one month. Those who are qualified may register up until 4pm on the day before the election, but applications received after writ day[8] are not included in the printed electoral rolls. All electors whose names are not included on a published roll must cast special votes on the day of the election.

The Electoral Enrolment Centre (EEC) undertakes continuous roll revisions. In election years the EEC's campaign is a substantial one, involving a registration mail-out to all persons on the electoral roll, extensive media advertising, and targeted campaigns to encourage those who are not registered to do so. However, although registration is compulsory, not all eligible electors do so—in 2005, 95.2 per cent of the estimated number of qualified electors were registered, a 1 per cent increase on the equivalent figure for 2002. Since 1987 (when data were first kept) the 18–29 year cohort has been consistently the most reluctant to register (see chapter 4.2 for a discussion on young voters). More refined data for the 2002 and 2005 elections reveals that the 18–24 year cohort, with an average registration of 83.9 per cent, is least likely to fulfil its statutory obligation. By contrast, the average registrations from the 25–29 year cohort were 96.3 per cent—fully consistent with registration data from all older cohorts. While penalties (a $100 fine for a first offence and a $200 fine for any subsequent conviction) are included in the Electoral Act, these have never been invoked, the EEC preferring to encourage electors to register rather than to impose penalties for non-compliance.

STANDING FOR ELECTION

Candidates must be both New Zealand citizens and registered electors. Constituency candidates need not be resident in the electorate they are nominated for, but they must consent to their nomination in writing and pay a deposit of (currently) $300 by cash, bank draft or bank cheque—no credit cards are accepted. This deposit is refunded to candidates winning at least 5 per cent of the total votes cast for constituency candidates. In 2005, a total of 597 candidates from eighteen registered parties plus seven unregistered parties, and eighteen independents, contested the sixty-nine constituency seats. Of these, 415 (69.5 per cent) forfeited their deposits.[9] A constituency candidate may not seek election for more than one electoral district, but there is nothing to prevent constituency candidates from also being included on a party list.

Registered parties may nominate lists of candidates to contest the party vote and, in practice, most do so.[10] Since 2002 registered parties submitting a party list to contest the party vote are required to deposit $1,000 with the Chief Electoral Officer, refundable if the party wins at least 0.5 per cent of all party votes cast for registered parties or if at least one of their candidates wins a constituency seat. In 2005, ten of the nineteen parties contesting the party vote forfeited their deposits.

THE CONDUCT OF ELECTIONS

The rules governing the conduct of elections are designed to ensure that the secrecy of each individual's vote is preserved and that the act of voting is made as simple as possible. Compared to many other countries, New Zealand's laws governing the casting of votes are very liberal. Electors are able to cast their votes at any polling place in the country, or at any designated polling place anywhere else in the world. Most electors vote at a polling place located within the electoral district in which they are registered and where their entitlement to vote can be confirmed immediately. In both 2002 and 2005 the Chief Electoral Office sent EasyVote cards to every person on the roll as at Writ day, an innovation that significantly speeded up the process when electors applied for a voting paper at a polling place.[11]

Compulsory registration means that persons not registered as electors are not entitled to cast a valid vote. Over the past eleven elections, between 10 and 13 per cent of all votes cast have been 'special votes', that is, votes cast at polling places where electors' entitlement to vote is not able to be verified immediately because they are away from their electorates on election day, or because their names do not appear on the printed rolls for the districts where they claim the right to vote. In these circumstances electors are required to complete a declaration, and the information provided is subsequently used to verify or reject the claim. Between 1972, when data were first made available, and 1999, 22.1 per cent of all special votes cast were disallowed, principally because the person voting was either not enrolled at all, or voted in an electorate other than the one in which he or she was registered.

A major change governing the eligibility of special votes—passed in 2002—has been the recognition that a significant number of electors who are correctly registered have had their party votes disallowed because they have cast their constituency vote for an electorate other than the one in which they were registered.[12] In the first MMP election in 1996, no fewer than 19,572 disallowed votes (38.9 per cent of those whose votes were disallowed because they were deemed to have been 'not enrolled') were actually correctly registered in an electorate other than the one for which they cast their constituency vote (Electoral Commission 1997, p. 2). Three years later this number exceeded 20,000 (Electoral Commission 2002, p. 1). As a result of the change, the number of special votes rejected because voters were deemed to be 'not enrolled' has been reduced by nearly two-thirds.[13]

WHEN ELECTION RESULTS ARE DISPUTED

One of the very great strengths of democratic elections is that they enable the peaceful transfer of power from one government to its successor. For this to happen the declaration of the result must be accepted as fair and honest, and, where doubt exists, mechanisms must be in place to achieve finality.

Where a constituency result is very close, and particularly where a returning officer's decisions concerning the admission or rejection of votes are disputed, a judicial recount may be sought. Supervised by a District Court judge, a full recount of all votes cast is carried out, including a review of the decisions made by the returning officer, to confirm that the law has been applied correctly and fairly. When completed, the judicial recount becomes the final result for the electorate. Following the 1999 election, judicial recounts were sought in two electorates, Tauranga and Rangitikei: neither resulted in any change to the returning officer's initial declaration. No judicial recounts were sought in either 2002 or 2005.

Political parties may also seek a judicial recount of all party votes cast, although the probability of this happening is slight. The only instance where this might occur is where a party just makes, or just fails to make, the statutory 5 per cent threshold entitling it to parliamentary representation. Since 5 per cent of the party vote entitles a qualifying party to six seats (whereas 4.99 per cent entitles it to none) all parties who secure representation, and any party right on the threshold, have a vested interest in satisfying themselves and their supporters that the declared proportions of the party vote are indeed correct.

There is one further avenue for challenging an election result. Once the final result has been declared any interested person—a candidate, a person claiming to be entitled to be declared elected, or a voter—may file an election petition challenging the election. At this point the focus shifts to an examination of corrupt and illegal practices as set out in the Electoral Act. Petitions are heard by the High Court, which must be guided by the substantial merits of the case. The court can admit any evidence it chooses, provided that the evidence is relevant to the issue before it. The court's decision may range from recounting the votes (after including or excluding votes that have been challenged), to declaring the election void, in which case a new election must be held. There have been few electoral petitions lodged in the past seventy years and even fewer have been successful. Since 1972, only six have been lodged: those in Hunua (1979) and Wairarapa (1987) succeeded, but those in Wellington Central (1972), Kapiti (1979), Taupo (1982), and Tauranga (2005) failed. (On this last-mentioned case, see HC TAU CIV 2005–470–000719.) Under MMP, electoral petitions seem even less frequent because a successful outcome is unlikely to alter the overall party balance in the House of Representatives in any way.

CONCLUSION

New Zealand's adoption of MMP in 1993 represented a fundamental change to an electoral system that had operated largely unquestioned for most of the previous 140 years. Even so, the 1993 Electoral Act was not a completely new piece of legislation—much was derived from the earlier 1956 Act, which set out the structure and rules governing the former FPP electoral system.

In most instances electoral systems develop incrementally, with politicians generally controlling the pace of change (for it is they who ultimately control the content of the electoral laws). Since its passage in 1993 the Electoral Act has been amended no fewer than eight times. Even before the first MMP election in 1996 the Act was amended twice: once to reverse the original order of the two parts of the ballot paper so that the party vote appeared in the left-hand column (the side of the page where people commence reading) thus emphasising, almost subliminally, the primacy of the party vote, and then—in the face of opposition from the Electoral Commission—the Commission's membership was augmented by the addition of two 'political' representatives whenever the Electoral Commission determined the allocation of state funding to qualifying political parties to meet the costs of election programmes broadcast on television and radio.

An even more obvious attempt by MPs to reassert control over the electoral system occurred immediately following the 1999 general election. Shortly after the 1996 election Alliance list MP, Alamein Kopu, resigned from her party but continued to sit as an independent MP. During the 1999 election campaign the Labour party promised to introduce legislation to prevent 'party-hopping' by requiring MPs who left their party during a parliamentary term to also resign from parliament, a move that was supported by the Alliance. The Electoral (Integrity) Amendment Act was finally passed in December 2001 but it quickly proved to be unworkable in practice—when Jim Anderton and three of his colleagues were expelled from the Alliance in May 2002, ways were quickly found to avoid the Act's intent. The only time that this provision was invoked before it expired on the night of the 2005 general election occurred when ACT MP, Donna Awatere-Huata, was suspended from her party 'for flouting caucus guidelines' (*Sunday Star-Times*, 26 January 2003). Awatere-Huata fought what was effectively an expulsion from the ACT party, all the way up to the Supreme Court which unanimously found against her (NZLR CA34/04 [2004]; SC CIV 9/2004 [2004]).[14]

An important and long-overdue legislative change was the decision to allow Māori electors to cast an ordinary vote at any polling place rather than having to seek out a designated Māori polling place. Previously, if Māori electors voted at a polling place that was not so designated, they were required to cast a special vote with all its attendant obstacles (Levine 1978, p. 278). The impact of this change was significant: in 1996, 37.5 per cent of all Māori special votes were disallowed, compared to 11.4 per cent for non-Māori special votes; three years later Māori special votes that were disallowed totalled 27.3 per cent compared with 11.5 per cent for non-Māori. Following the law change in 2002 the proportion of Māori special votes disallowed was much closer to that for non-Māori—13.5 per cent compared to 10.5 per cent— and in 2005 Māori special votes disallowed accounted for 16.5 per cent (of which 98.3 per cent were for persons not registered as electors) compared with 6.3 per cent for non-Māori voters (of which 90.3 per cent were cast by persons who were not registered). This, coupled with a law change that allows Māori to cast ordinary votes at any polling place (Māori or General) in their own electorate has made it very much easier for Māori to cast an ordinary vote with the result that many fewer votes are now disallowed.

The contentious issue of political representation on the Representation and Electoral Commissions still requires revisiting. Although it was considered by the MMP Review Committee in 2001 no change was recommended to parliament because the committee was sharply divided: the Labour and National parties (who, effectively, appoint the political representatives to the two commissions) supported the status quo, while the smaller parties favoured the removal of all political representation from both commissions (Electoral Commission 2001, pp. 2–3).[15] The need for complete transparency in decision-making in an MMP environment will ensure that this matter will be revisited at some future date.

Consideration should be given to altering the basis on which electoral districts are defined. By using total population as the key arithmetical determinant, quite wide variations in the number of electors—and, therefore the equality of the vote—result. At the time of the 2005 election, for example, 88.7 per cent of the Wellington Central electorate's population were registered as electors compared with only 71.7 per cent for Mangere, and an average of 56.0 per cent in the seven Māori electorates. Although some of this discrepancy can be explained by the lower number of eligible persons registering as electors in Mangere and the Māori electorates, a more significant factor is that some electorates have many more persons under the age of eighteen living in them than do others. Ideally, electorates based on the number of registered electors would best meet the concept of 'one person–one vote–one value' but since voter enrolments are not carried out until after electoral boundaries have been established, this is not practicable. Alternatively, electorates based on adult population (i.e. those eligible to register and vote) would better meet the objective of 'one vote–one value'.

New Zealand has now experienced four MMP elections. The first resulted in the formation of a majority coalition (National–New Zealand First) government which held together for less than two years. Those of 1999, 2002, and 2005 have all been minority coalition governments headed by Labour, with confidence and supply being secured as a result of agreements with one or, as in 2005, two minor parties. In each case coalition-forming negotiations took between two (1999) and nine (1996) weeks to conclude. Many New Zealanders, used to knowing which party will form their new government in the former FPP environment late on election night, have still not adjusted to the MMP environment and are frustrated at the length of time that elapses between election day and the announcement that a new government has been formed.[16]

In 2005 all registered parties recognised that campaigning emphasis should be on the party vote; while both major parties campaigned for both the electorate and party vote, apart from a few very minor exceptions, all other parties campaigned only for the latter. In this regard the 2005 election may be considered as completing the transition from FPP to the MMP environment.

It is clear that voters welcome the greater opportunity afforded by MMP to vote for their preferred candidate as their electorate representative, regardless of party affiliation, before casting their party vote for their preferred party. Although, at 28.1 per cent, the number of split votes in 2005 is 11.2 percentage points lower than in 2002, it is still very high compared with Germany's experience under MMP, where the average percentage of split votes in that country's first four elections was 6.9 per cent, and across the fourteen elections between 1953 and 2002, 11.4 per cent.[17]

One somewhat disturbing aspect of the 2005 election is that despite the much more intense competition for the party vote, voter turnout, at 80.3 per cent, remains significantly below the long-term average of 87.8 per cent.[18] While some of this may be attributed to better statistics and an increased proportion of eligible electors actually registering, voter turnout in the last two elections has been at an historically low level. One of the claims made for proportional representation electoral systems—that they encourage higher voter turnout (Vowles et al. 1998, p. 6) and enhance public participation (Royal Commission 1986, pp. 55–7)—does not appear to be being borne out in this country.

Even so, some of the benefits predicted by the Royal Commission have eventuated. The number of women MPs has risen from sixteen (16.5 per cent) in 1990 to thirty-nine (32.2 per cent) in 2005, and the number of Māori MPs from five (5.1 per cent) to twenty-one (17.4 per cent) in the same period. Pacific Islands and Asian MPs now account for 4.2 per cent of parliament's total membership.

When measured by accepted liberal democratic standards, New Zealand's electoral system stands up well. Over a long period of time it has shown itself to be robust, and it broadly meets the criteria for free, fair, competitive, and regular elections. Nevertheless, there are areas where practice could be significantly improved. The challenge over the next few years is to continue to refine its details so that it comes closer to the ideal than it is at present.

DISCUSSION QUESTIONS

1   To what extent do you think that New Zealand's electoral system meets the goal of 'one person–one vote–one value'?
2   How might political input into the electoral redistribution, and the taxpayers' contribution to campaign financing, be achieved without giving the largest parliamentary parties an apparent advantage?
3   Are the rules for allocating public money to qualifying political parties for campaign broadcasting fair to all, or should the total amount allocated be divided evenly between all qualifying parties?
4   At present New Zealand's electoral administration is divided between the Chief Electoral Office, the Electoral Enrolment Centre, and the Electoral Commission. What advantages might accrue from consolidating the entire electoral administration into a single authority. On the other hand, what disadvantages might arise?
5   Should would-be voters whose votes have been disallowed for whatever reason, be advised of this by the Chief Electoral Office?
6   What are the arguments, for and against, for including a provision in the Electoral Act to prevent elected MPs from deserting the party under whose banner they were elected, during the ensuing parliamentary term?

NOTES

1   The term 'general' refers to all electoral districts (or constituencies) other than the separate Maori electoral districts. Prior to 1975 the general roll was known as the 'European' roll.
2   Introduced in 1881 the country quota provided that rural electorates should have smaller populations (and, therefore, fewer electors) than urban electorates. Its purpose was to compensate rural dwellers for the inconvenience of larger electorates and more difficult communications. For most of its existence the country quota meant that rural electorates were 28 per cent smaller than urban electorates.
3   'Treating' is an offence involving the provision of, or payment for, food, drink, entertainment, or other inducements intended to influence electors to vote for or against a particular candidate, or to refrain from voting.

4   Canada adopted the concept of an independent commission in 1964. Australia did likewise in 1983.

5   C/f Electoral Act 1993, s 35 and s 45 with s 268.

6   This amount includes the Goods and Services Tax (GST), currently 12.5 per cent. For a commentary on the rules for disclosing political donations see Electoral Commission's annual reports to Parliament, esp. *AJHR* 2002, E.57, pp. 14–16, and *AJHR* 2003, E.57, pp. 19–22.

7   The Māori Party, which did not exist at the time of the 2002 general election, received 3.9 per cent, while the Progressive Party (renamed Jim Anderton's Progressive) received 2.3 per cent. Four of the parties allocated public funding did not ultimately contest the election.

8   A writ is the legal instruction issued by the Governor-General to the Chief Electoral Officer, authorising him or her to conduct an election. Writs set the nomination date, the date on which the election is to be held, and the last date for the return of the writ endorsed with the name of the successful candidate.

9   The comparable figures for 2002 were: 593 candidates from twenty-eight parties plus independents, of whom 364 (61.4 per cent) lost their deposits; and for 1999: of the 678 candidates from thirty-two parties plus independents, 457 (67.4%) forfeited their deposits.

10 To obtain registration a party must demonstrate that it has at least 500 financial members who are eligible to register as electors. In 1996 there were twenty-two registered parties; in 1999 there were twenty-seven, of which twenty-two contested the party vote; and in 2002, twenty-four, of which fourteen contested the party vote; and in 2005 there were twenty-two of which nineteen contested the party vote.

11 Chief Electoral Office research indicates that 84 per cent of voters used their EasyVote cards when applying to vote.

12 This problem, which arose because the adoption of MMP significantly altered the electoral environment by giving each elector two votes—a party vote as well as a constituency vote—was first drawn to public attention in an article that appeared in the *National Business Review* on 8 March 1996.

13 In 2002 18,133 electors had their party votes counted even though they had cast their constituency vote for the wrong electorate. In 2005 the number of votes 'saved' by this provision was 25,520 (*AJHR* 2002 'The General Election, 2002' Part X; *AJHR* 2005, 'The General Election 2005' Part X).

14 This was the first case to be heard by the newly established Supreme Court. Interestingly, in mid-2003 National MP, Maurice Williamson, was suspended from his party's caucus 'until the next election' and placed on a good behaviour bond (*The Press*, 5 August 2003) but no attempt was made to invoke the Electoral (Integrity) Amendment Act. Following the 2005 election Winston Peters demanded that the Electoral (Integrity) Amendment Act be reinstated in return for New Zealand First's support for the Labour-led minority government on confidence and supply. The bill, without any sunset clause, was introduced in December 2005.

15 Alternatively, if complete removal of political representation was unacceptable, all smaller parties other than the Green Party supported extending the membership of each commission to include representation from all parties represented in Parliament.

16 The 2005 German federal election was held on 18 September, the same weekend as New Zealand's general election. The final results did not become available until

2 October, and the new Grand Coalition government was not officially appointed until 22 November, thirty-four days after New Zealand's Labour–Progressive Government was sworn in.

17　The frequency of split-ticket voting in Germany has risen gradually over the past fifty years. In both 1998 and 2002 the percentage was 20.9. Although data on the 2005 election was not available at the time of writing, analysts were predicting that it would exceed 21 per cent. It should be noted that, unlike New Zealand, Germany's data on split-ticket voting are estimates.

18　Comparable turnout data for the three previous MMP elections were 86.0 per cent in 1996, 83.1 per cent in 1999, and 76.4 per cent in 2002.

REFERENCES

Atkinson, N. 2003, *Adventures in Damocracy: A History of the Vote in New Zealand*, University of Otago Press, Dunedin.

Bogdanor, V. & D. Butler (eds) 1983, *Democracy and Elections: Electoral Systems and Their Political Consequences*, Cambridge University Press, Cambridge.

Butler, D., H.R. Penniman & A. Ranney (eds) 1981, *Democracy at the Polls: A Comparative Study of Competitive National Elections*, American Enterprise Institute, Washington DC.

Butler, D., & A. Ranney 1994, *Referendums Around the World: The Growing Use of Direct Democracy*, Macmillan Press, Basingstoke.

Electoral Commission 1997, Electoral Brief, no. 7, September.

Electoral Commission 2001, Electoral Brief, no. 20, September.

Electoral Commission 2002, Electoral Brief, no. 21, March.

Harrop, M. & W.L. Miller 1987, *Elections and Voters: A Comparative Introduction*, Macmillan, London.

Institute for Democracy and Electoral Assistance (IDEA) 2005, *Electoral System Design: The New International IDEA Handbook*, Stockholm.

Levine, S. (ed.) 1978, *Politics in New Zealand: A Reader*, George Allen & Unwin, Sydney.

Lijphart, A. 1984, *Democracies*, Yale University Press, New Haven & London.

Mackenzie, W.J.M. 1958, *Free Elections*, George Allen & Unwin, London.

McRobie, A. 1996, 'When Votes May Go to Waste: A Disenfranchising Glitch in the Old Electoral Law Will Carry Through to the MMP System', *National Business Review*, Wellington, 8 March, pp. 24–6.

McRobie, A. 1989, *New Zealand Electoral Atlas*, Government Printer, Wellington.

New Zealand Law Reports (NZLR), Court of Appeal CA34/04 [2004]; Supreme Court, SC CIV 9/2004 [2004].

Quintel, D.P. 1970, 'The Theory of Electoral Systems', *Western Political Quarterly*, December.

Rae, D.W. 1971, *The Political Consequences of Electoral Laws*, revised edn, Yale University Press, New Haven & London.

Schumpeter, J.A. 1976, *Capitalism, Socialism and Democracy*, 5th edn, George Allen & Unwin, London.

Taylor, P.J. & R.J. Johnston 1979, *Geography of Elections*, Penguin, Harmondsworth, Middlesex.

Weiner, M. & E. Özbudun (eds) 1987, *Competitive Elections in Developing Countries*, American Enterprise Institute, Washington DC.

FURTHER READING

Dahl, R.A. 1989, *Democracy and its Critics*, Yale University Press, New Haven & London.

Electoral Act 1993 (June 2005 reprint).

Electoral Act 1956.

Electoral Commission, Annual Reports, 1995–2002 (*AJHR* E.57)

Farrell, D.M. 2001, *Electoral Systems: A Comparative Introduction*, Palgrave, Basingstoke.

Inquiry into the Report of the Royal Commission on the Electoral System, Report of the Electoral Law Committee, Government Printer, Wellington, 1988.

Inquiry into the Review of MMP, *Report of the MMP Review Committee*, New Zealand House of Representatives 2001.

Joseph, Philip A. (ed.) 1995, *Essays on the Constitution*, Brooker's, Wellington.

Penniman, H.R. (ed.) 1980, *New Zealand at the Polls, The General Election of 1978*, Appendix A, American Enterprise Institute, Washington DC.

Royal Commission on the Electoral System 1986, *Towards a Better Democracy*, Government Printer, Wellington.

Taagepera, R., & M.S. Shugert 1989, *Seats and Votes: The Effects and Determinants of Electoral Systems*, Yale University Press, New Haven & London.

Vowles, J., P. Aimer, S. Banducci & J. Karp 1998, *Voters' Victory: New Zealand's First Election Under Proportional Representation*, Auckland University Press, Auckland.

Voting

Jack Vowles

Studies of voting usually ask: who voted for what parties and why? There are other important questions. Why do some people vote, and others not? Not voting has consequences, although not necessarily the obvious ones. International evidence indicates that the effects of higher or lower turnouts on party vote shares are weak, if any.[1] Higher turnout may be associated with greater Labour successes in New Zealand, although the evidence is mixed (Nagel 1988). There is better evidence for turnout effects in terms of agenda-setting. Where particular groups of people are less likely to vote than others, government decisions are less likely to reflect their needs and wishes.[2]

ESTIMATING TURNOUT IN NEW ZEALAND

Estimating turnout is not as easy as it seems. The official figures are a percentage of the number on the electoral rolls. Despite compulsory enrolment in New Zealand, non-enrolment has no penalty. Roll accuracy differs between elections. Included in the calculations are disallowed special votes and informal votes, some perhaps cast as a protest. Some special votes are disallowed because those who cast them are not on the electoral rolls, so using the rolls as the base is misleading. Given these problems, valid votes should be put on a base of the age-eligible population, those people who could be enrolled to vote on the basis of residency and age. The size of that group is now estimated before each election for the Electoral Enrolment Centre. It can be estimated from census data for the years before this data was generated (Nagel 1988).

Table 4.2.1: Roll coverage, and two estimates of turnout 1999–2005

	1999	*2002*	*2005*
Percentage enrolled	91.06	94.17	95.22
Enrolment change		+3.11	+1.05
Percentage official turnout	84.77	76.98	80.92
Official turnout change		−7.79	+3.94
Percentage valid vote/age-eligible turnout	75.00	71.70	76.10
Age-eligible turnout change		−3.3	4.4

Table 4.2.1 shows why these differences in estimation matter. In 2002, roll coverage increased by about 3 percentage points. At the same time, official turnout registered nearly an 8-point decline. The real decline was only about 3 points because increased enrolment in 2002 simply meant that more people who did not vote were enrolled. In 2005 the roll went up again, but this time so did turnout, with the result that the official figures slightly underestimate the turnout increase.

Turnout used to be very high in New Zealand. Despite claims otherwise, the picture has changed. New Zealand turnout probably remains in the top third of countries with available data, a performance better than in Britain, the USA, and Canada. But of twenty-two advanced democracies, recent research indicates that up to 1999 New Zealand's turnout decline since 1945 was the eighth steepest, and well above average (Franklin 2004, p. 11).

THEORIES OF ELECTORAL TURNOUT

Developing his rational choice theory of voting, Antony Downs (1957) argued that it is more useful to consider why people vote than to ask why they do not. The probability of vote (pV) is conditioned by, first, and negatively, the costs to an individual involved in casting a vote (C); second, positively, the benefits the individual expects if their party or candidate were to be elected (B); and third, the probability that vote of the individual concerned might determine the result (P). The relationship between B and P is assumed to be multiplicative, that is: $pV = (B*P) - C$ (Blais 2000).

Some models add a fourth variable, D, which stands for civic duty (Riker and Ordeshook 1968). This appears inconsistent with a rational choice model, which rests on the assumption of self-regarding individuals single-mindedly maximising their utilities without any concern for others. But it has logic as a solution to a Prisoners' Dilemma. After repeated games within which players fail to cooperate and therefore achieve suboptimal common results, individuals learn that cooperation is better than competition in maximising their long-run utilities (Schelling 1978; Shepsle & Boncheck 1997). Democracy is worth supporting by casting a vote as it benefits everyone including oneself. One may, or may not, be convinced by this logic. The leap from enlightened self-interest to a sense of civic duty is a long one. A sense of 'civic duty' that one must vote is very close to the act of voting. To say that it explains voting is close to tautology. The habit of voting helps generate civic duty. Sceptics argue that civic duty is 'endogenous', caused as much by voting as it is a cause of voting.

RECENT DEVELOPMENTS IN THEORY AND RESEARCH

There are two main thrusts in recent empirical literature. Costs associated with voting are not just the time and effort needed to cast a vote at the polling place (Milner 2002). More significant costs concern information. Voting without information is risky. Psychologically, it might be better not to vote and therefore not to influence the outcome than to cast a vote that one might later regret. There is evidence that people in the USA now know less about politics than did their counterparts in previous generations. If this is more generally the case, this could explain why turnout is declining in other countries. Historical data with which to test this claim is lacking in New Zealand.

Competitiveness is the other thrust in the literature. A study of voting turnout covering twenty-two countries since 1945, including New Zealand, develops a provocative thesis (Franklin 2004). It argues that the main driver of turnout is electoral competitiveness. There is a related question: 'Do elections matter?' If institutional arrangements make it difficult to translate votes into accountable and responsible government, one might expect turnout to be low. Extreme low-turnout cases fit the model well: the USA, where federalism, the separation of powers, and divided government conspire against responsive government; and Switzerland, where the same parties have formed a coalition government since 1959.

A related argument is based on generations, or age cohorts. Young people are less prone to vote and older people more likely to do so, findings that were first interpreted as a life cycle effect. The growing consensus is that the age effects are generational in the USA,[3] Canada,[4] and several European countries.[5] Young people are less likely to vote than their counterparts at the same age in earlier generations. As they grow older they may continue to vote less than previous generations at the same ages. The study's main author, Mark Franklin (2004), argues that the effects of competitiveness act most strongly on young voters. He found, for example, that as Swiss governments failed to change, older voters conditioned to vote under earlier more competitive conditions continued to do so, whereas those coming of age to vote were less likely to vote. With generational replacement, turnout gradually declined.

Franklin also argues that a key driver of turnout decline has been the lowering of the voting age. Voting is learned behaviour facilitated by social cohesion incorporating young adults into social networks. Persons twenty-one and older are more likely to be in stable and society-sustaining relationships than those between eighteen and twenty.

If first-time voters fail to vote, this leaves a 'footprint'. Their probability of voting at later elections is lower than if their first opportunities to vote had been taken up.

MODELLING NEW ZEALAND ELECTIONS SINCE 1949

Franklin's model has been fitted to New Zealand's election-level turnout data since the late 1940s on an enrolment basis (Franklin 2004, p. 242). However, as argued above, an enrolment base for turnout is problematic. On an age-eligible base, turnout change trends are clearer. But these raise problems for the analysis, which is a time series characteristic of much economic data. The trends turn out to be 'non-stationary', which means a statistical model based on turnout election by election could be misleading.[6] Turnout is more safely recoded as a change variable from one election to the next.

To retest the Franklin theory, a statistical model explaining and predicting New Zealand turnout since 1949 is reported in table 4.2.2. It contains four explanatory/predictor variables: change in the proportion of new voters (the increase in the age-eligible population at the election in question compared to that before, plus deaths

Table 4.2.2: Explaining and predicting turnout change in New Zealand, 1949–2005

OLS Regression suppressing constant term	1	2	3	4
	r	B (SE)	Variable Values 2002–2005	Effects in 2005**
Change in percentage new voters	0.11	0.08 (0.22)	3.3	0.26
Change in competitiveness***	0.39	0.25* (0.09)	18.7	4.69
Change in competitiveness x new voters	0.30	0.04 (0.03)	61.7	2.24
Lagged change in competitiveness	0.10	0.28* (0.11)	−12.2	−3.40
Predicted Change				3.78
Previous turnout (2002)				71.7
Predicted turnout				75.5
Actual turnout (2005)				76.1
Adjusted R^2		0.23		
N		20		
Durbin Watson	1.9			

*   Significant at .05 or better.

** The figures in column 4 are the result of multiplying B (from column 2) by the variable values in column 3. These sum to the predicted change figure of 3.78.

*** Competitiveness is at its maximum at 100 (no difference between the two main parties). A 20-point difference would therefore score at 80.

Figure 4.2.1: Actual and predicted turnout in New Zealand, 1949–2005

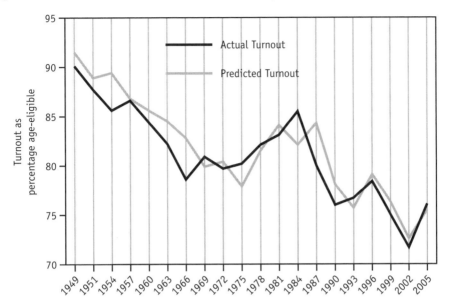

Source: New Zealand Electoral Commission 2003; Nagel 1988.

between the two elections, less net immigration, as a percentage of the current election's age-eligible population); change in competitiveness, measured in terms of the percentage distances in votes between the two major parties at that election and the one before; change in competitiveness between the election before and the election before that; and an interaction of these changes between new voters and competitiveness to test whether new voters respond more to competition.[7]

Not as expected by Franklin, column 1 shows that an increase in new voters correlates with increasing turnout. (These figures are Pearson's r correlations, where 1 equals complete sameness, 0 no relationship, and −1 complete opposition). But in the regression model results in column 2 the actual effects of change among new voters turn out to be very small and quite probably illusory, particularly given a lack of statistical significance and the size of the standard error term next to it.[8]

Supporting Franklin, when new voters are influenced by competitiveness, the effect is much stronger, falling only slightly short of conventional statistical significance. Competitiveness itself has quite strong and significant effects on people of all ages, for the current election, and the one before. In general, the model can predict turnout change with some confidence. There are some elections where it fails conspicuously: 1966, 1975, 1984, and 1987 in particular, elections that many would agree stand out as exceptional in New Zealand political history. Aspects of these elections outside the compass of the variables in the model can be said to have 'reset' turnout trends and the model can only adapt afterwards. As for other differences between the predicted and actual values, we

Figure 4.2.2: Competitiveness in New Zealand elections, 1949–2005

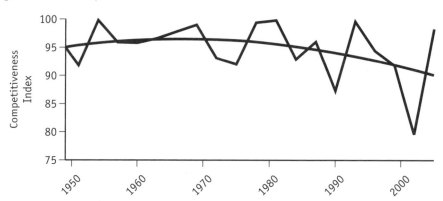

would not expect such a model to be completely accurate. It cannot take into account other factors such as party efforts to mobilise voters and the campaign in general.

In general, as figure 4.2.2 indicates, competitiveness between Labour and National has varied over time. (Where National and Labour gained the same vote shares exactly, the index would stand at 100, where they were, say, 20 points apart, the score would be 80). But the second order polynomial trend line drawn through the figure shows the general trend has been towards less competition—hence, lower turnout.

While all this supports some of Franklin's claims, further analysis does not find evidence of effects of the lowering of the voting age. Nor do the new voter effects operate over the first three elections at which people become eligible to vote, as Franklin assumes, but only on the first. Nor, considering claims from other literature, does further analysis find any effects of MMP on turnout. With only twenty elections as cases, some smaller effects could be too small to register at the macro or aggregate level, but might be discerned at the micro or individual level.

INDIVIDUAL LEVEL EVIDENCE

New Zealand election survey data, sampled at the level of the individual voter, can be used to further test these claims. The data is from 1963, 1975, 1981, and 1987 through to 2002 all combined in a single dataset, giving a combined respondent total of about 25,000. Data from the 2005 election was not ready for inclusion in this chapter. The data from 1963 to 1987 is imperfect, as surveys usually over-report votes. That said, after much international research there is a general consensus that this tends not to bias findings seriously. From 1990 onwards, respondent turnout is validated by inspection of the marked rolls. The hypothesis that age effects are primarily generational, not life-cycle, is well supported, although there is some evidence of the latter.

Figure 4.2.3: Per cent probabilities of not voting by generations, at elections 1963–2002

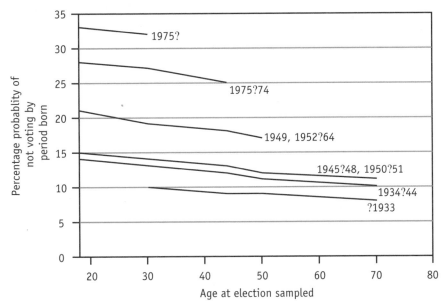

Source: Victoria University Studies 1963, 1975; 1981 Study; NZES 1987–2002. Pooled Sample, derived from Model I, see Appendix.

Based on a logistic regression model reported in Appendix A, figure 4.2.3 shows that about the age of 30—the age at which all component samples contain an overlap—a person born in 1970 and after is about 22 per cent less likely to vote than a person born in 1933 or earlier. The model includes controls for the special circumstances of all elections, compared to 2002. There is evidence of an effect for the reduction of the voting age. The group affected—those born in 1949 (with the lowering of the age to twenty) and from 1952—are 5 to 6 per cent less likely to vote than their immediate predecessor cohort. A significant gap opens up at this point. Yet there is obviously more going on. No more affected by the lowering of the voting age than those who first experienced it, later cohorts are even less likely to vote.

The first model setup reported in figure 4.2.3 uses dummy variables (1 or 0) for each election except 2002 to stabilise the estimates (this makes little difference to the slopes for each cohort). An alternative version substitutes competitiveness for each election—the absolute difference in vote percentages between the two main parties—in place of the election dummies (see Appendix A). Adding this control for competitiveness indicates that half the generational effects can be accounted for by the competitiveness of the election at which respondents were sampled. No generational effects prior to the suffrage reduction cohort remain significant. But differences still remain between the post suffrage extension age cohorts.

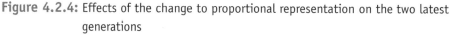

Figure 4.2.4: Effects of the change to proportional representation on the two latest generations

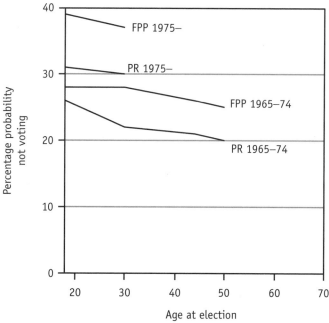

The question of the effects of MMP from 1996 onwards can be addressed by introducing a proportional representation (PR) code of 1 for the elections from 1996 onward, 0 for those before. Adding this to the competitiveness, cohort, and life cycle model replicates the consistent finding in the international literature that PR facilitates higher turnout, albeit a small but significant effect of about 4 per cent (see Appendix A). More important, the shift to PR appears to facilitate even higher turnout than would otherwise have been the case under first past the post, among those born after 1975: an 8 per cent effect. The effect reduces in the older generations to only a marginal difference in the oldest cohort (see Appendix B).

Depending on the model setup, the negative effect of belonging to the post-1974 generation on turnout is between 20 and 30 per cent. Report of the findings that follow is based on the effects of the changes other variables make to that probability when added to the model, thereby 'decomposing' the effects of the age generations, and thereby seeking to explain them. (Similar albeit smaller effects are generally found on the other later generations as well.)

1 As an aspect of social cohesion, we would expect trends of later marriage among more recent generations to partly explain lower turnout. *This has the expected effect, although it is small (about 3 per cent).*

2 High proportions of more recent generations with university education should increase apparent age effects when added to the model, that is, this should act against the generational trends toward lower turnout. *However, no such effect is found.*

3   Persons in more recent generations will be less likely to identify with political parties than persons in older generations at the same point in the life cycle; if so, this may partly explain generational effects. *Party identification strongly influences turnout but not through generational differences as hypothesised.*

4   Those in manual households are less likely to vote, and declining proportion of manual occupations available to people in recent generations will make them more likely to have higher status non-manual jobs making them more disposed to vote, thus acting against generational effects on turnout. *But there are no such occupational or class effects associated with the generations.*

5   Māori are less likely to vote in the absence of electoral competition in their electorates (except in 1996 and 1999) and because they are less integrated into the political system, and with lower levels of political knowledge and education. An increasing proportion of the electorate among more recent generations will be responsible for some of the generational effects on turnout. *There is an effect, but it is very small, of the order of only 2 per cent.* However, data on ethnicity is available only in the 1975 and datasets from 1987 and after.

6   Immigrants will be less likely to vote, again for reasons of lower political integration. As the proportion of immigrants rises, their higher concentration in more recent generations will partly account for generational differences in turnout. *No such effects are found.*

7   The effect of generational change on turnout will run through interest in politics, that is, the younger generations are less interested in politics and therefore adding interest in politics to the model will apparently reduce the generational effects. *This is supported moderately well, with about a 9 per cent effect.*

8   Younger generations will have a lower sense of civic duty, thus adding this to the model will also apparently reduce the generational effects. *This has the strongest effects of all, about 13 per cent, roughly half of the generational effects.*

After all this analysis, about half the generational effects are still unaccounted for in the most comprehensive model that can be constructed, drawing only on the post-1990 datasets.

CONCLUSION

Structural effects (marriage, changing demography) on voter turnout are weak. Lower interest in politics and a more attenuated sense of civic duty provide most of the available explanation for lower turnout in the more recent generations. This may or may not be associated with lower knowledge about politics among those in the recent generations: there is no comparable data about levels of political knowledge from the earlier election studies that can be used to test this hypothesis. More education about politics in schools and tertiary institutions might help boost turnout. Currently, while education is associated with turnout, increasing levels of education have not boosted turnout as one might expect if the effects of education were to significantly enhance political knowledge.

Reduction of the voting age explains about 6 per cent (the difference between the turnout probability of baby-boomers affected or not affected by the change). Yet the ebbing of voting turnout among the younger generations does begin to take hold at about this time, 1969–72. Perhaps reduction of the voting age overlaps with cultural changes that began during this period, the effects of which have intensified on those coming to maturity later. Later generations probably have a more privately focused and apolitical political culture, the effects of which may be intensifying. Offsetting this, the shift to proportional representation also could have slightly offset the tendency of the youngest generation not to vote. Above all, the effects of competitiveness loom the largest. If elections are competitive, people are indeed more likely to vote, younger people even more so. Turnout decline is not an inexorable process. It can be halted and reversed.

DISCUSSION QUESTIONS

1   Why is electoral turnout in New Zealand higher than in many other democracies, such as the USA and Britain?
2   Account for the decline in turnout in the postwar period.
3   Do you agree with the Franklin argument that the main driver of turnout is electoral competitiveness?
4   What can be done to increase turnout rates among the young?

NOTES

1   For discussions in the relevant international literature, see: Grofman, Owen & Collet 1999; Highton & Wolfinger 2001; Citrin, Schickler & Sides 2003; and Marsh & Bernhagen 2005.
2   See, for example: Husted & Kenny 1997; Hill & Leighley 1992; Hill, Leighley & Hinton-Andersson 1995; Brady 2003; and Mueller & Stratmann 2003.
3   See, for example, Miller & Shanks 1996; Lyon & Alexander 2000; and Putnam 2002.
4   For a discussion on Canada, see Blais, Gidengil, Nevitte & Nadeau 2004.
5   European countries are discussed in Franklin 2004, pp. 59–89.
6   Simply, this means that there are different trends over different sections of the series influenced by exogenous 'shocks'. This is exactly the shape of the turnout data. For a standard statistical explanation of the problem see, for example, Gujarati 1995, pp. 709–21.

7   As is conventional in the literature, we assume that polls gave voters a good idea of how competitive the election result would be, and therefore data from the result itself is a good proxy for their expectations. Prior to the early 1970s there were no regular polls, which may explain the less satisfactory fit of predictions for elections before this period.

8   The model suppresses the constant term because theoretically, as a model on change, its constant term (with all explanatory change variables at 0) should also be 0. A model including a constant had a slightly higher R-squared, and a constant of -0.93 (standard error 0.53) which was not statistically significant. Given this, the theoretical assumption of a constant of 0 is more plausible than a statistically dubious marginally negative estimate.

REFERENCES

Blais A. 2000, *To Vote or Not to Vote? The Merits and Limits of Rational Choice Theory*, University of Pittsburgh Press, Pittsburgh.

Blais, A., E. Gidengil, N. Nevitte & R. Nadeau, 2004, 'Where Does Turnout Decline Come From?' *European Journal of Political Research*, 43, pp. 221–36.

Brady, D. 2003, 'The Politics of Poverty: Left Political Institutions, the Welfare State, and Poverty', *Social Forces*, 82/2, pp. 557–88.

Citrin, J., E. Schickler & J. Sides 2003, 'What If Everyone Voted? Simulating the Impact of Increased Turnout on Senate Elections', *American Journal of Political Science*, 47/1, pp. 75–90.

Downs, A. 1957, *An Economic Theory of Democracy*, Free Press, New York.

Franklin, M.N. 2004, *Voter Turnout and the Dynamics of Electoral Competition in Established Democracies since 1945*, Cambridge University Press, Cambridge.

Grofman, B., G. Owen & C. Collet 1999, 'Rethinking the Partisan Effects of Higher Turnout: So What's the Question?' *Public Choice*, 99, pp. 357–76.

Gujarati, D.N., *Basic Econometrics*, 3rd edn, McGraw Hill, New York.

Highton, B. & R.E. Wolfinger 2001, 'The Political Implications of Higher Turnout', *British Journal of Political Science*, 31, pp. 179–223.

Hill, K.Q. & J.E. Leighley 1992, 'The Policy Consequences of Class Bias in State Electorates', *American Journal of Political Science*, 36/2, pp. 351–65.

Hill, K.Q., J.E. Leighley & A. Hinton-Andersson 1995, 'Lower-Class Mobilisation and Policy Linkage in the U.S. States', *American Journal of Political Science*, 39/1, pp. 75–86.

Husted, T.A. & L.W. Kenny 1997, 'The Effect of the Expansion of the Voting Franchise on the Size of Government', *Journal of Political Economy*, 105/1.

Lyons, W. & R. Alexander 2000, 'A Tale of Two Electorates: Generational Replacement and the Decline of Voting in Presidential Elections', *Journal of Politics*, 62, pp. 1014–34.

Marsh, M. & P. Bernhagen 2005, 'Turnout Matters: Sometimes', Paper presented at the CSES Conference, Taipei, 10–11 March.

Miller, W.E. & J.M. Shanks 1996, *The New American Voter*, Harvard University Press, Cambridge, MA.

Milner, H. 2002, *Civic Literacy: How Informed Citizens Make Democracy Work.* University Press of New England, Hanover NE.

Mueller, D.C. & T. Stratmann 2003, 'The Economic Effects of Democratic Participation', *Journal of Public Economics*, 87, pp. 2129–55.

Nagel, J. 1988, 'Voter Turnout in New Zealand General Elections 1928–1988', *Political Science*, 40/2, pp. 16–38.

New Zealand Electoral Commission 2003, *The New Zealand Electoral Compendium*, New Zealand Electoral Commission, Wellington.

Putnam, R. 2002, *Bowling Alone. The Collapse and Revival of American Community.* Simon and Schuster, New York.

Riker, W.H. & P.C. Ordeshook 1968, 'A Theory of the Calculus of Voting', *American Political Science Review*, 62, pp. 25–44.

Schelling, T.C. 1978, *Micromotives and Macrobehaviour*, W.W. Norton, New York.

Shepsle, K.A. & M.S. Boncheck 1997, *Analysing Politics: Rationality, Balance, and Institutions*, W.W. Norton, New York.

FURTHER READING

Blais A. 2000, *To Vote or Not to Vote? The Merits and Limits of Rational Choice Theory*, University of Pittsburgh Press, Pittsburgh.

Blais, A., E. Gidengil, N. Nevitte & R. Nadeau, 2004, 'Where Does Turnout Decline Come From?' *European Journal of Political Research*, 43, pp. 221–36.

Franklin, M.N. 2004, *Voter Turnout and the Dynamics of Electoral Competition in Established Democracies since 1945*, Cambridge University Press, Cambridge.

Milner, H. 2002, *Civic Literacy: How Informed Citizens Make Democracy Work.* University Press of New England, Hanover NE.

Nagel, J. 1988, 'Voter Turnout in New Zealand General Elections 1928–1988', *Political Science*, 40/2, pp. 16–38.

Campaigning

Chris Rudd & Janine Hayward

Political campaigning at election time has undergone significant changes in form and function during the postwar period. But this transformation has, for the most part, added new campaigning styles and tools, rather than replacing the original principles of the political campaign. Ironically, as campaigning techniques have become more sophisticated, public disengagement from politics has also increased. With more voters than ever before uncertain as to whom they will vote for, and whether or not to vote at all, campaigning is all the more important for the success of any political party.

'Political campaigning' essentially refers to the activity of political parties attempting to engage with potential voters. New Zealand has an 'official' campaign period which begins four weeks before the general election, traditionally launched with the opening addresses of the incumbent and opposition parties. While this chapter will focus on the official campaign period, we acknowledge, however, that political parties are often in a constant state of campaigning (the 'permanent' campaign) between one election and the next.

THE PHASES OF ELECTION CAMPAIGNING

Various theories and models have been developed to explain the changes in political campaigning in the last hundred years or so. Farrell and Webb (2000) identify three phases of pre-television, television, and new technologies; Norris (2000) similarly talks of pre-modern, modern, and postmodern campaigning. These theorists concur on the fundamental principles of campaigning through time, although they debate some of the finer details. Their common conclusion is that the developments in campaigning techniques, such as television and new technology, have added to, as opposed to replacing, the traditional principles of election campaigning established in very early years. Norris says, 'changes in campaign communications can best be understood as evolutionary processes of *modernization* that simultaneously transform party organizations, the news media, and the electorate' (2000, p. 137).

1. Pre-modern/pre-television campaigning

The pre-modern or pre-television campaigning period in New Zealand extended up until about 1969, and describes a period when mass membership of political parties was common. New Zealand had some of the highest party membership in the Western world during this period (Miller 2004, p. 7). This membership acted as campaign volunteers, whose contributions to organise and finance campaign events, mobilise voters and monitor public opinion overwhelmingly characterised the campaign style of the time. These campaigns were limited in planning, and informally coordinated and orchestrated. Volunteers canvassed door-to-door and distributed leaflets, essentially using direct methods of appeal and communication, as mass communication was not at their disposal. This period is often considered a 'golden age' in campaigning, when candidates worked hard and voters really seemed to care about the issues.

In the 1920s and 1930s radio started to have some impact in terms of simultaneously communicating the campaign message to larger audiences than the campaign meetings could reach. But it is important not to romanticise this campaign era; the party leader often played a central 'larger than life' role in the campaign, not unlike the widely criticised 'presidential style' campaigning we see today.

As Norris summarises, the pre-modern campaign organisation was 'based on direct forms of interpersonal communications between candidates and citizens at the local level, with short-term, ad hoc planning by the party leadership' (2000, p. 137).

2. Modern/television campaigning

With the introduction of television, the dynamics of the pre-modern campaign were forever changed. Party member volunteers were replaced by professional advisers and consultants, leading to a dramatic decline in party membership (Miller 2004, p. 10). A more professionalised, media-focused campaigning style emerged, and parties shifted their focus from local, face-to-face canvassing to advertising, public relations campaigns, and media performance. Miller argues that this shift also replaced the party's ideology and policy platform with a greater concern for mass marketing, party branding, and promotion of the leader's qualities and characteristics (2004, p. 9). Moreover, the traditional ideological Labour/National split was replaced by both parties' efforts to be inclusive and have mass appeal. The most important shift in dynamic was, of course, the ability for leaders to convey their message to mass audiences without the assistance of party members and volunteers. Campaigns became an integrated, planned, ensemble of logos, brands, and jingles; parties made use of focus groups to test ideas and formal opinion polling also began to emerge.

As Norris explains, in modern campaigns, 'party organization [is] co-ordinated more closely at a central level by political leaders [and] advised by external professional consultants like pollsters' (2000, p. 139). As a result, she concludes 'campaigns have become more distant from most voters leaving them disengaged spectators outside the process' (2000, p. 140).

3. Postmodern/new technologies campaigning

Given the impact television had on campaigning style and impact, the arrival of new technologies such as telecommunications, satellite transmission and the Internet might be expected to herald significant changes in campaigning style. More importantly, it provides the potential for voters to re-engage in the election campaign at the individual level, as the channels of communication are open from candidate to voter, and vice versa—a 'virtual world' version of the street-corner campaign and door-to-door canvassing of another era. But can new technologies deliver on these very high expectations of increased voter engagement? Certainly, the postmodern campaign has further centralised the campaign organisation, as parties capitalise on the ease of communication. But, as Farrell and Webb observe, it has also allowed the targeting of sections of the electorate, in a more sophisticated campaign than the 'one size fits all' mass media televised campaign (2000, p. 106). It has also introduced the concept of the 'permanent' election campaign, with spin doctors and public relations consultants working constantly between elections, not just before elections, to promote the party brand. In a further centralisation, the campaign is now generally conducted and organised by the political wing of the party, with the party leader playing a particularly central role. Senior politicians who will be in the campaign spotlight are assisted with speech writing and media performance, and the maintenance of the party website design and content becomes an important campaigning dimension. The continuity of the website also contributes to the 'permanent campaign' that parties run in the postmodern era, rather than the limited campaigning seen in earlier days.

HOW MUCH HAS CAMPAIGNING REALLY CHANGED?

Despite the emergence of new technologies, and the potential they are seen to offer in terms of re-engaging voters in the election campaign (and voting), how much has really changed in the postmodern era? As Norris notes (2000, p. 140), '[f]or some citizens, the election may represent a return to some of the forms of engagement found in the pre-modern stage, as the new channels of communication potentially allow greater interactivity between voters and politicians'. But Norris, along with Farrell and Webb, conclude that the case that campaigning has changed dramatically throughout any of the era discussed above, can be overstated. For Norris, 'direct forms of campaigning have essentially been supplemented but not replaced' (2000, p. 142) and instead of there 'being a linear development, the postmodern campaign symbolises a return to some of the more localized and interactive forms of communication that were present in the pre-modern period' (2000, p. 149). It is still important for the local candidate to be seen by his/her constituents, despite the fact that 'direct forms of communications have become ancillary to mediated channels of party-voter communication' (2000, p. 142). Furthermore, with the introduction of television in the modern era, newspapers have not declined in importance, but rather have been supplemented by television, like, as Norris describes it, 'another layer of the onion' (2000, p. 145).

In fact, the theorists agree that some fundamental principles of election campaigning evident in the very first election campaigns, remain central to the most recent campaign. First, it has always been essential for a party to communicate or advertise itself in the campaign. Second, the campaign is a full-time focus for whichever branch of the organisation is responsible for it. And third, a campaign is leadership and personality driven. What has undoubtedly changed is the manner in which these principles are expressed. Campaigns are now much more centralised and professionalised, and public attendance at and engagement in the electoral campaign has suffered as a result. Can this trend be reversed by the new technologies that potentially offer the individual a way to re-engage with politicians directly? Perhaps the most critical ingredient will be the desire for politicians themselves to *want* to re-engage with the voter and allow them to set the agenda with the issues they raise and engage with.

CAMPAIGN STRATEGIES AND TECHNIQUES

Although the aim of campaigning is 'to influence the outcomes of political decision-making by shaping public opinion' (Farrell & Schmitt-Beck, 2002, p. 3), the ways by which parties seek to achieve this aim may differ considerably depending on a number of factors. Three factors of relevance to the New Zealand situation are: the type of party; incumbent v opposition status; and the nature of the electoral system. The type of party refers to the position of the party in the electoral marketplace. Parties that occupy a dominant position in the marketplace or realistically aspire to such a position will adopt a campaign that seeks to appeal to as wide a cross-section of voters as possible. Such parties are often referred to as catch-all parties or, in the political marketing literature, as market leader and challenger parties (Collins & Butler, 1996). The Labour and National parties would fit this categorisation in New Zealand. Other parties, ones that can only hope to win a small segment of the vote, have a more targeted approach to their campaign. Such minor or 'niche' parties in New Zealand would include ACT, New Zealand First,

United Future, the Greens, and the Māori party (note that none of these parties would too openly declare that they had only limited aspirations as to their voting appeal).

In 2002, New Zealand First campaigned around the three issue areas of crime, the Treaty, and immigration. All three issues were of particular concern to New Zealand First's elderly target group. In 2005, economic nationalism and superannuation were added to the party's list of key issues—again both of specific concern to older generations of New Zealanders. ACT's image since its inception has been as a party for less government, less tax, and greater individual freedom and personal responsibility. While such values could have wide appeal, in reality ACT has focused its campaign efforts on small businessmen, rural voters, and urban free-market liberals. United Future was labelled the 'family-friendly' party in 2002 and since then has tried to capitalise on this image by presenting itself as a moderate, sensible party that represented 'good-hearted middle New Zealand'. The Greens would seem to be the niche party par excellence, something the party acknowledged and tried to turn to its advantage during the 2002 campaign where its newspaper advertisements carried the headline 'Our single issue is the future of New Zealand' and went on to state 'Single issue politics? *We wouldn't have it any other way*'. However, by the 2005 campaign, the Greens were trying to widen their appeal beyond the issues of the environment and safe food by adding 'social justice' which encompassed calls for a higher minimum wage, extra help for beneficiaries, and more state housing.

With regard to the two main parties, National's 2005 conference slogan was 'Tackling the issues of mainstream New Zealand'; the intention was to contrast with Labour's catering to minority and special interest groups. This appeal to mainstream New Zealanders was also reflected in the iconic red and white billboards that went up around the country early in the election campaign. Even the choice of a Neil Diamond song for the conference and the appearance of comedian Jim Hopkins could be viewed as appeals to mainstream New Zealanders.

Labour was conscious of National's efforts to portray the party as not in sync with mainstream New Zealand—although Helen Clark was able to at least define 'mainstream', unlike Don Brash! Labour's campaign strategy was to adopt a multifaceted approach that involved specific appeals to a wide range of targeted audiences, for example, families with the Working for Families package; students with the scrapping of student loans; and the elderly with rates rebates and the promise of extra cataract operations and major joint procedures. Labour also sought to appeal to New Zealanders' sense of national pride with the use of celebrity endorsements by Peter Jackson and Michael Campbell in party ads, while actor Sam Neill was the master of ceremonies at the opening of the party conference.

The problem facing niche parties is that for their appeal to remain distinctive or differentiated from other parties, the larger parties must not encroach on their targeted segment of the electorate. In 2005, ACT faced the problem of National adopting a policy of across-the-board tax cuts; New Zealand First faced National taking a hardline stance over the Treaty, immigration and crime, while both National and Labour engaged in a bidding war to win over the elderly vote. Even United Future's apparent monopoly over family policy was blurred by Labour's Working for Families package. As for the Greens, by trying to widen their appeal outside their core constituency, they may have diluted their message and weakened their brand image. Furthermore, the Greens, like all the minor parties in 2005, found that when the major players in the electoral market increase their brand awareness (and this was certainly the case for National), small players tend to get less recognition.

Whether the party is incumbent or in opposition will also affect the party's campaign strategy. Incumbent parties are most likely to adopt a positive campaign—for example, use positive rather than negative advertising—basing their campaign around their achievements while in office. There has also been an increasing tendency in New Zealand for the incumbent party to use the perquisites of office to bolster their campaign efforts. In the 2002 and 2005 elections, the Labour party strongly campaigned on what they had achieved in office with specific reference to the delivery on the credit card pledges. The Progressive party, as a formal coalition member between 2002 and 2005 also campaigned on its achievements with the party's slogan in 2005 being 'What Jim says, Jim does'. United Future, which provided support to the Labour-led government on confidence and supply, issued frequent press statements detailing what United Future had achieved between 2002 and 2005.

Opposition parties, on the other hand, are much more prone to conduct negative or attack campaigns and this was certainly evident in much of the National party's 2005 advertising campaign, while New Zealand First ran a campaign that was critical of both major parties. The ACT party's attacks on Labour were to be expected; more surprising was its criticism of National, which was undoubtedly a reflection of National's lukewarm response to ACT's overture for an electoral agreement over the seat of Epsom (where ACT leader Rodney Hide was a candidate).

The third factor influencing the nature of a party's campaign is the electoral system. Under New Zealand's Mixed Member Proportional (MMP) electoral system, the party vote determines a party's share of seats (but with some important exceptions to be discussed below). As such, a party will focus on maximising its party vote. In some cases this may lead parties to not even campaign for the electorate vote at all (the Greens) or only in a selected crucial seat (ACT and New Zealand First in 2005). In such a situation, national campaigns become the focus of a party's energy, ensuring a consistent and stable message is put across nationwide. One of the criticisms of the National party campaign in 2002 was that it failed to effectively pursue the party vote and even its advertising varied widely from electorate to electorate.

Another aspect of the MMP electoral system has been that it invariably produces coalition governments. This means that parties, especially the minor ones, are campaigning in the knowledge that some of the other parties are potential partners in a post-election coalition while others are potential rivals. This was particularly apparent in the 2005 election.

United Future's coalition prospects were threatened both by the Greens and New Zealand First, and both these parties were subject to strident attacks by United Future for most of the campaign. Peter Dunne in his speech at the launch of United Future's campaign, set the tone when he exclaimed that if MMP was to be made to work, 'Swaggering bluster based on personal ego and either designer suits or a gold chain as the case may be, or a discredited "me first" ideology will not do it, nor will aged hippies on a drug fetish'. Later press releases by Dunne labelled a Labour–Green coalition as a 'recipe for lunacy and disaster'. The Greens likewise were aware of the danger posed by United Future and New Zealand First to a future Labour–Green coalition and Green party co-leader Rod Donald, in his keynote address to the party's 2005 national conference, referred to New Zealand First leader Winston Peters as the 'ugly face of New Zealand politics' and as a 'consummate showman ... a snake-oil merchant'. As for United Future, Donald attacked them for wanting to flog and castrate criminals and repeal the civil unions bill. The Greens also campaigned to create a closer link with Labour, culminating during the third week of the 2005 campaign in which Green co-leader Jeanette Fitzsimons and Labour leader Helen Clark spent a morning campaigning together in Auckland. Fitzsimons also stressed at the party's campaign opening that the Greens and Labour animosity to each other during the 2002 campaign was regrettable.

On the centre-right, ACT's relationship, or lack of relationship, with National, forced it not only to attack National on occasion—its only feasible coalition partner—but also to focus its campaign on winning an electorate seat, Epsom. Other than the Māori party, whose natural campaign focus was the seven Māori electorate seats, ACT was the only party in 2005 to channel its resources into winning an electorate rather than party votes. The party succeeded in winning Epsom but its party vote fell far short of the 5 per cent party vote threshold and only one other MP was returned with the party leader, Rodney Hide, the winner in the Epsom contest. ACT's campaign was also influenced by considerations of alternative coalition partners, arguing that if ACT failed to cross the 5 per cent threshold, National would be forced into a coalition with New Zealand First—which in turn meant that National would not be in a position to deliver on lower tax promises. Thus, ACT MP Kenneth Wang organised a 'Stop Peters by ACTion' campaign that used billboards depicting Peters holding hands with Brash and Clark with the warning that a deal with either of them would mean chaotic government. A message (in Chinese) said, 'Peters has time and again proven himself to be a racist xenophobe and will do and say anything to win votes'.

WAS 2005 A POSTMODERN CAMPAIGN?

If we examine the 2005 election campaign within the framework set out by Norris, it is clear that there are elements present from all three campaigning types. We can also see that some parties tend to utilise postmodern characteristics to a greater degree than other parties and that the reason for this can, in part, be linked back to the position of the party in the electoral market (as discussed above).

A central feature of the modern campaign is the focus on the main evening news on television as *the* medium for 'getting out the message' to voters. All parties at the 2005 election used television in this way and staged events and photo opportunities were designed to (hopefully) appear on the evening news on TV One and TV3. In a postmodern campaign, television is still *the* medium for a party's campaign but there is a shift in focus from 'broadcasting' to 'narrowcasting' where television audiences are segmented and targeted. Television in New Zealand has not yet reached the level of development where narrowcasting would produce any significant returns to the parties. In the US, for example, morning television has a large, predominantly female, audience, and candidates vie to appear on morning TV shows to provide positive insights into their personal/family life. In New Zealand, morning television has yet to reach a level of popularity that would warrant that much attention by parties. Māori television and Māori radio stations were naturally a focus of the Māori party although it is likely that TVNZ and TV3 were the main media for reaching the party's desired audience.

The use of specialist advisers and professional consultants is a characteristic of both modern and postmodern campaigns; the difference is that 'more' are used in the latter than the former. All parties make use of professional public relations consultants and advertising agencies although the costs involved often mean the smaller parties only do this on a limited scale. ACT used the services of an Australian public relations consultant and Australian and American polling companies. For the National party, the Australian firm Lynton Textor was used for polling and National's iconic billboards were the brainchild of former radio advertising specialist John Ansell and Auckland-based designer, Phil O'Reilly. Labour used the expensive advertising company 'Assignment' for its TV ads, and UMR for its polling.

The use of websites as an interactive device for parties to obtain feedback from voters is clearly located in the postmodern campaign. All parties maintained websites and in some cases, individual candidates had their own websites or blogs and many had their own electronic newsletters. But it is questionable to the extent parties used these for other than top-down campaign communication. The New Zealand First, United Future, and National party websites gave little, if any, opportunity for active involvement by either members or non-members. The Greens and ACT were partial exceptions to this. ACT's top five candidates on the party list all had their own website and the party's website not only allowed people to join online, donate and subscribe to mailing lists, but also to comment on news releases and fill in online surveys. The Greens claimed over 12,000 daily visits to their website and almost 5,000 daily visits to the Greens 'frogblog'. The party had also set up earlier in the campaign year a members' discussion forum (forum.greens.org.nz) designed to facilitate member-to-member communication.

We find considerable evidence of segmentation and targeting in the 2005 campaign and it is perhaps here that the postmodern campaign is most evident. The major parties spent considerable resources in segmenting the electoral market according to some criteria (e.g. socio-demographics) and then tailoring mailouts accordingly; the smaller or niche parties tended to target their core voters. Winston Peters was a regular speaker at Grey Power meetings; the Greens on university campuses. When niche parties tried to make appeals outside their core constituencies, this either appeared incongruous (as with Rodney Hide's attempt to portray ACT as a party of 'workers' and United Future's electoral alliance with the WIN party) or risked undermining the unique brand of the party (as with the Greens trying to broaden their support base by encompassing social issues).

Norris notes that the postmodern campaign may fall somewhere between the local activism of the pre-modern campaign and the national-passive forms of communication characteristic of the modern TV campaign (2000, p. 149). While a party may maintain tight centralised control of the campaign, a recognition of the need to take account of local conditions led to what has been termed 'localising the national' (Ward 2003) where local candidates and party organisations adapt national messages to make them have relevance at the local level especially in crucial marginal seats. In a small country like New Zealand, it is debatable as to the extent that the local and national can be separated in this way or, at least, its relevance under MMP where there are no 'marginal' electorates as such. In fact, there is evidence that in New Zealand, parties increasingly are trying to centralise control of campaigns. A major criticism of National's 2002 campaign was the ineffectiveness of the central party machine at ensuring that the electorates campaigned for the party vote rather than the electorate vote. There was not even a central party direction that all party material be printed in the party's colour of blue! Nor were there any generic hoardings until the last week. Learning from these mistakes, the campaign manager, Steven Joyce, made it clear during the regional conferences in the run-up to the election that there would only be one campaign, one uniform party brand, one party colour and uniform hoardings (with an operations manager wholly responsible for hoardings). At each regional conference from 2004 onwards, party president Judy Kirk asked party delegates to repeat (three times) after her: 'It is the party vote that is the most important'.

Even the Greens, with their traditional image of grassroots and local activism, advertised for local campaign managers who would 'ensure that local campaign teams, strategies and materials are consistent with the national campaign's style and standards'. The Greens campaign manager, Russel Norman, together with Sue Bradford the campaign committee convenor, implied greater centralised control when they announced that the national campaign would be more 'proactive and decisive' in 2005 compared to 2002. Following the disastrous 1999 election campaign, New Zealand First centralised its campaign strategy. Party president, Doug Woolerton, told local electorates prior to the 2005 campaign that the local candidate's job was to sell the core message of the party and that while local candidates should take control of local issues, these should not conflict with national policies—local candidates should always have 'empathy' with the national campaign.

CONCLUSION: THE EPSOM CAMPAIGN

The campaign conducted by Rodney Hide showed that pre-modern campaigning is alive and well in New Zealand. Hide used volunteer party workers as well as existing ACT MPs (and the party president) to conduct an intensive door-knocking campaign, to deliver thousands of brochures (over 20,000 in one weekend), and to erect hoardings. Hide was seen on early morning commuter buses handing out leaflets. However, not only was this labour-intensive style of campaigning forced upon a party short of funds to finance anything more capital intensive, postmodern techniques were still combined with more traditional ones. For example, there was the (postmodern) targeting of voters in the electorate, most crucially the estimated 4,000 Asian voters in Epsom who were then delivered leaflets in the traditional (pre-modern) style by a group of Mandarin-speaking volunteers organised by Kenneth Wang, the ACT MP.

There is, therefore, no one phase of campaigning that neatly fits all aspects of campaigning for a party; different types of parties in different circumstances and under different political systems, will 'pick 'n' mix' campaign strategies and techniques accordingly. There may be a *tendency* for parties to become more professional and high tech in what they do but there are no hard and fast rules as to what constitutes a correct way to campaign. And as the National party found in 2005, you can win a campaign but still lose the election.

DISCUSSION QUESTIONS

1   Why has the change in campaign technique (from pre-modern to postmodern) led to an increase in public disengagement from the process?

2   What might be done to reverse the trend of public disengagement?

3   Which party ran the most successful election campaign at the 2005 general election, and why?

4   What might be the most essential features of a successful campaign strategy at the next general election?

FURTHER READING

Collins, N. & P. Butler 1996, 'Positioning Political Parties', *Harvard International Journal of Press/Politics*, vol. 1, pp. 63–77.

Farrell, D. & R. Schmitt-Beck (eds) 2002, *Do Political Campaigns Matter?*, Routledge, London and New York.

Farrell, D. & P. Webb 2000, 'Political Parties as Campaign Organizations', in R. Dalton & P. Wattenberg (eds), *Parties Without Partisans*, Oxford University Press, Oxford, pp. 102–28.

Miller, R. 2004, 'Parties and Electioneering', in J. Hayward & C. Rudd (eds), *Political Communications in New Zealand*, Pearson Education, Auckland, pp. 2–19.

Norris, P. 2000, *A Virtuous Circle. Political Communications in Postindustrial Societies*, Cambridge University Press, Cambridge.

Ward, I. 2003, 'Localizing the National', *Party Politics*, vol. 9, pp. 583–600.

The General Election of 2005

Stephen Levine & Nigel S. Roberts

On Monday, 25 July 2005, Prime Minister Helen Clark called a press conference the day before parliament reconvened after a four-week parliamentary recess. She announced that the general election would be held fifty-five days later on 17 September. The announcement came after a period when the Labour party had been behind in opinion polls, a predicament that gave the prime minister ample motivation to delay the election date almost until the last possible moment. While it would have been possible to have postponed the election until the following Saturday, 24 September happened to be the start of the state school holidays as well as the sixty-fifth birthday of the National party's leader, Don Brash, and scheduling an election on that date was considered a rather risky choice.

Perhaps ironically, the reason for delaying the election date began to disappear almost as soon as the date was announced. New opinion polls suddenly put Labour back in front, once again holding a substantial lead over National in the aftermath of Labour suggestions that National's policies were being influenced by Washington and that, as a consequence, New Zealand's iconic anti-nuclear policies and independent foreign policy posture were under threat. Labour gained further momentum with its announcement of a new policy towards student loans, with its promise of no-interest loans likely to save thousands of students tens of thousands of dollars in interest, taking years off the life of their loans. Following the announcement the Labour party's website was very heavily visited and the policy took the initiative away from National, which had already announced a much less generous student loan policy and which had been losing its tax policy advantage by failing to announce it.

In reality, the election campaign began two months earlier, with National party billboards being erected all across the country. The 2005 billboards were of a uniform format—a photograph of an anguished Helen Clark against a red background, side by side with a picture of a cheerful and avuncular Don Brash set against a blue backdrop—with a simple message above each of their images. These messages— sometimes no more than a word apiece—reminded voters of problems, scandals, and embarrassments associated with Labour in contrast with National's intended approach.

National's 2002 campaign had been much criticised for its lack of flair and its failure to understand MMP—some advertising had concentrated on winning individual (and, in some cases, unwinnable) electorates, and neglected to ask voters to give National their party vote—but the party's 2005 campaign was innovative and effective. Advertisements also called upon voters to give National 'two ticks', as Labour had done in 2002 and previously. The party's television advertisements were also simple yet clever, deploying caricature and musical gimmickry to highlight unpopular cabinet ministers and controversial policies. In all this National stayed on message, emphasising its view that New Zealanders were overtaxed and that National would put things right.

Indeed, Labour's progress towards a third successive term in office began to come unstuck when Minister of Finance, Dr Michael Cullen, introduced the government's 2005 budget on 19 May. Mixed signals had given an impression that the budget might hold attractive surprises for voters, raising expectations of tax cuts, but the most that Dr Cullen had been prepared to do was to raise tax thresholds—the income levels at which higher tax rates commenced—in three years' time. New Zealand First leader Winston Peters' jibe that these would eventually give New Zealanders enough extra money for half a packet of chewing gum each week provided a focal point for public disappointment, even anger, and reflected the public relations failure of an election year budget perceived to be excessively parsimonious rather than merely prudent.

Labour's campaign, although hard-fought and aggressive, nevertheless saw it often on the defensive. The main issues of the campaign—tax policy; policies towards Māori; police emergency services; education; health—were ones emphasised by National. When National finally released its tax policy, offering substantial cuts to personal and corporate income tax, Labour argued that the tax cuts would require reductions in public services and a resumption of government borrowing. Labour's own election policy called for an increase in state-funded benefits of one kind or another—the Working for Families policy—which, with the student loans policy, gave the impression that Dr Cullen's strictures about the unavailability of surplus funds had either been disingenuous or that they were being tossed aside in a desperate bid to retain office.

THE 2005 CAMPAIGN

The formal campaign normally has a predictable structure. It begins with televised opening presentations from each of the parties, using allocations of broadcast time provided by the Electoral Commission using criteria found in the Broadcasting Act.

During the three- or four-week campaign there are various leaders' debates on both television and radio. The campaign closes with televised closing presentations on the Friday evening before the election. By midnight Friday all billboards and election hoardings must come down, and on Saturday the voters go to the polls.

In 2005 the format was disrupted at the outset with a TV3 leaders' debate on Thursday evening, 11 August, several days prior to the Monday night opening addresses. The TV3 debate became more controversial—and acquired a larger viewing audience—when the network decided to exclude two of the party leaders from participating, initially on the basis that the studio was too small. Legal action was initiated on behalf of the two party leaders—Progressive leader (and coalition partner) Jim Anderton and United Future leader Peter Dunne—two days before the broadcast. On Wednesday, 10 August, a judge in the High Court issued a ruling ordering TV3 to include Anderton and Dunne in the debate,[1] with which the network reluctantly complied. The debate had seemed especially important to Peter Dunne, as this was the only leaders' encounter to use the 'worm'—a method of recording the reactions to leaders' statements from a sample of uncommitted voters—which had proved so decisive in dramatically increasing United Future's parliamentary representation in 2002.[2]

The use of the 'worm' in 2005, however, produced nothing comparable. New Zealand First leader Winston Peters, often the centre of attention at elections as in parliament, was marginalised. Peter Dunne's 'common sense' message was no longer new and other party leaders also learned to speak positively about the need to help New Zealand families. The other minor party leaders likewise failed to make a strong impact. The Greens used one of their co-leaders, Jeanette Fitzsimons, and her performance, while earnest, was often wooden. The Progressives' Jim Anderton appeared simply as an adjunct to Labour—indeed, with Anderton's approval, Helen Clark went so far as to say during the campaign that they were a 'job lot': they went together—promoting his own experience as a long-serving cabinet minister who knew how to get things done.

Three MPs were leading their parties in an election campaign for the first time. ACT's Richard Prebble had announced his intention to retire from parliament at the end of the 2005 term and had stepped down from the leadership. The privilege of succeeding him was contested by much of the ACT caucus, with Rodney Hide narrowly being selected. The Māori party leader Tariana Turia was first elected as a Labour MP in 1996, but she left the party in 2004 over the government's foreshore and seabed legislation—a statute designed essentially to forestall litigation (following a court decision granting Māori the right to take such action) by placing ownership in Crown (i.e. public) hands. Turia was easily returned to parliament in a virtually uncontested by-election and in 2005 she was standing as co-leader of a new party expected to make strong inroads into the Labour-held Māori electorates. As the campaign progressed, however, co-leader Dr Pita Sharples often appeared as the party's spokesperson, and his more effervescent approach won praise.

The principal campaign newcomer was the National party leader. Don Brash was not entirely new to campaigning. He had been a National candidate on two occasions in the early 1980s, but with no success.[3] Since then he had been the long-standing Governor of the Reserve Bank (originally appointed by Labour and subsequently reappointed by National). He was recruited to stand for parliament in 2002 by then National party president Michelle Boag. National's overwhelming defeat at that election cost Boag her presidency and Bill English his leadership. An October 2003 challenge to English saw National's parliamentary caucus elect Brash by a narrow margin after having served only 15 months in parliament.

The inexperienced Brash committed various gaffes and blunders during the campaign. Whereas Clark seemed never at a loss for words, Brash was at times tongue-tied. He was unable to evade difficult questions and his knowledge of the details of National policy was at times less than thorough. At the same time, many voters appeared to forgive him his shortcomings and as the campaign progressed Brash seemed more confident and more capable.

While it has become commonplace for New Zealand elections to be characterised as increasingly 'presidential', this campaign was even more focused on the leaders than previous contests. In particular the focus of media coverage was on the two major party leaders, Clark and Brash. Very few other Labour or National figures received much, if any, attention.[4] They were absent from advertisements and played little role in their party's campaign. The leaders of the smaller parties also found themselves largely outside the spotlight. Part of the problem was that, the Māori party aside, there seemed little new on offer. Anderton, Dunne, Fitzsimons, and Peters had each been around for a very long time. Even ACT's advertisements, highlighting Rodney Hide, at times drew attention to the party's founder, former Labour Finance Minister Roger Douglas, and to Ruth Richardson, a former National Minister of Finance—controversial individuals whose periods of popularity and public esteem lay years in the past.

The contrast between the experienced Clark, fluent and competent, and the novice Brash, at times hapless and besieged, was an important feature of Labour's campaign. The prime minister was aggressive, arguing that everything that Labour had been trying to achieve would be put at risk if National were elected. In the aftermath of one debate, Brash stated that he had felt some unease about debating against a woman, a glimpse into his outlook that was objectionable to some, understandable to others. When in difficulty, Brash was able to benefit from uncertainty about the cause of his problems—whether naivete or something more sinister. Over the course of the campaign there was a sequence of stories that raised questions about his judgment and purpose. Leaked emails from his office showed that he had been receiving advice from the Business Roundtable, a neo-liberal group that had been especially influential when Douglas and Richardson were Finance Ministers. The emails also showed that one parliamentary party, ACT, had been at least vicariously involved in the choice of the leader of another. Indeed, Brash had been characterised by ACT's president and by its leader as the party's '10th MP', and he had been welcomed enthusiastically to ACT's conference after becoming National leader.

Revelations of involvement by a small and obscure Christian sect, the Exclusive Brethren—a group whose members do not vote—midway through the campaign also raised questions about both National and its leader. Leaflets produced by the Exclusive Brethren, attacking the Greens and the government, were not the full extent of the sect's involvement in the campaign. It was also claimed that the church had offered to provide at least some National party candidates with financial contributions and with campaign workers.[5] All this would already have been awkward for National, but became even more so when Brash's initial denials of prior knowledge of the church's activities were followed by admissions that he had had several meetings with leaders of the group.[6]

Clark had campaign problems that were also largely of her own making. Six years in office had done little to soften her image. Indeed, her image itself—the 'air brushed Helen', as the straight-teeth youthful photo of the prime minister used in Labour advertising came to be known—increasingly drew mocking comment. The tendency towards arrogance that had emerged from time to time during her tenure as prime minister began to take its toll on voters. The 2002 election had had 'paintergate'[7]—the prime minister's signing of a painting that she had not herself painted—and the 2005 election had 'speedgate'. This affair found the prime minister attacked not only for a high-speed motorcade that had swept along South Island roads in July 2004 to get her to Christchurch airport in order for her to attend a rugby match in Wellington, but also for the prime minister's unwillingness to accept any responsibility for the incident. Her claim that she had been reading in the back seat of the car and had had no idea of its speed defied credibility. The timing of the trial of police officers and staff could not have been worse—it was held in the lead-up to the campaign, with the verdict delivered in mid-August—and the prime minister's unwillingness to testify on behalf of the police officers showed a lack of loyalty to staff and an indifference to the consequences that was not ameliorated by a subsequent 'whip around' among cabinet ministers of $120 each towards the cost of the fines—effectively an admission of responsibility, but one that was tacit and without apology.

Clark experienced more campaign travel difficulties when an Air New Zealand pilot used his intercom system to complain to passengers that their flight had been delayed to accommodate the prime minister. In fact, the pilot was mistaken, but Clark's response—to go to the cockpit and have words with the pilot, reminding him at the same time of the government's financial stake in the airline—was extraordinary, widely reported, and seemed to many to be consistent with an image of arrogance. The pilot was required by the airline to apologise—which he did several times—and to undergo communications training, effectively a form of counselling.

As a result, both Brash and Clark displayed shortcomings of personality and character that caused misgivings among voters. While Clark sought to focus solely on leadership, competence and trustworthiness, her own behaviour reduced the clarity of that message. The two leaders' sharply contrasting personalities were accompanied by significant differences in outlook and policy.

Brash had characterised National's policies as aimed towards 'mainstream' New Zealand and, when challenged in a televised debate between the two major party leaders to explain who in New Zealand was not 'mainstream', he identified Clark herself and those who supported her ideas and policies. Brash's campaign targeted 'political correctness', associated with measures on behalf of gays and Māori, and he also emphasised the need for major changes in relation to Māori policy. Departing from National's previous policy towards the Māori parliamentary seats—first established in 1867 as a temporary measure, but continued ever since,[8] and under MMP allowed to rise in proportion to the increasing numbers on the Māori rolls—Brash pledged to abolish the seats whether or not Māori still wanted to retain them. He also rejected the idea that the Treaty of Waitangi represented an ongoing 'partnership' with Māori and said that the education curriculum would be revised accordingly. By the end of the campaign he was promising to do away with all special government provisions for Māori, which would have involved the abolition of government departments and the cessation of government programmes, many of them of long duration.

Brash's campaign against what he portrayed as special entitlements for Māori had begun earlier, when he gave a January 2004 speech at Orewa (north of Auckland) that immediately propelled National ahead of Labour in the polls.[9] The net effect of his comments—and their resonance with many voters—was to move Labour towards an acceptance that a more determined effort was needed to resolve historic Treaty of Waitangi grievances. There were differences in tone, and in the specific dates suggested both for filing and resolving Treaty claims, but both major parties were signalling their awareness that a never-ending process was unattractive to electors.

Throughout the campaign there were conflicting opinion polls, on an almost day-by-day basis, some giving the lead to National, others to Labour. Some polls showed the race as close; others projected substantial leads for one or the other. What all of the polls showed, however, was that the proportion of the vote going to the two major parties was going to be the largest that it had been since the introduction of MMP. From the campaign on through to the counting of the votes themselves, the 2005 election represented something of a return to two-party politics, albeit under MMP rules.

THE RESULTS

The results of the 2005 election are presented in table 4.4.1. The most significant change in the share of the vote was achieved by the National party, which nearly doubled its party vote from 2002. A political party that raises its representation in parliament from twenty-seven seats to forty-eight has clearly waged a successful campaign. It is noteworthy, however, that the collision between National and Labour

Table 4.4.1: Results of the 2002 and 2005 general elections in New Zealand

	2002						2005					
	Party votes %	Total seats	Total seats %	Elec. votes %	Elec. seats	List seats	Party votes %	Total seats	Total seats %	Elec. votes %	Elec. seats	List seats
Lab	41.3	52	43.3	44.7	45	7	41.1	50	41.3	40.4	31	19
Nat	20.9	27	22.5	30.5	21	6	39.1	48	39.7	40.4†	31	17
NZF	10.4	13	10.8	4.0	1	12	5.7	7	5.8	3.5	0	7
Grn	7.0	9	7.5	5.4	0	9	5.3	6	5.0	4.1	0	6
UnF	6.7	8	6.7	4.6	1	7	2.7	3	2.5	2.8	1	2
Mao	–	–	–	–	–	–	2.1	4*	3.3	3.4	4	0
ACT	7.1	9	7.5	3.6	0	9	1.5	2	1.6	2.0	1	1
Pro	1.7	2	1.7	1.8	1	1	1.2	1	0.8	1.6	1	0
Des	–	–	–	–	–	–	0.6	0	0.0	0.8	0	0
LCP	0.6	0	0.0	0.2	0	0	0.3	0	0.0	0.1	0	0
ChH	1.4	0	0.0	2.1	0	0	0.1	0	0.0	0.1	0	0
Aln	1.3	0	0.0	1.7	0	0	0.1	0	0.0	0.1	0	0
Out	1.3	0	0.0	0.0	0	0	–	–	–	–	–	–
Oth	0.3	0	0.0	1.4	0	0	0.2	0	0.0	0.7	0	0
Total	100.0	120	100.0	100.0	69	51	100.0	121*	100.0	100.0	69	52
Turnout:	77.0 %						80.9 %					

† It should be noted that although the National party won 45,506 fewer party votes in 2005 than did the Labour party, at the same time National won 802 more electorate votes than Labour did throughout the country as a whole.

* Includes 1 overhang seat.

Key: ACT = ACT; Aln = Alliance; ChH = Christian Heritage NZ; Des = Destiny New Zealand; Elec. = Electorate (that is, the equivalent of constituency in the UK and district in the USA); Grn = Green Party; Lab = Labour Party; LCP = Aotearoa Legalise Cannabis Party; Mao = Māori party; Nat = National Party; NZF = New Zealand First Party; 0th = Others (which in both 2002 and 2005 consist only of parties with less than 0.5 per cent of the party vote); Out = Outdoor Recreation NZ (which worked in conjunction with United Future New Zealand in 2005); Pro = Jim Anderton's Progressive; UnF = United Future New Zealand.

had little effect on the latter's vote when compared to 2002. Labour won fifty-two seats in 2002, and fifty three years later.

The principal losers in the election were the smaller parties, as Labour and National together had won 80.2 per cent of the party vote, their largest combined proportion in any MMP election and their highest share of the vote since the 1990 general election.[10] New Zealand First saw its share of the vote nearly halved, its representation dropping from thirteen to seven. The Greens also lost support and, more dramatically, so too did United Future. Even Jim Anderton's Progressives managed to slip further, declining to only one seat in parliament. ACT's precipitous drop below the 5 per cent threshold saw its representation fall from nine to two, the party retaining its position in parliament only as a result of an energetic campaign by its leader, Rodney Hide, who managed to win the National-held Epsom electorate by persuading enough National voters that a vote for Hide was, in effect, a vote for National—as it would give National an essential coalition partner.[11] In this argument Hide was assisted by MMP's rules. These allow electorate candidates to be given places on party lists, an option accepted by most of them. Incumbent MPs are frequently given high rankings on the lists, allowing Hide to claim, correctly, that his victory would have no effect on the continued presence in parliament of Epsom's incumbent electorate MP, National's Richard Worth (who was ranked at sixteen on National's list).[12]

Indeed, the availability of dual candidacy saved many MPs in addition to Worth from parliamentary retirement after they were defeated in their electorates. In the 2005 election, National took ten electorate seats from Labour, defeating a cabinet minister (Jim Sutton) and a number of experienced MPs. Every one of them was able to return to parliament as a result of their list rankings. The new Labour team was to have four new MPs, all elected off the party list. By contrast, including replacements for two retiring MPs, there were twenty-three new MPs in the National caucus, reflecting the party's substantially improved performance.[13]

Ranked number one on National's list, Brash was seeking to become the first list-only candidate to become prime minister. Clark easily retained her Mount Albert electorate, but another long-standing party leader was not so fortunate. Winston Peters, MP for Tauranga for twenty-one years, lost his seat to National's candidate Bob Clarkson in a colourful, if at times unseemly, campaign.[14] Clarkson's tendency to refer to his more private body parts led the National party leader to make one of the more unusual statements in the history of New Zealand politics: 'I don't want any candidates to be talking about their testicles, to be quite frank'.[15]

With Brash as leader, National was able to occupy much of the political space previously taken up by ACT, New Zealand First, and United Future. While these parties could take some comfort in the acceptance by National of policies and themes that they had placed on the agenda, they were deprived of their distinctive messages and thus had difficulty articulating why voters should continue to vote for them. United Future's position in parliament was secure, given Peter Dunne's pre-eminence in his

Ohariu-Belmont electorate, but his capacity to bring two other MPs into parliament together with him was in part attributable to both Clark and Brash identifying Dunne as a person with whom they could comfortably work—in Brash's case, a benediction given by way of a much publicised meeting at an Auckland café.

With the Alliance gone from parliament as a result of the 2002 general election, and the party's former leader, Anderton, safely ensconced within the Labour coalition, Labour was in little danger of being outflanked on its left. The Green party offers a distinctive message, and appeals to a particular constituency on a somewhat separate issue dimension.[16] The Māori party, born out of the foreshore and seabed controversy, made inroads into Labour's support, yet in six of the seven Māori electorates Labour was able to win a majority of the party vote (and in the seventh, Te Tai Tokerau, won by Hone Harawira, Labour won 49.3 per cent of the party vote to the Māori party's 31.0 per cent). On the other hand, the Māori party was able to win four out of the seven seats, an impressive achievement for a party formed only fifteen months earlier. The party's challenge to Labour is but one facet of its wider challenge to New Zealand's political and legal arrangements. The substantive effect of its victories will be felt in due course in parliament, but the party's triumphs have already produced an impact on the outcome not experienced in previous MMP elections.

MMP's rules give pre-eminence to the party vote, but—as Anderton (who held his seat in Wigram), Dunne, and Hide showed—an electorate victory can be vital, preserving representation for parties receiving less than 5 per cent of the party vote. The Māori party's electorate successes, however, had different consequences. Its four seats were one more than it was entitled to according to its overall share of the party vote. As a result, for the first time, parliament has an 'overhang'—a party winning more seats in parliament than its proportion of the party vote would have entitled it to—so that the parliament elected in 2005 has 121 MPs, one more than the 120 found in the three previous MMP parliaments. This was a result not likely to be popular among electors taking the view that, at 120, there were already too many MPs.[17]

ELECTORAL AFTERMATH

The immediate consequence of the election was uncertainty. Election night saw Brash unable to claim victory but refusing to concede defeat. There were nearly a quarter of a million special votes (10.8 per cent of the total votes cast) still to be counted, including 27,482 cast overseas.[18] He foresaw several weeks of discussions with other party leaders in an effort to form a government. A chastened Helen Clark acknowledged the closeness of the result, and the divisions that the campaign had revealed, but looked forward to forming a new government. Initially she had the advantage. Her previous minority government had been a Labour–Progressive coalition supplemented by further agreements with United Future and the Greens. She had said throughout the campaign that her preference was to continue with those arrangements and the election results suggested that it might be possible for her to do so because of campaign commitments made by the Greens (who had pledged to support a Labour–Progressive government), as well as by both United Future and New Zealand First.

Peter Dunne had been the first of the latter two to state his party's stance towards coalition discussions, promising to consult at the outset with the party that held the largest number of seats in parliament. While this did not represent an unequivocal offer of support, so long as the Greens were not given ministerial portfolios there was little in United Future's outlook to prevent a coalition agreement with Labour from speedily being completed.

Winston Peters' approach to coalition arrangements took longer to make itself known. During the course of the campaign, voters were reminded of his role in the protracted discussions that followed the first MMP election. In 1996, Peters bargained simultaneously with both Labour and National until, after nine weeks, he announced that he would be going into coalition with National.[19] He had lost ground in opinion polls in 2005 when he engaged in an ill-judged televised stunt in which he held two telephones, one in each hand, one red and one blue, pretending to keep both 'Don' and 'Helen' on hold.

Finally, less than two weeks before the election, Peters gave undertakings clearly indicating that he would not form a coalition with either Labour or National, and that he would refuse 'the baubles of office' (Peters 2005). He pledged that New Zealand First would talk first with the party with the most seats in parliament. Subsequently, when necessary, New Zealand First would support whichever coalition was in power (whether led by Labour or National) on confidence and supply in order to ensure stable government. Although the speech was dismissed at the time by both Brash and Clark—each claiming it to be ambiguous—both were ready to rely on Peters' assurances after the election.

The closeness of the result—fifty to forty-nine on election night—and the possibility of further adjustments as a result of special votes (including even the possibility of the Greens falling below the 5 per cent threshold) meant that only at best preliminary discussions could take place in the immediate aftermath of the 17 September poll. After the counting of special votes was completed, and the final result confirmed Labour's position as the single largest party in parliament, the pace of coalition negotiations quickened. The election night results had been altered, but only slightly: National's share of the vote slipped sufficiently so that its already tenuous claim to a possible mandate to govern appeared to have vanished with its forty-ninth MP. At a fifty to forty-eight advantage, the prime minister announced her readiness to complete negotiations with possible coalition and support parties. Her task was eased somewhat by the reduction in the size of the 'overhang', as National's loss of a seat brought the numbers of MPs down to 121 (from the election-night 122), making sixty-one votes (rather than sixty-two) sufficient for a parliamentary majority.

Don Brash conceded defeat on Saturday, 1 October, following the confirmation of the special votes. In fact, however, National made one last effort to put together a government, with Brash sending a letter to Winston Peters on 14 October advising 'that in the event that New Zealand First wishes to consider an alternative to supporting a Labour-led Government, there are parties representing 57 seats in Parliament'—National, ACT, United Future, and the Māori party—'willing and able to enter into discussions with New Zealand First to form a National-led Government'. The invitation to Peters to discuss 'the key policy platforms that would, with New Zealand First's involvement, form the basis of such a Government' was not taken up.[20] Instead, Peters concluded his negotiations with the prime minister, agreeing to support the Labour–Progressive coalition on confidence and supply, with the coalition adopting a number of New Zealand First policy positions and with Peters obtaining a ministerial position outside cabinet as New Zealand's Minister of Foreign Affairs, the first Māori to hold the appointment. United Future also agreed to support the government on a comparable basis, with Peter Dunne likewise accepting a ministerial appointment outside of cabinet.

With two ministers outside cabinet yet holding ministerial warrants as part of the executive—free to a considerable extent from the confines of traditional collective responsibility (so much so that parts of *The Cabinet Manual*, the guardian of orthodoxy in such matters, were likely to be revised to take the 2005 governing arrangements into account)—the prime minister characterised her new government as a further innovation in the evolution of New Zealand's voting system. This view was reflected in the government's statement of its programme, the Speech from the Throne: 'Of necessity, the longstanding constitutional conventions associated with the consequences of the old electoral system are evolving to respond to the challenges of MMP'.

Formation of the new government, which was announced on 17 October, was not lacking in controversy. Dunne's and Peters's objections had excluded the Greens from office, although the Greens' support was acknowledged through acceptance of some of the party's policy initiatives and the offer of spokespersonship roles to its two co-leaders. The likely long-term stability of the new arrangements, involving an executive cobbled together from a group of disparate and in some ways feuding parties, was questioned by many commentators.

As for the opposition, there was immediate speculation about whether Brash would be replaced before the next election, possibly by National's Finance spokesperson John Key. There were also doubts raised about whether Prime Minister Clark would see out the three-year term, and Labour's prospects for a fourth successive term in office seemed weak at the outset of its new tenure. Peters's involvement, and initial uncertainty about whether he and his party were considering themselves to be part of the government or the opposition, emphasised the government's fragile position.

In the end, however, it was an election that may have given New Zealand's voters more or less what they had been seeking. The government had been returned, but it had been reprimanded for its 'social engineering', the new coalition arrangements moving the Clark-led regime towards the centre rather than towards the left (as a coalition with the Greens and the Māori party would have done). The National party had been considerably strengthened, but not sufficiently to win office with its large number of untested MPs and aging leader. The Labour–Progressive agreements with the Greens, New Zealand First, and United Future had adopted some of the more attractive and uncontroversial components of those parties' programmes—solar power heating for homes (Greens), a rise in the minimum wage (New Zealand First), greater use of private hospitals to reduce waiting lists (United Future)—perhaps adding value to a government's programme in the way that voters intended when they adopted MMP. As for Prime Minister Helen Clark, she had accomplished what no previous New Zealand Labour prime minister had been able to do. She had led her party to three successive election victories[21]—no mean feat in a country where, it is said, 'tall poppies' exist solely for the purpose of cutting them down.

DISCUSSION QUESTIONS

1   Why did New Zealand voters give the two major parties a significantly higher degree of support in 2005 than in any of New Zealand's three previous MMP elections?

2   Helen Clark won a third term as prime minister in 2005—a unique achievement for a Labour leader in New Zealand. Why?

3   Why didn't National win the 2005 general election?

4   People thought they adopted a 5 per cent threshold when they voted for MMP in 1993. In 2005, however, all the parties in New Zealand that won more than a mere 1 per cent of the party votes gained representation in parliament. Why?

NOTES

1   See oral judgment of Justice Ronald Young, 11 August 2005, in the High Court of New Zealand, Wellington Registry (CIV 2005 495 1596): blog.greens.org.nz/wp-content/TV3Judgment.pdf.

2   For analysis of the consequences of the introduction of the 'worm' into New Zealand leadership debates, see Sowry (1997), pp. 29–30, 32; James (2003), pp. 50–1, 56–7; Donnelly (2003), pp. 121–2; Morrison (2003), p. 214; Bale (2003), pp. 230–1; and Hayward and Rudd (2003), pp. 254, 263–4.

3   Don Brash contested the September 1980 East Coast Bays by-election for National and lost to Social Credit's Garry Knapp. He was defeated again by Knapp in the November 1981 general election.

4   National's Finance spokesperson, John Key, was a partial exception.

5   See, for instance Tracy Watkins (2005), noting 'offers of assistance [that] extended to half a million dollars' worth of questionable campaign material and a seemingly nationwide grassroots campaign'.

6   The incident produced an extraordinary statement from Dr Brash, reminiscent of US President Richard M. Nixon's famous remark assuring the American people that he was 'not a crook': 'I can assure the New Zealand people I am not a liar' (quoted in *Sunday-Star Times*, 11 September 2005, p. A11).

7   For commentary on 'paintergate' and the 2002 election, see Church (2003), p. 37; James (2003), pp. 48–9; and Morrison (2003), pp. 209–10. Such was the notoriety surrounding the painting (which was destroyed) that a colour photograph of it was reproduced on the cover of a book on the election—*New Zealand Votes: The General Election of 2002.*

8   A recent history of New Zealand's electoral system, including its system of separate Maori electorates, has been provided by Atkinson (2003).

9   For a perceptive and critical analysis of the Orewa speech, see Johansson (2004).

10   The results of the three previous MMP elections are analysed in Levine & Roberts (1997b; 2001; and 2003). The circumstances leading to the introduction of the new electoral system are reviewed in Levine & Roberts (1997a).

11   For instance, an ACT party billboard in Epsom displayed the following equation: 'Hide = Hide + ACT + Worth; Worth = Only Worth'.

12   The National party list 'front-end loaded' its incumbent MPs who were standing for re-election in precisely the same order as their party's parliamentary ranking. The only newcomer who broke into that bloc of twenty-five MPs was New Zealand's World Trade Organization negotiator, Tim Groser, who was ranked number thirteen.

13   Strictly speaking, not all of them were 'new MPs'. Tau Henare (list) had previously served two terms as a New Zealand First MP (1993–99); Anne Tolley, elected in East Cape, had previously been a National party list MP (1999–2002); and Eric Roy, elected in Invercargill, had been elected for Awarua in 1993 and was a list MP for the 1996–2002 period.

14   Peters did not concede defeat and subsequently a motion was filed on his behalf against Clarkson, claiming that the National candidate had overspent on his campaign. Peters had originally entered Parliament as MP for Hunua in 1979 as a result of an electoral petition after the 1978 general election. He had also been instrumental in another successful petition, one that saw the 1987 result in the Wairarapa electorate overturned in favour of National's Wyatt Creech. His 2005 legal action proved futile.

15   See, for example, *New Zealand Herald*, 15 September 2005, p. A1. The quote was reprinted frequently in newspaper columns and was also rebroadcast on numerous occasions on television programmes about the election.

16   See Boston, Levine, McLeay & Roberts, 1996, pp. 58–60.

17   For an analysis of a citizens-initiated referendum in 1999 calling for the number of Members of Parliament to be reduced to ninety-nine MPs—the same number as had been found in the final first-past-the-post Parliament—see Church (2000), in Boston, Church, Levine, McLeay & Roberts (eds), chapter 18.

18   Official voting statistics are from Chief Electoral Office (2005).

19   The still-controversial 1996 post-election negotiations process—described by a then newly elected New Zealand First MP as 'a healthy thing for this country' (Bloxham 1997), p. 42—was viewed less positively by the media and public (as well as by many New Zealand First voters). A thorough analysis of this first exercise in MMP-generated post-election coalition negotiations is given by Boston (1997), chapter 18.

20   For the text of the letter, see www.nzherald.co.nz, 19 October 2005.

21 The 1935–49 Labour government was achieved through four election victories, 1935, 1938, 1943 and 1946, two under the leadership of Michael Joseph Savage and two with the party led by Peter Fraser. Four National party leaders won three in a row Sidney Holland (1949, 1951 and 1954), Robert Muldoon (1975, 1978 and 1981) and Jim Bolger (1990, 1993 and 1996) and one, Keith Holyoake, led his party to victory four successive times (1960, 1963, 1966 and 1969).

REFERENCES

Atkinson, N. 2003, *Adventures in Democracy: A History of the Vote in New Zealand*, University of Otago Press, Dunedin.

Bale, T. 2003, 'News, Newszak, New Zealand: The Role, Performance and Impact of Television in The General Election of 2002', in J. Boston, S. Church, S. Levine, E. McLeay & N.S. Roberts (eds), *New Zealand Votes: The General Election of 2002*, Victoria University Press, Wellington, pp. 217–34.

Bloxham, J. 1997, 'New Zealand First: Ready for Responsibility', in J. Boston, S. Levine, E. McLeay & N. S. Roberts (eds), *From Campaign to Coalition: New Zealand's First General Election Under Proportional Representation*, Dunmore Press, Palmerston North, pp. 39–43.

Boston, J. 1997, 'Forming the First MMP Government: Theory, Practice and Prospects', in J. Boston, S. Levine, E. McLeay & N. S. Roberts (eds), *From Campaign to Coalition: New Zealand's First General Election Under Proportional Representation*, Dunmore Press, Palmerston North, pp. 207–46.

Boston, J., S. Levine, E. McLeay & N.S. Roberts 1996, *New Zealand under MMP: A New Politics?*, Auckland University Press, Auckland.

Chief Electoral Office 2005, 'Part X—Return of Special Votes', in E-9 Reports: The General Election 2005: available at www.electionresults.govt.nz/e9/html/e9_part10_1.html

Church, S. 2000, 'Crime and Punishment: The Referenda to Reform the Criminal Justice System and Reduce the Size of Parliament', in J. Boston, S. Church, S. Levine, E. McLeay & N.S. Roberts (eds) 2000, *Left Turn: The New Zealand General Election of 1999*, Victoria University Press, Wellington, pp. 184–99.

Church, S. 2003, 'Going Early', in J. Boston, S. Church, S. Levine, E. McLeay & N.S. Roberts (eds), *New Zealand Votes: The General Election of 2002*, Victoria University Press, Wellington, pp. 28–44.

Donnelly, B. 2003, 'The New Zealand First Campaign', in J. Boston, S. Church, S. Levine, E. McLeay & N.S. Roberts (eds), *New Zealand Votes: The General Election of 2002*, Victoria University Press, Wellington, pp. 118–122.

Hayward, J. & C. Rudd 2003, ' "Read All About It!": Newspaper Coverage of the General Election', in J. Boston, S. Church, S. Levine, E. McLeay & N.S. Roberts (eds), *New Zealand Votes: The General Election of 2002*, Victoria University Press, Wellington, pp. 254–69.

James, C. 2003, 'Two Million Voters in Search of a Rationale', in J. Boston, S. Church, S. Levine, E. McLeay & N.S. Roberts (eds), *New Zealand Votes: The General Election of 2002*, Victoria University Press, Wellington, pp. 45–58.

Johansson, J. 2004, 'Orewa and the Rhetoric of Illusion', *Political Science*, vol. 56, no. 2, pp. 111–29.

Levine, S. & N.S. Roberts 1997a, 'MMP: The Decision', in R. Miller (ed.), *New Zealand Politics in Transition*, Oxford University Press, Auckland, pp. 25–36.

Levine, S. & N.S. Roberts 1997b, 'The 1996 General Election', in R. Miller (ed.), *New Zealand Politics in Transition*, Oxford University Press, Auckland, pp. 223–33.

Levine, S. & N.S. Roberts 2001, 'The 1999 Election Results', in R. Miller (ed.), *New Zealand Government and Politics* (2nd edn), Oxford University Press, Auckland, pp. 213–23.

Levine, S. & N.S. Roberts 2003, 'The 2002 General Election', in R. Miller (ed.), *New Zealand Government and Politics* (3rd edn), Oxford University Press, Melbourne, pp. 219–32.

Morrison, A. 2003, ' "Constructing Something from a Few Crumbs": A Journalist's View of the Campaign', in J. Boston, S. Church, S. Levine, E. McLeay & N.S. Roberts (eds), *New Zealand Votes: The General Election of 2002*, Victoria University Press, Wellington, pp. 209–16.

Peters, W. 2005, 'Who Will New Zealand First Go With?', speech to a public meeting in Rotorua, 7 September: available at www.nzfirst.org.nz/content/display_item. php?t=1&i=2092

Sowry, R. 1997, 'The National Campaign: Tactics and Strategies', in J. Boston, S. Levine, E. McLeay & N. S. Roberts (eds), *From Campaign to Coalition: New Zealand's First General Election Under Proportional Representation*, Dunmore Press, Palmerston North, pp. 25–32.

Speech from the Throne 2005, delivered by Governor-General Dame Silvia Cartwright, 8 November: available at www.beehive.govt.nz

Watkins, T. 2005, 'Under the Blowtorch', *Dominion Post*, 12 September, p. B7.

FURTHER READING

Boston, J., S. Levine, E. McLeay & N.S. Roberts 1996, *New Zealand under MMP: A New Politics?*, Auckland University Press, Auckland.

Boston, J., S. Levine, E. McLeay & N.S. Roberts (eds) 1997, *From Campaign to Coalition: New Zealand's First General Election Under Proportional Representation*, Dunmore Press, Palmerston North.

Boston, J., S. Church, S. Levine, E. McLeay & N.S. Roberts (eds) 2000, *Left Turn: The New Zealand General Election of 1999*, Victoria University Press, Wellington.

Boston, J., S. Church, S. Levine, E. McLeay & N.S. Roberts (eds) 2003, *New Zealand Votes: The General Election of 2002*, Victoria University Press, Wellington.

Jackson, K. & A. McRobie 1998, *New Zealand Adopts Proportional Representation: Accident? Design? Evolution?*, Ashgate, Aldershot.

Vowles, J., P. Aimer, S. Banducci & J. Karp (eds) 1998, *Voters' Victory? New Zealand's First Election under Proportional Representation*, Auckland University Press, Auckland.

Vowles, J., P. Aimer, J. Karp, S. Banducci, R. Miller & A. Sullivan 2002, *Proportional Representation on Trial: The 1999 New Zealand General Election and the Fate of MMP*, Auckland University Press, Auckland.

Vowles, J., P. Aimer, S. Banducci, J. Karp & R. Miller (eds) 2004, *Voters' Veto: The 2002 Election in New Zealand and the Consolidation of Minority Government*, Auckland University Press, Auckland.

5.0 Parties

Labour Party

Peter Aimer

The Labour party was formed in July 1916, in what now seems like a fictional setting. In the politics of the time, notions of class and class conflict were prominent. They were an expression of the deep poverty and insecurity of livelihood that many experienced, while others prospered amid allegations of wartime profiteering (Gustafson 1980, pp. 95–104). There had been bitter industrial disputes in the coal mines of Westland (1908), the gold fields of Waihi (1912), and on the Wellington wharves (1913). In Waihi and Wellington there was violent confrontation and even death (King 2003, pp. 306–13). The strikes, though heroic, achieved little, and the futility of such industrial action steered the leaders of the labour movement towards an alternative form of redress.

The Labour party was founded to be the political wing of the industrial labour movement, linked in its organisation and personnel to trade unions, and speaking for workers and their families (Gustafson 1980, pp. 92–4). Its goals were humanitarian. Its leaders, says Gustafson, 'sought an effective, independent, working-class voice in parliament as the key to legislation that would dramatically improve living conditions and provide security and equality of opportunity for all' (p. 151). The new party also took from one of its founding elements—the Social Democratic party—the classic, anti-capitalist objective of the socialisation of the means of production, distribution, and exchange, that is, state control of the economy.

TAMING OF LABOUR

Labour fought its first general election in 1919 on a platform of radical policies which called for the extension of the state into such activities as banking, insurance, shipping, and coal mining. While such policies were consistent with socialist practice,

Table 5.1.1: Labour leaders and prime ministers

	Leader	Prime Minister
Harry Holland	1919–33 (Di)	
Michael Joseph Savage	1933–40	1935–40 (Di)
Peter Fraser	1940–50	1940–49 (Df)
Walter Nash	1950–63	1957–60 (Df)
Arnold Nordmeyer	1963–65 (R)	
Norman Kirk	1965–74	1972–74 (Di)
Wallace (Bill) Rowling	1974–83	1974–75 (Df)
David Lange	1983–89	1984–89 (R)
Geoffrey Palmer	1989–90	1989–90 (R)
Michael (Mike) Moore	1990–93	1990 (Df)
Helen Clark	1993–99	1999–

Di = died Df = defeated R = resigned

they fell short of realising the party's avowed socialist objective, even if implemented. But there was no prospect of that in 1919 or later, as Labour's radicalism lacked broad enough appeal to be an election winner. Accordingly, while still waving the banner of the socialist objective, Labour turned down an alternative path of greater moderation and pragmatism, adjusting earlier policies to make them less threatening to farming and property-owning, middle-class communities, and more attuned to the specific problems of the time (Chapman 1969, p. 64). The prescriptive relevance of Labour's sweeping socialist objective was thus waning almost from the time it was adopted. Labour has never lived up to its socialist objective, even though it held onto it until 1951.

Since 1951, Labour has been associated with a variety of ideological labels. More recently, it has been depicted as an 'ideological coalition' of 'liberals and socialists' (Vowles 1987, p. 223). This combination, with its potential for a shifting balance between its two elements, is more commonly expressed as social democracy. As a social democratic party, Labour belongs to a 'family' of comparable centre-left parties in developed democracies, including the Labour parties of Australia, Britain, and Norway, the Social Democratic parties of Denmark, Finland, Germany and Sweden, and the New Democrats of Canada.

In countries like Britain and New Zealand, in which the recent imprint of neo-liberal theory and political practice is strong ('Thatcherism' and 'Rogernomics'), social democracy has tilted towards the liberal end of the scale. Now sometimes referred to as 'third way' politics, it is an open-ended prescription for a mixture of policies, some expressing the traditional humanitarian concerns of labourites and social democrats, others deferring to free-market reforms, fiscal caution, and the greater individualism and demand for choice that has permeated society (Miller 2005, pp. 163–6).

'Third way' politics rejects the notion that markets should be 'kept largely subordinate to government' (Giddens 1998, p. 99). More vaguely, it 'looks instead for a synergy between public and private sectors, utilizing the dynamism of markets but with the public interest in mind' (p. 100).

Labour now accepts the primacy of the free market, as National once espoused Labour's postwar mixed economy of separate public and private sectors. Indeed, it was Labour which provided the impetus to free-market reforms in the 1980s. Between 1984 and 1990, Labour's once radical potential re-emerged in a surprising direction when the fourth Labour government embarked on a programme of economic changes grounded in classical liberal thought. In defiance of the party's traditions, Labour politicians argued for a scaling back of the economic role of the state. Far from tilting at capitalism, as their predecessors once had, they lauded the disciplined efficiency of the private sector and the free market, deregulated the economy, imposed corporate structures and procedures on state enterprises, and sold others outright to private enterprise. 'Rogernomics' may have destroyed the fourth Labour government in 1990, but it set policy directions which the incoming National administration followed with zeal for the next decade. By 1999, when Labour returned to office, the economic middle ground—what people had become used to—had moved well towards the liberal end of the socialism–liberalism scale.

In this setting, 'third way' politics sprawls across the partisan divide and offers Labour considerable flexibility of policy and practice. Following Giddens, there is only slightly more room for the state in the economy under Labour compared to National. Labour returned to government in 1999 committed to checking the further encroachment of free-market principles into what remained of the public sphere. But it was not committed to turning back the economic clock. Labour's response was conservative. It restored the Accident Compensation Commission's monopoly, rejected bulk funding of schools, abolished market rentals for state housing, and reinvigorated the state housing programme. The generation and distribution of electricity, however, a vital resource, remain largely deregulated, and commercial imperatives still dominate public service broadcasting. In transport, the government bought back the rail tracks only, not the services on them, and it bailed out Air New Zealand, but unwillingly and only when the flagship airline was on the brink of collapse. While the establishment of Kiwibank marked the return of the state to banking, it was a reluctant concession to Labour's coalition partner on its political left, not a Labour initiative. Offshore, Labour has pursued free trade as fervently as National. At home, it has only slightly relaxed the inflation parameters within which the Reserve Bank had operated through the 1990s, and has pursued a cautious fiscal policy aimed at achieving budget surpluses.

ELECTORAL HISTORY

Labour's electoral history is shown in figure 5.1.1. From the first general election it contested in 1919 and through the 1920s, Labour was a significant minor party in a three-party system. Rapid growth in electoral support followed in the early 1930s as depression gripped the country, driving the two non-Labour parties (United and Reform) together, and establishing Labour as the main opposition party. Since then, Labour has retained its status along with National (formed 1936) as one of the twin pillars of New Zealand's two-party dominant politics. Figure 5.1.1 thus presents a profile of remarkably stable support across a broad slice of the electorate for the last seventy years. We should note, though, towards the end of the figure, Labour's catastrophic slump signposting the electoral collapse of the fourth Labour government in 1990, and subsequently compounded by the advent of MMP in 1996, and the emergence of a more multi-party system. Since Labour's electoral nadir in 1996, it has rebuilt a so-far stable electoral platform of about 40 per cent of voters.

The peaks of the bars in figure 5.1.1 mark the high points in Labour's electoral history—the elections it won. They are widely spaced, for after its rapid rise on the back of the depression, and a period of dominance through the late 1930s and 1940s, Labour has been electorally much less successful than National. In the second half of the century, Labour governed intermittently for a total of only twelve years—in 1957–60, 1972–5, and 1984–90. Hence the jubilation in Labour ranks as the party entered a third term of government in 2005.

Miller identifies Labour's 'modest office-holding record' as one of the 'paradoxes' surrounding the party, considering its longevity and major party status in a simple

Figure 5.1.1: Labour vote in elections 1919–2005

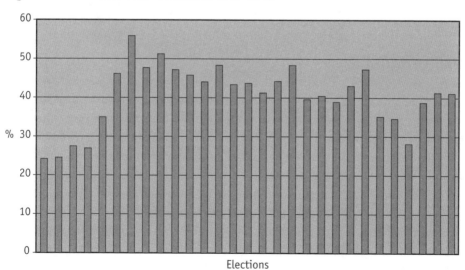

two-party system (2003, p. 235). Yet it is a record that is not so very different from that of kindred parties in Australia and Britain, where equally mature Labour parties spent many more years in opposition than government. Moreover, Labour's 'modest' record of years in government conceals the closeness of the contests between it and National. Across the twenty-three elections from 1938 (National's first election) to 2005, the average electoral 'gap' between the two parties was 5.6 per cent. In eleven of these elections, less than 4 per cent separated them (in two of which Labour won slightly more votes while losing the election).

These are important statistics, which bear on the character of both major parties. In the evenly balanced two-party system, the pull to the political centre has been strong. This means that the policy distance between Labour and National, like the electoral gap between them, is usually small, relative to the theoretical range of economic and social alternatives. The pull to the so-called moderate centre discourages radical change, so that the initiatives of one party may be modified, but rarely overturned, by the other. In this process of consensus building, National held the advantage during the last half of the twentieth century, having come to accept much of Labour's welfare state and Keynesian economic management, thus relegating Labour to the role of 'alternative conservative party' (Miller 2003, p. 239). It was this role that, against expectations, was rejected by Labour in the 1980s, with its programme of free-market reforms. The programme embracing such initiatives as GST, a flatter tax structure, a floating exchange rate, and privatisation or corporatisation of state utilities, were then safe under the incoming National administration. These once-radical policies were thus absorbed into a new consensus, which extended beyond economic policies to such issues as legalised homosexuality and questions of nuclear power and arms. The centre of politics had shifted. By the end of the 1990s, Labour was back in its familiar systemic role of 'alternative conservative' party.

ORGANISATION

Defined in great detail by the party's constitution, Labour's organisational structure has evolved to cater for a pluralistic membership. Within the party there are 'sectors' for women, youth, Māori, Pacific people, rural interests, gay, lesbian and transgender interests (the 'Rainbow sector'), local government interests, and trade union affiliates.

It is a three-tiered organisation—electorate, regional, central. At its base are individual members associated with local branches, which are represented on an electorate committee within the boundaries of each of the sixty-nine geographical electorates (in 2005). Where members are few the electorate committee may become the primary organisational unit in the place of branches.

Electorates are grouped into six regions—Auckland/Northland, Waikato/Bay of Plenty, Central North Island, Wellington, Northern South Island, Otago/Southland. The regional councils have a coordinating role in party organisational activities, while the regional conferences channel policy remits to the party's central organs, and play a part in the construction of the ranked candidate lists.

Higher up the party structure, the annual party conference is the most visible component of organisation, being the party's media showcase, and a platform for the leader and other prominent party figures or rising political stars. In party constitutional terms, it is 'the supreme governing body', where delegates consider and vote on party policy and constitutional changes, and elect the senior office-holders of the party. Informally, conference is a venue for socialising among activists, and rubbing shoulders with politicians. Proceedings are tightly managed in the interests of the smooth running of a potentially unwieldy event, and to avoid possible public relations disasters, as well as open displays of disunity or dissension. Policy remits, for example, once the source of raw emotion and rambling debate on the floor of conference, now arrive consolidated and refined via the regional conferences, the central Policy Council, and perusal by one of up to ten policy committees.

Among the central organs the two most powerful bodies are the Policy Council and the New Zealand Council. Two sets of interests, which may not always be in harmony, converge in the Policy Council—those of the amateur rank-and-file membership of the party, and those of the professional politicians. MPs and ordinary party members are both represented on the Policy Council, where they are joined by the party's top officials—the president and the general secretary—and representatives of the sector groups within the party. The Policy Council has the potentially sensitive task of shaping the party's election manifesto, revising old and developing new policies. The New Zealand Council is the governing body in between the brief meetings of conference. The council monitors the functioning of the party organisation at all levels, and initiates and manages significant procedures such as the selection of parliamentary candidates. Chaired by the party president, it is made up of the elected elites from across the various sectors of the party organisation.

LINKS TO THE UNIONS

A hallmark of Labour's organisation is the affiliation of trade unions to the party. It is a distinctive feature, connecting the party's past to its present, and contributing at times a colourful strand in its history. The intra-party role of unions has not always gone unchallenged. Some within the party have sought the uncoupling of Labour from the unions in the belief that it would enhance intra-party democracy by removing the elective weight of the card vote wielded by affiliated union delegates, and that it would broaden Labour's electoral appeal by lessening the perception of union dominance of the party, a theme much relished and exaggerated by cartoonists and the National party. But excommunication of the unions was always a provocative and radical proposal, which seemed to strike at the core of Labour's historical purpose as the party for working people. Through a period of significant constitutional changes in the 1970s, which established the format of the party's present organisation, affiliation survived (Strachan 1985, pp. 159–70).

Today, the presence of affiliated unions within the party structure raises few if any hackles. This may be partly a matter of numbers. Under the influence of the National government's Employment Contracts Act, and the introduction of voluntary unionism, total union membership in the workforce declined drastically in the 1990s (Street 2003, p. 381). Of this shrunken total, Vowles has estimated that by the end of the decade little more than 10 per cent were affiliated to Labour (Vowles 2002, p. 419). In 2005, Labour's Web page listed only three affiliated unions, the largest being the Engineering, Printing, and Manufacturing Union.

Affiliation, therefore, maintains in atrophied form an historical association with industrial labour that goes back to Labour's origins. That association, however, is also expressed in a variety of less atrophied ways, most commonly in the shared political interests that align unions with Labour. After disillusionment with the actions of the fourth Labour government, unions and Labour found common ground again in the party's drive to recover from its electoral drubbing in 1990, and the unions' determination to overturn the Employment Contracts Act, and also to nudge Labour away from its 1980s neo-liberal path. Practical expressions of alignment are unions contributing to Labour's election funds, or engaging in politically sympathetic advertising campaigns, and union members helping to swell the ranks of party workers on election days. Active alignment of this kind then shades off into a more passive form, which sees households with union links voting strongly for Labour (Vowles et al. 2002, p. 227). Even unions which do not overtly support Labour have a covert preference for election results that favour the centre-left over the centre-right, for policy reasons, or simply to keep out more hostile parties.

Once back in government after the 1999 election, the Labour–Alliance administration replaced the Employment Contracts Act with the Employment Relations Act, which restored the unions' collective bargaining rights, and set in train a recovery in the number of unions and union members (Street 2003, p. 381). Since then, Labour-led governments have attended to such issues as paid parental leave, workplace health and safety regulations, holiday entitlements, and minimum wage levels—not always to the satisfaction of union leaders, and sometimes pushed by other centre-left parties, but enough to sustain union alignment with Labour, if not to re-invigorate direct affiliation to the party's organisation.

Labour had begun as an arm of the trade unions and as the political mouthpiece for manual workers and their families. The background of its early politicians reflected this. But, as in comparable parties elsewhere, the number of MPs from wage-earner backgrounds dwindled (Gustafson 1985, p. 151). 'Where have all the workers gone?' asked Bruce Jesson more than twenty years ago when looking at Labour's 'lineup' on the eve of the election of the fourth Labour government (Sharp 2005, pp. 118, 122–3). Labour politicians (indeed like all others) now mostly arrive in parliament with a tertiary education and from non-manual occupations. The link between party and workplace remains, however, in the trade union background of a significant proportion of Labour MPs and candidates (Miller 2004, pp. 93–4). Rebuilding after the 1990 defeat, when Labour's caucus sank to only twenty-nine MPs, unionists were among those who sought and won selection as candidates. As a result, by the late 1990s 'the number of former union members and officials in Labour's parliamentary party' had increased (Vowles 2002, p. 419). Personifying this are the now senior politicians Rick Barker, Winnie Laban, and Mark Gosche, joined in 2005 by successful first-time candidates Sue Moroney and Darien Fenton.

CANDIDATE SELECTION

Since the introduction of MMP in 1996, candidate selection procedures have had to deal with two issues—who is picked to stand, and where will he or she rank on the party's nationwide list. Both are crucial decisions for candidates with serious political ambition and not merely cheerful party flag-bearers. Electorate candidates are sought and selected following a schedule determined by the New Zealand Council. Although the selection of a candidate is of high importance to local party members, especially in electorates likely to return a Labour MP, a key feature of Labour's selection procedure has been the factoring in of wider party interests. The electorate selection committee thus consists of three local representatives and three representing the New Zealand Council. A preferential ballot among local party members present at the meeting also counts as one vote. There is a potential for impasse and disagreement between central and local representatives, and this has occurred in the past. Yet selection crises are rare. Council representatives tend to defer to a strongly expressed local preference, rather than risk a standoff and damaging conflict. Moreover, the construction of the ranked list of candidates provides another way for wider party interests to be expressed in terms of gender, ethnic, occupational skills, and competency criteria.

The party's list ranking process occurs in two stages. At regional level delegates rank a number of candidates proportional to their region's population, having been enjoined to achieve lists which contain a 'spread' of groups, interests, and candidate criteria. The second and definitive stage is performed by a high-powered Moderating Committee, with a membership drawn from the New Zealand Council, the sector councils, the six regions, and the MPs, including the leader and deputy leader. Labour's constitution allocates the top two list positions to the leader and deputy. But below that, the role of the Moderating Committee, 'allows the party hierarchy to control the outcome in a number of significant ways', including safeguarding sitting MPs, having regard to their seniority, gender, ethnic, regional location, and the marginality of their seats (Miller 2003, p. 244).

In 2005, the leader and deputy leader, the Speaker (Margaret Wilson), ministers inside or outside cabinet, and two parliamentary under-secretaries accounted for nineteen of the first twenty places on Labour's list. Among the top forty on the list, thirty-eight were sitting MPs. For a new candidate to be ranked among sitting MPs is a sign of extraordinary approval and likely rapid promotion. The two candidates who broke the phalanx of MPs in 2005 were the highly regarded Harvard graduate and chair of the Treaty of Waitangi Fisheries Commission, Shane Jones (at number twenty-seven), and former Labour party president, Maryan Street (at number thirty-six). Placed immediately after the MPs were Sue Moroney and Darien Fenton, whose ranking was likely in part to have been an acknowledgment of political skills honed as union officials. A few MPs, usually in fairly secure Labour seats, and perhaps still believing in the greater worthiness of electorate over list representation, like Clayton Cosgrove (Waimakariri) and Ross Robertson (Manukau East), refused a place on the list. In 2005, eight MPs made this choice. Only one, John Tamihere (Tamaki Makaurau), who had stood aside from the list in 1999 and 2002 also, missed re-election. George Hawkins (Manurewa), however, broke ranks with his cabinet colleagues, turning down a list placing lower than in 2002, with its implied demotion after a troubled second term as police minister.

While the privileging of sitting MPs may appear self-serving and deferential, there is little alternative if value is placed on promoting a stable and therefore experienced caucus, and avoiding obvious grounds for intra-party dissension. Safeguarding MPs, however, is likely to constrain Labour's promotion of fair and diverse representation, a goal clearly written into its constitution, though having pursued this aim since the advent of MMP, Labour has already gone further than most other parties in advancing gender and ethnic representation. In 2005, its mix of candidates remained almost the same as in 2002 (Miller 2003, p. 244). Among its top thirty-five places there were thirteen women (down two since 2002), six Māori (unchanged), and three Pacific Islanders (up one). Ashraf Choudhary, the first Muslim MP, had also moved into this bloc of candidates where election was almost certain.

While the significance of such descriptive representation in mobilising electoral support should not be overstated, there is an obvious correspondence between the pluralism of Labour's list and its roots in the electorate, at least insofar as women more than men have favoured Labour in recent elections, while the Māori electorates and general electorates with large Māori and Pacific populations are Labour strongholds. Would Labour have won the close contest between it and National in 2005 without these disproportionate concentrations of Labour voters?

CONCLUSION

In 2005, for only the second time in its long history, Labour returned to government for a third consecutive term. For the party and for its leader, Helen Clark, it was a notable milestone. For immediate explanations we could assess the effects of a strong economy, qualities of leadership, a flexible style of government, a sufficient war chest, tactical campaigning, adequate grass-roots organisation, and some well-targeted election promises. But this chapter has mostly looked at Labour from a more historical perspective, to depict and explain its present political character.

Founded at a distant and unique time in New Zealand history, Labour's distinctive objectives, organisation, and practices have been adjusted in response to the vastly changing demands and political environments of the last ninety years. The final twenty years, including the term of the fourth Labour government, have been crucial. Labour has evolved into a 'third way', social democratic party, economically orthodox, socially liberal, flexible and mildly innovative, holding to a traditional focus on the material issues surrounding health, education, jobs, and the alleviation of poverty with one hand, while reaching out with the other toward more post-materialist concerns in arts, culture, and social identity. Through an organisation that has acknowledged the claims of gender and ethnicity, Labour has established multiple links to a pluralistic population, and reaped the electoral benefits. While cultivating diversity is necessary to Labour maintaining its major party status, it is not an easy strategy.

Harbouring different expectations and priorities, Labour's constituency is not naturally cohesive. In its recent second term, there were obvious strains between social liberals rallying to such initiatives as legalised prostitution, smoke-free environments, and provision for same sex unions, and those who, like their Labour-voting forebears, yearn for a fairer distribution of wealth, and the abolition of poverty. For them, however, there is the 'Working for Families' package. For Labour retains a stronger urge than the political right to redistribute the benefits of the economy more equitably through welfare spending. Yet in the contemporary setting, Labour's earlier egalitarianism has largely surrendered to an acceptance of the greater income inequalities of a competitive free market economy. Certainly, ninety years after the unity conference in Wellington in 1916, the language of class conflict is muted. 'Forward Together' was Labour's inclusive and conciliatory campaign slogan in 2005.

DISCUSSION QUESTIONS

1 Bruce Jesson has written: 'Labour treads a careful path in relation to where it sees the middle ground'. What does he mean, and does the record of Labour-led governments since 1999 bear him out?

2 What evidence is there that Labour is responding to the centripetal electoral effects of the continuing dominance of two major parties?

3 Can Labour now claim to be the 'natural party of government'? If so, why? If not, what do you think are the greatest electoral threats to Labour's continuing status as the dominant party?

4 Suggest another way of selecting and ranking parliamentary candidates. Weigh up the pros and cons of the method, and compare them with Labour's current procedure.

REFERENCES

Chapman, R. 1969. *The Political Scene 1919–1931*, Heinemann Educational Books, Auckland.

Giddens, A. 1998, *The Third Way*, Polity Press, Cambridge.

Gustafson, B. 1980, *Labour's Path to Political Independence*, Auckland University Press/ Oxford University Press, Auckland.

Gustafson, B. 1989, 'The Labour Party', in H. Gold (ed.), *New Zealand Politics in Perspective*, 2nd edn, Longman Paul, Auckland.

King, M. 2003, *The Penguin History of New Zealand*, Penguin, Auckland.

Miller, R. 2003, 'Labour', in R. Miller (ed.), *New Zealand Government and Politics*, Oxford University Press, Melbourne.

Miller, R. 2004, 'Who Stood for Office, and Why?', in J. Vowles, P. Aimer, S. Banducci, J. Karp & R. Miller (eds), *Voters' Veto. The 2002 Election in New Zealand and the Consolidation of Minority Government*, Auckland University Press, Auckland.

Miller, R. 2005, *Party Politics in New Zealand*, Oxford University Press, Melbourne.

New Zealand Labour Party, 2002. Constitution and Rules, New Zealand Labour Party, Wellington.

Sharp, A. (ed.) 2005, *To Build a Nation. Bruce Jesson Collected Writings 1975–1999*, Penguin, Auckland.

Strachan, D. 1985, 'A Party Transformed: Organisational Change in the New Zealand Labour Party', in H. Gold (ed.), *New Zealand Politics in Perspective*, Longman Paul, Auckland.

Street, M. 2003, 'Trade Unions', in R. Miller (ed.), *New Zealand Government and Politics*, Oxford University Press, Melbourne.

Vowles, J. 1987. 'Liberal Democracy: Pakeha Political Ideology', *New Zealand Journal of History*, vol. 21, no. 2, pp. 215–27.

Vowles, J. 2002, 'Parties and Society in New Zealand', in P. Webb, D. Farrell & I. Holliday (eds), *Political Parties in Advanced Industrial Democracies*, Oxford University Press, Oxford.

Vowles, J., Aimer, P., Karp, J., Banducci, S., Miller, R. & Sullivan, A. 2002, *Proportional Representation on Trial*, Auckland University Press, Auckland.

FURTHER READING

Gustafson, B. 1989, 'The Labour Party', in H. Gold (ed.), *New Zealand Politics in Perspective*, 2nd ed., Longman Paul, Auckland.

Miller, R. 2003, 'Labour', in R. Miller (ed.), *New Zealand Government and Politics*, Oxford University Press, Melbourne.

Miller, R. 2005, *Party Politics in New Zealand*, Oxford University Press, Melbourne.

Vowles, J. 2002, 'Parties and Society in New Zealand', in P. Webb, D. Farrell & I. Holliday (eds), *Political Parties in Advanced Industrial Democracies*, Oxford University Press, Oxford.

Vowles, J., P. Aimer, J. Karp, S. Banducci, R. Miller & A. Sullivan 2002, *Proportional Representation on Trial*, Auckland University Press, Auckland.

National

Colin James

The National party was the party of government through most of the second half of the twentieth century, holding power for thirty-eight of the fifty years from 1949 to 1999. Since 1999, however, it has been the party of opposition, unable to recreate the mix of policy, political skills, and spread of representation that accounted for its impressive record of electoral dominance.

The National party was formed in 1936 by the 'fusion' of two conservative parties, Reform and United, which had governed in coalition from 1931 to 1935. Reform, the vehicle of farmer and city merchant interests, dominated governments from 1912 to 1928 after supplanting the previously dominant Liberal party. Liberal went through a number of metamorphoses and name changes (including National) in the 1920s before taking office as United, with the Labour party unenthusiastically acquiescing, after a three-way split election in 1928. Overwhelmed by the international economic depression that followed the 1929 New York stock market crash, United formed a crisis 'national' government with Reform in which United was the junior partner in all but name.[1]

After its formation, National spent thirteen years in opposition to the first Labour government, losing elections in 1938, 1943 (during the Second World War) and 1946. It won office in 1949 under its second leader, Sir Sidney Holland, a Christchurch businessman. Holland won two more elections, a snap election in 1951 after a confrontation with the Waterside Workers Union during which he proclaimed a state of emergency and a routine triennial election in 1954 before being ousted by his deputy, Keith Holyoake, ten weeks before the 1957 election.

Holyoake lost that election narrowly to Labour but then won four elections in succession in the prosperous 1960s. In early 1972 he was replaced by his deputy,

John Marshall, in a vain attempt to halt a tide running the way of the Labour party, which won the election in November that year in a landslide.

In 1974 Marshall was supplanted as leader of the opposition by Robert Muldoon, who defeated Labour in a landslide in 1975, helped by a collapse in international prices for the country's exports. Muldoon himself was beset by the faltering economy and retained office in 1978 and 1981 only by quirks of the first-past-the-post voting system that awarded National more seats than Labour even though Labour on both occasions won more votes.

Muldoon lost office in a landslide in 1984 amid an economic crisis, in part of his own making. National did not regain office until 1990, after the Labour party split when its government introduced radical market-led economic reforms. Jim Bolger won that election, in yet another landslide, but survived only narrowly in the 1993 election after a 13 per cent loss of vote share. After the 1996 election he led the first government in the Mixed-Member-Proportional (MMP) period in coalition with New Zealand First, led by Winston Peters, whom he had sacked from the cabinet in 1991. This coalition proved unpopular with the country and with the National party and Bolger was ousted by Jenny Shipley in 1997. She could not save the 1999 election and was herself ousted by Bill English in 2001.

National's share of the vote declined sharply after 1990 (when it won 48 per cent), to 35 per cent in 1993, 34 per cent in 1996 and 31 per cent in 1999 before a disastrous 21 per cent of the party vote in 2002, the lowest vote for a major party since 1902 (though its 31 per cent in the electorate vote was probably a fairer indication of its true strength). In 2005, after yet another change of leader, to Dr Don Brash in 2003, the former Reserve Bank Governor (1988 to 2002), National recovered to a creditable 39 per cent of the party vote.

THE SOCIAL UNDERPINNING

The original National party was essentially a gathering of political forces opposed to the Labour party and the 'socialism' they believed the Labour government would introduce (see chapters 1.4 and 5.1). They included farmers, industrialists, merchants, those in commerce and professional people—those who might loosely be called 'bosses'—broadly those in the middle and upper middle classes. Many small farmers, struggling with high debt and low prices in the wake of the Great Depression, initially voted Labour in the 1930s. During the 1940s they returned to National. But National also began to acquire an increasing (and now creditable) share of the votes of wage-workers, particularly among the better paid.

A measure of National's activist base is the occupations of its MPs. Of all MPs elected from 1936–86, 40 per cent were farmers, 20 per cent in business, 17 per cent lawyers and 6 per cent accountants. Senior office-holders had a wider distribution:

16 per cent farmers, 25 per cent business, 12 per cent lawyers, 9 per cent accountants and 11 per cent teachers.[2] This was clearly the party of the farmer, business, and professional classes. By 2005, however, farmers had lost ground; of the forty-eight MPs elected in that year, six were farmers (eight if Bill English, who grew up on a farm, and Lockwood Smith, who bought a farm while an MP, are included), thirteen from business and eight lawyers.

National's success in the 1950s to 1970s was built on a low-fee broad membership recruited by face-to-face canvassing by elected officials and other active members, which by the early 1970s was claimed by party officials to be around 200,000, a high figure in a population of three million. While most members were passive— whole families were signed up—the large subscriber membership meant there were National party members in almost every society, association, club and special interest organisation, ranging from national and regional business lobby groups such as Federated Farmers, the Manufacturers and Retailers Federations and the Chambers of Commerce, through professional associations such as the Law and Accountants Societies to local business and ratepayers associations—and throughout the less formal local business network organisations such as Rotary and Lions clubs and informal sports and other clubs. These networks both informed a wide pool of people outside the party of government actions and reasoning and kept the party hierarchy and parliamentarians in touch with an extensive range of people of widely varying views and special interests. They provided a wide recruitment base and were in turn recognised by the National party through appointments to a vast range of boards and organisations. This two-way interaction affirmed National as the party of power and legitimacy to which people seeking decisions or a political career would naturally turn and, as a simple imperative of maintaining such varied and far-reaching networks, restrained National from too ideological an approach to decision-making. In this way National could validly claim to be the 'national' party, widely representative of the nation. Some called it the natural party of government.

But these dense interlocking networks broke down during the 1970s for several reasons: some of the groups lost vitality as society became more mobile and diverse from the 1960s onward; membership of the National party itself declined in step with the general decline of the mass party in similar democracies; and during Sir Robert Muldoon's term as prime minister, party members and supporters in business and other lobby groups increasingly felt National was not reflecting its traditional values, particularly in economic policy. By the late 1990s the membership had dipped to little more than one-tenth of its zenith.[3] In 2005, while membership numbers and vitality had revived somewhat, its conferences and its parliamentary caucus no longer reflected the ethnic and gender diversity of the nation. There were few brown or yellow faces and women were mostly in subordinate roles. It was no longer a truly national party and it was certainly not the natural party of government.

The National party is in a broad stream of 'centre-right' parties found in European, North American, and emerging Asian democracies and is an active member of the International Democratic Union of centre-right parties. It keeps in close touch with the Australian Liberal party, the British Conservative party, and the American Republican party, with which it has much in common in values and from which it learns campaigning and organisational techniques. The Australian firm of CrosbylTextor, headed by Lynton Crosby, campaign director of the Liberal party in 1998 and 2001 and Mark Textor, official Liberal pollster from 1996–2004, advised National before and during the 2005 election campaign. However, the National party is not a clone or twin of any of those parties. It has been shaped by the special social, political, and economic history and circumstances of New Zealand and reflects New Zealand instincts and values.

THE MAIN TENDENCIES

National is frequently described as 'conservative' or 'liberal–conservative', combining a liberal tendency and a conservative tendency. But it also has outlier libertarian (radical) and populist tendencies that occasionally are ascendant. More recently, a moral conservative tendency has also been evident. National can also be described as functionalist, a party that sees governing as an end in itself rather than in service of an ideology or principles.

The conservative tendency within National is concerned to 'conserve' (though not to freeze) what it sees as valuable and enduring (or valuable *because* enduring).[4] What this constitutes varies over time but some threads run through National's history, among them: the traditional political order, as inherited from Britain, including the monarchy, the Westminster parliamentary system, the rule of law and equality before the law; strategic defence alliances with 'kith-and-kin' countries such as Britain, the USA and Australia; individual freedom; the centrality of property rights and private enterprise in the economy; a discomfort with social and moral reform; and the importance of the family as the fundamental social unit.

The conservative tends to see society as an organism of different but mutually supporting parts, each with a place that is not to be disturbed without good cause. The conservative sees the past as integral with the present and thus the source of social and cultural wisdom and enduring institutions and customs that are therefore to be respected—in politics, the constitution must be respected. The conservative is sceptical of abstract theory and thus of proposals for change drawn from theory. The conservative is suspicious of reform unless to reinstate traditional values. Radical change and popular movements are anathema to the conservative. Bill English, leader from 2001–03 and a self-described 'modern conservative', said in an interview in 1999 that conservatism in the modern National party is 'about maintaining those things that work well, a sense of social order around values like commitment and respect, personal and community responsibility'.[5] Some trace the intellectual foundations of conservatism back to Edmund Burke, a late eighteenth-century English political philosopher who polemicised in favour of the existing order and against revolution, which he feared might spread from France. But New Zealand's conservatives seldom elevate their beliefs into doctrine.

National's conservative tendency has been tempered by a liberal tendency which has at times been ascendant, perhaps most notably in the liquor and legal reforms of Ralph Hanan in the 1960s, culminating in the passing of a remit sponsored by Young Nationals (the youth wing) at the 1970 conference to decriminalise homosexuality. The liberal values very highly the individual and liberty and is sceptical of government except insofar as it enhances freedom and preserves the rights of the individual. The liberal advocates tolerance in morality and religion and freedom of speech.[6]

Like conservatives, liberals within the National party seldom appeal to doctrine but some senior figures have, from time to time, cited two nineteenth-century English political philosophers, J.S. Mill and T.H. Green,[7] as fountainheads. Shades of their thinking can be discerned in the maiden speech in parliament in 1947 of a future leader, John Marshall. In what amounts to a credo for the party in the post-1945 period through to his own period of leadership, Marshall stated, reflecting Mill's famous essay, *On Liberty*:[8] 'The conditions of the good society are liberty, property and security and the greatest of these is liberty'. But, reflecting Green, Marshall rejected 'mere selfish individualism. The doctrine of *laissez-faire* passed out of liberal thinking 50 years ago'. Thus Marshall validated a degree of labour market regulation and profit-sharing as aids to 'the common man' achieving economic liberty and social security as making 'a considerable contribution to economic liberty' and 'planning to enable free enterprise to function without the evils that have attended its unrestricted development'. All that, however, depended on 'individual initiative under the spur of competition'.

The liberal and conservative tendencies are often linked: Marshall, in an interview[9] on his accession to the leadership in 1972, added 'conservative' to 'liberal' to describe his, and the party's, position at that time; Jim McLay, leader from 1984–86 and a self-declared liberal, quoted Mill at the 1997 conference as urging that '[a] party of order or stability and a party of progress or reform are both necessary elements of a healthy state of political life' and depicted National as encompassing both. And English in his 1999 interview talked of maintaining (though improving) the welfare state, a 'pluralistic' society and a need for 'an engine of ideas' to drive the economy, all notions nearer National's liberal than conservative end.

A third, though lesser, tendency within the National party is a variant of utilitarianism, traceable (in theory) back to Jeremy Bentham and some of J.S. Mill's writings and roughly summarised as 'the greatest good for the greatest number', though in National hands it has been more an electoral calculus—maximising votes—than a principle. Taken to its logical conclusion, this calculus amounts to populism. Sir Robert Muldoon did take it to that logical conclusion—he adopted as his pre-eminent criterion for decision-making what he divined the 'ordinary bloke' would approve, in whose interests he claimed always to be operating.

The fourth, also lesser, tendency within the National party is market-liberalism (also known, with variations, as economic libertarianism, classical liberalism, neo-liberalism, neo-classicism and New Right). This draws its intellectual underpinning from, among others, Adam Smith, Friedrich von Hayek and, in the 1970s and 1980s, the Chicago and Virginian 'schools' of what are sometimes called 'neoliberal' economic thinking. This thinking has been vigorously promoted since the late 1980s by the Business Roundtable through its director, Roger Kerr, who prefers to call it simply liberal. It argues for low taxes, small government, free trade, and light regulation of the economy.[10]

This tendency waxed from the late 1970s on, especially during the Labour government's market-oriented reforms of 1984–90, and gained ascendancy in the party briefly in 1989–92 during Ruth Richardson's time as finance speaker and then Finance minister, when she extended the economic and social reforms begun by the Labour government in 1984. There was a partial revival with the appointment of Don Brash, an economic libertarian, who came into parliament in 2002, as finance spokesperson in that year and leader in 2003. But in fact, though Brash argued the economic libertarian position in some early speeches, the policy the party adopted under his leadership for the 2005 election was relatively moderate and even, in some respects, populist (see 'the future' below).

Populism and libertarian radicalism are seldom ascendant. Their adherents usually spin off from National or develop parties outside it. The New Zealand First party in the 1990s and 2000s is an example of a populist party spun off from National, its leader, Winston Peters, having been a National cabinet minister in 1990–91. The Democrats in 1935, Liberal and Liberal Reform parties during the 1960s, the New Zealand party, which won 12 per cent of the vote in 1984, and the ACT party from 1995 on, which Richardson eventually joined, are examples of economic libertarian parties.

More recently, a moral-conservative tendency has emerged, based on a conservative reading of Christian values. An informal Christian Voice group, set up in 1998, puts this case within the National party, though without fanfare (and it was not on the official programme at the 2005 conference). Again, most people of this persuasion organise outside the party, including in the Christian Democrats, formed by an exiting National MP, Graeme Lee, in 1996, who joined Peter Dunne's United party in United Future in 2000. However, in 2005 National explicitly accepted help from the Exclusive Brethren Church, both in its canvassing and in separate advertising attacking Labour and the Greens. It is not clear whether this might develop into a more enduring, even if still arm's-length, relationship, similar to the Australian Liberals' links with the religious right. Two possible pointers are the predominant view within the parliamentary caucus against the legalisation of prostitution in 2003 and 'civil unions' (in effect, marriage) between same-sex couples in 2004 and the appointment of a spokesperson for 'political correctness eradication' in 2005.

The history of the National party can be seen, for the most part, as a continuous rebalancing of the liberal and conservative tendencies, with an occasional excursion beyond those tendencies, followed by a return to them. The balance is influenced in part by the interests of groups that support the party. The period from 1936–51 might be seen as the anti-socialist mobilisation stage, culminating in assuming office in 1949 and the defeat in 1951 of waterside workers in a six-month-long battle with their employers, backed by the new National government. There followed what might be called the party's 'classical' liberal–conservative period through to 1974 when it relegated Labour to two short periods in government and when some thought National might be the 'natural party of government'. Towards the end of that period a growing restlessness among younger liberals in part contributed to John Marshall's replacing of Sir Keith Holyoake in 1972.

Then under Robert Muldoon, after 1974 the party veered into populism. Liberals took issue with Muldoon's resort to extensive and intrusive economic controls more usually associated with 'socialists', his conservative positions on social, moral, race and foreign policy matters and his strong-arm tactics against opponents. Conservatives also took issue with his recourse to economic controls, and they did not share his celebration of the 'ordinary bloke'. Because many of 'Rob's Mob' were new to the party, they were accused by some long-term National members of disturbing the party's social order.[11] Far from preserving the party's traditions, Muldoon proved iconoclastic. As a result, the party was depleted and disoriented, the more so because of the growing influence, particularly among those under the age of forty (including in Muldoon's own caucus ranks), of market-liberal ideas, which were put into practice by the Labour government after 1984. Many of National's supporters deserted it for Labour in the 1987 election, including in its safest seats (Remuera was thereby made marginal). Ruth Richardson's ascendancy in the early 1990s pleased market-liberals but disturbed conservatives and populists—and, in any case, the radicalism entailed in her policy approach is anathema to liberals and conservatives. During this period many of 'Rob's Mob', including some who had become MPs, left. Then when Richardson left many of the market-liberals also left.

Since then the National party's recent history may be seen as an attempt to strike again a durable liberal–conservative balance that also has broad appeal to voters. This had not been achieved by the time of the 2005 election.

THE FUNCTIONALIST PARTY

The National party may be viewed through another lens. While it does have a set of guiding principles and values, even a 'vision' (to be discussed), it has usually (the Richardson ascendancy excepted) been more concerned with power than programmes.

And, in exercising power it attends to its supporting interest groups. Thus, by contrast with the programme-oriented Labour party, National seeks power to govern and then governs to stay in power. In that sense it is functionalist, rather than ideological.

In this it reflects a practical bent among New Zealanders, going back to the nineteenth century. The French sociologist, André Siegfried, visiting in 1899, concluded that pragmatism was the ideology of New Zealanders at that time, the essence of its democracy.[12] That is still essentially true. And it is the antithesis of radical change. After supplanting a Labour government in 1949 whose 'socialism' the National party had been formed to combat, National nevertheless maintained much of the apparatus of economic regulation and control, maintained the welfare state and expanded education. This gave it the appearance of being 'social democratic'.

This is a misreading. National was in effect managing the status quo. And to the extent it did make some modest changes, as in its mild relaxation of economic controls, it generally did so in favour of its supporting interest groups. It did not significantly extend the welfare state, as the Labour party would have done—and in fact did between 1972–75.

RESTRUCTURING THE PARTY

In April 2003, under Bill English as leader and Judy Kirk as president, the party restructured its organisation at a special constitutional conference. The semi-autonomous divisions were stripped of their offices and administration was centralised in Wellington (though the divisions still hold conferences and select list candidates). Membership subscription and management were also centralised. The governing board was slimmed down to nine and, apart from its two MP appointees, was elected at large instead of consisting of the divisional chairs and specialist section heads; the president was elected by the board instead of the conference as a whole.[13] A general manager was appointed on a business model. He also became the campaign manager in the 2005 election. A candidates' college was set up to train potential and actual election candidates. A more systematic effort was made to shoulder-tap able candidates.

This was in part in reaction to the disastrous 2002 campaign in which many electorate candidates had emphasised the electorate vote instead of the party vote. The central campaign committee was ineffective and at times dysfunctional and electorates were left to go their own way. In 2005, as a consequence of the organisational changes, MPs were required to go on the list[14] and to emphasise the party vote. The margin between the electorate vote and the party vote was thereby reduced from 10 per cent in 2002 to 0.5 per cent in 2005.

Still, there remains a significant degree of devolution of administration to the electorates. They choose their candidates, either at a delegated meeting or by an electorate-wide membership plebiscite (unless their membership is deemed too low, in which case the head office may step in). Electorate chairs are pivotal figures in the organisation and meet once a year at national conference time in a sort of national council, though without executive power.

The party also adopted at its constitutional conference a revised 'vision' that 'seeks a safe, prosperous and successful New Zealand that creates opportunities for all New Zealanders to reach their personal goals and dreams'.[15] The vision stated that 'we believe this will be achieved by building a society based on the following values: loyalty to our country, its democratic principles and our Sovereign as Head of State; national and personal security; equal citizenship and equal opportunity; individual freedom and choice; personal responsibility; competitive enterprise and rewards for achievement; limited government; strong families and caring communities; sustainable development of our environment'.

THE FUTURE

National fought the 2005 election essentially on two planks: 'one law for all' and the replacement of 'race-based funding' with a policy based on a 'partnership' under the Treaty of Waitangi; and large personal tax cuts. While both planks were based on principle consistent with the party's 'values', in the campaign they were essentially presented in a populist manner to win voters across the divide from Labour.

However, in essence, the numbers attracted from Labour were relatively small. Don Brash, the austere former Reserve Bank governor with a stiff speaking manner, made an improbable populist. More important was his personal authority (from his Reserve Bank days) and his record as favouring light regulation, low taxes, and limited government—but these appealed to people who had in the past leaned towards National but drifted off to other parties during the 1990s and early 2000s. So ACT and New Zealand First dropped 5 per cent and United Future 4 per cent, accounting for nearly all National's 18 per cent rise in party vote share—and in the process National limited its own options for post-election coalition/support partners. This return of lost sheep encouraged some long-experienced party officials to compare the surge of voters towards National with the landslide win in 1990 and to believe before the election that the party could reach 45 per cent. But a deregulated economy was not a centrist position and so was unlikely to challenge Labour's hold there. Moreover, there is some evidence the populist pitch on race worked against National by driving people in lower socio-economic strata who had not voted in 2002 to vote for Labour in 2005—especially Māori and Pacific Islanders. Polls also suggested a big difference in Labour's favour among women.

The question this poses for National is how to broaden its message to appeal to Māori, Pacific Islanders, and women—that is, how to regain its 'national' representativeness. The near-absence of Māori[16] and Pacific Islanders at National conferences and its paucity of such candidates and MPs are strikingly at odds with Labour's more broadly representative makeup. History suggests that a modernised version of the liberal–conservative position that served National effectively in the 1950s and 1960s might be the appropriate positioning.

DISCUSSION QUESTIONS

1   How can National recover its status as the 'national' party of New Zealand?
2   Is the National party primarily a pragmatic party or one guided by the interests of its support groups or one driven by ideology?
3   Why has National failed to promote more Māori MPs?
4   How has National adapted to the MMP system of voting?
5   Given that a party will seldom, if ever, govern on its own under MMP, to which parties can National reach for support? [Refer to the post-election negotiations in September–October 2005.]

NOTES

1   Bassett, Michael R, 1982, *Three Party Politics in New Zealand 1911–1931*, Historical Publications, Auckland, provides a brief summary of the changing parties and politics of this period.

2   Gustafson, Barry, 1986, *The First 50 Years: A History of the New Zealand National Party*, Reed Methuen; Auckland, p. 241.

3   While membership figures are not divulged, unofficial sources told the author that total membership in 2001 was little more than 20,000.

4   Roger Scruton, a noted authority on conservatism, describes it thus in 1996 *A Dictionary of Political Thought*, 2nd edn, MacMillan, p. 100: 'The social and political outlook which springs from a desire to conserve existing things, held to be either good in themselves or better than the likely alternatives or at least safe, familiar and the objects of trust and affection'.

5   Interview with Bill English by the author, published in the *New Zealand Herald*, 16 June 1999; this quote cited from the author's webpage, www.synapsis.co.nz/herald/Herald_1999/Herald_englishextra_jun_99.htm

6   For a critique of liberalism, see Gray, John, 1995 *Liberalism*, 2nd edn, Open University Press.

7   Green's 'expanded liberalism' is summarised in Curtis, Michael, (ed.), 1981, *The Great Political Theories*, vol. 2, Avon Books, New York, as: 'The aim of a liberal society must be to create the conditions necessary for the high moral development of its citizens … The function of the state was to create opportunity and freedom for the individual … [and] … this involved government action in industrial affairs, housing, education, alcoholism and health.'

8   Mill, John Stuart, 1991, *On Liberty and Other Essays*, Oxford University Press, Oxford.

9 *New Zealand Herald*, 2 February 1972.
10 A 'classical liberal' group held a breakfast at the 2004 conference but had not managed to establish itself as a fixture by 2005.
11 Gustafson, op. cit., p. 125: 'One long-term woman activist remarked that before Muldoon became leader, "I could have gone into a room and known it was a National party gathering just by glancing around but [after] I'd go to the National party gatherings and think I was at the local football club … He brought a whole new group in."'
12 Hamer, David, 1982, introduction to reprint of André Siegfried, *Democracy in New Zealand*, Victoria University Press, Wellington, p. xxxv.
13 This was in part a recoil from the high-profile, public campaign by Michelle Boag to oust John Slater from the presidency in 2001. Boag resigned shortly after the disastrous 2002 campaign.
14 The only exceptions were leader Don Brash and Georgina te Heuheu, who would logically have stood in a Māori electorate.
15 www.national.org.nz/About/vision.aspx
16 The party stood no candidates in the seven Māori electorates in 2005.

FURTHER READING

Clark, M. (ed.) 2003, *Holyoake's Lieutenants*, Dunmore Press, Palmerston North.
Clark, M. (ed.) 2004, *Muldoon Revisited*, Dunmore Press, Palmerston North.
Gustafson, B. 1986, *The First 50 Years: A History of the New Zealand National Party*, Reed Methuen, Auckland.
Gustafson, B. 2000, *His Way: A Biography of Robert Muldoon*, Auckland University Press, Auckland.
Miller, R. 2005, *Party Politics in New Zealand*, Oxford University Press, Melbourne.
Wood, A. 2003, 'National', in R. Miller (ed), *New Zealand Government and Politics*, 3rd edn, Oxford University Press, Melbourne.

New Zealand First

Raymond Miller

As the third-ranked party in parliament, New Zealand First attracts almost as much attention for the unpredictability of its stance on being in government as for its mercurial leader and populist agenda. In 2005, in an incongruous turn of events, Winston Peters was appointed Minister of Foreign Affairs, although outside of cabinet, the latter move designed to quell criticism that he had broken a pre-election promise not to enter a coalition. His repeated assertion that New Zealand First was not part of the Labour-led coalition reinforced public suspicion that Peters wanted to enjoy the 'baubles of office' while remaining outside of government. For any whose memory spanned the first four MMP elections, it was an all-too-familiar sequence of events. Following the 1996 election, the first under the new electoral rules, New Zealand First had been strategically placed to exercise the balance of power. Despite giving a clear promise both before and during the campaign that its preference was to form a government with Labour, in the end it decided to go with National. Significantly, Peters had extracted a promise from Prime Minister Jim Bolger that he would receive the plum positions of deputy prime minister and Treasurer. Two years later the party was out of office and in disarray.

Quite apart from any possible electoral fallout from these most recent events, there is merit in the argument that simply being in government irrevocably compromises a populist party's principles and beliefs. New Zealand First's policy agenda and ability to survive the ebbs and exploit the flows of public discontent will provide the focus of this chapter. Although New Zealanders' flirtation with populist politics is hardly new, the New Zealand First manifestation of populism reflects public concern over a range of social issues, in particular immigration, the growing incidence of violent crime, and the state of race relations. In 2005, Peters tapped into this rich vein of anxiety, although with less electoral effect than in some previous elections (the party's share of the vote and seats was halved, and it lost the cornerstone seat of Tauranga for the first time). Does this mean that the public is beginning to tire of Peters and his party? This chapter will conclude by considering the future viability of New Zealand First as an electoral organisation.

ORIGINS AND DEVELOPMENT

New Zealand First is a product of two major trends of the early 1990s—economic recession, and the government's commitment to economic liberalisation. Building on Labour's reforms of the 1980s, the incoming National administration adopted a radical agenda that included a strong commitment to the privatisation of state-owned assets and a range of measures designed to reduce the scope and influence of the welfare state. The resulting cutback in public spending would impact upon everything from health care and education to pensions. For example, contrary to National's explicit promise to voters, the superannuation surtax was not only retained, but increased. The cabinet and government caucus became increasingly unpopular and divided, with a former prime minister, Sir Robert Muldoon, charging the government with dishonesty and contempt for New Zealand's egalitarian tradition and values. Two government backbench MPs resigned in protest to form the Liberal party, which later became part of the Alliance. They invited disaffected colleagues, including the National's Minister of Maori Affairs, Winston Peters, to do likewise.

Peters' public criticisms of government policy were at first tantalisingly opaque. When condemning the effects of economic and social policy reform, for example, he was more inclined to blame the previous Labour government than National. Slowly but surely, however, and notwithstanding his hallmark protestations and disclaimers, Peters lost the support and goodwill of most of his cabinet and caucus colleagues. It had become clear that neither an appeal to his party loyalty nor the convention of collective ministerial responsibility was sufficient to keep the maverick minister in check.

Despite mounting media speculation that he was about to launch a new political movement, Peters remained with National until 1993. To all intents and purposes, however, his dismissal from cabinet in October 1991 marked the end of his career with that party. Seemingly unperturbed by frequent threats of expulsion from the prime minister and senior party officials, he developed an independent economic strategy, which included increased borrowing, reduced taxation, and more moderate welfare policies. He also launched a series of attacks on leading members of the business community, some of whom were backers of the government, accusing them of everything from profiteering to financial mismanagement and corruption. His campaign struck a respondent chord with the elderly and those on low incomes, many of whom felt that the major burden of reform had been born by those least able to afford it.

Following months of contrived suspense, New Zealand First was finally launched in July 1993. At the 1993 election it received 8.4 per cent of the vote nationwide. More importantly, Tau Henare won the seat of Northern Maori, thereby doubling the party's parliamentary representation. Three years later the party attracted an even more impressive 13.4 per cent of the vote, entitling it to seventeen of the 120 seats in the first MMP parliament. It won all five Māori seats, as well as Peters' seat of Tauranga. The other eleven MPs were elected from the party list.[1] Even more importantly, the distribution of seats in the new parliament gave New Zealand First the opportunity to exercise the balance of power.

In December 1996, after two months of negotiations, Peters announced his decision to form a coalition with his erstwhile enemy, National. This cynical disregard for the promises made to voters stands in stark contrast to the party's vaunted pledge to make New Zealand politics more democratic and accountable. But Peters' decision also flew in the face of public opinion—survey research showed that a vast majority of the party's voters favoured a coalition with Labour, and few wanted one with National (Miller 1997a). Not surprisingly, following the 1996 election New Zealand First's popularity went into sharp decline. By mid 1997, only one year after achieving its best-ever opinion poll result of close to 30 per cent, the party's level of support was below 4 per cent (One Network News/Colmar Brunton, 15 July 1997).

This dramatic fall-off in support, together with the negative publicity being given to some of its MPs (notably Tukoroirangi Morgan, who was accused of extravagant over-spending in his previous job with publicly funded Māori television), had a corrosive effect on relations between New Zealand First and National and, as a result, on the performance of the new government. Within months the National caucus had replaced the prime minister, Bolger, with Jenny Shipley, a move intended to stiffen the party's resolve in dealing with its politically inexperienced and increasingly feisty partner. When, in August 1998, Peters walked from the cabinet room in protest at the government's decision to sell its shares in Wellington Airport, the prime minister promptly dismissed him from cabinet, thereby precipitating the coalition's collapse. In subsequent negotiations, eight MPs, including several ministers, broke ranks with the New Zealand First party and its leader. These defectors then propped up the minority National government until the time of the 1999 election.

Table 5.3.1: New Zealand First's election results, 1993–2005

Election	Party vote (%)	Electorate vote (%)	Electorate seats	List seats	Total seats
1993		8.4	2	–	2
1996	13.4	13.5	6	11	17
1999	4.3	4.2	1	4	5
2002	10.4	4.0	1	12	13
2005	5.7	3.5	0	7	7

ORGANISATION

Winston Peters is not alone among the leaders of small parties in being the personification of his movement. Critics and media commentators alike initially referred to it as the 'Peters' party, and its electoral fortunes have always been inextricably linked to the personal popularity of Peters, with any fluctuations in its credibility and popular support tending to reflect those of its leader. What Peters lacks in tact and guile is more than made up for in determination and courage. Although he conveys great personal warmth and charm, with his followers frequently referring to his sincerity, integrity, and accessibility, Peters appears to thrive on being viewed as a political outcast, a trait that helps to reinforce the image of New Zealand First as essentially a one-man band.

As with other small parties of the personality driven type, the organisational structure took some time to develop, with the day-to-day decisions initially being made by Peters in collaboration with a small network of supporters. For example, at its first election those who wanted to contest a parliamentary seat under the party label were advised to submit their curriculum vitae, together with the names of six referees, to the Peters-appointed management committee. Candidates also had to provide a list of names of people willing to work for them in their electorate. Despite the party's call for greater democracy and accountability in politics, candidate selections were made by Peters and the management committee alone and in secret. It was even decided that the names of the unsuccessful nominees would not be made public. Three years later this high level of centralised control was still in evidence, with Peters and a close political adviser allegedly ranking the entire candidate list (Laws 1998, p. 342). Their personal intervention produced some interesting outcomes, including the demotion of prominent candidates who had dared to disagree with Peters and the dramatic promotion of several relatively unknown candidates.

In time, the party developed a more effective organisation and introduced measures to make senior office-holders more responsive to the membership. The management of the party became the responsibility of a Board, consisting of the leader, deputy-leader, director-general, national office-holders, seven elected directors, and two representatives chosen by the Māori electorates (New Zealand First Constitution, December 2001). The electorates are serviced by a committee and, in some cases, a network of local branches. The most active of these electorate committees help carry out the tasks of recruiting members, fund-raising, and assisting the candidate during election campaigns. In many of the weaker electorates, however, these functions are largely carried out by head office. Indeed, while the new structure gives the appearance of encouraging grass-roots participation, some party officials readily admit that many of the major decisions have been made in the parliamentary offices of Peters and, until his resignation in 2005, the party president (who is also an MP). This is not an uncommon practice among small parties. Along with the other parliamentary parties, New Zealand First receives taxpayer funds to cover the cost of administration, research, and other parliamentary expenses.

POPULISM

Given their appeal to popular discontent, it is hardly surprising that Peters and New Zealand First are often viewed as contemporary manifestations of populism. One of the central propositions of populism is that the power of 'the people' has been usurped by political, bureaucratic, and financial elites (Craig 1993). North American populism grew out of resentment over profiteering by large banks and business cartels, at the expense of independent farmers and traders; hence its association with anti-capitalism, conspiracy theories, and tirades against corruption (Rozenstone et al. 1984, pp. 67–75). As one commentator has pointed out, more recent expressions of populism embrace a wide variety of negative sentiments, or 'anti-attitudes', including 'anti-political-establishment', 'anti-modern', 'anti-foreign', 'anti-minority', 'anti-intellectual', and even 'anti-politics' (Schedler 1996, pp. 292–3).

Populism appeals to those who harbour feelings of powerlessness, perhaps even victimisation, and who cling nostalgically to what they perceive to be a simpler, more intimate, and caring past. Such people have a fear of outsiders, most commonly refugees, immigrants, and foreign investors, and are often associated with support for racial assimilation and strident nationalism. Since they trust neither the established political institutions nor elected officials to uphold democratic principles, it is hardly surprising that populist parties tend to support the instruments of direct democracy, such as referendums, citizens' initiatives, and the recall of members. While rejecting the motives and actions of political elites, populists express an abiding faith in the 'common sense of the common people' (Gibbins & Stewart 2002, p. 87).

Most prominent among contemporary populist parties are Jean-Marie Le Pen's National Front in France, Haider's Austrian Freedom party, the Norwegian Progress party, and, most notably of late, Holland's List Fortuyn. The latter party attracted international attention as a result of the extreme anti-immigration and anti-Muslim views of its founding leader, Pim Fortuyn. Best known among contemporary North American populist parties is the Canadian Alliance party, which, having merged with the Conservatives, is currently that country's governing party. As well as expressing a deep sense of 'western alienation' and adopting forthright positions on immigration, multiculturalism, and the perceived decline of Christian moral values (Laycock 2002), supporters of the Reform party, as the former Alliance was once named, are said to be resentful of 'welfare cheaters, uppity social activists, feminist rhetoricians and other minoritarian pleaders …' (quoted in Gibbins & Arrison 1995, p. 67).

But the roots of populism also run deep in the political culture of New Zealand. Several past prime ministers, including Richard John Seddon (1893–1906) and Sidney Holland (1949–57), were strident populists, and Robert Muldoon (1975–84) adopted the 'them versus us' language of populism in his appeal for the support of the 'ordinary bloke'. Assuming the role of political outsider, he frequently condemned 'establishment' figures, such as academics, journalists, and elements of the bureaucracy. At the 1975 election, he promised voters 'New Zealand the way you want it', and used overtly racist visual images in the National party's law and order advertising campaign. In later years, the Muldoon government employed 'dawn raids' to track down over-stayers within the Pacific Islands community. Better known still for its commitment to the principles of populism was the New Zealand Social Credit Political League (now Democrat party), which was founded in 1953. At the core of Social Credit's support was a small entrepreneurial class struggling for material independence and prosperity against the forces of big business, big foreign investors, big unions, and a big bureaucracy. The party claimed to stand for self-reliance, small enterprise, and the public observance of 'Christian' standards of morality. It argued that the nation's economic woes would be solved through an increase in the money supply, a view shared with some populist movements elsewhere, including the American People's party.

New Zealand First's early reputation was built on three of the most enduring pillars of populism, namely: economic nationalism, anti-corruption, and anti-immigration.

1. Economic nationalism

Peters established a clear link between the privatisation of state-owned assets and the wider issues of foreign ownership and national sovereignty. He warned that New Zealanders were in 'grave danger of losing economic control of their own country'.[2] Drawing on strongly patriotic sentiments, he opined that generations of soldiers who died on the battlefield could not have intended that New Zealanders become 'strangers in our own backyard; serfs in our own country' (*Dominion*, 22 July 1993). New Zealand First opposed all foreign ownership of land and promised to reduce overseas investment to less than a quarter of any New Zealand company. Even more controversially, Peters promised that a number of privatised state assets would be compulsorily repossessed from their foreign owners at the purchase price. He repeatedly threatened to use parliamentary privilege to expose details of any sale to foreign interests. 'Whose country is it? A country fit for the families of ordinary New Zealanders whose votes have placed the politicians in power, or a paradise for foreign take-over merchants looking for cheap gains at our expense?' (*New Zealand Herald*, 2 February 1996).

2. Anti-corruption

Peters made his early reputation as a maverick politician by attacking the integrity of some leading companies and their directors, most prominently the merchant banker Michael Fay and Selwyn Cushing of Brierley Investments. His allegation that Cushing had attempted to bribe him (Peters) into supporting policies that were advantageous to big business resulted in substantial damages being awarded to

Cushing in a defamation case against Peters in the District Court. Among the New Zealand First leader's prime targets was a group of companies that allegedly used the Cook Islands as a tax haven to 'swindle' New Zealand taxpayers of millions of dollars. The 'Winebox Inquiry', as the commission investigating these allegations came to be called, spent almost three years hearing evidence from leading business, legal, and financial institutions, as well as the Serious Fraud Office and the Inland Revenue Department. As John Roughan has aptly stated, 'Nothing stirs [Peters] like a whiff of corporate crime' (*New Zealand Herald*, 22 October 2005).

A second focus of Peters' attention was corruption in the bureaucracy and government. The 'relegated, denigrated and forgotten'[3] were encouraged to hold their politicians to account. Proposed changes included the creation of an anti-corruption commission, more direct democracy through the use of referenda, and a reduction in the numbers of bureaucrats and government consultants. To combat waste, he proposed salary reductions for politicians and a smaller parliament and cabinet. Peters has also accused successive governments of 'cronyism' in their statutory appointments.

3. Anti-immigration

Peters tapped into populist sentiment still further by launching an attack in 1996 on a range of immigrant groups, particularly business-investment migrants and refugees from Asia. For much of the postwar period, annual net immigration averaged approximately 10,000. During the previous five years, however, more than 200,000 immigration permits had been issued. In 1995 alone there were 55,000 new immigrants, most of whom were from Asia, particularly China, Taiwan, Hong Kong, and South Korea.[4] In a speech delivered to a mainly elderly audience in the Elim Christian Centre, in the heart of Auckland's Asian community, Peters described some Vietnamese refugees as people of 'unsound character' and condemned a policy 'which sees rows of ostentatious homes in this very suburb, occupied in some cases by children whose parents have no ties to this country other than the price they paid for the house, and who prefer to remain outside its shores' (*New Zealand Herald*, 14 February 1996). The classrooms, he said, were full of children who could not speak any English. A New Zealand First government would cut immigration to 'the bare bones',[5] and put immigrants on probation for the first four years. During this period, their visas would be reviewed annually to determine whether or not their commitment to New Zealand was genuine and satisfactory. Unless they became citizens, they would not be allowed to buy land other than that which lay under their house or business. His Māori ethnicity made Peters a difficult target for attack on this issue, with many liberal politicians and commentators preferring to cast blame in the direction of the Immigration Minister and his government.

With the election of the centre-left Clark government in 1999 much of the heat went out of the debate over the perceived link between privatisation, foreign ownership, and nationalism. Similarly, between 1999 and 2002, Peters's anti-corruption campaign was overtaken by a series of anti-corruption allegations from the ACT party, most of which were orchestrated by its perk-busting Auckland MP, Rodney Hide. Aware that the one remaining issue that gave New Zealand First its distinctiveness and had genuine electoral potency was immigration, Peters built his 2002 campaign around three straightforward and potentially related propositions: a drastic reduction in the number of immigrants; harsher sentences for violent crime; and a 'one-nation' solution to the problem of race relations. To the 'Bob the Builder' rhetorical question 'Can we fix it?' Peters's repeated assurance to voters was 'Yes we can!'

Peters's 2002 campaign strategies and rhetoric were virtually indistinguishable from those of six years earlier. The increase in immigrant numbers to an annual total of around 53,000, together with the government's controversial decision to accept approximately 140 refugees from the vessel *Tampa*, provided the New Zealand First leader with an opportunity to conflate the issues of nationalism, ethnicity, terrorism, and economic prosperity within the same argument. Immigrants were accused of being 'gate-crashers' from 'alien cultures and rigid religious practices' (*New Zealand Herald*, 1 July 2002). Why, he asked, was the government 'handing out citizenship like bus tickets'? In response to suggestions of racism and xenophobia, Peters accused the 'big city media' of stifling healthy debate and treating his followers as 'lepers' (*New Zealand Herald*, 26 June 2002).

The litany of offences allegedly committed by recent immigrants included: thwarting Māori economic development and reducing the availability of jobs; causing traffic jams on the nation's roads; spreading AIDS and other infectious diseases; putting house prices out of the reach of ordinary New Zealanders; and creating inflationary pressures that were likely to lead to an economic downturn. As this list of complaints suggests, there was little attempt to discriminate between the perceived dangers posed by wealthy Chinese immigrants, on the one hand, and impoverished Afghani and Somali refugees, on the other. Peters accused the *Tampa* asylum-seekers of not being genuine refugees, but rather political activists, and perhaps even potential terrorists. Along with the 20,000 over-stayers, they should be sent home. He later claimed that: 'We have an obligation to our own people, our own emerging culture and our own creeds … before that of any Tom, Dick, Harry, Mustaq, or bin Laden who wants to come here' (*New Zealand Listener*, 20–27 September 2002, p. 21).

While attracting less public attention than the issue of immigration, law and order gave New Zealand First its second major theme of the 2002 campaign. Buoyed by the overwhelming public support for tougher sentences for violent criminals, as evidenced by its 91.8 per cent endorsement in the Norm Withers' referendum of 1999, the party's law and order platform called for greater use of mandatory minimum sentences for violent crime, a 'three strikes and you're out' policy for repeat offenders, with a minimum sentence of ten years 'irrespective of the nature of their crime', and tightening of the laws on parole. Believing that society had degenerated into a state of 'rampant lawlessness' (*New Zealand Herald*, 27 June 2002), the party proposed that the drinking age be raised from eighteen to twenty years, there be an automatic prison term of six months for drink drivers convicted more than once, and that the unemployed young be required to undertake national military training or community service in order to 'foster discipline and self esteem and bring order into their lives' (New Zealand First 'Law and Order Policy' 2002). Although official party policy avoided any explicit reference to a causal link between more immigrants and rising crime, the same could not be said for the views of some of New Zealand First's supporters.

Completing the 'Can we do it?' trilogy were a clutch of policies designed to make Māori more self-reliant, address the 'grievance industry' with respect to the Waitangi Tribunal's settlements process, and stop efforts to allow Treaty principles to infiltrate the law and constitutional system of New Zealand (*New Zealand Herald*, 2 July 2002). As well as creating a financial elite of advisers and consultants, the Tribunal's work allegedly resulted in a waste of resources and a breakdown in social cohesion, with Māori being pitched against Māori, and Māori against European. Consistent with the party's belief in only one class of citizen, in 2002 it called for the abolition of separate Māori parliamentary seats and an end to the practice of treating Māori as if they continued to be victims of colonial occupation.[6]

Of course, being able to deliver on these three messages in the near future required that New Zealand First become a partner of Labour either inside or outside of government. Despite Peters's confident 'Yes we can!' promise to voters and the party's sharp rise in support during the course of the campaign, a trend that had much to do with some savvy electioneering by the New Zealand First leader, even before polling day Clark judged his views to be so 'deeply offensive' as to render him ineligible for any post-election pact with her government (*New Zealand Herald*, 24 July 2002).

'A MAN FOR A CHANGE': 2005 ELECTION

In receiving 5.7 per cent of the party vote in 2005, New Zealand First managed to remain in front of its traditional rivals for the third party vote, specifically the Greens (5.3 per cent), United Future (2.7 per cent) and ACT (1.5 per cent). More disappointing than the overall decline in its share of the vote (down from 10.4 per cent in 2002) and seats (from thirteen to seven), was its loss in Tauranga, an electorate that had served as an invaluable buffer in the event that the party dropped below the 5 per cent threshold that guarantees a party its proportional share of all the parliamentary seats (as happened in 1999, when the New Zealand First vote dropped to 4.3 per cent). In a personally bitter campaign against the National party candidate,

Bob Clarkson, a prominent local businessman, Peters' share of the vote dropped from 52.7 per cent in 2002 to 39.3 per cent (Clarkson 41.4 per cent). Peters subsequently took legal action against Clarkson for over-spending, a charge that was rejected by the Court.

What had gone wrong with New Zealand First's 2005 campaign? The populist themes that had worked so well for Peters in previous elections proved much less effective, as illustrated by his attempt to exploit fears about the threat of terrorism. Several months before the campaign began, he launched an attack on the country's Muslim community, accusing them of harbouring potential terrorists. Although the party subsequently enjoyed a lift in the polls, creating speculation that Peters was likely to hold the balance of power after the election, the bizarre nature of the claim, together with a spirited response from aggrieved members of the Muslim community, ensured that any impact was short-lived. Ironically, the subsequent decline in support may well have been a direct consequence of the rise, in media speculation about Peters's King (Queen)-making role in the event of a hung parliament. If anything was likely to hurt Peters's cause, then surely it was to remind the public of his unpredictable and self-serving performance in the coalition negotiations of 1996.

New Zealand First's election result must also be viewed in the context of the performance of the minor parties generally. Even before the campaign began, influential media commentators and journalists were predicting that the 2005 election would boil down to a two-way contest between Labour and National. Although such an assessment was hardly new, the 2002 pre-campaign polls having provided similar evidence of a two-horse race, what proved different in 2005 was the lacklustre performance of the minor parties in polls conducted during the course of the campaign—in 2002, combined support for the minor parties rose from approximately 18 per cent at the commencement of the campaign to 39 per cent on polling day. Frustrated by a lack of media attention, in 2005 the minor parties became excessively dependent on the televised leaders' debates and other staged events, with the result that they were barely noticed until late in the campaign, when attention understandably focused on the likely shape of the next government.

Having been challenged to divulge his preferred coalition partner during the early part of the campaign, approximately two weeks before polling day Peters declared: 'I am announcing today that New Zealand First will not be going into a formal coalition with either Labour or National … We are not the desperate lonely hearts of New Zealand politics, looking hopefully and forlornly for a suitor' (quoted in *Sunday Star Times*, 23 October 2005, C1). Given the potential loss of support encountered by a populist party when, having campaigned as an outsider it enters the inner sanctums of government, this announcement appeared to be an astute move. It might even reverse the party's slide in the polls. Lest there be any remaining doubt in the minds of potential voters, Peters reiterated his promise: 'Now, just to be sure there is no misunderstanding of what I am saying let me be clear—no coalition means just that, it is not a play on words'. (Ibid) Despite failing to restore the party's former support, the reassurance may have prevented a further slide to below the critical 5 per cent.

Peters's subsequent decision to enter a formal coalition with Labour led to the party president's resignation, and may well have been largely responsible for some unfamiliar criticism of Peters's campaign performance from leading party members and officials. For example, the party's policy and strategy director stated publicly that the party's campaign was tactically inept and lacked coherence (Post-election Conference, Wellington, 3 December 2005). He referred to the leader's personal attack on Clarkson in the final week of the Tauranga campaign as a mistake and criticised the party's billboards, which featured a formally suited Peters incongruously perched at the water's edge of an unnamed beach (could it be the Tauranga electorate's Mt Maunganui?). A feature of the billboards was the ambiguous caption 'A Man for a Change'. The party's deputy leader reportedly described the campaign as a 'stuff-up' and added, 'I don't think you'll ever see New Zealand First run a campaign like that again, I sincerely hope not' (*New Zealand Herald*, 4 December 2005).

SOURCES OF ELECTORAL SUPPORT

Polling results at successive elections confirm the popular stereotype of New Zealand First as a party predominantly of the middle-aged and elderly. Peters' early opposition to the superannuation surtax won the approval of those in retirement, a number of whom helped organise his public meetings and became founding members of New Zealand First. The elderly were also adversely affected by moves to cut back the welfare state, including the double decision of a previous National government to both freeze pensions and increase the age of entitlement from 60 to 65 years. As well as impacting upon elderly voters' sense of security and personal incomes, these reforms challenged traditional notions of fairness and equality. Having won over the support of an understandably nostalgic generation of New Zealanders, Peters built their loyalty on his populist agenda. Although this chapter was written before survey data on voting behaviour from the 2005 election became available, we know that, at the 2002 election, 52 per cent of all New Zealand First voters were over the age of fifty, and 34 per cent were over the age of sixty (New Zealand Election Study 2002). The proportions of middle-aged and older voters were higher than in any other party (for example, comparable figures for National were 37 per cent and 23 per cent respectively).

But New Zealand First also appeals disproportionately to those on low and low-middle incomes. Many of the latter are self-employed small business operators and manual workers, groups that were badly hit by the free-market reforms of successive governments. Areas of electoral strength include the northern half of the North Island,

Māori electorates, and the provincial towns and countryside. Less attracted to New Zealand First are the young, South Islanders, city-dwellers (with the exception of parts of Auckland), and high-income earners. There is a slight gender imbalance, with more men (53 per cent) than women favouring New Zealand First with their vote. The appeal to elderly and low-income voters caused a former Labour prime minister, Mike Moore, to characterise New Zealand First as a party of 'blue rinses' and 'blue jeans' (*New Zealand Herald*, 26 November 1996). However, the moderately well-off elderly, and unemployed or low-income Māori proved to be an irreconcilable mix, with most of the latter having gone back to supporting Labour in 1999 and 2002 (see chapter 4.1).

The social conservatism of New Zealand First's support base can be measured in several different ways. Three-quarters of all New Zealand First voters believe that the number of immigrants should be reduced, and almost 50 per cent are of the view that the reductions should be substantial (New Zealand Election Study 2002). Some 37 per cent of New Zealand First voters would like to place a total ban on immigration from Muslim countries, and one in five support a ban on all immigration from Asia. Not surprisingly, these anti-immigration sentiments are much more forcefully held within New Zealand First than the other parliamentary parties. In response to the question 'Should Māori be compensated for land confiscated in the past?' one in two New Zealand First voters say no, and three out of every four believe that all references to the Treaty of Waitangi should be removed from the law (again, the highest proportion of any party). Finally, although it is not New Zealand First policy, three-quarters of all New Zealand First voters want the re-introduction of the death penalty for some murders (New Zealand Election Study 2002). Their response on this issue, together with those on immigration and Māori and the Treaty, provide emphatic proof of Peters's astuteness in placing them at the centre of his recent campaigns.

CONCLUSION

The future of New Zealand First is likely to depend on how the party deals with two key issues:

1 As an anti-establishment movement, even an anti-political one, how can the party retain its electoral support while playing a constructive role in government?
2 Given that Winston Peters remains the personification of the party, can New Zealand First survive without him?

As we know from the party's experience between 1996 and 1998, there is some merit in the argument that simply being in government irrevocably compromised New Zealand First's populist principles and beliefs. The preference for National over Labour as coalition partner obviously had a significant bearing on the party's subsequent decline in the polls. However, it is pertinent to raise the speculative question as to whether a decision to coalesce with Labour would have spared Peters the accusation of betrayal and the subsequent unravelling of his party and its electoral support. While every attempt was made to extract a raft of policy concessions from National, in the end the conventions of cabinet government severely blunted Peters's ability to create space between his party's policies and those of the senior coalition partner. Rather than being a launching pad for a renewed appeal to the powerless and forgotten, the trappings of high office simply reinforced the impression that the former outcast had been transformed into a political insider. Given Peters's personality and New Zealand First's radical agenda, it remains to be seen if the party, having returned to government, will be able to retain and build on its 2005 level of electoral support.

A second issue concerns the ability of New Zealand First as a personality-based party to survive the inevitable departure of Peters from political life. Although New Zealand First has been in existence for over thirteen years, Peters remains its only publicly recognised figure (he first entered parliament in 1979). Several MPs can claim political experience (Brian Donnelly, Peter Brown, Ron Mark, and Doug Woolerton all entered parliament in 1996), but none shows any particular inclination or aptitude for leadership, with the result that they are largely anonymous figures to all but the party's rank-and-file. A common characteristic among dominant leaders is a failure to acknowledge or groom successors, as the increasingly difficult relationship between Peters and his former deputy leader, Tau Henare, in 1998 serves to illustrate. Despite his tendency to polarise opinion, Peters remains one of only two or three genuinely charismatic politicians to have graced the New Zealand parliament in the past two decades.

Yet there are signs that the New Zealand First leader is now in the sunset of his political career. While losing the seat of Tauranga was a bitter blow for Peters personally, breaching the 5 per cent threshold is likely to pose an even greater problem for the party at the next election. Still, in accepting the plum position of Foreign Minister, Peters might have been indicating that he does not anticipate having to defend the charge of broken promises at the 2008 election. Finally, there is the question of age (although there is no mandatory retirement age in politics, at the time of the next scheduled election Peters will be 63). Given the extent to which he single-handedly created the party's raison d'etre, shaped its policy agenda, and maintained its visibility from one election to the next, it is hard to see New Zealand First surviving long without him.

DISCUSSION QUESTIONS

1   To what extent can the 1998 split within New Zealand First be attributed to the costs of being in coalition?

2   In what conditions do minor parties flourish? Assess the chances of long-term survival for New Zealand First.

3 Assess the risks, benefits, and costs for New Zealand First of Winston Peters's decision to accept the position of Minister of Foreign Affairs in the 2005–08 Labour-led government.

4 Can New Zealand First survive without Peters at the helm?

NOTES

1   Currently, sixty-nine seats are electorate seats, and proportionality is achieved through having fifty-one list seats.

2   New Zealand First, 'Foreign Investment Policy', Wellington, 7 August 1996.

3   W. Peters, 'New Zealand First—A New Beginning', speech notes, Alexandra Park, Auckland, 18 July 1993.

4   Migration Section, Department of Statistics, Wellington, 1997.

5   In the 1995–96 financial year, 50,874 immigrants were admitted to New Zealand. In 1996–97 this was cut by the National government to 35,000. Peters advocated a target of no more than 10,000, *New Zealand Herald*, 28 June 1996.

6   W. Peters, 'Political Correctness and Treaty Grievances', public address, 7 March 2003.

REFERENCES

Betz, H. 1994, *Radical Right-Wing Populism in Western Europe*, St Martins Press, New York.

Boston, J. 1992, 'Redesigning New Zealand's Welfare State', in J. Boston & P. Dalziel, *The Decent Society: Essays in Response to National's Economic and Social Policies*, Oxford University Press, Auckland, pp. 1–18.

Craig, S.C. 1993, *The Malevolent Leaders: Popular Discontent in America*, Westview Press, Boulder, CO.

Gibbins, R. & S. Arrison 1995, *Western Visions: Perspectives on the West in Canada*, Broadview Press, Peterborough, Ontario.

Gibbins, R. & J. Stewart 2002, 'Wither or Whither the Populist Impulse in Western Canada?' in W. Cross (ed.), *Political Parties, Representation and Electoral Democracy in Canada*, Oxford University Press, Don Mills, Ontario, pp. 87–95.

Laws, M. 1998, *The Demon Profession*, Harper Collins, Auckland.

Laycock, D. 2002, *The New Right and Democracy in Canada: Understanding Reform and the Canadian Alliance*, Oxford University Press, Don Mills, Ontario.

Miller, R. 1997, 'Preparing for MMP: 1993–1996', in R. Miller (ed.), *New Zealand Politics in Transition*, Oxford University Press, Auckland, pp. 37–48.

Miller, R. 1997a, 'Coalition Government: The People's Choice?' in J. Vowles & P. Aimer (eds), *Voters' Victory: The 1996 Election in New Zealand*, Auckland University Press, Auckland, pp. 120–34.

Miller, R. 1989, 'The Democratic Party', in H. Gold (ed.), *New Zealand Politics in Perspective*, Longman Paul, Auckland, pp. 244–59.

Mulgan, R. 1997, *Politics in New Zealand*, Auckland University Press, Auckland.

Rozenstone, S., R. Behr & E. Lazarus 1984, *Third Parties in America: Citizen Response to Major Party Failure*, Princeton University Press, Princeton, NJ.

Schedler, A. 1996, 'Anti-Political-Establishment Parties', in *Party Politics*, 2/3, pp. 292–3.

Vowles, J., P. Aimer, H. Catt, J. Lamare & R. Miller 1996, *Towards Consensus: The 1993 Election in New Zealand and the Transition to Proportional Representation*, Auckland University Press, Auckland.

FURTHER READING

Boston, J., S. Levine, E., McLeay & N.S. Roberts (eds) 1997, *From Campaign to Coalition: The 1996 MMP Election*, Dunmore Press, Palmerston North (especially chapters 4, 18 & 19).

Boston, J., S. Levine, E., McLeay & N.S. Roberts (eds) 2000, *Left Turn: The New Zealand General Election of 1999*, Victoria University Press, Wellington (especially chapters 8, 18 & 22).

Miller, R. 2005, *Party Politics in New Zealand*, Oxford University Press, Melbourne.

Vowles, J., P. Aimer, S. Banducci & J. Karp (eds) 1998, *Voters' Victory: New Zealand's First Election Under Proportional Representation*, Auckland University Press, Auckland.

Vowles, J., P. Aimer, S. Banducci, J. Karp & R. Miller (eds) 2004, *Voters' Veto: The 2002 Election in New Zealand and the Consolidation of Minority Government*, Auckland University Press, Auckland.

The Greens

Tim Bale & John Wilson

The Green party of Aotearoa emerged relatively unscathed from the 2005 election. It lost three (or a third) of its MPs in a contest that saw other minor parties lose between half and three-quarters of the seats they won in 2002. Of course, the loss entailed a substantial reduction in the Green party's parliamentary funding—a reduction which may affect its ability to improve its electoral support, seemingly stuck in single figures. But this blow was in any case overshadowed by the loss of party co-leader Rod Donald, who died before parliament resumed in early November. Donald personified the Greens' determination to 'do politics differently', but at the same time was one of their most pragmatic and strategic thinkers. The Green party is certainly bigger than one person, but, as with many minor parties, in New Zealand, one person can sometimes make all the difference.

ORIGINS AND DEVELOPMENT

The immediate origins of the Green party date back to May 1990 when it was formed from the merger of a number of groups contesting local body elections under a green banner. Just six months later it put up seventy-one candidates to contest the ninety-seven seats in the 1990 general election and won 6.8 per cent of the vote. But the historical origins of the party can be traced further back to May 1972, when the New Zealand Values party was formed at Victoria University of Wellington. Indeed, those sharing the leadership of the Greens in the past, Jeanette Fitzsimons and Rod Donald, were Values party members in the mid to late 1970s. Values became the first green party in the world to contest a national election in 1972, winning 2 per cent of the vote.[1] Considering that it had formed just six months previously, this was a creditable result.

Table 5.4.1: New Zealand Green party's election results 1972–2005

Year	Electoral System*	Party	Party Vote (%)	Electoral Seats	List Seats	Total Seats
1972	FPP	Values	2.0	0	0	0
1975	FPP	Values	5.2	0	0	0
1978	FPP	Values	2.4	0	0	0
1981	FPP	Values	0.2	0	0	0
1984	FPP	Values	0.2	0	0	0
1987	FPP	Values	0.1	0	0	0
1990	FPP	Green	6.8	0	0	0
1993**	FPP	Alliance	(18.2)	(0)	(0)	(0)
1996**	MMP	Alliance	(10.1)	(0)	(3)	(3)
1999	MMP	Green	5.2	1	6	7
2002	MMP	Green	7.0	0	9	9
2005	MMP	Green	5.3	0	6	6

*   FPP: 'First-Past-the-Post' (single-member plurality system).

MMP: Mixed-Member-Proportional (proportional representation system).

** The Green Party contested these elections as part of a multi-party alliance winning 0 out of 2 Alliance seats in 1993, and 3 out of 13 Alliance seats in 1996.

The Values party raised issues that had been completely ignored by the traditional parties—those of ecology, resource and population limits, quality of life, the ethical rights of non-human species, and more democracy in decision-making practices. The Values party, for example, had the first female deputy leader of a New Zealand political party (1974), the first female leader (1979), and the first 'out' gay candidate (1978). But despite improving its performance to win 5.2 per cent in 1975, and 6.8 per cent as the renamed Green party in 1990, New Zealand's then electoral system did not allow such results to translate into seats in parliament (see table 5.4.1).

Realising that gaining parliamentary representation would require electoral reform and minor party cooperation, the Greens entered into a five-party alliance in 1991. As part of the Alliance, the Greens contested the 1993 general election and successfully campaigned to introduce MMP in time for the 1996 general election. MMP immediately produced results for the Greens—three Green MPs (Jeanette Fitzsimons, Rod Donald and Phillida Bunkle) were elected to parliament under the Alliance banner.

With MMP in place, the Greens contested the 1999 general election in their own right, capturing 5.2 per cent of the vote—an echo of their 1975 performance, but this time netting them seven seats. At 7 per cent of the vote, the Green party's 2002 performance was even better, giving it nine members of parliament. Its list of policy achievements since 1999 includes some notable—if indirect, inexpensive, and often incomplete—successes. Most obvious, perhaps, were: getting a much sought-after

Royal Commission of Enquiry into genetic modification; helping to ensure an end to the unsustainable logging of native forests on the west coast of the South Island; helping to pass the Māori Television Service Act and the Clean Slate Act; getting $3.2 million of the 2002–03 Budget allocated towards cleaning up and recording highly contaminated sites; and establishing a number of energy initiatives. The Greens also put resource limits back on the political agenda when they posed parliamentary questions on the issue of 'peak oil' (the suggestion that the world's oil reserves are now on a downward slope) and proposed steps to cope with coming oil shortages, higher prices, and increased geo-political tension. By mid-2005, the Greens and the Māori party were the only two national political parties worldwide that were openly concerned about peak oil (Bresee & Room 2005).

These achievements and arguably prescient warnings, however, appeared to do little to help increase support for the Green party in the 2005 general election—where it gained just 5.3 per cent of the vote and six seats. In part, this decline in support was due to a number of green voters who may have wanted to vote Green but, given the neck-and-neck polling by the Labour and National parties, felt they had to vote Labour to ensure Labour had the best opportunity to form a government. The Green party's fortunes were also not helped by extraordinary antagonism from the business press and from other political parties. United Future, for example described the Greens as 'dangerous', and as 'luddites' (*New Zealand Herald*, 19 September 2005). The Green party also came under attack from the Exclusive Brethren, a religious sect whose members are barred from voting but who nevertheless funded a $500,000 anti-Greens pamphlet that appeared to breach the Electoral Act. By the time the matter was referred to the police by the Chief Electoral Officer, the election campaign was over and the damage already done (*Dominion-Post*, 26 October, 2005).

Nevertheless, the Green party can count itself as one of the survivors of New Zealand's move to MMP. In four general elections, support for the Greens has always been above the critical 5 per cent threshold necessary to secure seats in parliament. And if MMP seems here to stay, then so, too, do the Greens. There was some hope that, following the counting of over 200,000 special votes (votes cast by those out of their electorate on polling day), the Greens would gain a seventh MP. Alas, this was not to be. Although their final share of the vote improved from the 5.07 per cent they held on election night, the party was about 1,200 votes short to return their seventh-ranked (famously Rastafarian) candidate, Nandor Tanczos, to parliament.

SUPPORT

Table 5.4.2 suggests that the Māori electorates were a significant source of the decline in the Green party's share of the vote at the 2005 election. While the party vote among general electorates declined on average by 1.4 per cent between 2002 and

Table 5.4.2: Green party vote share—top five electorates, 2005

Electorate	Party Vote Share 2002 (%)	Party Vote Share 2005 (%)	Change (%)	Enrolled Youth 2005 (%)*	Total enrolled 2005 (%)
Wellington Central	16.3	15.8	−0.5	75.5	89.1
Auckland Central	15.8	13.0	−2.8	51.6	69.9
Rongotai	13.0	12.6	−0.4	89.9	97.1
Dunedin North	12.4	10.8	−1.6	68.3	85.1
Banks Peninsula	10.2	10.4	0.2	87.3	98.9
General Electorates	6.8	5.4	−1.4	85.8	94.9
Māori Electorates**	10.7	3.3	−7.4	54.6	55.9
NZ Total	7.0	5.3	−1.7	87.3	95.2

*   Enrolled youth = Eighteen to twenty-nine-year-olds enrolled as a share of total eighteen to twenty-nine voting age population.

** Some electors of Māori descent enrol on General roll.

2005, the vote for the Greens among the Māori electorates declined 7.4 per cent. In total, just 21,729 fewer people voted for the Greens in 2005 than in 2002—yet, one third of these votes came from the seven Māori electorates. If the Māori electorates were a source of strength for the Greens in 2002 (polling 10.7 per cent), they were a source of weakness in 2005 (polling 3.3 per cent). With the Māori party (New Zealand's newest political party) now on the scene, attracting back previous support from Māori may prove challenging in coming elections.

As in past elections (and probably to their cost), the Greens did not stand candidates in all electorates. In 2005, seventeen electorates were not contested—eleven of which saw their share of the party vote decrease by more than the average 1.7 per cent decline for the party as a whole from 2002. More significantly, six of the electorates not contested were Māori electorates—precisely where a significant reduction in the Green vote has already been noted. This suggests that, as far as the Green party is concerned, standing an electorate candidate can have a beneficial impact on its overall party vote. While it clearly helps to have a high profile personality or an incumbent MP as the electorate candidate, this is not always essential. The 2005 election saw thirteen electorates record a higher candidate vote than the party vote compared with the four that did so in 2002.

Among the electorates it did contest in 2005, the Green party once again performed particularly well in the main urban areas. Wellington Central, Auckland Central, and Rongotai (in Wellington) were the three highest-polling electorates for the Green Party in both 2002 and 2005. These support figures resemble the vote profile of their sister parties in Europe, where Green voters on average tend to be younger, better educated, and living in larger urban areas rather than in small towns or rural areas. Indeed, according to the 2001 census, Wellington Central was the best educated electorate in the country, with 36 per cent of the population aged fifteen and over having either a bachelor degree or higher—three times the national average (10.1 per cent). On this same measure, Auckland Central and Rongotai ranked third-highest and fifth-highest respectively. Among general electorates in 2001, Wellington Central also had the highest proportion of twenty to twenty-nine-year-olds in New Zealand at 26.7 per cent (Parliamentary Library 2005).

Yet relying on young well-educated voters in urban electorates poses problems for the Greens. As table 5.4.2 shows, young voters (aged eighteen to twenty-nine years) are less likely to enrol than older voters. Barely half of this age group, for example, were enrolled in Auckland Central in 2005. Even when they do enrol, young voters are less likely to vote than their older counterparts. Recent research (see Dalton & Wattenberg 2000, p. 277) also suggests that younger people, especially when they are better educated, are also the most likely to forgo conventional participation in favour of more fluid, movement politics (be it intensely local or global). Perhaps, there is also an element of 'anti-establishment' appeal that attracts young voters to Green parties that inevitably wanes as these voters age. Thus, the Green party may face more problems than its competitors in holding on to, let alone growing, its 'core' support.

Green supporters also tend to have less traditional religious affiliations than other party supporters. Of those who voted Green in 2002, for example, half stated that they either had no religion or were non-Christians (Vowles, Aimer, Banducci, Karp & Miller 2004, p. 201). These tendencies do not mean, however, there is any such thing as the 'typical Green voter'. It is not true, for example, that Green supporters are drawn just from the ranks of the young. Coromandel, while the first electorate in New Zealand to elect a Green MP (in 1999), actually had the lowest proportion of fifteen- to twenty-nine-year-olds in the country in 2001. Or again, of Green voters in 2002, 55 per cent were aged thirty to forty-nine, the highest proportion of any political party (Vowles et al. 2004). There may also be a grain of truth, then, in the New Zealand media stereotype of the Green voter as a well-to-do thirty- or forty-something mother concerned about safe food and a safe environment for her children!

EXPLAINING GREEN SUPPORT

How do we explain the kind of concerns expressed by Green supporters? One explanation is Ronald Inglehart's theory of 'post-materialism'. This is the notion that increasing environmental concern is a product of both psychological mechanisms within individuals and increasing material (economic) affluence in society. Young people, socialised in affluent societies, are thought to be less concerned with satisfying their material wants than with a set of post-material ideals—a clean environment, civil liberties, and gender and racial equality. The implications of the theory for political parties is that the more affluent nations of the world are increasingly producing voters with post-materialist values who then support green political parties that cater to these sorts of demands.

The problem here is that post-materialism implies that environmental concern exists because people have changed, not because the environment has changed. Second, Green supporters are as concerned as anyone with many issues that impact their material well-being such as health, education, and unemployment. Third, environmental concern is not just a 'luxury' able to be indulged by the affluent middle class in rich Western nations. The developing world also sees much environmental activism from the 'Chipko' (literally 'tree-hugger') movement in India to environmentalists in Nigeria, such as Ken Saro-Wira, who was, it is claimed, executed by the Nigerian authorities for drawing attention to the environmental impact of oil drilling by foreign oil companies.

A more promising approach may be to explain Green support in terms of 'post-industrial' voters concerned with a 'risk society' mobilising to form 'New Social Movements'. The New Social Movements approach draws our attention to the fact that political conflict in post-industrial societies is not now simply about the relative distribution of power and wealth among the industrial classes of labour and capital. Rather, people are taking political action to mobilise against industrial practices that (a) take little account of the ecological services that the planet provides, (b) create global risks (climate change, genetic engineering, ozone depletion, oil depletion), and (c) cede control by democratically elected national parliaments to unelected, unrepresentative, and unaccountable global economic organisations (the IMF and WTO). Along with Green parties, NSM organisations such as Greenpeace and Friends of the Earth are adept at attracting environmental supporters through skilful use of the media to frame environmental issues as structurally problematic aspects of industrial society.

ORGANISATION

The New Social Movements (NSM) approach also suggests that the 'newness' of new political parties such as the Greens is to be found in the way they are organised—how they operate on a day-to-day basis, how they make decisions, and how they are structured (Dalton & Kuechler 1990). For example, despite being a parliamentary party, the Greens have continued to operate by using many unconventional forms of political participation such as mass petitions, street protest, and the new information and communication technologies (ICT). Green party MPs have protested on the steps of parliament, and the party as a whole exploits ICT to a much greater extent than most of its competitors. The party's website was voted the best of all political parties, its political 'blog' (web-log) is regarded as one of New Zealand's most popular, and, in what is believed to be a first for a New Zealand political party, its manifesto was published on a multimedia CD-ROM (Donald 2005b). ICT also plays quite a large part in the day-to-day operations of a party with a small active membership who, despite being widely spread geographically, are expected to (and indeed expect) to play quite a large role in both governance and policy making. Indeed, ultimate power in the party is exercised by the membership at the annual party conference that sets the political direction for the organisation.

In between times power is vested in the national executive. Partly made up of 'executive networkers' (elected by the membership of nine geographically-based 'provinces'), this body also comprises four 'counsellors' and one representative sent by Te Roopu Pounamu, the Green's Māori 'network', established in 2000. This is charged with supporting 'the inclusion of a Māori dimension in all Green party processes, policies and practices' in the light of the party's 'commitment to honouring te Tiriti o Waitangi'. Also on the executive are two policy co-convenors—one male and one female. Gender balance must also be maintained for the co-convenors who chair the executive and for the co-leaders, who also sit on the executive as of right, as does a representative of the caucus. The caucus itself comprises the co-leaders and Green MPs (who together make up its voting members) and others whose appointment (for example, by the executive) they agree to.

All decisions taken at any of the party's organisational meetings are made by consensus. If consensus on a motion is not achieved after reasonable attempts, a vote can be taken, but can only be carried with a 75 per cent majority of the votes cast. Because of its emphasis on membership participation, decision-making by consensus, gender balance, Māori representation, co-leadership, and candidate-selection procedures, the Green party is one of the most organisationally democratic political parties in New Zealand.

Nevertheless, there are inherent difficulties in such an approach. Striving for consensus, for example, can tend to stifle criticism by those not taking the majority view position on say, Māori sovereignty, drug law reform, or GE. Decision-making by consensus also intensifies the need for communication and trust between the parliamentary caucus and office located in Wellington and the membership as a whole. This is part of the aim of the summer gatherings that are usually held in holiday parks or places with rough and ready accommodation and where all share in the domestic tasks and in providing the entertainment. Such collective meetings help to break down the status differences between party members and create a sense of working together in a common political project. Maintaining a 'flat' organisational structure also has to be balanced against the demands of running a robust parliamentary operation capable of responding both rapidly and flexibly to the demands of events, other parties, and of course the media.

These competing demands intersect most obviously in the selection of candidates for the party list at general elections. The party uses the single transferable vote (STV) system to ensure that all ordinary members are given the opportunity (by post) to rank all candidates. This process means that incumbent MPs are reliant on nothing more than past performance and name recognition to differentiate themselves from a host of relative unknowns who are able to compete on what, at least procedurally, is a level playing field. Postal voting does not take place, however, until a 'selectorate' (consisting of the candidates themselves and the party executive) conduct an initial ranking using track-record, team-playing ability, and media appeal as criteria. This body also reserves the right to adjust the party list to ensure, for example, a reasonable geographical and age spread and, most importantly, a gender balance of at least 40 per cent.

Until 2005, any tensions between the demands of grassroots democracy and professional party management remained muted because the Greens were not in government. But with the position of Green MPs as government spokespeople and increased access to government ministers and confidential information, the Greens may find it challenging to maintain their full commitment to the democratic charter of their organisation. In the immediate aftermath of the 2005 election, for example, the 'grassroots' members were already questioning whether the support agreement negotiated by party leaders with the Labour government was worth it, and why the agreement was not subjected to a vote by party members. Similar tensions are likely to emerge over the coming parliamentary term.

PROSPECTS

Until they made it into parliament in their own right in 1999, the focus of the Greens was on winning sufficient public support to shift government policy in an environmentally friendly and socially focused direction rather than on actually entering government themselves. Since then, and especially at the leadership level, thoughts of potential coalition have begun to enter the equation. But the difficulty has been, and continues to be, finding a way through three interlinked dilemmas or (for the more pessimistic) catch-22s.

The first of these is rooted in the Green party's status as a 'post-industrial' party. While the Greens support much of the Left's aims on social and economic justice, they do not believe that this can be achieved through a process of economic globalisation that views environmental, health, labour, technology, and foreign investment regulations as barriers to free trade. Such a position may well attract votes, but it leaves the Greens in a poor position when it comes to getting into government. This is because it strands them to the left of a very strong Labour party firmly wedded to an industrial paradigm—the technological optimism of genetic engineering, limitless economic growth from 'free' trade and foreign investment, and a foreign policy intent on preserving a reasonably good (if not Australian-style 'special') relationship with Washington. These are just some of the most obvious examples of policies that Labour would have trouble watering down to accommodate the Greens around the cabinet table.

Yet compromise on some of these issues by Labour does not seem impossible. Indeed, some of New Zealand First's policy positions (opposition to a free trade agreement with China and support for raising the minimum wage by 2008), have not prevented Labour from working with New Zealand First in an 'enhanced' confidence and supply agreement. The fact that New Zealand First has marketed itself as a centrist party, able to join a coalition of the centre-right as well as one of the centre-left, clearly has advantages in terms of bargaining power. The likelihood of the Green party moving in this 'centrist' direction, however, is minimal. The Greens have ruled out working with the National party, preferring to assume the mantle of the Alliance as the 'alternative' but credible voice of the left on the New Zealand political scene. The first dilemma for the Greens then is that to get into government they are highly dependent on the calculations of a Labour party able to choose their coalition partners from among five minor parties and whose stance on some key issues is fundamentally at odds with their own post-industrial instincts.

The second dilemma for the Greens is that to be seen as a credible coalition partner for Labour requires them to both build relationships with that party as well as other potential coalition partners, and at the same time compete with all of them for votes. If MMP tends to lead to coalition government, coalitions tend to require more than one minor party to support them. For the Greens this means building working relationships with other minor parties so that Labour is able to put together a viable and stable centre-left coalition. The Greens have much in common with the Māori party, for example, in their determination to see not just the letter but the spirit of the Treaty of Waitangi embodied in the country's legislation and governance. But relationship building requires more than just policy similarities. It requires a degree of strategic cooperation over time to establish trust and credibility—precisely the qualities in short supply when it comes to the perceptions of the Green party held by the public, the media, and other political parties. In a survey undertaken after the 2002 election, the Greens were seen as 'not serious enough', as 'flaky', as 'not wanting to play too much of a role in Government', as 'wanting to cause trouble', and as 'a single issue party' (Faehrmann 2002). Overcoming these perceptions will require taking active counter-measures against a media all too willing to adopt the unsympathetic framing used by others to characterise the Green's policies, membership, organisation, and achievements. In this regard, the appointment of a professional media person has yet to show dividends. At the same time, attempts by the Greens to show the business community, for example, 'that we are not the devils they sometimes make us out to be' have met with limited success and show how far the Greens have to go in building relationships with those 'peak organisations' able to influence the wider community (Donald 2005b).

The third dilemma is how to achieve more credible policy gains by entering government without incurring a voter backlash. Although New Zealand's political culture is obviously still in transition, it remains hostile to minor parties that enter government, and who are seen, rightly or wrongly (and variously), as the 'tail that wags the dog', as 'selling out', as 'holding the government to ransom' (if indeed it is possible for part of the 'government' to hold another part hostage). While New Zealand voters support an electoral system that has replaced the executive dictatorship of a one-party-takes-all system, they also seem to overestimate the power it delivers (at least in theory) to small, more radical parties. The Greens have so far avoided the fate of other minor parties in government (such as New Zealand First and the Alliance), by (in)voluntarily choosing a halfway position—supporting a Labour-led government either by voting for it on confidence and supply motions, or not voting against it by abstaining on such motions. Between 1999 and 2002, the Greens did the former—giving Labour informal support on confidence and supply in return for promises of consultation and minor policy concessions on things that did not really matter to Labour, or that it would have done anyway, or that would not cost it too much (see Bale & Dann 2002). Between 2002 and 2005, the Greens had a 'co-operation agreement' with the minority Labour–Progressive government, but offered their votes on confidence and supply on a case-by-case basis (Bale & Bergman 2006). But, while this meant Labour took them less for granted, it provided them with little real leverage since the Greens' votes were not essential on such motions. In 2005 the Greens agreed to a 'comprehensive policy agreement' with a Labour-led government in exchange for an abstention on motions of confidence and supply. Ironically, this agreement promises to deliver more to the Greens than anything they have had before: consultation; ministerial access; involvement in the detailed development and implementation of specific policy proposals and budget initiatives; government spokesperson roles on energy efficiency and a 'Buy Kiwi Made' campaign (Green party 2005).

But the Green party's policy gains should not be overstated. They pale in comparison to what any self-respecting coalition partner would have expected in exchange for taking on the responsibility of office. This shortfall in policy gains is especially dramatic for a country like New Zealand where, despite MMP, what coalition theorists call the 'policy influence differential' (the difference between simply being in parliament and actually being in the executive), continues to be massive (Strøm 1990, pp. 38–44). Indeed, the long-term prospects for the Greens may suffer if they continue to be excluded (or exclude themselves) from government. With little real power they will be unable to achieve any of their more significant policy initiatives, they will continue to suffer from the lack of credibility and status that being in government would bring (among voters as well as other parties), and they may lose support from voters as a consequence. While Green arguments may indeed be historically inevitable, responding to them does not inevitably require a Green party.

Yet, despite such dilemmas and difficulties, the Greens still have reasons to be cheerful. First, they may see voter support increase as a result of what may turn out to be a strategic mistake by the Labour party. Resentment from left-leaning voters and among the union, public service, and education sectors is possible against a party who failed to pursue a viable centre-left coalition—a Labour–Progressives–Greens minority government supported by the Māori party on confidence and supply. Indeed, one-third of Labour voters indicated that they felt 'cheated' by getting a political grouping they didn't expect to get when they voted (3 News TNS Poll, 3 November 2005). Perhaps the compromises necessary to maintain stable coalition arrangements with two centre-right parties will likely provide a constant source of irritation for some Labour, Green, and Māori party supporters (let alone Labour MPs).

Second, although talk of a global 'Green wave' was always overblown (Mair 2001), it is unlikely that we have necessarily witnessed the height, let alone the end, of Green popularity in 'Western' countries like New Zealand. Green policy solutions will be required to address a range of problems facing New Zealand, such as energy security. The dependence of economic globalisation on endless economic expansion, a 'borderless' world, and cheap oil may well be exposed by stagflation, inequitable trading rules, oil depletion, and avian influenza.

Finally, party politics is a combination of agency and structure, of time and chance—a game in which Green parties in many other countries have proven themselves capable of getting into, and staying in, government. It would be foolish therefore to write off the Greens as somehow stuck in neutral. Their MPs are hard-working, effective, colourful, and philosophically united in their determination to create a sustainable green future. This is a huge advantage in New Zealand where the political scene is small and where the media seems intent on portraying politicians as cynical, ego-driven personalities obsessed with power. Doubtless the Greens will continue to champion the rights and interests of those whose voice seems to threaten the comfort zone of 'mainstream' or 'middle' New Zealand, such as the unemployed, refugees, and cannabis users. As National's Don Brash found, claiming to represent the mainstream is problematic and there are probably more than enough people living outside that sheltered construct to make it worth the Green party's while to stick up for them, at least in terms of votes. Under MMP this will translate into seats in parliament. Whether it translates into power is another matter.

DISCUSSION QUESTIONS

1 Why are a disproportionate number of Green party supporters younger? Is this a good thing?

2 What are the advantages and disadvantages of Green-style collective, consensual decision-making for a modern, nationwide political party?

3 Does the emergence of the Māori party present the Greens with a threat as well as an opportunity?

4 Is the Labour party the Greens' best friend or worst enemy?

5 What is it about New Zealand society, in terms of the issues that are or are becoming important to it, and in terms of its political institutions, that might favour the Greens in the future?

NOTE

1   Green party politics began in Australia in March 1972, when the United Tasmania Group (UTG) formed in Hobart. The UTG was the first environmental or green party per se to form in the world—but it was an Australian state party, not a party that contested a national election.

REFERENCES

Bale, T. & C. Dann, C. 2002, 'Is the Grass Really Greener? The Rationale and Reality of Support Party Status: a New Zealand Case Study', *Party Politics*, vol. 8, pp. 349–65.

Bresee, J. & D. Room 2005, 'Powering down America: Local Government's Role in the Transition to a Post-Petroleum World', *Global Public Media*, 20 October 2005, www.globalpublicmedia.com/articles/533

Bale, T. & T. Bergman 2006, 'Captives no Longer, but Servants Still? Contract Parliamentarism and the new Minority Governance in Sweden and New Zealand', *Government and Opposition*, forthcoming.

Dalton, R.J. & M. Kuechler 1990, *Challenging the Political Order: New Social and Political Movements in Western Democracies*, Cambridge, Polity Press.

Dalton, R.J. & M.P. Wattenberg 2000, 'Partisan Change and the Democratic Process', in R.J. Dalton & M.P. Wattenberg (eds), *Parties without Partisans: Political Change in Advanced Industrial Democracies*, Oxford University Press, Oxford.

Donald, R. 2005, 'Greens Build Bridges with Businesses', Green Party Press Release, 20 September 2005.

Donald, R. 2005b, 'Greens Virtually Win Election', Green Party Press Release, 16 September 2005.

Faerhmann, C. 2002, 'In hindsight—a Review of the Green Party's 2002 Election Campaign', Presented to Campaign Review Seminar, Parliament, 23 August 2002, www.greens.org.nz/searchdocs/other5552.html

Green Party 2005, 'Labour-led Government Co-operation Agreement with Greens', 17 October 2005. Available at www.greens.org.nz/searchdocs/other9314.html

Katz, R.S. & P. Mair 1995, 'Changing Models of Party Organization and Party Democracy: The Emergence of the Cartel Party', *Party Politics*, vol. 1, pp. 5–28.

Mair, P. 2001, 'The Green Challenge and Political Competition: How Typical is the German Experience?' *German Politics*, vol. 10, pp. 99–116.

Panebianco, A. 1988, *Political Parties: Organization and Power*, Cambridge University Press, Cambridge.

Parliamentary Library, 2005, *Electorate Profile: Wellington Central*, Parliamentary Library, July 2005. www.clerk.parliament.govt.nz/Publications/ResearchPapers/

Scarrow, S., P. Webb & D. Farrell 2000, 'From Social Integration to Electoral Contestation: The Changing Distribution of Power Within Political Parties', in R.J. Dalton & M.P. Wattenberg (eds), *Parties without Partisans: Political Change in Advanced Industrial Democracies*, Oxford University Press, Oxford.

Strøm, K. 1990, *Minority Government and Majority Rule*, Cambridge University Press, Cambridge.

Vowles, J., P. Aimer, S. Banducci, J. Karp & R. Miller 2004, *Voters' Veto: the 2002 Election in New Zealand and the Consolidation of Minority Government*, Auckland University Press, Auckland.

FURTHER READING

Burchell, J. 2002, *The Evolution of Green Politics: Development and Change within European Green Parties*, Earthscan, London.

Green Party of Aotearoa New Zealand, <www.greens.org.nz>.

Green Party, 'Labour-led Government Co-operation Agreement with Greens', available at www.greens.org.nz/searchdocs/other9314.html

Müller-Rommel, F. & T. Poguntke 2002, *Green Parties in National Governments*, Frank Cass, London.

Rainbow, S. 1993, *Green Politics*, Oxford University Press, Auckland.

Rüdig, W. 2002, 'Between Ecotopia and Disillusionment: Green Parties in European Government', *Environment*, vol. 44, pp. 20–33.

Māori Party

Kaapua Smith

The Māori party is a new and potentially significant phenomenon in New Zealand electoral politics. It was established in July 2004 in the wake of a hikoi (land-march) from the Far North to the steps of parliament in protest at the government's proposed Seabed and Foreshore legislation. Less directly influential in its formation was the 'Orewa I' speech by National's Don Brash on the future of race-based policies, the themes of which struck a chord with the New Zealand public and framed the debate over race relations and Treaty issues in the run-up to the 2005 campaign. Following the election, the party's sole representative in parliament, Tariana Turia, was joined by three other Māori party MPs, all of whom regarded themselves as representatives, not just of a party, but also of a wider social and cultural movement.

This chapter will examine the Māori party from two perspectives. The first places the party in the context of Māori political movements more generally, particularly those committed to the achievement of 'tino-rangatiratanga'. By providing a background to the development of Māori parties prior to 2004, the foundations will be laid for an understanding of some of the unique characteristics of Māori politics, especially those that impacted on the party's 2005 election campaign. A second perspective focuses on the organisational features and policies that contributed to the party's election success. Finally, we will consider the future of the Māori party, especially as it seeks to clarify its ideological position and working relationship with the two major parties.

KOTAHITANGA—UNITY

While there have been many attempts to advance the interests of tino rangatiratanga[1] (self-government) through such groups as iwi (tribes), hāpu (sub-tribes) and whānau (families), unifying Māori as a collective and homogeneous group has been a daunting task. One of the earliest examples of group activity was the Kingitanga movement of 1858, which was committed to the establishment of a Māori monarchy (Cox 1993, p. 44). Another was Paremata Māori, which was formed in 1892 as a separate and representative council serving Māori interests.[2] Both movements were born out of a series of hui (meetings) to express dissent at features of the political system, especially the lack of recognition for iwi autonomy, constitutional alienation from national government, and the detrimental effects of ongoing land alienation (Cox 1993, pp. 44–62).

While these movements reflected Māori political aspirations and activity, Māori were also engaged in the struggle for tino rangatiratanga through representation inside parliament. The Māori Representation Act, which was passed in 1867, saw the establishment of four Māori electorate seats.[3] While there have been many MPs occupying the Māori seats since that time, the first official Māori political party, Mana Motuhake, did not come into existence until 1979. A precursor, the Young Māori party, which had been formed in 1897, was less a political party than an interest group promoting Māori social development and cultural revival. One of its priorities was the promotion of increased Māori political participation and representation in parliament. This may help to explain why so many of the party's members were also members of parliament, including Sir Māui Pomare, Sir James Carroll, and Sir Apirana Ngata (Williams 1969, pp. 151–4).

Another notable political movement was Ngā Koata e Whā (four quarters), which was formed in 1928. It was born out of the Rātana faith, a Māori religious movement that was also engaged in the pursuit of Mana Māori Motuhake (autonomy). In alliance with the Labour party, it stood candidates in all Māori electorates, with the first successful candidate being elected in 1928.[4] While the Ngā Koata e Whā movement eventually disappeared, the essence of the relationship between the Rātana faith and the Labour party remained, with Rātana MPs sitting in parliament right up until the present time (Cox 1993, pp. 125).

In 1960, the Independent Māori Group was established. As the name suggests, it wanted Māori representation in parliament to be independent and free from the influence of party politics, hence its opposition to the Rātana/Labour alliance. The Group was primarily focused on promoting Māori land ownership (Foster 2005). In essence, it paved the way for independent Māori representation. In 1979 a disaffected Labour MP and former Minister of Māori Affairs, Mātiu Rata,[5] took its plea for independence one step further by establishing the first genuine Māori party.

Mana Motuhake was established with a view to protecting and representing Māori interests, promoting Māori autonomy, and diminishing Māori dependence upon the state (Walker 2004, p. 228). Although it garnered reasonable support from the Māori community, Mana Motuhake failed to win any seats until a strategic alliance was made with other minor parties[6] to form the Alliance in 1991. Although the coalition with the Alliance clearly strengthened the party's electoral chances, many Māori were still searching for autonomy and viewed the five-party Alliance as an impediment to the achievement of that goal (Hazelcraft 1993). Thus, following the coalition between Mana Motuhake and the Alliance a number of other minor Māori parties were established to fill the space that Mana Motuhake had vacated. One such party was Mana Māori, which was founded in 1991 by Eva Rickard, a political activist and former Mana Motuhake supporter.

The introduction of MMP in 1996 resulted in a significant increase in the level of Māori parliamentary representation and the formation of several new Māori parties, including Te Tawharau 1995, Mana Wahine Te Ira Tangata 1998, Mauri Pacific 1998, Ngā Iwi Morehu 2002, Aroha Ngia Tatou, 2002, and the Derek Fox party 2002.[7] While these parties generated some interest and Derek Fox came close to winning the eastern North Island Māori seat of Tairawhiti in 1999, none were able to muster sufficient support to reach the 5 per cent electoral threshold, although Mana Motuhake[8] and Tuariki Delamere's Te Tawharau[9] did manage to enjoy short bursts of parliamentary representation.

The reasons why Māori political parties have failed to make a greater impact until now have been the subject of debate. One explanation posits that Māori voters have yet to fully understand the MMP environment and the greater power held by minor parties in a multi-party parliament. Another is concerned with the limited appeal of political agendas that focus exclusively on perceived 'Māori' issues, especially given the widely varying needs of Māori voters. Perhaps most important of all, however, has been the continuing strength of a Rātana/Labour relationship that guaranteed that Labour would retain every Māori seat for all but a few of the previous seventy years.

TE PĀTI MĀORI—THE MĀORI PARTY

In 2003, a small South Island iwi, Ngāti Apa, made a case to the Māori Land Court claiming title over the seabed and foreshore within their tribal boundaries (Durie 2005, p. 87). The appeal signalled a realisation that ownership over the foreshore had never actually been assigned, and was therefore open to contest. The Labour-led government moved to remedy this by drafting legislation vesting all rights of ownership in the government. Its decision provoked strong opposition from Māori, who argued that it was a perversion of due process, since it prevented them from pleading their case in a court of law (see also chapter 8.4). The government's refusal to back down prompted a 40,000-strong land-march. The hikoi started at the very tip of the North Island, at Te Rerenga Wairua, and culminated in a gathering on the front steps of parliament. The hikoi was an expression of Māori organisation and unity—kotahitanga. Its symbolic leader was Tariana Turia, a Māori Labour MP who had been torn between representing the wishes of her electorate and obeying an ultimatum from Prime Minister Helen Clark to either support the government's legislation or step down as a minister. In the opinion of her supporters, Turia had become a political martyr. They called on her to resign from the Labour party and contest her seat in a by-election under the auspices of a new political party—a Māori party.

Turia sought the support of Pita Sharples and Whatarangi Winiata, two notable Māori leaders and academics. In a series of hui held in the wake of the hikoi, the decision to form a political party was confirmed. On 24 May 2004 the party had its first official hui at Turangawaewae, where the key positions of leader (Turia and Sharples) and party president (Winiata) were confirmed. At that time the party had no name and was simply dubbed the 'Māori party'.

The party's first order of business was to rally around Turia to ensure her re-election to parliament in the Tai Hauāuru by-election. The party campaigned and worked hard to establish some basic organisational structure, and was officially launched on 7 July 2004, three days prior to the by-election. Turia, who stood as an independent in a race not contested by the two major parties, was returned to parliament in a landslide victory (7000 votes separated her from the next closest candidate, Dun Mihaka of the Legalise Cannabis party). Having gained parliamentary representation, over the next year the Māori party incrementally established an organisational structure and the necessary policies, processes, and candidates to contest the 2005 election.

HE HUI, HE KŌRERO, HE HUI, HE KŌRERO ...

From the outset the party was driven by grassroots community support. This in turn underpinned and shaped its organisational structure, values, and policies. Since the movement was born out of the hikoi, an expression of kotahitanga, many Māori were prepared to support the 'kaupapa' (cause), despite an initial lack of policies or structure. Turia, Sharples, and Winiata, as the movement's official figureheads, had sufficient mana to be able to command strong pan-tribal support. However, in order to keep the momentum going, and to ensure ongoing commitment, the party leadership conducted a series of he hui and he kōrero (meetings and discussions). This process was part of a bottom-up approach to decision-making that is common among Māori political movements, with Kingitanga, Paremata Māori and Mana Motuhake being prime examples. Through this process, the party leadership tried to establish what the community wanted, how they wanted to be represented, and how the party organisation should be structured. The following statement, which was made at a national Māori party hui in Wanganui in July 2004, is fairly representative of the range of views expressed:

> I've been out this morning talking to gangs of forestry workers, trying to get them to vote. The support's there. But they ask us, 'where's your constitution? Where do we come in the chain? Where are your policies?' I think we need education. We need to keep New Zealand nuclear-free. I'd like to see us become a world leader in organic agriculture—not genetically modified. The Māori world-view complements the Western world-view. We need shared visions, not domination. We need different structures. The trust boards are killing us. They're taking money away from the marae and the hapu. They were set up by the Māori Trust Boards Act, by the Crown. We need structures based on tikanga. We need leadership. People love Tariana—and they do—because she takes our concerns into parliament (Nikora cited in Brookes 2004, electronic resource).

The hui were useful in a number of ways. As well as providing the opportunity for supporters to express their opinions on the proposed party structure and policies, the hui process enabled the communities to meet the party leaders who would be representing their interests during the forthcoming election campaign and in parliament. Many such hui were held 'off the beaten track' in small towns that no other political party had ever visited (C. Smith, pers.comm. 24 October 2005). This process both empowered the communities and the grassroots party membership. The membership mushroomed from 4,000 in July 2004 to 20,000 by the time of the election (D. Gardiner, pers.comm. 25 October 2005).

The party's organisational structure reflects its commitment to the community. While there is a national governing body, the power and drive comes from the electorates and branches. An example of this dynamic structure can be highlighted through the candidate selection process. This process is driven from the electorate, where nominees are identified and a majority vote of members is cast. Once the vote has been settled, and the electorate is happy with the decision, the national committee is left to provide official endorsement. The candidates chosen to stand in the Māori electorate seats in 2005 were a diverse group that included academics and activists, philosophers and pragmatists, seasoned politicians and novices. The 'magnificent seven' as they were dubbed, were Hone Harawira, Pita Sharples, Te Ururoa Flavell, Tariana Turia, Atareta Poananga, Angeline Grensill, and Monte Ohia. The first four went on to win seats.[10]

Because the party had few financial resources with which to contest the election, the bulk of the fundraising and workload had to be carried by the party members. Among the strategies adopted by individual volunteers and community groups were: comprehensive door-knocking campaigns, with canvassers visiting every house listed on the Māori electoral roll; market-day stalls to raise money, recruit new members and answer questions; and a 'communiqué', which resembled a pyramid scheme, where people would hold social events with a view to informing potential supporters of the party's progress and to solicit opinion on policies. While the party also used traditional campaign methods such as banners, flyers, and media advertising, much of its strategy was based around 'whanaungatanga' (relationships) and word of mouth. While the campaign may have been viewed as simplistic, the 'kanohi ki te kanohi' (face to face) approach was well suited to the needs of the party's target audience (C. Smith, pers.comm. 24 October 2005).

Another barrier that had to be overcome was mobilising Māori voters, especially the young, to participate in voting (Tamihere 2004, p. 158). In the month leading up to the election the party actively promoted the electoral registration process with a view to maximising its vote. One method of getting voters to the polling booths was to operate a system of car pools. Overall, the election campaign was not only about promoting the party, but also increasing turnout by removing some of the perceived barriers to participation (within the legal constraints placed upon them as a political party) (D. Gardiner, pers.comm. 1 November 2005).

One of the recurring criticisms was that, while the party was strong on enthusiasm and determination to get out its vote, it was weak on substantive policy proposals. Early on, the party released its underlying principles or 'Te Tāhuhu Herenga Kaupapa',[11] which used many Māori concepts derived from tikanga Māori. It soon became apparent, however, that voters could not relate to this framework and were growing restless waiting for the policies to be released. Reasons for the slow pace of policy production included the party's bottom-up approach to decision-making, as well as the complex consultative process that guided its development. As the leadership soon found, consensus is difficult to achieve, especially among large groups of strongly opinionated party members. Indeed, it was not until May 2005 that a stream of party policy began to be released.

TIKANGA, KAWA, KAUPAPA—POLICIES

By founding their party policies in tikanga, the leaders hoped to harmonise traditional Māori principles with contemporary values. Policies would reflect the priorities of Māori indigeneity, including the drive towards tino rangatiratanga, as well as the current and practical needs of a socio-economically disparate people. While the party had a comprehensive Treaty of Waitangi policy, which was intended to promote legal recognition and increase awareness of Treaty issues among all New Zealanders, there was also a determination to reflect a broader understanding and application of tino rangatiratanga. The drive towards recognition for mātauranga Māori (Māori knowledge) focused on developing holistic solutions to social issues and promoting culturally inclusive programmes. There was also a move towards empowering whānau as a means of restoring tino rangatiratanga, as can be seen through the whānau development policy, which cuts across many of the policy areas to develop stronger communities in a holistic manner.[12]

While the party's primary focus was on representing Māori issues, there was an attempt to broaden their appeal to the wider New Zealand community. As Sharples himself stated, 'The future of New Zealand is deeply intertwined with the future of Māoridom and is, in the eyes of the global community, uniquely intertwined with the idea of this nation' (Sharples 2005, p. A12). Among the policies deemed to be culturally inclusive were free early childhood and primary education systems, free primary health care for all children under the age of six, increased support for community-based initiatives, increased support for preventative health care and other such policies. While many of these promises were similar, if not identical, to those of other parties, they were conceived with quite distinctive goals in mind, such as empowering whānau and communities, inculcating culturally diverse value systems (with emphasis on Māori values), and increasing access to Māori culture for all New Zealanders. The party's policies resonated with the aspirations of earlier Māori political parties in focusing on a combination of socio-economic disparities and the search for self-determination. However, the policies were also distinctive in their drive towards an increased awareness of the value of Māori culture as an asset for all New Zealanders. In the words of Sharples:

> 'Our wish, and what I and the Māori party are working towards, is a society embracing Māori culture as well as the people; where Māori are able to enjoy their health, education, whilst also enjoying being Māori; where Te Reo Māori can be heard on the streets, in the shops, by all people—true equality for Māori' (Sharples 2005, p. A12).

TE MURA O TE AHI—THE HEAT OF THE FIRE

The contest for the seven Māori seats was at its most intense in the Auckland electorate of Tāmaki Makaurau, where Sharples was attempting to defeat the controversial Labour incumbent, John Tamihere. During 2005, the charismatic Labour MP had been the subject of considerable media attention, amid bitter criticism from some Labour colleagues over a series of incidents, including taking a 'koha' (gift, in this case a significant monetary gift) from his former employer, the Waipareira foundation, despite having suggested otherwise, together with a damaging interview in which Tamihere made derogatory comments about the prime minister, Labour colleagues, women, and homosexuals (Wishart 2005). Sharples, on the other hand, although a well-known community leader, was without experience as a political campaigner. The race between the pair was mostly cordial, although it was not without its bizarre moments, highlighted by an incident in the final week in which Tamihere's campaign manager allegedly paid a group of youths to smear

Table 5.5.1: Māori party's performance in the seven Māori seats, 2005

	Electorate vote (%)		Party vote (%)	
	Māori Party	Labour	Māori Party	Labour
Te Tai Tokerau	50.9	30.6	32.5	48.8
Tamaki Makaurau	51.4	40.5	27.2	54.6
Tainui	40.9	50.9	27.2	54.7
Ikaroa-Rawhiti	41.7	52.3	27.7	57.5
Waiariki	52.8	38.2	30.3	52.3
Te Tai Hauauru	60.9	32.4	31.3	52.4
Te Tai Tonga	33.0	45.7	17.4	57.3

Māori party billboards, and Sharples' supporters allegedly responded by kidnapping one of the culprits, holding him against his will until the damaged billboards were repaired.

The other electorates were not as controversial, although still very tense. Most Māori party candidates polled well during the campaign, apart from Poananga and Grensill, who were up against two Labour MPs with strong iwi electoral support bases. Despite the popularity of the Māori party's four successful electorate candidates, there was a substantial split in the vote, with the party vote favouring Labour in all electorates (see table 5.5.1). Perhaps this reflected a concern among some voters about the prospect of a National-led government. Their concerns may have been heightened by the Māori party's stance on preferred coalition partners, citing on many occasions that they would speak to any of the major parties, including National. This was not a popular statement with many Māori voters, as Brash and his stance on race relations ultimately threatened the existence of the Māori seats, the Treaty settlement process, and other targeted assistance for Māori.

The overall results generally supported the political polls leading up the election. Four of the seven Māori electorates went to the Māori party. The remaining Māori seats went to Labour, along with an overwhelming majority of Māori people's party votes. Nonetheless, the Māori party celebrated the fact that Flavell, Sharples, and Harawira were about to join Turia in parliament. The four made an interesting and yet balanced mix of talent: one an educationalist, one a community philosopher, one an activist, and one a seasoned politician.

Following the tight election results, with only two seats (fifty to forty-eight) separating the two major parties, coalition discussions began. At first it seemed possible that either party could become the government with the support of a group of minor parties (New Zealand First had seven seats, the Greens six, United Future three, ACT two, and the Progressives one). The Māori party, which decided to enter into negotiations with both major parties, held many hui around the country to consult with Māori over the ongoing coalition negotiations. During this period there was much speculation around Turia's relationship with the prime minister, Helen Clark (which somewhat soured after her resignation from the party during the hikoi), and the impact this would have on a coalition agreement with Labour. On the other hand, party members in the various Māori electorates were not happy with the idea of entering into a relationship with National. Despite this, the Māori party continued to negotiate with the centre-right party. As we know, Labour went on to become the government in coalition with the Progressives, and with a confidence and supply relationship with United Future and New Zealand First.

HE AO HOU—A NEW WORLD

The outcome of coalition negotiations saw the Māori party sitting out of government and alongside the other opposition parties, National, ACT and the Greens. While some people believe this is the best place to be in order to represent the interests of Māori without compromise, others believe that this position still presents only a minority voice in parliament. Many will watch with interest to see how the party fares in this new environment, especially considering its unique bottom-up organisational structure and relative inexperience. The challenge for the Māori party will be to solidify its position as a party that is here to stay by reinforcing its organisational structure and maintaining its base of support. The precedence set by past Māori political parties and movements has ensured a cynical outlook on the party's ability to succeed in this challenge. The Māori party members on the other hand are positive and hopeful, although ultimately their performance in parliament will determine their survival at the next election.

DISCUSSION QUESTIONS

1 What are the common themes that can be seen among Māori political parties and movements? Do these impact on their organisational and/or electoral successes and failures? Why or why not?

2 Account for the large party membership that the Māori party has acquired. How does this compare to party membership generally within New Zealand?

3 Discuss the positive and negative attributes associated with the 'bottom-up' approach that the Māori party uses.

4 What were the outcomes of the 2005 election in relation to the Māori party? Account for the Māori party's relative success and/or failure.

NOTES

1   Tino rangatiratanja is not simply about gaining access to political power for power's sake, but is the result of Māori indigenous rights, expectations implanted through the Treaty of Waitangi 1840, and a history of colonisation that has alienated Māori from decision-making processes, access to power, and the ability to exercise control over their own destiny (Walker 2004, p. 148).

2   Paremata Māori was established after the Māori Representation Act of 1867 and highlighted the frustration felt by Māori due to the limited powers of their parliamentary representation.

3   Due to the introduction of MMP and proportional representation in 1996 there are now seven Māori seats. In 1867 if the Māori seats were allocated according to population, Māori would have been entitled to twenty seats out of the seventy in existence at that time. See Cox, L., 1993, *Kotahitanga: The Search for Māori Political Unity*, Oxford University Press, Melbourne.

4   The Labour party values and advocacy for the rights of the working class were aligned with the aspirations and needs of the followers of the Rātana faith.

5   Rata entered into parliament in 1968, and for a short period of time held the position of Minister of Maori Affairs. He set in place legislation that had considerable impact on Māori, such as the Treaty of Waitangi Act 1985.

6   Those minor parties were the New Labour party, the Green party and the Democratic party.

7   The Derek Fox party was established in 2002 by Derek Fox who stood as an independent candidate for Tairāwhiti in the 1999 election. While the party was launched in 2002 it did not make it to an election as Fox ultimately decided to take up a position with the newly established Māori Television Service.

8   Sandra Lee entered into parliament in 1993, to be joined by another party member, Alamein Koopu, in 1996 who later left the Alliance party to establish Mana Wahine Te Ira Tangata.

9   Tuariki Delamere, who originally entered into parliament under the NZ First party, swore allegiance to Te Tawharau in 1998 after he resigned from his party. Delamere failed to be re-elected in the 1999 election.

10 The Māori party also put up candidates in a number of general seats.

11 Literally translated it can be understood as the backbone that binds the policies together.

12 See Māori Party Policy Manifesto at www.maoriparty.com.

REFERENCES

Alves, D. 1999, *The Māori and the Crown: An Indigenous People's Struggle for Self-Determination*, Greenwood Press, London.

Brookes, G. 2004, 'Māori Party reflects mood of resistance' in *Socialist Worker Monthly Review*, 21 September 2005, from www.monthlyreview.com.

Cox, L. 1993, *Kotahitanga: The Search for Māori Political Unity*, Oxford University Press, Auckland.

Durie, M. 1998, *Te Mana, Te Kāwanatanga: The Politics of Māori Self-Determination*, Oxford University Press, Auckland.

Durie, M. 2003, 'Mana Māori Motuhake', in R. Miller (ed.) *New Zealand Government and Politics*, 3rd edn, Oxford University Press, Auckland.

Durie, M. 2005, *Ngā Tai Matatū: Tides of Māori Endurance*, Oxford University Press, Auckland.

Farrell, M. 1992, *Te Pooti Māori: Māori Representation and Electoral Reform*, Centre for Māori Studies and Research, The University of Waikato, Hamilton.

Foster, B. 2005, 'Māori Political Parties' in *An Encyclopedia of New Zealand*, from www. eara.govt.nz/1966/P/PoliticalParties/MaoriPoliticalParties/en

Hazlehurst, K. 1993, *Political Expression and Ethnicity: Statecraft and Mobilisation in the Māori World*, Praeger Publishers, London.

Karp, J. & Banducci, S. 2002, 'Political Parties and Voter Mobilisation' in J. Boston (ed.) *New Zealand Votes: The General Election of 2002*, Victoria University Press, Wellington.

Kelsey, J. 1990, *A Question of Honour? Labour and the Treaty 1984–1989*, Allen & Unwin, Wellington.

Mana Motuhake 1980, Nga Kaupapa WhakaMāori i nga Tari a te Kawanatanga Na te Mana Motuhake: Institutional Transformation of Governing Bodies to include Māoritanga from Mana Motuhake, unpublished report printed by Mana Motuhake, Auckland.

Mana Motuhake 1980, 'Remits Passed at Mana Motuhake Policy Hui', *Tirahou Marae*, 29–30 March, Auckland.

Māori Party 2005, 'Te Tāhuhu Herenga Kaupapa: Our People Moving Forward', from www.maoriparty.com.

Miller, R. 2005, *Party Politics in New Zealand*, Oxford University Press, Melbourne.

Ministry of Social Development 2005, *The Social Report: Te Pūrongo Oranga*, The Ministry of Social Development, Wellington.

Schwimmer, E. 1968, 'The Māori and the Government', in E. Schwimmer (ed.), *The Māori People in the 1960's*, Blackwood & Janet Paul Ltd, Auckland.

Sharp, A. 1990, *Justice and the Māori: Māori Claims in New Zealand Political Argument in the 1980s*, Oxford University Press, Auckland.

Sharples, P. 2005, 'Tamihere V Sharples', in *New Zealand Herald*, 11 August.

Tahana, A. 1985, 'Māori Political Representation', in R. Walker (ed.), Nga Tumanako: Conference Proceedings for Māori Representation Conference, *Turangawaewae Marae*, 26–27 April, Centre for Continuing Education, The University of Auckland, Auckland.

Tamihere, J. 2004, 'Campaigning in a Maori Seat', in J.Vowles et al. (eds) *Voters' Veto: The 2002 Election in New Zealand and the Consolidation of Minority Government*, Auckland University Press, Auckland.

Tamihere, J. 2005, 'Tamihere V Sharples', in *New Zealand Herald*, 11 August.

Te Runanga Ko Huiarau. 1991, *Ko Huiarau*, Puriri Press, Auckland.

Vasil, J. 1990, *What Do the Māori Want?*, Random Century Publications, Auckland.

Walker, R. 1980, 'Mana Motuhake, Its Origins and Future', Unpublished Paper, 15 October, Auckland.

Walker, R. 1989, 'The Treaty of Waitangi: as the Focus of Māori Protest', in H. Kawharu (ed.) *Waitangi: Māori and Pakeha Perspectives of the Treaty of Waitangi*, Oxford University Press, Auckland.

Walker, R. 2001, *He Tipua*, Penguin Books, Middlesex, England.

Walker, R. 2004, *Ka Whawhai Tonu Mātou: Struggle without End*, Revised Edition, Penguin Books, Middlesex, England.

Ward, A. & J. Hayward 1999, 'Tino Rangatiratanga: Māori in the Political and Administrative System' in P. Haveman (ed.), *Indigenous People's Rights in Australia, Canada, & New Zealand*, Oxford University Press, Auckland.

Williams, J. 1969, *Politics of the New Zealand Māori: Protest and Cooperations, 1891–1909*, Oxford University Press, Auckland.

Wishart, I. 2005, 'Tamihere Comes Clean', in *Investigate Magazine*, Issue 51.

FURTHER READING

Durie, M. 2005, *Ngā Tai Matatū: Tides of Māori Endurance*, Oxford University Press, Melbourne.

Harris, A. 2004, *Hikoi: 40 years of Māori Protest*, Huia Publishers, Wellington.

Māori Party 2005, *Te Tāhuhu Herenga Kaupapa: Our People Moving Forward*, from www. aoriparty.com.

Miller, R. 2005, *Party Politics in New Zealand*, Oxford University Press, Melbourne.

Walker, R. 2004, *Ka Whawhai Tonu Mātou: Struggle without End*, Revised Edition, Penguin Books, Middlesex, England.

Minor Parties and the Religious Right[1]

Raymond Miller

The influence of America's Religious Right on that country's electoral politics has rekindled international interest in the nature of the relationship between religion and politics. Paradoxically, despite its constitutional commitment to the separation of church and state, the USA blends faith with politics to a degree not found in most other Western nations. Other Anglo–American societies may share America's democratic and religious traditions, but none has experienced a similar rise in the incidence or influence of 'faith-based' politics. This is not to say that the growth of secularism has gone unchallenged—indeed, some of the most secular Western societies have experienced an increase in the level of political activity among socially conservative Christian groups, whether in the form of Christian parties, organised rallies and protests, or faith-based interest groups and think tanks.[2] Attitudes adopted by Christian parties tend to focus on opposition to abortion and homosexuality (especially same-sex marriage), support for policies designed to combat dependency on tobacco, alcohol, and other drugs, and a commitment to the importance of the nuclear family as the 'basic building block of society'.

This chapter will consider what, if any, impact the rise of faith-based politics has had on the party system of New Zealand. The advent of MMP gave rise to the formation of a number of niche parties, mostly from within parliament, resulting in the consolidation of a multi-party system that had taken root during the neo-liberal reforms of the 1980s and early 1990s. Features common to these new parties include small and extremely fluid patterns of electoral support, together with a commitment to policy agendas that fall outside the mainstream of politics. This chapter will trace the development of that cluster of micro-parties that have branded themselves as

'Christian', specifically the Christian Heritage, Christian Democrat, Christian Coalition, and Destiny New Zealand Parties, together with United Future. While the latter party rejects any explicitly Christian identity, its policies and MPs have clearly appealed to some conservative Christian voters.

The discussion will consider reasons for the emergence of these small Christian parties and chart their development as electoral organisations. In assessing their chances of future success, the discussion will draw on survey data on attitudes to faith-based issues, especially among churchgoers and those who profess a religious faith. Of course, identifying what constitutes the Religious Right in the context of New Zealand is no easy task. Unlike its counterpart in the USA, it lacks a strong institutional structure, group consciousness or public profile, and there is little evidence of agreement over political strategies, tactics, and goals. Because of these difficulties, the major focus of this discussion will be on that discrete collection of morally conservative parties that compete for votes under the label 'Christian'.

RISE OF FAITH-BASED PARTIES IN NEW ZEALAND

In the heyday of the two-party system, the political values and aspirations of most religious groups were largely accommodated within the ideologies of the two major parties. While no attempt was made to incorporate an overtly religious perspective in their policy agendas, there was an implicit acknowledgment of the largely Christian character of postwar New Zealand society. Because social class, not religion, was considered to be the main determinant of voting behaviour, the party preferences of churchgoers attracted little attention among voting specialists. This said, there was an assumption that the National party enjoyed broad support among Anglicans, Presbyterians, Baptists, and other evangelical denominations, such as Plymouth Brethren and Pentecostals. On the other hand, Labour's more egalitarian and collectivist ideology was said to appeal to Catholics and Methodists (see, for example, Chapman, Jackson & Mitchell 1962, pp. 174–5). One of the few studies on religion and political participation is an unpublished survey-based thesis on religion and politics in Auckland. It found that an overwhelming majority of the nonconformist Christians it surveyed—that is, Presbyterians, Methodists, and Baptists—regularly voted National, with Baptist respondents proving to be the most conservative on a range of social and political values (Reynolds 1970, p. 181).

Although there were outlets for political activism among the more theologically liberal denominations, especially through such vehicles as the National Council of Churches and Student Christian Movement, prior to the 1980s evangelical and Pentecostal Christians appeared to be largely preoccupied with spiritual matters, especially questions surrounding the issue of personal salvation. In claiming that they were *in* this world but not *of* it, those with the most separatist tendencies were able to justify not voting and, in extreme cases, not even registering to vote (the best known contemporary advocates of this view are the Exclusive Brethren). It therefore came as something of a surprise when, in the mid to late 1980s, some evangelical church leaders began to mobilise their members to oppose a number of government and parliamentary initiatives, including abortion[3] and homosexual law reform, and the creation of a Ministry of Women's Affairs. Their actions, which included organised protests, the creation of a lobby group, the Coalition of Concerned Citizens, and the use of an evangelical journal, *Challenge Weekly*, as a vehicle for their opinions (see Guy 2002), marked the beginning of a period of growing politicisation on the part of some evangelical and Pentecostal churches.

1. Christian Heritage (1989–)

The Christian Heritage party, which was formed in 1989, was the first of the overtly Christian parties. While not a direct offshoot of the anti-gay movement, it reflected a wider concern among some Christians about the perceived breakdown of moral values and traditional family life in New Zealand. Like the African Christian Democratic party, which was formed some four years later, Christian Heritage New Zealand drew much of its early support from the New Zealand chapter of the theologically and socially conservative Dutch Reformed Church. Moreover, the name of the new party and many of its founding principles were borrowed from the Christian Heritage party of Canada, an organisation that has enjoyed some support among small pockets of fundamentalist Christians, mainly in Western Canada.

Although Christian Heritage New Zealand attempts to target all churchgoers, at its first general election in 1990 it drew disproportionate support from Pentecostal and evangelical congregations, notably Baptists, as well as from Catholics. Most of its vote came from National rather than from Labour (Vowles & Aimer 1993, p. 183). The party's policies were built around the needs of the family, with strong emphasis on the rights of parents with respect to moral education and the use of physical force to discipline their children. Not unexpectedly, Christian Heritage took a strong line on crime and punishment,[4] as well as on national security and defence. The party also adopted a right-wing position on economic and welfare policy, although in arguing that the rightful place for women is in the home, it expressed a commitment to something akin to the former family wage. At the 1993 election, Christian Heritage gained a mere 38,749 votes, or 2.2 per cent of the nationwide vote.

2. Christian Democrats (Future NZ) (1995–2000)

In the wake of the decision in a binding referendum in 1993 to adopt the MMP system of proportional representation, a number of new, largely opportunistic parties sprang up both inside and outside parliament. The Christian Democratic party was formed in 1995 by a Baptist lay-preacher, National MP, and former government minister,

Graeme Lee. Compared with Christian Heritage, it was a relatively moderate party, especially on the issues of abortion and homosexuality. It was also more inclusive in its choice of spokespeople and parliamentary candidates. For example, whereas Christian Heritage insisted that all its candidates subscribe to a strict set of moral and theological doctrines, the Christian Democrats spread their net widely to include all churchgoers, as well as those non-churchgoers who supported the party's policy agenda and willingness to be part of a National-led coalition after the 1996 election.

3. Christian Coalition (1996)

Following the left-wing Alliance's success in attracting 18.2 per cent of the vote at the 1993 election, the leaders of the Christian Heritage and Christian Democratic parties began to negotiate the terms of an electoral pact. Reaching the 5 per cent electoral threshold at the 1996 election was a formidable task for either Christian party, especially when competing for the same votes. While retaining their integrity as independent organisations, the two parties agreed to the formation of the Christian Coalition, with one candidate being chosen per geographical electorate (it contested thirty-six out of the sixty-five seats), and with a common party list. Christian Heritage did, however, produce its own separate manifesto with a view to drawing public attention to its more hard-line position on such issues as abortion and the death penalty (Rainbow & Sheppard 1997, p. 180).

Despite coming tantalisingly close in 1996 to winning seats in the new parliament, with 4.3 per cent of the party vote, the Christian Coalition failed to overcome several major obstacles, including allegations in the media of bigotry, especially on abortion and gay rights. More damaging still, however, was the perception, given impetus by some adverse public opinion poll results during the campaign, that a vote for the Christian Coalition was a wasted vote. At the election, the Coalition did best in rural and provincial town seats, especially those with significant numbers of evangelical and Pentecostal congregations, as well as in seats with a high proportion of retirement-age voters (for example, Rodney, Hamilton, Tauranga and Nelson).

Following the 1996 election the two Christian parties went their separate ways, with the Christian Democratic party renaming itself Future New Zealand. Apart from a brief period following the decision of an Alliance MP, Frank Grover, to break away from his party and join forces with Christian Heritage, it was becoming increasingly obvious that the two Christian parties had become something of an electoral irrelevance.

4. United Future (2000–)

Although Peter Dunne has consistently rejected suggestions that United Future is a Christian party,[5] the party did assume something of a Christian character at the 2002 and 2005 elections with its conservative views on social and family values, opposition to any relaxation in the cannabis laws, and promotion of a number of evangelical

Table 5.6.1: Party vote of regular churchgoers, 1996–2002

	1996 %	1999 %	2002 %	Comparison with nationwide party vote, 2002
Labour	22.8	31.5	30.6	41.3
National	23.8	20.2	14.4	20.9
NZ First	9.9	4.2	6.8	10.4
ACT	2.4	3.3	2.6	7.1
Green	-	1.4	3.3	7.0
United Future/Future NZ	0.2	5.7	27.3	6.7
CH/Christian Coalition	20.8	16.3	5.2	1.4
Other	20.1	17.4	9.8	5.2

Source: New Zealand Election Study, 1996–2002

Christians into the top few positions on the party list. In 2000, Dunne's party, United New Zealand, had merged with the Christian party, Future New Zealand. At the 2002 election, United Future received significant support from regular churchgoers (see table 5.6.1). As one study of the party observed: 'Religion and church-going play an especially important part in the lives of United Future voters' (Aimer 2002, p. 299). Drawing on the NZES data, Aimer discovered that four out of every ten United Future voters described themselves as 'very religious'. The party's negotiations with Labour after the 2002 election resulted in a 'good faith and no surprises' pact with the incoming government. Among the policy concessions extracted from Labour was the establishment of a special government-funded Families Commission (Miller 2004, p. 148). Despite its promise to offer confidence and supply for the next three years, United Future opposed several liberal legislative initiatives, notably the Prostitution Reform Bill 2003, Civil Unions Bill 2005, and Relationships Bill 2005. Dunne was particularly keen to distance himself from the Civil Unions Bill, describing it as 'more "Think Pink" from a government that imposes its prejudices on New Zealanders' (quoted in Miller, 2005, p. 58). Because the Bill gave legal status to a variety of civil unions, including those between same-sex couples, its passage through parliament was strongly opposed by conservative Christian voters.

5. Destiny NZ (2003–)

One of the most vocal critics of the Civil Unions Bill was the founder of the Destiny Church, an independent charismatic church that has quickly expanded from its Auckland base to include some twenty congregations scattered throughout the country. Pastor Brian Tamaki, who first came to prominence through his televised church services, condemned the 'secular humanism' of successive governments, which he blamed for same-sex marriages and 'mass' abortions, a reduction in the drinking age from twenty to eighteen, the condoning of de facto and same-sex relationships, and the breakdown of family life. In July 2003 he launched a new Christian party, the Destiny party of New Zealand. Shortly before the 2005 election it claimed to have some 7,000 members, most of whom attended the Destiny Church.[6] In terms of the social profile of the membership, some 60 to 70 per cent are Māori, although the party claims to have a strong presence in the Pacific Island community, with established networks in a number of Pacific churches.[7] Most party members are said to be in full-time employment but on relatively low incomes, often due to the limited nature of their formal education. A majority of members come from single-income families, either because the mother has stayed at home to bring up the children or as a result of family breakdown. Also, a significant number have not previously voted, although those that have tend to be former Labour voters.

Among the family-based policies being promoted by the Destiny party at the 2005 election were tax credits for marriages that last, more support for full-time mothers, and the removal of any financial benefits that might be seen to encourage parental separation. Destiny's particular brand of moral conservatism includes a sex education programme for its young members based on a commitment to abstinence before marriage. By mid-2005, some 400 members had signed a pledge to abstinence from sex before marriage, as well as from the use of drugs and alcohol.[8] The principles of the party include a belief in the infallibility and moral authority of the bible and a commitment to encouraging all New Zealanders to 'live within the parameters of God-honouring moral principles'.[9]

The leadership of the Destiny party is more apostolic than democratic. Although it has a ten-person National Management Board, all the important decisions, including the selection of electorate and list candidates, together with the ranking of the party list, are made by the leader, Richard Lewis, in consultation with the party's spiritual head, Brian Tamaki. With only three exceptions, all those chosen as electorate candidates at the 2005 election were members of the Destiny Church (the others were from the Metro Church and New Life Centre). Before being accepted, aspiring candidates are required to sign a statement of personal Christian faith and to declare any previous bankruptcy or criminal convictions.

6. Proposed Christian Coalition (2005)

Conscious of the damage the Destiny party could potentially inflict on Christian Heritage's small and ever-shrinking vote,[10] the leader of Christian Heritage, Ewen McQueen, proposed a coalition arrangement similar to that struck with the Christian Democrats in 1996.[11] According to the 'Coalition Proposal', the first draft of which was circulated in December 2004, the creation of a new Christian Coalition to contest the 2005 election would create 'one identity, one brand, one message'. While the two constituent parties would retain their separate structures and memberships, the overarching body would promote a joint policy and produce a common party list of parliamentary candidates. McQueen proposed that he would become the leader of the Christian Coalition, with the Destiny party leader, Richard Lewis, filling the position of deputy leader. The proposal was discussed at a meeting of the Association of Pentecostal Church leaders in December 2004.

It soon became obvious that the Destiny leadership was in no mood to play second fiddle to Christian Heritage. Having achieved nationwide publicity over their 'Enough is Enough' marches in Auckland and Wellington, as well as on the Treaty grounds at Waitangi, the leaders of the Destiny party rightly believed that their brand had greater public recognition and appeal than either 'Christian Heritage' or 'Christian Coalition'. They therefore proposed that the new coalition be called Destiny New Zealand. Nor would Brian Tamaki, who was about to assume the title of 'Bishop', readily submit to the authority of Christian Heritage and its leader, Ewen McQueen. As McQueen himself observed, Tamaki wanted nothing less than the 'subsuming of Christian Heritage into Destiny'.[12] But Tamaki and Lewis were also concerned that a formal relationship with Christian Heritage would undermine Destiny's chance of electoral success among Māori voters, especially in the seven Māori seats.

REASONS FOR THE EMERGENCE OF CHRISTIAN PARTIES IN NEW ZEALAND

Of the various reasons for the growth of Christian parties during the past ten to fifteen years, three stand out. The first concerns the extensive coverage in the New Zealand news media of the American Religious Right. At almost every presidential election since the defeat of Jimmy Carter by Ronald Reagan in 1980, the American media has drawn attention to the role of that country's Moral Majority and Christian Coalition movements in supporting faith-based political candidates, most of whom have been Republicans, and orchestrating the defeat of those who either oppose or fail to uphold conservative Christian values. The Religious Right's determination to set the political and social agendas is beyond question. During George W. Bush's 2000 presidential campaign, for example, the evangelical publication *Christianity Today* published the results of a poll of some 475 evangelical leaders. It revealed that 91 per cent advocated 'staying focused on politics'. The journal also referred to a survey taken in 1990, which showed that some 75 per cent of evangelical leaders cited abortion and homosexuality as the most important problems facing the USA.[13] Key figures in the conservative evangelical movement over the past two decades have included Jerry Falwell, James Dobson, and Paul Weyrich. Among the activities conducted by Falwell, for example, was a '52-week patriotic God Save

America national tour' that overlapped with the 1996 presidential election.[14] Given the continuing electoral influence of the Religious Right, with tens of millions of adherents living in the nation's most pivotal states, it is little wonder that the George W. Bush re-election campaign of 2004 targeted the movement for special support. Indeed, one of the features of his administration is the number of Christian Coalition leaders who gained key roles in the White House, as well as in the Bush campaign.

While the influence of America's Religious Right on New Zealand's Christian leaders should not be overstated, the agendas and many of the strategies that have been adopted here, including the growth of think tanks such as the Maxim Institute (see chapter 7.3), bare a strong resemblance to those developed in the USA in the past twenty-five years. When the question of possible influence is put to them, key personnel in New Zealand's Christian parties tend to state that, while they have followed developments in the USA, they have not been the principal motivation in their decision to become politically active.

A second, and probably more significant, influence on the emergence of Christian parties has been the advent of proportional representation. MMP has offered a more conducive electoral environment within which boutique parties can become established and grow. With the obvious exception of Christian Heritage, all of the explicitly Christian and Christian-oriented parties have been formed since the electoral referendums of 1992 and 1993. While the 5 per cent threshold and multi-party competition for votes might appear to some to be an almost insurmountable barrier to representation, Christian party leaders are supreme optimists, believing that the estimated 300,000 churchgoers in New Zealand provide a sufficiently large reservoir of potential voters to ensure their party's survival, if not electoral success.

A third explanation for the formation of Christian parties has been the growing activism of the New Zealand parliament on matters of personal and social morality. The reasons for this are complex, and may include the questioning of traditional norms by younger generations and the declining influence of institutional religion. The number and type of conscience issues that came before the New Zealand parliament in the period up to 1970 were vastly different from what they are today. As David Lindsey has found (see chapter 2.7), in the fifty-year period between 1900 and 1950 there were a mere nine conscience votes, mostly covering the sale of alcohol. In contrast, the next fifty-year period produced 112 votes. Most of these occurred in the period since 1980, and covered issues as diverse as abortion, homosexuality, the right of adopted children to know the identity of their birth parents, the advent of Sunday and Easter trading, euthanasia, prostitution reform, and the care of children. It is hardly a coincidence that a number of these issues have provided the necessary motivation for the formation of most, if not all, of the aforementioned Christian party organisations.

IDENTIFYING NEW ZEALAND'S CHRISTIAN CONSTITUENCY

In the USA, an astonishing 47 per cent of voters (and 59 per cent of Bush voters) attend religious services at least once a week (*Time Magazine* 21 June 2004, p. 19). To measure the size of the church constituency in New Zealand and to consider the voting dispositions and attitudes of churchgoers on a range of issues, we can draw on the findings of the New Zealand Election Study (NZES), which has surveyed voters by postal questionnaire, with a telephone top-up, at each MMP election.

According to the NZES, some 13.2 per cent of 2002 respondents claim to attend religious services at least once a week. If taken as a percentage of all registered voters, New Zealand would have some 330,000 regular churchgoers of eighteen years of age or over (a total only slightly higher than the 300,000 cited in news sources). If we turn the question away from church attendance and instead consider responses to the more inclusive question of whether or not respondents look upon themselves as being religious, response rates are broadly similar (for example, in 2002 11.7 per cent claimed to be very religious). As might be expected, women profess a stronger religious faith than men (50 per cent of women are 'somewhat' or

Table 5.6.2: Church attendance 1996–2002

	1996	1999	2002
Non-churchgoer	43.8	55.1	54.9
Occasional churchgoer	45.0	32.3	31.9
Weekly churchgoer	11.2	12.6	13.2

N = 4,063 (1996); 5,881 (1999); 4,537 (2002).

Table 5.6.3: Religious beliefs by gender, 2002

	Female	Male	Total
No religious beliefs	15.7	24.2	19.6
Not very religious	32.4	35.1	33.6
Somewhat religious	37.1	28.8	33.3
Very religious	13.1	10.2	11.7
Total	100.0	100.0	100.0

N = 4,447.

'very' religious, compared with 39 per cent of men). There are obvious differences between the two sets of responses, however, as illustrated by the position adopted by one of the staunchest critics of the Civil Unions Bill within parliament, National's Brian Connelly. While claiming that his opposition to the bill was due to deeply held religious beliefs, Connelly, a Catholic, freely admitted that he did not attend church.

When we consider attitudes to key social issues by religious denomination (see table 5.6.4), it is possible to detect similarities as well as differences in the responses of those from the explicitly evangelical and Pentecostal churches compared with non-churchgoers and those from the more established churches. Consistent with their strongly held preference for women staying at home to bring up their children, evangelical and Pentecostal respondents are lukewarm in their support for pay parity. On the question of stricter parental discipline, churchgoers are decidedly

Table 5.6.4: Attitudes to law and order and domestic issues, 2002

Strongly Per cent agree	No religion	Anglican	Catholic	Presby- terian	Baptist	Brethren	*Pente- costal
Women should stay at home with their children	11.8	17.0	18.9	19.2	23.8	45.0	32.2
Close pay gap between men and women	24.3	22.2	20.5	17.0	12.3	15.0	18.2
Reintroduce death penalty for some murders	31.4	31.2	29.2	30.7	24.8	25.0	22.3
Serious sex offenders should be flogged	17.4	17.3	21.3	16.5	14.1	15.0	15.7
Young people need stricter parental discipline	16.1	23.2	22.3	27.1	20.8	42.1	24.6

*   This includes the various charismatic denominations, such as Elim and Assemblies of God, as well as the independent fundamentalist churches.

more conservative than non-churchgoers. On the other hand, on law and order issues that lie outside the home, notably capital punishment, the differences are not particularly significant.

Whereas faith-based voters in the USA have an enthusiasm for individual self-help and the free market, the same cannot be said for their counterparts in New Zealand. Those who adopt a conservative position on family and law and order issues are likely to hold more moderate views on economic policy. For example, approximately two-thirds of such respondents support free government-funded health care for everyone, as well as free education from pre-school through to tertiary and university levels.

Although attitudes to gays were not measured in the most recent surveys, the 1996 survey does ask respondents if they consider homosexuality to be wrong. (During the 1996 campaign, a gay activist secretly taped comments about homosexuals and homosexuality from a home study group involving several Christian Coalition activists, including a former Police Commissioner, John Jamieson, who was ranked at number five on the Christian Coalition party list. The audiotape was the subject of an interview between the gay activist and Jamieson on Television New Zealand's *Holmes* show.) As the figures in table 5.6.5 show, opposition to homosexuality is much stronger among Baptist and Pentecostal respondents than non-churchgoers and those from established churches. The strength of their opposition is also in marked contrast to that expressed with respect to family and law and order issues (see table 5.6.4).

Having adopted an unambiguous position on a range of issues guaranteed to resonate with socially conservative Christians, it is hardly surprising that the Christian Coalition, Christian Heritage, and United Future parties did disproportionately well among regular churchgoers at the first three MMP elections. As the figures in

Table 5.6.5: Homosexuality is wrong (by religious affiliation), 1996[15]

	Strongly agree	Agree	Neither	Disagree	Strongly disagree	Don't know
No religion	7.7	7.6	17.9	22.7	41.7	2.5
Anglican	13.8	12.0	28.8	22.5	19.2	3.6
Catholic	17.6	13.0	23.3	22.1	20.7	3.3
Methodist	14.2	11.8	22.5	33.1	15.4	3.0
Presbyterian	14.4	13.1	30.8	23.8	14.1	3.8
Baptist	49.0	20.6	17.6	6.9	4.9	1.0
Pentecostal	71.4	14.3	7.1	3.6	1.8	1.8
Other Christian	46.9	11.8	16.9	8.3	11.8	4.3

N = 3,864.

table 5.6.6 show, at all three elections, support for the two major parties among churchgoers has been tracking at a significantly lower rate than the overall results nationwide. With less than half of all regular churchgoers supporting the two established parties, it is fair to conclude that churchgoers tend to be volatile voters with a marked capacity for experimentation with parties that are both new and untried.

This leads to the question of whether or not the current array of parties is perceived to be meeting the needs of the most deeply religious respondents. As the figures in table 5.6.7 show, in 2002 the most religious voters expressed the highest level of satisfaction with the existing parties—that is, they were the group least likely to be feeling a sense of grievance about the unrepresentative nature of the existing multi-party system.

FUTURE OF THE CHRISTIAN PARTIES

This brings us to the question of the sustainability of Christian parties in the short to medium term. It is possible to identify at least three related barriers to their future electoral success: first, the narrowness of New Zealand's social structure; second, the demands placed on small parties by the rules of MMP, in particular the 5 per cent threshold; and third, the absence of anything resembling the Religious Right movement in the USA, including a coherent organisational structure, group consciousness, significant support base, or public profile.

1. Narrow social structure

Scholars have argued that a nation's party system is a reflection of its social structure. Put simply, countries with narrow cleavage structures are likely to be dominated by two major parties, whereas those with a number of social divisions or cleavages tend to have pluralistic, and perhaps even highly fragmented, party systems. Examples of social cleavages include social class, ethnicity, language, regionalism, and religion. Belgium, and Israel are extreme examples of countries with complex cleavage patterns resulting in multi-party systems, whereas the party systems of the United Kingdom and the USA are products of a single dominant cleavage, that of socio-economic class.

New Zealand has long been regarded as having a one-dimensional social structure based on socio-economic class. Whereas National attracts most of its support from middle to upper income members of the business, professional, and agricultural communities, Labour has long been regarded as the party of blue-collar workers, beneficiaries, the low-paid, and those on fixed incomes. Following the electoral referendum of 1993, some scholars began to speculate that New Zealand was moving towards a more complex cleavage structure, with ethnicity and religion potentially offering additional strands to that of class (see, for example, Nagel 1994, Lijphart 1999, and Miller 2005). Together with those issue dimensions that are capable of sustaining new parties, including post-materialism (the Greens) and economic interventionism (the Alliance and ACT), one scholar predicted that New Zealand might have up to seven or eight parties holding seats at any one time.

Although the jury is still out on the medium- to long-term viability of a separate Māori party, evidence would suggest that, with up to 15 per cent of the population claiming Māori ancestry, and with a ready-made political issue in the form of the Foreshore and Seabed Act 2004, the new Māori party is capable of building on the four seats won at the 2005 election. In contrast, there is no evidence of an emerging religious cleavage of any size within the New Zealand social structure. While a conservative Christian party might be able to muster around 80,000 votes (the Christian Coalition's vote in 1996), sustaining that level of support beyond a single election, and keeping the disparate Christian elements united, will be a formidable challenge.

This chapter was written prior to the release of any 2005 post-election survey data. As a result, we can only speculate as to the reasons voters voted the way they did. Suffice to say that the size of the vote for National would suggest that a significant proportion of the conservative Christian vote is likely to have gone to the socially conservative National—for example, an overwhelming majority of National MPs voted against the Prostitution, Civil Union, and Relationships Bills during the term of the 2002–05 parliament (see chapter 2.7, especially table 2.7.2), a fact not lost on several Exclusive Brethren businessmen, who, during the 2005 campaign, ploughed an estimated $500,000 into a pro-National publicity campaign. Thus, with churchgoers splitting their 2005 votes between six or seven different parties (see table 5.6.6), and in the absence of significant dissatisfaction with the current

Table 5.6.6: How regular churchgoers cast their party vote, 1996–2002

	1996 %	1999 %	2002 %	Final election results nationwide 2002
Labour	22.8	31.5	30.6	41.3
National	23.8	20.2	14.4	20.9
NZ First	9.9	4.2	6.8	10.4
ACT	2.4	3.3	2.6	7.1
Green	–	1.4	3.3	7.0
United Future/Future NZ	0.2	5.7	27.3	6.7
CH/Christian Coalition	20.8	16.3	5.2	1.4
Other	20.1	17.4	9.8	5.2

Table 5.6.7: Do any of the existing parties represent your views? 2002

	No religious beliefs	Not very religious	Somewhat religious	Very religious
Yes	66.0	67.3	70.5	75.5
No	22.9	21.6	19.7	15.4
Don't know	11.1	11.1	9.8	9.1

N = 4,387.

array of parties (see table 5.6.7), the chances of building a viable conservative Christian party on New Zealand's small and fractured religious cleavage must be considered remote.

2. The rules of MMP

Although the advent of proportional representation was greeted with enthusiasm by the leaders of the small parties, the framers of the new electoral legislation (Electoral Act 1993) had taken the precaution of lifting the threshold from the 4 per cent recommended by the Royal Commission on the Electoral System (Wallace 1986) to 5 per cent. As well as making it unlikely that frivolous parties or those with extreme views would win seats in parliament, and potentially hold the balance of power, the threshold has had the discriminatory effect of applying to some parties but not others (parties winning an electorate seat are not required to reach the 5 per cent threshold). This has meant that a number of parties with fewer votes than the Christian Coalition gained in 1996—for example, United (Future) (1996, 1999, and 2005), New Zealand First (1999), the Progressives (2002 and 2005), and the Māori party (2005)—have been returned to parliament. Further assisting their chances of election success has been the availability of a range of financial, staffing, and other resources that are reserved for parliamentary parties. This has made it even more difficult for non-parliamentary parties to cross the threshold. It is hardly a coincidence, therefore, that no non-parliamentary party has been able to win seats at a general election since the introduction of MMP in 1996.

Of course, there are ways by which a Christian party can circumvent the 5 per cent threshold. One would be to persuade an incumbent electorate MP to defect from his or her party during the course of a parliamentary term, a method used by Graeme Lee and others from 1994 on. Alternatively, a nascent Christian party could join forces with an existing parliamentary party, an approach successfully adopted by Future New Zealand (formerly the Christian Democrats) when it joined forces with Peter Dunne and United New Zealand in 2000. Quite apart from the extra resources such a merger would bring, not having to breach the 5 per cent threshold weakens the force of the argument that a vote for a small party is simply a wasted vote.

Table 5.6.8: Party vote for 'Christian' parties, 1996–2005 elections

Party	1996 No.	%	1999 No.	%	2002 No.	%	2005 No.	%
Christian Coalition	89,716	4.3						
Christian Heritage			49,154	2.4	27,492	1.4	2,821	0.1
Christian Democrats			23,033	1.1				
Destiny NZ							14,210	0.6
United Future					135,918	6.8	60,860	2.7
Total	89,716	4.3	72,187	3.5	163,410	8.2	77,891	3.4

3. Absence of an organised Religious Right

Setting aside the social structural and electoral arguments, perhaps the greatest impediment to the success of a conservative Christian party is the absence of a movement that can make any claim to representing the interests of the Religious Right in New Zealand. As has been discussed, Fundamentalist Christianity has long been a significant religious and political force in the USA, partly because of the vast number of voters whose political values reflect their Christian beliefs, but also because the movement is extremely well organised, with groups such as the Christian Coalition of America and Focus on the Family utilising the new technology to good effect. Moreover, their party political activity is focused almost exclusively on influencing just one party, the Republican party. In New Zealand, in contrast, conservative Christians are not only poorly organised, but also deeply divided, weaknesses that have been exacerbated by their propensity for forming new parties, often in open competition for the same votes.

One course of action available to conservative Christians wishing to influence the political process would be to endorse United Future, a party with a strong legislative record of support for traditional family values and opposition to liberal reforms in such areas as prostitution, cannabis use, and same-sex civil unions. However, such endorsement is unlikely to be forthcoming from either of the two explicitly Christian parties, partly because of personal ambition and the high level of sectarianism that these small parties represent, but also because of a failure to accept that political influence inevitably involves compromise. Failure to cooperate with United Future on the grounds that it has supported some government measure or because of an alleged association between Dunne and the tobacco industry are merely illustrative of the all-or-nothing attitude that has crippled successive Christian parties since the advent of MMP.

DISCUSSION QUESTIONS

1   Account for the political influence of the Religious Right on US politics. Why has no similar movement taken root in New Zealand?

2 Imagine that you have been asked to offer professional advice to a small faith-based party on how to go about gaining parliamentary representation. What would you advise?

3 Had United Future branded itself a 'Christian' party and largely targeted the faith-based vote, in your view might it have done better or worse than it did at the 2005 election?

4 Is there a legitimate place for a Christian party in the new political environment of MMP?

NOTES

1 An early version of this chapter was presented at the Religion and Politics Colloquium, Carey Theological College, Penrose, 24–25 June 2005.

2 Recent examples of socially conservative Christian parties include Ireland's Christian Solidarity party, South Africa's Christian Democratic party, Canada's Christian Heritage and Family Coalition parties, and Australia's Christian Democratic and Family First parties.

3 Although an anti-abortion lobby group, the Society for the Protection of the Unborn Child (SPUC) sprang up in the 1970s, becoming particular active after the introduction of the Contraception, Sterilization and Abortion bill in 1977, its membership came largely from the Catholic Church.

4 In 2005, Christian Heritage's former leader, Rev. Graham Capill, a long-time advocate of Christian family values, was imprisoned for the indecent assault and rape of several under-age girls.

5 Interview with Peter Dunne, Parliament Buildings, Wellington, 16 July 2003.

6 Interview with Richard Lewis, Destiny Church, Auckland, 26 May 2005.

7 Interview with Richard Lewis, Destiny Church, Auckland, 26 May 2005.

8 Interview with Richard Lewis, Destiny Church, Auckland, 26 May 2005.

9 Destiny New Zealand, 'Manifesto', Destiny New Zealand, Mt Wellington, Auckland, 2005, p. 7.

10 Telephone interview with Ewen McQueen, 1 June 2005.

11 Personal email correspondence between E. McQueen (Christian Heritage) and R. Lewis (Destiny), 26 January 2005.

12 Telephone interview with Ewen McQueen, 1 June 2005.

13 R. Cizik, 'The Real Christian Coalition', Christianity Today, 12 June 2000 (www.christianitytoday.com/ct/2000/007/33.82.html).

14 J. Kennedy, 'Jerry Falwell's Uncertain Legacy', Christianity Today, 9 December 1996 (www.ctlibrary.com/ct/1996/dec9/6te062.html).

15 The 2005 survey responses on this issue came to hand after this chapter was completed. They show that attitudes have changed relatively little in the intervening nine years, with Baptists (61.9 per cent) and Pentecostals (91.7 per cent) agreeing that homosexuality is wrong. These figures compare with 69.6 per cent for Baptists and 85.7 per cent for Pentecostals in 1996.

REFERENCES

Aimer, P., 'United Future' 2003, in R. Miller (ed.), *New Zealand Government and Politics*, Oxford University Press, Melbourne, 3rd edition, pp. 293–304.

Chapman, R.M., W.K. Jackson & A.V. Mitchell 1962, *New Zealand Politics in Action: The 1960 General Election*, Oxford University Press, Wellington.

Cizik, R. 2005, 'The Real Christian Coalition: Evangelical Politics is Bigger than the Religious Right', *Christianity Today*, www.christianity today.com/ct/2000/007/33.82. html, 31 March.

Dunne, P. 2005, *In the Centre of Things*, Dunmore Press, Palmerston North.

Gibbs, N. 2004, 'The Faith Factor', *Time Magazine*, 21 June, pp. 16–21.

Guy, L. 2002, *Worlds in Collision: The Gay Debate in New Zealand, 1960–86*, Victoria University Press, Wellington.

Lijphart, A. 1999, *Patterns of Democracy: Government Forms and Performance in Thirty-Six Countries*, Yale University Press, New Haven.

Maddox, M. 2005, 'The Rise of Faith-Based Politics'. Paper presented to the Religion and Politics Symposium, Somerville Presbyterian Church, Remuera, Auckland, 21 May.

Miller, R. & J. Karp 2004, 'A Vote for Coalition Government?', in J. Vowles, P. Aimer, S. Banducci, J. Karp & R. Miller (eds), *Voters' Veto: The 2002 Election in New Zealand and the Consolidation of Minority Government*, Auckland University Press, Auckland, pp. 134–49.

Miller, R. 2005, *Party Politics in New Zealand*, Oxford University Press, Melbourne.

Nagel, J. 1994, 'How Many Parties Will New Zealand Have Under MMP?', in *Political Science*, 26/2, pp. 139–60.

Rainbow, S. & S. Sheppard 1997, 'The Minor Parties', in R. Miller (ed.), *New Zealand Politics in Transition*, Oxford University Press, Auckland, pp. 177–85.

Reynolds, P. 1970, 'Religion and Politics in Auckland: A Study of the Socio-economic Composition, Voting, and Religious and Political Attitudes of Activists in a Sample of Auckland Non-conformist Churches'. MA Thesis, University of Auckland.

Szajkowski, B. (ed.) 2005, *Political Parties of the World*, John Harper Publishing, London, 6th edn.

Tumulty, K. & M. Cooper 2005, 'What Does Bush Owe the Religious Right?', *Time Magazine*, 7 February, pp. 14–18.

Vowles, J. & P. Aimer 1993, *Voters' Vengeance: The 1990 General Election in New Zealand and the Fate of the Fourth Labour Government*, Auckland University Press, Auckland.

Vowles, J., P. Aimer, S. Banducci & J. Karp (eds) 1998, *Voters' Victory? New Zealand's First Election under Proportional Representation*, Auckland University Press, Auckland.

Vowles, J., P. Aimer, S. Banducci, J. Karp & R. Miller (eds) 2004, *Voters' Veto: The 2002 Election in New Zealand and the Consolidation of Minority Government*, Auckland University Press, Auckland.

Wallace, J. (Chair) 1986, *Towards a Better Democracy: The Report of the Royal Commission on the Electoral System*, Government Printer, Wellington.

FURTHER READING

Aimer, P. 2003, 'United Future', in R. Miller (ed.), *New Zealand Government and Politics*, Oxford University Press, Melbourne, 3rd edition, pp. 293–304.

Lineham, P. 1993, *Religious History of New Zealand: A Bibliography*, 4th edn, Department of History, Massey University, Palmerston North.

Maddox, M. 2005, *God under Howard: The Rise of the Religious Right*, Allen & Unwin, Sydney.

Miller, R. 2005, *Party Politics in New Zealand*, Oxford University Press, Melbourne (chapter 3).

Nagel, J. 1994, 'How Many Parties Will New Zealand Have under MMP?', in *Political Science*, 26/2, pp. 139–60.

Vowles, J., P. Aimer, S. Banducci & J. Karp (eds) 1998, *Voters' Victory? New Zealand's First Election under Proportional Representation*, Auckland University Press, Auckland.

6.0 Media

Democracy and the Media

Geoff Kemp

Starting at the very beginning is a very good place to start, so the new student of government is customarily informed of the antecedents of modern politics and democracy, both terms coined 2,500 years ago with reference to the Greek city-state, the *polis*, and its citizens, the *demos*. He or she is assured of a broad affinity with today—politics is about rule, democracy about rule by the people—while being alerted to the considerable differences between a classical democracy, like fourth-century BC Athens, and a modern democracy, like New Zealand. The comparison is often in our favour, given that ancient democracy was rule by only male people, relied on a slave under-class, and failed to impress the foremost thinkers of the age, Plato likening the *demos* to a beast happy with junk food.

Nevertheless, Athens can be glimpsed as thinkers of our time reflect on how to improve democracy. This suggests ancient democracy possessed something we lack, but the question can be turned around because it is equally significant what the ancients lacked and we have in abundance. Athens was essentially a democracy without media. It possessed the written word but was primarily an oral culture and an *unmediated* democracy. Its politics were face-to-face, not *Face to Face with Kim Hill*. Its public was not the dispersed audience of *Close Up* but 5,000 or so citizens assembled in the marketplace, the *agora*, or at their hillside meeting-place, the *Pnyx* (loose translation: 'close up'). Its Herald was not a newspaper but a man with a loud voice, who invited all to have their say from the *bema*, the speaker's platform, this *isegoria* or 'equal free speech' being taken as central to democratic self-government. As one contemporary observed: 'Can equality further go ... when the people piloteth the land'? (Euripides 1988, p. 535).

It is a long way from this idealised Athens to the modern world, but the recent 'deliberative turn' in political thinking has breathed new life into unmediated democracy, proposing that today's 'thin' democracy gain depth by bringing citizens face-to-face with each other and with decision-makers in a process of open discussion, seeking to bypass mediators. This is itself news, given that the media (taken as a unity) has traditionally been viewed as the essential counterpart to modern democracy. In 1840 the writer Thomas Carlyle famously labelled the press the 'Fourth Estate' of government, arguing in a London lecture that, for better or worse, printing made democracy inevitable because it ensured 'the nation was governed by all who had tongue in the nation'—'democracy is virtually *there*' (Carlyle 1993, pp. 141–2). Yet increasingly the mediation of politics is seen as a problem for democracy, limiting and distorting as much as fostering public deliberation, keeping 'we the people' quiet rather than giving us a voice, treating citizens as customers, making democracy 'virtual' *not* reality.

This chapter considers the accusation in relation to New Zealand's media, past and present, explaining why the media has an unavoidably ambiguous role but suggesting that something of its democratic promise is realised so long as there is continuing recognition that its role is underpinned by a 'promise' of service to the public to which it is accountable.

ATHENS TO AUCKLAND: CONNECTION AND ALIENATION

It is a long way from Athens to Auckland geographically as well as historically, as television viewers were reminded during the last Olympics. The satellite link between the Olympic media centre in Greece and TVNZ's studios would have impressed citizens of Plato's day but could not prevent a time lag in communication. 'It's weird, isn't it, the four-second delay,' remarked presenter Paul Holmes during TV One's 7pm current affairs slot, as he and New Zealand captain Beatrice Faumuina 17,500km away stumbled across the silences.[1] This fleeting television moment, which left much unsaid, actually said quite a lot about media, and not only about its preoccupation with sportspeople and celebrity presenters. More fundamentally, it illustrated how communications media transform human interaction, extending that connection across space and time but altering the relationship so it is often barely *inter*action at all.

The ability of Holmes and Faumuina to share with each other and with the audience the emotional bond of nationhood (despite the four-second delay) confirmed how the media links those not in physical proximity. 'Beatrice, we'll all be up very early in the morning,' declared Holmes, 'and we shall be watching you and nobody will be cheering louder for New Zealand than New Zealanders'. This stretching of connections seems obvious but the implications are immense, given that a condition for modern democracy is the linking of individuals so they can conceive of themselves as fellow members of a political community. In ancient Athens this was achieved by the physical co-presence of citizens in the agora or Pnyx, but after cohesive city–states gave way to sprawling kingdoms the creation of a democratic public required the development of representative political institutions and the growth of news media as a source of imagined community, sustained by shared information and mediated experience and with 'public opinion' as its expression. In performing this function, observed Carlyle's friend John Stuart Mill, the newspaper press became 'the real equivalent, though not in all respects an adequate one, of the Pnyx' (Mill 1977, p. 378).

Mill's point that the press was not an exact equivalent is important. Representative government and the media's political role emerged not simply as a technical fix but as an alternative to more direct 'people power', with democratic and aristocratic elements that harmonised not least with private commercial expansion. Indirect, mediated democracy links the people to political power and separates them from it, allowing media and governments the scope, within limits, to determine what counts as 'public opinion' and 'in the public interest'. This is *liberal* democracy, whose merits include a commitment to upholding liberties even against the *demos*, including the media's own freedom and property rights. The liberal state and media have their relative autonomy in part because we do not 'do' government together on a sunny hillside but more often share only the light of television pixels. This nonetheless makes us feel in communication with our fellow citizens and with government … at least so long as we do not feel too excluded from the conversation.

Which brings us back to the four-second delay. What it exposed, again often overlooked (literally), was the one-sidedness of the communicative relationship offered by media. A gap in the presenter–audience 'conversation' opened up but viewers were powerless to fill the silence as they might in a normal discussion, their status confirmed as bums on seats rather than speakers on the *bema*, spectators not participants. Plato once remarked that people in paintings seem real but if you ask them a question they ignore you. The cynic might say today's public is stripped of the impulse even to ask questions by a medium which is never silent, television plying the 'beast' with relentless audio-visual fodder in lieu of space for critical engagement. The viewer is part of a community of citizens that is imagined though not imaginary—it is a social fact—but is offered a semblance of dialogue that really does turn out to be imaginary. The media suffers a fear of open spaces, of ceding professional control, and agoraphobia often leaves little room for citizen involvement. The four-second delay was a small space in which a question was raised about the kind of media relationship the democratic citizen might have reason to expect.

DEMOCRACY AND DELIBERATION

There is no going back to (ancient) Athens, but holidaying there as a thought-experiment highlights the perceived problem with contemporary mediated democracy. This relates partly to a dearth of 'actual' dialogue but at root to a relative neglect of deliberation more broadly conceived: the process of forming considered judgments as a citizen on the basis of a diversity of viewpoints and credible information.

In Athens the ongoing deliberative process was the core of democracy; today, the focus is the infrequent decision mechanism, having a vote, with limited political interest outside elections. Eighteen-year-olds gained the vote three decades ago because it was felt 'political maturity' was being attained earlier, yet a system oriented exclusively or excessively towards voting and opinion polls is not inherently interested in the maturity of opinions. It aggregates individual preferences, counting your informed judgment as one and your flatmate's unconsidered prejudice as one. Relatedly, what pollsters declare to be 'public opinion', which dominates election coverage, appears in this light to be more like non-public opinion, an aggregate of private opinions. In fact, opinions are never wholly private or public but the balance is worth thinking about. Consider the televised 'worm debates' in the last two election campaigns, on TV One in 2002 and TV3 in 2005. Members of the studio audience ('the public') were exposed to party leaders' views but limited to responding as atomised private individuals, silently turning their reactor dials between 'good' and 'dull'. The issue is how far aggregated individual opinions of dullness really represent political *public* opinion, as suggested in reporting of the 'worm verdict'. And what about the election votes of those at home who responded to the worm verdict not the content of debate (or who were watching the game show on the other side)?

One response is to say public opinion or a democratic mandate just *is* this aggregate; another is to seek to turn the focus of democracy further towards the conditions of opinion formation and transformation such that improved deliberation leads to judgments that are duly mature and more truly public. This connects with the idea of the news media having a democratic mission to inform, represent and involve citizens, a 'public service' role not only applicable to a state-owned broadcaster like TVNZ but also to the broader media 'ecology' in a democracy. The complaint is that governments and media are often too preoccupied with anticipating, eliciting or reacting to bare preferences—via votes, polls, ratings or worms—to concern themselves seriously enough with the quality and quantity of public political deliberation. The charge is that in taking an 'economic' approach to democracy ('people buy, we care not why') they risk seeing the public good in terms of atomised self-interest not collective democratic goals.

An economic rather than democratic approach to communication readily becomes the default mindset in a heavily commercially driven media environment, as New Zealand's is. The defence is often offered that a media preoccupation with increasing customers is quasi-democratic, market forces enthroning the public as sovereign—media firms give audiences what they want or go bust, and television ratings show that the public wants soundbite-paced news not policy detail. Popularity is not to be sniffed at, but ratings do not show what people want, only what is viewed (I might watch *One News* not *3 News* but 'want' news with less advertising); the media does not really think individual choices are fixed and sacrosanct (otherwise promotion and advertising is money wasted); and it responds less to 'the public' than to demographics attractive to advertisers (viewers being 'currency' in ratings jargon, some virtually worthless). Moreover, reliance on ratings or circulation mirrors the problem of 'immature' democracy in assuming that individuals have an interest only in the satisfaction of existing preferences, however acquired. Critics are accused of arrogantly wanting to force people to watch 'worthy' programming, but arrogance would surely be rejecting the possibility that we may have an interest in an assessment of the adequacy of the conditions under which our preferences are formed. Indifference to the conditions of their own formation makes ratings a different currency to democratic public opinion.

PUBLIC SERVICE NORMS

What *are* adequate conditions of deliberation and opinion formation? The short and circular answer is that it is a matter for debate, but the most influential model in applying deliberative criteria to the media realm has been Jurgen Habermas's notion of the 'public sphere', conceived as the realm or process of free and open discussion in society, insulated from undue distortion by state and commercial power. In principle, it is open to all and oriented towards rational exchange and consensus, from which arises public opinion as a genuinely democratic guiding hand on government, legitimated by the process itself. This is a vague but intuitively appealing prescription, although some critics claim it privileges mainstream views ('rational consensus') and neglects the multiplicity of public spheres locally and globally. It is not simply a wishlist, however, but seeks to locate what could be called the 'ideal in the real', in that 'norms' or what *should* normally be the case are partially inscribed in what *is* the case, providing a critical yardstick for judging the 'fact' (Habermas 1996, p. 287).

Habermas points to norms of deliberation implied in ordinary conversation, which proceeds on a presumption of sincerity, openness to argument and so on. His earlier work suggested the way public sphere norms were articulated historically, legitimating political discussion outside traditional ruling circles inclined to censorship (Habermas 1989). For instance, the rise of the press as a private commercial enterprise was justified by claims of a more publicly persuasive 'universalist' kind. The defence of open access, downplaying of commercial motive (even if disingenuous), emphasis on non-partisan rational detachment (ditto), assurance that truth would emerge from the exchange of ideas—these were all staples of the early news media's self-justification, its enduring outcome being the freedoms the media enjoys today. These purposes became partly subordinated to commercial and political special interests with the growth of the 'mass media', but they subsist imperfectly as a normative underpinning, discernible in journalistic ethics of truth, fairness and so on, and more unsystematically in corporate media's self-image. When former All Black captain David Kirk became chief executive of media giant Fairfax he declared that its products, including the

Sunday Star-Times and seventy other New Zealand newspapers, were not just part of 'our market economies' but were 'fulfilling a critical role in the functioning of our democracies'.[2] Our cynic might say this was rhetoric masking corporate self-interest, but even if so it would not preclude 'the people' seeking to hold the media to its word. When Kirk later announced sixty-five redundancies, Fairfax workers alleged that the firm had betrayed principles of honesty and openness essential to any media operation in a democracy.[3]

A critical theory of this type suggests how an insistence on the media's democratic obligations is not erecting new obstacles in an empty landscape, because 'media freedom' is already a cluttered vista of principles, purposes, and practices. Media 'norms' are in this sense something like political concepts and practices generally, which are not invented anew each day but reproduced, recast, rejected, and partially recovered over time; hence the Athenian echo, and why history is relevant to political understanding.

MEDIATING AOTEAROA

New Zealand shares in this Western genealogy but affords its own insights into mediated and unmediated politics. The story could start three months before Carlyle's 'Fourth Estate' lecture, on 6 February 1840, when the written word enabled his nation to claim legitimacy for governing what he off-handedly called 'Felondom New Zealand', whose own oral, face-to-face society was encountering Western 'media' culture, the printing-press having arrived ten years before, the first newspaper only months earlier.[4] The encounter involved gains and losses, literacy and print being seen as gifts and weapons of colonisation, sharing the media's potential to connect and alienate politically. A 'medium effect' is suggested by the Treaty itself: without the written word there would be no Treaty, but its 'spirit' is deemed important partly because written words cannot entirely capture the understandings of signatories attuned to oral discussion and agreement not legal documentation. Differing conceptions of how political relations might be affirmed is suggested by Lieutenant-Governor Hobson's concern to arrange the printing of the Treaty even before it was signed (Colenso 1890, p. 28).

The written, printed, and promulgated Treaty was one of the imported institutional trappings of Western politics, the Fourth Estate and elections from 1853 being others. These were defended as Western civilisation's alternative to a dispersed and rudimentary aristocracy of tribal chiefs, although interestingly at least one colonial official characterised Māori political culture as democracy without media (like Athens, slave-holding and male-centred, although lacking Athenian institutions and democratic self-consciousness). 'The power of individual chiefs depends much on public opinion, and few matters of importance are undertaken, except after having been submitted to public discussion', observed Edward Shortland. '[T]he best idea to be given of the political constitution of their society will be to describe it as a democracy, limited by a certain amount of patriarchal influence' (Shortland 2001, p. 119). The core notion of democracy continues to be political accountability to public opinion but how public discussion can be transformed by media is suggested by the Aotearoan as well as Athenian example. Hobson's impulse to have the Treaty printed symbolised the transition—print addressed and modelled a public beyond ties of kinship or proximity, purposes superfluous to the political culture of iwi and hapu.

Government patronage along with commercial and philanthropic initiative would act as a spur to the first New Zealand newspapers, nine appearing over the next two years, each helping forge and inform the new community through news and official notices but each also a private concern with an ambivalent relationship to open discussion. The early press's self-justification was not as government or commercial mouthpieces, however, but advanced in broadly 'public sphere' terms as independent servants to the community they were also creating. The *New Zealand Advertiser* (15 June 1840) noted that promises were risky in a 'new society' but was typical in committing itself to 'promote the interests of the community' and 'do good to the *whole* population'. The press had been a 'mighty machine' of enlightenment in Europe, it added, and could now do the same in 'a country at the distance of half the Globe'. Importantly, the means by which newspapers vowed to serve the community coupled dissemination with a dialogic function in offering a public forum. Editors in effect promised Carlyle and Mill's virtual Pnyx as the equivalent of Shortland's democracy without media. Indeed, the first Auckland newspaper, the short-lived *New Zealand Herald and Auckland Gazette*, pointed out that in the absence of an elected assembly there was no colonial democracy 'except that of the public opinion' (Meiklejohn 1953, p. v). The advent of elections—for property-owning Pakeha males over 21—did not alter the undertaking to embody the ongoing public interest. Today's *Herald* first appeared on 13 November 1863, one of scores of newspapers launched during that decade, proclaiming itself 'an untrammelled exponent and supporter of public opinion' affording a forum 'open to free and independent discussion of all questions of public interest'.

New Zealand media's roots thus lay in a Western tradition of engaging to foster public deliberation, transplanted into a context which highlighted how the media could supplant as well as supplement collective discussion. The pioneer editors proffered 'equal free speech' but also cleaved to the liberal notion of press freedom as editorial autonomy, allowing the exertion of their own 'patriarchal influence' in determining what expression to include. The *Advertiser* opened its pages to debate while adding, 'We shall of course exercise our own discretion in the use of the materials'; the first *Herald* declared there would be 'careful surveillance' of contributions. The commitment remained to public deliberation but the balance between dissemination and dialogue, the choice of content and participants, was to be entrusted to editorial expertise and, at bottom, ownership prerogative. This represented both a limitation of discussion and a potential qualitative gain, in that a process of trustworthy selection, interpretation, and dissemination of information could serve the aspiration to be a cog in the 'machine' of enlightenment, a source for informed and coherent public opinion. This was not simply a European conceit: it was in a similar spirit that Māori-produced newspapers appeared from the 1860s, partly displacing direct dialogue but opening the door to knowledge, as one editor put it (Curnow 2002, p. 30). The ambiguous character of media persists. After the 2005 election the Māori party staged thirty hui, saying this represented a 'new style of politics', giving 'power to the people' by bringing them together and letting them have a say in the democratic process. But it took a party press release and media uptake for the suitably honed message to reach the rest of the *demos*.[5]

RE-MEDIATING NEW ZEALAND?

The 'genealogy' of New Zealand media yields a promise of public service in fostering deliberation and a dilemma of delivering on this commitment amid commercial, institutional, political, and technical pressures. How can it best provide a forum marshalling and reflecting differing views and expertise and generating a degree of consensus around the best outcome that represents and indeed sustains the political community? The detail of subsequent history lies outside this account, but major developments amplified the possibilities and problems. Most notably, the advent of broadcasting, first radio then television's dominance from the 1960s provided a vehicle particularly geared towards shaping and sustaining the identity of a national public, an important reason for the initial and continuing public ownership of what are now TVNZ and RNZ. Television's audio-visuality—its 'orality'—in many ways democratised access to information and experience, including bringing politics and politicians 'close up', but television also exacerbated media's monologic tendencies, lacked print literacy's ability to spur critical reflection, and always had to juggle public service and commercial objectives, being part-funded by advertising from the start. In addition, television oriented the media towards entertainment as much as news and information and over time towards news *as* entertainment (and vice versa), each contributing to the public's picture of the world and itself but in importantly different ways. The broader institutional, commercial and professional growth of the media, and to some extent political public relations, expanded the quantity of information and, given expert mediators, its quality; but it further distanced media discourse from grassroots input, and in commercial terms elevated audience and advertising maximisation and cost minimisation above wider goals, with market competition confused with information diversity.

More recently, of course, the major innovation has been digital technologies, with the Internet hailed by some as the new 'agora' for its online discussion forums and partial de-mediating of information. There is room only to remark that the Net's impact is hard to exaggerate but actually often is, with excessive claims for the demise of the nation–state and mainstream media, despite these still forming the basis for political affiliation and communication (for now at least). The Internet furnishes a world of facts but also embodies fiction, incoherence, and 'ghetto' deliberation: Babel as much as Pnyx. A more direct challenge for mainstream broadcast media is digital multichannel television's fragmenting of the audience and advertising market, although the full effects have been slow in reaching New Zealand and, as with the Net, can be overstated.

This rapid run-through shows the mainstream media as a public good experiencing successive changes and challenges rather than simple decline, clearly with parts too for variable performance and increased expectations. Across the range of news media, including the press and Internet, there remain resources for deliberation, but the pressing present challenge remains how to align a democratic role with an economic orientation reinforced by free market reforms including the restructuring of broadcasting in the late 1980s and 1990s and since marked by intensified commercial competition. Under the reforms TVNZ became subject to exacting commercial objectives in competition with TV3 and Sky, and less directly the deregulated broadcasting and press market came to be dominated by three major overseas groups. Economic constraints are a very real influence on media performance, with observable outcomes identified in the 'McDonaldisation' of television news and current affairs content (Atkinson 2004). At the same time, an 'economic approach' is inevitably ideological as well as practical, its sway depending in part on what society expects, because what it is possible to do is generally what it is possible to legitimise (in economic terms, credibility pays). The news media from its inception proclaimed the ability to foster public deliberation notwithstanding its commercial status, a purpose that legitimised its freedoms and still motivates conscientious journalists. Even if money talks loudest, public discussion *about* the media is not powerless to affect discourse *within* media, and can draw on the promise of service to the public—explicit and implicit, past and reiterated—as one resource in questioning the subordination of democratic to economic or other goals. Assuring media professionals and firms of their communicative obligations can help realign the balance between commercial and deliberative goals.

At the same time, it is hard to see how this can itself be an ideally free discussion, given that the main deliberative forum in which it might proceed is the media, reaching a judgment (public opinion) lacking expression apart from the media. A proposal to secure public access to private media, for instance, might struggle for a fair hearing. Moreover, the public is in a sense already partly 'de-liberated' in its judgment, in that advertising and ratings-talk position the audience on a daily basis as consumers rather than citizens. An analogous example is the use of the term 'shareholder value' to define the desired end in recent debates about TVNZ's identity crisis as public broadcaster and advertising-driven business—it appears to empower but in framing the public's self-image as that of individual shareholders prejudges the issue in favour of economic criteria. One response is to point out that the media is less of a unity than I have tended to portray, and *they* offer scope for differing individual views, but while critical voices filter into public debate this does not dissolve the disparities, still less prove the adequacy of deliberative conditions in general. 'Public opinion' is left needing an alternative embodiment to help secure those conditions—and the other public proxy is the democratic state.

The news media has a deep-seated resistance to governmental or legal intervention, its claim to freedom from external interest being rooted historically in opposition to censorship by the pre-democratic state and sustained by the need for independence as the public's watchdog on power. Today this is no straightforward matter, however. The media's rejection of external interest in effect includes freedom *from* the public except as individual consumers—it resists regulation by the organised public represented by the democratic state, yet it also relies on the state protecting its property rights against members of the public (or staff, the newsroom not being a democracy). It could also be said the news media *rests* on external interest in so far as it functions according to commercial imperatives logically external to its democratic function, making it a questionable watchdog on economic power. A democratic system of freedom of expression is therefore not one that excludes the state but a balance giving due regard to the potential of both government and media to serve and at times disserve the public interest. The Bill of Rights Act 1990 guarantees rights to free expression but subject to limitations 'demonstrably justified in a free and democratic society', and the real world of media is nowhere immune to legal limits and government policy. In New Zealand there have been around 2,000 media law cases over the past twenty years, and the Broadcasting Act 1989 makes all broadcasters subject to modest requirements of accuracy and balance through the Broadcasting Standards Authority, with additional rules for election campaign coverage. The state's media commitments include ownership but not direct control of TVNZ, and public funding of NZ On Air and Māori Television to address the failure of the market alone to satisfy local programming needs (buying overseas shows off the shelf costs a fraction of domestic production).

In this circumscribed way the state has an impact on the operation of the media, and concerns for public deliberation may suggest a case for further practical measures—making TVNZ (or TV One) non-commercial, imposing public service obligations on other broadcasters, and providing support for a range of diverse alternatives. However, such fundamental changes seem precluded by the current state of debate, reviving our problem of circularity, although official intervention can itself affect the terms of the debate, law and policy being not only of practical but also aspirational or exemplary effect. In this light the defence of public broadcasting takes on renewed relevance, contrary to its portrayal as an anomaly in a global, free-market, spectrum-rich media environment, because it makes a statement about what society expects from its media. The Labour government's introduction of the TVNZ Charter in 2003 represented a significant commitment to public service values as a yardstick for democratic media performance. The Charter characterised TVNZ's core role as that of a benchmark of quality, innovation, and integrity, its mission to provide a service that 'informs, entertains and educates', sustaining the public with 'shared experiences that contribute to a sense of citizenship and national identity', while ensuring a Māori voice and serving minority interests. Further objectives addressed the issue of public political deliberation more directly, requiring comprehensive news and current affairs coverage and programming that 'promotes informed and many-sided debate and stimulates critical thought' (TVNZ Charter 2003).

Aspiration does not equal achievement, and loosening of dividend expectations and limited 'Charter funding' did not resolve TVNZ's identity crisis; rather, it clarified the fact that it had one, as a public broadcaster and an advertising-driven, profit-conscious competitor in a deregulated market. This was confirmed by the calling of a select committee inquiry in late 2005 and TVNZ's chief executive resigning with the comment that advertising pressures made TV One's schedule increasingly 'incompatible with any recognisable model of public broadcasting'.[6] From an economic viewpoint, the Charter's social objectives were unrealistic, artificial impositions, but in 'public sphere' terms the Charter did not invent but simply made explicit the underlying media norms against which television's performance must be judged. From either perspective the Charter represented a contradiction, but whereas one side would see casting off the Charter as the solution, the other would argue that democracy demands imaginative institutional adaptation to realise Charter objectives. New Zealand lacks the resources to replicate that later British media tradition, the BBC, although the exemplary status of public broadcasting adds to the attractions of such a non-commercial 'full service' system compared to a 'market failure' model which yokes the image of public broadcasting to fringe programming. TVNZ itself points to the model of the Irish public broadcaster RTE, which serves a comparable population: TVNZ delivers a 9 per cent return and gets 90 per cent of revenue through advertising, RTE is not-for-profit and receives 58 per cent from advertising, due to licence fee income, meaning it carries half TVNZ's level of thirteen to fourteen advertising minutes per hour.[7] Easy solutions are unlikely, particularly given intensifying competition in a multi-channel market, but the poor showing of New Zealand's public broadcasting provision in international comparison suggests the availability of alternatives.

The Charter is routinely seen as TVNZ's particular concern. This overlooks the important point that its relevance is not only to TVNZ, however, but to the wider media realm, a core aim being the provision of a benchmark for others to emulate. The implied mechanism is the competitive advantage of quality, local programming but irrespective of this assumption, and TVNZ's variable actual performance, the Charter itself approximates to norms of public service applicable beyond publicly owned media. As such it arguably already represents a moral, if not enforceable, standard although the private media sector can tend to see public broadcasting less as an ethical benchmark than moral absolution from its own communicative obligations—serving democracy becomes someone else's problem. It is not unthinkable that a variation on the Charter could be imposed as a public service remit for private broadcasters, extending the scope of the Broadcasting Act; not least this would ease the competitive imbalance whereby TVNZ alone is 'hampered' by social objectives. Any such move would be resisted as political interference in 'media freedom', but this suggests how media's own use of the term tends to involve slippage between what might be called its 'democratic' and 'liberal' senses: between arguments in terms of enhancing public deliberation and those essentially concerned with property rights (or keeping the *demos* at bay). They are not always readily distinguished and both ask how far private companies have identifiable and possibly enforceable public responsibilities, but the answers will differ according to whether priorities are democratic or economic, with part of the challenge to have media order its priorities according to its status as part of democracy not just part of our shopping.

This was essentially the message of the High Court's ruling during the 2005 election campaign that the *TV3 Leaders' Debate*—the worm debate—should include two party leaders originally excluded from the line-up. The decision was criticised as an assault on media freedom, and certainly arguments oriented to improving deliberation were available, for instance that fewer speakers make for more intelligible debate. However, the strategy of TV3's owner Canwest was to insist on the key point being that as a private company it could not be held to be performing a 'public function' subject to review, its election programming a product like an electrician supplying a service. The judge disagreed, arguing that the court was justified in protecting the 'fundamental right of citizens in a democracy to be as well informed as possible before exercising their right to vote'.[8] TV3's strategy was partly directed by the exigencies of legal process, but in symbolic terms the court's ruling was a significant statement that a media born in New Zealand in 1840 proclaiming its public function was not to be readily relieved of the obligation a century and a half later.

BACK TO ATHENS

The message of Athens similarly concerned the importance of citizens in a democracy being well informed while emphasising that this came about by citizenship being exercised prior to voting through participation in the process of information exchange. Learning the first 'lesson'—the centrality of public deliberation to democracy—still leaves the problem of how the media best serves the cause of deliberation. Advocacy of deliberative democracy has contributed to a rise in face-to-face forums such as 'citizen's juries' as means to assist the political policy process, in New Zealand and elsewhere (see chapters 7.1, 7.4, and 7.5).

For instance, the select committee considering a possible review of constitutional arrangements called for deliberative procedures to be incorporated. To this extent deliberative democracy is a project of de-mediation, a return to Athens, yet clearly 'democracy without media' on a large scale is inconceivable, both because so much of our politics is communicated via the media and because any notion of democratic politics beyond small face-to-face communities must involve some medium. A question for mediated democracy is how far the dialogic conditions of the agora can or should be simulated, or whether public deliberation is better served by the media doing what it probably does best—dissemination more than dialogue, although dissemination that imagines its audience as partners in deliberation rather than as media 'currency'.

Existing forms of public access suggest the benefits and pitfalls, with newspaper letters columns, and more recently and conspicuously talkback radio, offering a space for grassroots opinion and sometimes diverse insights but one susceptible to appropriation by the immoderately and unrepresentatively opinionated which editorial intervention alternately invites and limits. Television's technical and institutional character—one-way communication driven by professional production values—aligns with the perceived pitfalls in leading to the 'agoraphobic' aversion to an unmediated public role noted earlier. TVNZ's Charter talked of 'enhancing opportunities for citizens to participate', but couched this in terms of empowering through information rather than granting direct access (although use of independent producers was urged in part to diversify viewpoints). In the event, however, TVNZ took its duty to encourage participation and 'many-sided debate' to justify including as Charter programming a series of prime-time studio debates, which provided an interesting if limited exercise in 'onscreen deliberation', akin to larger-scale experiments in the US and UK. *One News Insight* discussions of immigration, the family, the drinking age, and taxation accompanied *State of the Nation*, a live two-hour televised discussion of Māori–Pakeha 'race relations' involving 100 audience members taken as representative of the public. The format permitted a range of views to be expressed although the discussion was also subject to 'agoraphobic' constraints in having a presenter–moderator, video clips by co-presenters, phone-in polls, and multiple advertising breaks. These incursions can be criticised for curbing free discussion, as can structuring the discussion as a binary 'us and them' issue ('What do Māori *want?*'), but overall the programme confirmed the inherent problem of both widening debate and maintaining its ability to illuminate and advance the issue. Several members of the audience 'public' were actually prominent figures, unrepresentatively but usefully informed and articulate. While the expert did not inevitably provide superior insight to the non-expert, a speaker who fulminated that white people did not eat each other was cut short by presenter Anita McNaught saying 'that's not the kind of debate we want' (Phelan 2005, pp. 135, 142). Exclusion as well as inclusion, the trade-off between unity and diversity, or between free speech and a free-for-all, has always been a feature of democratic debate (ostracism was another term coined in ancient Greece).

Media controls, then, but also enables. Whatever the deliberative benefits or limitations of *State of the Nation* as a mini-agora, clearly they accrued only incidentally to participants, being intended more for the large viewing public as a means of providing a range of views on which to base their own discussions and judgments. The key contribution to public deliberation was the dissemination of dialogue, the potential strength of the media remaining primarily that of organising and packaging information and ideas so as to make them accessible to citizens at large. Even in Athens, 'people power' rested less on the opportunity for everyone to speak (5,000 Athenians × ten minutes each = thirty-five days) than securing the deliberative conditions most conducive to witnessing a diversity of viewpoints, a range of arguments, and the most useful and accurate information. Responsibility today falls on journalists and other media professionals to assist the democratic public through selection and explanation, as well as seeking to articulate public opinion; it today falls on policy-makers, media owners, and the public themselves. The example of Athens is a reminder that there is always scope for increasing public access and involvement, even if time and attention span are just two of the enemies of a fuller role for direct participation. Political deliberation takes place *within* the public of viewers and readers given suitable resources *as* viewers and readers: everyone 'talks television'. Deliberation as the considered judgment of pros and cons also ultimately takes place within the minds of the public, a process similarly enhanced by the provision of diverse viewpoints, credible information, and imaginative experience. The core material of democracy is political but reflecting the democratic community also implies extending the range of experience, whether through factual programming, drama or other means (a further reason for a 'full service' public broadcaster). The vision would be democracy and the media as a virtuous circle, an upward spiral in the quality of discourse as a deliberating public becomes more informed and discerning and the media respond. It's a dream, but not a new idea. Plato's philosophical successor Aristotle, in the book that coined the word 'politics', identified deliberation as its 'supreme element' and suggested there was a basis for workable government if suitable expertise and personal contemplation helped inform the people's voice of democracy (Aristotle 1988, p. 104).

DISCUSSION QUESTIONS

1 How does Athenian (or Aotearoan) 'democracy without media' compare to today's mediated democracy?
2 Why is public deliberation important in a democracy like New Zealand?
3 How do commercial pressures affect the operation of the 'public sphere'?
4 In what ways might the state legitimately intervene in the media realm?
5 What advantages and disadvantages can be claimed for the TVNZ Charter?

NOTES

1 *Holmes*, TV One, 12 August 2004.
2 www.fairfaxnz.co.nz/news/#ffxceo, accessed 20 April 2006.
3 *NZ Herald*, 7 November 2005.
4 Carlyle to Emerson, 2 July 1840.
5 Maori party press release, 11 October 2005.
6 *Herald*, Dec 13, 2005
7 TVNZ Annual Report 2005.
8 Dunne v Canwest TVWorks Ltd [2005] BCL 788.

REFERENCES

Aristotle 1995, *The Politics*, Cambridge University Press, Cambridge.

Atkinson J., 2004, 'Television', in J. Hayward & C. Rudd, *Political Communications in New Zealand*, Pearson, Auckland.

Carlyle, T. 1993, *On Heroes, Hero-Worship and the Heroic in History*, University of California Press, Los Angeles.

Colenso, W. 1890, *The Authentic and Genuine History of the Signing of the Treaty of Waitangi*, Wellington.

Curnow, J. 2002, 'A Brief History of Maori-Language Newspapers', in J. Curnow, N. Hopa, & J. McRae (eds), *Rere Atu, Taku Manu!*, Auckland University Press, Auckland.

Euripides 1988, *Suppliants*, Vol. 3, Harvard University Press, Cambridge Mass.

Habermas, J. 1989, *The Structural Transformation of the Public Sphere*, Polity, Cambridge.

Habermas, J. 1996, *Between Facts and Norms*, Polity, Cambridge.

Meiklejohn, G. 1953, *Early Conflicts of Press and Government*, Wilson and Horton, Auckland.

Phelan, S., J. Bernanke & S. Fountaine 2005, '"Heart to Heart on Race Relations": TVNZ's State of the Nation as Public Sphere Discourse', *Pacific Journalism Review*, 11/1, pp. 133–53.

Shortland, E. 2001, (1854), *Traditions and Superstitions of the New Zealanders*, Kiwi, Christchurch.

FURTHER READING

On democracy and the media generally:

Keane, J. 1991, *The Media and Democracy*, Polity, Cambridge.

Page, B. 1995, *Who Deliberates? Mass Media in Modern Democracy*, University of Chicago Press, Chicago.

Thompson, J.B. 1995, *The Media and Modernity*, Polity, Cambridge.

On New Zealand:

Comrie, M. & S. Fountaine 2005, 'Retrieving Public Service Broadcasting: Treading a Fine Line at TVNZ', *Media, Culture and Society*, 27/1, pp. 101–18.

Murdock, G. 1997, 'Public Broadcasting in Privatised Times: Rethinking the New Zealand Experiment', in P. Norris & J. Farnsworth (eds), *Keeping It Ours*, Christchurch.

Media Ownership and Control

Alan Cocker

A dramatic restructuring of media institutions has occurred globally since the 1980s. This was brought about in part by globalisation and new media technologies but most importantly by a major rethinking of public policy towards the sector. Governments throughout the world implemented neo-liberal or new right economic policies, the thrust of which was to create 'free market' conditions in all areas of economic activity. In the media, policies of deregulation led to the removal of government controls and restrictions, many of which had been implemented in the public interest to ensure a plurality of voices and sources in the media and to guard against the potential abuse of media power by monopolistic media owners. As a consequence of these policies of deregulation, far-reaching changes have occurred in media ownership and control. The theoretical blueprint for applying neo-liberal public policies to the media came largely from the USA. Although deregulatory change is most often associated with the USA and Britain, under prime minister Margaret Thatcher, New Zealand arguably went further in radically restructuring its broadcasting media according to the neo-liberal proscription.

Although the New Zealand government appeared to acknowledge the importance of media institutions in providing essential information to citizens and in the promotion of national identity and culture, the overwhelming focus of the new legislation was economic, concerned with deregulation and competition in the name of greater economic efficiency and the satisfaction of 'consumer' desires. This is an emphasis that gives secondary status to the media's political or cultural importance. It denies that media institutions have a distinct character that demands a differentiated and particular set of policies that take their political and cultural functions into account. In line with experience globally, deregulation and the application of market mechanisms and criteria have led to the almost complete dominance of commercially

452

driven broadcasting, and an accelerated trend of monopolisation, conglomeration, and overseas ownership in the print media industry.

The policy was driven by a belief that government intervention in the media industries had a negative economic impact. Intervention had included the mechanism of a Broadcasting Tribunal to police and impose standards on broadcasters by granting them warrants to broadcast that were renewable for fixed time periods. There was also public control over the rights to the radio frequency spectrum, legislation restraining levels of foreign and cross-media ownership, and other controls and regulations. These measures, policy advisers and ministers believed, had led to economic inefficiencies, restricted competition, hindered development, as well as slowing the introduction and adoption of new technologies. Freed of government supervision, the media businesses would be allowed to operate in an open and competitive market.

There is a certain irony in the move by politicians to lessen the government's involvement in the sector. The resources and effort that politicians and others now employ in 'news management' underscores the importance they place on their interaction with the media. They readily acknowledge the power of television to both inform and shape public opinion and set the agenda for political action. The shape of the election campaign, in particular, reflects the needs of the media, while its content is reflective of the politicians' understanding of how to pitch to a media audience—a television audience. Whether a potential leader is 'telegenic' and can 'handle the media' is now a fundamental factor when a political party makes its leadership choice. Political parties and their leaders rely on the media more heavily than in the past to reach individual citizens and cultivate or restore support for their policies. Decision-making always has one eye on the media, and is often based on 'how it will play in the media'.

If it is agreed that television and the other media institutions are critically important in the functioning and health of a democratic polity, then surely the pre-eminent task of media policy should be to ensure that the country's media meet the citizens' informational and cultural needs. A prescription for the nation's media institutions might include in-depth and impartial news and information coverage capable of supporting an informed public sphere. Our cultural rights may include the right to have our culture represented in national debate, and to have the diversity that exists within our society reflected in the media.

On the other hand, if media institutions are viewed purely as businesses operating in a free market, a number of the 'rights' we should expect from the media will not be forthcoming. The neo-liberal economic approach has presented an orthodoxy that insists that media policy must be assessed first and foremost in terms of its ability to match the subjective wants of consumers. According to this argument, consumers' interests can be measured simply in terms of their willingness to buy a newspaper or watch the programming offered on commercial television.

DEREGULATION OF BROADCASTING

As part of their agenda of neo-liberal reform, members of the fourth Labour government turned their attention to the institutions regulating broadcasting in New Zealand. In the first phase of reform, they sought to apply a 'more market' approach to the economy. In the second phase, beginning after their re-election in 1987, they sought to apply market reforms to government activities and enterprises. As part of this phase, public broadcasting was restructured into state-owned enterprises (SOEs). The Broadcasting Corporation of New Zealand (BCNZ) Restructuring Act 1988 disestablished the BCNZ and reorganised its constituent parts into two SOEs, Television New Zealand and Radio New Zealand.

The following year two key pieces of legislation, which determined the future development of the broadcasting sector, were enacted.

1. The Broadcasting Act 1989

The Act abolished the Broadcasting Tribunal, the regulatory body that had been responsible for issuing broadcasting warrants to operators and for monitoring their activities and quality of service. Broadcasters were to be freed from regulatory supervision by government-appointed bodies, except for the role of the new Broadcasting Standards Authority, which monitored standards of 'good taste and decency'. Although the general thrust of the legislation was to leave the sector's outcomes to be determined by the market, there was some recognition that this may not initially provide for all service needs. Therefore, the Broadcasting Act also established the Broadcasting Commission (New Zealand On Air) with the role of collecting the public broadcasting fee, and distributing its proceeds as grants to achieve certain social objectives in broadcasting. These were identified in s 36 of the Act in terms of three areas:

- to reflect and promote New Zealand identity and culture, including Māori language and culture
- to extend the coverage of television and radio signals to New Zealand communities that were commercially unattractive to private operators
- to ensure that a range of broadcasts was available to meet the needs of women, children, persons with disabilities, and minorities in the community, including ethnic minorities.

Although the New Zealand Broadcasting Commission was assigned the task of meeting these various social objectives, it was given very limited powers to achieve them. The final decision as to whether local, minority, or special interest programming is aired lies with the broadcaster, who has complete control over where the programme is placed, or, indeed, if it is played at all. An independent New Zealand programme producer must gain the agreement and interest of a broadcaster before the Broadcasting Commission will fund any proposal.

Over the first ten years of its existence the Broadcasting Commission, or, as it prefers to be known, New Zealand On Air, operated with the income from the public broadcasting fee. The fee was set in 1989 and was not adjusted from that point until its abolition, announced in mid 1999. At that point the government declared that, from the year 2000, New Zealand On Air would be funded from general taxation.

Operating within the constraints of its funding, New Zealand On Air sought to try and satisfy the demands from numerous supplicants: the independent television and radio production sector seeking programming finance; public radio; television operators seeking support for 'uncommercial production' and the extension of their coverage to regions not considered commercially viable; and community groups seeking to establish specialist or non-commercial radio and television stations. In general terms, New Zealand On Air has ignored funding requests from the last of these, seeing itself as assisting programmes on broadcasters with 'universal' coverage. The body has also identified its key role as 'presenting popular images of New Zealand for New Zealanders'. In determining its funding priorities, the first executive director saw the main goal in television as backing local mass audience programmes with prime-time potential, rather than highly specialist shows that few would watch. Minority and special interest programmes have struggled to find a place in the deregulated television market, while news and current affairs have become influenced by entertainment values.

2. Radiocommunications Act 1989

The second piece of legislation passed in 1989, the Radiocommunications Act, replaced the Broadcasting Tribunal's warrant system of regulating and allocating broadcasting frequency licences with a market-based system. The practical effect of this was that, except for portions of the spectrum reserved for specified uses, any broadcaster willing to pay the market price for licences could enter the industry. The Radiocommunications Act established tradeable property rights in the broadcasting spectrum. These are offered for sale to the highest bidder who then has rights for twenty years over those frequencies. The successful tenderer can use, sell, or lease this spectrum.

It is notable that the market in broadcasting spectrum in New Zealand is not constrained by any significant conditions or regulations governing the use of the frequencies whereas in Britain where a similar deregulatory thrust was experienced prospective tenderers still have to submit programme proposals and business plans to the public regulatory agency, the Independent Television Commission.

CROSS-MEDIA AND FOREIGN OWNERSHIP

Two other foundations of media regulation in New Zealand were dismantled as part of the new economic prescription. As part of the Broadcasting Act 1976, one of the functions of the Broadcasting Tribunal when determining broadcasting warrants was to consider 'the desirability of avoiding monopolies in the ownership or control of news media'. There was no such provision in the Broadcasting Act 1989, although mild restrictions on market dominance are contained in the Commerce Act 1986. The removal of specific regulatory supervision by the Broadcasting Tribunal in this area has seen the steady advance of cross-media ownership in this country.

Foreign ownership was also subject to regulation in the provisions of the News Media Ownership Act 1965, and the Overseas Investment Act 1973 and Regulations 1985. This legislation had been stringent in its restriction of overseas ownership of New Zealand media. Foreign investment in local broadcasting companies had been restricted to no more than 5 per cent until 1989, when this was lifted to 15 per cent. However, the collapse of TV3 in May 1990 and the inability to find a local investor saw the government remove all restrictions on foreign ownership in 1991. This enabled the Canadian company, Canwest, to take control of the country's first private television network, and opened the doors to foreign control of our major press, magazine, and commercial radio entities. For example, Canwest today operates the largest private free-to-air television channel (TV3) and, through its RadioWorks group, controls around half of the private radio market.

RETHINKING DEREGULATED BROADCASTING

In the decade of the 1990s New Zealand operated one of the most deregulated broadcasting environments in the world. A National-led government signalled to the Board of Television New Zealand in the middle of the decade that the next step was the privatisation of the state-owned enterprise and to prepare the organisation for sale. However, an incoming Labour administration in 1999 announced a policy shift away from the neo-liberal approach of privatisation and deregulation that successive governments had pursued since 1984. Labour's broadcasting policy acknowledged the cultural importance and democratic role of the medium and pledged not to sell TVNZ or any of its main constituent parts: TV1, TV2, and Broadcast Communications Ltd (BCL). Yet, although restructured as a Crown-owned company (CROC), TVNZ was still required to return a dividend to government and remained in essence a commercially driven broadcaster.

1. TVNZ Charter

The public service considerations were to be delivered principally through the introduction of a Charter. After much debate over its wording, the TVNZ Charter was formally implemented in March 2003. The first clause indicates a return to the language of public service television when it states that TVNZ shall 'feature programming across all genres that informs, entertains and educates New Zealand audiences'. However, the demands that TVNZ's commercial strength and profitability be maintained and the value of the government's asset not diminished have clearly been restraining factors limiting the changes ushered in by the Charter. An October 2005 memorandum written by TVNZ's then chief executive Ian Fraser to his board noted that, after more than two and a half years experience with the Charter, TVNZ had not measured any significant increase in viewer satisfaction—nor any marked public conviction—that the company was more of a public broadcaster than before it was introduced. He stated that the best TVNZ had managed to achieve under the new model was the 'pepper-potting' of some Charter programmes into the schedule. The outlook was that even this was not sustainable. As a result, the company would continue to give priority to commercially driven programmes that 'deliver maximum commercial value and maximum audience share and protect our channel shares from competitive erosion'.

2. Māori broadcasting

The relation between broadcasting, identity, and culture is at the cornerstone of the debate over the future role of Māori broadcasting. The fight for Māori broadcasting services saw Māori challenge the deregulation of broadcasting in New Zealand through the courts. The restructuring of the public radio and television services was stalled as Māori interests drew on the Treaty of Waitangi to claim a right to provision of services and spectrum to preserve their language and culture. Although they did not finally win their case on appeal to the Privy Council, they gained significant concessions and funding from the government. This led to the establishment of Te Mangai Paho, a Māori broadcasting funding agency under an amendment of the Broadcasting Act in 1993.

The first development phase of Māori broadcasting funded by Te Mangai Paho led to the establishment of twenty-five iwi (tribally)-based radio stations. The most successful of these is Auckland's Mai FM, which claims to be the city's leading youth station. However, some critics claim that this success is built on providing the largely imported cultural product of hip-hop, R & B and dance music to its young Polynesian audience at the expense of its role in promoting Māori language and culture.

With the establishment of iwi-based radio stations, attention then turned to a Māori television service, and in May 1996 an experimental Māori television service broadcasting with a low-power transmitter went to air in the Auckland area. However, Aotearoa Television Network ceased operations just over a year later after claims of financial impropriety concerning some of its directors. Seven years later a more securely resourced and national Māori Television channel was launched. In its first annual report released in November 2005, Māori Television claimed that over 90 per cent of its schedule was made up of locally made programmes and 71 per cent was in the Māori language. The chief executive of the channel stated that an obvious measure of viewer satisfaction was ratings. However, the figures cited were for monthly cumulative audiences, which measured only those who had tuned in at least once for that month. These figures were not comparable with the ratings used on other television services and the National party questioned whether, without comparative data, taxpayers would know whether they were receiving value for money out of their significant financial support for Māori Television.

3. Sky TV

One service that could claim to have grown from a very low base to securing around 20 per cent of all television viewing in New Zealand by 2005 was the subscriber satellite television operator Sky TV. After registering more than $230 million in losses since going to air in 1990, the service grew steadily to reach 600,000 subscriber households in 2005 and record its first profits. In November 2005 Sky announced that it had purchased New Zealand's third largest free-to-air television network, Prime Television. Controlled by media mogul Rupert Murdoch, Sky TV's dominance with its television set-top digital decoder raises the spectre that it could hold sway over the transmission and reception of digital television services.

RADIO OWNERSHIP AND CONTROL

Within five years of the passing of the legislation deregulating broadcasting, radio stations had increased in number three-fold. The key factor was the relatively low capital cost of establishing radio stations, compared to television. In 1989 there were sixty-four stations broadcasting separate programmes on a continuous basis; by late 1993 there were 170 radio stations and by the end of that decade over two hundred. Most of the new operators were operating on the favoured FM frequencies. Growth was greatest in the main metropolitan markets with twenty-four commercial stations in Auckland.

A highly competitive radio market developed, with a number of operators either failing or being taken over by larger competitors. The most prominent casualty was the publicly owned Radio New Zealand (RNZ). At the beginning of 1989 RNZ operated more than half of the radio stations in the country. By 1993 private operators owned three-quarters of the stations.

Although the number of stations in the market had increased dramatically, advertising revenue for radio was relatively static during this period. In March 1992 RNZ required a government rescue package worth $5.6 million to enable it to keep operating. As part of the rescue deal, the state-owned enterprise was restructured, with the three non-commercial divisions (National Radio, Concert FM, and RNZ News and Current Affairs) forming the wholly owned subsidiary, New Zealand Public Radio. In 1996 RNZ's commercial radio stations were sold to interests led and controlled by the Irish media magnate Tony O'Reilly, and they now operate as The Radio Network.

Other radio operators also found the deregulated market a very difficult environment. The increase in stations squeezed the revenue per station, and cost-cutting measures were implemented so they might survive. As part of this exercise on-station journalists were considered a disposable luxury. Independent Radio News, now also part of The Radio Network, supplies most of the commercial stations with news from a small centralised news operation. Another significant development has been the increase in 'networking', where radio programming originating in one centre is relayed to other stations through the country that are owned by the same operator. These stations play only a limited amount of their own locally produced material, or none at all. Where one company owns a number of stations in one market, the multiplex radio studio has been developed—a studio 'supermarket' where stations share staff, recordings, and facilities.

By 2006 the radio market had consolidated around two dominant overseas-controlled radio groups. The Radio Network (TRN) is jointly owned by an Australian arm of Tony O'Reilly's interests, APN News and Media (ANM), together with Clear Channel Communications of the USA. The other major operator dividing up the market is the Canadian-controlled Canwest group. Thus the radio 'market' since deregulation could be characterised as having passed through phases of rapid expansion, consolidation and then concentration or conglomeration. It is estimated that 90 per cent of New Zealanders listen to commercial radio and 90 per cent of that listening is to TRN or Canwest stations with the two groups roughly dividing this audience between them. Commercial radio's share of the advertising cake was 14 per cent or $250 million New Zealand dollars in 2004. This share is high by international comparison with the figures for Britain and Australia for the same year being 5 and 10 per cent respectively.

Although competing for the commercial radio audience, the two groups show the traits of operating as an oligopoly. They have formed an equal partnership in a radio-advertising agency, The Radio Bureau (TRB), which generates almost all of the large account radio revenue in New Zealand. Furthermore, the two companies are the predominant force in the radio industry lobby group, the Radio Broadcasters Association (RBA). The government has been effectively lobbied by this group on issues such as digital audio broadcasting policy, spectrum management, local content quotas, the possible expansion of public broadcasting and liberalising advertising restrictions, especially in the cases of alcohol and pharmaceutical advertising.

Despite the proliferation in the number of commercial radio stations, there has not been a corresponding expansion in the diversity of their output. There are two main categories of station: music stations playing popular music from the 1960s to the present day, with niche markets within this spectrum being catered for; and 'Newstalk' and talkback radio. A classical station supported by advertising was tried in the Auckland market but was not a success. Other forms of music or information radio are provided by public, access, or student radio. Clearly, without a public or non-commercial sector, the 'market' will leave a number of interests or needs from radio unsatisfied. In the political sphere, National Radio provides a depth of news coverage and analysis not found on any commercial service. Recognition that a purely market provision in radio would not provide the important services represented by the public radio networks, the National Programme, and Concert FM, has led the government to indicate its acceptance of their continuing role by granting them status under a more protective Public Radio Charter.

NEWSPAPER OWNERSHIP AND CONTROL

The New Zealand government has never channelled public funding in such a way as to ensure that a plurality of voices is represented in the press. In some European nations[1] public funding has been used to maintain a diverse newspaper structure by providing financial support to newspapers to ensure that a range of owners, ideological viewpoints, and social interests are able to exist in the publishing marketplace.

A degree of newspaper diversity occurred in the early colonial years in New Zealand, during an intense competitive struggle among newly established titles. Between 1860 and 1879, 181 newspapers[2] were founded in the colony, fuelled by a hunger for news as to what was happening in the other isolated settlements, and in the countries from where the colonists had recently emigrated. However, this phase of growth in the number of titles, and the competition between them, was short-lived. The establishment of the United Press Association in 1879 enabled a relatively inexpensive coverage of events in the country by providing 'pool' stories that all member newspapers had access to. But this also provided a barrier to entry for new titles, because they had to gain the approval of existing members of the Press Association before they could join. By the 1880s the Press Association newspapers had gained a long-term monopoly over news collection and dispersion. The established papers would only face competition among themselves, and they moved to lessen this by carving out provincial or city monopolies in either the morning or evening newspaper markets.

The 1880s to the 1980s was a period of relative stability for the New Zealand press. Local monopolies were further consolidated and newspaper companies generally refrained from encroaching on each other's interests. It was a 'free market', but not one characterised by open competition or diversity. The one attempt by an overseas press baron to buy a major local newspaper was successfully countered by the industry when it pressured the government to enact legislation to restrict overseas interest in the ownership of New Zealand news media.[3] Global trends were reflected locally with the steady demise of evening titles while morning papers were generally very profitable.

The 1980s brought momentous change for the press in this country. At the beginning of the decade the cosy understandings between regionally-based newspaper interests were shaken by competition to enter the electronic media sector. Two rival newspaper groupings, made up of alliances of most of the country's newspaper interests, emerged to pitch for New Zealand's first private enterprise television channel. The decade also saw the attempt by the owners of the *Auckland Star*, the failing evening paper in that city, to launch a morning paper in competition with the *New Zealand Herald*. The failure of a morning paper, the *Sun*, led to its owners Brierley Investments selling off all their publishing interests. This left two major press groups in the country, Wilson and Horton Ltd and Independent Newspapers Ltd (INL). The former were the owners of a number of provincial and suburban papers, and the *Herald*, the country's largest daily. INL had similarly taken over a number of provincial papers over the years, and also controlled a large number of suburban papers. This group's metropolitan papers are in Wellington and Christchurch. By 1991 INL controlled just over 50 per cent of newspaper circulation in New Zealand, and Wilson and Horton 32 per cent.

The deregulation of the broadcasting sector in this period also impacted on the press. The removal of foreign ownership regulations opened the door to foreign media owners. By the end of the 1990s the Wilson and Horton group was controlled by the interests of Irish media magnate Tony O'Reilly through the APN News & Media group (ANM) and had 43.8 per cent (2003) of the daily newspaper circulation. Its flagship title is the *New Zealand Herald* with the associated *Herald on Sunday* and it also publishes nine provincial daily newspapers. John Fairfax Holdings, the second largest newspaper publisher in Australia, bought INL newspapers in June 2003 to hold 47.4 per cent of the daily newspaper circulation in New Zealand. The main titles in this group are the *Dominion Post* in Wellington and *The Press* in Christchurch with the national Sunday papers the *Sunday Star-Times* and the *Sunday News*.

New Zealand's magazine market is also dominated by Australian interests. ACP Media, a company owned by Australia's Packer family, publishes over forty titles including *North and South* and *Metro*, giving the group a much greater presence in the magazine market than its two main competitors Fairfax and ANM.

THE NEW ERA

By the new millennium New Zealand's media institutions were characterised by a high degree of foreign ownership and control, limited diversity in ownership or content, and subject to the prime demand of profit generation in a commercially competitive market.

The shape and the nature of the media institutions have been fundamentally affected by government policies since 1984, which have been driven by a particular economic model. This economic policy blueprint was the touchstone against which the media institutions in public ownership were assessed, found wanting, and made to conform. However, at the beginning of the twenty-first century government policy has acknowledged that this model does not fully address the New Zealand public's needs as citizens rather than as consumers. The government has determined to retain a public radio and television component as part of this country's media mix, although it struggles to find a workable 'public service' prescription for public television.

The deregulation era for the media reflected a frame of reference that views all human activity through the narrow and exclusive lens of economics. Abstract economic ideas determine outcomes in core institutions that impact on social and political life. The neo-liberal economic schema followed in New Zealand since 1984 placed faith in the ability of largely unfettered market forces in the media to produce optimum societal benefits.

Another feature of this economic plan was the belief that a media market might operate beyond the regulation of the politicians. Yet right from the birth of mass media politicians have been notoriously sensitive to its content. The notion that governments might shed the responsibility for supervision of the sector is an absurdity. They may have relabelled their involvement, but the importance of the media to them ensures that they will continue to impose their will—either formally through policy-making and regulation, or informally by the techniques of news management and the wiles of their 'spin doctors'. Finally, the key outcomes of these economic policies have seen accelerated trends towards the aggregation of media in fewer hands and increased cross-media ownership and foreign control of New Zealand media. The new patterns of ownership and control raise questions relating to the adequate provision by the media for the social and cultural needs of New Zealanders as well as the impact on our democratic processes of a less diverse and plural media sector.

DISCUSSION QUESTIONS

1   In what ways are the media important for the functioning of a democratic state?
2   Consider the different roles of a media that serves our needs as consumers and one that serves our needs as citizens.
3   Consider whether more media necessarily means more diversity in media services.

4   For what reasons did the government in New Zealand deregulate broadcasting?
5   Does it matter that our media institutions are characterised by a high degree of foreign ownership and control?

NOTES

1   For example, Austria, France, Norway, and Sweden.
2   For an account of this period see Day (1990).
3   Lord Thomson, the Canadian newspaper magnate, was thwarted in his attempt to take over the *Dominion* newspaper by the passing of the News Media Ownership Act 1965.

FURTHER READING

Day, P. 2000, *Voice and Vision: A History of Broadcasting in New Zealand*, Volume 2, Auckland University Press, Auckland.

Mulgan, R. (with P. Aimer) 2004, *Politics in New Zealand*, 3rd edn, Auckland University Press, Auckland.

New Zealand On Air website, www.nzonair.govt.nz

Rosenberg, B. 2004, *News Media Ownership in New Zealand*, <canterbury.cyberspace.org.nz/community/CAFCA/publications/Miscellaneous/mediaown.pdf

Politics of Spin

Joe Atkinson

The concept of 'spin' is ubiquitous in the news and entertainment media these days, but its meaning blurs as the diversifying perspectives of its users stretch the core notion to incorporate both old and new activities, mainly in order to de-legitimise them. The original notion identifies a subset of political public relations (PR) dealing with the management of political messages (and public impressions) at the interface of politics and journalism. But political spinning is not 'a coherent, homogeneous [industry] geared to a single goal' (Louw 2005, p. 298). Its practitioners ('spin doctors') are both disparate from, and competitive with, each another. A partial listing of roles within the wider 'spin industry' would include public relations advisers, mass marketers, opinion pollsters, focus group researchers, targeted mass mailers, media-trainers, legislative lobbyists, campaign managers, corporate advertising executives, celebrity publicists, and speech-writers. Whatever its constituency, however, the term 'spin' is consistently pejorative, connoting 'spinning yarns,' weaving webs of deceit, hyping, deflecting, leaking, planting and concealing.

The 'demonisation' of spin has distinctly equivocal origins.[1] Ostensibly a journalistic reaction to the external political environment (e.g., neo-liberal policy-making, campaign professionalisation, populist scandal-mongering and information management) it does double duty as a coping response for difficult industrial conditions: multimedia convergence, hyper-competition, accelerated news cycles, fragmented news audiences, and understaffed newsrooms. Its industrial function is almost never acknowledged, however, for that would underscore the extent to which journalists are co-opted into a symbiotic relationship with the politicians and spin doctors upon whom they depend as sources, and whose efforts are intended to furnish precisely those stories the commercialised media are willing to cover. Deeper self-reflection might also induce news producers to acknowledge the degree to which their own media antics resemble—sometimes to the point of caricature—those they so patronisingly disdain.

NEWS DISDAIN

Mark Levy (1981) was the first to note a new kind of 'strategic ritual' performed by journalists under competitive pressure to accept 'tainted' (i.e., spin doctored) news. He saw a growing tendency for professional norms of newsworthiness to be challenged by 'soft news' coverage of celebrities, by stereotyped reporting of diplomatic summits, and by stage-managed 'pseudo-events' such as campaign walkabouts, party conventions, and candidate press conferences. When commercial rivalry urged publication of 'tainted' news, journalists tried to reassert their professional autonomy by rhetorically distancing themselves from the 'tainted' item. Although such journalistic responses could be 'highly critical, scornful, or derisive', they were much more likely to offer exculpatory explanations or apologies, or to invoke 'a comic or mocking tone … to suggest the offense is relatively trivial' (Levy 1981, p. 29).

Since Levy's groundbreaking article, the 'autonomy and relevance of professional journalism's training, ethics, and truth claims' (Altheide 2004, p. 295) have been significantly compromised by media logics developed in the face of over-the-shoulder competition between news organisations, channel fragmentation, shrinking audiences for conventional news formats, and newsroom cutbacks. The advent of 'a less top-down news order, and a more distributed information system' has produced 'a feedback system that pushes tawdry stories into competing channels' and induces even serious-minded news executives to fall into line (Bennett 2003, p. 133).

The epistemology of tabloid news differs from that of serious investigatory journalism in prizing 'juicy' stories over verified truth or social significance. This overrides routine processes of 'scientific' journalism: checking source credibility, weighing evidence, seeking balance, and so on (Ettema & Glasser 1985, pp. 192–201). Thus, whereas Levy (1981, p. 31) saw news disdain as 'by and large conservative behaviour, reinforcing existing rules for newswork', its contemporary modes are more cavalier about standards of balance, fairness, and accuracy.

Tabloid journalism and news disdain thrive under social conditions that also encourage political populism; that is, 'in times of increased competition in the news industry as well as in times of rapid social change' (Ehrlich 1996, p. 2). Irony and disdain are standard tabloid devices for elevating presenters, journalists, and viewers 'into a position of "ironic knowingness", superior to the stories themselves and safely detached from their more sordid aspects' (Ehrlich 1996, p. 6). Savvy talk about politics slips easily across the ill-defined border between serious and popular journalism, particularly in relation to strategy and horse-race coverage of elections, as Louw (2005, p. 69) elaborates:

[B]ecause the strategic interpretive frame is premised on the sports model, it encodes the (unjustified) assumption that winning the game is the (only?) motivation driving politicians ... This slides easily into the watchdog notion of journalism—providing journalists with a justification for mistrusting politicians; reaffirming their need to adopt adversarial postures towards politicians; and boosting journalists' egos because they see themselves as the defenders of democracy against Machiavellian politicians. This causes the journalists to become patronising towards their audiences because they believe they have special insight into the political process and the motivations of politicians.

Campaign news and current affairs stories thus mix extreme cynicism about politicians and public officials with utopian or fantasised views of the media as fearless 'watchdogs' hounding the powerful: as 'inside dopesters', guardians of truth and justice, infallible spin-detectors, duty-bound to intervene in the political process against politicians and their spin doctors on behalf of a gullible public (Nimmo and Combs 1990, p. 226). These Manichaean perspectives hide a more convoluted political reality that the triangular relationship between journalists, spin doctors, and politicians is basically symbiotic and co-dependent. Neither genuine 'political insiders nor fully in control of the story-telling process', serious journalists cannot do without source collaboration (Louw 2005, p. 90). The conventional 'watchdog' notion of journalist autonomy misconstrues even serious newswork practice. Lacking independent power 'to make policy or allocate resources' and yet well positioned to embarrass those with such power, the media opt for negative tactics: seeking 'to frighten politicians and to mobilize "moral panics" and "groundswells of hostility" to policies.'

An irony of the negotiated relationship between journalists and their sources is that it is largely opposition politicians, especially minor party populists—in temporary alliance with scandal-mongering media due to their mutual need to discredit the ruling bloc—who drip-feed most of the anti-spin stories. Since politicians are both the most prolific producers of spin and its most energetic critics, under-resourced journalists learn to survive, first by repurposing opposition meta-spin, and second by deriding the sources they are both beholden to and expected to hold accountable.

Misgivings about over-reliance on some politicians thus transmutes into ostentatious moralising about the deviousness of others and, implicitly, of all politicians. The extension to all political news of a strategic ritual, initially developed to indicate scepticism about specific and transparent instances of 'tainted' news, is facilitated by the cynical but productive assumption that everything democratic politicians and their attendant minions do is *ipso facto* dishonest. While some journalists readily confess their reluctance to report about political PR professionals in a 'neutral and educational way' and their tendency 'to use the term spin doctor indiscriminately to demonise any kind of professional PR' (Esser et al. 2002, pp. 39–40), others wrap themselves in a protective cocoon of self-aggrandising myths. The performative character of the journalism in question, as distinct from the amount of spin faced, is one factor affecting the perceived need for self-protection.

SPIN IN NEW ZEALAND

With one notable exception (Esser et al. 2005), recent scholarly accounts of demonised spin focus on British and North American cases to the exclusion of smaller and more egalitarian polities (such as New Zealand or Sweden). McNair's (2004) assessment of British anti-spin journalism, for example, is preoccupied with the activities of a landslide majority government on a war footing, within an authoritarian culture and class system and a two-and-a-half-party electoral system which produces strong but relatively inaccessible executives, and which confronts an aggressively competitive and diverse but centralised media system predisposed to cynicism by a long and tawdry history of official secrecy.

Even under these more extreme circumstances, spin journalism displays tabloid propensities. McNair (2004, p. 333) concedes that British journalism is 'at times … alarmist and self-righteous in counter-posing the class of selfish, self-interested spin doctors with the noble, disinterested journalists (who are sometimes reluctant to concede that they have always found much of what spin doctors do immensely useful to their work)'. In Blairite Britain, however, McNair sees 'a clear public interest in alerting potential voters to the fact that political rhetoric [is] rarely the same thing as political reality' (2004, p. 333). Similarly, in Bushite America, it could be argued 'that if the story is important, a little [media feeding] frenzy becomes a good thing' (Bennett 2003, p. 132; Sabato 1993, p. 6). But since when did democratic voters ever trust their politicians to speak unvarnished truths? And are media feeding frenzies more likely to deter than incite unjustified foreign policy adventures? In New Zealand, moreover, 'a quiet little country where genuine news is often lacking, [where] the media are forever rushing to attach the "-gate" suffix to relatively minor incidents', and where politicians are often 'caught up in scandals that would not make it past breakfast in other countries' (Dusevic 2005, p. 16), the case for either counter-spin or feeding frenzy is much weaker.

Prime Minister Helen Clark wisely resisted pressure to join the Iraq invasion, and 'most government leaders would die for her approval, competence and preferred prime minister ratings' (James 2005). In a recent survey (Ellis 2005), half of New Zealand gallery correspondents recorded positive relations with Prime Minister Clark and her cabinet ministers, with all the rest recording neutral relations (and none negative). This reinforces Clark's reputation as one of the democratic world's most approachable and candid leaders. Her long-time television trainer, Dr Brian Edwards, tells his clients 'to be straightforward, truthful and admit any mistakes', counselling those 'who can't tell the truth or find their position indefensible' to turn down all requests for interviews. 'Spin, if it means the distortion of the truth', he claims, 'doesn't work and it's not what we do' (Bland 2005).

Clark continues to accept this kind of advice and to conduct personally weekly televised prime ministerial press conferences, and more frequent radio interviews. She also makes herself freely available to journalists for one-on-one interviews and informal meetings. One quarter of the press gallery respondents reported regular interviews with Clark, while 60 per cent had occasional sessions. Less than a fifth said they were restricted to formal contacts via press secretary, press conference, or press release. Finally, while 57 per cent of gallery respondents agreed with the survey's suggestion that the media were 'manipulated' by the government, a full third concurred with the opposing suggestion that the government was 'at the mercy of the media' (Ellis 2005).

By the testimony of New Zealand's elite corps of political journalists, therefore, New Zealand political principals—up to and including the prime minister—look exceptionally accessible. Other survey evidence confirms a healthy balance of power between government and media. One respondent interviewed at length by Ellis (2005, p. 10), underscored this relatively benign view of politicians with empathy for politicians' increasing suspicion of journalists:

> As a generalisation I think politicians are more wary and perhaps less trusting of journalists than they were. One of the factors affecting that is a steady lowering of the threshold of what constitutes a story, especially a moral story or scandal. I think it is an effect of the increasingly competitive nature of the news media combined with an increasingly competitive political environment. It is all the more intriguing because while society's morals that apply to politicians are tightening, society's morals, generally speaking, become more liberal.

Implicit in both this comment and the Press Gallery survey data is a view of political spin as a reaction to scandal journalism. The critical literature on political communication also permits this interpretation (Cottle 2003; Louw 2005; Lloyd 2004; Meyer 2004; McNair 2004). This is hardly a new conclusion, for as Entman (1989, p. 20) observed of US media politics sixteen years ago:

> Elites who want to succeed politically cannot afford to debate complicated truths in a marketplace of ideas. Nor can officials volunteer information for the public to use in holding them to account, in the naïve faith ordinary people will understand the complexities. If politicians do make a mistake, their competitors will almost certainly pounce and seize the advantage. So news organizations wind up depending upon elites whose primary goal when talking to reporters is to manage publicity rather than illuminate truth ... the media system encourages elites to fashion rhetoric and to take actions that accord with journalistic values and limitations rather than with responsive public policy.

The theoretically independent institutions of politics and the media have since become even more intricately enmeshed in each other's routines and practices, and the boundaries between journalism, politics, and public relations have grown even more opaque (Esser et al. 2001, p. 22).

JOURNALISTS AS SPINNERS

Spin is not just something being done to journalists by politicians, because roughly equivalent procedures are followed on both sides. The prevalence of 'pack journalism', for instance, helps to explain why politicians feel the need to spin in the first place. Furthermore, the dogmas of 'press freedom' make journalists, if anything, more impervious than politicians to calls for public accountability. On the use of confidential sources, for instance, Tiffen (2005, p. 7) writes:

> Journalists are the most ardent proponents of Brandeis's view that the best disinfectant is sunlight. Nevertheless, while deploring others' secrecy and its social costs, they insist that the secrecy surrounding their interactions with sources is essential to their work, and greatly enhances the public's knowledge and hence the quality of democracy. However, there is no reason to think that journalistic transactions alone are immune from the pitfalls and abuses which attend secrecy in other areas of social and political life.

Spin instruments are stitched deeply into television newswork practice. Much of what television does is concealed from audiences to achieve a seamless sheen of professionalism. The front-stage antics of presenters are scripted and auto-cued to convey spontaneity and friendliness. Comparable modes of relaxed informality are unattainable by politicians without comparable training and preparation, but where evidence of media training is taken to signify evasion and held up as a pretext for attack interviewing, politicians work at a distinct disadvantage.

While trumpeting the hostility and power of politicians, broadcasting journalists are more reticent about their own manipulations. The standard television practice of pre-recording video interviews to produce edited soundbites that confirm a (usually predetermined) story line, for example, is heavily biased against considered viewpoints and iterative elaboration of the kind favoured by experts, intellectuals, or subject specialists. Those who submit themselves to pre-recorded interviews do so at a clear disadvantage. Repeat soundbitees implicitly accept their views will be misrepresented, if only by decontextualisation. 'Story of the day' spin techniques represent a counteractive response by politicians faced with an invidious choice between media disdain for spinning and public invisibility.

'Source professionalization' (Blumler & Kavanagh 1999) and the associated habits of defence and control that politicians build around their public appearances, are merely sensible coping responses. If both the relevant critical literature and New Zealand journalists working closest to the political coalface support this account of spin, and if the New Zealand political culture is relatively free of it anyway, what prompts Edwards to describe New Zealand broadcasting as harbouring 'the most aggressive, rude and disruptive interviewers in the world' (Bland 2005), and why was New Zealand television coverage of the 2002 election campaign so widely lambasted by academic observers (Atkinson 2004; Bale 2003; Church 2004)?

THE NEW ZEALAND TELEVISION CAMPAIGN

Given its relatively benign political circumstances and unusually open government, New Zealand's 2002 television campaign was exceptionally combative, even by the adversarial standards of contemporary Britain. Preliminary data from the University of Auckland's Marsden-funded content analysis of 2002 campaign coverage confirm that 70 per cent of all television debate sections were 'often interrupted,' and that 76 per cent of moderator interjections were of a sceptical or cynical nature. Media cynicism was prevalent in campaign news coverage as well, with 40 per cent of all political news items featuring media mockery and/or cynicism directed at politicians (with half of these items featuring both). Furthermore, this mockery and cynicism was most frequent in news items dealing with issues of strategy or campaigning rather than policy—in other words, it focused on party leaders' spin.

A *cause célèbre* of the 2002 campaign was the so-called 'Corngate' interview of Prime Minister Helen Clark by TV3's John Campbell. The interview was occasioned by *Seeds of Distrust*, a book by journalist Nicky Hager claiming a government cover-up of a release of contaminated corn. The interview was conducted on the day *before* the book was publicly released, so that Clark was questioned without an opportunity to read it. When an edited version of the pre-recorded interview was broadcast the following evening, it was preceded by an eleven-minute documentary supplying a racy and melodramatic summary of Hager's dubious claims.[2] Without knowledge of the book or the preceding documentary, and given only a vague and misleading idea of what she would be asked, Clark was seriously under-briefed. She was then questioned at length on a specific event of some scientific complexity that had occurred almost two years previously and occupied a policy field where she was not the responsible minister. This carefully staged ambush was clearly predicated on the presumption of spin. When Clark avowed herself unable to recall details of the case, for instance, Campbell countered 'I think you *do* remember' and persevered with his remorseless line of questioning. Following the election, the Broadcasting Standards Authority (BSA) found the programme lacked accuracy, balance, fairness, impartiality, and objectivity (Vowles et al. 2004). Rather than accepting accountability, both Campbell and TV3 head of news and current affairs, Mark Jennings, were adamantly unrepentant and disdainful of the BSA.

The cynical and mocking character of New Zealand anti-spin discourse is further illustrated by post-mortem commentary on one of the milder and more policy-oriented debates of the television campaign: the second TV3 debate between the two major party leaders, Bill English and Helen Clark, and moderated by John Campbell. To exemplify the carnivalesque tone of Campbell's approach, here is a typically flamboyant provocation to English on why he was lagging in the polls: 'You never took it on the chin. You were sent to do time out by the country. You know when a naughty boy does time out, the only way they can get out of their bedroom is to apologise to Mum and Dad. Ya never did! Ya should've!'

The debate concluded with a panel discussion between 'a trio of senior journalists': TV3's political editor Jane Young, *Dominion-Post* television critic, Jane Bowron, and *Listener* editor Finlay Macdonald, chaired by Campbell. An excerpt illustrates the patronising 'inside dopester' tone often evident when backstage journalistic gossip moves frontstage (Carpignano et al. 1990). An emphasis on spin tactics is notable, as is Campbell's disappointed expectation of a post-Corngate retaliation from Clark:

Bowron:	I thought it was incredibly disappointing because we didn't get to see Helen Clark savage you, you know, 'the little creep'. (Clark's angry description of John Campbell after the 'Corngate' interview).
Campbell:	Yeah, I was ready to cop it like a chook in the interests of democracy Jane, I was.
Bowron:	Yeah, and it didn't happen. No, she was incredibly sweet and statesmanlike and just kept her cool and you were I thought just slightly harder on Bill English … Come on this was what all New Zealand was waiting for tonight was that to happen, and it didn't happen.
Macdonald:	Yeah, John [Campbell], you failed man.
Campbell:	Yeah, yeah, yeah.
Macdonald:	Bummer!
Campbell:	Why didn't she have a go at me fafa Finlay [Macdonald], have you got a theory about that?
Macdonald:	If I were her media minder, if I were a spin doctor, god forbid, I would have had her on autopilot as regal, composed, dignified and pleasant, and I think that's what she [inaudible].
Campbell [interrupting]:	And did she achieve that tonight?
Macdonald:	Very much, yeah! […]

Campbell
[interrupting]: I have to say, when I look at the Nats campaign, they're so sort of nonchalant in some respects that I wonder if they somehow forgot that the election comes around every three years, and you knooow?

Young: Well this one didn't, it took them quite by surprise.

Bowron: He [English] was more subdued too. He'd lost that vaguely hooligan attitude that he had earlier in the week with [TV1's Paul] Holmes.

Campbell: He [English] tried aggression didn't he? He tried aggression with Holmes as we all would wouldn't we when confronted by Holmes? [laughter]

Bowron: Yes, he was much softer.

Young: I tell you though, that was also a lesson that they would have seen this come through in the [negative] type of advertising. That the derogatory, the negative and the aggressive just does not go down well. People don't want to be shouted at and we've had I think in all of the debates in this campaign we have had times when the shouting has been to such a degree you've got no idea what on earth is going on. You hear nothing, you see nothing and all you have is the … every now and then you might pick up some little, you know, quick one-liner to the side …

Notable in this exchange (and in other journalist discourses scattered throughout the 2002 campaign) is the uncritical approval of Campbell's stagey and self-centred performance and the contrastingly cynical disdain for politicians' quieter accomplishments. Since the media's role in the 'hear nothing … see nothing' outcomes described by Young was unexamined, the impression was left open that the politicians were the main offenders. As detailed elsewhere, however, their differential treatment did not reflect their behaviour. A 'bad faith' model of politicians also prevailed on TV1's Sunday current affairs programme, where presenter Mike Hosking urged spin panellists to satirise campaigning candidates, ramped up conflict in the Law & Order and Post-Election specials with hectoring, quick-fire questioning, and then tried to hold party leaders responsible for outcomes that were mostly due to his own behaviour and the condensed format of his show. Demonisation of spin was evident in Hosking's belief that any hesitation in answering one of his questions—even if it was incomplete, being talked over, or otherwise unclear—signified deliberate avoidance (Atkinson 2004).

As the foregoing examples suggest, in the 2002 election campaign New Zealand television interviewers, debate moderators and postmortem panellists acted in ways they roundly condemned in theory. By a curious process of inversion, savvy talk about spin was transmuted into a cynical rejection of any serious form of political speech, and thus of the very political engagement it purported to uphold.

EPISTEMOLOGY OF SPIN

A recent *New Zealand Listener* cover story on 'The Spin Slayers: The Tricks and Tactics of Getting Honest Answers from Politicians' (Black 2005) confirms that the empathy for politicians shown by working Press Gallery journalists, is not replicated by their more performance-oriented colleagues, such as radio and television current affairs interviewers. The high-profile New Zealand broadcasters interviewed by the *Listener* during the 2005 election reaffirmed the 'bad faith' mantra of the 2002 television debates, by assuming that:

- Any power imbalance between journalists and politicians works invariably in favour of the latter.
- No causal relationship holds between the media's standard operating procedures and the politicians' apparent coping responses.
- Apparent attempts by politicians to redress an imbalance of power they see as working against them are abuses of power rather than admissions of weakness.

National Radio's Morning Report co-presenter Sean Plunket occupies a pivotal position in the New Zealand media. Together with the major urban dailies, but in the absence of a nationwide newspaper, his morning radio programme helps to set the news agenda for the daily and evening radio and television bulletins. Despite his status as a senior public service broadcaster, Plunket's favoured 'bulldog' style of political interviewing entails, as one observer notes, 'not letting people finish and automatically assuming they are liars' (Judy McGregor, quoted in Black 2005). Yet his incongruous self-image is that of a neutral conduit of information for an active and powerful audience:

> I don't think I'm powerful as an individual. I might conduct an interview which contains information that radically alters something in New Zealand society or a view of some political party or affect the outcome of an election, and I guess you hope that every interview in a small way does do that, but that's not my power, that's the power of information. The other power Morning Report has is its listenership …

But when Plunket is challenged about treating politicians more harshly than other interview subjects, he resorts to a crude watchdog saga where savvy journalism sometimes prevails over devious and better-resourced politicians:

> The politicians have planned everything. They work out their strategies and what to expect and how to respond to such-and-such, but there's still the possibility of

> tripping … Politicians have hundreds of thousands, if not millions of taxpayer dollars to speak to the public. Every MP has a budget to send out what the Attorney-General (sic) rightly recognises as ill-disguised political statements. We're a public broadcaster … and maybe our job is to redress that balance. It's definitely not to duplicate.

Either the denial of personal power, or the watchdog turn, could supply useful escape clauses for otherwise culpable behaviour, but together they are simply contradictory. Furthermore, Plunket fails to take account of qualifying counter-arguments: that interview planning is both mutual and justifiable, that some government persuasion is necessary and legitimate, that advertising is a poor substitute for balanced news coverage, and that the Auditor-General's critique is limited to specific instances. All of his fellow broadcasters offered similar responses: deflecting implied criticism by ascribing primary responsibility to others—politicians, audiences, or other media—anyone, it would seem, other than themselves.

Thus, the doyen of New Zealand radio and television interviewers, Kim Hill, finessed any personal complicity by highlighting extreme examples and blaming audience bias. Incredulous that a politician once termed her 'the single most important force in the media for bringing down the New Zealand economy', she implied that criticism and praise were both tainted and thus extraneous to her performance: 'Practically every interview I do with any heat in it half the people will say, "Ah, you lost that one, you nasty bitch" and the other half say, "Good on ya, you got them" and I'm thinking, "Was I there?"'

The other radio and television broadcasters interviewed were equally impenitent and oblivious to counter arguments: the fact that faster news cycles, to say nothing of ambush interview techniques, make adequate briefing increasingly problematic; or that information overload and the growing complexity of modern government make it unavoidable; or that rigid time constraints are imposed by media and advertisers, not by politicians. The demonology of venal and power-hungry politicians brought down by brave and selfless servants of the people was virtually impregnable.

DEMOCRATIC IMPLICATIONS

Is political spin really the grave threat to democracy that populist or tabloid journalism would have us believe, or is spin journalism more a matter of backstage gossip moving frontstage to fill new commentary spaces created by channel proliferation? The latter interpretation gains credence from our evidence that performative journalists are comparatively rabid demonisers, whereas their backstage colleagues are more inclined to regard spin as a minor inconvenience. The main difference between the two groups is that celebrity broadcasters are more in the public eye whereas other working journalists work mostly behind the scenes—having as a consequence, less need for self-protective myth-making as well as fewer opportunities for self-aggrandising showmanship. In ironic mimicry of the politicians they demonise, broadcaster interviewers, debate moderators, and panelists melodramatise their private selves when they go onstage.

Striking similarities in the working procedures of media and political institutions also suggest: a) that journalists are not as powerless or under-resourced as their frontstage colleagues claim; b) that restraints on journalistic autonomy are scarcely greater than parallel restraints on politicians; and c) that such restraints are only distantly related, if at all, to political spin doctoring. To the extent that it exists, spin is a counter-reaction to the growing centrality of the media in political communication and the related expansion of democratic accountability and transparency: the growing accessibility of political actors to public scrutiny; more conditional media access; less deferent, more anti-authoritarian popular cultures; more hypercompetitive and extensive public attention markets; shorter electoral tenures and policy cycles; more fragmented parties and multi-party governments; and a loss of political and national power to global capitalism.

If disdain of 'spin' and 'spin doctors' is indeed, as argued here, the favoured rhetorical device to restore, defend, or distract attention away from the news media's diminishing independence and legitimacy by demonising the media manipulators on which cut-price commercial journalism is forced to depend, then the complaint seems both disproportionate to the offence, and ill-suited for its repair. Particularly where, as in New Zealand, the purported offence is relatively slight, spin demonisation is likely to be counterproductive in displacing genuinely useful democratic discourse. By elevating the concerns of the bored and indifferent, the attendant convoy of 'worms', spin panels, and focus groups lines up formulaic villains for ceremonial roasting, while promoting the plebiscitary myths of the professional marketers it makes such a public show of spurning. The associated cult of spontaneity—evident in quick-fire debate formats and ambush interviews—elevates top-of-the-head preferences and knee-jerk reactions over more stable partisan viewpoints or well-considered political responses.

In short, recent antipodean modes of spin demonisation represent a form of journalistic theatre involving 'laddish' culture and associated rhetorics of selfishness and *faux* anti-elitism. The attitudes and priorities of television journalists, as evident in both the 2002 campaign and 2005 *Listener* interviews, are incompatible with any liberal democratic notion of 'principled autonomy' involving the giving of reasons in public (O'Neill 2002, p. 19). They are largely congruent, however, with paternalist neo-liberal conceptions of individualised autonomy that privilege self-expression and privatise communicative action by reducing public debate to 'argument-free acclamation' (Barnett 2003, p. 200).

DISCUSSION QUESTIONS

1   How faithfully does New Zealand news coverage of elections reflect the efforts of party sources, and how much does it reflect the efforts of journalists and the news media?

2   What range of factors influence negotiated relationships between journalists and political sources? Which of these factors affect both journalists and their sources, and which tend to be exclusive to one rather than the other?

3   In what ways is the relationship between journalists and political sources mutual and cooperative, and in what ways is it rival and conflictual? What political circumstances tend to encourage cooperation or conflict?

4   In what ways do the news media operate as unified institutions with goals opposed to democracy, and in what ways and with what effects do the various branches of the media differ in terms of both goals and operating procedures?

5   Discuss the proposition that the term 'spin doctor' is used in a one-sided and problematic way when it is used to discredit the legitimate interests of politicians, parties, and governments in asserting themselves against an autonomous and powerful journalism with its own self-interested agenda and at variance with the public welfare.

NOTES

1   De Luca and Buell (2005, p. 4) define demonisation as 'use of language or symbols ... to strongly imply or directly suggest others have very bad, immoral, or evil qualities ... [and] to do so without sufficient evidence, inquiry, justification, or consideration of the consequences'.

2   One issue in dispute concerned the meaning of 'statistical confidence'. New Zealand has a policy of zero-tolerance for GM content as determined by statistical tests with a .05 (5 per cent) confidence level. The stringency of the test (its confidence level) is determined by the consequences of error. A higher confidence level of 1 per cent is common for life-critical products such as pharmaceuticals or aircraft parts, but New Zealand's 5 per cent level was an atypically stringent test for GM corn. A confidence level (or interval, or threshold) represents the extent to which a sample can be relied on to accurately represent the batch from which it was taken. Thus a 0.05 per cent confidence level means there is a 5 per cent chance that a result is incorrect; that is, that it is a false positive (saying something is there when it's not) or a miss (saying something is not there when it is there). The only way to achieve 100 per cent confidence is by testing the whole batch (which in this case would destroy all the corn seed). Hager and Campbell shared the misconception that a test showing a (false) positive with a 5 per cent confidence level meant 5 per cent of the sample was contaminated, which they extrapolated to tens of thousands of corn plants being grown and harvested. Campbell mistook a 5 per cent confidence level to mean 'up to 5 per cent' contamination was possible. It is true that the 5 per cent confidence level was introduced after the fact, but at the time there was no international standard for a suitable confidence level for

testing. If Hager's book really had the scientific credibility it claimed, it would have been able to withstand the kind of critical scrutiny from independent scientific experts that TV3 persistently denied it.

REFERENCES

Altheide, D.L. 2004, 'Media Logic and Political Communication', *Political Communication*, 21/3, pp. 293–6.

Atkinson, J. 2004, 'The Campaign on Television', in J. Vowles, P. Aimer, S. Banducci, J. Karp & R. Miller (eds), *Voters' Veto: The 2002 Election in New Zealand and the Consolidation of Minority Government*, Auckland University Press, Auckland, pp. 48–67.

Bale, T. 2003, 'News, Newszak, New Zealand: The Role, Performance and Impact of Television in The General Election of 2002', in J. Boston, S. Church, S. Levine, E. McLeay & N.S. Roberts (eds), *New Zealand Votes: The General Election of 2002*, Victoria University Press, Wellington, pp. 217–34.

Barnett, C. 2003, *Culture and Democracy: Media, Space and Representation*, Edinburgh University Press, Edinburgh.

Bennett, W.L. 2003, 'The Burglar Alarm That Just Keeps Ringing: A Response to Zaller', *Political Communication*, 20, pp. 131–8.

Black, J. 2005, 'The Spin Slayers', *New Zealand Listener*, 200/3407, 27 August–2 September, pp. 16–20.

Bland, V. 2005, 'How to Handle the Media', *New Zealand Herald*, 5 November, C11.

Blumler, J.G. & D. Kavanagh 1999, 'The Third Age of Political Communication: Influence and Features', *Political Communication*, 16/3, pp. 209–30.

Carpignano, P., R. Anderson, S. Aronowitz & W. DiFazio 1990, 'Chatter in the Age of Electronic Reproduction: Talk Television and the Public Mind', *Social Text*, Nos 25–26, pp. 33–55.

Church, S. 2005, 'Televised Leader Debates', in J. Hayward & C. Rudd (eds), *Political Communications in New Zealand*, Pearson Education, Auckland, pp. 159–77.

Cottle, S. (ed.) 2003, *News, Public Relations and Power*, London, Sage.

De Luca, T. & J. Buell 2005, *Liars! Cheaters! Evildoers! Demonization and the End of Civil Debate in American Politics*, NYU Press, New York.

Dusevic, T. 2005, 'A Victim of Success?' *Time Magazine*, 19 September, pp. 14–19.

Ellis, G. 2005, 'Media, Manipulation and Politics: Power and the Press Gallery', Paper delivered to the Anatomy of Power Symposium, Auckland, University of Auckland, 26 November.

Entman, R.M. 1989, *Democracy without Citizens: Media and the Decay of American Politics*, Oxford University Press, Oxford.

Ettema, J.S. & T.L. Glasser 1985, 'On the Epistemology of Investigative Journalism', *Communication*, Vol. 8, pp. 183–206.

Ehrlich, M.C. 1996, 'The Journalism of Outrageousness: Tabloid Television News vs. Investigative News', *Journalism & Mass Communication Monographs*, Columbia, February, Vol. 155, pp. 1–15.

Esser, F., C. Reinemann, & D. Fan 2001, 'Spin Doctors in the United States, Great Britain, and Germany: Metacommunication about Media Maznipulation', *Harvard International Journal of Press/Politics*, 6/1, pp. 16–45.

James, C. 2005, 'Labour Fix-it Requires Ministers to be on the Ball', *New Zealand Herald*, 14 December, p. 19.

Levy, M.R. 1981, 'Disdaining the News', *Journal of Communication*, 32/3, pp. 24–31.

Lloyd, J. 2004, *What the Media Are Doing to Our Politics*, Constable, London.

Louw, E. 2005, *The Media and the Political Process*, Sage, London.

McNair, B. 2004, 'PR Must Die: Spin, Anti-spin and Political Public Relations in the UK, 1997–2004', *Journalism Studies*, 5/3, pp. 325–38.

Meyer, T. 2002, *Media Politics: How the Media Colonize Politics*, Polity, London.

Nimmo, D. & J.E. Combs 1990, *Mediated Political Realities*, Longman, New York.

O'Neill, O. 2002, 'Licence to Deceive', BBC Reith Lecture 5, downloaded from www.bbc.co.uk/radio4, pp. 1–6.

Sabato, L. 1993. *Feeding Frenzy*, Free Press, New York.

Tiffen, R. 2005, 'Why Political Plumbers Fail: Hypocrisy and Hyperbole in Leak Control', Unpublished paper, University of Sydney, Sydney.

FURTHER READING

Esser, F., C. Reinemann & D. Fan. 2001, 'Spin Doctors in the United States, Great Britain, and Germany: Metacommunication about Media Manipulation', *Harvard International Journal of Press/Politics*, 6/1, pp. 16–45.

Ewen, S. 1996, *PR! The Social History of Spin*, Basic Books, New York.

Lloyd, J. 2004, *What the Media Are Doing to Our Politics*, Constable, London.

McNair, B. 2004, 'PR Must Die: Spin, Anti-spin and Political Public Relations in the UK, 1997–2004', *Journalism Studies*, 5/3, pp. 325–38.

Meyer, T. 2002, *Media Politics: How the Media Colonize Politics*, Polity, London.

Media and Political Communication

Janine Hayward & Chris Rudd

Political communication refers to words, images, and actions that attempt to influence the political environment. Three sets of political communicators take part in this process: political parties and candidates; the mass media; and citizens and voters. The communication between these groups establishes and challenges power relationships, and raises questions about the nature of modern democracy. What is the appropriate role of the media in political communication? How can voters communicate with political parties? How effectively do political parties respond to voters' concerns, if they hear these concerns at all? Political communications is also an important area of study because who communicates, what they say, how they say it, and with what effect, are central questions relating to the political system.

This chapter takes a very broad approach to media and political communications. It begins by briefly identifying the three main actors in the political communications process, and the 'reciprocal relationships' between them (Kleinnijenhuis & Rietberg 1995, p. 97). The remainder of the chapter then looks in more detail at these reciprocal relationships based on the 2005 election. It should be noted that we focus only on communications involving the three traditional media of television, newspapers, and radio.

THREE MODELS OF POLITICAL COMMUNICATIONS

The political elite—parties, candidates—are the major source of information on politics and they attempt to set the agenda for political debate through their controlled release of information either to the public directly (through party manifestos and party websites, for example) but more often, indirectly via the media (press releases, staged media events, leaders' debates). This 'top-down' process of political communications is in contrast to the 'bottom-up' process whereby the public attempt to transmit their political messages to the political elite—and again, this can be done directly (asking questions at candidate meetings) but more often indirectly via the media (letters to the editor, talkback radio). Finally, the media is often accredited with playing an independent role in the political communications process and not just being passive transmitters of views from above or below. The idea of a 'mediacracy' involves powerful gatekeeping roles for media organisations in deciding what information to transmit, and what prominence or slant to give to such news.

1. Top-down communication

Advertising

Advertising is an excellent 'top-down' opportunity for parties to control the message they send to voters. At each election campaign, parties are faced with choices as to what type of advertising to engage in to achieve the greatest effect on voters. Negative advertising, which has been on the rise in the USA and Britain in recent elections, describes ads that attack an opposing party without providing the voter with information about the party running the ad. Contrast advertising, on the other hand, will attack the opposition, at the same time giving positive information about the party responsible for the ad. This contrast may be direct, where both parties are named, or indirect, where the attack party's identity is strongly implied but not made explicit. Finally, positive advertising avoids references to other parties at all, and focuses instead on the achievements of the advertising party in a positive light.

Newspaper advertising in New Zealand has undergone considerable evolution since the postwar period, but studies have shown that it bucks the international trends towards increasingly trivial, negative advertising by parties (Hayward & Rudd 2002). Generally speaking, New Zealand political parties have pursued a positive campaign strategy in newspaper advertising from the 1930s to 2002. The introduction of the MMP voting system, which encourages a multi-party campaign, may encourage parties to prefer more positive campaigns. In the previous two-party system, a party could be confident that a negative campaign would attract voters to the only alternative party; in the multi-party system parties have to be more careful about using negative advertising as voters have greater options in shifting their vote.

Contrary to the assumption that newspaper advertisements contain less policy information for voters than they have in the past, newspaper advertising campaigns in recent decades contain significant voter information. Although these advertisements appear more 'slick' than in earlier eras, with slogans, logos, and effective use of colour and imagery, they nevertheless serve voters reasonably well as an effective form of direct political communication between political parties and media audiences (Hayward & Rudd 2004, p. 50).

Newspaper advertising in the four metropolitan newspapers at the 2005 election was remarkable in a number of respects. First, in terms of sheer number, there were more ads in 2005 than for many previous postwar elections. Second, there was extreme variation between newspapers and between the parties. Labour, on the one hand, accounted for nearly half of all party ads, with most of its ads half- or full-page ones calling for the party vote. National, on the other hand, had *no* ads at all in the *Dominion Post* or the *New Zealand Herald* and most of its ads were by local candidates asking for the electorate vote. Third, the number of ads by interest groups was high compared with previous elections. Finally, unlike previous elections, many of the party ads contained implied or direct criticism of other parties, particularly the case with the Labour party which, as the incumbent party, is fairly unusual (as incumbents tend to promote their record in office rather than attack the opposition).

With regard to television advertising, New Zealand has very strict rules and regulations governing the amount of money parties can spend on their advertising on television. Although television advertising itself is not a new phenomenon in New Zealand (the famous 'dancing Cossacks' campaign in the 1970s is evidence of that), the study of televised advertising as a form of direct political communication from party to voter is a recent development. Claire Robinson (2004) notes that television advertising has the potential to communicate with large numbers of late-deciding voters, which makes the televised advertising marketplace particularly intense (2004, p. 70). She cautions that this sort of influential communication from party to voter is not a cause for concern or alarm; her study reveals that if voters in 1999 and 2002 only had the information channelled to them through television advertising to make their voting choices, they would nevertheless have sufficient policy information to make an informed voting choice. Moreover, it is highly unlikely that television advertising would have manipulated them into making irrational voting choices.

News stories (press releases, staged events, spin doctors)

Newspaper coverage of election campaigns is a tradition dating back to some of the earliest elections in New Zealand. There is a popular perception that a 'golden age' in campaigning existed in yesteryear when newspapers gave politicians a fair hearing by reporting manifestos, policy announcements, and public meetings verbatim, without interference or 'spin' by the journalists. The reality is that although newspaper coverage since about the 1940s has become more leader-focused ('presidentialised') and less localised (elevating national campaign news), voters are relatively well served by newspapers at election time. A study of the *Otago Daily Times'* election coverage since the 1940s revealed that, although leaders are of increasing interest, the local candidate and party has not been seriously neglected in news coverage. More importantly, despite the concern that election news is increasingly trivial at the expense of important policy information, this was not found to be the case in the *Otago Daily Times* (Hayward & Rudd 2002, pp. 18–19).

Turning to the newspaper coverage of the 2005 election, there was little evidence of great trivialisation of campaign coverage compared to previous elections, with the four metropolitans devoting on average more than one-fifth to stories of substance. There was, however, a trend towards more presidentialisation in terms of the focus on the leaders of the two main parties. This presidentialisation, of course, to a certain degree reflected the strategy of the two main parties who made it clear from the outset that the personal qualities of their leaders (and lack of such qualities in their opponent) would be at the forefront of their campaigns. This links to an important point in the relationship between the newspapers (and the media in general) and politicians: newspapers rely heavily on the press releases put out by the parties which provide the parties' media managers ('spin doctors') the opportunity to set the news agenda. However, this is something the newspapers are keenly aware of. The *New Zealand Herald* in particular expressed its intention to both cover the events of the campaign trail but also to 'examine vigorously the issues, policies and character of those aspiring to lead the nation' (18 July 2005).

It is also interesting to note that the editors of the four metropolitan newspapers all claimed that they had decided against publicly endorsing any political party. The only major newspapers to openly advocate a voting preference were the *Sunday News* and the *Sunday Star-Times*, both of which gave qualified editorial endorsement to Labour.

Television coverage of the election, in terms of 'quantity', provided plenty of opportunity for viewers of TV One and TV3 to follow the election campaign. In addition to the early and late evening news, there were the various current affairs programmes including *Campbell Live, Closeup, Agenda,* and *Face-to-Face* which devoted considerable time to the election campaign. But in terms of 'quality', compared to the newspapers, television coverage was more 'game' and this was more so with the news programmes than current affairs. There is the tendency for television to succumb to the need to create compelling, visual entertainment best epitomised with the dramatic stories constructed around the results of opinion polls commissioned by the television channels. Television also is driven by the need to be the first with breaking news stories that led to the absurdity of TV One's election night programme calling the election (for National) less than thirty minutes after the polls had closed.

Leaders' debates

The televised leaders' debates are a major source of information for voters, and concern has been increasing in recent elections that serious debate about policy is being sacrificed for trivial and entertaining banter between host and leaders, for the sake of ratings. The inclusion of the 'worm'—a graphic which tracks audience response to politicians' statements on the screen—in the 2002 leaders' debate, became a focus of the debate about how to strike an appropriate balance between entertainment and information. Stephen Church's study of televised debates concludes that, despite the important tension between format and presentation of debates, their influence on the voter should not be overestimated. It is oversimplifying a range of complex influences on voters to assume that an election result can be overwhelmingly influenced by who 'won' or 'lost' any particular debate (Church 2004, p. 176).

The leaders' debates in 2005 took place both on Radio NZ as well as TV One and TV3. Labour leader Helen Clark refused a request for a live Sky TV debate and she also refused to participate in a Radio NZ debate with National party leader Don Brash if, as planned, it was to be simultaneously broadcast on Sky TV. (The official reason given was that the two formats were too different to be accommodated in one programme.) Commentators generally agreed that comparing the performance of the two main party leaders in the debates, Clark 'won'. Brash made a number of mistakes—most notably over his party's assets sales policy in the all-leaders debate on TV3, when he also called himself a 'listener' rather than a 'leader' and referred to student loans as being tax deductible for pre-schoolers. After the subsequent TV One debate between Brash and Clark, where Clark had been particularly assertive, Brash implied he had 'gone easy' on Clark because it was 'not entirely appropriate for a man to aggressively attack a woman' (*Press*, 24 August 2005). Although a gentlemanly attitude may have won Brash support in some segments of New Zealand society, it appeared a lame excuse for a poor performance in the debate.

Although Brash's performance did improve throughout the debates, overall he did little to dent Clark's image as someone very competent and on top of her job. As for the minor party leaders, the debates were an opportunity for them to shine, but there was no replication of the big impact Peter Dunne made at the 2002 'worm' debate. The presence of live audiences probably did little to engender considered debate between the leaders. This was especially the case at the TV One debate between Clark and Brash when a vociferous crowd led Clark to subsequently claim that National had brought in a mob of hooligans who had shouted personal abuse at her—'no-kids lesbo', 'scrubber', and 'liar'.

2. Communication from the bottom up

Letters to the editor and talkback radio

Traditional methods of bottom-up communication are talkback radio and letters to the editor. But how much attention does, and should, politicians take of the communication they can receive through these media? How representative are the views reported in these sources? Letters to the editor are, theoretically, a mechanism for readers to respond to issues raised in the paper (particularly in editorials) and more importantly to attempt to 'set the agenda' by raising matters of concern which the newspaper has neglected to report. Presumably, the newspaper can then choose to respond to the public agenda in its editorials and articles. But how often does the public control communication in this manner? The newspaper can easily control the letters it chooses to print, and it may be wary of letters that appear to be part of an orchestrated letter-writing campaign on the part of political parties or other interest groups. During the 2005 election campaign the letters editor for the Christchurch *Press* obtained a copy of a National party memo detailing lines of argument and phrases members should use in letters to editors when attacking Labour's student loans interest rebate. National was certainly not the only party to prepare party members in this way.

Talkback radio, on the other hand, is a potentially less mediated form of bottom-up communication than the letters to the editor. Talkback radio provides opportunities for the public to voice concerns in a less structured and more spontaneous way, potentially giving voice to those who do not wish to commit to the premeditated written word. But how much credence should politicians and political parties give to the views they hear on talkback radio? How representative are these views of the general public? Generally speaking, talkback radio in New Zealand and overseas (particularly America) is considered to be more conservative and right-wing than the liberal mainstream media sources. Certainly the various talkback shows on *NewstalkZB* (such as those hosted by Paul Holmes, Leighton Smith, Danny Watson, Larry Williams, Bruce Russell, and Justin du Fresne) and *Radio Pacific* (John Banks), would be considered extremely conservative and right of centre. Yet while politicians may reject the views expressed in talkback as unrepresentative and atypical, at the same time, political parties monitor talkback radio, and letters to the editor, to sense the mood, perhaps not of mainstream New Zealand, but of certain segments of New Zealand society. This may be very useful for niche parties who want to reach a specific target audience. Many politicians and former politicians have had their own talkback shows or been guest presenters (examples being John Banks, Pam Corkery, David Lange, Michael Laws, Rob Muldoon, and John Tamihere).

Opinion polls

Pollsters can manipulate opinion polls to elicit opinion where none may exist or to 'manufacture consent'. But it is also the case that politicians are keenly interested in poll results, with the major parties conducting their own polls throughout an election campaign. The media are also interested in what public opinion polls have to say using poll results as a basis for news stories. At the 2005 election, all the major media outlets joined forces with commercial polling agencies to produce regular polls throughout the four-week campaign: TV One with Colmar Brunton; TV3 and Maori TV with TNS; National Business Review with UMR and Philips Fox; Fairfax Ltd (owners of the *Press*, *Dominion Post*, and *Sunday Star-Times*) with AC Nielsen; *New Zealand Herald* with DigiPoll; and the *Sunday Star-Times* with BRC. The *Otago Daily Times* had an agreement with the *New Zealand Herald* to use the results of its Digipoll. Both the major TV channels and all the metropolitan newspapers gave some prominence to poll results in their news stories.

But how effective were these polls in communicating the views of voters upwards, to politicians? In one respect, there is a limited amount of information that comes out of opinion polls, especially those conducted during election campaigns. Respondents are usually asked only for their vote preference and their 'preferred prime minister', with possibly a further question on 'most important issues'. Thus, opinion polls are very blunt instruments for expressing the views of citizens. On the other hand, politicians and parties do react to some degree to these broad sentiments—witness the Labour party's response to the increased popularity of the National party following the Orewa speech of January 2004. The role of polls as reported in the media was highlighted in the 2005 election with regard to the campaign in the seat of Epsom. Rodney Hide, leader of ACT, was seeking to win this seat off the incumbent National candidate. Opinion polls reported in the mainstream media consistently put Hide well behind the National party candidate, and at times, even the Labour candidate. Hide's own independently commissioned polling, however, showed him in the lead but this was either ignored by the media or given negative coverage, with the *New Zealand Herald* referring to ACT's 'jack-up polls' in Epsom and commenting that polls that suggested Hide could win were the 'biggest slice of baloney' of the campaign. Hide himself criticised TV One's poll in Epsom for not mentioning the name of the candidates when asking whom people would vote for in the electorate. So, while the media can attempt to give voice to voters through the polls they commission, there are some grounds for thinking that polling is a channel of communication open to use and abuse by the media.

As if reacting to perceived inadequacies of opinion polls, the major newspapers at the 2005 election endeavoured to elicit more qualitative data from a small sample of readers. The *Press* had an 'Election Jury' of twelve readers who were asked to judge the election campaign and say 'which policy, or outburst, caught their attention' and who they thought 'won the week' (this latter point indicating the newspaper still wanted to have a 'race horse' element). The *Otago Daily Times* had a 'Voters' Panel' of readers. The *Dominion Post* invited readers to send in their comments and feedback on what they thought of the campaign, 'who performed well and what policies were vote winners'. The *Sunday Star-Times* had a readers' panel that commented on parties' policies. The *New Zealand Herald* began its campaign coverage with a week-long series of articles based on 600 interviews conducted by one of its reporters who 'travelled the length of the country', to go beyond 'the polls' bald numbers' and find out what was 'really on New Zealander's minds'. None of these efforts constitute 'in-depth' interviewing, but they did represent efforts by one section of the media to give voters the chance to move beyond 'yes–no' or one-word responses to opinion polls.

MEDIACRACY

Mediacracy is the view that media have an independent role in determining the nature of political communication. The media decide *what* is communicated by deciding what gets reported. The media also decide the prominence to be given to news stories—a front-page story or inside page, in the case of newspapers. And, of course, the media may exhibit a particular partisan bias in their political coverage.

Since around the 1970s, there has been little overt partisanship in the major newspapers and television channels. Editorials have on occasion expressed preferences for a party or, more often the case, disaffection with all parties! At the 2005 election, editors of the metropolitan newspapers claimed political neutrality in their editorials. However, there was clearly negative coverage of some parties in the editorials and news columns—ACT in particular. After the election, the Greens also bemoaned the fact that the media did not give the party fair coverage with co-leader Rod Donald saying that the party's media coverage was 'simply shut out by Bob the Builder's private parts' (*New Zealand Herald,* 12 October 2005).

Do the media set the agenda via political communication? It is difficult to determine cause and effect over the question of agenda setting—are the media reporting on what they think voters consider the most important issues or are voters' interests a reflection of the issues they have seen, read, and heard about in the media? Putting this difficulty to one side, at the 2005 election the major issues covered by newspapers were very similar to the ones identified in opinion polls: tax, health, education, the economy, and law and order being among the top half-dozen important issues for both. There were some discrepancies, however, with the issue concerning the elderly more prominent in opinion polls than in newspaper coverage, while newspapers gave significant coverage to the issue of transport and more prominent coverage to race issues, than found in the survey of voters.

CONCLUSION

When examining the reciprocal relationship between the three main actors in the political communications process, it is clear that the media play an important role either as the channel through which parties and voters communicate with each other or as independent actors in their own right. It is equally evident that the bottom-up flow of political communication, from citizens to the political elite, is not a very vigorous path of communication. Politicians do take note of what is said on talkback radio and newspaper editors do follow the topics dominating letters pages. And both track what is being reported in opinion polls (despite usual disclaimers by politicians that the only poll that matters takes place on election day). However, these efforts of political communication are largely overwhelmed by the flood of press releases, staged media events, and photo-opportunities orchestrated by the political parties, and the preoccupation by the media with ensuring their audiences are first and foremost entertained (more so for television than public radio or newspapers).

Whether this state of affairs is a failing in the political system will depend upon one's opinion regarding the desirable degree of involvement of citizens in the political process. For elitists, the minimal involvement of citizens is not a problem and political communications should be primarily top-down with the media largely an uncritical channel for this to be achieved. For participationists, the lack of effective channels for citizens to communicate their views is a weakness endemic of 'representative' democracy. For both schools of thought, an independent media that overplayed its role as gatekeeper for bottom-up and top-down flows of communication would represent the worst of both worlds by distorting the political communications between the ruled and the rulers. Fortunately there is little to suggest that New Zealand has reached the point of becoming a mediacracy despite the occasional outbursts from politicians from across the political spectrum that at times this might appear to be the case.

DISCUSSION QUESTIONS

1 Do you consider New Zealand to be a mediacracy?
2 How do you think the bottom-up flow of political communications could be made more effective?
3 Is it appropriate for voters to decide who to vote for on the basis of, say, the leaders' debates, or should voters be informed on policy detail before making their voting choices?
4 Do you think the political communications process in New Zealand helps citizens make informed choices at election time?

FURTHER READING

Church, S. 2004, 'Televised Leaders' Debates', in *Political Communications in New Zealand*, eds J. Hayward & C. Rudd, Pearson Education, Auckland, pp. 159–82.

Hayward, J. & C. Rudd 2002, 'The Coverage of Post-War Election Campaigns: The Otago Daily Times', *Political Science*, vol. 54, pp. 3–19.

Hayward, J. & C. Rudd 2004, 'Party Advertising in Newspapers', in J. Hayward & C. Rudd (eds), *Political Communications in New Zealand*, Pearson Education, Auckland, pp. 38–51.

Kleinnijenhuis, J. & E. Rietberg 1995, 'Parties, Media, the Public and the Economy', *European Journal of Political Research*, vol. 28, pp. 95–118.

Robinson, C. 2004, 'Televised Political Advertising', in J. Hayward & C. Rudd (eds), *Political Communications in New Zealand*, Pearson Education, Auckland, pp. 52–73.

Political Marketing

Jennifer Lees-Marshment

Political marketing is a hot topic in academic study and political practice around the world. Increasingly voters are referred to as consumers; political systems as markets; policies as a product; and politicians continually talk of achievable pledges and the need to deliver in government. Political marketing may offer the means to respond to a more consumerist, demanding, and heterogeneous electorate. It was traditionally associated with the use of snazzy technical methods during election campaigns usually led by the US. However, the significant electoral success of Tony Blair's New Labour party turned attention to the UK, where marketing was used to inform the design of policy, leadership, and organisation, rather than just sell the candidates during US-style campaigns. This more comprehensive use of political marketing is more applicable to other party-based political systems, prompting the global sharing of political marketing ideas and consultants. This chapter will explore the nature of political marketing, how it has been used in New Zealand, and the wider democratic issues it raises.

MORE THAN JUST SPIN

Political marketing is often conceived as being about selling techniques used to persuade the voter that your party is the best one to vote for. In business, however, while public relations campaigns, and new sales techniques remain a substantial activity, marketing is used not to persuade, but to create a product the market will want, thereby making selling almost unnecessary. Political marketing is no different. Even Alastair Campbell, Tony Blair's former communications chief, implied this. When asked on the 1997 election night 'Why, though, do you think you've won, what was it about the campaign—did you do so well, did the Conservatives' do so badly—what was it?' he stated 'Well, I don't know whether the campaign in the end made that much difference'. After he left his post, Campbell was asked on his television show, *An audience with Alastair Campbell*, 'What is political marketing?' He refused to answer, saying 'that's a PhD thesis; it's too complicated to do in twenty-five seconds'. Clearly he was not about to agree with his critics, most of whom equate political marketing with spin doctoring.

MORE THAN JUST TECHNIQUES

Political marketing is not just a bag of tools of techniques that parties can adopt in a campaign. Activities such as polling, focus groups, segmenting the market, consumer data, targeting, and direct mail are what tend to attract the attention of the media and public. There is no doubt that the use of market intelligence in whatever form is a crucial part of political marketing, but only if the results are then used to help guide politicians as to what issues voters care most about, and what kind of policy positions they should take. Segmentation can help parties decide who they should focus on representing, rather than simply trying to appeal to everyone. However, such tools cannot make up for a long-term, strategic use of marketing. Voters are highly discerning and critical, and political parties are complex organisations with ideological traditions. The simple use of computerised data and research techniques will not be sufficient to help parties either respond to voter demands in a manner that is mature, reflective, and wholehearted or produce a realistic, believable, and unified product. Political marketing is more a *way of thinking*. While it certainly involves the use of communication techniques, political marketing is also concerned with the nature of the party product and how this relates to the predispositions and needs of voters (see table 6.5.1).

Table 6.5.1: Political marketing

IS NOT...	IS...
• just about political ads	• about the design of the political 'product'
• just about political communication	• how political organisations and actors behave in relation to their 'market'
• just about campaigns	• the application of marketing concepts as well as techniques
• about spin-doctoring	

THE PRODUCT TO BE MARKETED

A party's product encompasses many characteristics, is ongoing, and is offered at all times (not just elections) and at all levels of the party. The product includes aspects such as those listed below, although this will vary from one country to another:

- **leadership:** powers, image, character, appeal, relationship with the rest of the party organisation, and with the media
- **Members of Parliament** (existing or candidates)
- **membership:** powers, recruitment, loyalty, and behaviour
- **staff:** researchers, professionals, advisers etc.—their role, influence, office powers, and relationship with other parts of the party organisation
- **symbols:** name, logo, and anthem
- **constitution:** formal, official rules
- **activities:** party conferences, rallies, and meetings
- **policies:** those proposed for when in office and those enacted once in office.

Parties using comprehensive political marketing can therefore alter their product to suit the nature and demands of their market.

THE MARKET-ORIENTED PARTY

The Lees-Marshment (2001) model of Market-, Sales- and Product-Oriented Parties is the most widely used framework in political marketing. It combines knowledge from both political science and marketing disciplines in a 'marriage' of theory, accepting that marketing is not just about selling, but that parties are very complex organisations, with some quite different characteristics from those of business. A Market-Oriented Party uses party views and political judgment to design its behaviour to respond to and satisfy voter demands in a way that meets their needs and wants, is supported and implemented by the internal organisation, and is deliverable in government. Political marketing is used to understand the public, rather than manipulate it. Parties may use their ideology as a means to create effective solutions to public demands, but ideology and the beliefs of party elites do not drive policy. They try to respond to market demand, rather than trying to shape it.

The market is more complex than just voters. The electorate may be segmented so that the party does not just focus on the middle ground. The market also includes members, related think tanks, and politicians. Needs, not just wants, must be considered, in the long as well as the short term. Therefore, a market orientation is not about simply giving people what they want, because a party needs to ensure that it can deliver the product on offer. It also needs to ensure that the new product will be accepted within the party and so needs to adjust its product carefully to take account of this. A market orientation in politics is not about removing all ideology, or just following public fashion, but about being responsive; respecting voters and reflecting on the party's own behaviour. Market-Oriented Parties (MOPs) should not all become the same, or assume the characteristics of

Figure 6.5.1: The political marketing process for a Market-Oriented Party

---
STAGE ONE: MARKET INTELLIGENCE

The party aims to understand and ascertain market demands. Informally it 'keeps an ear to the ground,' talks to party members, creates policy groups, meets with the public. Formally it uses methods such as polls, focus groups and segmentation to understand the views and behaviour of its market, including the general public, key opinion-influencers, MPs and members. It uses market intelligence continually and considers short and long-term demands.

STAGE TWO: PRODUCT DESIGN

The party then designs 'product' according to the findings from its market intelligence, before adjusting it to suit several factors explored in Stage 3.

STAGE THREE: PRODUCT ADJUSTMENT

The party then develops the product to consider:
Achievability: ensures promises can be delivered in government.
Internal reaction: ensures changes will attract adequate support from MPs and members to ensure implementation, taking into account a party's ideology and history, retaining certain policies to suit the traditional supporter market where necessary.
Competition: identifies the opposition's weaknesses and highlights own corresponding strengths, ensuring a degree of distinctiveness.
Support: segments the market to identify untapped voters necessary to achieve goals, and then develop targeted aspects of the product to suit them.

STAGE FOUR: IMPLEMENTATION

Changes are implemented throughout the party, needing careful party management and leadership over an appropriate timeframe to obtain adequate acceptance, to create party unity and enthusiasm for the new party design.

STAGE FIVE: COMMUNICATION

Communication is carefully organised to convey the new product, so that voters are clear before the campaign begins. Not just the leader, but all MPs and members send a message to the electorate. It involves media management but is not just about spin-doctoring; it should be informative rather than manipulative, and built on a clear internal communication structure.

STAGE SIX: CAMPAIGN

The party repeats its communication in the official campaign, reminding voters of the key aspects and advantages of its product.

STAGE SEVEN: ELECTION

The party should win not just votes but attract positive perception from voters on all aspects of behaviour including policies, leaders, party unity and capability, as well as increased quality of its membership.

STAGE EIGHT: DELIVERY

The party then needs to deliver its product in government.

Source: Lees-Marshment 2001

catch-all parties, or simply move to the Downsian centre-ground.[1] In order to ensure this, there is a process of activities—known as the market-oriented party political marketing process—which parties should carry out to achieve a market orientation (see figure 6.5.1).

SALES-ORIENTED PARTY

Where parties do not follow the market-oriented model, they have been prone to adopt a sales-orientation. Sales-oriented parties aim to sell what they decide is best for the people, utilising effective political marketing communication techniques. Market intelligence is used not to inform the product design, but to help the party persuade voters it is right (see figure 6.5.2).

In PR (proportional representation) electoral and multi-party political systems there is a greater tendency for parties to be sales-oriented, especially for minor parties. Minor parties, with little chance of winning power, will predominantly want to influence the agenda and potential coalition partners, and therefore a sales orientation is a rational option to use marketing to present their argument most effectively to the segments most

Figure 6.5.2: The political marketing process for a Sales-Oriented Party

STAGE ONE: PRODUCT DESIGN
The party designs its behaviour according to what it thinks best.

↓

STAGE TWO: MARKET INTELLIGENCE
Market intelligence is used to ascertain voters' response to its behaviour, identify which voter segments offer support, which do not, and which might be persuaded. Research can also explore how best to communicate with target markets.

↓

STAGE THREE: COMMUNICATION
Communication is devised to suit each segment, targeting presentation on the most popular aspects of the product whilst downplaying any weaknesses. Communication is highly professional and organised, using modern marketing communication techniques, such as direct mail, leaflets, posters, direct-mail videos, party-election broadcasts and mobile phone texts to persuade voters to agree with the party.

↓

STAGE FOUR: CAMPAIGN
The party continues to communicate effectively as in Stage 3.

↓

STAGE FIVE: ELECTION
The general election.

↓

STAGE SIX: DELIVERY
The party will deliver its promised product in government.

Source: Lees-Marshment 2001

open to persuasion. Like any approach, the use and effectiveness of political marketing depends on the goals of the organisation and the nature of the environment.

POLITICAL MARKETING IN NEW ZEALAND

There is no doubt that the main parties in New Zealand use elements of marketing, such as employing pollsters, using advertising agencies, and considering how best to present and position their policies. The extent to which they have employed comprehensive political marketing in the form of the Market-Oriented Party is more debatable.

1. Global New Labour: Copy-Cat Clark

There are significant similarities between the behaviour of the New Zealand Labour party and its UK counterpart: Clark not only used marketing tools but copied the idea of a Labour Listens process to be more in touch, adopting pledge cards to make the product more tangible. Rudd's (2005) case study found that Labour's behaviour in the 1990s fitted the MOP model to a significant degree. The party engaged in internal market intelligence and external quantitative polling (e.g. UMR Insight), utilised management consultants to create strategic plans and subsequently assessed performance against objectives. It responded to market intelligence in policy development, especially in key areas identified as of particular importance to voters such as health, pensions, jobs, and law and order, as well as the general desire for positive vision and achievable proposals.

Copying Tony Blair and the UK New Labour party in response to voter desire for credibility and believable promises, Clark offered clearcut policy pledges appearing on a 'credit card' in 1999 (see figure 6.5.3).

Figure 6.5.3: New Zealand Labour party's 1999 pledges

1. Create jobs through promoting New Zealand industries and better support for exporters and small business.
2. Focus on patients not profit and cut waiting times for surgery.
3. Cut the cost to students of tertiary education, starting with a fairer loans scheme.
4. Reverse the 1999 cuts to superannuation rates. Guarantee superannuation in the future by putting a proportion of all income tax into a separate fund which cannot be used for any other purpose.
5. Restore income-related rents for state housing so that low-income tenants pay no more than 25 per cent of their income in rent.
6. Crack down on burglary and youth crime.
7. No rise in income tax for 95 per cent of taxpayers earning under $60,000 a year. No increases in GST or company tax.

Like Blair, Clark's pledges were created to suit the target market of middle-income New Zealanders and focused on issues voters cared most about. They were also, as Rudd noted, worded to make them relatively easy to produce evidence of their delivery, and created to suit the target markets to which the Labour party was trying to appeal. In campaigning terms, the party copied British New Labour again and created a 'virtual Millbank'. The New Zealand Labour party also copied the UK in making vigorous efforts to tell the electorate that it was keeping its election promises, issuing progress reports and lists of achievements in government, a practice continued in the 2005 election.

2. The New Zealand hybrid model

Rudd also noticed a number of differences in political marketing practice by New Zealand Labour compared with the UK. As Rudd noted, coalitions 'may lead to a party sacrificing, or at least de-emphasising, policies that it knows are attractive to its own supporters but are anathema to a potential coalition partner's voters'. This makes the product adjustment stage even more complex. He asserted that it could be possible that the New Zealand system fosters a hybrid form of political marketing, which combines the market and sales orientation. For example, on certain major issues, the Labour party was clearly not poll-driven, but instead offered leadership up-front, such as when the Labour–Alliance coalition decided to become more pro-active in economic development. The party was market-driven in responding to issues such as cutting hospital waiting lists, reducing the costs of tertiary education, tougher sentencing, and stricter immigration controls. The more sales-oriented, leadership-driven policy stance in some areas might be a natural result of the system which produces a coalition government, and therefore even if Labour wanted to be completely market-oriented it had to adapt to its coalition partner in order to stay in government.

Learning lessons from abroad: A superior version of the Market-Oriented Party

However, it can also be argued that there are elements of leading rather than following in Clark's Labour party. This has taken the form of a comprehensive adoption of a market-orientation in politics. The MOP should take into account ideology, as this allows the party to be distinctive and appeal to its traditional base, and it needs to adjust to the competition—therefore in a system such as New Zealand, adopting some policy stances to suit your coalition partner is part of a market-oriented strategy.

In many ways Clark may have learnt from Blair's mistakes as much as his success. UK New Labour was more market-driven than a Market-Oriented Party: Blair neglected internal analysis and careful implementation, alienating traditional supporters in the process. He also adopted many policies close to identical to that of the opposition

Conservative ideology without supplementing it with distinctive Labour policies. A fully Market-Oriented Party should not exclude ideology from political debate or completely override traditional supporters. It is a complex balance of different demands. It could therefore be argued that New Zealand Labour has implemented the MOP more effectively than its UK mentor. Clark herself asserted that 'Labour didn't start as a party of the Centre, it has no desire to be a party of the Centre … its traditions lie in the desire of working men and women'. Nevertheless, because New Zealand remains a multi-party, PR-based electoral system, we would expect other smaller parties to adopt the sales-oriented approach, because parties with 5 per cent or less of the overall votes can have a role in government. As Rudd (2005) noted, in a multi-party system the raison d'etre of many smaller parties is 'the principled position—the leaders have a faith in their product and are not prepared to follow public opinion'—and so will make full use of marketing techniques 'to persuade and convert'.

3. The 2005 election

The 2005 election in New Zealand saw the continuing development of political marketing. Looking firstly at the wider product rather than how it was sold, both major parties did make certain changes reflective of a market-orientation. As in previous elections, Labour emphasised its achievements in government (in 2005, low unemployment, 10,000 modern apprentices, spending on health and educations and the Working for Families package), but added clear new pledges for its third term (see figure 6.5.4).

National abandoned previously unpopular policies on superannuation, anti-nuclear legislation, and four weeks' leave, and successfully focused on the 'Super blues', creating groups, newsletters, an individual website as well as policy and campaign events aimed at this target market.

Both Labour and National focused on the salient issue of tax, providing tax calculators on their website during the campaign for voters to gauge whether they would be better off or not. When National launched plans to cut income tax, it enjoyed a sudden rise in polled support. Labour's slogan under its commitments, 'You're better off with Labour' tried to suggest that the party would be good for voters financially as well as in terms of the public sector.

Figure 6.5.4: Labour's 2005 pledges: 'My Commitment to You'

```
1. No interest on student loans
2. Final date for Treaty claims 2008
3. Increase rates rebate
4. Kiwi Saver
5. 250 extra community police
6. More cataract and major joint operations
7. 5,000 more modern apprenticeships
```

Looking at the product more broadly, however, National failed to convince a sufficiently large proportion of the voting public that its proposals were either credible or achievable. Its highly negative billboard campaign against Clark, while cleverly conceived and eye-catching, with highly detailed and unrealistic promises underneath sensationalised slogans, may have failed to convey the image of a unified, mature party capable of government. Clark attracted significantly higher poll ratings as leader than Don Brash. Unlike Blair, Clark was on the side of public opinion in opposing New Zealand military involvement in the Iraq War—an easier position for a country such as New Zealand to take perhaps, but nonetheless one that won support. Clark also succeeded in projecting a highly pragmatic and cooperative approach towards the small parties—necessary skills for any leader wishing to form a stable and effective coalition government. This involved campaigning as an ally of Jim Anderton, leader of the Progressive party, as well as the co-leaders of the Greens.

The close election results, however, also suggested weaknesses in Labour's behaviour and strategy, with neither major party satisfying voters' demands enough to win a clear lead. This was despite—or maybe even because of—the extensive use of marketing communication techniques during the campaign. The *New Zealand Herald* (24 September 2005) argued that 'advertising was the winner'. Advertising may have been dominant, but this did not mean that political marketing was used effectively. One of the media stories was National importing Australian public relations and polling consultants Lynton Crosby and Mark Textor, and the consequent emergence of insights-driven, scare-mongering marketing which plays on voters' deepest psyche and fears, using issues such as immigration and race. Crosby also advised the UK Conservative party and employed similar means with limited effect (see Lees-Marshment & Roberts 2005). The other weakness with this approach is its focus on selling a policy stance suited to traditional support rather than new voters (including first-time young voters and new immigrants).

The use of such techniques is indicative of a sales rather than a market orientation. National undoubtedly benefited to the extent that it gained significantly more votes than at the 2002 election, but perhaps at the expense of some long-term damage to its image as a positive, credible alternative. This negative image is perhaps why National came close, but in the end not close enough to be in a position to form government. Voters were dissatisfied with Labour, particularly on its perceived policy delivery, but perhaps were not sufficiently confident in the alternative. In this respect, it was a missed opportunity for National, although one that was hardly surprising. As predicted, while marketing techniques may help to boost turnout among the party faithful and gain attention for their negativity, they rarely provide sufficient impetus to win the hearts and minds of those voters in the moderate centre. This is a point that National, as well as parties in other countries, need to pay heed to when importing global political marketing practitioners, tactics, and trends.

IMPLICATIONS OF POLITICAL MARKETING

Political marketing is a global phenomenon, and New Zealand is no exception. The use of political marketing raises a number of normative questions, such as:

- How do we balance listening with leading? Unpopular policy decisions might be in the interests of the public in the long term.
- How do we distinguish between want and need?
- Delivering the political product is highly complex: can the political consumer ever be satisfied?
- Should the public be treated as consumers or citizens?
- Parties and other public organisations are different to business. Practitioners that go from commercial to political marketing are often surprised by how different it is. New Zealander Simon Walker, who became the Queen's communication secretary, noted that 'dealing with the media at Buckingham Palace is a very different job to working with them at British Airways'.
- How does market-oriented politics relate to theories of representative democracy, direct democracy, and deliberative democracy?

There are a number of arguments in defence of political marketing. A market-orientation needs to incorporate judgment, leadership, professionalism, and ideology, as long as these attributes are executed in response to voter concerns: it does not mean simply following public opinion. Ideology is part of the political product and needs to be marketed accordingly. The political consumer has responsibilities as well as rights; they are part of the delivery process. Other questions about want and need, which market segments tend to focus on, relate back to classical political questions of how to distribute resources. Political marketing does not cause the problem in New Zealand or elsewhere, but effective analysis and improved practice may help find new perspectives and solutions.

DISCUSSION QUESTIONS

1 Should the public be treated as consumers?
2 How similarly positioned ideologically and electorally was the New Zealand Labour party in 1999 to the British Labour party in 1997?
3 In what way is political marketing used differently in New Zealand to other countries such as the UK?
4 Has Helen Clark's Labour party delivered on its promises? Can any government ever satisfy the public?
5 Does political marketing improve or undermine democracy?

NOTE

1   For a discussion on the main features of catch-all parties and the application of the Downsian model, see Miller 2005, pp. 70–1, 79–80, and 160–3.

FURTHER READING

Lees-Marshment, J. 2001a, *Political Marketing and British Political Parties*, Manchester University Press, Manchester.

Lees-Marshment, J. 2001b, 'The Marriage of Politics and Marketing', *Political Studies* 49/4, pp. 692–713.

Lees-Marshment, J. & J. Roberts 2005, 'Why It Didn't Work for Labour … Political Marketing and the 2005 Election: And the Importance of Thinking before You Target', Debate paper published online by the Chartered Institute of Marketing, see www.cim. co.uk/cim/ser/html/knoFactFile.cfm?KCTopicID=5ED7B46F-E13F-DEF8–8FABA D6086295D16&objectID=57FBF065-BA82–7E99–167F340E8502143D.

Lilleker, D. & J. Lees-Marshment 2005 (eds), *Political Marketing: A Comparative Perspective*, Manchester University Press, Manchester.

Miller, R. 2005, *Party Politics in New Zealand*, Oxford University Press, Melbourne.

Rudd, C. 2005, 'Marketing the Message or the Messenger? The New Zealand Labour Party, 1990–2003', in D. Lilleker & J. Lees-Marshment (eds), *Political Marketing: A Comparative Perspective*, Manchester University Press, Manchester, chapter 5.

Media, Politics, and Sport

Wayne Hope

This chapter initially explores the symbiosis of media, sport, and advertising in a global context. Attention is then given to the global absorption of national media and the impact this has had on national sporting culture. America's Cup yachting and All Black rugby are provided as pivotal case studies. This is followed by a normative consideration of the changing relationship between sport and television in New Zealand.

GLOBAL MEDIA-SPORT

Recent decades have witnessed the emergence of a global media system dominated by Time-Warner, Disney, News Corporation, Viacom, Bertelsmann, Vivendi-Universal, and Liberty Media. Meanwhile, outside conglomerates AT&T, Sony, and General Electric have acquired multiple assets in film, television, recorded music, print media, and Internet services (McChesney 2000, p. 91; unattributed 2002b). Corporate concentration across all communications industries has been accelerated by the neo-liberal policy agendas of governments and supra-national institutions (WTO, World Bank, IMF). Government relaxations of media ownership regulations have enabled the expansion of transnational media empires. These developments undermine the principles of public communication and public access (to communication infrastructures). Instead, knowledge, information, and cultural activity have become branded products of consumption and market exchange.

In this context, sports products have enormous commercial value. Media-entertainment corporations insert sporting spectacles into their programming schedules to build audiences and generate advertising revenue. Mass-mediated sport is easy to pre-schedule, relatively inexpensive to produce, and attractive to demographic groups which are otherwise elusive (in particular, high profile male sport appeals to eighteen- to thirty-five-year-old males). Furthermore, major sporting contests have distinctive features, which are commercially exploitable. These can be summarised as follows:

1   *Cultural centrality*: Various sports reflect deep-rooted personal, regional, and national identifications. Games, tournaments, and competitions involving teams and/or individual athletes are imbued with long-standing social rituals of participation, spectatorship, and fandom.
2   *Unpredictability*: Although sporting contests are structured according to codified rules, time limits, and traditions of conduct, results are often unpredictable. When this is so, spectators and mass audiences strongly engage with the live action as it unfolds.
3   *Drama*: Like popular drama productions, live sporting events feature heroes, villains, and bit players who advance themes and plot lines. What takes place is described and interpreted by various commentators.
4   *Strategy and tactics*: Sporting contests display strategic and tactical conflicts, which are recognisable to supporters and commentators. Their responses to a given contest add to social knowledge of the sport.
5   *Spectacle*: The sound and colour of major sporting events have always engaged assembled crowds. For spectators today, such occasions are supplemented by ground announcers, electronic billboards, and video screen replays. Simultaneously, mass media and multimedia technologies project sporting spectacles into private lives and public places.
6   *Eroticism*: The physical attributes and activities of accomplished athletes attract widespread erotic attention. How this occurs depends on the sexual orientation and desires of particular spectators. In this regard, promotions of sporting contests and sports people often exploit masculine, feminine, and racial stereotypes.

The preceding features have been systematically exploited by Disney-backed ESPN (Entertainment and Programming Sports Network). ESPN International telecasts in twenty-one languages to 182 nations and 155 million households via twenty networks (across Asia, Australia, and Latin America) (Miller, Lawrence, McKay, Rowe 2004, pp. 91–2). Within the USA, the Disney-owned ABC holds rights to over US$6 billion worth of sports coverage in college football, PGA golf, the National Hockey League (NHL), National Football League (NFL), and Major League Soccer. The live rights to soccer and golf are shared with ESPN. From Disney's perspective, sport is a lucrative addition to its collection of globally recognisable entertainment products and symbols. Their commercial value is realised through control of advertising-driven media outlets (publishers, free-to-air television networks, subscription channels, radio stations, and Internet services) and major sports teams. Additionally, Disney's entertainment-sport products and symbols are cross-merchandised through stores, theme parks, and websites (Harvey, Law 2005, pp. 194–6).

During the 1990s Rupert Murdoch's News Corporation drew from its US-based print, television, and film studio revenues to acquire satellite delivery systems and subscription channels in the United Kingdom (BSkyB), Germany (Vox), Australia (Foxtel), New Zealand (Sky), Japan (JSkyB), India (ZeeTV), and East Asia (Star TV) (Andrews 2004, pp. 101–2). The profitability of News Corporation's worldwide, pay television holdings depended upon the acquisition of live broadcasting rights to popular sporting contests. The United Kingdom experience illustrates the general strategy involved. In 1990, News Corporation gained 50 per cent of BSkyB following the merger of Murdoch's pay television with chief competitor British Satellite broadcasting. In 1992, BSkyB secured exclusive live broadcast rights for English Premier League Soccer. This newly formed division of elite clubs was the most valuable sports product in Britain. News Corporation's initial outlay of £305 million over five years paid immediate dividends—within a year subscriber numbers doubled to three million. BSkyB subsequently moved to quash future rivals by agreeing to pay £670 million for an extra four years' coverage. The 2001–05 television rights attracted rival bidder NTL, an American cable television corporation financed by Bill Gates. BSkyB eventually prevailed with a repurchase bid of £1.1 billion. From here, News Corporation set out to purchase other sporting contests including England soccer internationals, England's overseas cricket tests, major rugby union games, Ryder Cup golf, and the whole of professional rugby league including team franchises in England and Australia (Andrews 2004, p. 107). These developments were part of an international strategy. Murdoch used live sport to build subscriber bases for his pay-television channels. Major events could be broadcast, simultaneously, to multiple audiences worldwide. This maximised advertising revenue and weakened the position of free-to-air broadcasters in national markets.

The globalisation of media corporations was intimately associated with the globalisation of advertising. By 1996, the ten largest agencies had offices in more than fifty countries. McCann-Erikson was the pre-eminent global player with over two hundred offices in 130 countries. The leading world advertising and broadcasting associations had devised a single global standard for the purchase and production of television advertising. These developments signify the emergence of a vast media-advertising complex with the capacity to absorb cultural practices, public places, electronic spaces, and everyday life routines (Jackson, Andrews & Scherer 2005, p. 4). Today, the very definition of advertising blurs with public relations, sponsorship, celebrity marketing, brand building, and event management. Under these circumstances, sport offers advertising a myriad of opportunities. Thus, the clothing and equipment of prominent teams and athletes reveal corporate logos. Sport celebrities are promoted to fit brand values. During televised events, virtual advertisements are projected onto fields and stadia. Overall, the rich cultural traditions of particular sports provide a consumer base for the media-advertising complex. Truly international sports, such as athletics or soccer, attract global media and global advertisers. Consequently, top athletes and teams become vehicles for transnational brand building. The commercial lure of international sport is especially apparent during global events, such as the summer Olympics, World Cup soccer, and World Cup rugby union. These are mass-mediated occasions designed to fit the time schedules and commercial imperatives of television networks, major advertisers, and corporate sponsors (Roche 2004, pp. 165–81).

At this point, one must add a cautionary note; the resilience of national cultures precludes the prospect of a single global market for consumer durables, fashion, music, or sport-related products. Consequently, transnational corporations seek to represent national cultures in ways designed to engage the national sensibilities of local consumers. In this regard, David Andrews and Michael Silk argue that domestic constructions of national identity are refashioned to fit the promotional strategies of transnational corporations (Andrews & Silk 2005, p. 178). In particular, 'sport is mobilised as a major cultural signifier of nation that can engage national sensibilities, identities and experiences' (p. 181).

1. Global media-sport arrives in New Zealand

From 1987, national infrastructures of banking, energy, power/telecommunications, and rail transport were incorporated within the balance sheets of global corporations. As part of this trend, the New Zealand media system was hollowed out by transnational media corporates. Four key developments accelerated this process: the deregulation and corporatisation of broadcasting (1989), the entry of private and pay television (1989), the sale of Telecom (1990), and the removal of all restrictions on foreign media ownership (1991). Thus, TV3, which began as a nationally-based private consortium of investors, was taken over by Canada's largest television broadcaster, CanWest Global Communications Corporation. Pay-television operator, Sky Network Television Ltd, was founded by Craig Heatley (an ACT party founder), Terry Jarvis (a former New Zealand test cricketer), and Tappenden Construction (headed by Alan Gibbs and Trevor Farmer). For most of the 1990s, 51 per cent of Sky's shares were controlled by Bell Atlantic (an original purchaser of Telecom), American Information Technologies Corporation, Tele-Communications Inc and Time-Warner Inc. The other shareholders included ESPN, and Television New Zealand (Rosenburg 1994). In 1999, most of Television New Zealand's share was bought out by Newscorp-controlled Independent Newspapers Ltd. At that time it also owned 49 per cent of New Zealand's daily newspaper circulation along with extensive holdings in magazines, national weeklies, community titles, and websites. By 2001, INL controlled 66 per cent of Sky shareholdings (Rosenburg 2002).[1] Local advertising agencies have also become part of global empires. Thirty-five years ago,

80 per cent of New Zealand advertising was booked with locally owned agencies. By the early 1990s, almost 75 per cent was booked with subsidiaries of overseas-based firms (Perry 1990, p. 28).

The global absorption of corporate capitalism, national infrastructures, and media organisations and the advertising sector has redefined national culture. The transformation of New Zealand sport has been a cause and consequence of this process. This general argument can be explained via two strategic case studies.

2. America's Cup yachting

Offshore yacht racing had been a popular sport since the 1960s. New Zealand yachtsmen had won Olympic golds in the Sydney to Hobart race, the One Ton Cup, and the Whitbread Round the World race. The America's Cup, however, seemed beyond the country's resources. When merchant bankers Michael Fay and David Richwhite bankrolled the *KZ7* Fremantle challenge, they initiated an historic passage of events. From 1987, successive campaigns promoted entrepreneurial nationalism, equated national identifications with consumerism, and erased the distinction between sporting activity and commercialisation. In the first instance, Fay and Richwhite regarded the *KZ7* challenge as a marketing vehicle. They sought to promote their company and subsidiary holdings among the global financiers and corporate directors involved with the contest. Fay Richwhite also developed a sponsorship structure whereby the BNZ gained naming rights and raised public money through its branch network. Lion Corporation contributed funds through Steinlager sales, and a host of subsidiary sponsors raised cash in return for a commercial profile. As Bryn Evans observes, advertising, public relations, and sports marketing companies designed a publicity campaign to 'convince sponsors that their investment was worthwhile' and to 'legitimise the place of the new breed of financial high flyers at the top of New Zealand's national economy' (Evans 2004, pp. 85–6). For the latter purpose, corporate, entrepreneurial nationalism was equated with national unity. Most notably a BNZ television commercial featured the campaign theme song 'Sailing Away', a reworded version of 'Pokarekareana'. It was performed and recorded by a massed choir of New Zealand entertainers, sportspeople, and television personalities. Meanwhile, the mainstream media were saturated with sponsors' advertising and daily material from Fay Richwhite's public relations department.

The *KZ7* episode ended with the challenger's final loss to Denis Conner's *Stars and Stripes*. One year later, Fay Richwhite's failed attempt to wrest the cup with a giant monohull effectively changed the rules and commercial requirements for later challengers. At this point, TVNZ became involved as a restructured, commercially-oriented broadcaster. It needed a ratings booster to stave off growing competition from TV3. By vigorously promoting the new challenge, TVNZ could enlarge audience share and increase advertising revenue. Other sponsors could be secured with the guarantee of blanket television coverage (Atkinson 1995, pp. 40–1). Thus was born the family-of-five comprising TVNZ, Lion Nathan (Steinlager), Toyota, Telecom, and the Apple and Pear Marketing Board (ENZA). The campaign was unsuccessful, but in 1995 Team New Zealand's *Black Magic* won the America's Cup from *Stars and Stripes*. The family-of-five sponsorship model underwrote the successful challenge with Lotto replacing Telecom. Bryn Evans succinctly outlines the convergence of interests from a television perspective.

> In performing the simultaneous roles of supporter, investor and journalist, TVNZ's schedule was saturated with Cup coverage. Appeals to national sentiment were continually utilized to build public interest, and all of the broadcasts were saturated with sponsors' logos and products. Pseudo-documentaries and advertorial promotional clips blurred the lines between event coverage and advertising. They contained intermingling discourses of sport, business and nationalism. The general objective was to establish a shared national history centred on the America's Cup event and its sponsors (Evans 2004, p. 161).

Post-victory coverage fused national self-congratulation with corporate sector triumphalism. The euphoria exemplified a broader process whereby a seamless web of media, sport, and advertising obscured transnational corporate absorption of the New Zealand economy. After Team New Zealand successfully defended the America's Cup in 2000, skipper Russell Coutts, chief tactician Brad Butterworth, and other crew members joined Ernesto Bertarelli's *Alinghi* syndicate. During the 2003 Challenger series, all major syndicates employed New Zealand sailors, builders, and designers. After *Alinghi* won the America's Cup from Team New Zealand, Bertarelli announced that he would relax nationality rules for future competing teams. Future regattas thus became a showcase for inter-corporate rather than international rivalry (True 2003, pp. 10, 13–24). This passage of events effectively destroyed the family-of-five sponsorship and publicity system, which had driven previous New Zealand campaigns. The transnational corporate absorption of domestic business enterprise eventually included the personnel and expertise of Team New Zealand itself. The ensuing recriminations involving Team New Zealand and *Alinghi* supporters[2] revealed an underlying principle—the full commercialisation of a sport undermines its value as a catalyst for corporate nationalism.

3. Rugby Union

During the 1980s, the growing commercialisation of rugby union threatened its traditional amateur status. Elite players expected financial payment and they pressured the NZRFU to professionalise the game. After the inaugural World Cup of 1987, key All Blacks signed rugby league contracts with English and Australian clubs. Consequently, the 1991 World Cup All Blacks suffered a semi-final loss to Australia.

As the 1995 World Cup approached, global media-sport developments forced the New Zealand, Australian, and (post-apartheid) South African unions to embrace professionalism.

The first and most pressing of these developments was Super League, a rugby league organisation incorporating club competitions in Britain, France, and Australasia. This was a News Corporation vehicle to generate revenue from the purchase of live television rights and various team franchises. In Australia, News Ltd (a regional subsidiary of News Corporation) obtained control of the Brisbane Broncos club and offered big salaries to players already contracted to the incumbent Winfield Cup competition. This would enable the development of a twelve- to fourteen-team Super League competition for News Corporation's pay-television network, Foxtel. However, the Australian Rugby League (ARL) managed the Winfield Cup and the free-to-air Channel Nine network held live broadcasting rights. Channel Nine was part of Kerry Packer's conglomerate, Publishing and Broadcasting Ltd (PBL) (Mirams 2001, p. 52). Not surprisingly, the ARL publicly opposed Super League and, with PBL support, took legal action against News Ltd. During the interim, the ARL's defence of the Winfield Cup competition led to a bidding war for player contracts. Consequently, certain All Blacks were made lucrative offers to switch codes. The prospect of a depleted national team compelled the NZRFU to seriously consider the introduction of professionalism.

A second media-sport development eventually served to hasten the NZRFU's decision. During 1995, the World Rugby Corporation (WRC) initiated by a group of sports-minded Australian businessmen sought to sign elite rugby union players of various nationalities for a new global competition. This professional structure would benefit all parties once television rights for the matches were sold to global media. The international establishment of WRC franchises would then generate advertising and sponsorship support. By mid-July, immediately after the 1995 World Cup final, the WRC had signed up most of the New Zealand, South African, and Australian squads. Welsh, French, Scottish, and Western Samoan players had also committed themselves to the WRC (Fitzsimons 1996, p. 144). Packer's PBL made a speculative offer for broadcast rights if the WRC competition eventuated. In return for an initial outlay of A\$4 million, PBL also accepted an option to acquire majority ownership of World Rugby Corporation Ltd (Fitzsimons 1996, p. 214). As these events unfolded, the South African, Australian, and New Zealand unions (SANZAR) resolved to introduce professional contracts. This brings us to a third media-sport development. Contracts could only be financed from the sale of television rights and the only plausible buyer was News Corporation. Rupert Murdoch's interest in adding rugby union to his collection of sports was reinforced by the 1995 World Cup's obvious commercial success.

A deal was subsequently drawn up in which SANZAR received \$555 million over ten years in return for exclusive television rights to a yearly, international tri-series and a provincial 'super 12' competition (Fitzsimons 1996, p. 96). Each national union was thereby compelled to repurchase their squads from the WRC. To this end NZRFU officials and sympathetic journalists publicly aligned the News Corporation proposal with the national traditions of All Black rugby. The players eventually returned and the WRC collapsed but the new professional competitions broke with a central rugby tradition—free-to-air live telecasts of international matches. News Corporation onsold their broadcasting rights to the Sky network and TVNZ could only purchase delayed match coverage. As I have indicated Sky became, increasingly, a News Corporation-controlled enterprise. Televised rugby was thus a global media product only available to those with disposable income and good reception. Rugby's newfound commercial value was also exploited by advertisers, merchandisers, sponsors, and elite players themselves. All Blacks became marketable celebrities and/or salesmen pitching to consumers rather than players representing their supporters.

Global media's commercial influence over professional rugby was accompanied by transnational corporate sponsorship. In October 1997 German sportswear company, Adidas agreed in principle to a NZ$130 million contract with the NZRFU. Their mutual strategy was to co-brand the All Blacks. As apparel supplier to a team with global media exposure Adidas could expand the rugby sportswear market. Correspondingly, the NZRFU obtained a business partner with global marketing and distribution channels (Motion, Leitch & Brodie 2003, p. 1091). The promotional objective was to bring together core brand values. According to a Saatchi and Saatchi executive the 'All Blacks exuded excellence, tradition, inspiration, and respect' (for the black jersey, the country, and its people). The Adidas mission was to become the world's best and most authentic sports brand. In this context the All Black values of tradition, inspiration, and respect were matched with Adidas authenticity. For this purpose Saatchi and Saatchi were hired to undertake a multi-million dollar advertising campaign from July 1999. As Judy Motion, Shirley Leitch, and Roderick Brodie observe this was an exercise in corporate nationalism:

> The NZRU and its leading brand, the All Blacks, were positioned within the discourses of sport, national identity and, to a lesser extent business whereas Adidas was positioned within sport and business. For the articulation to succeed in New Zealand Adidas had to enter the discourse of national identity and rugby had to enter the discourse of business as a professional sports organization (Motion, Leitch & Brodie 2003, p. 1088).

The new All Blacks jersey exemplified these strategic objectives; a bright Adidas logo appeared opposite the left breast silver fern. The collarless neck resembled that worn by the 1905 'originals'. Adidas was thus positioned as new, yet natural inheritors of the All Black legacy. This branding strategy was complemented by the promotion of black-ness at each home test match. Fans were encouraged to wear black face paint and clothing to 'black out' the ground (Motion, Leitch & Brodie 2003, p. 1089). However, the centrepiece of the Saatchi and Saatchi campaign was a rebranded haka. From a Māori perspective, the All Black haka originated from that composed in the 1820s by Te Rauparaha, chief of the Ngati Toa tribe (Jackson & Hokowhitu 2005, p. 71). From 1905, this haka became appropriated as a generic symbol of racial integration and national unity. For Adidas, the haka was relaunched as an authentic, primal war dance and the All Blacks were promoted as 'the last authentic warriors' (Motion, Leitch & Brodie 2003, pp. 1087–8). This matched and reinforced the 'authentic' quality of the Adidas brand. For some observers the 'Adidasification' of the haka undermined the right of Māori to represent their cultural identity (Jackson & Hokowhitu 2005, pp. 77–9). Previously, the rugby–haka association had been a distinctive, contested feature of national history. Under corporate nationalism, such nuances were marginalised. The haka was repositioned to generate global commercial leverage from the All Black brand.

4. Sport and commercial television: Normative considerations

As the preceding case studies indicate, the commercialisation of television is inseparable from the commercialisation of sport. This dual process has reduced the capacity of sport to foster a public broadcasting culture. The TVNZ charter, implemented in March 2003, declares that 'programming should provide shared experiences that contribute to a sense of citizenship and national identity' (corporate.tvnz.co.nz/tvnz_detail). Clearly, this public broadcasting principle has been undermined by the migration of live sports coverage to pay television. At present, the Sky Network holds exclusive live rights to rugby union (All Black tests, Super 14, and the National Provincial Championship), rugby league ('Kiwi' tests and NRL matches featuring the New Zealand Warriors) and cricket ('Black Cap' test and one-day matches). Additionally, Sky programming features live sporting events not involving New Zealand. These include all other NRL matches, the State of Origin, all 'grand slam' tennis and golf tournaments, plus selected cricket and one-day internationals (usually involving Australia).[3] TVNZ retains live rights to 'Silver Fern' netball and international men's basketball featuring the 'Tall Blacks'. The reduction of public access to televised sport extends beyond live events and matches. In 1999, TV3 replaced TVNZ as Sky's delayed coverage partner for rugby union and cricket. Compared to 1998, roughly half as many rugby matches were shown and cricket coverage was restricted to highlights only (Norris 2002, p. 51). Thus, public television lost a lucrative source of advertising revenue, and free-to-air audiences were provided with less televised sport. Since then, cricket and delayed coverage of New Zealand Warriors rugby league matches has shifted to the Prime Network. This was formerly owned by Kerry Packer's PBL conglomerate, but, in November 2005, Sky announced its intention to buy Prime for NZ$30 million (Chan 2005). The purchase eventually took place and was approved by the Commerce Commission. With this deal, Sky could deny or curtail delayed sports coverage to rival networks. And, Prime would become a promotional vehicle for Sky programming. Such an arrangement has no parallel in other countries.

In the United Kingdom, BSkyB's acquisition of key sporting events precipitated government legislation to protect eight events deemed to be of national importance. These were the soccer World Cup, the Olympic Games, Wimbledon, the English and Scottish FA Cup Finals, the Epsom Derby, the Aintree Grand National, and home test matches for the England cricket team (Andrews 2004, p. 122).[4] In Australia, anti-siphoning laws protect international cricket, Bledisloe Cup rugby union, rugby league test matches and State of Origin, the NRL final, netball tests, the Formula One Grand Prix, and Olympic and Commonwealth Games coverage. In New Zealand, such regulations have been promised but never implemented. In 1996, Labour MP Steve Maharey called for protection of rugby matches of 'national significance', such as the Bledisloe Cup and World Cup (Bain 1996, p. 1). And New Zealand First deputy leader Tau Henare sought leave in parliament to introduce 'the Live Broadcast of All Black Test Matches Act' (unattributed, *The Dominion* 1996, p. 2). In April 1998, after TVNZ lost live cricket coverage to Sky, broadcasting spokespersons from the Alliance (Pam Corkery) and Labour (Marion Hobbs) attacked the National–New Zealand First coalition government for failing to honour its promise to protect live sport. Hobbs also proposed the establishment of a broadcasting code with provision for leading sports events to be televised free-to-air (unattributed, *The Dominion,* 1998, p. 2). However, after the election of the 1999 Labour–Alliance government, this proposal was never activated. As successive Ministers of Broadcasting and proponents of the TVNZ charter, Marion Hobbs and Steve Maharey failed to enhance the contribution of sport to public broadcasting.

In a deregulated broadcasting environment, ratings-driven free-to-air networks and subscription television reinforce the prominence of major sports. Corporate sponsors finance those sports with high television exposure, and television networks favour such sports because of the commercial revenue they provide. Meanwhile, minor sports are forced to pay for television access. In 1996, New Zealand-On-Air, the Health Sponsorship Council, and the New Zealand Assembly for Sport organised the telecast of a smoke-free minor sports series to better reflect the diversity of sporting activity (Cameron & Gidlow 1998, p. 141). However, recent sports policy developments have undermined this objective. In June 2000, the Labour–Alliance government established the Ministerial Taskforce on Sport, Fitness and Leisure. Following the release of its report, the Hillary Commission, the Sports Foundation, and the Office of Tourism and Sport were merged to form a new Crown agency—Sport and Recreation New Zealand (SPARC). Its strategic plan for sport prescribed more targeted funding and stated that future allocations would depend upon 'the likelihood of receiving a return on investment'. On this basis 'priority' sports were identified (Jackson 2004, p. 218). Sports that provide a return on investment are those which already enjoy corporate sponsorship and television exposure. The net result is likely to be the marginalisation of minor sports (in terms of funding and television coverage), and a reinforcement of traditional gender biases in sports programming (McGregor & Melville 1992, pp. 18–27).

All of those developments fracture the relationship between sport, broadcasting, and the fostering of an inclusive national identity. As I have argued, the predominant trend in New Zealand has been for commercial media-sport to expedite the commercialisation of national identity.

DISCUSSION QUESTIONS

1   Is it true to say that media corporations have no inherent interest in sport?
2   What kinds of sport are most vulnerable to commercial exploitation?
3   How has the corporate branding of New Zealand sport contributed to the commercialisation of national identity?
4   Is the coverage of sport on New Zealand television consistent with the principles of public broadcasting?

NOTES

1   I have not the space here to further detail the global media absorption of New Zealand print and radio holdings. For more information see Cocker 2003, 2006 and Rosenburg 2002. Bill Rosenburg's regularly updated website documents the evolving patterns of global media ownership within New Zealand.
2   When the *Alinghi* syndicate hired Russell Coutts, Brad Butterworth and other sailors, national sentiment was mobilised against them. Team New Zealand marketing equated nationalism with loyalty and an unofficial 'Blackheart' campaign financed by Auckland businessmen branded Coutts and Butterworth as traitors (True, 2003, pp. 10–12). The latter development can be seen as a last-gasp expression of a corporate nationalism originally devised for the 1986 *KZ7* campaign.
3   Sky does not hold exclusive live rights to the Olympics, the Soccer World Cup, or the Rugby World Cup. The organising bodies for these global mega-events stipulate that free-to-air broadcasters must not be denied live coverage. This maximises worldwide audience sizes for major-event sponsors.
4   Home cricket test matches in the United Kingdom are no longer subject to anti-siphoning laws.

REFERENCES

Andrews, D. 2004, 'Speaking the Universal Language of Entertainment: News Corporation, Culture and the Global Sport Media Economy' in D. Rowe (ed.), *Sport Culture and the Media*, Open University Press, London, pp. 99–128.

Andrews, D. & M. Silk 2005, 'Global Gaming: Cultural Toyotism, Transnational Corporatism, and Sport' in S. Jackson & D. Andrews (eds), *Sport, Culture and Advertising*, Routledge, London, pp. 172–91.

Atkinson, J. 1995, 'Cup Fever', *North and South,* July, pp. 40–1.

Bain, H. 1996, 'PM and Williamson at Odds on Pay TV Sport', *The Dominion,* 10 February, p. 1.

Cameron, J. & B. Gidlow 1998, 'Sociology of Leisure and Sport', in H Perkins & G. Cushman (eds), *Time Out? Leisure, Recreation and Tourism in New Zealand and Australia,* Longman Paul, Auckland, pp. 127–50.

Chan, K. 2005, 'Sky Television Buys Prime New Zealand', *New Zealand Herald,* 19 November.

Evans, B. 2004, 'Commercialising National Identity: A Critical Examination of New Zealand's America's Cup Campaigns of 1987, 1992 and 1995', MA Thesis, Auckland University of Technology.

Fitzsimons, P. 1996, *Rugby War,* Harper Collins, Sydney.

Harvey, J. & A. Law 2005, ' "Resisting" the Global Media Oligopoly? The Canada Inc. Response', in M. Silk, D. Andrews & C. Cole (eds), *Sport and Corporate Nationalisms,* Oxford, Berg, pp. 187–226.

Hope, W. 1996, 'A Short History of the Public Sphere', in *Aotearoa-New Zealand Continuum,* 10/1, pp. 2–32.

Hope, W. 2002, 'Whose All Blacks?', *Media, Culture and Society,* 24/2, pp. 235–53.

Jackson, S. 2004, 'Sport Policy Development in New Zealand', *International Review for the Sociology of Sport,* 39/2, pp. 205–22.

Jackson, S., D. Andrews & J. Scherer 2005, 'The Contemporary Landscape of Sport Advertising' in S. Jackson & D. Andrews (eds), *Sport, Culture and Advertising,* Routledge, London, pp. 1–23.

Jackson, S. & B. Hokowhitu 2005, 'Sports, Tribes and Technology: The New Zealand All Blacks Haka and the Politics of Identity', in M. Silk, D. Andrews & C. Cole (eds), *Sport and Corporate Nationalism,* Oxford, Berg, pp. 35–66.

McChesney, R. 2000, *Rich Media, Poor Democracy,* New Press, New York.

McGregor, J. & P. Melville 1992, 'The Invisible Face of Women's Sports in the New Zealand Press', in *Australian Journal of Leisure and Recreation* 2/4, pp. 18–27.

McLean, T. 1990, *Silver Fern: 150 Years of New Zealand Sport,* Hodder Moa Beckett, Auckland.

Mirams, C. 2001, *Beleaguered!—The Warriors—from Dream to Nightmare,* Hodder Moa Beckett, Auckland.

Motion, J., S. Leitch & R. Brodie 2003, 'Equity in Corporate Co-branding: The Case of Adidas and the All Blacks', *European Journal of Marketing,* 37/7/8, pp. 1080–94.

Norris, P. 2002, 'News Media Ownership in New Zealand', in J. McGregor & M. Comrie (eds), *What's News?,* Dunmore Press, Palmerston North, pp. 33–55.

Perry, M. 1990, 'Some implications of the internationalization of commercial capital for New Zealand', in *New Zealand Geographer,* 47/1, pp. 26–31.

Roche, M. 2004, 'Mega-events and Media Culture: Sport and the Olympics' in D. Rowe (ed.), *Sport, Culture and the Media,* Open University Press, London, pp. 165–81.

Rosenburg, B. 1994, 'News Media Ownership in Aotearoa', *The Word,* 6, July–August.

Rosenburg, B. 2002, 'News Media Ownership: How New Zealand is Foreign Dominated', *Pacific Journalism Review,* 8, June, pp. 59–95.

True, J. 2003, 'The Rebranding of National Identity', in R. Miller (ed.), *New Zealand Government and Politics,* 3rd edn, Oxford University Press, Melbourne pp. 3–15.

Unattributed, 1998, 'McCully to Seek Answers after TVNZ Drops Cricket', *The Dominion,* 16 April, p. 2.

Unattributed, 1996, 'Rugby Broadcast Bill Blocked', *The Dominion,* 22 February, p. 2.
Unattributed, 2002, 'The Big Ten', *The Nation,* 7–14 January (special supplement).
Watkin, T. 1998, 'Hit for Six', *Listener,* 2 May, pp. 22–4.

FURTHER READING

Collins, C. 2000, *Sport in New Zealand Society,* Dunmore Press, Palmerston North.
Maguire, J. 1999, *Global Sport: Identities, Societies, Civilisations,* Polity, Cambridge.
Roche, M. 2000, *Mega Events and Modernity: Olympics, Expos, and the Growth of Global Culture,* Routledge, London.
Wenner, L. 1998, *MediaSport,* Routledge, London.

7.0 Participation

7.1

Public Participation

Bronwyn M. Hayward

This chapter examines how the public participates in local and national decision-making in New Zealand and questions why increasing numbers of people, especially younger voters and ethnic minorities, appear to be switching off from traditional politics. Among the factors that help to explain declining participation are voter choice and political culture, political mobilisation, and the availability of opportunities to participate. The discussion concludes by exploring the implications of declining voter turnout for the future of democracy in New Zealand.

DECLINING PUBLIC PARTICIPATION

In the closing months of 2005, two events highlighted the problems of public participation facing many established democracies. In September, a significant US report was released which documented a pattern of declining voter turnout and increasing political disengagement which, the authors argue, puts the legitimacy of American democracy 'at risk' (Macedo et al. 2005). In November, riots broke out across France, with media commentators claiming that the rioters were predominantly young, the children of Muslim African and Arab immigrants, and lacking in employment opportunities, education, or a belief they could effect political change.

New Zealand seems far removed from international problems of public participation. Historically, New Zealanders have turned out to vote in droves, and our enthusiasm for community organisations once prompted a commentator to describe New Zealand as a nation of 'joiners' (Mitchell 1969, p. 179). However, more recently, New Zealand's record of participation has proved less robust. Ignoring the warning signs now may contribute to a more serious crisis of participation in the future.

Voter turnout remains high by international standards, but in the election 2002 the 'voting age population turnout' rate fell to a one-hundred year low of 72.5 per cent (Atkinson 2003, pp. 244–5). Between 1945 and 1999, New Zealand recorded the eighth steepest overall decline in turnout among OECD countries (Vowles et al. 2004, pp. 3–4). The 2005 turnout of 77 per cent of age-eligible voters (see chapter 4.2) is a surprisingly modest increase on the previous low figure, given the 'record' numbers who pre-registered to vote, and the highly competitive nature of the 2005 election campaign (Electoral Enrolment Centre 2005). At the level of local government, turnout is worse. The average turnout for mayoral elections in 2004 was 46 per cent, down from 61 per cent in 1989 (Justice and Electoral Committee 2005, p. 1.7C.)

While we may once have been a nation of 'joiners', New Zealanders are increasingly opting out of public life. In 1991 nearly half the country was estimated to belong to a sports club, but by 2003 this had fallen to 36 per cent (Cushman & Laidler 1991; SPARC 2001, pp. 3–4) and only approximately 2.4 per cent of voters belong to a political party (Miller 2005, p. 14).

When New Zealanders do participate in politics, we prefer passive forms of participation: voting, signing petitions, phoning talkback radio, writing letters to the editor (Vowles et al. 1995, p. 138), or informal discussion about politics with friends and family (Hayward 2005). Fewer New Zealanders participate more actively. The New Zealand Study of Values (1999) reported that 89 per cent of respondents had signed a petition, but only 19 per cent had attended lawful demonstrations, 17 per cent had joined a boycott, 4 per cent had joined unofficial strikes, and 1 per cent had occupied buildings or factories (Perry & Webster 1999, p. 88).

While most New Zealanders may prefer to participate in politics from the comfort of their couch, there are disturbing indications of more significant political disengagement. Following rapid economic and social policy changes of the 1980s, trust and confidence in government plummeted (State Services 2001). In the 1960s, about 66 per cent of survey respondents had agreed 'you can trust the government to do what is right most of the time', but by 1993 only 31 per cent agreed with this statement (Vowles et al. 2004, p. 173). While the figure recovered to 44 per cent by 2002 (Vowles et al. 2004), disturbingly few citizens express *strong* confidence in government (State Services Commission 2001). While some scepticism is healthy in a democracy, pervasive cynicism or mistrust is not. Of particular concern is a survey that found that 69.5 per cent of respondents agreed 'a few big interests, looking out for themselves are running New Zealand' (Perry & Webster 1999 cited in Henderson & Bellamy 2002, p. 92).

Rates of public participation in New Zealand are uneven. Some groups are participating less often than others. Young New Zealanders are notably less likely to vote, and voting abstention among young people seems to be lasting longer (Catt & Hayward 2005; Vowles 2004). Pacific and Māori voters are also more likely to stay at home on polling day (Vowles et al. 2004, p. 201). But staying at home is not a sign of satisfaction or complacency. A 2005 survey revealed that 18 per cent of New Zealand-Pacific people and 16 per cent of New Zealand-Māori strongly agreed that they would like more say in central and local government decision-making (Gravitas 2005). Similarly, a recent survey of Asian political opinion revealed two-thirds of the respondents believed 'it is harder for Asians to participate in NZ politics' and nearly 90 per cent of respondents agreed that Asian New Zealanders 'had very little or no influence on government policies in NZ' (*Rural Bulletin* 2004).

These patterns of declining participation and alienation are troubling, and what is particularly concerning is how little we know about who participates and why (Vowles et al. 2004). If New Zealand is to avoid a significant participation crisis in the future, we need to try to understand who is and who isn't taking part in public life, what issues matter to these communities and what factors might affect future participation.

DEFINING KEY TERMS

In a *representative democracy* voters choose a party or political candidate to make key decisions on their behalf. But even within a representative democracy, there are significant opportunities for citizens to participate in politics beyond voting. These opportunities range from commenting on proposals and policies, to actively making decisions where the representative government has delegated authority to a community, iwi (tribe) or other organisations. Techniques for eliciting participation include: tele-polling/free phones; citizen juries or public submissions (for select committees, commissions, or local councils); petitions and citizens' initiated referenda; public meetings; multi-stakeholder workshops; and a variety of online forums (Hayward 2005). Representative democracies that provide extensive opportunities for public participation are sometimes called '*thick*' or '*strong*' democracies (Barber 1984).

A narrower term, *public consultation*, is also used in legislation (Chen 1994). Effective public consultation is more than simply telling the public what the government plans to do. In a landmark ruling in 1992, Chief Justice McGechan defined public consultation as: 'The statement of a proposal not yet fully decided upon, listening to what others have to say, considering their responses, and then deciding what will be done' (Wellington Airport 1994). McGechan went on to say that consultation does not '... necessarily involve the negotiation toward an agreement, although the latter not uncommonly can follow ... consultation is an intermediate situation involving meaningful discussion'. The Chief Justice's ruling highlights the essential elements of effective public consultation, these are: providing *sufficient information* to consulted parties, ensuring *adequate time* for public consultation and deliberation, *genuine consideration* of any advice given, and a *willingness to change*.

Democracies that go beyond public participation or consultation, enabling citizens to make decisions first-hand, are referred to as '*direct*' or '*participatory*' democracies (Pateman 1970). In a '*direct*' or '*participatory*' democracy, citizens make binding decisions, for example, through referenda, town hall meetings, or community voting (Hayward 1995). The term '*deliberative*' democracy is used to describe a particular vision of participation where communities engage in open and tolerant public discussions rather than simply participating through voting (Young 2000).

WHY DOES PARTICIPATION MATTER?

Not everyone agrees that extensive public participation is necessary or even desirable. Some argue that low rates of participation indicate public satisfaction with government or that public involvement in politics should be limited to voting for competing parties in periodic elections (Schumpeter 1942). Public participation can be cumbersome and time consuming in large modern societies. Many people are just not that interested in politics, or lack the time to get involved. Advocates of participation are also criticised for looking back nostalgically to Athens of the fifth century BC, an oft-cited example of participatory democracy. In reality, Athenian citizens were carefully vetted, with all women, slaves, immigrants, and men under twenty being denied the privileges of citizenship (Beetham 1993).

Despite these criticisms, there are significant benefits associated with encouraging public participation. First, a high level of public involvement in democracy gives legitimacy to government policy and, furthermore, the level of voter turnout can impact on the content of policy. Vowles (2004, p. 27), for example, argues that in '... jurisdictions where turnouts are low, governments spend less on welfare'. Second, public participation often produces better decisions. Local communities can contribute valuable local knowledge or new perspectives (Hayward 2005). Third, the experience of first-hand involvement in government can strengthen the public's commitment to the principles of democracy (Barber 1984). Fourth, the adversarial, representative style of New Zealand's Westminster parliamentary debate often results in point-scoring and short-sighted policies designed to win elections rather than to solve collective problems. Wider public deliberation can aid collective problems by providing new opportunities for collaboration. Citizens can become 'transformed', no longer thinking solely of their own needs, but rather becoming 'other regarding' citizens, with a strengthened commitment to applying principles of democracy to public life (Warren 1992; Young 1997, pp. 67–8). Finally, public participation is also valued for intrinsic reasons, as an end in itself, as part of the 'good life'. Advocates argue that participation is a duty of citizens in a democracy, that is, our rights as free democratic citizens are matched by a corresponding duty to participate (Barber 1984).

WHAT FACTORS INFLUENCE PARTICIPATION?

As we have seen, those least likely to participate are young, and/or members of ethnic minorities and those people who are already economically or socially disadvantaged (Vowles & Aimer 1993). A social profile developed by Vowles and Aimer identifies three interrelated characteristics of non-voters:[1]

- an association with relative economic deprivation (low incomes, working class occupations and beneficiary status)
- an association with lower integration into the community (younger age, renters, never married, not church attendees)
- membership of a minority culture.

While voting is a useful indicator of participation, it does not capture all forms of political participation. Pippa Norris argues that public participation is not declining so much as rearranging. She describes it as a 'phoenix' effect as people find new ways to participate in politics (Norris 2002). New Zealand research has found some evidence to support her claim. Younger citizens vote less often but they are more likely to participate in consumer boycotts and Internet forums (Vowles 2004). To understand changing patterns of public participation we need to examine a complex range of factors. The factors discussed in this chapter that affect public participation are: *voter choice and political culture* (political socialisation and education); *political mobilisation* (the role of parties, trade unions, and interest groups); and *political opportunity* to participate (at the macro and micro level).

VOTER CHOICE AND POLITICAL CULTURE

Franklin (2004) argues that patterns of public participation are influenced by the rational choices of individual voters. In his view, voter attitudes and habits are influenced by the nature of the elections (how competitive they are), the extent to which parties successfully appeal to voters, and the way these factors interact to influence people at the time they first vote. Franklin suggests the experience of first-time voting is 'vital' because it sets a pattern for the rest of your life. Those who do not vote are more likely not to vote in subsequent elections. However, Franklin argues that young people do not lack a sense of civic duty or civic virtue. Rather they are affected by the conditions that influence their decision-making (Franklin 2004, p. 215). Franklin controversially concludes that the decision to lower the voting age to eighteen was 'a really bad idea' (Franklin 2004, p. 213; also see discussion in chapter 4.2 of this volume) claiming that, at eighteen years of age, most people have left formal schooling but are not usually fully integrated into society (e.g. through work and relationships). As a result, he argues, they are ill-prepared to make their first vote. Franklin concludes: 'ironically almost any other age from 15 to 25 would be a better age for individuals to first be confronted with the need to acquire the skills and knowledge required for casting a vote' (2004, p. 213).

In New Zealand, there are indications that younger voters are disadvantaged by a lack of formal voter education (Catt & Hayward 2005). What we teach young people about politics and how we teach it matters (see chapter 7.5). The more education a person has, the more likely they are to vote and to have a positive perception of their own 'personal efficacy', or competence, to participate (Morrell 2005). Furthermore, education that provides experience in decision-making also increases a citizen's sense of external efficacy, or belief that his or her participation will make a difference (Catt & Hayward 2005).

Beyond education, other aspects of political culture are also thought to influence participation. The impact of the media on voter behaviour has been studied extensively. Researchers have examined the way the length of news items, style of presentation, the adversarial nature of interview formats, content, and advertising can influence turnout and public attitudes (Boston et al. 2003, pp. 221–82). Other studies have examined the relationship between social capital and political participation. Social capital is a broad term covering general participation in social networks and community groups and the levels of cooperation, trust, and reciprocity generated by this participation (Putnam 2000, p. 420). Robert Putnam argues that 'declining electoral participation is merely the most visible symptom of a broader disengagement from community life' (Putnam 2000, p. 35). But the relationship between social capital and political participation is problematic. Community disengagement does not entirely explain political disengagement. For example, in New Zealand, Māori and Pacific communities have high rates of social capital, yet low voter turnout (Ministry of Social Development 2005).

POLITICAL MOBILISATION

Research has been conducted on how groups, especially political parties and interest groups, mobilise the public. A decline in political party membership is thought to reinforce declining voter turnout (Miller 2005). Slimmed-down political parties have focused their campaigns on leadership and mass advertising at the expense of grass roots voter mobilisation (Miller 2005, pp. 192–3.). With the exception of the Greens, there has also been a particularly noticeable decline in party mobilisation of young voters (Miller 2005, pp. 91–2). Young people may be a particularly difficult group for traditional parties to target because when they do vote, younger voters tend to be motivated by particular issues rather than being aligned with particular parties (Duncan 2004, p. 107; Boston et al. 2003, pp. 140–4).

Many local interest groups have also struggled to mobilise participation in the wake of membership decline. The collapse of trade union membership was particularly dramatic in New Zealand after the introduction of the Employment Contracts Act 1991 (Duncan 2004, pp. 222–3). Research suggests that the decline of unions depresses voter turnout for parties on the left, but that parties on the right of the political spectrum are not affected as greatly because their supporters tend to remain as core members of church, agricultural, and business groups and are more easily mobilised through these groups (Bowler & Donovan 2005).

POLITICAL OPPORTUNITY

Public participation is also affected by the presence or absence of opportunities to participate. Macro-level opportunities include the institutional arrangements and legislative provisions for participation. New Zealand's most significant institutional opportunity is the electoral system. Systems of proportional representation are generally associated with higher voter turnout as the public perceives their votes are less likely to be wasted (Vowles et al. 2004). In New Zealand, the introduction of MMP was associated with a temporary recovery in declining voter participation and, while voter turnout has fallen again, it is likely that voter turnout is still higher than it would be if a first-past-the-post system had remained (Vowles et al. 2004, pp. 150–66).

There are also significant legislative opportunities for public participation, for example, under the Resource Management Act (RMA) 1991 and the Local Government Act (LGA) 2002. The purpose of the RMA is to promote the sustainable management of New Zealand's natural and physical resources. Any group or individual can make submissions on a resource application if the application is publicly notified. Business interests have criticised the RMA for slowing development; however, in reality fewer than 5 per cent of all proposals are notified for public comment each year.[2] The Local Government Act 2002 also introduced new public participation procedures. The purpose of the Act is to 'enable democratic local decision making' (LGA 2002 part 2, s 1). In particular, the Act requires local councils to identify stakeholders and consult communities of interest about their long-term values and priorities in the preparation of 'long term community plans'. These provisions are new and not yet implemented effectively. A 2005 survey reported that less than half of the respondents understood how local government decisions are made (Gravitas 2005). These legislative opportunities are complemented by other initiatives, including opportunities for public submissions to parliamentary select committees or commissions of inquiry, together with the opportunity to petition parliament to hold a Citizens' Initiated Referendum (CIR Act 1993).

The extent to which the public takes up these institutional and legislative opportunities is affected by a number of *micro-level factors* including context, conditions, and resources. Turning first to the context of participation, factors such as the time of day, presence or absence of competing events, provision of childcare, and advertising can significantly encourage or deter people from participating (Hayward 2005). Other influential conditions include how comfortable and welcome participants are made to feel. For example, women and members of minority cultures often report feeling intimidated by large adversarial public meetings or meetings where there is a lot of technical jargon (Hayward 2005).

Access to resources, particularly free time, knowledge, and finances also affect the extent to which communities can take up opportunities to participate. Many people, especially women, report having less time to take part in community events, particularly those who work longer hours for less income (Ministry of Social Development 2005). Many minority groups report consultation fatigue, due to being over-surveyed or over-consulted. Other resource limitations include expertise or finances; making a submission or appeal can be a costly exercise. For example, under the RMA developers often stand to gain tangible financial rewards from a proposal, and therefore have added incentive to participate. While environmental legal assistance is provided to those support groups that represent the wider environmental or public interest, any funding is limited to $30,000 per case, and only $1 million was available in total in 2005/6.[3]

IMPROVING PUBLIC PARTICIPATION: PREVENTING A FUTURE CRISIS?

In summary, while public participation in New Zealand is declining, the pattern of decline is uneven. Young people, members of ethnic minorities, and those with the lowest levels of education and income are least likely to participate by voting. Some groups do not vote but are involved in public life in other ways, for example, by participating in the local Pacific church or through consumer boycotts or Internet forums. However, voting is the primary method by which we choose a government and legitimate those decisions that are made in a democracy. Those who do not vote are silenced in the policy process. Furthermore, many non-voters may be doubly disadvantaged by any trend towards new forms of political participation. Low income Pacific communities, in particular, lack the economic resources to have their say via consumer boycotts, and these same groups have the lowest household penetration of Internet technologies, making new forms of e-democracy comparatively inaccessible (Ministry of Social Development 2005).

Voter turnout is likely to decrease further as New Zealand's population changes and younger New Zealanders, particularly those from ethnic minorities, reach voting age. There is much we don't know about who participates and who doesn't. Are particular generations less likely to vote than others, or is non-voting a symptom of wider social change? What political issues matter to people? These fundamental questions need to be understood if New Zealand is to avoid a future crisis of public participation. We need to act now to enable new voices to be heard in New Zealand politics.[4]

DISCUSSION QUESTIONS

1 As a tutorial group, stand up and arrange yourselves in a continuum, ranging from those who most strongly agree, to those who most strongly disagree with the following statement: 'I find joy and fulfilment in private life rather than public activity'. In what ways and to what extent do you think changing patterns of public or community participation reflect changes in wider lifestyle and community values?
2 Do you agree with Franklin that it was a 'really bad idea' to lower the voting age to eighteen and that almost any age between fifteen and twenty-five would be better? Why or why not?
3 Have you participated in politics? If so, how?
4 How important is voting as a form of political participation in your view?

NOTES

1   The choice of indicators of community integration could be debated. For example, rates of heterosexual marriage or of church attendance may not be universally accepted as valid indicators of an individual's sense of integration into the community. However, Vowles and Aimer argue that, taken together, their results are 'consistent with international evidence about non-voting' (1993, p. 53).The belief that 'my vote won't count' and 'disbelief in the importance of voting as a civic duty' are also factors associated with recent patterns of non-voting in New Zealand (Vowles 2004).
2   For a discussion of the RMA and public provisions see the Ministry for the Environment website at www.mfe.govt.nz/issues/resource/participation/
3   Ibid.
4   While any errors within this chapter are the responsibilities of the author, I am grateful to Victoria Craw and Timothy Milne for research assistance, and to Therese Arsenau for helpful comments.

REFERENCES

Atkinson, N. 2003, *Adventures in Democracy, A History of the Vote in New Zealand*, Otago University Press, Dunedin.
Barber, B. 1984, *Strong Democracy: Participatory Politics for a New Age*, University of California Press, Berkeley.
Beetham, D. 1993, 'Liberal Democracy and the Limits of Democratization', in D. Held (ed.), *Prospects for Democracy; North, South, East, West*, Polity Press, Cambridge.
Boston, J., S. Church, S. Levine, E. McLeay & N.S. Roberts (eds) 2003, *New Zealand Votes, The General Election of 2002*, Victoria University Press, Wellington.
Bowler, S. & Donovan, J. 2005, 'State Level Barriers to Participation', Paper presented to the American Political Science Association, 1–4 September, Washington DC.
Catt, H. & B. Hayward 2005, 'Now or Never: The Impact of Political Education on Civic Participation', Paper presented to Australasian Political Studies Conference, 28–30 September, Dunedin.

Chen, M. 1994, 'The Impact of MMP on Public Consultation', Paper presented to Public Consultation Process Conference, Wellington.

Dominion Post 2005, 'Rioting for their Rights', 14 November www.stuff.co.nz/stuff/dominionpost/0,2106,3477483a6483,00.html

Duncan G. 2004, *Society and Politics*, Pearson, Auckland.

Electoral Enrolment Centre 2005, 'Young People Don't Care about Voting: Yeah Right!' www.elections.org.nz/news/eec_media_young_120505.html

Electoral Enrolment Centre 2005, 'Enrolment Passes the 95 Per cent Mark', 21 September www.elections.org.nz/news/article_410.html

Franklin, M. 2004, *Voter Turnout and the Dynamics of Electoral Competition in Established Democracies since 1945*, Cambridge University Press, Cambridge.

Gravitas Research and Strategy Limited for Christchurch City Council 2005, 'Quality of Life in New Zealand's Largest Cities', Local Government Association, Wellington.

Hayward, B. 1995, 'The Greening of Participatory Democracy; Reconsideration of Theory', *Environmental Politics*, 4/4, pp. 215–36.

Hayward, B. 2005, 'Effective Citizen Engagement and Social Learning in Environmental Policy: The New Zealand Experience', Paper presented to the American Political Science Association, 1–4 September, Washington DC.

Hayward, J. (ed.) 2003, *Local Government and the Treaty of Waitangi*, Otago University Press, Dunedin.

Henderson, J. & P. Bellamy 2002, *Democracy in New Zealand*, Macmillan Brown Centre for Pacific Studies and International Institute for Democracy, Christchurch.

Justice and Electoral Committee 2005, 'Inquiry into the 2004 Local Authority Elections', otherpublications.clerk.parliament.govt.nz.clients.intergen.net.nz/attachments/FileForWeb-20050826–123722-I7C.pdf

Knauf, J. 2005, 'From the Scrum to the Chamber: Social Capital, Public Confidence and the Parliamentarian's Dilemma', *Political Science*, 57/1, pp. 21–38.

Lamare, J. 1991, 'Crisis in Confidence: Political Powerlessness in New Zealand', in E. McLeay (ed.), *The 1990 General Election: Perspectives on Political Change in New Zealand*, Oxford University Press, Auckland, pp. 164–6.

Macedo, S. 2005, *Democracy at Risk*, Brookings Institution Press, Washington DC.

McVey, A. & J. Vowles 2005, 'Virtuous Circle or Cul De Sac? Social Capital and Political Participation in New Zealand', *Political Science*, 57/1, pp. 5–20.

Miller, R. 2005, *Party Politics in New Zealand*, Oxford University Press, Melbourne.

Ministry for Social Development 2005, The Social Report 2005, 'Social Connectedness', Wellington. www.socialreport.msd.govt.nz/

Mitchell, A.V. 1969, *Politics and People in New Zealand*, Whitcombe and Tombs, Christchurch.

Morrell, M. 2005, 'Deliberation, Democratic Decision-Making and Internal Political Efficacy' in *Political Behaviour*, 27/1.

New Zealand Human Rights Commission 2005, 'Action Plan for Human Rights' www.hrc.co.nz/report/index.html

Norris, P. 2000, *Democratic Phoenix: Reinventing Political Activism*, Cambridge University Press, New York.

Parliamentary Library 2005, 'Final Results: 2005 General Election', in Information Briefing Service for Members of Parliament, Wellington.

Pateman, C. 1970, *Participation and Democratic Theory*, Cambridge University Press, Cambridge.

Perry, P. & A. Webster 1999, *New Zealand Politics at the Turn of the Millenium,* Alpha Publications, Auckland.

Putnam, R. 2002, *Bowling Alone,* Simon and Schuster, New York.

Rural Bulletin 2004, 'Asian Political and Social Attitudes', Ministry of Agriculture and Forestry, Wellington, www.maf.govt.nz/mafnet/publications/ruralbulletin/oct-04/oct-04–02.htm#P54_10041

Schumpeter, J. 1942, *Capitalism, Socialism and Democracy,* Allen & Unwin, London.

SPARC (Sport and Recreation New Zealand) 2001, Key Facts, www.sparc.org.nz/research-policy/research-/sparc-facts-97–01

Spellerberg, A. 2001, 'Framework for the Measurement of Social Capital in New Zealand', Statistics New Zealand, Wellington.

State Services Commission 2000, 'Working Paper No. 9: Declining Government Performance? Why Citizens Don't Trust Government', www.ssc.govt.nz, Wellington.

Vowles, J. 2004, 'Civic Engagement in New Zealand: Decline or Demise'? Inaugural professorial address delivered at Conference Centre, University of Auckland, www.nzes.org/docs/papers/Inaugural_2004.pdf

Vowles, J., P. Aimer, S. Banducci, J. Karp & R. Miller (eds) 2004, *Voters' Veto: The 2002 Election in New Zealand and the Consolidation of Minority Government,* Auckland University Press, Auckland.

Vowles, J. & P. Aimer 1993, *Voters' Vengeance: The 1990 Election in New Zealand and the Fate of the Fourth Labour Government,* Auckland University Press, Auckland

Vowles, J., P. Aimer, H. Catt, J. Lamare & R. Miller 1993, *Toward Consensus? The 1993 Election in New Zealand and the Transition to Proportional Representation,* Auckland University Press, Auckland.

Warren, M. 1992, 'Democratic Theory and Self Transformation', *American Political Science Review,* 16/1, pp. 8–23.

Wellington International Airport Ltd vs. Air New Zealand, High Court Registry CPN0 403/91, 1994, Cited in Ministry for the Environment and Local Government Commission, *Taking up the Challenge of Agenda 21: A Guide for Local Government,* Ministry for the Environment, Wellington, p. 25.

Young, I. 2002, *Inclusion and Democracy,* Oxford University Press, New York.

FURTHER READING

Boston, J., S. Church, S. Levine, E. McLeay & N.S. Roberts (eds) 2003, *New Zealand Votes, The General Election of 2002,* Victoria University Press, Wellington.

Franklin, M. 2004, *Voter Turnout and the Dynamics of Electoral Competition in Established Democracies since 1945,* Cambridge University Press, Cambridge.

Macedo, S. 2005, *Democracy at Risk,* Brookings Institution Press, Washington DC.

McVey, A. & J. Vowles 2005, 'Virtuous Circle or Cul de Sac?' Social Capital and Political Representation in New Zealand', *Political Science,* 27/1, pp. 5–20.

Putnam, R. 2002, *Bowling Alone,* Simon and Schuster, New York.

Vowles, J., P. Aimer, S. Banducci, J. Karp & R. Miller (eds) 2004, *Voters' Veto: The 2002 Election in New Zealand and the Consolidation of Minority Government,* Auckland University Press, Auckland.

Interest Groups

Tim Tenbensel

Imagine, for a moment, that you are the proud but poor owner of an apartment that suffers from 'leaky building syndrome'. You and your fellow residents face high renovation costs and you might want to take legal action against the developer, but you discover that the developer's company doesn't exist any more. You could take legal action against the government's Building Industry Authority that approved the use of untreated timber in new buildings. However, such actions have so far been unsuccessful. What else can you do? According to a conservative estimate, around 15,000 homes in New Zealand are affected by leaky building syndrome. That means that 15,000 homeowners are experiencing similar problems. A potentially more productive approach would be to band together as a group to put pressure on the government to provide compensation for your losses. Such a group exists and is known as Leaky Homes Action. In December 2005, its spokesperson claimed that '... people are sitting in the leaking, rotten, poisonous homes. The government should step up, acknowledge it's a national disaster and provide compensation or assistance to enable safe and sanitary repairs'.[1]

The fact that organised groups attempt to influence government policy and decision-making has significant implications for how we think about politics in a democratic society. Clearly, political participation is not simply a matter of voting in periodic elections. When citizens organise themselves into groups they are often capable of exerting considerable influence.

Typically, when we hear about the efforts of a group such as Leaky Homes Action, we are likely to be interested in their chances of success. Political scientists have some useful tools for investigating this type of question. Political scientists who study such groups (we typically refer to them as interest groups or pressure groups) will pose questions such as:

- Are there different types of interest group, and do some types have more influence than others?
- What types of relationship are there between interest groups and government, and between different interest groups?
- Is interest group influence in a democratic society desirable or not?

As students of New Zealand politics, there is also the question of how interest groups fit into this country's broader political environment. This chapter outlines some of the key ways in which these questions have been answered.

DEFINING INTEREST GROUPS

Interest groups can be defined as groups who organise in order to influence public policy decisions, but do not do so in the form of political parties. This may appear to be a simple definition, yet it needs to be unpacked a little more. The first key point to note is that interest groups are organised. This means that the focus of interest-group study is on identifiable and specific groups. For example, the environmental movement is not an interest group, but National Forest Action is.

Second, the definition states that the purpose of interest groups is to influence policy. This does not mean that influencing policy is a group's sole or even primary purpose, just that it may seek to do so under particular circumstances. In addition to obvious groups such as business councils and trade unions, many organisations, including churches, sports clubs, and welfare agencies, can become interest groups if and when they perceive that their interests, and the interests of those whom they represent, might be advanced or threatened by political developments.

Finally, a line needs to be drawn between interest groups and political parties as types of political organisations. The distinction is usually made along the lines that political parties operate primarily in the electoral arena, while interest groups operate in a range of non-electoral areas, such as bureaucratic forums and public inquiries, or on coordinated social protests. Thus, if a new group forms and decides to put up candidates and contest an election, it is regarded as a party. The distinction between interest group and party highlights difficult choices of political strategy. Within the green movement for example, it is a mistake to consider the Green party as having the same political objectives as environmental organisations. They have different, and sometimes conflicting, priorities that are largely shaped by the political milieu within which they operate.

TYPES OF INTEREST GROUPS

The category 'interest groups' covers a richly diverse range of organisations. Political scientists often make a distinction between 'sectional' and 'promotional' groups. Sectional groups are those that represent identifiable economic interests. For instance, the Federated Farmers of New Zealand represents the economic interests of farmers in the policy process, and the Council of Trade Unions represents workers' economic interests.

The contrasting category, promotional groups, refers to those organisations that promote particular value-based causes such as independence for Tibet, or the rights of the unborn child. Greenpeace and Amnesty International are considered to be classic promotional groups because the benefits of the policy objectives they pursue are not limited to their membership. Other distinctions follow from this basic one. Sectional groups typically have 'closed' or limited membership, whereas promotional groups typically have 'open' membership. Anyone can join National Forest Action, but only registered medical practitioners can be members of the New Zealand Medical Association.

An obvious way for interest groups to exert influence in political processes is to be closely tied to a major political party. For example, unions have often preferred to pursue their interests through the New Zealand Labour party, as have farmers through National. While there are obvious benefits from adopting such a strategy, there is also an equally obvious downside. Forming a connection with a particular party means that times are likely to be lean for the group concerned when its party is not in office. For this reason, some interest groups may prefer the durability of a relationship with the more permanent institutions of government, particularly the bureaucracy.

A related characteristic of interest groups concerns the extent to which they can be considered to be political insiders or outsiders. Insiders 'have the ear' of government—they are typically involved in the formulation of policy, and are consulted over any changes that may affect their constituency. Insider status brings with it access to information about policy. It also confers a formal role on such groups. Insider groups also become more aware of the opposing political forces within government. The Employers' Federation is a good example of an insider interest group. (It should be remembered, however, that government does not always do what insider interest groups want.) The Water Pressure Group, which opposes user charges for household water, exemplifies an outsider group that has no channels of access to government.

We should not presume, however, that all interest groups aim to become insider groups. Being on the inside attracts significant costs as well as benefits. Insider status can limit the capacity of the group to speak out, either because of fear of losing status or the favour of the government, or because they are 'locked in' to decision-making processes, even though they may disagree with decisions that are made. In the end, access to decision-making and policy influence may be deemed not worth the cost of compromising the group's broader values.

It is also misleading to equate interest-group influence with media profile. Despite enjoying substantial media coverage, some of the most prominent groups have relatively little influence with the government. Indeed, the major reason why some groups are so vocal is simply because of a lack of influence over governmental decision-making and policy. High media visibility may be an indicator of outsider status. In contrast, insider groups are less inclined to make a big media splash, particularly if they have contributed to the policy of the day. Greenpeace is a good example of an interest group that has gradually shifted from an outsider to an insider strategy. In the 1970s and 1980s Greenpeace pioneered many highly effective, symbolic actions that attracted media and public attention. Such outsider strategies were very effective in putting new issues on the political agenda. However, once Greenpeace's issues (such as whaling) were successfully established on the agenda, it tended to follow more of an insider strategy.

While these distinctions between sectional and promotional, closed and open, insider and outsider, are all useful, they are best used as defining the ends of spectrums rather than as black-and-white categories. Many groups will pursue both sectional interests and values (in practice it is sometimes difficult to draw a line between these). Interest groups can also be insiders on one issue and outsiders on another.

There are a number of important organisational characteristics that contribute to the capacity of interest groups to exert influence. Virtually every political activity engaged in by interest groups costs money, whether it be organising rallies or acquiring the services of a professional lobbyist. The level of membership may significantly determine the level of financial resources available to an interest group. Membership also provides a pool of committed, voluntary labour for crucial campaigns. For groups such as Amnesty International, strong membership can overcome financial obstacles.

Expertise is also an important political resource. Many interest groups choose to establish a permanent office or secretariat that employs staff. Other groups are more reluctant to do so, as this frequently leads to differences in priorities between the membership and the staff.

Another significant resource is the commitment of members and/or staff. Commitment is often the major strength of small community and promotional interest groups. The reverse side of this coin, however, is that groups may risk 'burn-out' of their best members and activists if they rely on commitment too much.

MODELS OF INTEREST-GROUP POWER

Pluralism is a theoretical approach to the study of politics that situates interest groups at the centre of the political process. Pluralism was at its most influential in the USA during the 1950s and 1960s, and its most important exponents were David Truman and Robert Dahl. Pluralists contend that interest groups are the building blocks, the active forces, of politics. Governments, on the other hand, tend to act as the independent arbiter between the various competing claims of interest groups, thus occupying a more reactive role in political processes, responding to the demands of interest groups rather than initiating their own demands.

Pluralists also argue that political power is generally fragmented rather than concentrated. This means that no particular interest group dominates political processes across the board. So, for example, while it may be true that one group is most influential in educational politics, and another group dominates defence issues, the same group does not dominate both. Although pluralists claim that political power is widely dispersed, this does not imply that it is distributed equally between interest groups. The actual power of interest groups is dependent upon their capacity to mobilise their resources and exploit political opportunities available to them. Pluralists such as Truman do claim, though, that any interest group has the potential to influence political outcomes, and that there is equality of opportunity between groups (Truman 1951).

Many critics of pluralism took issue with the way in which pluralism treated the role and significance of government. In contrast to the pluralist view of government as reactive to social forces, a number of writers (Skocpol 1985; Nordlinger 1988) have sought to re-emphasise the role of government as a proactive force. These 'state autonomists' argued that governments have identifiable interests of their own, and are, in many cases, capable of acting autonomously from the demands and pressures of interest groups. Governments may choose to involve interest groups when and where it suits, but the choice to include or exclude is more a reflection of government's power rather than a reflection of the power of the interest groups concerned (Christiansen & Dowding 1994).

An intermediate position between pluralist and state autonomist views of interest groups is that of corporatism. These commentators argue that there are only a small number of powerful interest groups whose input is essential to the conduct of government (Lembruch & Schmitter 1982). In this model, key insider groups (usually business, and sometimes labour unions) are at the centre of government. Policy is set by negotiation and agreement between government and the representatives of key interest groups. Meanwhile, other groups that may have a reasonable interest in economic policy (such as welfare groups or environmental groups) are likely to be excluded from the policy process. The idea that some types of groups are more important than others was also suggested by Charles Lindblom, a close academic colleague of Dahl's. Lindblom claimed that business interests had a 'privileged position' in the policy process in a way that other groups did not (Lindblom 1980).

ANTI-SMOKING GROUPS AND GOVERNMENT

Most political scientists studying interest groups over the past twenty years have concentrated on understanding dynamics within particular 'policy subsystems'—such as food policy or transport policy. One thing that is very clear from a range of studies in this area is that the nature of these relationships varies significantly between policy areas, and over time.

One of the most important findings of research into relations between interest groups and government is that there are many differing and competing interests *within* government. One of the most influential ideas about interest groups that has gained acceptance in the past twenty years is that interest groups and government agencies work closely together on a range of issues, often in opposition to other constellations of interest groups and government agencies. The arena of tobacco policy is one where this dynamic has been clearly charted in the UK (Read 1992).

Similar dynamics can be observed in New Zealand (Thomson & Wilson 2001). There was a close relationship between anti-smoking groups such as Action for Smoking and Health (ASH) and the Smoke-free Coalition, and the Ministry of Health in the development of the Smoke-free Amendment 2003 that banned smoking in bars, clubs, and restaurants. This relationship between the Ministry and anti-tobacco interest groups has persisted and grown over some time. Many anti-tobacco proposals were resisted in the 1990s by a combination of tobacco industry groups and the most powerful government agency, namely Treasury. These different combinations, which are held together by similar interests, values, and world views, are sometimes referred to as 'policy communities' (Marsh & Rhodes 1992), or 'advocacy coalitions' (Sabatier & Jenkins-Smith 1993), or 'discourse coalitions' (Hajer 1995).

The relationship between the Ministry of Health and ASH was an interesting side issue to the debate about the Smoke-free Amendment. The interest group representing the hospitality industry (HANZ) objected to the fact that a substantial proportion of the money used by ASH to conduct its campaign for smoke-free bars and clubs was provided by the Ministry of Health. This example shows the close ties that can exist between government organisations and interest groups. However, New Zealand's political institutions also make it possible for governments to marginalise interest groups from the political and policy process. New Zealand is a unitary rather than a federal country, and it has only one house of parliament (a very unusual feature among OECD countries). This concentrated institutional power has the potential to reduce the opportunities for interest groups to influence the decision-making process because governments have a greater capacity to drive through changes. In the USA, where institutional power is much more fragmented, an interest group that is cut out of the political process at one level, or loses a political battle in one arena, can usually find other arenas in which to launch a fresh challenge. From New Zealand's bedrock of concentrated power, governments of the 1980s and 1990s took steps to reduce the role of interest groups in political processes even further. Some reforms, such as those in education and workplace relations, were specifically designed to curtail the influence of particular interest groups, such as unions.

INTEREST GROUPS AND GOOD GOVERNANCE

These different patterns of relationship between interest groups and government are partly underpinned by different evaluations of the role of interest groups in policy. Do interest groups facilitate better political decisions, or are they impediments to good government? Should governments aspire to including interest groups in policy deliberations, or should they try to minimise their influence? The following sections of this chapter give a broad outline of the positive and negative evaluations of interest groups.

1. The positives

Pluralists such as Truman and Dahl clearly thought that interest groups actually provide the glue that connects the concerns of individual citizens to the task of governing society. A number of arguments have been advanced in favour of interest groups:

- They are essential to a healthy democracy because they provide viable avenues for political participation. Without interest groups, participation in democratic processes would be limited to the ballot box.
- Interest groups counteract the dominance of parliament by the executive government. In the event that parliament has become a less viable channel to articulate democratic concerns, then interest groups can assume some responsibility for such a task. In other words, when the parliamentary opposition is weak or inept, interest groups can act as watchdogs or whistle-blowers on executive government.
- Interest groups can act as sounding boards for new policy proposals. They can contribute creative input and fresh angles on particular problems.
- Interest groups perform crucial roles in providing feedback to government, and in helping to ensure that implementation of government policy is successful. Interest groups can inform government that a particular course of action will adversely affect the constituency of that interest group.

2. The negatives

Critics of interest groups, on the other hand, question their democratic credentials and challenge any suggestion that they enhance the goals of fairness and efficiency. Their arguments are as follows:

- A society that emphasises the role of interest groups is condoning the principle that 'whoever shouts the loudest is given the most attention'. It gives the advantage to those who are capable of organising themselves, those who are articulate, and those who have access to key resources, and disadvantages those who do not possess these skills and resources (Lowi 1969).

- Interest groups clog up the machinery of government. The proliferation of demands from interest groups make it more difficult for governments to govern, because too many demands must be satisfied if a government is to remain electorally viable. Interest groups also slow down the process of government because of the degree of consultation that is necessary to include them in the policy process.

- Interest groups do not serve the public good. Rather, they are only concerned with looking after the interests of their members and constituencies at the expense of the broader good of the community. Interest groups only ever represent minority interests. To the extent that they are successful in having their interests taken into account, they can be considered as 'vested' interests—the word 'vested' indicating that they would have something to lose if policies that genuinely reflected the common good were pursued.

- Interest groups may not really represent their constituencies. Those who make this argument question the degree to which unions engaged in corporatist policy processes actually represent the interests of the workers they represent, and suggest they may simply represent the combined interests of government, business, and union leadership.

INTEREST GROUPS IN NEW ZEALAND POLITICS

If we turn the clock back to the late 1970s and early 1980s, New Zealand exhibited many of the characteristics typical of Western democracies of that era. Economic policy was based on a dominant consensus between the major political parties and major producer interests such as the Federated Farmers. Vowles (1993) identified a long-standing tendency towards corporatism in New Zealand, particularly when Labour was in power. Similarly, it was not difficult to trace the growing significance during this period of promotional groups such as Greenpeace and HART (Halt All Racist Tours).

From the perspective of reformers within Treasury, the Business Roundtable, and some influential ministers in the fourth Labour government, all interest groups, regardless of whether they claimed to be representing sectional or non-sectional interests, were really in the business of securing benefits for their members at the expense of the rest of society. Consequently, between 1984 and 1999, New Zealand's political elite took on board the view that the role of interest groups in the political process should be minimised. They instituted a range of reforms that have quite clearly reduced and constrained the political space within which interest groups can operate.

Since the election of the Labour-led government at the end of 1999 there has been a noticeable reduction in anti-interest-group rhetoric from government ministers and agencies. In contrast, the Clark government has adopted much of the style and substance of the 'Third Way' in its emphasis on 'inclusion', 'partnership', 'networks', and 'stakeholder involvement' in policy development and implementation. This certainly does indicate an ideological shift to accepting the legitimacy of interest groups in general. More important, however, is the fact that the shift back to consultation and involvement of interest groups was a pragmatic response to the legacies of the previous era of reform. In many cases the attempt to freeze out interest groups in the 1990s created significant practical problems for government.

Many of the health reforms of the 1990s foundered on the rocks of implementation because government policy-makers in Wellington had little understanding as to how health services were actually run. Had health interest groups been consulted, many implementation problems could have been averted, but their involvement would also have diluted the extent of reforms. In practice, the Labour-led government of the 2000s oscillates between exclusion and inclusion of interest groups.

For example, the government largely excluded a key interest group of general practitioners—the Independent Practitioners Association Council (IPAC)—from the formulation in 2001 of its cornerstone health policy, the Primary Health Care Strategy. This was because the government wanted to ensure that the interests of general practitioners did not dominate the policy. However, when the establishment of Primary Health Organisations, a key part of the policy, ran into difficulties in 2003, the Ministry of Health engaged in consultation and compromise with IPAC to smooth out some of the implementation problems.

The radical reform period of 1984–99 continues to have a considerable impact on the capacity of interest groups to shape governmental decision-making and policy development. As a result of reforms to the state sector, many more government-funded services were contracted out to non-government organisations. Many of these non-government organisations also act as interest groups representing the constituency they serve. For example, the Plunket Society not only provides services to new mothers and their children, but also acts as a lobby group for this category of the population. However, the more dependent such organisations are on government funding, and the more they are required to account for the delivery of services within frameworks defined by government, the less they are able to be critical of government policy in that area. In the face of sustained criticism, the government has the power to reduce the organisation's funding.

Clearly though, interest groups remain vital players in politics and policy development in New Zealand. Indeed, it is likely that they will become even more significant due to developments in information technology. These developments help to narrow the 'knowledge gap' between interest groups and government agencies. The development of the Internet also allows for rapid international dissemination of information, and thus enables interest groups with similar concerns in different countries to network more effectively and learn from each other's arguments, strategies, and experiences. Interest groups, therefore, are changing the ways in which they attempt to influence government policy, with a greater emphasis on research. This means that more and more arts and social science graduates—people with skills in constructing arguments and interpreting evidence—are likely to find themselves on the staff of an interest group at some time in their careers. Sophisticated arguments alone, however, will not necessarily lead to increased influence, as the core interest group skills will continue to be those of networking, persuasion and persistence. The nineteenth century social theorist Max Weber's description of political activity as the 'slow, boring through hard boards' applies well to the work of interest groups.

DISCUSSION QUESTIONS

1 Imagine that you have a cause that you wish to advance through the political process and for which there is no existing interest group. First, discuss the pros and cons of establishing a new interest group. Second, consider whether, as a key member of a new interest group, it would be better for you to adopt insider or outsider strategies in order to advance your cause.

2 How feasible is it for governments to govern without input and feedback from interest groups?

3 Should some interest groups be able to influence government policy more than others? On what bases would you make distinctions between acceptable and unacceptable interest-group influence?

NOTE

1 *NZ Herald*, 'Leaky home owners "out on limb"', 5 December 2005.

REFERENCES

Christiansen, L. & K. Dowding 1994, 'Pluralism or State Autonomy? The Case of Amnesty International (British Section): The Insider/Outsider Group', *Political Studies*, 42/1, pp. 15–24.

Dahl, R. 1961, *Who Governs?: Democracy and Power in an American City*, Yale University Press, New Haven.

Hajer, M. 1995, *The Politics of Environmental Discourse: Ecological Discourse and the Policy Process*, Oxford University Press, Oxford.

Lembruch, G. & P. Schmitter 1982, *Patterns of Corporatist Policy-making*, Sage, Beverly Hills.

Lindblom, C. 1980, *The Policy Making Process*, Prentice Hall, New Jersey.

Lowi, T. 1969, *The End of Liberalism*, Norton, New York.

Marsh, D. & R. Rhodes 1992, *Policy Networks in British Government*, Oxford University Press, Oxford.

Nordlinger, B. 1988, 'The Return to the State: Critiques', *American Political Science Review*, vol. 82, pp. 875–85.

Read, M.D. 1996, *The Politics of Tobacco: Policy Networks and the Cigarette Industry*, Avebury, Aldershot.

Skocpol, T. 1985, 'Bringing the State Back In: Strategies of Analysis in Current Research', in P. Evans, D. Reuschemeyer & T. Skocpol, *Bringing the State Back In*, Cambridge University Press, Cambridge.

Thomson, G. & N. Wilson 2001, 'Tobacco Control Policy', in P. Davis & T. Ashton (eds), *Health and Public Policy in New Zealand*, Oxford University Press, Melbourne.

Truman, D.B. 1951, *The Governmental Process*, Alfred Knopf, New York.

Vowles, J. 1993, 'New Zealand: Capture the State'? in C. Thomas (ed.), *First World Interest Groups*, Greenwood Press, Westport, Connecticut.

FURTHER READING

On definitions and types of interest groups

Jordan, G. & J. Richardson 1987, *Government and Pressure Groups in Britain*, Clarendon Press, Oxford, chapter 1.

On pluralism and corporatism

Smith, M.J. 1993, *Pressure, Power and Policy: State Autonomy and Policy Networks in Britain and the United States*, Harvester Wheatsheaf, London, pp. 15–37.

On the view that interest groups inhibit effective government

Mitchell, W.C. & R.T. Simmons 1994, *Beyond Politics: Markets, Welfare and the Failure of Bureaucracy*, Westview Press, Boulder, pp. 62–3.

On interest groups in New Zealand

Mulgan, R. (with P. Aimer) 2004, *Politics in New Zealand*, Auckland University Press, Auckland, chapter 9.

Policy Entrepreneurs, Think Tanks, and Trusts

Michael Mintrom

Since the late 1980s, a class of actors who are neither elected politicians nor government policy advisers have come to play an increasing role in promoting and shaping policy debate in New Zealand. These non-partisan, non-governmental actors have established organisations with the purpose of promoting particular ideas for policy change. Such actors differ from traditional interest group leaders, business lobbyists, and union representatives because they have not started out with predefined constituencies of supporters, and they profess to seek policy change in the national interest. I call such actors *policy entrepreneurs* (Mintrom 2000). Like entrepreneurs in the marketplace, policy entrepreneurs begin with ideas. They make arguments to others and work to build coalitions that can transform those ideas into something tangible. In the marketplace, that tangible thing is a new product. In the world of politics and policy-making, the intended product is policy change.

In this chapter, I discuss the emergence, actions, and influence of three entities that each owe their success to the efforts of specific policy entrepreneurs. They are The New Zealand Business Roundtable (led by Roger Kerr), The Maxim Institute (led by Bruce Logan), and The New Zealand Institute, which evolved from the Knowledge Wave Trust (led by John Hood). Although these organisations differ in their goals and activities, all have sought to gain high levels of attention and change minds. At the end of the chapter, I suggest directions for further analysis of this new class of political actor and the organisations they use to place their ideas in the public domain.

AMERICAN PRECURSORS

While they are relatively new in New Zealand, policy entrepreneurs and think tanks are an established part of the policy community in the USA. There, they supply policy proposals, arguments, analyses, and research-based evidence to what is commonly termed 'the marketplace of ideas' (Smith 1991; Rich 2004). The truck and barter of policy ideas is most intense in Washington, DC, the national capital. The emergence of a market for ideas in that city can be traced back to the mid 1970s, when the near-universal faith in the ability of government to solve a range of economic and social problems started to break down. Prior to that, think tanks were fairly scarce on the ground. The Brookings Institution, founded in the late 1920s, had for a long time served as a broker of social science research to the policy-making community. By the mid 1970s, its reputation was set as a collective of policy researchers with close connections to the welfare-state-supporting Democratic Party. Meanwhile, the American Enterprise Institute, founded in the 1940s, had developed as a more business-oriented counterpart to Brookings and as a source of policy advice for the conservative Republican Party. Both think tanks used their own endowments and gifts from donors to support in-house policy researchers, publish policy-relevant work by university-based researchers, hold seminar series for policy-makers, and offer safe havens to partisan political advisers when their parties were out of office. They continue to do so today.

Another Washington player, the Heritage Foundation, proclaims the virtues of the free market and conservative social values. Like other think tanks, it survives largely on gifts from donors who are sympathetic to its values and policy goals. Its emergence in 1973 shook up the old world of think tanks in Washington. Unlike its established counterparts, the Heritage Foundation placed a great premium on the marketing of policy ideas, so that the means by which ideas were presented was given equal billing to evidence and analysis. Heritage achieved unprecedented influence in both the incoming Republican Administration of President Ronald Reagan and among Washington's chattering classes when late in 1980 it supplied a massive blueprint for market-oriented policy reform to the White House transition team. The work was direct in style, containing clearly argued proposals for major policy change. This action, and the influence that came with it, led many people to realise the merits of supplying well-packaged, easily digested policy proposals to politicians and their advisers. Thus, in subsequent years, many new think tanks were established in Washington, and that trend has shown no signs of abating. These organisations cover the spectrum of substantive policy interests, partisan loyalties, and political ideologies (Smith 1994).

Beyond Washington, policy think tanks focusing on local issues can be found in most states in the Union. The states have long served as important sites for policy entrepreneurship and for the emergence of policy ideas that have then spread from state to state or been adopted by the national government. Since the 1980s, concerted efforts have been made by well-financed policy entrepreneurs to establish a network of pro-market, socially conservative, state-level think tanks across the USA (Covington 1997). These developments have extended the marketplace of ideas, so that in America today spaces and support for policy entrepreneurship can be found in many locations. Further, these many local actors and organisations are tightly linked to one another through a variety of networks that facilitate the sharing of policy ideas, political war stories, and strategies for achieving policy influence (Hird 2005; Mintrom & Vergari 1998).

NEW ZEALAND'S CHANGING CONTEXT FOR POLICY DEBATE

Over the past twenty years, changes in the organisation of New Zealand's public sector have created gaps in the traditional Westminster system of giving advice. In particular, it is now fairly widely acknowledged that reductions in the number of staff employed in the public sector, along with fragmentation of advice-giving and service-delivery roles have reduced the capacity of government departments and ministries to develop policy advice that raises and assesses fundamental, strategic, and long-term policy concerns. Further, the introduction of contractual relationships between ministers and the chief executives of government agencies has reduced the degree to which agency staff are willing to offer policy advice that could be politically risky. Thus, the time is long past when, for example, the Treasury could produce briefing papers for the incoming government that included lengthy expositions on the appropriate role and structure of government with an assessment of the current economic situation.[1]

The introduction of the Mixed Member Proportional (MMP) electoral system in 1996 significantly increased demand for high-quality policy advice. The demise of the National party and Labour party duopoly in parliament has led to more political parties and members of parliament seeking to be well informed on emerging policy issues and problems than ever before. Thus, at the same time as both the quantity and scope of policy advice supplied to ministers by government agencies and quasi-governmental organisation have diminished, overall demand for high-quality policy advice has increased. This shortfall between the supply of policy advice from traditional government sources and its demand has created exciting opportunities for new voices to enter the broader policy conversation.

NEW ZEALAND BUSINESS ROUNDTABLE

The New Zealand Business Roundtable comprises around 50 chief executives of major New Zealand firms, who assemble several times a year to discuss the policy directions of the country and desirable policy changes. Membership is by invitation and the annual fee is $40,000. The executive director, Roger Kerr, maintains an office in Wellington where he is joined by one policy researcher plus secretarial staff. Each year, the Roundtable produces submissions to parliament on proposed legislation, releases books and policy reports commissioned from local and overseas policy researchers, contributes opinion pieces and letters to newspapers, gives speeches, and sponsors visits by overseas speakers.[2]

The Business Roundtable was established in 1986, but it had its genesis in the Economic Summit held in parliament in 1984, shortly after the fourth Labour government assumed office. Sir Ronald Trotter, then chief executive of Fletcher Challenge, chaired the Summit. It was through discussions with other business leaders in the aftermath of the Summit that the idea for the organisation emerged (Trotter 1999). Roger Kerr, then a senior manager in the Treasury, was approached to lead it. The Roundtable is always chaired by a business leader. In addition to Trotter, they have included Sir Douglas Myers of Lion Nathan, Ralph Norris of the Auckland Savings Bank and Air New Zealand, and Murray Horn of the ANZ Bank, a former Secretary of the Treasury. But Kerr has great influence over the organisation's agenda. Its statement of purpose captures its philosophical orientation: 'The NZBR is committed to contributing to the overall development of New Zealand and to promoting the interests of all New Zealanders ... In an open and free domestic and international market environment, the interests of the business sector are closely aligned with those of the community at large'. Since its inception, the Business Roundtable has been a clear and consistent voice for limited government and greater reliance on markets for the allocation of resources in society. This position places it at odds with many people and groups—including some business groups—who believe a strong governmental hand is needed to nudge 'the invisible hand' of the market towards a range of socially desirable outcomes.

In terms of affinities with political parties and politicians, the philosophy of the Business Roundtable is close to that of ACT, and also to that of Don Brash and his ideological allies on the right of National. Essentially, this organisation would like policy-makers to keep working away at the 'unfinished business' of former minister of finance Roger Douglas (Douglas 1993). How much influence has the Roundtable had on policy-making in New Zealand? Policy changes adopted in the late 1980s and the early 1990s appear to have been consistent with positions taken by the Business Roundtable. But those changes might have occurred with or without its presence, since the ideological predispositions of finance ministers and their advisers then were broadly consistent with the Roundtable's. Since Helen Clark has been Prime Minister and Michael Cullen has served as Minister of Finance, the views of the Business Roundtable have not been well received by the government. However, the position taken by Kerr is '... [w]hat matters over time in terms of influencing politics and where governments go is the quality of arguments. If the arguments are sound, sooner or later they will be taken up'.[3] This view is consistent with Weiss's (1980) contention that policy-makers most often form their preferences for policy change based on the slow accretion of evidence and argument.

While the Business Roundtable has not always achieved its short-term policy goals, it has often served to limit the advancement of the alternatives, simply by being a voice of opposition. As the current chairman, Rob McLeod, has observed: 'Even when the Government asserts in the media that it is frustrated or concerned with the Roundtable, the fact is that it is actually focused on the Roundtable and what it's saying'.[4] That said, McLeod has also expressed an interest in improving the reputation of the organisation among a broader set of stakeholders, such as Māori, families, and young people. But, so far, that effort has met with limited success. For all his energy and efforts, which have certainly given the Business Roundtable a high profile in New Zealand, Roger Kerr has burned a lot of bridges over his almost twenty years at the organisation's helm. Kerr's dogmatic views on what constitutes good public policies have frequently alienated him and the organisation from people who could otherwise have been allies in a coalition for more market-oriented policy reform. A common view of the Business Roundtable is that it has now run its course, that it no longer generates fresh or interesting contributions to policy debate, and that few politicians wish to be publicly associated with it. At the same time, newer think tanks have begun to attract attention.

MAXIM INSTITUTE

The Maxim Institute has offices in both Auckland and Christchurch. Like the Business Roundtable it claims that government should be limited and that, as far as possible, the allocation of resources should be left to the market. However, there are relevant—if not articulated—differences in the issues each organisation works on. If the Business Roundtable were consistently libertarian, it would call for government to minimise its interventions into people's personal affairs as well as their economic ones. If it were consistently conservative, it would match its calls for economic liberalism with calls for the greater legislation of morality. Yet the Business Roundtable has avoided morality issues, perhaps because embracing them would invite critics to draw unwelcome contrasts between the organisation's prescriptions for the good life and the business (and personal) morality of its members. But whatever the reasons, the Roundtable's focus on economic policy has left a space for other think tanks to address broader social issues. This is the space Maxim has entered. Like the Heritage Foundation in the USA, the Maxim Institute is a neo-conservative organisation. That is to say, it espouses limited government and reliance on markets in the economic sphere, but it believes that government should intervene in the private lives of individuals and families whenever such action would serve to advance conservative social values.

Established in 2001, the Maxim Institute claims to be 'committed to promoting the principles that underpin a free, just, and compassionate society'. It seeks to connect with other New Zealanders who value a 'society built on the foundation of family along with individual and corporate character'.[5] The Institute is formally constituted as a charitable trust, with a board of trustees who serve as fund-raisers, a board of advisers who set its policy agenda, and a group of media advisers. John Graham, a former All Black captain and principal of Auckland Grammar School and presently Chancellor of the University of Auckland, leads the Board of Advisors. In contrast to the Business Roundtable's elitism, Maxim seeks the financial support and involvement of like-minded individuals and community trusts. The Keith Hay Trust has given the Institute free use of a property that serves as its Auckland office. Similarly, the Tindall Foundation (formed by Stephen Tindall, the founder of the Warehouse retail chain) covers the salary of a policy researcher. Bruce Logan, a former secondary school principal, Director of the New Zealand Education Development Foundation, and evangelical Christian, is without doubt the central figure at Maxim. The organisation emerged out of conversations in early 2001 that Logan had with Greg Fleming, then general manager of an Auckland group called Parenting with Confidence. Upon its founding, Maxim incorporated the activities of Logan's Education Development Foundation.

As well as mirroring the philosophical views of many conservative American think tanks, the Maxim Institute has also learned many operational lessons from the likes of the Michigan-based Mackinac Center for Public Policy.[6] The Institute has used several innovations to get its message out and to gain support. First, it routinely supplies briefing notes by fax to talkback radio hosts and television news programmes. Second, its website offers a template that individuals can use to write email messages to members of parliament on issues raised by Maxim. Third, it has an annual essay-writing contest for tertiary students, and the winners are offered summer internships at the Institute. Fourth, it publishes its own magazine, *Evidence*, which is sent to subscribers and sold at newsstands. Further, the Institute makes submissions to parliamentary committees and frequently contributes opinion pieces and letters to newspapers. It also publishes commissioned research papers, organises forums, and arranges speaking tours for invited overseas guests.

According to the Maxim Institute, a well-functioning market economy requires a strong, self-regulating civil society. Few would disagree. But, for Maxim, the cornerstone of that civil society is 'the natural family', by which it means the two-parent family unit, with Dad as the breadwinner and Mum at home raising the children. Thus, the organisation has made a variety of arguments for preserving this 'male breadwinner' family, some calling for less government, others for more. Among its policy positions, the Institute has opposed any ban on smacking children, because that encroaches on the rights of parents. It opposed decriminalisation of the sex industry, because that opens the way for greater exploitation of vulnerable women and legitimates sex outside the family. The Institute opposes the Domestic Purposes Benefit because it makes it easy for men and women to avoid forming or staying in families. It opposes pay equity because wages should be set in the market and, also, by giving more status to women's paid employment, pay equity would further reduce the incentives for women to stay home. Also, the Institute opposed giving gay couples equal status to married couples, arguing that this undermines the claim that there is a 'normal' family form. These policy positions reveal Maxim's ambivalence toward government and its role in shaping and constraining individual choices.

THE NEW ZEALAND INSTITUTE

The New Zealand Institute was launched in July 2004. Auckland-based, and headed by former Treasury economist David Skilling, the institute currently has an operating budget of around $1 million. Besides Skilling, it has three staff: a communications director, a research associate, and an executive assistant. To understand the origins and purpose of this think tank, it is vital to recognise the linkages it has to the Knowledge Wave trust. That Trust, established in 2001, sought to engender widespread appreciation of the pivotal role that research-based knowledge will play in securing New Zealand's future economic and social well-being. The trust formalised relations among a group of individuals who began talking in 2000 about the country's future directions. John Hood, then vice-chancellor of the University of Auckland, was at the centre of that group. Concerned at the lack of public discussion on how to improve the country's chances in the global economy, Hood sought to move beyond partisan politics and create opportunities for a diverse group of stakeholders to begin talking seriously about New Zealand's future. His efforts led to the planning and execution of the national conference held at the University of Auckland in October 2001, called 'Catching the Knowledge Wave', which Hood co-chaired with Prime Minister Helen Clark. Half of the conference costs were covered by commercial sponsors, a quarter by the government, and the remainder by delegate fees. The event's success led to the creation of the Knowledge Wave Trust.

John Hood served as the chair of the Knowledge Wave Trust's nine-member Executive Board of Directors. The board was charged with setting the Trust's strategic direction and securing sponsorship. It was an amalgam of business, academic, and media interests, and members included the editor-in-chief of the *New Zealand Herald*, and Stephen Tindall of the Warehouse and the Tindall Foundation. The Trust also had a thirty-five-member advisory board, containing high-profile politicians, academics, business leaders, government officials, and community leaders. Like the Business Roundtable and the Maxim Institute, the Trust's overarching purpose was to change minds and promote policy change. Its organisational form and the activities it promoted represented novel approaches to influencing both policy-makers and the public.

In February 2003, the Knowledge Wave Trust held a second major conference, designed as a follow-up to the event of 2001, 'Knowledge Wave 2003—The Leadership Forum'. Like its predecessor, this was a three-day event hosted by the University of Auckland. It was attended by 450 invitation-only guests, people chosen for their roles as opinion leaders in government, business, education, Māoridom, and the wider community. The conference proceedings were broadcast live on television. Like the conference of 2001, it came with a price tag of several million dollars, a large amount of which was required to cover the costs of bringing in high-profile thinkers and leaders from overseas to give the keynote addresses. The Knowledge Wave Trust took the view that events of this kind fill a gap, offering forums 'where people from all sectors, age groups, and geographies can meet on an equal footing … to create lasting national networks to lead change and move the national agenda forward'.[7]

The New Zealand Institute was established to serve as a permanent source for the generation of ideas and argument of the kind the Knowledge Wave conferences had evoked. The Institute runs as a private, not-for-profit organisation funded primarily through an annual membership fee. It is governed by an executive board containing thirty-three members, seven of whom served on the nine-member Executive Board of Directors of the Knowledge Wave Trust. More so than the Knowledge Wave Trust, the Executive Board of the Institute is heavily populated by members of the Auckland business elite. According to its website, the institute takes the view that:

> New Zealand is a country with vast potential and opportunity ahead of it. But we have to overcome a number of challenges if New Zealand is to face up to its full potential. Those challenges won't be met by recycling the same old solutions. We need new solutions and new ideas. We need a new generation of thinking.

Having been around for only a short time, it is difficult to assess the influence of the New Zealand Institute. But if the accomplishments of the Knowledge Wave Trust are taken as a guide, then the Institute appears to have great potential to influence policy debate in New Zealand. So far, the Institute's work, and the efforts of its chief executive David Skilling, have both received strong support from media commentators. The Institute's argument that New Zealanders must save more has been shared by the Minister of Finance and the Governor of the Reserve Bank, among others. Like the other think tanks discussed here, the fortunes of the New Zealand Institute will rest on two qualities. First, it must be able to produce a steady stream of creative, well-supported reports that have the potential to change people's minds about the direction of the country. Second, it must market those reports in ways that ensure broad exposure of the keys ideas to opinion-leaders and decision-makers. With the views of the Business Roundtable and the Maxim Institute having become predictable and somewhat tired, the present times offer unique prospects for the New Zealand Institute to contribute to the country's intellectual life.

CONCLUSION

The think tanks and trusts discussed in this chapter represent important vehicles for policy entrepreneurship. Through them, individuals with strong convictions and high energy have promoted ideas for policy change, and created coalitions of supporters to help them achieve such change. These players on New Zealand's political scene have emerged at a time of transition in the institutions supporting policy discussion, policy advising, and policy-making. They represent early entrants into an emerging marketplace of ideas. Other policy entrepreneurs are in operation, many of whom use private wealth, channelled through charitable trusts, to sustain their efforts. The concept of the policy entrepreneur—a non-traditional political actor who seeks to sell ideas to others—alerts us to new forms of political participation, and gives us a starting point for interpreting those activities. The study of policy entrepreneurship, think tanks, and trusts represents fertile ground for scholars of politics and public policy in New Zealand. Thus, I conclude by suggesting three directions for future research.

First, there are issues of power and persuasion. The argument is often made that good ideas will themselves be sufficient to prompt policy change. But surely there are inextricable ties between the messenger and the message. Exploring relationships between ideas, identities, and interests, with the purpose of assessing what matters most in the making of political arguments, could yield useful insights into the dynamics of contemporary New Zealand politics. Second, the individuals and organisations featured in this chapter have all used overseas experts to promote policy approaches that they would like New Zealand to adopt. Yet ideas and approaches that seem well suited to one locality are often inappropriate for use elsewhere. Exploring how ideas from abroad get reworked for local consumption could offer new insights into those aspects of New Zealand's policy settings that can or cannot be easily changed, and how the lines of demarcation here distinguish this country's political culture from that of others. Finally, the work of local policy entrepreneurs, think tanks, and trusts takes place in a global context. But little is known about how local policy actors engage with their foreign counterparts, and whether the sharing of ideas goes both ways. Among political scientists, transnational policy learning is both under-theorised and under-studied. The investigation of policy learning among policy entrepreneurs in New Zealand and their overseas counterparts could contribute in interesting ways to our broader understanding of political processes.

DISCUSSION QUESTIONS

1 Does policy discourse in New Zealand approximate a 'marketplace of ideas'?

2 How do New Zealand think tanks and trusts promote their policy ideas?

3 What are the pros and cons of non-partisan, non-governmental policy entrepreneurs seeking to influence policy debate in New Zealand?

4 John Maynard Keynes once said the power of ideas is greater than the power of vested interests. What do you think?

5 Do New Zealand opinion-leaders give more credence to the knowledge and advice of overseas experts or to local knowledge and policy research?

NOTES

1   See The Treasury (1984; 1987).

2   For a discussion of the linkages between the Business Roundtable and individuals and organisations with similar political dispositions and goals in the USA and Australia, see Janiewski (2002).

3   Quoted by Speden (1988).

4   Quoted by Taylor (2002).

5   These statements come from the 'Frequently Asked Questions' section of the Institute's website, www.maxim.org.nz

6   In October 2005, evidence emerged that passages in some of Bruce Logan's opinion pieces published in New Zealand newspapers had been lifted from the writings of other authors, including Lawrence W. Reed, president of the Mackinac Centre. In his defence, Logan said that Reed's words had become 'just part of the way we talk here' (Thompson, 2005).

7   This quote is taken from publicity on 'Knowledge Wave 2003—The Leadership Forum' contained in the University of Auckland's staff circular, *Next Week*, February 2003. See also Grant (2003).

REFERENCES

Covington, S. 1997, *Moving a Public Agenda: The Strategic Philanthropy of Conservative Foundations*, National Committee for Responsive Philanthropy, Washington, DC.

Douglas, R. 1993, *Unfinished Business*, Random House, Auckland.

Grant, A. 2003, 'Leaders from All Sectors Pool Ideas', *New Zealand Herald*, 17 February.

Hird, J.A. 2005, *Power, Knowledge, and Politics: Policy Analysis in the States*, Georgetown University Press, Washington DC.

Janiewski, D.E. 2002, 'New Right Networks: The New Right as a Transnational Enterprise Linking the United States, New Zealand, and Australia', paper prepared for the Networks in History Conference, Brisbane, 1 July, History Department, Victoria University of Wellington, Wellington.

Mintrom, M. 2000, *Policy Entrepreneurs and School Choice*, Georgetown University Press, Washington, DC.

Mintrom, M. & Vargari, S. 1998 'Policy Networks and Innovation Diffusion: The Case of State Education Reforms', *Journal of Politics*, vol. 60, pp. 126–48.

Rich, A. 2004, *Think Tanks, Public Policy, and the Politics of Expertise*, Cambridge University Press, New York.

Smith, J.A. 1991, *The Idea Brokers: Think Tanks and the Rise of the New Policy Elite*, The Free Press, New York.

Speden, G. 1998, 'The Roundtable's One Knight Stand', *The Independent*, 14 October.

Taylor, K. 2002, 'Roundtable Out to Win Over Public', *New Zealand Herald*, 16 November.

The Tindall Foundation, 2001, *The Tindall Foundation Annual Report*. The Tindall Foundation, Auckland.

The Treasury 1984, *Economic Management*, Government Printer, Wellington.

The Treasury, 1987, *Government Management: Volumes I and II*, Government Printer, Wellington.

Thompson, W. 2005, 'Copied Quotes Backfire on Think-tank', *New Zealand Herald*, 19 October.

Trotter, R. 1999, 'The New Zealand Business Roundtable and What It Stands For', speech to the Harbour City Rotary Club, 10 March.

Weiss, C. 1980, 'Knowledge Creep and Decision Accretion', *Knowledge*, vol. 3, pp. 381–404.

FURTHER READING

Hird, J.A. 2005, *Power, Knowledge, and Politics: Policy Analysis in the States*, Georgetown University Press, Washington DC.

Mintrom, M. 2000, *Policy Entrepreneurs and School Choice*, Georgetown University Press, Washington, DC.

Smith, J.A. 1991, *The Idea Brokers: Think Tanks and the Rise of the New Policy Elite*, The Free Press, New York.

Direct Democracy

John Parkinson

'Direct democracy' is a term for processes that allow people to decide on public issues, as opposed to indirect democracy, which merely allows them to choose representatives who then make the decisions. It is sometimes claimed that this is the most genuinely democratic form of government; indeed, some say that the arguments against it are arguments against democracy itself (Bogdanor 1981). This chapter argues that we need to treat such claims with caution. It describes the range of direct democratic devices in use around the world, outlines the arguments for and against direct democracy, and discusses the New Zealand experience. It is in the New Zealand setting that we see some of the best and worst features of direct democracy, so it makes an interesting testing ground.

DIRECT DEMOCRATIC DEVICES

Although the term 'direct democracy' could refer to a great range of methods, nine times out of ten it refers to referendums—large-scale, mass voting on specific questions—and it is that more restricted usage that is the topic of this chapter.[1]

Referendums go by a variety of names. In the USA, for example, the word 'referendum' means a government proposal which is sent for a vote by the people before it becomes law; a proposal which the people themselves generate is called an 'initiative'. Regardless of the different terminology from country to country, pretty much all referendums can be classified according to whether they are

547

Figure 7.4.1: Types of referendums

		SOURCE	
		Citizen	**Government**
AIM	**Prospective**	• Initiative (Switzerland, twenty-four states in the USA); Citizen-initiated referendum (New Zealand)	• Referendums on decrees, treaties, and constitutional amendments (numerous); taxation (some US states)
	Reactive	• Recall (USA) • Referendum (twenty-four states in the USA); Facultative referendum (Switzerland)	• Counter-proposals (Switzerland and USA)

government or citizen-initiated, and whether they propose a new idea or react to an existing one.

The most widely-used form of referendum is the prospective, government-initiated variety, and it is most often used to decide constitutional or territorial issues (Butler & Ranney 1994). These include changes to voting qualifications or the electoral system, such as New Zealand's electoral system referendums in 1993; or relations between central and local institutions, such as the 2005 referendums on the European Union constitution in many member states; or decisions whether to join or leave a given state or federation, such as the referendums in 1898–1900 which led to the creation of Australia. Newly formed or reformed states frequently send their constitutions to the people for approval in a referendum—Iraq did so in 2005; Taiwan is due to do so in 2006. From the point of view of social contract theory, this is exactly what one would expect—at the very least, citizens should consent to the terms of association of the state that governs them, if the acts of that state are to have any legitimate force (Ackerman 1991). However, sometimes governments also refer to the people other questions on which the legislature cannot reach agreement, or on which they think there should be wider public debate. This has been the case with some moral issues like abortion, of which there have been examples in Portugal and Italy; although in some places, like Ireland, these are constitutional matters as well.

Much less common than government-led processes is the citizen-initiated referendum (CIR), often called the 'initiative'. CIR attracts a lot of interest from democratic theorists and campaigners alike in many countries, but it is much more rare in practice, with only Italy, New Zealand, and Switzerland using the device nationally. Other notable examples occur at the sub-national level: of the fifty states in the USA, twenty-four use some form of CIR, with California's attracting most of the academic attention. Many counties and towns use them too, but there has never been a national referendum of any kind in the USA. Swiss cantons and communes also use direct devices regularly.

Direct democracy can be used not just to propose a new idea, but also to react to an existing one. For example, revenue-raising bills in some American states must be sent to the voters for approval, while voters in Switzerland can launch what they call 'facultative' referendums to challenge laws that have been passed by the Federal Council. Citizens (in some US states) and governments (in the USA and Switzerland) also use 'counter-proposals' to react to citizens' initiatives. This can cause some complications when multiple questions on the same topic appear on a ballot, and different jurisdictions have different rules for handling this situation. In the USA, the usual rule is that if conflicting propositions win majorities, the one with the biggest majority is the overall winner. In Switzerland, a 'double yes' is permitted to both an initiative and the government's counter-proposal, the final result being determined by further consultation between the Federal Council and interest groups.

Although it affects elected representation, and thus could be seen as a more indirect device, it is also worth noting that voters in fifteen US states can subject elected state officials to a 'recall' vote. The best-known recent example comes from California in 2003, when the incumbent governor Gray Davis lost a recall vote and was replaced by 'the Governator', Arnold Schwarzenegger. However, recall votes are relatively rare, even in California, where of 118 attempts to date, only eight have attracted enough support to qualify for the ballot, and only five succeeded in unseating their targets: governor Davis, two state senators in 1913 and 1914, and two state assembly members in 1994 and 1995.

NEW ZEALAND REFERENDUM TYPES

New Zealand has a long history of government-initiated referendums, going back to polls on the establishment of new provinces between 1858 and 1861; and local polls on liquor licensing, one version of which was established in 1893. National, triennial liquor referendums were held between 1911 and 1989. Otherwise the use of the device has been sporadic. Seven other national referendums have been held— table 7.4.1 gives a summary. Their sporadic use is partly due to the fact that there is no constitutional requirement to hold referendums on certain issues, as there is in countries like Switzerland or Australia that have codified constitutions. Instead, the New Zealand government can decide to hold a referendum whenever it likes, but must pass specific enabling legislation before it can proceed. This ensures at least

Table 7.4.1: National referendums in New Zealand, 1949–2005

Date	Topic	Turnout	Result	
9/3/49	Off-course betting	54.3	For:	68.0
			Against:	32.0
3/8/49	Compulsory military training	63.5	For:	77.9
			Against:	22.1
23/9/67	Term of parliament	69.7	3 years:	68.1
			4 years:	31.9
27/10/90	Term of parliament	85.2	3 years:	69.3
			4 years:	30.7
19/9/92	Voting system	55.2	*Part A*	
	Part A: retain First Past the Post		Retain:	15.3
	Part B: preferred alternative:		Change:	84.7
			Part B	
	Supplementary Member,		SM:	5.6
	Single Transferable Vote,		STV:	17.4
	Mixed Member Proportional,		MMP:	70.5
	Preferential Voting		PV:	6.6
6/11/93	Voting system	85.2	FPP:	46.1
			MMP:	53.9
26/9/97	Compulsory Retirement Savings Scheme	80.3	Yes:	8.2
			No:	91.8

Source: Electoral Commission, www.elections.govt.nz/voting/referendums. 'Turnout' is total votes cast as a percentage of enrolled electors

some parliamentary scrutiny of the issue, and the precise wording of the question to be asked, minimising the risk of more blatant abuses of power by asking leading or otherwise manipulative questions (see Butler & Ranney 1994, pp. 6–7).

Since 1993, New Zealanders have also been able to launch Citizens' Initiated Referendums (CIR). A total of thirty-three petitions have been launched (see table 7.4.2) on topics ranging from battery hens to criminal justice, the size of parliament, health spending, and forest management. However, only three have come to a vote because all the other proposals failed to gain enough signatures to force a referendum. This signature target is one of the key variables in how different referendum systems work around the world, and it has a significant impact not only on how easy it is to qualify a proposition for a vote, but also on what kinds of people tend to launch them.

Table 7.4.2: New Zealand CIR petitions, 1993–2005

Year	Topic	Sponsor	Result
1993	Should the production of eggs from battery hens be prohibited within five years of the referendum?	Royal New Zealand Society for the Protection of Cruelty to Animals	Failed signature target 10/95
1993	Should a Judge sentencing a person convicted of murder to life imprisonment be empowered to order that the person be imprisoned for his or her natural life and not be eligible for parole?	Christian Heritage Party	Lapsed 6/95
1993	Should the size of Parliament be reduced from 120 Members of Parliament to 100 by reducing the number elected from party lists?	Michael Laws MP, Hon Winston Peters MP, Geoff Braybrooke MP	Lapsed 8/95
1994	Should there be a legally enforceable requirement that political parties observe their constitutions and their manifesto promises?	William Maung Maung	Lapsed 11/95
1994	Do you agree that the laws of New Zealand should not discriminate against or give preference to citizens or permanent residents of New Zealand on the basis of their ethnic origins?	One New Zealand Foundation	Lapsed 3/96
1994	Should all New Zealanders have access to comprehensive health services which are fully government funded and without user charges?	Next Step Democracy Movement	Failed signature target 3/96
1994	Should all New Zealanders have access to public education services, from early childhood to tertiary level, which are fully government funded and without user charges?	Next Step Democracy Movement	Failed signature target 3/96
1994	Should full employment with wages and conditions that are fair and equitable be the primary goal of government economic policy?	Next Step Democracy Movement	Withdrawn 2/96
1994	Should all New Zealanders on income support and benefits get an income based on what it actually costs to live?	Next Step Democracy Movement	Withdrawn 2/96
1994	Should increases in New Zealand's electricity demand be met from energy conservation and from the use of sources that are environmentally sustainable?	Next Step Democracy Movement	Withdrawn 2/96
1994	Should New Zealand's defence expenditure be reduced to half its 1994/95 level by the year 2000 with the savings spent on health, education, conservation and the promotion of full employment?	Next Step Democracy Movement	Withdrawn 2/96

(Continued)

Table 7.4.2 (Continued)

Year	Topic	Sponsor	Result
1994	Should the number of professional fire-fighters employed full-time in the New Zealand Fire Service be reduced below the number employed on 1 January 1995?	New Zealand Professional Fire-fighters Union	**Vote held 2/12/95** Turnout: 28% Yes: 12% No: 88%
1995	Should people aged 18 years and over who are terminally or incurably ill be permitted to have their lives ended if they request this, in a humane manner and in accordance with procedures to be established?	Voluntary Euthanasia Society	Lapsed 12/96
1996	Should the forestry licences to 188,000 hectares of Crown forest land which are currently held by the Forestry Corporation of New Zealand Limited remain in State ownership (subject to the determination of any Treaty of Waitangi claims)?	Jim Anderton MP	Lapsed 12/96
1996	Should all tree felling and clearing on any indigenous land (except in plantation forests and already protected conservation areas) be prohibited, unless such tree felling or clearing is in accordance with Maori customary use?	Nga Kaitiaki o Te Waonuia Tane o Aotearoa	Lapsed 10/97
1997	Should there be a Written Constitution, taking precedence of the Treaty of Waitangi and all other sources of law, which guarantees the right of all people without favour or discrimination?	Mark Whyte	Withdrawn 7/98
1997	Should the Government increase its annual spending on health services to at least 7% of GDP, funding the increase, if necessary, from personal income tax?	Cancer Society of New Zealand	Withdrawn 12/98
1997	Should the size of the House of Representatives be reduced from 120 members to 99 members?	Margaret Robertson	**Vote held at general election 28/11/99** Turnout: 82.8% Yes: 81.5% No: 18.5%
1997	Should there be a reform of our Justice system placing greater emphasis on the needs of victims, providing restitution and compensation for them and imposing minimum sentences and hard labour for all serious violent offences?	Norm Withers	**Vote held at general election 28/11/99** Turnout: 82.9% Yes: 91.75% No: 8.25%

Table 7.4.2 (Continued)

Year	Topic	Sponsor	Result
1998	Should members of Parliament be elected by single transferable vote (STV) with constituency-based, multi-member electorates?	Frederick Richards	Lapsed 6/99
1998	Should there be no further compulsory school closures until comprehensive criteria have been established by law for the Minister of Education to follow when deciding to close a school?	Gavin Hugh Piercy	Lapsed 3/00
1999	Do you support the request that the Government of New Zealand reduce the number of unemployed people to below 1% of the working population by the year 2004?	Julie Waring	Lapsed 8/00
1999	Should New Zealand adopt direct democracy by binding referendum whereby ideas for laws would be submitted and voted upon as of right by the public and, according to the result, submissions collected from the public and then assessed by opinion poll, resulting in draft law alternatives being prepared by independent groups, from which one opinion would be chosen by majority vote by the public; the resulting legislation to be binding?	The Free New Zealand Party Society	Lapsed 10/00
2000	Should Parliament enact legislation to ban the sale and distribution of tobacco?	Raymond Lorenzen	Lapsed 7/01
2000	Should the Shared Parenting Bill introduced by Dr Muriel Newman (which creates a presumption that parents who are separated or divorced will have equal rights to custody of their children) be passed by Parliament?	Tim Hawkins	Lapsed 8/01
2000	Do you believe New Zealand should hold a binding referendum on whether we should replace MMP by a return to first-past-the-post election?	Dennis Crisp	Withdrawn 2/01
2000	Should a binding referendum be held to decide the future voting system, based on a Parliament of 99 MPs?	Stuart FE Marshall	Lapsed 3/02
2001	Should New Zealand adopt a written constitution expressly vesting sovereignty in the people and protecting fundamental human and civil rights?	Ian Wishart on behalf of the Constitution Trust of New Zealand	Lapsed 10/02

(Continued)

Table 7.4.2 (Continued)

Year	Topic	Sponsor	Result
2003	Should all rights of appeal to the Privy Council be abolished?	Dennis J Gates	Lapsed 7/04
2003	Should the Prostitution Reform Act 2003 be repealed?	Larry Baldock MP and Gordon Copeland MP	Lapsed 11/04
2003	Should the law be amended to make the results of Citizens' Initiated Referenda binding on the New Zealand Government?	Steve Baron	Withdrawn 2/04
2004	Should the design of the New Zealand flag be changed?	NZFlag.com	Withdrawn 08/05
2005	Should the proprietor of licensed premises be able to determine whether those premises are smoke-free?	John van Buren	Signature deadline 6/4/06

The question is that agreed by the Clerk of the House, which in some cases may be quite different from the original. 'Withdrawn' means that the proposal was withdrawn by its sponsor by the signature deadline. 'Lapsed' means that the petition was not presented to the Clerk on time. 'Failed target' means that the petition presented on time, but checks revealed that there were insufficient valid signatures.

Source: Clerk of the House of Representatives (1993–2005)

HOW REFERENDUMS WORK

There are many variables in the workings of referendums around the world, but five of the most important are: scope; qualification hurdles; the time limits for a vote; the decision rule used; and the effect or decisiveness of a referendum. These variables have more to do with citizen-initiated polls than government-initiated ones, simply because most government polls are one-off events requiring specific enabling legislation.

The first variable, scope, refers to the kinds of law that can be affected by a referendum, particularly whether the referendum addresses the nation's constitution or statute law. In the USA, fifteen states allow initiatives that propose both constitutional amendments and specific laws; six allow legislative proposals but not constitutional amendments; and two (Florida and Mississippi) allow constitutional amendments but not legislative proposals. Switzerland is the same as the last two, but this has caused some problems because every little proposal for a law change must be phrased as a constitutional amendment. The constitution soon became a hotchpotch of fundamental principles and specific statute, such that the entire constitution had to be redrafted and approved in another referendum in 1999. A proposal to allow the Swiss to launch initiatives to influence statute law at the federal level was, however, rejected, so it is possible that the document will become clogged up with day-to-day law once again. In New Zealand there are no restrictions on the type of law that can be created or modified by referendum.

The qualification hurdles vary by type of referendum and by country. The lowest hurdle is in Switzerland where initiative proponents have eighteen months to gather just 100,000 signatures, roughly 1.75 per cent of eligible voters at a rate of just over 182 per day. That compares with California's threshold for statute initiatives of 5 per cent of voters in the previous elections for governor, which must be gathered in 150 days, a rate of 2,492 a day based on 2002 figures. The threshold is even higher for constitutional amendment initiatives: 8 per cent, or 3,987 signatures per day. It should not be surprising, therefore, that a signature-gathering industry has sprung up in the USA given the enormous resources needed to gather that many signatures in such a short time; but this is also true in Switzerland, even with its very low hurdle and long time limit. Compare New Zealand's threshold of 10 per cent of registered electors in twelve months, with two-month extensions possible. Based on the number of electors on the roll for the 2005 general election, this means that a would-be referendum initiator needs to gather 284,740 signatures, or 780 a day. Even well-funded campaigns can struggle, as the NZFlag.com organisers found when they managed to gather barely more than a third of that number in 2004–05 (see table 7.4.2).

As well as there being different time limits for gathering signatures, there are different time limits by which a vote must be held. In the USA, referendums are almost always held at the same time as a state or federal election, which means that once a proposition qualifies for the ballot it can come to a vote within two years. In New Zealand, the vote must be held within a year of a successful petition being presented to parliament, unless 75 per cent of MPs vote to defer it. However, it is a great deal cheaper, and increases turnout, if a vote is held with a general election; compare the high turnouts for the 1999 referendums with the low turnout on the Firefighters' referendum in 1995—see table 7.4.2. In Switzerland, by contrast, initiatives *cannot* be held at the same time as a general election, and the Federal Council has four years in which to consider the proposal. It can then set any date it likes for the vote, a delaying tactic which can serve to take the heat out of an issue so that by the time it comes to a vote, it is frequently old news and the proposal is defeated.

When a vote is held, the decision rule can vary as well, from a simple majority (more than 50 per cent) to various kinds of qualified majority. In several referendums in New Zealand before the Second World War the decision rule was 60 per cent, a hurdle that prohibitionists just narrowly failed to reach in 1919. Initiatives in Switzerland have to pass a 'double majority' test, that is, a proposal has to win the votes of a majority of individual voters, and it has to win in half the cantons, in order to protect small cantons from the 'tyranny of the majority' in the larger, more populous ones. The same is true of constitutional referendums in Australia: a referendum not only has to be approved by 50 per cent of the total population, but must win a majority in every state as well, to ensure that it is not just Sydneysiders and Melburnians determining the constitutional rules for the rest of Australia.

Finally, what happens after a vote can vary, even when a proposal wins the necessary majority, because they may or may not be binding on government. In New Zealand CIR are non-binding and the government can determine for itself how to respond to the outcome. Although it is true that this makes New Zealand something of an oddity in the world of CIR, this can be overstated. First, many so-called 'binding' referendums in the USA are struck down by the courts on constitutional grounds. Second, it is not uncommon for government-initiated referendums to be non-binding. In many places, New Zealand included, questions are broad statements of principle, and so the legislature still needs to draft and debate a law that puts the general idea into effect. Australia has held three non-binding, government-led referendums, which it calls 'plebiscites': two on military conscription in 1916 and 1917, and one on the national song in 1977. Given its constitutional tradition of parliamentary sovereignty, British votes are not formally binding on government either, and do not have immediate force because parliament still needs to draw up and debate legislation after the vote.

EVALUATING DIRECT DEMOCRACY

Given that variation, whether we think that direct democracy is a good thing or not depends on the precise form we are talking about, and the institutional setting in which it is embedded. This means that broad arguments about the value of an institution in principle need to be treated with caution. Nonetheless, political scientists tend to make three kinds of arguments in favour of direct democracy: that it promotes responsiveness; that it provides better signals than elections about voters' policy preferences; and that it enhances the legitimacy of decisions.

Government responsiveness is taken by some authors to be what defines democracy, and the referendum is a device that creates responsiveness *par excellence*: 'What better way to maximise responsiveness of rulers to the ruled than by fostering a system in which the ruled themselves make the decisions'? (Saward 1998, p. 83). It has been argued that concerns over a lack of responsiveness of the 1984–90 Labour government is what led the National party to promote CIRs in New Zealand, hoping to make themselves appear more responsive to people's wishes after years of dramatic and unannounced reform (Church 2000), although the specific trigger may well have been the failure of some groups to stop the Homosexual Law Reform Bill in 1985 (Parkinson 2001).

Ranged against that claim are two problems. The first is that the enormous cost of launching and sustaining a CIR campaign, from signature gathering to winning the public debate, means that they tend to be used not by 'ordinary' people at all, but by established interest groups or political parties. Indeed, there is evidence that the

Figure 7.4.2: CIR petitions launched by year, 1993–2002

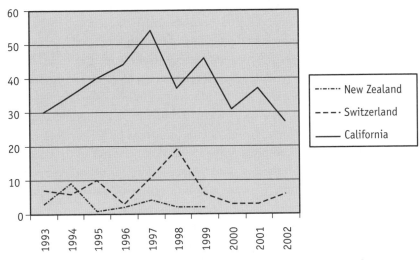

In each case, the count is of those petitions that have had their titles approved by the relevant state authorities before the signature-gathering stage.

Sources: California Secretary of State (2002); Federal Authorities of the Swiss Confederation, www.admin.ch; Clerk of the House of Representatives (1993–2005). In each case, the count is of those petitions that have had their titles approved by the relevant state authorities before the signature-gathering stage.

primary purpose of many initiatives is not the substantive issue but to enhance the electoral fortunes of the party promoting it—the Swiss People's party has become the second largest in the National Council by promoting a series of anti-immigrant initiatives over many years. Furthermore, the best-funded side has a better chance of winning. In the USA, Magleby (1984) shows that while well-funded sides only win support for about half of their proposals, they have around a two-thirds success rate in shooting down others. That is, money cannot buy a 'yes', but it can more easily buy a 'no', regardless of the substantive merits of the different positions. In New Zealand the CIR rules include a spending cap of $50,000 in the signature-gathering stage, and another $50,000 during the campaign in order to equalise power between the two sides of a question. But these amounts are extremely low given the actual costs of national advertising and promotion, and probably serve to keep people uninformed about petitions and the laws they propose. The spending cap in New Zealand may have some positive role in that a wider variety of people attempt to use CIRs than is the case elsewhere—politicians and established interest groups certainly, but also many private individuals. However, given the relative powerlessness of the device in New Zealand, it may be that established elites choose to put their energies into activities that are more likely to bear fruit. Overall, the number of petitions launched in New Zealand is very low, especially compared with California where a successful initiative has immediate legislative effect and the time lag between launch and vote is very short (see figure 7.4.2). The long time lag, and deliberate delaying tactics, may explain why Swiss enthusiasm for the device at the federal level in recent years has been comparable to New Zealand's, but this is speculation.

The second problem is known as 'the tyranny of the majority'. Because referendums tend to be majoritarian devices that award victory to the largest number, dominant groups in society will use referendums against the interests of minorities, no matter how just the claims of those minorities might be. Dominant groups—generally those who are older, male, well-off, well-educated and, in certain countries, of European background—are also much more likely to vote. The risk of CIR being used by Pakeha New Zealanders to stop programmes aimed at improving the lot of Māori was one of the reasons given by the Royal Commission on the Electoral System (1986) for not recommending the widespread use of referendums. We have seen how Switzerland and Australia manage geographical differences by requiring regional majorities; Canada has in some cases required majorities within ethnic groups as well to help manage this problem.

In systems with traditions of parliamentary sovereignty, the criticism is often made that governments are elected to govern, and they renege on their responsibilities if they simply set up a referendum every time they come across an issue that is 'too hard' (see Palmer 1986, p. 256). Enthusiasts of direct democracy respond with a second major point in favour: policy preference signalling. They argue that elections are very poor guides to people's actual policy preferences: the issues that are salient at the time of an election may not be the critical issues a year or two later; and parties increasingly market themselves as 'good managers' rather than on the basis of specific manifesto pledges. Other methods of judging public opinion tend to be unreliable in part because they appear to respondents to be relatively costless—nothing obviously changes as a result of an opinion poll—whereas a referendum can change the law of the land and thus gets taken more seriously by voters. For these reasons, some argue that referendums are useful for democratising the specifics of policy rather than just trusting leaders on the basis of vague managerial promises.

That might be true often, but there are cases where even a referendum result can be difficult to interpret. A famous recent case is the Australian republic referendum of 1999, which seemed to endorse the monarchy (see also chapter 2.3). However, research revealed that for many voters it was actually a rejection of the parliament-dominated republican model they were being offered; the popularly elected presidential model that rated better in opinion polls was not included on the ballot (Uhr 2000). The same has been said of New Zealand's 1997 referendum on the Compulsory Retirement Savings Scheme. A postal-only ballot, it attracted an impressive turnout but was crushingly defeated (see table 7.4.1). However, it has been argued that this was more to do with the personal unpopularity of its chief architect, Winston Peters, than the substantive merits of the proposal.

Related to this point is the issue that most (but not all) referendums present a stark, yes/no choice on a specific question, when people's views on that question may be a great deal more complex. An obvious example is the 1999 referendum on criminal justice in New Zealand. The question was, in fact, four questions: placing more emphasis on needs of victims, giving them compensation, imposing minimum sentences, and imposing hard labour for 'serious violent offences'. Now, this appears to breach the requirements of the Citizen Initiated Referenda Act 1993 which states that CIRs must ask one question that admits of a yes/no answer, but correspondence between the Clerk of the House and the proposer, Norm Withers, reveals a long battle in which the Clerk simply gave up fighting, perhaps safe in the knowledge that, being non-binding, the vote did not matter very much anyway. Regardless, the four-fold nature of the question caused difficulties for voters who were in favour of one part but not others. If the proposal had been split into separate questions, it would have allowed voters to give a more considered response, and given the government a more clear recommendation to consider.

Finally, opponents of referendums, especially CIRs, attack them on rationality grounds. Some variants of this argument denigrate popular capacities—people are just too ill-informed and self-interested to make sensible collective choices—although that, if true, would seem to count against any kind of democracy, elitist democracy included. Some states try to increase voter awareness and knowledge, not just by encouraging the proponents and opponents to slug it out in the media, but also by distributing detailed voter information pamphlets, sometimes with detailed policy costings. Clearly the quality of the media is crucial here. However, there are other variants of the argument that are not about the capacities of *people* but about the features of *institutions*. Kateb (1981) famously argues that representative, deliberative institutions like parliaments are superior because they consider a large number of issues and thus build up more experience of how issues interlock and affect one another. Referendums, on the other hand, encourage a kind of political myopia, considering issues out of context and without weighing them against other, equally important considerations. One of the most famous cases of this is Proposition 13 in California in 1978 which dramatically cut property taxes, but thereby crippled state funding of education (Smith 1998).

Nonetheless, a mass, popular vote on a specific proposal has one enormous strength—it confers an authority and legitimacy on a policy that no other institution can match. There is some debate whether a just-over-50-per cent victory is enough to convey legitimacy—the closer the result, the more hard-done-by the losers feel. Still, if public debate has been extensive and relatively well-informed, if the question is well-crafted and turnout is reasonably high, a referendum can legitimate a course of action more effectively than any other political institution.

CONCLUSION

When considered against problems of unresponsive governments or the vague signals that elections send, referendums seem like a more democratic alternative. However, there are reasons to be cautious. Referendums are inherently majoritarian devices which empower already-dominant groups, although there are ways of modifying them to give a crude kind of balance. They cost a great deal and, in the case of CIRs, are often used for tactical ends by parties and interest groups on the fringes of power, not 'ordinary people'; this is less of a problem in New Zealand, but that may have more to do with the non-binding nature of the vote and the spending cap which renders the whole exercise less worthwhile. Referendums sometimes send vague or hard-to-interpret signals themselves, and may encourage political myopia. But, when used cautiously, they are powerful legitimating tools, especially useful for considering major constitutional questions about how the people of a given place should live together.

DISCUSSION QUESTIONS

1 Bogdanor (1981) writes, 'in the final analysis, the arguments against referendums are arguments against democracy'. Is he right?
2 Should governments use referendums more often than they do?
3 Who should initiate referendums: governments, citizens, both, or neither?
4 Should CIRs be made binding on government in New Zealand?
5 Is New Zealand's 10 per cent signature threshold too high, too low, or about right? What are the pros and cons of New Zealand's $50,000 spending caps?

NOTE

1 Fishkin (1991, pp. 21–5) is one author who uses the term in a broad sense. For a survey of other direct devices, often small-scale and deliberative rather than large-scale and aggregative, see Smith (2005). On the deliberative/aggregative distinction, see Shapiro (2003).

REFERENCES

Ackerman, B. 1991, *We the People 1: Foundations*, Harvard University Press, Cambridge MA.
Bogdanor, V. 1981, *The People and the Party System: The Referendum and Electoral Reform in British Politics*, Cambridge University Press, Cambridge.
Butler, D. & A. Ranney (eds) 1994, *Referendums Around the World: The Growing Use of Direct Democracy*, AEI Press, Washington DC.
Church, S. 2000, 'Crime and Punishment: The Referenda to Reform the Criminal Justice System and Reduce the Size of Parliament', in J. Boston, S. Church, S. Levine, E. McLeay & N. Roberts (eds), *Left Turn: The New Zealand General Election of 1999*, Victoria University Press, Wellington, pp. 184–99.
Clerk of the House of Representatives 1993–2005, *Parliamentary Bulletin*, Office of the Clerk of the House of Representatives, Wellington.
Fishkin, J. 1991, *Democracy and Deliberation*, Yale University Press, New Haven.

Kateb, G. 1981, 'The Moral Distinctiveness of Representative Democracy', *Ethics*, 91/3, pp. 357–74.

Magleby, D. 1984, *Direct Legislation: Voting on Ballot Propositions in the United States*, Johns Hopkins University Press, Baltimore.

Palmer, G. 1986, *Unbridled Power*, 2nd edn, Oxford University Press, Wellington.

Parkinson, J. 2001, 'Who Knows Best? The Creation of the Citizen-initiated Referendum in New Zealand', *Government and Opposition*, 36/3, pp. 403–21.

Royal Commission on the Electoral System 1986, *Report of the Royal Commission on the Electoral System*, Government Printer, Wellington.

Saward, M. 1998, *The Terms of Democracy*, Polity Press, Cambridge.

Secretary of State, California 2002, *A History of California Initiatives*, Secretary of State, Sacramento, California.

Shapiro, I. 2003, *The State of Democratic Theory*, Princeton University Press, Princeton.

Smith, D. 1998, *Tax Crusaders and the Politics of Direct Democracy*, Routledge, New York.

Smith, G. 2005, *Beyond the Ballot: 57 Democratic Innovations from Around the World*, The Power Inquiry/Short Run Press, London.

Uhr, J. 2000, 'Testing Deliberative Democracy: The 1999 Australian Republic Referendum', *Government and Opposition*, 35/2, pp. 189–210.

FURTHER READING

Catt, H. 1996, 'The Other Democratic Experiment: New Zealand's Experience with Citizens' Initiated Referendum', *Political Science*, 48/1, pp. 29–47.

Kobach, K. 1993, *The Referendum: Direct Democracy in Switzerland*, Aldershot, Dartmouth.

Parkinson, J. 2001, 'Deliberative Democracy and Referendums', in K.M. Dowding, J. Hughes & H. Margetts (eds), *Challenges to Democracy: Ideas, Involvement and Institutions*, Palgrave, London, pp. 131–52.

Simpson, A. (ed.) 1992, *Referendums: Constitutional and Political Perspectives*, Department of Politics, Victoria University of Wellington, Wellington.

Walker, M. 2003, *The Strategic Use of Referendums: Power, Legitimacy and Democracy*, Palgrave, Basingstoke.

WEBSITES OF INTEREST

c2d.unige.ch/—Centre d'études et de documentation sur la démocratie directe, University of Geneva, in English, featuring a searchable database of every national and many sub-national referendums around the world; details of referendum rules in different countries; links to local resources; and news of recent and upcoming votes.

hwww.iandrinstitute.org/—Initiative and Referendum Institute at the University of Southern California, a website that focuses on US experience, with a useful set of pages comparing different states' use of various devices, except the recall.

Participation and Citizenship

Helena Catt

Citizenship, in political terms, is normally defined as a relationship between the individual and the state that involves reciprocal rights and responsibilities and encompasses civil, political, and social rights. While this definition seems straightforward, different concepts are emphasised by writers from different political orientations. Currently one of the key areas of divergence is whether citizenship means that people need to participate and if so what kind of participation is implied.

The three types of rights included in the definition are often described as having been an historical progression in the developed democracies, with the different rights won by people over time. *Civil* rights protect citizens from state interference when they are doing a range of things that are needed for a democracy, for instance, freedom of speech and of association. *Political* rights relate to more formal participation by citizens, again in ways that are needed for democracy, for instance, the right to vote or to form a political party. *Social* rights are positive rights and ensure that people can use the other two rights because they are on an equal footing. The last of these three is the most controversial and is often omitted in discussions of citizenship. These three components of citizenship were first identified by T.H. Marshall in 1950 in his seminal work *Citizenship and Social Class.* While they are still referred to, different aspects are stressed depending upon the political orientation of the writer.

The relationship aspect of citizenship is commonly described in terms of rights and responsibilities, meaning that both the state and the individual citizen have obligations and duties because of citizenship. However, different approaches to citizenship tend to use different emphasis. Generally, ideas based on liberal and individualist beliefs emphasise the rights of the individual that are inherent in citizenship. So an individual has a right to say what they think, to meet with others, and to express views in print. Not only do individuals have these rights but they expect the state to uphold and protect those rights. Another component of the rights of the citizen was the tendency to see the citizen as a consumer of the services provided by the state. This viewpoint found its clearest formal expression in the series of citizen charters established in Britain by the Conservative government of John Major in the 1990s. Such charters specified standards that people could expect from state-funded services, such as hospitals or trains, and also specified the redress or compensation that citizens could expect when these standards were not met. So the rights of the citizen are akin to the rights of a shopper and thus participation is as a contract. Here the emphasis is on what an individual can do and the importance of the law in guaranteeing those rights.

In contrast, the responsibilities of citizens are emphasised by those writers who can loosely be described as communitarian. While communitarians are more varied than liberals, they share a central interest in individuals as part of a community, shaped by that community and with responsibilities towards the community. So, for these writers citizenship is a particular relationship with the community, in this case the state, and refers to the responsibilities that individual citizens have to the wider community and the greater good. Here the emphasis is on the impact that rights have upon the community, in this case in the strength of democracy.

This difference in emphasis has clear implications for the ways in which we think about political participation, both as citizens and as political scientists. For example, according to the rights-based approach voting is something that citizens are entitled to do and the state may only remove this right in specific circumstances, such as incarceration. According to the responsibility-based approach, on the other hand, citizens are expected to vote because it is an important part of the workings of democracy. Another example is the right to have your crimes heard by a jury and the responsibility of sitting on a jury to enable trial by your peers. Clearly when citizenship is viewed primarily as a right, the levels of participation become irrelevant. However, when citizenship is seen as having a strong component of responsibility then declining participation levels cause concern.

Note that both the liberal and the communitarian ideas concentrate on the citizen part of the relationship rather than on the roles of the state. Although the definition of citizenship given at the start talks of a reciprocal relationship, much more is said about the role of citizens than of the role of the state. Much of the state's side of the relationship refers to ensuring that citizens can enjoy the three types of rights. Again, there are partisan differences in emphasis. So those who believe in a small state or government see the state's side of the relationship as being the upholding of rights and the rule of law. At the other end of the spectrum, welfarism charges the state with responsibility for ensuring that social rights and equality between citizens are upheld.

Discussion so far has been of citizenship within a political and political science framework. There is also a more narrow legal definition of citizenship in that a person who is eligible to hold a passport from a nation is a citizen and others are not. Such a status is often granted to someone rather than being automatic. In the past the status of citizen was not conferred on whole sections of the population in an area, such as women or slaves. The extent to which children are citizens in this legal sense varies across different countries. In the past, many of the rights of citizenship were limited to those with this legal status, but now people who are not citizens of New Zealand have most of the rights of citizens. New Zealand is unique in extending the right to vote to all permanent residents rather than restricting voting to legal citizens. However, only legal citizens can stand for election to local bodies and to parliament. Non-citizens who live in New Zealand pay taxes, have to obey the law, can send their children to local schools, can join a political party, and make a submission to a select committee.

Traditionally citizenship has been used exclusively to refer to the relationship between people and a nation–state, though increasingly it is used both more broadly and more narrowly. As part of the political integration of the European Union, people are now citizens of the EU and not just of one of the member countries. This is an example of citizenship that is still related to a geographical and political entity, just not a nation–state. However, globalisation and acceptance of the idea of universal rights mean that many talk of global citizenship. While much of the rhetoric relates to the rights that are conferred by UN charters, this expansion of citizenship is not closely tied to a geographic area and political body. Instead the idea is based on the human sharing of rights and responsibilities, as defined in the UN charters. Taking this view further, ideas of commonality and a sense of belonging to the group have led to increasing use of the term to refer to people who are active members of a particular community or group. So people may be referred to as citizens of a school or a workplace or a community. With this usage the link to a political organisation that can ensure rights is lost, as well as the geographic connection. In these circumstances citizenship is being used to describe a form of behaviour or relationship between the individual members of a group rather than between each individual and the organised or formal part of the group. Implied in this use of the term is behaviour that would have been described in ancient Greece as civic virtue or being an active citizen.

ACTIVE CITIZENSHIP

Inherent within the concept of active citizenship or civic virtue is the idea that people should participate in civic life for the good of the community, or nation–state. Citizenship in this case is primarily a role and responsibility. The argument is that individuals benefit from being part of a democratic society or nation and therefore have a duty to do those things that are necessary to ensure that the society continues. In exchange for enjoying the rights of citizenship, citizens should be involved in public affairs, that is, take part in debate and the making of decisions that impact on everyone. For instance, one important aspect of democracy is competition between parties and political views. If there were not a number of political parties with different views, all seeking election and acting as the opposition in parliament, then we would not have the choice and scrutiny that is central to democracy. Likewise only if people vote does the elected legislature and executive have the legitimacy to rule. If people do not exercise the right to speak out and comment, or the right to access information, then there is no real scrutiny of the government. Each of us has the right not to vote, not to express views, not to take political action, but if everyone decided not to use that right then we would not have a democracy. The idea of the active citizen applauds those who use their citizenship rights and embrace the responsibilities to the community and the various political roles that go with democratic citizenship. Such roles range from taking an interest in politics, reading the news, asking questions, expressing views, seeking to change a law or policy, or standing for election.

The core components of active citizenship are a sense of belonging, recognition of the values of democracy, and participating in collective decision-making. Clearly participation is vital in the eyes of those who promote and seek active citizenship. Participation in political activity is obviously important. However, community involvement of all kinds is also seen as vital. Doing things with other people is one of the important ways in which social capital is built and social capital is seen as crucial to a healthy democracy.

Robert Putnam is most closely linked with the idea that social capital is in decline and that this is a major cause of declining political participation and of trust in government. In his book *Bowling Alone*, Putnam argues that when social capital is high, people feel part of society and are interested in what happens to others. In other words, politics matters to them. If you and your family live in an area without traffic congestion then you are less likely to pay much attention to government actions in relation to roading. But if you know people who talk about the impact that traffic jams have on their lives, then you are more likely to take note of government plans because the problem has more relevance and meaning. Social capital depends upon people interacting, doing things in a variety of groups, getting to know a wide range of people, and experiencing being involved with others. The interaction does not need to be political engagement. Joining groups of any kind —for instance, sports clubs, music groups, churches, unions, social groups—is important because it brings people together and everyone has experience, and hopefully some understanding, of the lives of others and how political issues affect them. Social capital is in decline in Western democracies as people focus on self and family and are less involved in group activity. As the title of his book suggests, people go ten-pin bowling alone or with family now rather than with work colleagues or friends and thus have less social interaction.

Active participation has not always been seen as a good part of citizenship and vital for a healthy democracy. In the 1960s, Almond and Verba studied the type of culture that is needed to uphold democracy. They argued that a participant culture, full of active citizens, most closely met the ideals of democracy. For a stable democracy to exist and prosper, however, there needs to be a mix of subject and participant culture. In a subject political culture most people recognise that they are unlikely to be able to influence what government does, with the result that they take no active part in politics. Voting and following the news are generally the only political actions of the subject political culture.

ATTEMPTS TO STRENGTHEN ACTIVE CITIZENSHIP

In the past decade there have been a range of moves to encourage active citizenship. Two related, but sometimes contradictory, observations about the relationship between citizens and the nation–state have been important in prompting these moves. On the one hand there is concern at the decline in participation levels and a desire to encourage greater participation on the grounds that it is a necessity in a strong democracy. On the other hand there's a perception of threats to the nation–state as an entity because of a decline in an exclusive relationship between the state and its citizens. Identity and belonging are central to conceptions of active citizenship. No longer identifying primarily with the nation–state has implications for how and if people participate as citizens. A number of different identities and relationships are challenging the exclusivity of the nation–state.

The renaissance of indigenous identity and culture is a clear example of identity that is not exclusively with the nation–state. Rather than a single identity, many people now think of themselves with multiple identities: Tainui, Māori, and New Zealander; or Polynesian, Mormon, and New Zealander; or Somali, refugee, and New Zealander. In an immigrant nation, cultural and ethnic ancestry increasingly contributes to the identity of many, along with that of being a Kiwi. Perceptions of what it is to be a New Zealander and the dominant views and norms are changing and being contested, as the 2005 election campaign demonstrated with arguments around what constitutes 'mainstream New Zealand'. Campaigns to change the flag are also part of this debate about identity.

Identity is also changing in an international sense. More people travel, live, and work in other countries, and hold multiple passports, making them legally citizens of more than one nation. Even for those who do not travel, a large number of global and regional organisations are able to communicate directly with citizens without the mediation of nation–states. These aspects of globalisation have changed the ways in which people think about their identity, about ways in which they might participate and about citizenship (for fuller discussions on ethnicity and globalisation in relation to identity, see chapters 1.3 and 1.7).

The arguments related to opportunity stress the responsibilities of being a citizen, while those prompted by threat focus on values associated with citizenship. Both seek a change in the way that citizens think about the nation–state and their relationships with it. The challenge for the government is how to change the ways that individuals think about citizenship and the impact that this has on their participation.

One example of a government attempt to strengthen the idea that citizenship is more than a legal status is the introduction in Australia of a celebration of Australian Citizenship Day on 17 September each year. The explanation on the website demonstrates the different strands of citizenship that have been discussed. The importance of belonging and identity is very strong:

> Australian citizenship symbolises our unity as a nation. It represents commitment to Australia and its people, the values we share and our common future. It also symbolises the sense of belonging to the country where we have been born or where we have decided to make our home. (www.citizenship.gov.au)

The common values of democracy are also emphasised: 'Most importantly, Australian Citizenship Day is also an occasion to celebrate our democratic values and commitment to a fair go, equality and respect for each other'. Finally, the active role of people in shaping the nation is recognised: 'It is a chance for all of us to think about the changes that have shaped our nation and the role all citizens have played in building Australia and shaping our future'.

CITIZENSHIP EDUCATION

Another common move aimed at encouraging active citizenship is that of strengthening citizenship education. In August 2005, two New Zealand select committee inquiries included a recommendation for citizenship education in schools. Neither was the education select committee. Both were considering aspects of New Zealand's democracy and seeking ways of encouraging active citizenship.

The Constitutional Arrangements Committee considered a range of issues relating to the constitution, including how much people know and think about New Zealand's constitutional arrangement. They recommended that, in order 'To foster greater understanding of our constitutional arrangements in the long term … increased effort should be made to improve civics and citizenship education in schools to provide young people with the knowledge needed to become responsible and engaged citizens'. The Inquiry into the 2004 Local Authority Elections considered details of the conduct of the election, but also the low turnout and if anything could and should be done to encourage higher participation. In the interests of increased participation, they recommended that 'the Ministry of Education should be encouraged to strengthen the place of citizenship education in the curriculum and make more teaching resources available for this purpose'.

New Zealand is not alone in reaching this conclusion. In England and Wales, for example, citizenship education was introduced as a compulsory part of the school curriculum in 2002, with the aim of creating active and responsible participation from citizens. It was expressly promoted as education for citizenship rather than just an end in itself (Crick 1998). Canada and Australia have introduced citizenship as an explicit part of the school curriculum and it is present in most countries within the European Union. Civics has been part of the school day in the USA for decades, although its content is currently being questioned by those concerned with the low levels of political participation (for example, just over 50 per cent of eligible American electors vote in a presidential election, well below the historically low voter turnout found in New Zealand).

Before the 1990s, citizenship education was rarely mentioned by political scientists. The fact that the USA was well known for both teaching civics and for a very low turnout in elections seemed to indicate that civics in schools was not the way to encourage participation. The resurgence of interest in citizenship education as a means of encouraging participation marks a change in thinking about what should be taught, as well as the growing concern about the relationship between the state and individuals discussed above. It reflects a move away from the ideas of Almond and Verba towards a desire for more participation from active citizens, and a need to increase social capital. Education is seen as central to fostering a shared sense of belonging and in equipping people 'with the political skills needed to change laws in a peaceful and responsible manner', and to 'distinguish between law and justice' by 'forming through learning and discussion, concepts of fairness, and attitudes to the law, to rules, to decision-making, to authority, to their local environment and social responsibility' (Crick 1998).

In studies in the USA, three of the four strongest predictors of whether school students voted when they were adults occurred while they were at school: first, the student's level of civic knowledge; second, the confidence they gained in their efficacy of participation at school; and third, the extent to which they discussed and wrote about elections and voting in their class (Torney-Purta & Amadeo 2003, p. 271). Of course, school is not the only important forum for learning citizenship. The fourth important factor in this study was talking about politics in the family.

If citizenship education is an important part of the answer to worries about declining levels of active citizenship, then what exactly does it entail? What lessons and experiences will encourage people to participate in politics throughout their life? If we want more young people to have an interest in politics and the confidence to participate'then we have to persuade them that politics matters to them and that they can make a difference. Of course, we must also ensure that they know how to participate. Education that encourages people to behave as active citizens is not just concerned with knowledge, but also values, skills, and understanding. One component is fostering a sense of belonging and being part of society and sharing the common values of that society. Another is knowledge, or 'political literacy' as it is now called in the curriculum in England (Crick, 1998). However, this knowledge is not just another subject to be learnt, examined on, and forgotten. Instead, the information needs to be meaningful so that students will remember it, or how to access it in adult life as needs arise. The final component is the confidence to be an active citizen, or, put another way, the efficacy necessary to participate. Efficacy is most easily nurtured through the experience of participation. The Crick report that led to citizenship education in the UK argued that the three strands of education for citizenship were social and moral responsibility, community involvement, and political literacy.

Writers and researchers in the study of education argue that children learning about citizenship need to have meaningful opportunities to develop concepts of belonging to groups and communities, and of decision-making. Budding citizens need to learn how to participate and when to exercise dissent and resistance to illegitimate exercises of power. Schools need to learn to foster participatory and consultative curriculum development and teaching methods. These issues are undeniably political and there is no neutral way forward.

New Zealand schools within a 'Tomorrow's Schools' framework of teacher and community partnership may be well placed to achieve this participatory and consultative approach to curriculum development in ways that parallel the current health curriculum. Admittedly, students acting as active citizens of their school and community may appear somewhat threatening to some schools, teachers, and communities.

New Zealand citizenship education has been a poorly defined part of the social studies curriculum since 1942 (Olssen 2001). The social studies curriculum aims 'to enable students to participate in a changing society as informed, confident and responsible citizens ... by developing knowledge and understandings about human society as they study ... people's organisation in groups and the rights, roles and responsibilities of people as they interact within groups ... the contribution of culture and heritage to identity and the nature and consequences of cultural interaction ...'. In terms of the three components highlighted in the Crick report, the missing aspect is community involvement and actually experiencing participation. The Crick report was adamant that this was important because 'volunteering and community involvement are necessary conditions of civil society and democracy. Preparation for these, at the very least, should be an explicit part of education'. Active citizenship is learnt and nurtured through action, not just knowledge.

DISCUSSION QUESTIONS

1 Is citizenship as an idea used in so many different ways that it has lost real meaning?
2 Which aspects of a democracy need high levels of citizen participation?
3 What did you learn at school that prepared you for being an active citizen?
4 Do you think New Zealand should introduce 'citizenship day' and what should be done to celebrate citizenship?

REFERENCES

Almond, G.A. & S. Verba 1989, *The Civic Culture*, 2nd edn, Little Brown, Boston.
Crick, B. 1998, *Education for Citizenship and the Teaching of Democracy in Schools: Final Report of the Advisory Group on Citizenship*, QCA, London.
Inquiry into the 2004 Local Authority Elections: Report of the Justice and Electoral Committee 2005, Forty-seventh Parliament, Tim Barnett (Chairperson), New Zealand House of Representatives.
Marshall, T.H. 1950, *Citizenship and Social Class*, Cambridge University Press, Cambridge.
Olssen, M. 2001, 'Citizenship and Education', *Alfred Educational Philosophy and Theory*, 33/1, pp. 77–94.
Putnam, R. 2000, *Bowling Alone*, Simon & Schuster, New York.
Report of the Constitutional Arrangements Committee 2005, Forty-seventh Parliament, Hon Peter Dunne (Chairperson), New Zealand House of Representatives.
Torney-Purta J. & J. Amadeo 2003, 'A Cross-National Analysis of Political and Civic Involvement among Adolescents', *PSOnline*, April, pp. 269–74.

FURTHER READING

Almond, G.A. and S. Verba 1989, *The Civic Culture*, 2nd edn, Little Brown, Boston.
Crick, B. 1998, *Education for Citizenship and the Teaching of Democracy in Schools: Final Report of the Advisory Group on Citizenship*, QCA, London.
Putnam, R. 2000, *Bowling Alone*, Simon & Schuster, New York.
UK Electoral Commission 2002, *Political Engagement and Young People*, Electoral Commission, London.

PART E

Policy

Process

Public policy has been described as 'Anything a government chooses to do or not to do' (Thomas Dye). It covers the full spectrum of government activity, including economic policy, employment policy, environmental policy, and welfare policy (chapter 8.1). Every time a leading politician advocates tax cuts, there is a rekindling of the same debate over policy priorities and outcomes that divided the country during the period of social and economic restructuring in the 1980s and early 1990s. However, as has been argued elsewhere in this volume, policy priorities are largely determined by context, as illustrated by the rise in the importance of international security in the aftermath of the 9/11 terrorist attacks in the U.S. The attention given to regional security, immigration, and refugee policy in this volume reflects that reality.

Among the policy areas considered in Part E are:

- **Social Policy**. How best to provide for the welfare of citizens is a central question facing any government. Chapter 8.2 explores the challenge of finding ways to address the consequences of child poverty and low-paid employment in an increasingly diverse society, and within the context of an open economy. One area of perennial public concern is the state of the health system. Chapter 8.5 investigates the reasons why the problems of health care are so expensive and unsolvable. As well as describing the current structure of the health system, it considers some tough options, including the rationing of health services.

- **Indigenous Policy**. Chapter 8.3 casts a critical eye over National's proposals to complete historical Treaty claims by 2010; remove any legislative references to the Treaty; end race-based funding arrangements for educations and health; and abolish the separate Māori seats. Chapter 8.4 provides a background discussion on the development of Māori policy from assimilation to the devolution of delivery to tribal groups. The attacks on Māori by the National party leader, Dr Don Brash, and the dispute over the Foreshore and Seabed Act (2004) are described as having had a polarising effect on race relations in New Zealand.

- **Global and Regional Policy**. Although New Zealand enjoys a 'clean and green' image internationally, chapter 8.6 claims that this reputation is undeserved. Among the problems that have not been adequately addressed are water pollution, energy inefficiency, and high vehicle emission levels. Chapter 8.7 describes New Zealand as one of only a few countries that actively seek out new immigrants. That said, the public has not always been as convinced of the benefits of immigration as government politicians, with the New Zealand First party making its opposition to immigration a major campaign issue at every election since 1993. Refugee settlement has been a similarly controversial issue (chapter 8.8), as illustrated by the case of Ahmed Zaoui, an asylum-seeker who faced imprisonment after his arrival in 2002. The final chapter looks at security in the Pacific, particularly in light of the Bali bombings, the growth of trans-national crime, and political instability in such countries as the Solomon Islands and Fiji.

The Policy Process

Claudia Scott

Policy can be defined as a broad orientation, an indication of normal practice, a specific commitment, or a statement of values (Colebatch 2002, p. 7). The nature and scope of public policy can be described in a number of ways. Some definitions focus on the role of government. Public policies encompass both what a government chooses to do and what it prefers to ignore—the so-called 'no-policy' policy. Public policies also include the frameworks of laws and regulations that influence the behaviour of private individuals, groups, and organisations.

Public policy can be divided into a set of categories and subcategories for policy action. These include the areas of economic policy, social policy, employment policy, and so on. Social policy can be subdivided into the subcategories of health, education, social security, and housing. Policy areas may also be identified with particular groups, for example, women, Māori, the elderly, the disabled, and the unemployed.

THE POLICY PROCESS

The existence of a diverse literature and traditions concerning public policy has led to some different ways of portraying the public policy process. One popular way is to try to simplify the policy process, and to present this as a series of stages. Portraying the policy-making process as a set of stages is common; it is often assumed that policy-making is evolutionary and ongoing, with feedback loops, rather than being something which is linear, with a definite life cycle.

Theories about the policy process allow a complex area to be simplified into discrete stages. There is lively debate among scholars of public policy concerning the roles and relative importance in the policy process of various actors and economic, social, and

Table 8.1.1: Link between problem-solving and policy cycle stages

Phases of applied problem-solving	Stages in the policy cycle
1. Problem recognition	1. Agenda setting
2. Proposal of solution	2. Policy formulation
3. Choice of solution	3. Decision-making
4. Putting solution into effect	4. Policy implementation
5. Monitoring results	5. Policy evaluation

political institutions. Some theories place great emphasis on the role of individuals and groups (be they bureaucrats, politicians, or the private sector) as the driving forces behind public policies. Others focus on the important role of institutions in shaping the choices of policy actors.

There are many different versions of the policy process. Some authors refer to the policy 'cycle' and others to the policy 'framework'. Howlett and Ramesh (1995) make connections between the stages of the policy cycle and the phases of applied problem-solving (see table 8.1.1). It is useful to discuss each of these stages of the policy cycle and to identify the role of politicians, public servants, individuals, and groups and institutions at various points in this process. The concept of agenda-setting refers to the way in which problems become identified by government as requiring attention. Questions that arise are issues surrounding whether or not the agenda is internally or externally generated, and, if internally, the role of the politicians and analysts in shaping it.

If a problem exists, there is a need to distinguish the symptoms from root causes. Policy advisers need to focus clearly on the particular issues, policy objectives, and context of the perceived problems. The policy adviser may seek guidance from various government policy statements, election manifestos, previous cabinet decisions, and discussions with ministers.

Policy formulation refers to the definition of policy options by government for addressing the agenda. In examining various options, it is important to consider the status quo (do nothing) option. Defined options should provide decision-makers with real alternatives. They should address both the symptoms and the root cause of the problem, and should influence factors that promote the government's desired outcomes or strategies in this area. In defining the options, it is useful to address some of the problems of putting such a policy in place, including various transitional problems that may arise.

Decision-making refers to the way in which alternatives are evaluated and form the basis of a decision by government. Good analysis requires that clear criteria exist to evaluate different policy options. In looking at the costs and benefits of these alternatives, it is important to consider the costs to government and to private individuals and organisations. The impact on other policies in the sector and on other government policy objectives should be considered. It is also important to look at distributional equity considerations, to see the way in which the choices affect particular sectors, regions, and groups in society, and their implications for legal issues and for constitutional and human rights issues (e.g. the Human Rights Act and the Privacy Act).

Decision-makers make choices among the alternatives. The choice of a preferred alternative often involves trade-offs among conflicting policy objectives and criteria (e.g. efficiency versus equity). In analysing options, it is important for policy-makers to draw on available experience and evidence from New Zealand and overseas, to assist their analysis.

Policy implementation refers to the way in which particular policies are put into effect. This stage involves the development of the operational details of policy, the preparation of legislation or regulations (if required), the establishment or modification of administrative structures and systems, and the communication and promulgation of the policy. The literature on implementation concerns the particular perspective of policy implementation that is conveyed, as well as the debate about the selection of appropriate instruments. The 'top-down' approach sees implementation as an aspect of policy design, whereas 'bottom-up' approaches put emphasis on both formal and informal policy networks in designing a proposal for implementation.

The debate about the choice of instrument may sometimes reflect the disciplinary orientation of the policy specialist. Instruments may be usefully classified in terms of the degree to which they are voluntary or compulsory. The economics literature is oriented towards the use of voluntary rather than compulsory approaches; for example, freeing or facilitating markets as instruments for overcoming market and government failure. The political science literature tends to be more sympathetic to the use of regulation, public enterprises, and direct provision as valid and effective instruments for achieving public policy strategies.

Policy evaluation refers to the various ways in which policy results are monitored and evaluated, and the results reintroduced into the policy cycle. Policy monitoring is done to ensure that the policy has achieved what was intended. Research and evaluation techniques are used to assist analysts to make judgments concerning the merits of maintaining, modifying, or terminating the policy.

The introduction of Mixed Member Proportional representation (MMP) has brought some changes to the agenda-setting and policy-adoption stages of the policy process. Under the former First-Past-the-Post (FPP) electoral system the government agenda was firmly in the hands of the cabinet, working with department officials and advisers. Under MMP, the range of parties and interests that are able to affect the agenda, and whose support is required, is much greater. The importance and influence of these groups depends on the composition of a particular government and on the degree to which minor parties and interest groups support or oppose the government's policies. (For fuller discussions, see chapters 3.1 and 3.5.)

In addition to a wide literature on the various stages of the policy process, there are several broad theories concerning the policy-making process as a whole. These theories comment, in particular, on different approaches to decision-making. Three broad approaches can be identified: the rational model, the incremental model, and the garbage-can model.

The rational model suggests a process and set of procedures that will lead to the choice of the most efficient means of achieving policy objectives. Rationalist theories place the policy analyst in a technical role, in which advice is given as to the most appropriate strategy to achieve given ends. The incremental model grew up as a response to the rational model. It portrays decision-making as a political process, involving bargaining and compromises among key self-interested stakeholders. Political scientist Charles Lindblom (1959, pp. 79–88) is associated with this approach and in his well-known article, 'The Science of Muddling Through', he discusses reasons that much policy change is incremental. Lindblom does, however, see ways in which incremental decision-making can peacefully coexist with efforts to make policy analysis and decision-making more 'rational'. Nevertheless he is sceptical of analysis that suggests that decisions involve welfare maximisation and optimisation.

The *garbage-can model* of policy decision-making aims to strip away the emphasis on rationality in previous models, and to acknowledge that public decisions are often quite ad hoc. While hardly a theory of its own, it nevertheless serves to open up what had become a somewhat sterile debate between the rationalists and the incrementalists, and to focus attention on the study of actual decision-making processes by governments.

THE ROLE OF GOVERNMENT

When considering public policies, it is important to acknowledge the different roles which governments can perform; for example, the role of funder, purchaser, provider, regulator, and owner. Sometimes these different roles are used as the basis for the organisation and administration of a policy area. Health sector reforms, both in New Zealand and in many other countries, have often involved changes to institutions and arrangements surrounding the role(s) of government and the private sector in the health care system. Regulation of purchasers and providers in the health sector is done by the Ministry of Health and also through various professional bodies and organisations.

Important influences on the role of government and the public policy environment of a country include ideology, international trends and experiences, and historical and cultural factors. Though public policies extend beyond the direct activities of governments, it is not uncommon for policies to be generated, or at least processed, within the framework of government procedures, influences, and organisations. Thus a public policy involves a key role, but not necessarily an exclusive or dominant role, for public sector agencies. Sometimes policies are embodied in legislation, but they need not be.

Public policy can be conducted in a way that is descriptive and/or prescriptive. Descriptive public policy is concerned with examining 'what is', while prescriptive public policy gives emphasis to 'what should be'. Students of public policy often consider the way in which policies are influenced by various actors and institutions. Governments require policy analysts and advisers to assist elected members of central or local government in making decisions about the nature of public policies. Increasingly, the public policies in a country are being influenced by developments in other countries. In designing policies, it is important to draw lessons from the experiences of other jurisdictions and provide advice to decision-makers which is 'evidence-based' (Nutley 2003).

TOPIC OR DISCIPLINE?

There is widespread debate within the field of public policy about the degree to which public policy is a topic or a discipline. Public policy as a discipline implies that the area is unique by virtue of having its own concepts, frameworks, and theories. Public policy as a topic implies that the area is a field to which a number of separate disciplines contribute.

Public policy draws on several disciplines and is very closely linked to both economics and politics. Economics is an important discipline because of its concern with the alternative use of scarce resources. Politics provides valuable insights concerning the distribution of power in society and the appropriateness of different organisational structures.

Philosophy, sociology, and social science methodologies all support investigations in the field of public policy, as does law. Constitutional and administrative law explore relationships among the organs of the state and share an interest with politics in fostering democratic principles, such as liberty, justice, and rights.

Those who see public policy as comprising a unique discipline commonly link the area of public policy to the 'policy sciences', an area that emerged after the Second World War. The policy sciences were concerned with the content of policy as well as processes for policy-making. The area was multidisciplinary, normative, and very much centred on addressing the priority policy issues of the government of the day.

The various disciplines that contribute to the study of public policy provide a rich body of theory to shape the discussion and analysis of public policy issues. These theories vary across a number of dimensions. Some develop their analysis in a deductive way, whereas others use an inductive approach. Deductive approaches and theories build on a number of assumptions (or postulates) that are given universal status and provide overall shape to the study. Inductive theories begin by recording observations of different phenomena and then make generalisations that become the basis of theories. Theories can also be distinguished in terms of the units of analysis they adopt. Some theories are based on individuals, whereas others focus on organisations and institutions.

Universities that specialise in the study of public policy vary in the relative emphasis they place on particular disciplines. For example, programmes in Australasia put particular emphasis on the study of politics. In New Zealand, the study of public policy can be traced to the establishment of a Diploma of Public Administration (DPA) at Victoria University, Wellington, in 1940. The programme was developed in response to requests by the New Zealand Institute of Public Administration. In 1975 the diploma was converted to a Master of Public Policy Degree, which provides for multidisciplinary study in economics, politics, and law within the context of the New Zealand public sector. Programmes in North America commonly combine the study of politics with that of economics. A few programmes give greater emphasis to economics rather than the politics, and many employ the use of various quantitative techniques as an important input to policy analysis.

POLICY ANALYSIS AND THE POLICY FRAMEWORK

Policy analysis is a procedure for the design and evaluation of the merits and demerits of a specific policy proposal. It encompasses:

- client-oriented advice relevant to public decisions
- a means of synthesising information and research results to produce a format for policy decisions
- those activities aimed at developing knowledge relevant to the formulation and implementation of policy
- the evaluation of options in terms of explicit criteria. Such criteria should be normative and prescriptive, not descriptive.

Policy analysis consists of analysing options available to the government for solving policy problems. Time pressures, and the need to acknowledge particular constraints, mean that there is rarely scope to consider all possible alternatives. Rather, policy research consists of applying formal methodology to policy-relevant questions. Variables used are often those that can be altered by policy-makers.

Economics and political science have been influential in the evolution of the area of public policy and in the development of alternative views of the policy analyst. One view portrays the policy analyst as an objective technician and scientist. A contrasting view challenges the ability of the analyst to remain detached and to ignore politics, human nature, and the institutional structures that are in place. A third view sees a reconciliation of these two opposing positions, in which scientific knowledge and political power are no longer seen as deathly antagonists.

In order to make recommendations to governments as to what they should and should not do, the policy analyst must have the ability to understand and predict the likely impact of policy actions. These predictions should be based both on theory and on the use of appropriate empirical analysis.

Theories are often simplifications and abstractions of the real world. The analyst aims to understand and describe changes to that world that are caused by the public policy under investigation, and to separate these changes from those caused by other factors. All theory is an attempt to simplify a complex reality, and no scientific theory should be judged solely in terms of its underlying assumptions. The usefulness of a discipline to the analysis of public policies should be linked to its capacity to provide explanations and predictions.

The methodological debates within public policy often reflect the differing views inherent in the disciplines of politics and economics. One example of this in the literature is the debate about the extent to which public policy is based on technical or formal rationality (meaning the selection of appropriate means for achieving given ends). Individuals vary in their views as to whether formal rationality is possible and desirable. While economists often put greater emphasis on the importance of rationality in public policy, political scientists suggest that formal techniques of analysis and theory are mediated by processes of political interaction, and are no substitute for them.

Economic approaches to the examination of public policy questions commonly draw on theories of market failure and government failure. Market failures were traditionally seen as justification for state intervention. Government failures occur when policy interventions end up being less welfare-enhancing than the market failures they were designed to overcome.

In judging market outcomes and balancing the merits of government intervention, the broad criteria of efficiency and distributional equity play important roles. The criterion of efficiency can be divided into allocative and technical efficiency. Allocative efficiency is achieved when the level and mix of resources devoted to different activities produce maximum benefits to society and no rearrangement would be able to put these to better use. Technical efficiency is a narrower concept in which an output of a given quality is produced at least cost. Also important when judging policy is the criterion of equity or fairness. Policy impacts often have outcomes that are not evenly distributed among different groups. In making policy recommendations, it may be necessary to explore the relationships between the criteria of efficiency and equity. Some degree of efficiency may need to be sacrificed in order to get greater distributional equity. Other criteria used to judge policy are the administrative efficiency of different policy arrangements, the extent to which there is consumer choice and voice in policy decisions, and the nature of the accountability arrangements.

POLICY ADVISING

Policy advising is a profession requiring a multidisciplinary approach and knowledge, skills, and competencies which span the arts and sciences. Some use the word 'craft' to describe policy analysis, drawing attention to the way in which it is undertaken in a specific context and tailored for a particular client and purpose. Public sector advisory services are more contested than in the past. The focus of government action is shifting from outputs to outcomes, which is challenging departments and ministries to deliver ambitious policy outcomes, and to reconcile multiple (often conflicting) policy goals. Some governments are extending their roles in service delivery and giving emphasis on the leadership and governance roles.

Forces of globalisation are changing individual and community expectations about government and civil society. The phenomenon of 'globalisation' is linking citizens more closely with international trends and developments, while also creating demands for greater responsiveness and tailoring of public services provision in local and community settings.

Public sector agencies are being asked to tackle the so-called 'wicked issues'. The phrase refers to challenging policy areas where there is little agreement on the nature of the problem, and whether the public sector can assert jurisdiction over the area and secure the necessary buy-in and support from citizens and key stakeholders.

New paradigms and ideologies are shaping public action. External threats to security, whether arising from terrorism or public health risks, are creating new roles for governments and requiring a more seamless and comprehensive approach to policy and service delivery. Greater attention is being given to place-based policies concerning social, environmental and cultural well-being and to policy goals which pursue equity and sustainability.

The need to develop policies from a 'whole-of-government' perspective is requiring greater collaboration and partnerships between government agencies and other organisations, institutions and stakeholder groups. The concept of separate policy design and implementation stages is being increasingly discredited and there is growing evidence that successful implementation is associated with joint ownership and agreement on problems and proposed public policy solutions.

IMPROVING THE QUALITY OF POLICY ADVICE

A good policy process is likely to improve the formulation of policy advice. However, quality policy advice requires more than a good process. Like any production process, quality policy advice is made up of inputs, processes, and outputs. The quality of inputs is influenced by the human resource practices of government agencies: staff development, working conditions, and support. The quality of outputs is enhanced by establishing good systems for internal and external peer review, ministerial feedback, and policy advice quality audits.

It is difficult to get agreement about the qualities and features of value-adding policy advice within the context of the Westminster tradition of government. There are many guidelines, templates, and checklists setting out the qualities of good policy advice. Most of these relate to inputs and processes and are, at best, necessary rather than sufficient conditions for ensuring that advice is fit for purpose.

Fundamentally, quality policy advice must assist decision-makers to make informed choices about policies which support strategic directions and desired policy outcomes. The issue of measuring the quality and value-adding nature of policy analysis and advising will always be a difficult one. Benchmarking and measurement needs to be done over long timeframes and cannot be judged by simple measures such as 'proportion of advice taken' or 'ministerial satisfaction' on a day-to-day basis.

All policy is value-based, but value-creating advice is transparent and explicit regarding the values and assumptions which underpin the analysis. The specification of alternative credible options is required and criteria developed to allow comparisons to be made and recommendations to be prepared for decision-makers (Scott 2005).

Value-added policy advice requires well-argued policy frameworks and the application of research analysis to underpin recommendations. Alternative credible choices are provided and the pros and cons of alternative choices are made explicit, so that the analysis can be debated and challenged.

Getting more value-added policy analysis and advice is dependent on a more robust and engaged public. Policy analysts and advisers can play value-adding roles in fostering democratisation and mediation on specific issues. One of the most difficult areas to address concerns the relationships between elected members, policy advisers, and various stakeholder groups. The move to greater emphasis on consultation and engagement is supporting more participatory styles of policy-making that can potentially challenge the role of politicians in providing policy leadership. It is important to ensure that the abilities of both advisers and decision-makers are being developed to maximum potential.

Making a policy advisory system more innovative and transformational will require effort and commitment. While maintaining an apolitical role in policy advice, the public sector can nevertheless play a key role in encouraging more deliberation on medium-term issues. Policy leadership in the public sector can be enhanced by anticipating policy issues and by building the capabilities and resilience of governments to respond to and shape future challenges and opportunities.

Value-added policy advice also requires innovation and risk-taking. Like any other industry, the public sector needs significant investment in building the capability and performance of policy advisers, including appropriate investments in research and development to drive performance improvement. Without such investments, the public sector's ability to exercise its comparative advantage in policy analysis and advising will suffer.

DISCUSSION QUESTIONS

1 During which stages of the policy cycle is it important for a policy analyst to consult with citizens and stakeholder groups?
2 Identify factors that are likely to influence a person's view about the appropriate role(s) for government in society.
3 Discuss the merits and demerits of the view that policy analysis should be carried out in a way that is objective and scientific.
4 Make a list of six areas of knowledge or skills which will assist policy analysts to provide quality policy advice to decision-makers.

REFERENCES

Colebatch, H.K. 2002, *Policy*, Open University Press, Buckingham.

Howlett, M. & M. Ramesh 1995, *Studying Public Policy*, Oxford University Press, Toronto.

Lasswell, H. 1956, *The Decision Process: Seven Categories of Functional Analysis*, University of Maryland, College Park.

Lindblom, C. 1959, 'The Science of Muddling Through', *Public Administration Review*, vol. 19.

Nutley, S. 2003, 'Evidence Based Policy and Practice, Cross Sector Lessons from the UK', Paper for the Social Policy and Research Evaluation Conference (mimeo).

Scott, C. 2001, *Public and Private Roles in Health Care Systems: Reform Experiences in Seven OECD Countries*, Open University Press, Buckingham.

FURTHER READING

Bardach, E. 2000, *A Practical Guide for Policy Analysis*, New York, Chatham House.

Scott, C.D. 2005, 'Value-Adding Policy Analysis and Advice: new roles and skills for the public sector', *Policy Quarterly*, 1/3, pp. 10–15.

State Services Commission 1999, 'Essential Ingredients: improving the quality of policy advice', Occasional Paper No. 9, State Services Commission.

Weimer, D. & A. Vining 2005, *Policy Analysis: Concepts and Practice*, Prentice-Hall, New Jersey.

Social Policy

Patrick Barrett

Is there anything distinctive about the social democratic approach to the management of social risks in New Zealand in the early twenty-first century? The social policy rhetoric of the Labour-led governments since 1999 has drawn on the language of the 'Third Way' (see chapter 1.5), but this is renowned for being frustratingly vague. After six years of power by the centre-left, though, it is timely to ask, 'what is different?' Are there signs of a new welfare edifice based on distinctive social policies under Labour-led governments? Exploring these themes involves tracing the emergence of new social risks in New Zealand and exploring the evolving interface between the state, the family, and the market.

SOCIAL POLICY

Questions about social policy and how to provide for the welfare of citizens are at the heart of much analysis of government and politics. While the term 'social policy' is used frequently today, it is not always easy to have an image of what social policy is in the same way as one might have an image of, say, foreign affairs or health policy. Social policy has an applied dimension and is something that governments, private organisations, and communities do (Blackmore 1998, p. 1). It is also a distinctive branch of research and teaching—and an interdisciplinary field of study, drawing on the methods and insights of other disciplines such as politics, sociology, economics, and philosophy. Like public policy, social policy is concerned with analysis of the process and substance of public decisions and non-decisions. Social policy is characterised by its orientation towards social action—actions taken by decision-makers in both government and non-government organisations, including voluntary groups—in the pursuit of individual and social well-being[1] (Alcock 1998, p. 7).

Social policy as an academic discipline was originally concerned with the study of the administration of social services such as health, poverty relief, and housing assistance. It was called social administration. As the discipline evolved, definitions of social policy recognised that decisions about the distribution of resources and life opportunities across a much broader sphere of societal activity affected individual and social well-being. Titmuss (2001, pp. 67–9) recognised this in terms of occupational welfare (benefits in cash or in kind through the workplace), fiscal welfare (tax relief or allowances), and social welfare (benefits and services provided by the state). So, while social policy is concerned with the study of ameliorative social services,[2] it is not simply an appendage to the economy or a supportive system that provides welfare services for people. The separation between the social and the economic in both academic analysis and in government administration is therefore artificial. Titmuss (2001) recommended understanding social policy as involving a wide array of government and community activity that included corrective regional economic development policies, retraining and education initiatives, and other measures to improve the standard and quality of life. In this view, the distinction between economic development and social development is blurred, with social policy both an enabling force for change and a means of ameliorating social risks.

It is also worth noting that we cannot avoid making moral judgments or applying normative criteria when studying social policy (Mullard & Spicker 1998, p. 2). Thus, questions about how best to pursue individual and social well-being cannot be approached as purely technical or scientific matters, but rather as matters of interpretation. Interpretations of social problems are, at root, value judgments and involve applying moral codes to situations. Moral values traditionally served by welfare states are: the reduction of poverty; the promotion of social equality; the avoidance of social exclusion; the promotion of social stability; the promotion of economic efficiency; and the promotion of autonomy (Goodin et al. 1999, p. 22). Value judgments might be thought of as the reasons governments and non-government organisations concern themselves with the well-being of individuals and groups. They influence how we interpret questions of individual and social well-being and the importance we give to issues of equality, poverty, risk, freedom, and justice. The notion of risk, for example, has received closer attention in social research from the 1990s and, according to Kemshall (2002), has become a key theme in framing social policy concerns. How a society understands and responds to social risks is determined by the relative importance it gives to particular values.

We encounter value judgments within the context of the various normative frameworks which provide alternative visions of the 'good society'. While competing visions of the good society recognise the legitimacy and importance of similar values, they interpret them differently and give them different emphases. Furthermore, they group values together with distinctive programmes and policies (Goodin et al. 1999, p. 5). For example, the neo-liberal welfare framework favours individualism and liberty, the latter negatively defined as the freedom from interference, and markets. In this framework, the government is assigned a minimal and residual role in the pursuit of social well-being. The social democratic framework favours social equality, inclusion, and comprehensive social citizenship—the notion of everyone having the wherewithal to participate fully in the life of the community. These frameworks emphasise particular social risks. In the neo-liberal framework, the risk is primarily that of the inefficient operation of markets, including the labour market, and the tendency for people who do not participate in markets to become dependent on governments which provide assistance.[3] In the social democratic framework, working people face risks by their position in the economy and there is less optimism that unfettered markets can deliver well-being. Each framework allocates different responsibility to the state, the family, and to the market in providing livelihoods and producing well-being; each represents a system with its own internal logic that prescribes what policy options can fit coherently together (Goodin et al. 1999, p. 37).

Our task as students of social policy is to adopt a critical stance which identifies the normative frameworks upon which policy is developed. Recognising the normative frameworks of social policy orients us towards seeing social problems from more than one perspective. Furthermore, a critical stance allows us to identify the assumptions about both facts and values that are not usually made explicit in policy politics when competing political actors describe problems and propose solutions (Stone 1997).

HISTORICAL RESPONSES TO SOCIAL RISKS

The history of social policy in New Zealand is characterised by periods of intense reform followed by more extended periods of consolidation. During the periods of reform there has been an intensification of ideological debate between competing normative frameworks. The first of these periods of reform in New Zealand occurred during the final decade of the nineteenth century when path-breaking innovations in industrial relations and social policy were constructed in response to social risks from low wage levels and harsh employment conditions. The welfare system that evolved over the next three decades was based around meeting income needs for male breadwinners through the wages system, and providing highly selective income assistance for the aged and, later, widows.

The second period of reform occurred during the term of the first Labour government between 1935 and 1949 when a Keynesian response to prevailing social risks was constructed. The Keynesian welfare state was built on high levels of employment, achieved through a combination of market regulation and protectionism, and demand stimulation through spending in social policy areas of education, the health sector, housing, and infrastructure. Keynesian social policies were based around the full employment of male breadwinners and around addressing social risks arising from interruptions to employment income through frictional unemployment, retirement, ill-health, or widowhood.

Changes that occurred during the 1970s undermined the effectiveness of the Keynesian response to social risks. The integration of domestic markets with international markets resulted in changes in the structure of domestic industry and pressure on the state to foster local competitiveness. Declining economic growth led to a shrinking base of resources from which to fund welfare programmes at a time when new programmes were initiated in the form of accidental injury compensation, income support for lone-parents, and an expensive universal superannuation scheme. Unemployment also began to rise, further increasing demands on social welfare spending. The efficacy of the social policy measures built around providing welfare through fully employed male breadwinners was further reduced by change in the family structure. The 1970s witnessed growth in divorce; non-marital childbearing; change in gender norms with a greater number of women pursuing lifelong careers, or at least greater participation in the labour market; declining fertility; and deferred childbearing.

Loss of confidence in Keynesian measures led to a resurgence in normative debate over rival visions of the good society. What followed was another period of intense policy reform between 1984 and 1993 inspired by the neo-liberal blueprint for a more residual role for the state, recommodification of many social services, and greater emphasis on individual and family responsibility (Boston, Dalziel & St John 1999). From the neo-liberal perspective, social risks primarily had their origin in large government and excessive regulation, which was responsible for declining economic growth and rising unemployment. If markets were permitted to operate more freely, it was assumed, the economy would better adjust to the new global economic environment, and problematic obstacles to individual initiative and mobility would be removed. This optimism in the capacity of the neo-liberal policy mix to address questions of economic development, however, was not realised.

NEW SOCIAL POLICY CHALLENGES IN THE TWENTY-FIRST CENTURY

Many of the neo-liberal initiatives actually exacerbated the old risks from the Keynesian era and led to historically high levels of unemployment, peaking in 1992 at 10.4 per cent, and poverty. New risks emerged associated with an increased threat of unemployment or employment in low-end precarious jobs that did not guarantee a living wage. These changes were linked with changes in the family and constitute new challenges for social policy-makers.

Foremost among these were the effects of the social and economic restructuring of the 1980s and 1990s. They had differential impacts on working people according to skill, occupation, ethnicity, age, gender, and geographical location (Singley & Callister 2003, p. 137). The unskilled and the low-skilled experienced redundancy and job loss at a much higher rate than others and, from the mid-1980s, the gap in the employment prospects of those with low skill levels and those with high skill levels began to widen. Certain occupational groups were more vulnerable and population sub-groups, especially Māori and Pacific Island people, were over-represented in some of the hardest-hit sectors, leading to a new form of social dualism. Improved economic growth in the first years of the twenty-first century has resulted in declining unemployment across all population groups to a level of 3.7 per cent in 2005. Disparities between ethnic groups have reduced, but Māori continue to be the most disadvantaged, concentrated in semi-skilled work, unemployment, or not in the labour force. Māori remain more than three times more likely to be unemployed than Pakeha New Zealanders, while Pacific Island people and 'other' ethnic groups (most often ethnically identifiable migrants) are more than twice as likely (Department of Labour 2005). The income inequality which increased sharply from 1987 to 1991 has not declined significantly (Ministry of Social Development 2005).

While there have been 'winners' through recent growth in employment, then, there continue to be 'losers'. We can see this through the ongoing need for food banks, a phenomenon which first emerged during the mid-1980s. Demand for food banks has not fallen from the mid-1990s despite declining unemployment. Food banks have become an essential part of the social service sector, responding to a degree of deprivation that cannot be met through the benefit system. In many cases food banks deal with people referred straight from the Department of Work and Income (Cheyne, O'Brien & Belgrave 2005, p. 175). The Poverty Indicator Project (New Zealand Council of Christian Social Services 2004), which surveys a range of indicators related to the use of food banks, reports there has been little change in demand since their research began in 2000. Most food bank recipients are those on benefits, but up to 30 per cent of those who receive assistance are in paid employment (this varies according to geographical location). New Zealand now has a new group of 'working poor'—those who have made it into the labour market but who earn incomes insufficient to meet basic needs. One explanation for this is that much of the job-rich economic growth of the past six years has been in the services sector, a sector in which there are large gaps between skilled, professional jobs and low-end, routine jobs. Additionally, financial constraints and job insecurity have had a far-reaching impact, not least in the area of home ownership. They are the largest impediments to first-home purchase, and it is not surprising that with growth in income differentials has come a decline in rates of home ownership over the past two decades. Meeting the income needs of those in low-end jobs has become one of the primary welfare challenges of the twenty-first century.

Significant changes in demographic structure and family behaviour from those underpinning the era of the Keynesian welfare state present a further social policy challenge. The Ministry of Social Development's (2004, p. 9) review of families in New Zealand observes that families today are more evenly distributed across a wider variety of forms that include:

> ... couples with children, sole parents, parents who don't live with their children but are still involved, same sex couples (some with children), and many family members who have ties of support across households and generations.

These changes are accelerating. For example, younger men and women are partnering, dissolving relationships, and re-partnering more frequently. While these changes in family and household arrangements reflect greater freedom and choice, they also present new forms of insecurity and risk. The much wider diversity of family forms and decreasing family stability presents new social policy challenges in ensuring household income needs are adequately met.

A related point is that risk is becoming concentrated at a household level, given the propensity for individuals to live with others in similar circumstances and this has implications for all family members, especially children. The winners and losers in post-industrial economies are likely to 'bundle in households', and household formation and stability has particular implications for the life chances of children (Esping-Andersen 2002, p. 3). In their review of child poverty in New Zealand, St John and Craig (2004, p. 12) assert that growing gaps in income and wealth distribution have occurred alongside a 'de-greying of poverty'. Growth in child poverty rates date from the recession of the early 1990s and the benefit cuts of 1991, and have been higher in New Zealand than in other OECD countries, despite falling unemployment (Perry 2005, p. 13). By far the largest number of children below the poverty line are from lone-parent families, this group the most likely to be dependent on a benefit, followed by families with three or more children (Ministry of Social Development 2005).

A stark indicator of the effects of child poverty is the development of significant gaps in the achievements of the best and worst performing students. The Programme for International Student Assessment study shows New Zealand performing among the top six countries in mathematical, scientific, and reading literacy. However, New Zealand also has a 'long tail' of underachievement, one of the longest in the OECD, comprising a greater number of Māori and Pacific Island students (Sturrock & May 2002). The study's analysis clearly associated poverty, or socio-economic status, with the widening gap. In an economic environment where education and skills are central to determining later employment prospects, the accumulation of human capital and educational achievement is now more critical. Social inheritance in childhood frames access to those opportunities and determines many later life chances.

In sum, the challenge facing social policy-makers in the early years of the twenty-first century has been to find ways to address problems associated with a more highly dualised society, within the context of an open economy. The issue has become one of how to reduce the risk of family entrapment in unemployment or low-paid employment how to address problems associated with inferior life chances for all family members.

A NEW WELFARE ARCHITECTURE?

We might ask, therefore, after six years of Labour-led governments, can we detect a new direction in social policy to meet the new welfare challenges? On the one hand, many of the economic policy settings of the neo-liberal era remain in place (Duncan 2004, p. 213). There has been no return to the policies of market regulation and control, although the Employment Relations Act has given greater recognition to the place of unions and accident compensation has been re-nationalised. Furthermore, there has been a more activist approach to the support of business development and employment growth in the regions through the establishment of the Ministry of Economic Development and Industry New Zealand.

Alongside regional economic development initiatives to promote employment growth have been changes to the way benefits are administered. Rhetorically, the shift is from 'tightly-targeted income assistance' to 'investment in social development' with clear assumptions around 'reciprocal obligations'. The Community Wage and the 'job seeker contract', put in place when Work and Income New Zealand (WINZ) was established in 1998, were abolished under the Labour–Alliance government. The work-test was removed for those receiving the domestic purposes and widows' benefits. The 'job seeker contract', which was the tool to require participation in the work-for-the-dole scheme, was replaced by what might be described as 'activation' policies. Activation policies involved more intensive case management of people on benefits to address specific barriers to getting a job, such as support for access to childcare, education, skill development, or work placement. The rationale has been one of investment to facilitate transitions into 'real jobs'. The obligations on benefit recipients specifying required job-seeking behaviours, such as a preparedness to move, with assistance, to a centre where jobs were available, were made explicit in a 2003 Jobs Jolt programme. The planned shift to a Single Core Benefit in 2007 or 2008, as a replacement for the unemployment, sickness, invalids, domestic purposes, and widows benefits, is designed to simplify benefit administration and increase potential for case management. What defines these initiatives, is an approach that supports citizens meeting their basic income, and therefore basic welfare, needs within the market.

This approach is also evident within the flagship 'Working for Families' package which is explicitly oriented towards encouraging people into the labour market and which uses fiscal welfare (the tax system) to address the issue of low incomes among the working poor. Working for Families will lead to a major redistribution of income in support of poorer New Zealanders, the first such initiative in thirty years (St John & Craig 2004, p. 4). The timeframe for introducing the package was brought forward as a part of Labour's response to National's tax cuts promised in the 2005 election campaign, and from 2006 it will give a sizeable financial boost to many families on borderline incomes. It involves the extension of Family Support, first introduced in 1986, as a targeted tax credit based on combined parental income and the number of children. It also provides an 'In Work Payment' and assistance with accommodation costs and childcare subsidies. It will guarantee working families a net income of approximately $17,000 from 2006 (St John & Craig 2004, p. 43).

Initial assessments are that the increase of Family Assistance is likely to lower poverty and improve the incomes of in-work families with children (Perry 2004). The major beneficiaries will be working families with relatively low incomes, but middle-income families will also have their incomes boosted. It improves access to childcare and provides assistance with housing. The point here is that the programme is designed to orient people towards market employment. Working for Families is criticised for its neglect of out-of-work families with children. Critics suggest it will entrench 'an underclass even further by leaving the most vulnerable behind; even worse-off than before, relatively speaking' (St John & Craig 2004, p. 4). It is clear that its orientation is towards enhancing labour market participation and addressing problems that stem from a low-wage market.

The other area of social policy that might be described as typically Third Way has been increased investment in training and lifelong learning (Giddens 1998; Duncan 2004, p. 219). This represents a policy of 'capacity building' to develop human resources and furnish citizens for success in the market. Public investment in education, skills, apprenticeships, and lifelong learning has been oriented towards providing a bridge into further education, training, or employment. Again, the emphasis is on promoting social inclusion through employment, and on promoting an entrepreneurial culture, especially for Māori and Pacific peoples, as a way of reducing disparities.

CONCLUSION

Since 1999 there has been a shift away from an explicitly ideological programme. Governments have been more pragmatic, concerned with remaining electable and avoiding the perception of extreme ideological devotion. While it has been difficult to decipher precisely what successive Labour-led governments have intended from vague and generic Third Way rhetoric, it is possible to discern the building blocks of a new welfare edifice oriented towards actively equipping individuals and families to engage in the market. Rather than intervene in markets, the role of the state under Labour-led governments has been to accept responsibility for preparing people for markets. It is an approach based on social investment or social development, activation, building up individuals' capacities, and ensuring they have opportunities to enter markets. The guarantee of minimum incomes through the Working for Families programme is perhaps the first concrete evidence of a serious re-distributory intent, providing liveable income guarantees for those at the lower-end of the labour market. The well-being of out-of-work families with children remains at risk. Taken together, though, the income guarantees, the accent of activist approaches to integrating people into employment, and the provision of assistance for childcare, resemble the social policy instruments employed in Scandinavian countries. Helen Clark is known to admire the Scandinavian approach to welfare and it just may be that a similar model is being fashioned in New Zealand.

DISCUSSION QUESTIONS

1   What values should underpin a nation's approach towards addressing poverty? List them in order of priority.
2   After the decades of social reform through the 1980s and 1990s, can it be said that New Zealand is a better place? Why? Why not?
3   In what way have growing income disparities affected New Zealand society? Should we be concerned about social equality?
4   Imagine you are a cabinet minister making a case to your fellow ministers for a universal child benefit. What would your argument be?

NOTES

1   For a discussion on the meaning of 'well-being' see Duncan (2005) and the Ministry of Social Development (2005, p. 6).
2   You can gain a sense of these by noting the key functions performed by the Ministry of Social Development. As well as providing social policy advice to the government, it also provides social services including: income support, employment services, and superannuation through Work and Income; student allowances and loans through StudyLink; services to rural clients through Heartland Services; and coordination of services that support families through Family and Community Services. The Ministry is also responsible for the Ministry of Youth Development, the Office for Disability Issues, the Office for Senior Citizens, the Office for the Community and Voluntary Sector, and the Office of the Families Commission.
3   See Mullard and Spicker (1998, pp. 176–80) for a critique of this assumption about dependency.

REFERENCES

Alcock, P. 1998, 'The Discipline of Social Policy', in P. Alcock, A. Erskine & M. May, *The Student's Companion to Social Policy*, Blackwell Publishers, Oxford, pp. 7–13.

Blackmore, K. 1998, *Social Policy: An Introduction*, Open University Press, Buckingham.

Boston, J., P. Dalziel & S. St John 1999, *Redesigning the Welfare State in New Zealand: Problems, Policies, Prospects*, Oxford University Press, Auckland.

Cheyne, C., M. O'Brien & M. Belgrave 2005, *Social Policy in Aotearoa New Zealand: A Critical Introduction*, 3rd edn, Oxford University Press, Melbourne.

Department of Labour 2005, *Employment and Unemployment—June 2005 Quarter*, Department of Labour, Wellington.

Duncan, G. 2004, *Society and Politics: New Zealand Social Policy*, Pearson, Auckland.

Esping-Andersen, G. 2002, Towards the Good Society, Once Again? in G. Esping-Andersen (ed.) *Why We Need a New Welfare State*, Oxford University Press, Oxford, pp. 1–25.

Giddens, A. 1998, *The Third Way: The Renewal of Social Democracy*, Polity Press, Cambridge.

Goodin, R., B. Heady, R. Muffels & H. Dirven 1999, *The Real Worlds of Welfare Capitalism*, Cambridge University Press, Cambridge.

Kemshall, H. 2002, *Risk, Social Policy and Welfare*, Open University Press, Buckingham.

Ministry of Social Development 2004, *New Zealand Families Today: A Briefing for the Families Commission*, Ministry of Social Development, Wellington.

Ministry of Social Development 2005, *The Social Report*, Ministry of Social Development, Wellington.

Mullard, M. & P. Spicker 1998, *Social Policy in a Changing Society*, Routledge, London.

New Zealand Council of Christian Social Services 2004, *Poverty Indicator Project, Foodbank Study, Summary Report, First Quarter*, New Zealand Council of Christian Social Services, Wellington.

Perry, B. 2004, 'Working for Families: The Impact on Child Poverty', *Social Policy Journal of New Zealand*, Issue 22, pp. 19–54.

Perry, B. 2005, *Social Report Indicators for Low Incomes and Inequality: Update from the 2004 Household Economic Survey*, Ministry of Social Development, Wellington.

Singley, S. & P. Callister 2003, 'Work Poor or Working Poor? A Comparative Perspective on New Zealand's Jobless Households', in *Social Policy Journal of New Zealand*, Issue 20, pp. 134–55.

St John, S. & D. Craig 2005, *Cut Price Kids: Does the 2004 'Working for Families' Budget Work for Children*, Child Poverty Action Group, Auckland.

Stone, D. 1997, *Policy Paradox: The Art of Political Decision Making*, W.W. Norton & Company, New York.

Sturrock, F. & May, S. 2002, *PISA 2000: The New Zealand Context: The Reading, Mathematical and Scientific Literacy of 15 year olds*, Ministry of Education, Wellington.

Titmuss, R. 2001, 'The Social Division of Welfare: Some Reflections on the Search for Equality', in P. Alcock, H. Glennerster, A. Oakley & A. Sinfield, *Welfare and Wellbeing: Richard Titmuss's Contribution to Social Policy*, The Policy Press, Bristol, pp. 59–70.

FURTHER READING

Cheyne, C., M. O'Brien & M. Belgrave 2005, *Social Policy in Aotearoa New Zealand: A Critical Introduction*, 3rd edn, Oxford University Press, Melbourne.

Esping-Andersen, G. 2002, 'Towards the Good Society, Once Again'? in G. Esping-Andersen (ed.), *Why we Need a New Welfare State*, Oxford University Press, Oxford, pp. 1–25.

Ministry of Social Development 2005, *The Social Report*, Ministry of Social Development, Wellington.

Stone, D. 1997, *Policy Paradox: The Art of Political Decision Making*, W.W. Norton & Company, New York.

Treaty Policy

Janine Hayward

Western liberal democracies, such as New Zealand, regularly debate the appropriate recognition and protection of minority rights within a majoritarian system. Treaty of Waitangi policy is a very good example of the issues surrounding minority rights that cause controversy for a modern democracy like New Zealand. Treaty policy refers to the laws and principles that guide government interaction with Māori (specific examples are discussed below). The debate surrounding Treaty policy can be simplified thus: when, if ever, should minority rights be protected from (and specifically differentiated from) the rights of the majority?

During New Zealand's 2005 general election campaign, a stark contrast emerged between the status quo approach to Treaty policy, and the opposition National party's proposed policy. The status quo approach has been emerging since the 1970s under Labour and National-led governments, which, to a varying degree, have acted on the basis that the minority indigenous Māori population can and should legitimately be differentiated in law and policy in order to receive appropriate treatment by the state. By contrast, in 2005 the National party proposed abolishing what it described as 'race-based policy' in favour of 'one law for all'. The party advocated that Māori should not be specifically identified in law and policy under any circumstances, because this is inappropriate and unjustified. The changes National proposed would occur through majority will, and without specific Māori consent. In the event, National was not successful at the 2005 general election, leaving the elected Labour-led government to continue to support policies that in some manner identify or target Māori.

This chapter considers several examples of Treaty policy within a theoretical context of minority rights in a liberal democratic state. Treaty policy in this discussion is narrowly defined as the Treaty settlement process, the principles of the Treaty of Waitangi, and the guaranteed Māori seats in parliament. The theoretical framework proposed to consider the debate is that of Canadian theorist Will Kymlicka (1995). Kymlicka gives useful insights into the power relationship between minorities and majorities in liberal democracies, an approach that can be applied to questions raised in the 2005 election debate, and which will no doubt be raised in various forms in the future.

MINORITIES IN THE LIBERAL STATE

In March 2004, Don Brash, leader of the National party, made a speech at Orewa that prompted the most significant surge in National party support since the party's crushing defeat at the 2002 general election. His speech, entitled 'Nationhood' focused on what he described as the 'dangerous drift toward racial separatism' in New Zealand. This drift included, among other things, references to the 'principles of the Treaty' in legislation, and the 'anachronism of the Māori seats in parliament'. Brash concluded: '[t]here can be no basis for special privileges for any race'.[1]

During the 2005 general election campaign, Brash and the National party reiterated and expanded on this policy position that seemed to have resonated with a large section of the population (see chapter 8.4 for a discussion on the same theme). The party proposed, with regard to Treaty policy, to complete historical Treaty claims by 2010, to remove inappropriate references to the 'principles' of the Treaty from legislation, to give all citizens an equal say in decision-making, to remove race-based funding from education and health, and to abolish the guaranteed Māori seats in parliament.[2] This constituted a radical departure from the approach governments had taken to Treaty policy since the 1970s, whereby Māori and the Treaty have, over time, been afforded specific recognition in policy and law, often despite public resistance or dissatisfaction. With the National party's departure from this policy position, voters at the 2005 general election were presented with a clear ideological choice: either Māori and the Treaty should be afforded explicit policy recognition by the state, or, all references to Māori and the Treaty should be removed to eliminate special privilege. Although other political parties of the centre-right (ACT, New Zealand First, and United Future) shared National's concerns regarding Treaty policy, the National party went one step further in proposing that these radical changes to Treaty policy be introduced without Māori consent.

How can we make sense of the diverse approaches to Treaty policy evident at the 2005 election? Kymlicka provides a helpful starting point. He contends that there is much diversity within the liberal tradition regarding the appropriate treatment of minorities (such as Māori). Some liberal governments (or political parties) argue that a system of universal individual rights, or 'one law for all', accommodates cultural difference. In this context, 'liberalism' is interpreted to mean that individuals have the freedom to associate with whichever culture they choose. By extension, it is unnecessary to benefit or privilege any particular culture through law or policy because each can survive on its own strengths. Moreover, it is unfair to do so because some people's cultures and preferences are given priority over others. Kymlicka concedes that there is one law for all—the protection of individual civil and political rights to freedom of association, religion, and so forth—which is fundamental to the protection of rights, and is the basis of liberalism (Kymlicka 1995, pp. 107–8). But some forms of liberalism, such as that expressed by the National party, extend the concept of 'one law for all' past this fundamental premise to all laws and policies. These liberals argue that the state should neither promote nor inhibit the maintenance of any particular culture (by specific reference in legislation or policy), but rather should respond with 'benign neglect' to multicultural societies with neutral laws which identify (and thereby privilege) no specific group(s) (Kymlicka 1995, p. 108).

Other forms of liberalism take a different approach to minorities. These political parties and governments believe that liberalism requires some kind of state recognition and protection of minorities in order for minorities to sustain themselves. These liberals recognise that, beyond the provision of fundamental human rights, there can be no 'one law for all' because laws are not neutral and will impact on different individuals and groups in different ways. Even the laws and policies on internal boundaries, holidays, national symbols, institutional arrangements and voting systems, unavoidably recognise, accommodate, and support the needs and identities of particular groups (the vocal majority) even if they do not actually name this group. Consequently, these laws and policies will disadvantage minorities who do not share the majority's cultural, social, and political identity. In other words, a state that institutes one law for all unavoidably promotes the desires of the majority and potentially disadvantages minorities (Kymlicka 1995).

Between these two divergent interpretations of liberalism, there is a range of views that can be articulated. For example, those who support the liberal notion of one law for all need not (and indeed often do not) deny that a minority (such as Māori) has the right to express and retain a deep attachment to its own languages and cultures. Nevertheless, the state should not offer special protection in order for that group's culture to survive. If the law treats all equally, and allows freedom of association and other basic rights to all citizens, then people are free to choose for themselves which groups, cultural or otherwise, they choose to associate with, and therefore which cultures flourish and which do not.

Kymlicka, in considering these various expressions of liberalism, argues that benign neglect (or 'one law for all') is a mistaken and incoherent position to articulate and defend. He concludes (p. 108) that it is naïve to talk of one law for all, because this denies the influence of the majority will in shaping law as an expression of political, cultural, and moral assumptions. Policies and laws that make special provision for minorities reflect the liberal tradition that minorities require protection to a degree within a majoritarian democracy, and that to ignore minorities creates greater inequality rather than promoting equality. Kymlicka also points out that the majority culture is advantaged by the fact that it cannot be outvoted or overruled by the minority in asserting its cultural and political preferences, while the reverse cannot be said in favour of minority cultures (Kymlicka 1995).

Kymlicka's ideas offer a way of assessing the practical implications of the National party's proposed change in Treaty policy. Specifically, he provides a way to assess the claim that New Zealand society will be *more equal* when Māori are not specifically identified in policy and legislation, as opposed to the current tradition, which assumes that equality is achieved through policy which specifically recognises Māori and the Treaty. Before considering how Kymlicka's argument can be applied to the Treaty policy debate, however, we need to take one step back and consider a prior question. On what basis are Māori currently differentiated in legislation and policy? Or, differently stated, what is the Māori claim for recognition by the state?

MĀORI AND THE TREATY OF WAITANGI

The relationship between Māori and the state formally began in 1840, when leaders of Māori hapu (sub-tribes) and British representatives signed a treaty at Waitangi in the Bay of Islands. At the time, Māori vastly outnumbered British settlers and traders, and the agreement was presented to, and accepted by, many Māori as an act of the Queen's love and extension of her protection to Māori culture and lifestyle. The Treaty also secured for Māori the advantages British settlers brought with them in terms of trade and technology. Many British settlers, traders, and missionaries at the time spoke Māori and relied heavily on the alliance with Māori communities to engage in successful trade. The Treaty was an exchange to benefit both parties which Māori signatories appear to have understood thus: British governance was established in New Zealand (under article one) in exchange for the protection of Māori resources (most notably land) and treasured possessions (under article two).

By the 1860s, the settler pressure for access to Māori land was intense and attitudes toward Māori and the Treaty were beginning to change. When London handed over responsibility for Māori affairs to the growing settler government, significant changes occurred. Where previously accommodation had been made for Māori based on the Treaty guarantee, by 1877 the courts had declared the Treaty a simple nullity and the settler government's law-making authority undermined Māori ability to protect lands, resources, customs, and cultures. The various land confiscations Acts which forcibly removed Māori from their land, and the individualisation of Māori land tenure instituted by the Native Land Court have been recognised by government as breaches of the Treaty.

These grievances and many others are now being investigated by the Waitangi Tribunal and government agencies and redressed through the Treaty settlement process.

In terms of Treaty policy, the Treaty settlement process is perhaps the least contentious aspect; political parties across the spectrum seem to accept that redress for genuine grievances is appropriate. There is debate, however, about the length of time the process should take, and the amount of money that should be spent on it. But it is important to be clear on the issues surrounding settlements. The Waitangi Tribunal is not responsible for the settlement of Treaty grievances. It is a commission of inquiry with the authority to inquire into claims, determine whether those claims are well founded, and make recommendations for redress. Therefore, the Tribunal is just one (albeit vital) part of the Treaty settlement process. Other key players in the process are the Crown Forestry Rental Trust, which provides certain claimants with assistance to research claims; the Office of Treaty Settlement, which is the government unit responsible for the actual negotiation of Treaty settlements; and the Crown Law Office, which provides legal representation for the Crown throughout the process.

The current challenge to the Treaty settlement process is increasing political pressure to speed up the Treaty settlement process. In 1998, the ACT party introduced to parliament the Treaty of Waitangi (Final Settlement of Claims) Bill. This proposed that all historical claims be lodged with the Tribunal by 31 December 1999. Further, the Waitangi Tribunal would hear and report on all claims by 2005. Under the Bill, the government would take action within five years of receiving the Tribunal's recommendation. Although the Bill languished in the House, the ACT party has resuscitated the Bill on several occasions since then, also to no effect. Winston Peters, leader of New Zealand First, gained considerable mileage out of attacking the 'Treaty industry' at the 2002 general election campaign. Peters, like other politicians, is critical of the time and money spent on Treaty claims. In 2005, the Brash-led National party also advocated an end to the settlement of historical claims. Many other parties have put forward similar policies, with the exception of the Māori party and the Green party, who believed that limiting the time available for claims created the potential for further injustice against Māori.

Therefore, the claims that Māori make to state recognition extend from their relationship with the state established in 1840. Beyond the broad political acceptance that genuine historical grievances should be redressed, Māori claims of a special contemporary relationship with the state is a matter of debate and contention between political parties. In particular, the National party attacked two specific aspects of Treaty policy in its 2005 campaign: the principles of the Treaty in legislation; and the guaranteed Māori seats. Applying Kymlicka's arguments about the different ways to conceive of minority rights in a modern democracy allows us to consider the implications of the choice that faced New Zealand at the 2005 election.

ONE LAW FOR ALL: THE PRINCIPLES OF THE TREATY IN LEGISLATION

As discussed above, benign neglect assumes that the state does not (indeed should not) offer specific protection for any cultural group, because individuals can choose for themselves to support any group through voluntary membership and association. This is the logic underpinning the National party's proposal to remove legislative and policy references to the Treaty principles. As discussed above, Kymlicka would question whether removing such references makes Māori and non-Māori *more*, or *less*, equal before the law. To answer this, we must establish what the Treaty principles are, how they came to be in policy and legislation, and what the implications would be of removing all references to the Treaty.

In 1975, the Treaty of Waitangi Act was passed, allowing for the establishment in 1977 of the Waitangi Tribunal to investigate alleged Treaty breaches against the Crown. This was the first piece of legislation that spoke of the 'principles of the Treaty of Waitangi'. When the legislation was passed, there was little consideration of what the principles entailed; that was seen to be the task of the Waitangi Tribunal. The Tribunal described the principles as flowing from the Treaty's words and from 'the evidence of the surrounding sentiments, including the parties' purposes and goals'.[3] But it is important to note that the text of the Treaty itself was not integrated into legislation; this would have had dramatic consequences. Instead, to appease increasing Māori protest, a compromise was reached that the intention of the Treaty would be recognised and protected in law. From 1977 to 1987 the Waitangi Tribunal considered many claims and developed a body of reasoning against which to judge the Crown's actions. The early principles the Tribunal established included: the principle of partnership, active protection of Māori by the Crown, and good faith (Hayward 2004). It established these principles through close examination of the intentions and actions of Māori and the Crown when the Treaty was signed, and used those ideas to judge the appropriateness of the subsequent actions of both parties.

In 1987, the courts became intimately involved in the articulation of Treaty principles in the landmark case New Zealand Maori Council v Attorney-General, otherwise known as the 'Lands case'. This was a significant opportunity for the Court of Appeal to consider the principles of the Treaty in relation to the State Owned Enterprise Act 1986. As Cooke J noted: 'This case [was] perhaps as important for the future of our country as any that has come before a New Zealand Court'.[4] The Court held that: 'The Treaty signified a partnership between Pakeha and Māori requiring each to act towards the other reasonably and with the utmost good faith. The relationship between the Treaty partners creates responsibilities analogous to fiduciary duties. The duty of the Crown is not merely passive but extends to active protection of Māori people in their use of their lands and waters to the fullest extent practicable'.[5] Each judge in the Lands case delivered his own judgment, but all were in general agreement that the most important principle for the purposes of this case was the duty of the Treaty partners to act towards each other reasonably and with the utmost good faith.[6]

This case had a tremendous flow-on effect in terms of Waitangi Tribunal reporting. From this point there developed a reasonably consistent body of reasoning which identified (particularly following the Ngai Tahu Reports in 1991) the fundamental principle of exchange. This means that both Māori and the Crown benefited from the Treaty, but those benefits brought obligations to both parties. Other principles to emerge in the 1990s included the right of development, and the need for consultation. The Tribunal has not always upheld these principles in favour of Māori; dissenting opinions in various claims question the extent to which principles can be applied, and the Tribunal has rejected some claims outright when tested against the Treaty principles (Hayward 2004).

While this explains what the Treaty principles are, it does not explain how legislation and policy other than the Treaty of Waitangi Act 1975 came to include references to Treaty principles. It was during the 1980s in particular, when the Labour government was radically reforming the shape of New Zealand's resource management law and institutions, that the State Owned Enterprise Act 1986, the Environment Act 1986, and the Conservation Act 1987 made reference to Treaty principles. This was again a compromise; the government recognised that many Māori grievances concerning the loss of access to natural resources were likely to be upheld by the Tribunal. By including the Treaty principles in important environmental legislation, Māori concerns were likely to be appeased without the government having to commit to the actual terms of the Treaty. The understanding reflects the fact that Māori have a particular stake in environmental management that is different from the interests of other New Zealanders, because of the 1840 Treaty agreement.

The Resource Management Act 1991 (RMA) is perhaps the best example of the controversy surrounding the principles of the Treaty. When the Act was being drafted, Māori expressed concern that the Crown was assuming ownership of resources without the moral authority to do so—that many claims before the Tribunal would test the Crown's right to assume such authority. The Labour government recognised that Māori had a particular interest in the law reform process, but argued that it would not delay the passage of the legislation in order to deal with the complex matter of resource ownership. Therefore, the RMA directs decision-makers to take into account the principles of the Treaty to recognise specific Māori interests. Most often, this has been interpreted as the need to consult with Māori on decisions that affect them.

The debate about this provision is a good example of Kymlicka's argument about minority rights. If you accept that the RMA implicitly privileges non-Māori values and assumptions, then you may also accept that Māori values and needs require explicit recognition in order to protect the right for Māori to hold divergent views. If, on the other hand, you think that the legislation is neutral and can be applied to Māori and non-Māori without disadvantaging Māori, despite Māori protest to the contrary, then you will prefer to opt for 'benign neglect' advocated by the National party.

The latter position is, according to Kymlicka, naïve and incoherent. He would argue that the Resource Management Act privileges non-Māori because it endorses the values and assumptions of the non-Māori community, at the expense of Māori. How can the fundamental human right for Māori to choose to express themselves as Māori be upheld if other legislation, such as the RMA, denies them access to their own cultural, political, and moral identity? Kymlicka might say that if the National party removed the Treaty references, Māori would be less equal under the RMA because they would have lost the fundamental (albeit limited) right to express and protect their own cultural, social, and political beliefs.

It is not only environmental legislation which contains references to Treaty principles; since the 1980s a range of social policy has also come to incorporate references to the principles. The assumption supporting this is, once again, that in order for Māori to express their fundamental human right and freedom to be Māori, laws and policies must allow them the opportunity, and protect their right, to do so. Otherwise, not all cultures have equal access to their basic civil liberties. On a more practical level, specific recognition of the Treaty in social policy is also an attempt to redress the inequality that historical grievances have caused in terms of socio-economic development of Māori generally.

To recap, the National party advocated that a fairer, more equal, society would be created by removing the Treaty references from social policy; Kymlicka would argue that this would make Māori *less* equal and create disadvantage. Moreover, the fact that the majority can revoke Māori rights in law and policy without Māori consent (which Māori cannot do to the majority in return) is further indication of the fact that Māori are *less* than equal before the law, where their rights are not recognised and protected.

'RACE-BASED SEPARATIST POLICIES': GUARANTEED MĀORI REPRESENTATION

In addition to wishing to create 'one law for all', the National party proposed abolishing the guaranteed Māori seats in parliament. This is not a new debate; in fact, the future of the Māori seats in parliament has been under question since they were first created in 1867 (see chapter 8.4). National claimed that the seats are separatist race-based policy that privileges Māori inappropriately, divides New Zealand society and is intolerable in a modern liberal democracy.

The debate about the seats has always been heated, which makes the historical context in which the seats were created particularly surprising. In 1867 four Māori seats, overlaying the general constituencies and voted for by Māori on the Māori roll (not the general roll), were introduced to parliament. The motivation for the seats was pragmatic rather than an assertion of indigenous rights; with the burgeoning numbers of gold-miners in the South Island requiring representation, Māori seats largely in the North Island would ensure a balance of MPs was retained between the North and South Islands. Recently, the number of Māori seats has increased to seven, with the opportunity for more seats to be added as more Māori join the Māori roll.

MPs who passed the legislation in 1867 were obviously sufficiently comfortable with the idea of identifying communities of interest, such as gold miners, to see the logic of extending geographical representation to Māori also. This was not considered inconsistent with the liberal tradition of representation held at that time. So what has changed since 1867? If the liberal tradition could tolerate, indeed support, Māori representation in 1867 (even for pragmatic reasons) why is the issue debated so vehemently now? Kymlicka would argue that the liberal tradition (or at least an element within that tradition) has become less tolerant of group recognition of minority rights, particularly with regard to representation (1995, p. 139–51). As an extension of 'one law for all', specific recognition of minorities is seen to be 'separatist' and raises questions of special treatment for some groups at the expense of others, leading to hostility and racial division.

In presenting an alternative conception of the issue, Kymlicka argues that group representation is consistent with the liberal tradition of identifying 'communities of interest in an effort to make sensible geographical boundaries' (p. 133). Fear that group-differentiated minority rights will cause disunity in society assumes that unity is achieved through undifferentiated citizenship. A group-differentiated society, by extension, cannot be integrated and united. But ironically, the demand by Māori to retain the Māori seats is a fight for *inclusion* in society, not *exclusion*. It is illogical to assume that Māori are seeking this right in order to exclude themselves in a sort of self-inflicted separatism—it is in fact a desire to be included in government that brings this debate to prominence. Therefore, the liberal attitude should be to recognise Māori as a legitimate community of interest in order to promote civic participation and harmony. In other words, the *means* to achieve civic unity requires differentiated recognition, but the *end* is to ensure social cohesion. According to this logic, abolishing the Māori seats is more likely to create disunity than to avoid it.

CONCLUSION

Despite the fact that National did not gain office in 2005, the debate the party's policy raised about the Treaty and Māori rights is an important one that requires careful consideration. Does specifically identifying Māori and the Treaty in legislation and policy unfairly privilege Māori, or would removing these references make Māori *less* equal before the law? Kymlicka's argument provokes deeper consideration of the issues facing policy-makers in the future. He would argue that, beyond the fundamental human rights we all share, it is incoherent to argue that one 'neutral' law will cater equally and indiscriminately with all groups in society. In order for groups to be treated equally before the law, some cultural, political, and social differences must be explicitly articulated in the law to avoid disadvantage to minorities. Moreover, laws and policies that advocate for differentiated citizenship, such as special representation, are not causing disunity, but rather overcoming potential disunity by ensuring that all groups have equal access to participate in society's development.

If Kymlicka is to be believed, then the viability of Māori society may be undermined by policies such as those proposed by the National party in 2005. Māori can easily be outvoted by the majority on the issues of the Māori seats and legislative recognition of Treaty principles, despite the fact that Māori claim these protections are crucial to the survival of the Māori culture. The majority culture in New Zealand does not face this threat; this is a significant inequality which, if not addressed, can create serious injustice for all.

DISCUSSION QUESTIONS

1   Do you agree with Kymlicka that laws and policies are not neutral, and that 'benign neglect' therefore disadvantages some groups, such as Māori?

2   Which other minorities or groups might make a case for specific recognition and protection in policies and laws?

3   What other examples of Treaty policy can you think of that test Kymlicka's ideas about liberal approaches to minority rights?

4   What do you think would have happened to Treaty policy if National had been elected in 2005, and what might the implications have been for Māori and all New Zealanders?

NOTES

1   Don Brash, 'Orewa speech—Nationhood', www.national.org.nz 26 March 2004, (accessed 6 September 2005).

2   'National's 2005 Treaty Policy', www.national.org.nz (accessed 6 September 2005).

3   Waitangi Tribunal, *Report of the Waitangi Tribunal on the Muriwhenua Fishing Claim*, Department of Justice, Wellington, 1988, p. 388.
4   *New Zealand Maori Council v Attorney-General* [1987] 1 NZLR, p. 643.
5   *New Zealand Maori Council*, p. 642.
6   *New Zealand Maori Council*, pp. 664, 673, 703.

REFERENCES

Kymlicka, W. 1995, *Multicultural Citizenship*, Oxford University Press, Oxford.
Hayward, J. & N. Wheen (eds) 2004, *The Waitangi Tribunal*, Bridget Williams Books, Wellington.

FURTHER READING

Durie, M. 1998, *Te Mana, Te Kawanatanga: The Politics of Maori Self-determination*, Oxford University Press, Auckland, pp. 149–74.
Orange, C. 1987, *The Treaty of Waitangi*, Allen & Unwin Port Nicholson Press, Wellington.
Sharp, A. 1997, *Justice and the Maori*, 2nd edn, Oxford University Press, Auckland.
Walker, R. 1990, *Ka Whawhai Tonu Matou: Struggle without End*, Penguin Books, Auckland.
Ward, A. 1999, *An Unsettled History: Treaty Claims in New Zealand Today*, Bridget Williams Books, Wellington.

Māori Policy and Politics

Ann Sullivan

The restructuring of the welfare state in the 1980s included radical public sector reforms to Māori affairs. Government policy changed from assimilation and integration to devolving service delivery to tribal authorities. When a National government was elected in 1990 the emphasis was on contracting service delivery from mainstream organisations to tribal organisations. This was developed into a programme aimed at closing the gaps between Māori and non-Māori when Labour took over the Treasury benches in 1999, but was soon transformed into a social equity framework that targeted policies based on need rather than ethnicity. Following the National party's defeat at the polls in 2002, race-based policies became a major target of opposition politics. When the foreshore and seabed issue became a serious matter of contention between Māori and the government, the race politics of the National party struck a chord with a considerable number of non-Māori and National's poll rating correspondingly improved. The formation of the new Māori party and its electoral success was a direct response and reaction of Māori to both the Foreshore and Seabed Act 2004 and race-based politics. Māori are struggling for equality and Treaty settlements and while Māori investment in education and proactive self-determination of tribal organisations has contributed to the improved well-being of Māori, the socio-economic gaps between Māori and non-Māori have not improved.

DEVOLUTION

In 1984, a government-sponsored Māori economic summit/hui taumata promoted a new policy strategy for the delivery of social services and programmes to Māori. The former policy eras of assimilation and integration had not improved the socio-economic standing of Māori and there was a significant gap between Māori and non-Māori well-being. Māori advice to government was that Māori and their resources were underutilised by government, that if Māori were empowered to define and determine their own needs then more positive outcomes were likely to result from government expenditure on Māori health, education, training schemes, and similar areas of welfare need. The new Labour government, which was led by David Lange, was receptive to finding a new way forward for Māori, and the ensuing policy of devolution, a process by which service delivery was devolved from the centre (government agencies) to the periphery (tribal authorities) signalled a significant change to Māori affairs. For Māori, devolution provided some functional transfer of powers. Iwi (tribal) authorities were able to assert some autonomy on the delivery of programmes and services directly impacting on Māori. Devolution required that tribal organisations have good infrastructure and management systems in place to deliver government programmes, and in this respect enhanced Māori efforts to become more self-managing and self-determining. For the government, devolution fitted well with its neo-liberal objectives, which prioritised a reduction in the role of the state in the lives of the citizens. Succeeding governments have adapted the devolution concept, but fundamentally, initiatives arising out of the 1984 economic summit/hui taumata have influenced ongoing Māori policy direction and policy development.

MAINSTREAMING

When the National party regained power from Labour in 1990, mainstreaming and Treaty settlements were the major elements of its Māori policies. The policy document *Ka Awatea* determined that, while mainstream government departments would be held accountable for the needs of Māori, the contracting of specific services to Māori organisations was an acceptable means of service delivery. Throughout the 1990s successive National governments supported the contracting of health programmes, training initiatives, and similar government services to tribal organisations, and Te Puni Kokiri/Ministry of Māori Development was charged with providing policy advice on reducing disparities between Māori and non-Māori and monitoring mainstream delivery of services to Māori.

Treaty settlements were the second component of the 1990s policy programme. Although it is the function of the Waitangi Tribunal to make recommendations to government on Māori grievances relating to breaches of the Treaty of Waitangi, the 1990–96 National government by-passed much of this process by directly negotiating three major settlements—the Fisheries Settlement 1992 ($170 million), Tainui Settlement 1995 ($170 million), and the Ngai Tahu agreement 1996 ($170 million). The settlements fitted within a fiscal cap of $1 billion for all Treaty

Table 8.4.1: Māori labour market rates

	1986	1992	2003	2004
Employment	134,400	108,900	186,800	
Participation	67%	59.6%	65.7%	
Unemployment	11.3%	25.4%	10.2%*	9.5%*

* In 2003–04 non-Māori unemployment rates were 4 per cent.

Source: (Department of Labour 2005).

settlements, and although Māori protests surrounding the arbitrary financial limit were vociferous, all Treaty settlements to date have fitted within that paradigm. Both mainstreaming and the fiscal cap accorded with the governments' economic reform programme of downsizing government responsibilities and transparency in future fiscal management.

The restorative justice approach to Treaty settlements helped mitigate some of the social consequences of the recession that was a consequence of the radical reforms of the 1980s. Rolling back the state had included the downsizing, restructuring, and corporatisation of many government departments and enterprises, the privatising of state-owned commercial activities and major social policy reforms which included a tightening of eligibility criteria, and a reduction in payment levels of welfare benefits (see Kelsey 1993; Kelsey 1995; Rudd 1997). The severe impact of the recession disproportionately affected Māori as shown in table 8.4.1 because of the large numbers of Māori laid off work in manufacturing and meat processing industries, along with big numbers in state sector employment such as railways, the post office, and forestry. Māori unemployment rates peaked at 25.4 per cent in 1992. This had reduced considerably to 10.2 per cent by 2003 and further declined to 9.5 per cent in 2004, but it is still more than two and half times the unemployment rate of non-Māori.

CLOSING THE GAPS/SOCIAL EQUITY

The 1999–2005 Labour-led coalition governments' policies of 'closing the gaps' and 'social equity' have also built on the self-help model of the 1980s, using Māori organisations not only as service providers, but also as policy advisers. In 1998, Te Puni Korkiri/Ministry of Māori Development released a report *Progress Towards Closing Social and Economic Gaps Between Māori and Non-Māori*. The report highlighted significant socio-economic gaps between Māori and non-Māori and drew attention to the need to more directly target disparities between Māori and non-Māori. The Labour-Alliance government, which was formed in 1999, initially set up a Closing the Gaps cabinet committee that was chaired by the prime minister, thereby signalling the importance of centralising government strategies and policies focused on 'closing the gap'.

The committee was disestablished a short time later amid negative public reaction to policies that were directly targeting Māori (Tamihere 2001); Māori were perceived as receiving preferential treatment because of health policies that specifically targeted Māori in areas of diabetes, smoking, and hepatitis B. Since 2002, the Labour–Progressive government has focused on social equity, a more politically acceptable strategy, given that its emphasis is on needs; reducing inequalities through class-based, low-decile needs rather than ethnicity (or race). Successive post-1999 Labour-led governments have also promoted capacity-building in Māori communities (local solutions to local problems). The focus of this programme has been to enhance Māori self-determining efforts, with some limited support to whanau, hapu, and iwi for skills, business, strategic planning, and development initiatives.

As the New Zealand economy recovered and employment opportunities increased, the relative position of Māori in the post-2002 period has been better than a decade earlier, albeit that the socio-economic gaps between Māori and non-Māori have not been reduced. For example, Te Puni Kokiri has shown that, for more than a decade now, Māori participation in education has improved. Māori are more likely to attend early childhood education than in the past, more likely to stay at school past the compulsory leaving age, and more likely to leave with qualifications. There has also been considerable growth in the number of Māori attending tertiary institutions, and correspondingly more Māori with post-school qualifications. However, these increases must be viewed in the context of increasing participation and achievement among the population as a whole. This means that Māori will need to make significant advances in all educational categories if educational disparities are to be reduced (Te Puni Kokiri 1998a).

The inequalities of life chances between Māori and non-Māori are marked. On virtually all health indicators, such as health outcomes, preventive services, modifiable risk, and treatment services the disparities between Māori and non-Māori are pronounced. When comparing Māori health with Native Americans and their respective majority (non-indigenous) populations, the Māori/non-Māori disparities are even more pronounced (Bramley et al. 2005). According to the director of Otago University's health inequalities study, the only area of health that Māori do not fare worse than non-Māori is melanoma (Walsh 2005).

Statistics New Zealand data (2005) show Māori are still more likely to be employed in lower skilled occupations than non-Māori, and for any given level of qualification, Māori earn on average less than non-Māori. Māori home ownership is only 47 per cent compared with 71 per cent for non-Māori. Māori mobility is greater than non-Māori, because of lower home ownership rates, the youthful age structure of the population, and economic factors. Census data (Te Puni Kokiri 1998b) shows Māori households are more likely to depend on welfare benefits (22 per cent) than non-Māori households (6 per cent), with the sole exception of superannuation. Life expectancy for a Māori male is only sixty-eight years compared to seventy-seven years for a non-Māori male (with a similar gap for females, seventy-two to eighty-one), so most Māori males do not live long enough to collect an old age pension (Bryant 2003). Targeting policies by ethnicity is a practical and effective means of addressing recognisable inequalities.

A POLARISED NATION: THE FORESHORE AND SEABED

Immediately following its worst-ever performance in the 2002 election, the National party determined that it would focus on Māori issues and undermine government policies that specifically targeted Māori inequalities as a means of trying to boost electoral support. In particular, it targeted the place of the Treaty of Waitangi in the social and political framework of New Zealand. Using the rhetoric of 'one rule for all', the former National party leader Bill English (2002) began a series of attacks on Māori. His early 2002–03 speeches[1] on race relations gained little media attention, nor much public support. However, when the new leader, Don Brash (2004), picked up on the 'race' theme and used it in his 'Nationhood' speech at Orewa on 27 January 2004, the National party's ratings in the polls hugely improved. Why? In the interim, the Labour–Progressive government had reacted to the Court of Appeal decision that Māori should be allowed the opportunity to establish in the Māori Land Court the status of Māori customary rights to the foreshore and seabed (2003).

The government determined that Māori would not be allowed to go to the courts for a ruling on the issue by passing new legislation that provided for Crown ownership of the public foreshore and seabed—the Foreshore and Seabed Act 2004. The government's stated objective was to preserve the public foreshore and seabed on behalf of all New Zealanders (Department of the Prime Minister and Cabinet 2003). Māori were seriously aggrieved at not being allowed the opportunity to prove (or otherwise) in court, their claim to Māori customary rights; they had sought legal recourse to test article two of the Treaty of Waitangi rights, which guarantee Māori 'the full and exclusive and undisturbed possession of their lands and Estates Forests Fisheries and other properties'. It followed the decision of several sub-tribes of the Marlborough Sounds, which had been denied marine farming licences by the local council for a number of years, to seek clarification from the courts as to their customary ownership of the seabed.

The foreshore and seabed issue polarised the nation. The dominant public view was that access to beaches is an inalienable right of all New Zealanders and that, if Māori were given customary rights to the foreshore, public access would be denied. The government promoted its foreshore and seabed legislation as protecting public access to the foreshore and surrounding waters with ownership vested in the Crown. There was little public discussion or government dissemination of information regarding the already considerable amount of foreshore in private ownership—about one-third of the New Zealand coastline is in private ownership (Tamihere 2004), and one-third of the land adjoining the foreshore is under the control of territorial local authorities (Ansley 2004), with the remainder in Crown ownership. Ironically, local authorities lease out considerable tracts of the foreshore and seabed to private companies for commercial activities such as ports (e.g. Ports of Auckland), marinas (e.g. Westhaven and Whangaparoa's Gulf Harbour), and marine farming. The public are routinely denied access to these and other parts of the foreshore and seabed of New Zealand. Also not widely known is the fact that some two-thirds of the privately owned coastline is the private property of non-Māori, mostly farmers. Indeed, there is very limited land adjacent to the foreshore that is in collective Māori ownership. But where Māori do have customary rights, public access had not hitherto been an issue. For example, Ngati Whatu have customary title to Okahu Bay, one of the most popular inner Auckland harbour beaches. The public have never been denied access; indeed, exclusion is not tikanga Māori.[2]

Māori were not alone in condemning the government's action. A number of law professors warned of the difficulties associated with the legislation (Brookfield 2005; Evans 2004; McHugh 2004), and the United Nations General Assembly pointedly stated that the legislation clearly discriminated against Māori (United Nations General Assembly 2005).

The first major protest action by Māori was a hikoi (land march). Tens of thousands of Māori participated in the symbolic 'march' from Hapua in the Far North to parliament's buildings.[3] The prime minister refused to meet with the protestors, who she had earlier described as 'haters and wreckers' (Kiriona & Berry 2004). Her attitude was probably indicative of how quickly and how badly race relations in New Zealand had deteriorated. The culmination of the hikoi was the formation of a new political party, the second and most significant protest action by Māori (see chapter 5.5). The creation of the Māori party was a direct response to the government's foreshore and seabed legislation. With only eighteen months to build an electoral movement, field candidates, and fight an election, the success of the Māori party was nothing short of remarkable. At the 2005 election, it won four of the seven Māori electorates, which the Labour party had historically held, aside from a short period in the late 1990s.[4] There could not be a clearer indication of Māori disillusionment with government.

THE RACE CARD

Although the right-wing ACT and more centrist New Zealand First parties had periodically attempted to use the race card to further promote their individualist 'we are all one people' ideals, the 'nationhood' speech by Brash as the new leader of the National party struck a chord with mainstream New Zealand. As Walker has pointed out, it 'tapped into public fatigue with and ignorance of the Treaty of Waitangi' (2004, p. 394). Simmering resentment had been fuelled by a range of perceived benefits enjoyed by Māori, including Treaty settlements, Māori service providers,

Māori television, proportional Māori parliamentary representation, references to Treaty principles, and 'privileged' access to special educational and other benefits through targeted scholarships, quota schemes, and (amazingly) health-care screening programmes. When this was coupled with enormous vocal and visible Māori unity in response to the foreshore and seabed legislation, the portrayal by Brash (2004) of Māori as a privileged people with special rights caused an immediate and significant upsurge in support for National. It also signalled a marked deterioration in race relations. National's use of race politics during 2004 and in the lead-up to the 2005 election gave legitimacy to overt expressions of racism (see Walker 2004, p. 397). It also sparked a policy u-turn on the part of the Labour-led government.

In 2004, a new post of Minister of Race Relations had been created and given to a Pakeha minister, Trevor Mallard. One of Mallard's main tasks was to review all government policies and give an assurance that future policies targeted need, not race (Mallard 2005). Despite denials by the government, the initiative was in direct response to public opposition to welfare need being determined by ethnicity or race. The resulting effort to provide a 'colour blind' social policy agenda had the insidious effect of making Māori less visible. It meant that important historical relationships of subjugation, dispossession, marginalisation, and exclusion could be more easily dismissed.[5] As we have seen, the decision also flew in the face of statistics, which show that race *is* relevant. While the needs or class-based approach does address Māori well-being, with Māori appearing at the bottom of nearly all socio-economic indicators, it fails to make provision for Māori as an identifiable group (Jacobsen et al. 2002). Nor does it provide explanations, as Durie (2005) points out, for ethnic-specific causes, such as genetic disposition.

MĀORI REPRESENTATION

Changes to the electoral system in 1993 resulted in Māori, for the first time in New Zealand's electoral history, gaining parliamentary representation in proportion to the size of the Māori population. The change of the New Zealand electoral system from First-Past-the-Post (FPP) to Mixed-Member-Proportional (MMP) provided for Māori electorates to be determined by the number of Māori who choose to enrol on the Māori electoral roll. Following the passing of the Electoral Act 1993, the Māori electorates immediately increased from four to five (out of sixty-five). At the 1999 election the number of Māori electorates increased by one to a total of six (out of sixty-seven), and at the 2002 and 2005 elections there were seven (out of sixty-nine). Additionally, most political parties have given a favourable party list position to at least one Māori candidate, resulting in at least 15 per cent of the 120-member parliament identifying as Māori.

There has been recurring debate regarding the retention, or otherwise, of the Māori electorates from the time they were introduced in 1867. This debate resurfaced in the post-2002 period, but was broadened to include local government representation.

Basically the arguments used by the National and ACT parties centre on the notion that separate representation privileges Māori. Brash (2004), for example, claimed that separate Māori representation violates the democratic 'one person, one vote' principle. Māori on the other hand argue that separate representation guarantees Māori a voice in parliament. Prior to the introduction of MMP, Māori were always under-represented in parliament. While the Māori electorates guaranteed Māori representation in parliament, that representation remained limited mainly because political parties generally failed to support Māori candidates in the general seats. With the advent of MMP in 1996, Māori quickly gained representation proportional to their share of the population. In the event that the Māori seats are abolished, there are no guarantees that political parties will value the Māori vote sufficiently to guarantee representation equivalent to their share of the population. The Māori seats are an incentive for political parties to include Māori in favourable positions on their party lists.

A pattern of under-representation persists in local government elections that still favour the FPP system. Local government elections have always resulted in less than 5 per cent of elected councillors identifying as Māori (Sullivan 2003). In 2001, local governments were given the option of using a form of proportional representation (Single Transferable Vote, STV), having separate Māori electorates, or staying with the status quo of FPP elections. In the 2004 local government elections only ten of the eighty-six local government authorities opted to use STV. Results show that neither women (Vowles 2005) nor Māori increased their representation on councils (Sullivan 2005).

CONCLUSION

Since the 2002 general election, 'race' has been a major component of party politics in New Zealand. Rather than uniting the nation, the 2004 Orewa Nationhood speech by Don Brash provoked a highly emotive response. That Māori now have a political party in parliament representing Māori issues is a direct result of both the National leader's provocative stance on race and the Labour-led government's response in legislating away the rights of Māori to pursue their claims to the foreshore and seabed through the courts. Solely targeting public policies by socio-economic determinants rather than specific ethnic/race needs will not reduce the socio-economic gap between Māori and non-Māori. The long history of policies designed to assimilate, then integrate Māori into the dominant Pakeha way of life did not improve the social and economic positioning of Māori. Noticeable improvements in Māori development and Māori well-being have only become evident since the 1980s, when (among other factors) service delivery began to include Māori in policy design, formulation, and implementation. Statistics show that, far from being privileged, Māori are not a people with special rights that run counter to the rights of all New Zealand citizens. Separate representation does not give Māori a greater voice in parliament than non-Māori, but it does allow Māori to participate as equal citizens in decision-making forums.

References to the Treaty of Waitangi in legislation have not given Māori any special privileges, but have allowed Māori to seek recourse through the courts when it is alleged that an injustice has occurred. Treaty settlements have enabled some tribes to invest in their local economies and, as Māori-owned trusts, to have growing influence over local and regional economic development. This said, there is considerable potential for greater involvement in local and regional development. Since the 1984 hui taumata/economic summit, Māori self-determination has progressed to a point where there is an emerging Māori economy that is robust, albeit small at only 1.4 per cent of the New Zealand economy (New Zealand Institute of Economic Research 2003). Prior to the shift to a needs-based policy agenda, one positive influence on Māori development was the government's willingness to recognise and support specific programmes and policies that targeted race. Whether this policy reversal has a positive or negative impact on Māori development and well-being, time alone will tell.

DISCUSSION QUESTIONS

1 Who is Māori and why does it matter?
2 Discuss the differences and similarities between individual rights and needs and collective rights and needs.
3 Discuss Treaty of Waitangi implications or obligations on public policies.

NOTES

1 B. English 2002, 'One Standard of Citizenship—One Rule for All', Speech to the New Zealand Institute of Directors at The Wellington Club, Wellington. 19 November; B. English 2003a, 'The Treaty Grows another Leg'; B. English 2003b, 'Unity and Development Are Better than Division and Dependency', Speech delivered at the Channel View Lounge, Takapuna, Auckland, 22 January.
2 See submission by Sir Hugh Kawharu in Waitangi Tribunal. 2004, 'Report on the Crown's Foreshore and Seabed Policy', Waitangi Tribunal, Wellington (Wai1071).
3 The hikoi was modelled on the 1975 Land March led by Whina Cooper, except much of the hikoi procession was by motor vehicle whereas the land march walked all the way to Wellington.
4 See A. Sullivan and J. Vowles 1998, 'Realignment? Maori and the 1996 Election' in Vowles et al. (eds) *Voters' Victory*, Auckland University Press, Auckland.
5 A perceptive analysis of this issue has been written by K. Barber 2005, 'Indigenous Rights or "Racial Privileges": The Rhetoric of "Race" in New Zealand Politics', Paper presented to European Society of Oceanists, 6–8 July 2005, Marseille, France.

REFERENCES

Ansley, B. 2004, 'Stakes in the Sand', *Listener*, 1 May, pp. 16–21.

Barber, K. 2005, 'Indigenous Rights or "Racial Privileges": The Rhetoric of "Race" in New Zealand Politics', Paper delivered at European Society of Oceanists, 6–8 July, Marseille, France.

Bramley, D., P. Hebert, L. Tuzzio & M. Chassin 2005, 'Disparities in Indigenous Health: A Cross-Country Comparison Between New Zealand and the United States', *American Journal of Public Health*, 95/5, pp. 844–50.

Brash, D. 2004, 'Nationhood', An address by the leader of the National party to the Orewa Rotary Club, 27 January.

Brookfield, F. M. 2005, 'Māori Claims and the Special Juridical Nature of the Foreshore and Seabed', *New Zealand Journal of Public and International Law*.

Bryant, J. 2003, 'The Ageing of the New Zealand Population, 1881–2051', New Zealand Treasury, Wellington.

Department of Labour 2005, 'Trends in Māori Labour Market Outcomes 1986–2003', Department of Labour, Wellington.

Department of the Prime Minister and Cabinet 2003, 'Protecting Public Access and Customary Rights', New Zealand Government, Wellington.

Durie, M. 2005, 'Race and Ethnicity in Public Policy: Does it Work?' *Social Policy Journal of New Zealand*, 24/1, pp. 1–11.

English, B. 2002, 'One Standard of Citizenship—One Rule for All', Speech to the New Zealand Institute of Directors at The Wellington Club, Wellington, 19 November.

English, B. 2003a, 'The Treaty Grows another Leg', XXXXXXXX

English, B. 2003b, 'Unity and Development Are Better than Division and Dependency', Speech delivered at the Channel View Lounge, Takapuna, Auckland, 22 January.

Evans, J. 2004, 'Untangling the Foreshore', Unpublished paper, Law School, University of Auckland. publicaddress.net/default,1248.sm#post1248.

Jacobsen, V., N. Mays, R. Crawford, B. Annesley, P. Christoffel, G. Johnston & S. Durbin 2002, *Investing in Well-being: An Analytical Framework*, New Zealand Treasury Working Paper, Wellington.

Kelsey, J. 1993, *Rolling Back the State: Privatisation of Power in Aotearoa/New Zealand*, Bridget Williams Books, Wellington.

Kelsey, J. 1995. *The New Zealand Experiment*, Bridget Williams Books, Wellington.

Kiriona, R. & R. Berry 2004, 'Call for Peaceful Protest', *New Zealand Herald*, 5 May, A2.

Mallard, T. 2005, 'Release of final set of reviews (the reports and results from the government's review of targeted policies and programmes)', Wellington: www.beehive. govt.nz/Print/PrintDocument.aspx?DocumentID=23469

McHugh, P.G. 2004, 'Aboriginal Title in New Zealand: A Retrospect and Prospect', *New Zealand Journal of Public and International Law*, Volume 2.

New Zealand Institute of Economic Research 2003, 'Maori Economic Development. Te Ohanga Whanaketanga Maori', Report prepared for Te Puni Kokiri, Ministry of Maori Development, Wellington.

Ngati Apa v Attorney-General 2003, in Elias CJ, Gault P, Keith, Tipping, Anderson JJ. Auckland: CA173/01.

Rudd, C. 1997, 'The Welfare State', in R. Miller (ed.), *New Zealand Politics in Transition*, Oxford University Press, Auckland.

Statistics New Zealand 2005, *Māori Population: Looking out to 2021*, Statistics New Zealand, Wellington.

Sullivan, A. 2003, 'Māori Representation in Local Government', in J. Hayward (ed.), *Local Government and the Treaty of Waitangi*, Oxford University Press, Melbourne.

Sullivan, A. 2005, 'Racism and Ethnicity: The Invisibility of Indigeneity in Public Policy', Paper delivered at Australasian Political Science Conference, Dunedin, 28–30 September.

Sullivan, A. & J. Vowles 1998, 'Realignment? Māori and the 1996 Election', in J. Vowles, P. Aimer, S. Banducci & J. Karp (eds), *Voters' Victory*, Auckland University Press, Auckland.

Tamihere, J. 2001, 'Inquiry into the auditing and monitoring of "closing the gaps" programmes', Report of the Māori Affairs Select Committee, Wellington.

Tamihere, J. 2004, 'Foreshore and Seabed—Private Ownership', in *Parliamentary Questions and Answers*, New Zealand Parliamentary Debates, Wellington.

Te Puni Kokiri 1998a, 'Progress Towards Closing Social and Economic Gaps Between Māori and non-Māori', Te Puni Kokiri/Ministry of Maori Development, Wellington.

Te Puni Kokiri 1998b, 'Trends in Māori Employment, Income and Expenditure', Te Puni Kokiri/Ministry of Māori Development, Wellington.

United Nations General Assembly 2005, 'Decision 1 (66): New Zealand Foreshore and Seabed Act 2004', United Nations, Geneva.

Vowles, J. 2005, 'Submission to the Justice and Electoral Committee on the Inquiry into the 2004 Local Authority Elections', Justice and Electoral Committee, Wellington.

Waitangi Tribunal 2004, 'Report on the Crown's Foreshore and Seabed Policy', Waitangi Tribunal, Wellington (Wai1071).

Walker, R. 2004, *Ka Whawhai Tonu Matou, Struggle without End*, (revised edn). Penguin Books, Auckland.

Walsh, R. 2005, 'Signs of Hope Grim in Māori Health', *New Zealand Herald*, 11 August.

FURTHER READING

Cheyne, C., M. O'Brien & M. Belgrave 2004, *Social Policy in Aotearoa New Zealand: A Critical Introduction*, 2nd edn, Oxford University Press, Melbourne.

Durie, M. 2005, *Nga Tai Matatu: Tides of Māori Endurance,* Oxford University Press, Melbourne.

Durie, M. 2005, 'Race and Ethnicity in Public Policy: Does it Work?' *Social Policy Journal of New Zealand,* 24, pp. 1–11.

Fitzgerald, E. 2004, 'Development since the 1984 Hui Taumata', in P. Spoonley, C. MacPherson & D. Pearson (eds), *Tangata Tangata: The Changing Ethnic Contours of New Zealand.* Thomson/Dunmore Press, Palmerston North.

Kukutai, T., 2004, 'The Problem of Defining an Ethnic Group for Public Policy: Who is Maori and Why Does It Matter?' *Social Policy Journal of New Zealand,* 23, pp. 86–108.

Health Policy and the Health System

Robin Gauld

The national and international significance of health policy has increased in recent years due to institutions such as the World Health Organization and World Bank issuing reports advocating healthy populations and health service access as integral to economic and social advancement (World Bank 2001; World Health Organization 2000). Similarly, the United Nations' Millennium Development Goals explicitly cite a range of health outcome improvements as crucial to world development (United Nations Development Programme 2003). The emergence of new diseases such as SARS and the H5N1 'bird flu', and expectations of ever-improving service quality, also underscore the importance of robust health policy and systems.

Few public policy areas are as complex as health. Health policy-makers and service providers must deal with:

- issues of life, death, and comfort, and associated questions of justice and equity
- difficulty defining causal links between any one health or other policy intervention (for example, employment, housing, welfare, or education) on improving the health of the nation
- the fact that patients rarely have sufficient information available to them with which to make informed decisions about who should deliver their care and how
- powerful interests, such as the medical profession and pharmaceutical industry
- ever-increasing health care demand, propelled by medical advances, demographic changes, and 'lifestyle' diseases such as obesity, diabetes, and heart disease

- a voting public who deem health care to be one of the most crucial policy issues
- changing ideas about what constitutes an appropriate structure and focus for health care delivery.

Thus, for the student of politics and policy, the health sector provides fascinating case study material. For policy-makers, health presents an expanding array of highly politicised, and potentially expensive and unsolvable, dilemmas.

Recent New Zealand health policy might be described as chaotic and driven by political preference. Through the 1990s, New Zealand had four different public health system structures, making it the 'most restructured' in the developed world (Gauld 2001). The structures include Area Health Boards (1989–91), a competitive market system (1993–96), the Health Funding Authority (1997–01), and District Health Boards (2001–present). Through these restructurings health policy became increasingly politicised, largely as espoused advantages failed to materialise, but also because of political failure to adequately justify the need for restructuring. While District Health Boards now seem relatively secure, the government continues with restructuring, most recently presiding over primary care reforms.

This chapter has four main goals: first, it provides summary information on health and the New Zealand health sector; second, it overviews the changes of the 1990s; third, it outlines the District Health Board system; and finally, it considers key challenges currently facing health policy-makers.

HEALTH AND HEALTH CARE IN NEW ZEALAND: A SUMMARY

In 2002, life expectancy for a New Zealand male was 76.3 years; for females it had reached 81.1. A Māori male could expect to live 7.2 years fewer than a non-Māori; a Māori female, 9.2 years. There were also significant life expectancy differences between socio-economic groups. In 2004, the government spent almost $10 billion on health, or around 20 per cent (and the largest portion) of its entire budget. Of this, 76.8 per cent went to personal health services, 18.2 to disability support, and 1.8 per cent to public health (Ministry of Health 2004a).[1]

In an often uncomfortable mix, government dominates hospital services provision, while private providers dominate general practice and primary care. New Zealand has a high concentration of spending (around 59 per cent) in public hospitals; other advanced OECD countries average 42–46 per cent. New Zealand's general practice part-charges are among the developed world's highest and pose access barriers to many. There remains a lack of integration between the public and private sectors, and general practice and hospital care (see generally Gauld 2001; Ministry of Health 2002a).

HISTORY OF NEW ZEALAND'S HEALTH SYSTEM AND RESTRUCTURINGS

New Zealand's present health system has roots in the Social Security Act 1938, details of which are available elsewhere (Davis 1981; Hay 1989). The system remained largely untouched until initiation by the National government of Area Health Boards (AHBs) in 1983. The 1984–90 Labour government continued with the AHB model, but commissioned a health system review, *Unshackling the Hospitals* (Gibbs, Fraser & Scott 1988), that would later be influential. This suggested 30 per cent efficiency gains were attainable in public hospitals if the government:

- established Regional Health Authorities to purchase health services
- separated health purchasing from services provision
- made public hospitals and private providers compete for public funding.

Considering such options too radical, Labour sided with AHBs. AHBs were semi-elected bodies, funded by central government, to allocate resources within their districts. A key function was to integrate various service providers—primary, secondary, and tertiary[2]—and develop suitable local services. Formation of AHBs was not compulsory, and it was 1989 before all fourteen were established. In 1989, Labour instituted several AHBs changes. General managers were appointed to run hospitals and a series of financial performance and public health goals were created (Clark 1989).

1. The 'Health Reforms'

Despite Treasury advice that AHBs were performing positively (Treasury 1990), and the fact health expenditure was under control (Ministry of Health 2001), reform was pursued by the National government elected in 1990. In 1991, National established a taskforce that drew recommendations from *Unshackling the Hospitals*. New health structures, implemented by 1 July 1993, included:

- four Regional Health Authorities (RHAs) to decide which publicly funded services were required and purchase these from public, private, and non-profit providers
- formation of public hospitals into twenty-three Crown Health Enterprises (CHEs), expected to compete for service contracts offered by RHAs and return a profit to government on its health services investment
- a Public Health Commission to purchase public health services and provide public health advice to the government
- commencement of public consultation over 'core services', which might include either a list of people or services to be publicly funded (Upton 1991).

The 'health reforms', as they came to be known, expected by politicians to produce widespread efficiencies, reduce waiting lists, and improve service quality, achieved few gains. On the upside, and unenvisaged, was the emergence of independent practitioner associations (IPAs), general practitioner networks formed to ensure bargaining power in contract negotiations with RHAs. By the end of the 1990s, IPAs had over 70 per cent of general practitioners affiliated, with many managing pharmaceutical and laboratory services budgets (Malcolm, Wright & Barnett 1999). The RHAs funded Māori-run services (Barrett 1997), which continue to flourish. RHAs created Pharmac to manage the pharmaceutical schedule. Pharmac remains in existence and has controlled pharmaceutical costs (Davis 2004). There were also service management improvements. There were some productivity gains, but these commenced under AHBs (Devlin & O'Dea 1998).

On the downside, the reforms were imposed on a health community opposed to competition. This undermined morale and staff turnover rates throughout the sector soared. Second, health expenditure escalated, despite efficiency improvements, while waiting lists continued to expand.[3] Third, competitive contracting for services required protracted negotiations between RHAs and providers, promoted insularity throughout the sector, and eroded service standards (Stent 1998). Fourth, few competing providers emerged, meaning CHEs predominated. Fifth, politicians failed to allow 'unprofitable' hospitals to close, instead providing extra funding. Sixth, when Public Health Commission advice conflicted with business interests and government housing policy, the agency was disbanded (Bandaranayake 1994; Hutt & Howden-Chapman 1998). Finally, the core services debate achieved little, other than establishing that the public opposed rationing.

2. Reforming the reforms

Following formation of the National-led coalition government in 1996, and health reforms difficulties, further changes were enacted. These included creating a central purchaser, the Health Funding Authority (HFA), to replace RHAs. CHEs were renamed Hospital and Health Services (HHSs) and expected to focus on 'public service', while remaining 'businesslike'. HFA purchasing goals included national consistency and equity in service funding and access, and it moved toward 'benchmarking' contracts to ensure safe funding levels and regional service comparability.

Nonetheless, inequities and confusion encouraged by the 'health reforms' proved difficult to rectify, and many policies inherited by the HFA were implemented through the competitive era. For example, each CHE had developed different scoring systems for prioritising elective surgery patients, meaning it was impossible to compare funding levels or access thresholds in different regions. Thus, a good deal of the HFA's work was attempting to develop national systems (Health Funding Authority 1999). By the end of its reign, the health sector had central direction and a strategy for the way ahead. However, the HFA model brought criticisms of lacking understanding of local populations. Service contracting and tendering, which remained central to HFA operations, were also denounced for perpetuating competition.

THE DISTRICT HEALTH BOARD SYSTEM

Following the 1999 election the new Labour-led government announced that the HFA system would be replaced by twenty-one District Health Boards (DHBs). As noted in Labour's pre-election manifesto, DHBs 'have the primary objectives originally established for area health boards' (Labour party 1999).

DHBs were constructed around HHSs (hence, the rationale for twenty-one DHBs), with a crucial difference: HHSs were hospitals; DHBs have a much broader ambit with responsibility to provide health care for, and improve the health status of, their regional populations. Following this, each DHB must conduct local health care needs assessments and plan and purchase an appropriate range of local services including personal health, public health, disability support, and mental health. DHBs must also focus on reducing inequalities among different populations, on increasing service access particularly at the primary care level, and on prioritising services within government funding. DHBs are funded using a population-based formula.[4] Community consultation is central to all DHB work.

A range of notions underpin the DHB system. Labour argued that public confidence in the health system, recognised as low (Donelan et al. 1999), needed to be restored; that there was a need for a health sector vision; and that there was a lack of community input into decision-making. The government chose to give the Ministry of Health responsibility for leading the health sector and monitoring its performance. The 'vision' is provided by the *New Zealand Health Strategy* (King 2001) which contains key health priority areas, goals and targets to guide DHB planning and performance assessment.

Each DHB has a governing board served by a chief executive and management staff. Each board has seven elected members, with a further four (including the chair) appointed by the Minister of Health. In keeping with government commitment to the Treaty of Waitangi, two members are Māori. DHBs are required to establish formal iwi relationships. For most, this means the development of multiple iwi relationships; there is a similar situation for many iwi whose boundaries cross two or three DHBs. Each DHB has sub-committees for primary care, hospital management, disability support, and finance. DHBs must produce, in consultation with the community, a five-year strategic plan, as well as an annual service funding plan. For economies of scale DHBs have themselves created five inter-district 'shared services' agencies. Similar in some ways to the former RHAs, these provide for their parent DHBs services such as information and contract management, needs assessments, and legal, financial, and human resources.

A key question is whether such transformation was needed. It may be that Labour's changes were a delayed reaction to the 'market' structures preceding the HFA model, and some of the hangovers from this. Labour's desired directions for health services could have been achieved within the existing institutions, lessening the disruption of restructuring. For example, it would have been possible to have added elected representatives to HHS boards, and to have devolved greater numbers of staff, levels of funding, and responsibility for service planning to HFA locality offices to achieve the desired 'closeness' to local populations and providers. The HFA could have been required to consult more widely in its work. HHSs could have shifted their focus beyond the hospital through increased attention to service integration strategies and collaboration with other providers and sectors on initiatives aimed at improving health. As indicated above, some of Labour's policies were already emerging under the HFA, such as development of a population-based funding formula, longer-term strategic planning, and a focus on the determinants of health and health inequalities (Creech 1999).

PRESENT TENSIONS AND FUTURE CHALLENGES

In campaigning for the 2005 general election, no political party proposed health restructuring. With Labour retaining power the DHB system should remain for the foreseeable future. This said, a range of policy challenges exist.

1. DHBs

It is arguable that twenty-one DHBs is too many, creating administrative complexity and repetition of activities between regions that stretches scarce resources. Small DHBs such as West Coast (serving 32,500 people) have the same functions as larger urban ones such as Counties-Manakau (population 400,000), but substantially less capacity to conduct needs assessments, prioritisation exercises, community consultations, and service planning, contracting and coordination. Despite shared services agencies (see above) performing some functions mergers are possible. Ten to fourteen DHBs may be a more appropriate number, similar to the AHBs. Why the government did not initially seek a smaller number of DHBs remains an important question.

Enabling legislation unequivocally states that the Minister of Health is in charge of DHBs and that DHBs are accountable firstly to the government. Yet DHBs are dominated by elected members and required to respond to local needs. Moreover, government policy has implicitly driven expectations that the community will have a say in how and what sorts of services will be provided. However, with restricted funding DHB members are in the difficult position (previously performed by the HFA at arms-length from the community) of delivering the government's message that restrictions and certain policies are required.

The DHB elections, which occurred in conjunction with the 2001 and 2004 local government elections, raise substantial questions over 'democratisation' of health care decisionmaking (Gauld 2005). Voter turnout in 2001 was 50 per cent, dropping to

42 per cent in 2004. Due to large candidate numbers, successful candidates were predominantly elected on a fraction of the vote. Few Māori were elected, meaning most Māori board members are appointed.

2. Too many strategies?

The *New Zealand Health Strategy* (see above) and a host of accompanying strategies,[5] have produced suggestions that the health sector is 'over-strategised'. While the strategies do guide DHB strategic planning, in an austere funding environment, and with increasing demand for elective and acute services, DHBs and providers are limited in the extent to which they can develop practical responses. It remains to be seen whether all the strategic planning will produce health improvements.[6] Compounding this is the fact that many health determinants fall outside of health sector influence (National Health Committee 1998). DHBs are expected over the longer term to work with health influencing sectors and agencies, but most presently lack such capacity.

3. Primary Health Organisations

In keeping with its aims of advancing primary care and shifting care away from hospitals, the government has promoted formation of Primary Health Organisations (PHOs). PHOs extend the IPA model (see above) and are intended to incorporate various primary care providers—general practitioners, nurses, community workers, physiotherapists, etc. PHOs are non-profit organisations that engage the community in planning and service delivery. Patients are required to formally enrol with a PHO, and patient information is used to devise disease prevention strategies.

PHO funding is based on two capitated formulas.[7] First, an 'access' formula providing increased funding for PHOs with over 50 per cent of enrolments being Māori, Pacific, or from deprived areas as measured by the New Zealand Deprivation Index. 'Access' PHOs offer reduced fees for all patients. Second, an 'interim' formula for PHOs in less deprived areas. These PHOs have largely retained existing fees. In addition, there are new subsidies for all patients six to twenty-five and over sixty-five years.[8] By 2007, as further subsidies are implemented, all patient fees and prescription charges should reduce. Extra money is also available for 'care plus' programmes, to provide care for people with chronic illnesses, and 'services to improve access', as well as for health promotion. Research suggests the access and interim funding formulas are not delivering equitably. Around 41 per cent of access PHO patients are not from the targeted 'most deprived' groups, while nearly 20 per cent of interim patients should receive access funding but do not (Hefford, Crampton & Foley 2005).

PHO development was swift, commencing mid-2003 and largely complete by late-2004, and propelled by around $500 million additional per annum for primary care (6–7 per cent of the health budget) from 2002–08. Presently, there are seventy-nine PHOs of various shape and size. Thirteen PHOs (covering around 5 per cent of the population) are affiliated with Health Care Aotearoa, a network of non-profits whose focus on deprived populations and community governance foreshadowed the PHO concept. Thirty-four PHOs (61 per cent of the population) are IPA-associated, in that twelve core IPAs provide infrastructure support. Most large PHOs are IPA-supported. A third group of PHOs (6 per cent of the population) contracts 'management services' from IPAs, generally for a price per enrolled patient. A further set of fifteen PHOs (23 per cent of the population) sits outside the aforementioned. In parallel, fourteen organisations (including the twelve IPAs) provide information technology services for all PHOs. The largest PHOs have 350,000 enrolments; the smallest, from 3,000. Half the PHOs are categorised 'small', with under 20,000 enrolments, serving only 20 per cent of New Zealanders. Small PHOs tend to be located in remote or deprived areas, catering to specific communities.

Many small PHOs struggle to perform all activities expected of them. This is partly due to their infancy, but also restricted capacity. Their limited enrolments mean proportionately small administrative and other services budgets. Staffing has also been a problem. From the late 1980s until recently there was no health workforce planning in New Zealand. Assessments show an undersupply of most health professionals, the solution to which is a considerable policy challenge in its own right (Health Workforce Advisory Committee 2002). The new layer of PHOs has created an unmet demand for skilled staff particularly in administration, public health, and community services. Smaller PHOs also spend disproportionately on management. A 2004 government-commissioned study found management costs were up to 21 per cent, with small PHOs 'struggling to remain viable' (Capital Strategy Limited 2004). The government subsequently increased management funding.

PHOs are involved in developing many new and innovative services that promise to curtail disease and promote health (Ministry of Health 2005). However, while allowing for 'local solutions to local problems', the multiple initiatives coming out of seventy-nine PHOs are perplexing to those seeking best practice. There have been debates about the need for mergers and greater use of IPA and other management services. The government's dilemma is that mergers would affect mainly PHOs serving populations such as Māori, which would counter their autonomy. It could also undermine community embeddedness. Moreover, advocating management services and IPA involvement would countenance a layer of administration currently not formally recognised by government.

Despite such complexity, PHO development could reshape the health sector. PHOs are gradually increasing services available in primary care settings and may naturally inherit various DHB planning and purchasing functions—for instance, by managing patient hospital funding and admissions. In turn, the need for DHBs could diminish. This raises the issue of whether a careful analysis of the PHO policy was conducted prior to implementation. For instance, if DHBs are ultimately unnecessary, restructuring strain could have been minimised if the HFA had been retained and PHOs developed instead of DHBs.

4. Rationing

Prioritisation (or rationing) of services within limited funding remains a central challenge for the DHB system. DHBs have all developed prioritisation methods, as required by statute. Through this process, which corresponds with population needs assessments, DHBs have routinely revealed new service needs. However, acute services, by nature, cannot be rationed, elective services are prioritised using an imperfect points scoring system (Gauld and Derrett 2000), and demand for all services continues to grow. Consequently, DHBs continue to struggle with deficits (or underfunding), while the government continues to expand the health budget at more than double the inflation rate (Ministry of Health 2004b).

5. Public health

Public health challenges are possibly the greatest facing policy-makers and the health system today. A key concern is the growth of costly 'lifestyle' diseases such as diabetes, obesity, heart and respiratory illnesses. The causes of these are largely poor nutrition, poverty, smoking, and obesogenic environments (i.e., increasing fast-food consumption, car usage, and sedentary behaviour). While the government can warn of spiralling rates of lifestyle disease, and the health system can seek to treat increasing incidences, the challenge is to cultivate healthy culture. To do so requires a range of inter-sectoral strategies (Crawford 2002).

Another concern is the disparity of health outcomes between ethnic groups. Data shows that life expectancy for Māori and Pacific people has remained static since 1980, but improved for other New Zealanders. The reasons for the growing differences are complex. Suggestions include the impact on lower socio-economic groups, in which Māori and Pacific Island people are over-represented, of market-oriented public policies introduced through the 1980s that affected access to health services, housing, income and education (Blakely et al. 2005). This adds weight to the need—which many PHOs are designed to deliver—for culturally appropriate health services for disadvantaged groups, particularly Māori and Pacific people. It also underscores the importance of the government's health inequalities reduction and social development policies (Ministry of Health 2002b; Ministry of Social Development 2001), and of cross-sector strategies and service coordination required of DHBs, PHOs, and government social policy agencies per se.

DISCUSSION QUESTIONS

1   Should health care be funded privately by you when you need it, or through the tax system? Why/why not?

2   There is not enough government money to provide for all health care needs, and services need to be rationed. Two ways of doing this are to limit service coverage to those least able to pay, or make a limited range of services available to all. Which option is the more desirable? How else might services be rationed?

3   Which of New Zealand's health care systems do you prefer and why: the competitive market system (1993–96), the central HFA system (1997–2000), or the localised DHB system (2000–present)?

4   How should the government deal with 'lifestyle' diseases? Are these an individual or public responsibility?

NOTES

1   'Personal health' services are provided to individuals, including general practice, hospital services and maternity services. 'Public health' aims to prevent illness and injury and improve community health. Services include health promotion and community development, health protection, and disease surveillance and control.

2   These commonly used definitions describe the 'levels' at which health care is delivered. Primary care includes general practice, public health, optometry, physiotherapy, podiatry, etc. Secondary care includes standard hospital services: general medicine, general surgery, paediatrics, and obstetrics. Tertiary care includes advanced hospital specialties and some rehabilitative care.

3   From 1980–89, government expenditure on health increased 23 per cent. In 1989, total GDP health spending was 6.6 per cent. From 1990–99, public spending increased by 36 per cent. By 1999, health accounted for 8.1 per cent of GDP. Post-1996, there was considerable pressure to increase health expenditure in recognition that between 1988/89 and 1992/93 'real per capita funding fell by 16 per cent' (Ministry of Health, 1996). In 1992, 64,000 people were awaiting surgery. By 1995, there were 85,574 on waiting lists. Numbers peaked in 1998/99 at around 95,000.

4   Used from 2002–03, this calculates district funding based on demographics, disease incidence, ethnic composition, and health service utilisation rates. The formula has been controversial as some regions, particularly those with declining population, have lost funding to those whose populations are growing.

5   Individual strategies have been issued for primary care, Māori health, Pacific health, mental health, child health, disability support, older people, quality improvement and public health.

6   DHB plans are available on individual DHB websites, accessible via the Ministry of Health website (www.moh.govt.nz).

7   Since 1938, general practice has been subsidised by government on a per-patient basis.
    No matter how many times an eligible patient sees a doctor, a subsidy is paid; patients
    also pay a part-charge to the doctor at point-of-service. Capitation sees doctors being
    paid a per annum amount per patient.
8   Those up to six years were already heavily subsidised.

REFERENCES

Bandaranayake, D. 1994, 'Public Health and the Reforms: The New Zealand Experience',
    Health Policy, vol. 29, no. 1–2, pp. 127–41.
Barrett, M. 1997, 'Maori Health Purchasing: Some Current Issues', *Social Policy Journal of
    New Zealand*, vol. 9, pp. 124–30.
Blakely, T., M. Tobias, B. Robson, S. Ajwani, M. Bonne & A. Woodward 2005, 'Widening
    Ethnic Mortality Disparities in New Zealand 1981–99', *Social Science & Medicine*,
    vol. 61, no. 10, pp. 2233–51.
Capital Strategy Limited 2004, *Review of Primary Health Organisation Management Services.
    Report to the Ministry of Health. 11 August*, Capital Strategy Limited, Auckland.
Clark, H. 1989, *A New Relationship: Introducing the New Interface Between the Government
    and the Public Health Sector*, Department of Health, Wellington.
Crawford, D. 2002, 'Population Strategies to Prevent Obesity', *British Medical Journal*,
    vol. 325, pp. 728–9.
Creech, W. 1999, *The Government's Medium-term Strategy for Health and Disability Support
    Services 1999*, Ministry of Health, Wellington.
Davis, P. 1981, *Health and Health Care in New Zealand*, Longman Paul, Auckland.
—2004, 'Tough But Fair? The Active Management of the New Zealand Drug Benefits
    Scheme by an Independent Crown Agency', *Australian Health Review*, vol. 28, no. 2,
    pp. 171–81.
Devlin, N. & D. O'Dea 1998, 'The Hospital Industry', in M. Pickford & A. Bollard (eds), *The
    Structure and Dynamics of New Zealand Industries*, Dunmore Press, Palmerston North.
Donelan, K., R. Blendon, C. Schoen, K. Davis & K. Binns 1999, 'The Cost of Health System
    Change: Public Discontent in Five Nations', *Health Affairs*, vol. 18, no. 3, pp. 206–16.
Gauld, R. 2001, *Revolving Doors: New Zealand's Health Reforms*, Institute of Policy Studies
    and Health Services Research Centre, Wellington.
—2005, 'Delivering Democracy? An Analysis of New Zealand's District Health Board
    Elections, 2001 and 2004', *Australian Health Review*, vol. 29, no. 3, pp. 245–352.
Gauld, R. & S. Derrett 2000, 'Solving the Surgical Waiting List Problem? New Zealand's
    "Booking System" ', *International Journal of Health Planning and Management*, vol.
    15, no. 4, pp. 259–72.
Gibbs, A., D. Fraser & J. Scott 1988, *Unshackling the Hospitals: Report of the Hospital and
    Related Services Taskforce*, Hospital and Related Services Taskforce, Wellington.
Hay, I. 1989, *The Caring Commodity: The Provision of Health Care in New Zealand*, Oxford
    University Press, Auckland.
Health Funding Authority 1999, *Briefing Papers for the Incoming Minister of Health*, Health
    Funding Authority, Wellington.
Health Workforce Advisory Committee 2002, *The New Zealand Health Workforce: A
    Stocktake of Issues and Capacity*, Health Workforce Advisory Committee, Wellington.

Hefford, M., P. Crampton & J. Foley 2005, 'Reducing Health Disparities Through Primary Care Reform: The New Zealand Experiment', *Health Policy*, vol. 72, no. 1, pp. 9–23.

Hutt, M. & P. Howden-Chapman 1998, *Old Wine in New Bottles: The Public Health Commission and the Making of New Zealand Alcohol Policy*, Institute of Policy Studies, Wellington.

King, A. 2001, *The New Zealand Health Strategy.*, Minister of Health, Wellington.

Labour Party 1999, *Labour on Health. Policy—September 1999*, New Zealand Labour Party, Wellington.

Malcolm, L., L. Wright & P. Barnett 1999, *The Development of Primary Care Organisations in New Zealand: A Review Undertaken for Treasury and the Ministry of Health*, Ministry of Health, Wellington.

Ministry of Health 2001, *Health Expenditure Trends in New Zealand 1980–2000*, Ministry of Health, Wellington.

—2002a, *Doing Better for New Zealanders: Better Health, Better Participation, Reduced Inequalities: Advice to the Incoming Minister of Health*, Ministry of Health, Wellington.

—2002b, *Reducing Inequalities in Health*, Ministry of Health, Wellington.

—2004a, *The Health and Independence Report 2004*, Ministry of Health, Wellington.

—2004b, *Health Expenditure Trends in New Zealand 1990–2002*, Ministry of Health, Wellington.

—2005, *A Difference in Communities: What's Happening in Primary Health Organisations*, Ministry of Health, Wellington.

Ministry of Social Development 2001, *The Social Development Approach*, Ministry of Social Development, Wellington.

National Health Committee 1998, *The Social, Economic and Cultural Determinants of Health in New Zealand*, National Health Committee, Wellington.

Stent, R. 1998, *Canterbury Health Limited: A Report by the Health and Disability Commissioner April*, Health and Disability Commissioner, Wellington.

Treasury 1990, *Briefing to the Incoming Government*, Government Printer, Wellington.

United Nations Development Programme 2003, *Human Development Report 2003: Millennium Development Goals: A Compact Among Nations to End Human Poverty*, Oxford University Press, New York.

Upton, S. 1991, *Your Health and the Public Health: A Statement of Government Health Policy*, Government Print, Wellington.

World Bank 2001, *World Development Report 2000/2001: Attacking Poverty*, World Bank and Oxford University Press, Washington, DC.

World Health Organization 2000, *The World Health Report 2000: Health Systems: Improving Performance*, World Health Organization, Geneva.

FURTHER READING

Dew, K. & P. Davis (eds) 2005, *Health and Society in Aotearoa New Zealand*, Oxford University Press, Melbourne.

Gauld, R. 2001, *Revolving Doors: New Zealand's Health Reforms*, Institute of Policy Studies and Health Services Research Centre, Wellington.

Gauld, R. (ed.) 2003, *Continuity amid Chaos: Health Care Management and Delivery in New Zealand*, University of Otago Press, Dunedin.

Ministry of Health 2004, *The Health and Independence Report 2004*, Ministry of Health, Wellington.

Environmental Policy

Ton Bührs

The environment only became a subject of public policy in the 1960s. Although environmental problems have existed for as long as humanity, it was only from that time that governments started to 'see the environment as a policy framework within which many specific problems can best be solved' (Caldwell 1963, p. 37). Before then, environmental problems were mostly seen and dealt with as separate and unrelated issues. Increasingly, awareness grew that such problems were all part of how humans interacted with their surroundings, and that how they shaped their environment also impacted on them.

Environmental policy, in theory, constitutes an effort by governments to deal with environmental problems in an encompassing and integrated way. This is easier said than done, however, and even some three-and-a-half decades after many governments started to appoint ministers of or for the environment, and to create government agencies responsible for developing and implementing environmental policy, dealing with environmental problems comprehensively and effectively remains a formidable challenge, for many reasons. New Zealand, despite, or perhaps because of, its 'clean and green' image, is no exception in that respect.

This chapter will, first, provide a sketch of the environmental situation in New Zealand. How 'clean and green' is the environment? Is the environment getting better or worse? This provides a background against which, in the second section, the environmental policy efforts of New Zealand governments are discussed and evaluated. Third, the present institutional framework, and how it affects New Zealand's capacity to deal with environmental problems comprehensively and effectively, is assessed. Finally, the prospects for environmental policy are reflected upon in the light of the 'politics of environmental policy'.

'WHO IS THE CLEANEST AND GREENEST OF THEM ALL?'

New Zealand may win many a contest as the most favoured holiday destination, but it is strongly at risk of losing its image as a 'clean and green' country. Domestically, the proportion of New Zealanders who believe that their country is 'clean and green' dropped from about two-thirds in 2002 to just over 50 per cent in 2004, and a growing number express doubts or concern (Hughey et al. 2004, p. 14). There are good grounds for this growing scepticism, or perhaps realism, about New Zealand's image, and unless New Zealanders, and particularly governments and the business sector, are prepared to give up their exercise in collective self-deception, it is just a matter of time before New Zealand will lose its high place in the environmental beauty stakes.

That it is actually not so easy to determine the nature, scale, and seriousness of New Zealand's environmental problems is itself indicative of the collective denial syndrome. New Zealand's first State of the Environment report, published in 1997, brings to light the many gaps that exist in our knowledge and information of environmental matters. This same point was made one year earlier in a review of New Zealand's environmental performance conducted by the OECD. The situation is only slightly better now, but still New Zealanders are not being well-served with information about the state of their environment, and far less so, for example, than about the state of their economy. In fact, people who want to find out about trends in New Zealand's environmental conditions have a hard task doing so. Since the publication of the first State of the Environment report, no other comprehensive publication or data base has been put together, and made available, about the state of the New Zealand environment.

What can be gleaned from a variety of sources and reports does not create a pretty picture. Perhaps most concerning is the state of New Zealand's waterways, which are under pressure from a growing demand for water for irrigation, especially in the South Island, and pollution, making a staggering 95 per cent of lowland streams and rivers unfit for swimming, based on health department guidelines (Larned et al. 2004; Collins 2004). Several major lakes, including Lake Taupo, Lake Rotorua, and Lake Ellesmere, are already in a precarious ecological condition. An apparently growing barrage of introduced species adds to the threats to indigenous plants, animals, and ecosystems, in the water as well as on the land. Some of the more recent imports, such as the painted apple moth, the varroa mite, and the clubbed tunicate or sea squirt, have caused significant concern because of their (potential) economic costs (and, in the case of the first, possible risks to human health associated with control efforts). The recent discovery of an introduced alga, *Didymosphenia geminata* (more graphically labelled 'rock snot') poses an additional threat to riverine ecosystems. Although some species appear to have been saved from the brink by extra protection measures in some areas, little is known about the overall trend in the state of health of New Zealand's biodiversity and ecosystems. In its 2004 Annual Report, the Department of Conservation noted that 'Only about 6,000 of the more than 90,000 known indigenous species have been investigated and categorised thus far and of these, approximately 2,400 are listed as threatened'. Of the 2,400 threatened species, around 25 per cent are acutely threatened (Department of Conservation 2004, p. 29).

As for the extent to which physical environmental conditions affect the health and well-being of humans, New Zealand has traditionally been regarded as well-off and lucky compared with many other countries. With a relatively small population and low population density, few heavy industries and large industrial zones, spacious urban areas, and lots of outdoor recreational opportunities in most people's backyards (figuratively and often literally speaking), it has been, and still is, an attractive destination for immigrants. However, New Zealand's comparative advantage in terms of 'quality of life' derived from these features is also eroding, and in some respects becoming very relative indeed. In many urban areas, air pollution is damaging the health of citizens. In Auckland, concentrations of carbon monoxide and nitrogen dioxide are found to be higher than in European cities (Auckland Regional Council undated). It has been estimated that in New Zealand over 900 people above the age of thirty die from air pollution each year. Of these, some 400 die from emissions from vehicles, and a further 400 from road accidents (Fisher et al. 2002, pp. i, 43). As noted above, many water bodies are unsafe for swimming, and the quality of some 70 per cent of the drinking water supplies (mainly in smaller communities) is unknown (New Zealand Ministry for the Environment 1997, p. 7.70). As for pollution on land, estimates made in 1992 put the number of potentially contaminated sites at 7,800, 1,550 (22 per cent) of which were thought to pose a high risk of harming human health or the environment (New Zealand Ministry for the Environment 1992), although a later survey indicated that the actual number is higher (Organisation for Economic Co-operation and Development 1996, p. 81). Ongoing urban expansion and growth in traffic in most urban centres, but especially in the Auckland region, are adversely affecting the quality of life of many people, following similar trends in other countries. Although there are no slums as in many poor countries, housing conditions in some areas are poor, and contribute to health problems, due to overcrowding, inadequate insulation and heating, and poverty. The sharp rise of house prices in recent years further aggravates these problems by putting house ownership beyond the reach of many young people.

Although the list of environmental issues could be expanded, the discussion above suffices to illustrate the paucity of claims to New Zealand being 'clean and green'. Although much of New Zealand looks green and beautiful, the quality of its environment (even in the national parks) has been severely eroded, increasingly so since European settlement. Largely because of its relatively small population and the scenic splendour of much of the country, it has been possible for a long time to overlook or even deny the existence of environmental problems. The clean and green syndrome has also affected New Zealand's environmental policy performance, as we will see next.

ENVIRONMENTAL POLICY PERFORMANCE: HOW DOES NEW ZEALAND STACK UP?

Environmental policy can be defined as what governments do (or deliberately don't do) to address and/or prevent environmental problems. It comprises policies directed at protecting nature or ecosystems, policies aimed at protecting resources (to enhance or ensure their long-term availability), and policies that affect human well-being by means of changing the physical and natural environment (the quality of the human habitat). Environmental issues often fall into all three categories, demonstrating the interconnected nature of the environment itself. Resource use (a human necessity) will often impinge on ecosystems, and the way humans modify or shape their (urban and rural) environment will impact on their own well-being as well as on that of other species, and on the quality and quantity of resources available for the future. To effectively address environmental problems, or even better, to prevent them, requires an encompassing, integrated, and anticipatory approach, directed foremost at causes rather than effects ('end-of-pipe' solutions).

To do that in practice remains a formidable challenge, and there are no countries that can be said to have been fully successful. However, since the late 1980s, the development of more comprehensive and integrated environmental policies has been the subject of increased attention on the part of environmental theorists, practitioners, and governments, both at the national and international levels. Following the call in 1987 upon governments by the World Commission on Environment and Development (better know as the Brundtland Commission) to adopt sustainability as a leading principle or goal, and a growing recognition by environmental analysts and administrators that the fragmented and reactive approach to environmental problems was not delivering the desired outcomes, many governments started to adopt sustainable development strategies or some other form of 'green planning' (Jänicke & Jörgens 1998). Some countries, in particular the Netherlands, have been leaders in this field, setting specific targets and timeframes for most environmental problems, sharing responsibility for meeting those with target groups in proportion to their contribution to the problems, and taking implementation seriously (De Jongh & Captain 1999).

When taken seriously, green planning is based on and accompanied by the 'greening' of policies in areas that are responsible for many of the sources of environmental problems, such as the industrial, energy, transport, and agricultural sectors. The integration of environmental concerns into all sectors that (potentially) impact on the environment has come to be recognised as imperative if environmental problems are to be prevented rather than mitigated. The European Union has made environmental integration a legal obligation for all member countries. These moves are inspired and underpinned at the theoretical and scientific level by ideas that production and consumption, and transport and energy systems, need and can be modernised based on ecological or natural principles, as reflected in the notions of ecological modernisation and natural capitalism. Some countries, notably Germany, Sweden, the Netherlands, and Japan have taken the lead in this direction.

New Zealand has been a leader neither in green planning nor in environmental integration. In 1996, under National, the rudimentary basis for a first comprehensive and strategic environmental policy was laid with the adoption of *Environment 2010 Strategy*. The strategy hardly deserved that label, however, as it was more in the nature of an inventory of environmental problems facing New Zealand than an action plan based on an analysis of driving forces; it put forward very few specific objectives, targets, and strategic priorities, and was not supported institutionally in the form of the creation of a dedicated agency for its implementation and/or a legal basis (Bührs & Bartlett 1997).

When Labour came to power in 1999, the *Strategy* was quietly set aside. Labour's performance on this front can hardly be called any better, however. Strategic environmental policy development simply did not connect with the philosophy of Labour's environment minister, who was more interested in making things happen 'on the ground'. Consequently, and perhaps also because the minister's views were quite complementary to the approach advocated by the new chief executive of the Ministry for the Environment, green planning simply dropped off the political agenda. Only in 2001, with the World Summit on Sustainable Development looming, did the government announce that it was going to develop a sustainable development strategy. Given the short timeframe, however, the strategy was not completed on time for the Summit, leaving New Zealand one of the few countries without either a sustainable development strategy or some other form of green planning.

In 2003, a new environmental policy statement, *Sustainable Development for New Zealand. Programme of Action* (referred to hereafter as the *Programme*), focused on just four issues: water quality and allocation; energy; sustainable cities; and youth development. Although the *Programme* mentions the need for an integrated, holistic, and 'whole-of-government' approach, there is little evidence of effective translation of this in the form of environmental integration across all policy areas. Arguably environmental integration is most evident, be it still at a modest level, in energy policy, where specific objectives and targets for improving energy efficiency and conservation and increasing renewable energy supply have been adopted. However, it is much less evident in most other policy areas, such as transport, agriculture and, most importantly, economic policy. Although policies and strategies formulated in these areas may refer to 'sustainability' as a principle, this still has to be translated into concrete objectives and targets that imply *environmentally* sustainable resource use, and into effective actions that produce outcomes in that direction. The importance of economic growth and development as a dominant value and objective is reflected in almost all policy areas, including social and environmental policies. They reflect, and at times express, confidence that economic growth can be accompanied by a *reduction* of resource use and adverse environmental impact to levels that are environmentally sustainable ('absolute decoupling'). However, as yet, there is no evidence of this happening in New Zealand.

With economic growth remaining the dominant and overriding concern, and green planning and integration still being in a stage of infancy, environmental policy development has remained largely reactive. Environmental standards have not been adopted until recently, or are still in the process of being developed. Energy efficiency and conservation, and the promotion of renewable energy, have only recently been given stronger support (and still only modestly so) because of growing concerns about future energy supply and security. Growing transport problems and rising social and environmental pressures associated with ongoing urban development, especially in the Auckland region, have only just started to provoke policy responses that incorporate environmental considerations. But in most cases environmental policies are directed more at mitigating the effects of development rather than controlling the forces behind it.

GETTING THE INSTITUTIONS RIGHT ... OR NOT?

The reforms of the public service sector introduced by the Labour government in the 1980s aimed at creating an institutional framework that would enable or support the 'right' policies. For instance, policy and regulatory functions were, in most cases, allocated to separate agencies to avoid agency 'capture' and enhance transparency and accountability. Productive and commercial activities were split off from government departments and assigned to State Owned Enterprises (SOEs) that were expected to operate as corporations, and/or privatised, to get the government out of business and to enhance economic effectiveness and efficiency. Most responsibilities for day-to-day environmental management were devolved to regional and local government based on the assumption that this was a more appropriate level for making decisions on environmental matters. In short, creating the 'right' institutions would lay the basis for the 'right' policies to be developed.

In 1986, the Ministry for the Environment was established as the central government's main environmental policy agency. The ministry's role was mainly to develop and advise on matters of policy, leaving implementation, regulation, and enforcement mostly to local government. This foreshadowed the adoption of local government reform in 1989. It rationalised local government and created regional councils, with mostly environmental responsibilities. In 1991, these arrangements were corroborated by introduction of the Resource Management Act (RMA), which also amalgamated a raft of environmental legislation into one statute, thus providing for an unprecedented level of integration in environmental decision-making in New Zealand. In line with dominant thinking at the time, the Act did not prescribe environmental objectives, targets, or standards (apart from the general goal of the sustainable management of resources), but enabled regional and local government to adopt these in their own policy statements and plans. Conflicts about environmental decisions were to be resolved by the Environment Court, and only in exceptional cases to be 'called in' by the Minister for the Environment.

Although these reforms and arrangements have caused central government to take a back seat in day-to-day environmental management decisions, especially with respect to development proposals, they did not automatically bring forth 'better' environmental decisions, or even create the basis for more effective environmental protection. Many of the assumptions on which the reforms were based have proved to be problematic or unrealistic. First, they assume that regional and local governments have sufficient knowledge and information about existing environmental conditions to decide on whether the effects of proposals are environmentally sustainable. As noted above, this is still a problem today, given the considerable gaps in New Zealand's environmental information basis. Second, they assume that regional and local councils have the power, administrative, and resource capacity to deal effectively with the broad range of environmental issues in their area, an assumption that has proved to be unrealistic. This is especially so in the case of many smaller councils, but even with better resourced councils, as demonstrated in the Auckland region and, in Canterbury—a prime example being the issue of water management. In large part, the inadequacy of regional and local government can be attributed to the fact that they have no control over the driving forces and decisions behind development, such as those relating to the rising demand for energy and transport, population movements, and economic development. Third, it assumes that all councils have the political will to take environmental issues seriously. As 'environmental politics' occurs as much at the local as the national level, and as the playing field on which decisions are made is far from level, this assumption has also shown to be unrealistic.

What all these shortcomings point to is the need for strengthening environmental capacity at all levels of government. At the central government level there is a need for an agency (ideally at arm's length from line government agencies) that has the capacity to collect and build environmental information and to take responsibility for (annual and 'real time') environmental reporting. Given the complexity, costs, and expertise associated with developing environmental standards, there is a case to be made for the establishment of a central Environmental Protection Agency with the power to set and enforce standards. This would also enable the development of a more integrated approach to pollution control directed at controlling *sources* rather than at mitigating effects. Perhaps most important, there is a need for creating a central agency (such as a Sustainable Development Council) that builds and strengthens the capacity for green planning. To ensure the continuity of green planning, such a Council would need to be given legal backing and have broad community representation (Bührs 2002).

At the regional and local levels, there is also a need to strengthen the environmental capacity of councils, with financial assistance and guidance from central government.

There is a need to strengthen the capacity of councils for anticipatory planning rather than simply mitigating the effects of environmental pressure. This implies integrated urban design, zoning, building, and transport policies that give primacy to environmental and social concerns, a requirement which is incompatible with the *ad hoc*, incremental approach to development that has become common practice under the RMA. Regional councils, given the scale of many environmental problems, may be a better source of local green planning than city or district councils. But as noted above, this also assumes the existence of national policies that address the sources of environmental pressure. Although, in theory, the RMA provides for a hierarchy of planning efforts, in practice, it has produced or even encouraged planning that is vague and weak, lacking teeth, at the regional and local level, and devoid of planning at the national level. Reinstating a proper institutional framework that moves from a preoccupation with *effects* towards a concern with *design* will require more fundamental amendments to the RMA than those that have been adopted thus far.

While New Zealand has two significant environmental advocates in the form of the Department of Conservation and the Parliamentary Commissioner for the Environment, their influence on environmental policy, and especially environmental pressures, is quite limited. By the nature of its mandate, the Department of Conservation focuses primarily on the management of protected natural areas, although it does play an advocacy role for conservation in non-protected areas. The size of the challenges that it faces almost guarantees that it will always be underfunded and understaffed, and that it will be preoccupied with heading off more immediate and growing pressures associated with proposals for development within the conservation estate (for instance, for hydro power generation, mining), and rising numbers of tourists and demands for recreational facilities. The Parliamentary Commissioner for the Environment, although venturing boldly into critiques of energy and other policies, which is, strictly speaking, beyond its brief, does not appear to have been very effective in having his advice translated into policy changes, or in having brought about changes at the institutional or systemic level like the ones suggested above.

Apart from the 'clean and green' syndrome, New Zealand also suffers from 'institutional superiority' syndrome. Few people in New Zealand, other than those with a pro-development interest, argue in favour of a fundamental review of the RMA, or indeed for institutional reforms designed to better protect the environment. To some extent, this could be attributed to the phenomenon of 'reform fatigue'. More worrying, however, is the widely held idea that there is nothing fundamentally wrong with New Zealand's existing (economic and environmental) institutional framework, and that nothing more than tinkering might be needed to improve environmental performance. Whether New Zealand will continue to bask in this sense of achievement depends on the politics of the environment.

THE CONTINUING POLITICS OF 'CLEAN AND GREEN'

The politics of clean and green refers to the use of New Zealand's image of a 'clean and green' country to deny or downplay the existence of serious environmental problems and threats, or to support calls for stronger environmental policies. It is also used to project the idea that New Zealand is a 'world leader' in environmental management and policy, or at least should be. Both aspects of the clean and green image are often considered to be important for economic reasons: it provides a green edge to New Zealand's exports and makes it attractive as a destination for tourists and investments. In a report commissioned by the Ministry for the Environment, the monetary value of New Zealand's clean and green image, based on a range of exports alone, was estimated to be worth at least hundreds of millions, if not billions of dollars (New Zealand Ministry for the Environment 2001).

How much weight is given to environmental matters in government decision-making depends to a large extent on the effectiveness of environmental advocates both inside and outside of government. Unfortunately, successive Ministers for the Environment have had a relatively low ranking in the cabinet hierarchy, which has had a detrimental effect on their ability to advocate for their portfolio. In the 2005–08 Labour–Progressive government, for example, the Minister for the Environment, David Benson-Pope, ranked fourteenth in cabinet, and the associate minister, Nanaia Mahuta, nineteenth. To some extent these rankings reflect the importance assigned to the environment portfolio by the prime minister and other senior members of the government. The Conservation portfolio was slightly better off, with Chris Carter being ranked twelfth.

While Labour has generally expressed a stronger commitment to the environment than National, the Green party has been the strongest environmental advocate in parliament. The exclusion of the Greens from the government limits their influence on decision-making, apart from some concessions won in exchange for their support on confidence and supply. The influence of the Greens is also constrained by the government's reliance on two parties, New Zealand First and United Future. Both oppose a carbon tax and United Future wants New Zealand to pull out of the Kyoto agreement. Overall, the political support base of the Clark government does not bode well for improving New Zealand's environmental policy, capacity, and performance over the next few years.

That does not mean that the need and demand for strengthening environmental performance will decrease. As environmental pressures and problems continue to mount, in New Zealand and internationally, the demand for more effective action at all levels is likely to intensify. Growing concerns about the mismatch between New Zealand's clean and green image and environmental reality may lead to stronger calls for more effective environmental policies. International environmental politics has become an important driving force of its own, increasingly influencing New Zealand's environmental policies, especially on climate change. Unfortunately, though, it seems that New Zealand's reactive and fragmented approach to environmental policy development is likely to continue for some time yet.

DISCUSSION QUESTIONS

1 Is the 'clean and green' image a burden or an asset for environmental advocates?
2 If environmental problems are getting worse, as the author suggests, will this necessarily lead to stronger demands for more effective environmental policy?
3 Why have some countries become leaders in green planning and others, including New Zealand, not?
4 To what extent, and how, is the rapidly growing demand for oil in the world, and rising energy prices, likely to affect environmental policy in New Zealand?

REFERENCES

Auckland Regional Council Undated, 'Health Effects of Motor Vehicle Air Pollution', Auckland Regional Council, www.arc.govt.nz/arc/index.cfm?CE7B88F3-BCD4–1A24–97EF-5F814BD6EFE5.

Bührs, T. 2002, 'New Zealand's Capacity for Green Planning: A Political–Institutional Assessment and Analysis', *Political Science*, 54/1, pp. 27–46.

Bührs, T. & R.V. Bartlett 1997, 'Strategic Thinking and the Environment: Planning the Future in New Zealand?' *Environmental Politics*, 6/2, pp. 72–100.

Caldwell, L.K. 1963, 'Environment: A New Focus for Public Policy', *Public Administration Review*, vol. 23, pp. 132–9.

Collins, S. 2004, 'Water Fails Clean, Green Test', *New Zealand Herald*, www.nzherald.co.nz/category/story.cfm?c_id=39&objectid=3576307.

De Jongh, P. & S. Captain 1999, *Our Common Journey: A Pioneering Approach to Cooperative Environmental Management*, Zed Books.

Department of Conservation 2004, *Annual Report for the Year Ended 30 June 2004*, Department of Conservation, Wellington.

Fisher, G.W., K.A. Rolfe, P.T. Kjellstrom, P.A. Woodward, D.S. Hales, P.A. Sturman, D.S. Kingham, J. Petersen, R. Shrestha & D. King 2002, *Health Effects Due to Motor Vehicle Air Pollution in New Zealand*, Ministry of Transport, Wellington.

Hughey, K.F.D., G.N. Kerr & R. Cullen 2004, *Public Perceptions of New Zealand's Environment: 2004*, EOS Ecology, Christchurch.

Jänicke, M. & H. Jörgens 1998, 'National Environmental Policy Planning: Preliminary Lessons from Cross-National Comparisons', *Environmental Politics*, 7/2, pp. 27–54.

Larned, S.T., M.R. Scarsbrook, T.H. Snelder, N.J. Norton & B.J.F. Biggs 2004, 'Water Quality in Low-Elevation Streams and Rivers of New Zealand: Recent State and Trends in Contrasting Land-Cover Classes', *New Zealand Journal of Marine and Freshwater Research abstracts*, vol. 38, pp. 347–66.

New Zealand Government 2003, *Sustainable Development for New Zealand: Programme of Action*, Department of Prime Minister and Cabinet, Wellington.

New Zealand Ministry for the Environment 1992, *Potentially Contaminated Sites in New Zealand: A Broad Scale Assessment*, Government Printer, Wellington.

New Zealand Ministry for the Environment 1997, *The State of New Zealand's Environment*, Ministry for the Environment, Wellington.

New Zealand Ministry for the Environment 2001, *Valuing New Zealand's Clean Green Image*, Ministry for the Environment, Wellington.

Organisation for Economic Co-operation and Development 1996, *Environmental Performance Reviews. New Zealand*, OECD, Paris.

FURTHER READING

Barnett, J. & J. Pauling 2005, 'The Environmental Effects of New Zealand's Free-Market Reforms', *Environment, Development and Sustainability*, vol. 7, pp. 271–89.

Bührs, T. 2002, 'New Zealand's Capacity for Green Planning: A Political-Institutional Assessment and Analysis', *Political Science*, 54/1, pp. 27–46.

Bührs, T. 2002, 'New Zealand', in H. Weidner & M. Jänicke (eds), *Capacity Building in National Environmental Policy a Comparative Study of 17 Countries*, Springer, Berlin, pp. 329–46.

Bührs, T. & R.V. Bartlett 1993, *Environmental Policy in New Zealand. The Politics of Clean and Green?*, Oxford University Press, Auckland.

Dryzek, J.S. 1997, *The Politics of the Earth: Environmental Discourses*, Oxford University Press, Oxford.

Eckersley, R. 2004, *The Green State. Rethinking Democracy and Sovereignty*, MIT Press, Cambridge, Massachusetts.

Roberts, J. 2004, *Environmental Policy*, Routledge, New York.

Immigration Policy

Kate McMillan

Along with Australia, Canada, and the USA, New Zealand is often described as one of the 'traditional' countries of immigration, meaning that the overwhelming majority of the population in these countries are either descended from immigrants or are themselves immigrants. New Zealand, moreover, remains one the few countries in the world to seek out immigrants for permanent settlement. Although there have been restrictive aspects to immigration policy in New Zealand, the historical trend has been one of growth in the numbers and diversity of migrants. This reflects the belief held by successive New Zealand governments that properly managed immigration can further New Zealand's economic, social, and foreign policy interests. Five broad migratory periods are discernible in New Zealand's history.

POLYNESIAN SETTLEMENT

The first period of migration to New Zealand commenced with the earliest known discovery of its landmass. Polynesian explorers from the Society, Marquesas, and Cook Islands are thought to have landed and settled in New Zealand during their explorations of the Pacific Ocean in the thirteenth century AD (King 2003, pp. 48–60). From these early settlers and their descendants developed the unique people, cultures, and language known today as Māori. Geographic isolation meant it was over five hundred years before the next phase of migration to New Zealand was launched, beginning with British colonial migration.

MIGRATION 1840–1945

European colonialism created a number of highly significant migratory flows (Castles & Miller 2003, pp. 50–62) whose social and political legacies are today felt in every corner of the globe. Chattel slavery, the system of indentured labour that replaced it, and the huge outflow of temporary and permanent migrants from Europe to the various European colonies in Africa, Asia, the Americas, and later Australasia and the Pacific resulted in the inter-continental migration (forced and voluntary) of many millions of people between the late seventeenth and nineteenth centuries.

By the early nineteenth century New Zealand too was being spun into the web of empire. Early European visitors and sojourners to New Zealand included whalers and sealers, missionaries, mariners and merchants, attracted, as James Belich has put it, by New Zealand's 'flax, timber and whales; seals, sex and souls' (Belich 1996, p. 129). They hailed from England and France, but also from Portugal, the Netherlands, Germany, Denmark, America, and Canada. While some of these early visitors stayed on—only sometimes through choice—it was not until the mid-1800s that New Zealand began to be seen as a desirable destination for permanent mass migration from Europe.

Britain, by that time the mightiest of all the European imperial powers, had come under pressure to extend its empire into New Zealand. Plans for a French colony based in Akaroa, along with petitioning from the profit-hungry New Zealand Company and from a Church Missionary Society anxious about the spread of both lawlessness and French Catholicism, spurred the British into proclaiming sovereignty over New Zealand in 1840. The organised migration of settlers from Britain and Ireland to New Zealand began in earnest shortly thereafter. Already by 1861 there were nearly 100,000 English, Scottish, Irish, and Welsh settlers living throughout New Zealand (Belich 1996, pp. 179–90). Also among the early settlers to New Zealand were a number of Scandinavians (Danes, Swedes, Norwegians), Europeans (Dalmatians, Poles, French, Italians), Chinese and Indians (King 2003, pp. 175–6), but British settlers made up the vast majority, and continued to do so for the next 150 years.

The conviction held by colonial administrators that New Zealand society should be made up predominantly of those of either British or Māori descent, alongside the growing popularity of racialist thinking, influenced immigration policy for all of the nineteenth and much of the twentieth centuries. Around the turn of the twentieth century, for example, New Zealand went through a period of particularly virulent anti-Asian sentiment following the arrival of a number of Chinese to work the Otago goldfields. Between 1888 and the 1920s a series of legislative acts were passed with the intention of limiting 'Asiatic' migration to New Zealand, and preventing Asians from naturalising once they were here (Ip 1995, pp. 182–3). Similar anti-Asian legislation was passed in Canada, Australia, and the USA at this time.

POSTWAR MIGRATION

A third, more diverse and less discriminatory, period of migration is evident from the end of the Second World War, much influenced by the international human rights legislation developed under the auspices of the United Nations. After the war New Zealand accepted about 5,000 refugees and displaced persons from Continental Europe, and more than 1,100 Hungarians between 1956 and 1959 (Schroff 1989, p. 196).

Refugees aside, postwar immigration policy was generally cautious, tailored to meet New Zealand labour shortages and still strongly loyal to the concept of the British Empire. A population advisory committee established in 1945 recommended that migrants should only be encouraged to come to New Zealand if they were able to meet shortages in the New Zealand labour market (Schroff 1989, p. 197). Free and assisted passages were introduced in 1947 to try and encourage immigrants from the United Kingdom, a scheme expanded by the National government in 1950 in response to acute labour shortages. When it became apparent that Great Britain could not be relied upon to fill all vacancies, the official advice was that the next best option would be to recruit from Northern European countries (McKinnon, pp. 37–8). A bilateral immigration agreement was thus concluded with the Netherlands, leading to the arrival of a large number of Dutch migrants. These were joined in the late 1950s by a smaller number of occupational specialists recruited from Denmark, Germany, Switzerland, and Austria.

New Zealand's racially exclusionary immigration policies meant that in 1961 an overwhelming 98.7 per cent of New Zealanders were either Māori or European. By the mid-1960s, however, New Zealand's desire for cheap, unskilled labour had led to an ethnic diversification of immigration flows. In the 1950s and 1960s migrants from the South Pacific were encouraged to migrate to New Zealand to meet the growing need for semi- or unskilled labour in the New Zealand manufacturing sector. Pacific communities thus became established in a number of New Zealand cities. As long as New Zealand continued to experience labour shortages, migration from the Pacific Islands was accepted as economically beneficial, and a blind eye was turned on those Pacific Islands people who overstayed their work visas. But once the boom times were over many Pacific Islands people were branded as 'overstayers' and blamed for the recession then affecting New Zealand. Most infamously, Pacific peoples were subjected to 'dawn raids' from 1974, as officials conducted random checks on their immigration status.

A record number of migrants arrived in New Zealand in the 1970s (70,000 in 1973–74), including small numbers of assisted migrants from Belgium, France, Italy, the Netherlands, Switzerland, West Germany, and the USA, along with refugees from Vietnam, Laos, Cambodia, Chile, Uganda, and Iran. Yet a preference for migrants from 'traditional sources' still underlay New Zealand's immigration policy.

THE END OF 'TRADITIONAL SOURCE' MIGRATION AND THE INTRODUCTION OF A POINTS SYSTEM

Among the great raft of legislative and policy changes introduced by the fourth Labour government, elected in 1984, were those pertaining to immigration. Most significantly, in 1986 Labour terminated the preference for migrants from the 'traditional source countries' of Northern and Western Europe and North America. Instead, immigrants were to be selected on criteria that evaluated their 'personal qualities, skills, qualifications, potential contribution to the New Zealand economy and society, and capacity to settle well' (Burke 1986, p. 15). A new Immigration Act, embodying these changes, was introduced in 1987.

A number of political and economic events had precipitated this change in thinking about immigration. Britain's entry into the European Economic Community in 1973 had alerted New Zealand to an urgent need to diversify both its export products and its markets. Asia, the Middle East, and the Soviet Union were identified as important potential export markets and sources of investment capital, and there was an awareness that these new relationships might be jeopardised by an impression that New Zealand was willing to take the money, but not the people from these countries (Burke 1986, p. 15). The government also began to realise that, along with the skills, qualifications, and capital that migrants brought, were the personal links with and cultural understandings of the regions they came from, each of which could help New Zealand further develop its relationships with these regions.

Labour was voted out of office in October 1990 but the new National government was equally, if not more, persuaded by the argument that net migration increases had beneficial economic effects. In November 1991 National adopted a points-based immigration system, similar to that used in Canada. Under this system immigrants were no longer required to fill specific occupational vacancies identified by the Department of Labour but were allocated points for a combination of skills, education, capital, qualifications, age, and offers of employment. All those who reached a pre-determined number of points were granted residence permits. The government could control the number of migrants gaining residence by raising or lowering the number of points needed to 'pass'. During the period immediately after the 1991 policy changes, and before amendments were introduced in 1995, the number of people approved for residence in New Zealand grew rapidly: 26,000 people were approved for permanent residence in 1992, 35,000 in 1994, and 54,811 in 1995 (New Zealand Immigration Service 1994, 1996). This last number was over twice the minimum target of 25,000 residence approvals set in 1991. And, following the 1987 changes, they were a very diverse group, from over a hundred and twenty countries.

As was to be expected, the unprecedented arrival of a comparatively large number of visibly ethnically and culturally differentiated migrants met with some resistance from those New Zealanders who felt the new migrants somehow breached the cultural boundaries of the New Zealand community (McMillan 2005, pp. 73–80). A great deal of public and media attention focused on the fact that Asians now dominated the flow of migrants into New Zealand: 57 per cent of all residence approvals were granted to those from Asian countries in 1994 (New Zealand Immigration Service 1994, p. 2) and by 1995–96, Taiwan had overtaken Great Britain as the largest single country of origin of migrants (New Zealand Immigration Service 1996, p. 4). Some, but by no means most, of this coverage was quite negative (Booth & Martin 1993). In response, National introduced a number of minor policy amendments, one of which, an English language 'bond' introduced in 1995, was seen as racist in Asia, and had the effect of greatly reducing immigration from that region. Nonetheless, in 1996 the New Zealand First leader, Winston Peters, made political mileage out of anti-immigration feeling in the lead-up to New Zealand's first election using the Mixed Member Proportional (MMP) electoral system. Following a heavily nationalistic and anti-immigration campaign, in which Asian migration was implicitly if not explicitly singled out for criticism, New Zealand First won 14.4 per cent of the national vote, and all of the Māori seats. Having found himself in the happy position of kingmaker following the election, Peters went on to form a coalition government with the National party (see chapter 5.3 for fuller discussion). Despite his pre-election rhetoric, however, immigration policy continued relatively unchanged after 1996, although the unpopular language bond was dropped.

Upon entering office in 1999, the Labour–Alliance coalition government, and the Labour–Progressive government that succeeded it in 2002, retained the broad legislative framework outlined by the 1987 Act, and, with some amendments, the policy framework outlined by the 1991 policy. By 2005 60 per cent of successful applicants were accepted under the Skilled/Business stream that awarded points to migrants either for their qualifications and work experience, or their business experience and the funds they had available to invest in New Zealand (a minimum of $2 million was required for the investor category in 2005). And, in a return to pre-1991 policy, points were awarded to those able to fill pre-identified gaps in the labour market. Every year New Zealand also accepted up to 750 UN-mandated refugees under the Refugee Quota; 650 citizens from Fiji, Tuvalu, Kiribati, and Tonga combined under the Pacific Access Category; and 1,100 Samoan citizens under the Samoan Quota scheme. Once resident in New Zealand, migrants and refugees could apply to bring other family members to New Zealand under the Family Sponsored stream. By accepting immigrants through these various channels, New Zealand sees itself as fulfilling its humanitarian responsibilities.

In the 2004–05 year a total of 48,815 people were approved for residence, most of whom came under the Skilled/Business stream. While this number was slightly above the target of 45,000 set by the New Zealand Immigration Service for the 2004–05 year and representing 1.5 per cent of the total population, net migration (permanent and long-term arrivals minus permanent and long-term departures) for the year was actually much lower: at 10,000 it represented less than 0.25 per cent of the total population. Nonetheless, the cumulative effects of an increasingly expansive postwar immigration policy were beginning to show. In 2005 nearly 20 per cent of New Zealand's population had been born overseas, one of the highest proportions of overseas-born as a percentage of total population of any country in the world.

Following the formation of a Labour-led coalition government in October 2005, the new Minister for Immigration, David Cunliffe, reiterated the view that the New Zealand economy needed skilled and talented migrants, and, clearly convinced that low birth rates will force developed nations to compete for migrants of working age to support their aging populations, argued that New Zealand was 'in a global race for talent and we must win our share' (Cunliffe 2005).

This view of immigration as critical to New Zealand's economic development, characteristic of much of New Zealand's immigration policy since 1840, has more recently operated within an international environment of heightened concern about security and terrorism. This concern is the defining feature of a fifth, overlapping, period of immigration in New Zealand.

IMMIGRATION AFTER 9/11

The events of 11 September 2001, and the ensuing American-led 'War on Terror', have led to a new focus, particularly within Western nations, on 'border security'. Central to this focus has been an acute and sometimes hostile scrutiny of international migrants—especially those of an Islamic faith (International Organisation for Migration 2002, pp. 26–7). For New Zealand, the immigration policy implications of this security focus are yet to be fully realised, but were foreshadowed by the government's decision in 2005 to conduct a 'fundamental review' of the 1987 Immigration Act (Department of Labour 2005).

Measures already implemented to improve New Zealand's border security include a reduction in the period for which a New Zealand passport is issued (from ten to five years), an increase in the amount of time spent in New Zealand required before an application for citizenship can be made (from three to five years), the inclusion within New Zealand passports of a microchip containing biometric information about the passport holder's face, and the introduction of an 'Advanced Passenger Processing' (APP) facility. APP allows New Zealand border agencies to screen travellers before they get on planes destined for New Zealand by sharing information with border agencies in other countries. Those travellers thought to pose a risk to New Zealand border security can be prevented from embarking.

Much of the threat from migration is thought to come from irregular migration (those who are smuggled, trafficked, travel on fraudulent travel documents, overstay their visas, or claim asylum), as states have difficulty monitoring the backgrounds, identity, activities, and reasons for travel of such migrants. Although New Zealand's geographic isolation has insulated it from much irregular migration, the government does not want New Zealand to be, in perception or reality, a weak link in the international attempt to reduce irregular migration. It has, therefore, participated in a range of processes (the Bali Process, the International Organisation for Migration) established to minimise the risks associated with international migration. Participation in these processes, along with the adoption of more sophisticated information and surveillance technologies, is likely to increase New Zealand's capacity to monitor its borders. Inevitably, it will also tie New Zealand more closely into the processes used by other states to control irregular migration.

IMMIGRATION POLICY DEBATES

The central question preoccupying immigration policy-makers is whom to let in, and whom to keep out. Answering this question, however, generates a plethora of others, including whether the benefits of immigration outweigh the costs, and, if so, what governments can do to maximise the benefits and minimise the costs. These lead in turn to further questions, such as which kinds of people make the 'best' migrants, what is the optimal number of migrants to let in, and what kind of obligations does New Zealand have towards migrants once they arrive in New Zealand?

At the beginning of the twenty-first century there seems to be broad agreement within policy circles that continued immigration is, indeed, desirable. Research on the fiscal impact[1] of immigration to New Zealand conducted in 2003 found that, in the previous year, migrants had a 'positive net fiscal impact of $1.7 billion', and that the net contribution of migrants to central government revenue was 'slightly higher than that of the New Zealand born' (Department of Labour 2003, p. 10). This research is in line with international findings. However, Poot and Cochrane found in 2004 that many other aspects of the economic effects of migration to New Zealand, such as the impact of immigration on wages, employment, productivity, and housing costs, remain under-researched (Poot and Cochrane 2004).

There also seems to be widespread agreement that immigration is most likely to benefit New Zealand when migrants are chosen for their skills, experience, and capital, particularly where those skills can fill existing labour shortages. The family reunification and humanitarian streams, meanwhile, are seen as important ways in which New Zealand can fulfil its obligations both to migrants already in New Zealand, and to the international community.

In the 1990s, successive National governments tended to assume that selecting the right migrants was the hard part of immigration policy, and that suitably skilled and resourced migrants would, because of their resources, settle well in New Zealand. Since 1999, however, greater emphasis has been placed on the experiences of migrants post-arrival. A range of employment, English-language tuition, and information services are now provided to new migrants and refugees, on the assumption that such assistance will help migrants settle well, and thus improve migration outcomes (Department of Labour 2004). A longitudinal study of immigrants, piloted in 2003 by the New Zealand Immigration Service and Statistics New Zealand, aims to establish more clearly what factors contribute to successful migration outcomes.

The New Zealand public has not always been as convinced about the benefits of immigration as recent policy-makers, and immigration remains an issue capable of generating considerable political heat—never more so than during election year. As has been discussed, Winston Peters has consistently, and successfully, used the immigration issue as a major plank in all of New Zealand First's election campaigns since 1993. Recent evidence seems to suggest, however, that many New Zealanders now accept the current rate of immigration, and do not feel as threatened by the arrival of immigrants from diverse backgrounds as they appeared to in the 1990s (Levine & Roberts 2005). An appeal by Winston Peters to anti-refugee and anti-Islamic sentiment in the 2005 campaign did not seem to resonate strongly with the public (Peters 2005).

Nonetheless, one of the most profound effects of immigration policy in New Zealand since 1987 has been the rapid ethnic and cultural diversification of New Zealand's population. While this has, as discussed above, on occasion led to strained relations between members of the host population and new migrants, New Zealand has not experienced the level of ethnic conflict seen in a number of other states. Interestingly, the countries which seem to have dealt best, although by no means perfectly, with the ethnic diversity brought about by immigration are two other traditional countries of immigration: Australia and Canada (Castles & Miller 2003, pp. 220–54). These states' willingness to extend full citizenship rights to a diverse range of migrants, and their public recognition of and support for ethnic difference, seems to have been a more successful way of managing ethnic relations than the state-imposed assimilation of migrants practised in France, or the exclusionary citizenship policies practised until recently in Germany, which denied full citizenship to second- and even third-generation Turks resident in Germany. To argue that Australia and Canada still have a long way to go in dealing with indigenous issues in their countries—and indeed, with ethnic issues more generally—does not necessarily undermine the argument that granting full citizenship rights to long-term migrants, and recognising and supporting diversity in the public realm, is less likely to lead to conflict between migrants and the host community.

A recurrent theme of debate in recent years is whether New Zealand too ought now to move from an official policy of 'biculturalism' to one of 'multiculturalism'. Some non-Māori, non-Europeans have argued that the term 'bicultural' appears to exclude from an understanding of the national community those who are neither 'Pakeha'[2] nor Māori. Māori, for their part, have often opposed talk of 'multiculturalism' for fear it would dilute their claims to a special and unique status in New Zealand (Fleras & Spoonley 1999, pp. 218–24), and Māori were among those who most vociferously opposed the new Asian migration in the 1990s. Ranginui Walker, for example, argued that Māori workers would be among those most marginalised by the entry of skilled and business migrants from Asia (Walker 1995, pp. 301–2).

Demographically New Zealand is clearly multicultural: over two hundred ethnicities were recorded in the 2001 census. Asians now comprise 6.6 per cent of the total population, Pacific peoples 6.5 per cent, Māori 14.7 per cent, and Europeans around 80 per cent.[3] Those who fall into the 'other' category still comprise less than 1 per cent of the population (Statistics New Zealand 2002, p. 11).

In many respects New Zealand is also already multicultural in policy: Pacific and 'Ethnic' peoples have institutional representation in government through the Ministry of Pacific Islands Affairs and the Office of Ethnic Affairs; a range of social policies are targeted directly at specific ethnic groups; and, as mentioned above, a range of services are made available to new migrants from non-English-speaking backgrounds. But it would be inaccurate to say that multiculturalism has replaced biculturalism; rather, multiculturalism and biculturalism can be seen to operate simultaneously. Both bi- and multiculturalisms can take a wide variety of forms, each of which is likely to be contested by different groups in society (Fleras & Spoonley, pp. 218–50), but the questions and debates associated with biculturalism are, in significant ways, separate from those associated with multiculturalism, and the two should not be seen as either inherently oppositional or mutually exclusive. What does seem clear, however, is that both Māori and non-Māori ethnic minorities feel the need for an inclusive narrative of national identity that embraces and acknowledges their identity and status.

CONCLUSION

Economic, social, political, and environmental forces have long acted as incentives for people to move from one place to another. While the decision by an individual or family to move from one country to another may be intensely personal—and often somewhat traumatic—it is usually informed and influenced by factors and processes that operate at a national, regional, or even global level. An examination of New Zealand's immigration history and policy-making reveals that although New Zealand is geographically isolated, it has nonetheless been subject to and part of the wider forces that have shaped the international movement of people. Global and regional forces seem destined to exert an even greater influence over New Zealand's immigration policy in the future as the number of international migrants in the world increases, and as states begin to work together to try and better manage international migratory flows.

Nonetheless, policy-makers in New Zealand will undoubtedly continue to see immigration as a means of meeting New Zealand's wider economic, demographic, humanitarian, and foreign policy goals. A better understanding of the factors that contribute to successful migration outcomes, achieved through detailed research, will assist policy-makers in developing policy to meet those goals, while regional and global 'migration management' practices will increase New Zealand's capacity to enforce those policies. It is to be hoped that immigration policy continues to be informed by an ever-improving understanding of what makes migration work—both for migrants and for the host community—and not by the desire of politicians to gain political support by inciting xenophobia and a mistrust of particular migrant groups.

DISCUSSION QUESTIONS

1   On what grounds should immigrants into New Zealand be selected? How widely should different sectors of the community (e.g., Māori, trade unions, business groups) be consulted about immigration policy?
2   What obligations, if any, does the government have towards immigrants and refugees once they are in New Zealand?
3   Should immigrants be required to conform to a set of 'core' New Zealand values? If so, what might such values be? If not, why not?
4   In what ways do the debates about biculturalism and multiculturalism differ, and in what ways are they similar?

NOTES

1   Defined as 'the contribution of migrants to central government revenue less government expenditure attributable to the migrants population' (Department of Labour 2003, p. 5).
2   'Pakeha' is a term commonly used to refer to New Zealanders of British or European descent.
3   Because of the number of respondents who identified themselves as having multiple ethnicities, the total does not equal 100 per cent.

REFERENCES

Belich, J. 1996, *Making Peoples: A History of the New Zealanders From Polynesian Settlement to the End of the Nineteenth Century*, Allen Lane, Penguin Press, Auckland.
Booth, P. & Y. Martin 1993: 'The Inv-Asian', *Eastern Courier*, 16 April, pp. 7–9.
Burke, K. 1986, *Review of Immigration Policy August 1986*, Department of Labour, Wellington.
Castles, S. & M.J. Miller 2003, *The Age of Migration: International Population Movements in the Modern World*, 3rd edn, Palgrave Macmillan, Hampshire.
Cunliffe, D. 2005, 'Where From: Where to for Immigration', Speech to Auckland Public Meeting, Titirangi War Memorial Hall, 19 November, www.beehive.govt.nz/ViewDocument.aspx?DocumentID=24425.

Department of Labour 1990, 'Ministerial Brief, October 1990, Wellington', Department of Labour, Wellington.

Department of Labour 2004, 'Our Future Together: The New Zealand Settlement Strategy in Outline', New Zealand Immigration Service, Wellington.

Department of Labour 2003, 'The Fiscal Impacts of Migrants to New Zealand 2003', New Zealand Immigration Service, www.immigration.govt.nz/NR/rdonlyres/09503445-D634–491C-BAC6–20D42282B3C7/0/Fiscalimpacts2003FINAL.pdf.

Department of Labour 2005, 'Terms of Reference: Review of the Immigration Act 1987', www.immigration.govt.nz/NR/rdonlyres/8E0A2C30–231F-408E-A7B3–55070C22D8C6/0/termsofreference.pdf.

Fleras, A. & P. Spoonley 1999, *Recalling Aotearoa Indigenous Politics and Ethnic Relations in New Zealand*, Oxford University Press, Auckland.

International Organization for Migration 2002, *World Migration 2003. Managing Migration Challenges and Responses for People on the Move*, Volume 2, IOM World Migration Report Series, International Organization for Migration, Geneva.

Ip, M. 1995, 'Chinese New Zealanders', in S.W. Greif (ed.), *Immigration and National Identity in New Zealand. One People—Two People—Many Peoples?*, Dunmore Press, Palmerston North, pp. 161–99.

King, Michael 2003, *The Penguin History of New Zealand*, Penguin, Auckland.

Levine, S. & N.S. Roberts 2005, 'Mixed messages: Voting Behaviour in New Zealand in 2005', Paper presented to the Post Election Conference, 2 December, Parliament Buildings, Wellington.

McKinnon, M. 1996, *Immigrants and Citizens: New Zealanders and Asian Immigration in Historical Perspective*, Institute of Policy Studies, Victoria University of Wellington, Wellington.

McMillan, K. 2005, 'Immigration and Citizenship Debates of the 1990s' in A. Trlin, P. Spoonley & N. Watts, *New Zealand and International Migration: A Digest and Bibliography*, No. 4, Massey University, Palmerston North, pp. 70–85.

New Zealand Immigration Service, 1994, *Immigration Fact Packs*, Department of Labour, December, Wellington.

New Zealand Immigration Service 1996, *Immigration Fact Packs*, Department of Labour, February, Wellington.

Peters, W. 2005, 'The End of Tolerance', Speech to Grey Power, 28 July, Kaitaia.

Poot, J. & B. Cochrane 2004, 'Measuring the Economic Impact of Immigration: A Scoping Paper', New Zealand Immigration Service, Wellington, www.immigration.govt.nz/NR/rdonlyres/CC67A9CF-CDF5–4F87–9790-C6F61EBEEB18/0/ScopingpaperontheEconomicImpactsofImmigration.pdf.

Schroff, G. 1989, 'New Zealand's Immigration Policy', in *Department of Statistics, The New Zealand Official Yearbook 1988–9*, Department of Statistics, Wellington.

Statistics New Zealand, 2002, '2001 Census of Population and Dwellings Ethnic Groups', Wellington, www.stats.govt.nz/NR/rdonlyres/988C1E07–45FD-4A14–8164–393B5CFDF513/0/EthnicGroups01.pdf.

Walker, R. 1995, 'Immigration Policy and the Political Economy of New Zealand', in S.W. Greif (ed.), *Immigration and National Identity in New Zealand. One People—Two People—Many Peoples?*, Dunmore Press, Palmerston North, pp. 282–302.

Working Party on Immigration 1991, Report of the Working Party on Immigration, Wellington.

FURTHER READING

Fleras, A. & P. Spoonley 1999, *Recalling Aotearoa: Indigenous Politics and Ethnic Relations in New Zealand*, Oxford University Press, Auckland.

Greif, S.W. (ed.) 1995, *Immigration and National Identity in New Zealand. One People—Two People—Many Peoples?*, Dunmore Press, Palmerston North.

New Zealand Immigration Service homepage: www.immigration.govt.nz/migrant/general/generalinformation/research/

Pearson, D. 1990, *A Dream Deferred: The Origins of Ethnic Conflict in New Zealand*, Allen & Unwin in Association with Port Nicholson Press, Auckland.

Spoonley, P., C. MacPherson & D. Pearson (eds) 2005, *Tangata Tangata: The Changing Ethnic Contours of New Zealand*, Thomson/Dunmore Press, Victoria, pp. 109–94.

Trlin, A.D. & P. Spoonley, *New Zealand and International Migration: A Digest and Bibliography*, No. 4, Massey University, Palmerston North.

Refugee Policy

Jane Verbitsky

[A refugee is a person who] owing to well founded fear of being persecuted for reasons of race, religion, nationality, membership of a particular social group or political opinion, is outside the country of his nationality and is unable or, owing to such fear, is unwilling to avail himself of the protection of that country; or who, not having a nationality and being outside the country of his former habitual residence as a result of such events, is unable or, owing to such fear, is unwilling to return to it (Art. 1(A)(2), Convention Relating to the Status of Refugees).

This definition of a refugee used by the international community derives from the 1951 United Nations Convention relating to the Status of Refugees. The Convention, later updated by the 1967 Protocol relating to the Status of Refugees, is the key international instrument on refugees. New Zealand was an early signatory, acceding to the Convention in 1960, and refugee policy is based on New Zealand's obligations to protect refugees in accordance with the Convention. The text of the Convention is set out in the Sixth Schedule to the Immigration Act 1987, which forms the statutory framework for assessing and determining claims made by people in New Zealand seeking refugee status.

New Zealand's involvement in refugee resettlement, though, predates the Convention. New Zealand accepted 1,100 Jewish refugees during the 1930s, but the first major refugee group to be resettled in New Zealand was a group of 837 Polish refugees, mostly children, who arrived in 1944 (Brooking & Rabel 1995, p. 33). While the original intention was for these refugees to return home at the end of the Second World War, the political situation in Poland by that time had changed and repatriation was no longer a feasible solution. New Zealand also accepted 4,500 other war-time refugees from Europe for resettlement between 1949 and 1952 (Campbell 2003, p. 2).

The arrival of refugees in New Zealand is typically precipitated by political or ethnic conflict, humanitarian crisis, war and repression in their home countries, and the roll-call of refugee groups accepted by New Zealand over the next five decades reflects these circumstances. Hungarian refugees arrived here following the 1956 Hungarian revolution, and in the 1960s New Zealand became the new home for Czechoslovaks driven out of their country after the failure of the Prague uprising of 1968. Persecuted Chinese also began arriving during this period. In the 1970s Asians fleeing the Uganda of Idi Amin, Chileans seeking refuge from the regime of General Pinochet, and Jews and East Europeans escaping the Soviet Union or one of its satellite states arrived in New Zealand. The largest refugee groups, though, came from Indo-China. Wars in Vietnam, Cambodia, and Laos produced waves of refugees throughout the 1970s and 1980s. Refugees from the Middle East, notably Iran, Iraq, and Afghanistan, began to arrive in the 1990s. They were joined as the decade wore on by others from Burma, Somalia, Ethiopia, Sri Lanka, Sudan, and the former Yugoslavia. Since 2000, New Zealand has also become home to refugee groups from Burundi, Eritrea, and Djibouti (Devere, McDermott & Verbitsky 2005; RefNZ Statistics 2005).

NEW ZEALAND AND REFUGEE RESETTLEMENT

Fewer than twenty countries worldwide provide refugee resettlement programmes, and many have only recently instituted these programmes. New Zealand, however, has operated a refugee quota system for more than two decades. Each year up to 750 refugees are resettled in New Zealand. This quota recognises the fact that within the global refugee community some refugees are at particular risk, and cannot be either repatriated to their home country or integrated into the country in which they first sought asylum. For these refugees, permanent resettlement in a third country, such as New Zealand, is the only durable solution. Refugees accepted by New Zealand under the quota system are those whose status as refugees has been authenticated, or 'mandated', offshore by the United Nations High Commissioner for Refugees (UNHCR).

New Zealand is not just one of the few countries to accept refugees for resettlement, but one of only a handful which reserves places within its refugee resettlement quota for women at risk, medical/disabled, and emergency protection cases. These categories represent refugees who, among an already vulnerable and marginalised group, are the most imperilled and most difficult to place of all refugees. New Zealand's willingness to accept these refugees has brought it international respect for its humanitarianism.

In exceptional circumstances, New Zealand will also accept groups of refugees who are in immediate danger. In 1999, for example, as a consequence of the humanitarian crisis in Kosovo, the UNHCR asked Convention states to take in as many Kosovo refugees as possible. New Zealand responded by accepting for resettlement over four hundred Kosovars who had family in New Zealand. Similarly, in 2001, New Zealand accepted for resettlement more than a hundred and thirty Afghani asylum-seekers picked up by the freighter, MS Tampa, after their craft capsized in the Indian Ocean.

In addition to accepting up to 750 quota (or 'UNHCR-mandated') refugees per year, New Zealand also accepts spontaneous asylum-seekers ('Convention refugees') whose claim to refugee status is validated by the Refugee Service Branch of the New Zealand Immigration Service, or by the Refugee Status Appeals Authority. The number of asylum-seekers who claim refuge in New Zealand annually is relatively small, and reflects New Zealand's geographically isolated position and lack of shared territorial borders. An average of 1,585 Refugee Status applications is received each year with around 12.5 per cent of these applications being approved (RMS 2003, p. 2).

Convention refugees apply for refugee status when they arrive in New Zealand, or before their temporary visa expires. Those in the former group with uncertain identities may be detained at the Mangere Refugee Resettlement Centre in Auckland, or in prison, while their claim to refugee status is investigated. The non-refoulement principle of the Refugee Convention prevents refugees being returned to states where their lives or freedoms could be endangered. The 1984 UN Convention against Torture and Other Cruel, Inhuman or Degrading Treatment or Punishment, to which New Zealand is also a signatory, imposes a similar requirement to prevent any person being returned or extradited to another state where there are substantial grounds to believe that person might be tortured.

UNHCR-mandated refugees arrive in New Zealand in groups of around a hundred and twenty, and stay for their first six weeks in the country at the Mangere Refugee Resettlement Centre. The Centre provides a six weeks, on-arrival, residential orientation programme which includes medical evaluations, English language classes, and education about New Zealand. At the end of the six weeks, refugees leave the Centre for one of New Zealand's five major resettlement areas (Auckland, Hamilton, Napier, Wellington, and Christchurch) to begin their new lives in New Zealand.

REFUGEES AND INTEGRATION INTO NEW ZEALAND SOCIETY

Both UNHCR-mandated refugees and Convention refugees receive permanent resident status in New Zealand, and that status enables them to access the range of welfare services and benefits provided by the state. However, assistance which directly addresses the specific needs of refugees as they attempt to integrate into society is limited, and refugees confront well-documented difficulties in adjusting to life in New Zealand. These difficulties include: ongoing trauma and stress associated with the reasons for flight from their home country; learning English as an Additional Language; prejudice and overt racism in the host community; non-recognition of qualifications gained in their home country and concomitant inability to gain similar jobs to those occupied in their home country; lack of support structures within the local community; cultural shock; separation from family members; and inadequacy of state provision in the early period of settlement transition (Elliott 1997; NZ Immigration Service 2004; Altinkaya & Omundsen 1999; Nash & Trlin 2004).

These problems are considerable. In addition, the scattered nature of service provision means that refugees have historically had to negotiate an array of government departments and agencies, as well as a range of non-government, and voluntary service providers in order to access needed services. This task is obviously made more difficult when refugees have limited English, and are still adjusting to life in a new land. 'One stop shops', such as the Auckland Regional Migrant Service, have recently been set up, and this has been a helpful innovation. Nevertheless, problems of access remain for refugees who do not have their own transport, or who live outside the larger cities.

Until recently, the problems faced by refugees in attempting to establish a life in New Zealand were exacerbated by a lack of coordination and direction in government strategies. The National Immigration Settlement Strategy for migrants, refugees, and their families announced in May 2004 is intended to remedy this. The Strategy's five goals are that migrants and refugees:

- obtain employment appropriate to their qualifications and skills
- are confident using English in a New Zealand setting, or can access appropriate language support to bridge the gap
- are able to access appropriate information and responsive services that are available to the wider community (for example, housing, education, and services for children)
- form supportive social networks and establish a sustainable community identity
- feel safe in expressing their ethnic identity and are accepted by, and are part of, the wider host community; and participate in civic, community, and social activities (NZ Immigration Service 2005).

The Strategy acknowledges the multiple and inter-related problems, such as unemployment and lack of English skills, faced by refugees. Employment and English language proficiency are both important means of integration, and employment is a key indicator of resettlement. Yet, in 2004 an Immigration Service survey revealed that nine out of ten refugees still depend on a benefit for their main source of income two years after their arrival, and that 78 per cent of refugees who had lived in the country for five years were still reliant on government support (*The Press* 22 July 2004; NZ Immigration Service 2004). This state of affairs has, in part, been attributed to discrimination in the community, including discrimination by potential employers. The *Social Report 2005* (2005) confirmed that refugees are one of the three groups— the others being 'Asian' and 'Recent immigrants'—most perceived to experience discrimination in New Zealand.

Underlying these problems is the diversity of refugees' backgrounds, and their varying levels of English-language abilities. To fully participate in New Zealand society, refugees must have English-language competence. However, 'many refugees come from countries where English may not be spoken at all' and few 'can become full participants in New Zealand society without formal English education and/or skill upgrading' (Altinkaya & Omundsen 1999, p. 35). Recent research on the English-language needs of migrants from non-English-speaking backgrounds reaffirms the need for support 'in the form of both coordinated educational provision and community involvement' to assist adult immigrants and refugees to gain acceptance and become fully functioning members of society (White, Watts & Trlin 2002, p. 160).

REFUGEE POLICY: BALANCING COMPETING INTERESTS

Since 1960 the number of refugees in the world has risen exponentially. By the 1980s the increases in global refugee numbers had reached large enough figures to be characterised as a 'crisis'. Although the numbers of refugees have declined since the high point of 18.2 million in 1992, the number remains substantial. In 2005 the UNHCR stated that the global refugee population was 9.2 million (UNHCR 1993, 2005).

Refugee flows have major political, economic, social, cultural, and personal consequences, and no continent has been immune from these impacts (Ager 1999, p. 1). While the suffering of refugees evokes sympathy and humanitarian concern, refugee situations have also been recognised as a 'potential threat to the social, economic, and political fabric of host states, and ultimately a threat to peace' (Loescher 1999, p. 2). Governments, consequently, must try to balance these competing interests of humanitarianism and national security. However, in the aftermath of escalating refugee crises during the 1980s and 1990s, and fearful of the impact of the borderless world promised by globalisation, the reaction of many developed states was to implement restrictive interventions to try and reduce the number of asylum-seekers who entered their borders.

The tension between the competing interests of humanitarianism and national security is exemplified by two divergent models of refugee policy: the security, or statist, model; and the individual rights model. The security model is based on the concept of sovereignty, and seeks to control refugee movements because these present a potential threat to individual national security, and also to wider regional or international security. There are two dimensions to the model. The internal dimension is represented by deterrence and 'control mechanisms directed at people moving or seeking to move' across borders, and is 'accompanied by a certain rhetoric in public discourse, which serves to heighten a sense of national alarm, or claims to protect new and established communities, or raises the spectre of social tensions' (Goodwin-Gill 2001, p. 14). The external dimension is to be found in foreign policies, in 'support for solutions by resolution in the Security Council, in support of interventions and in the more or less effective "steering" of international, particularly UN agencies' to provide protectionist measures against refugee movements (Goodwin-Gill 2001, p. 14).

The individual rights model, by contrast, is centred around the idea that refugees, asylum-seekers, and migrants should be considered as individuals, each with potentially justifiable claims to protection, and that these claims must be determined on their merits. This model stands in opposition to the security model in its emphases on rights protections, the rule of law, and limits to state action where such action would violate human rights. The model is founded on the core international human rights treaties: the 1948 Universal Declaration of Human Rights; the 1965 International Convention on Elimination of All Forms of Racial Discrimination; the 1966 International Covenant on Civil and Political Rights; the 1966 International Covenant on Economic, Social and Cultural Rights; the 1979 Convention on Elimination of All Forms of Discrimination Against Women; the 1984 UN Convention against Torture and Other Cruel, Inhuman or Degrading Treatment or Punishment; and the 1989 Convention on the Rights of the Child.

The security model has, in recent years, been perceived to be dominant in state–refugee interactions, and in the ways in which states construct refugee policy. Human Rights Watch, commenting on the fiftieth anniversary of the establishment of the UNHCR against the backdrop of increasingly restrictive interpretations of the Refugee Convention in Western Europe and even more restrictive border control policies, noted that unlike 'most other areas of human rights where it is possible to chart progress over the last decades, states have largely regressed in their commitment to protecting refugees over the last fifty years' (Human Rights Watch 2001).

REFUGEE POLICY: THE DEBATES

According to Ager, the 'growth of global refugee numbers through the past three decades has established an increasingly high profile for the issue of forced migration within political and public debate' (1999, p. 1). This has been the case in New Zealand. Refugee policy has become a source of much contention over the last decade.

The political debate surrounding refugee policy is generated by competing beliefs about: who should be eligible to resettle as a refugee in New Zealand; how many refugees New Zealand should allow to resettle in the country; how much resource allocation should be devoted to refugee policy; and whether resources would be better spent on New Zealanders than on foreigners. The issue of national identity, too, has often been raised. There have been concerns expressed that allowing in too many refugees will unfavourably alter New Zealand's national identity. Since 9/11 and the spate of global terrorist attacks attributed to the Al-Qaeda network, security concerns have become pre-eminent in the debate.

The arguments raised in the debate mirror the perspectives expressed in the security and individual rights models. On one side, proponents reflect the priorities of the security model. They talk about the abuse of the refugee system by 'rogues', and those who see New Zealand as a rich, 'soft touch' welfare state ripe for exploitation (Jones 2004; *The Press* 2005; Espiner 2005). As well, arguments are made about the need to address domestic problems within New Zealand, particularly issues of poverty and inequality, ahead of global refugee problems (Ryall 2005). Arguments are made, too, about the need to preserve the national identity and heritage, lest it be swamped by alien cultures, and about the need to ensure that those refugees who come to New Zealand are not attempting to camouflage criminal or terrorist identities (McLoughlin 2004; Newman 2005; *NZ Herald* 2005) Tighter border controls and security measures are advocated, as are cuts to the refugee quota and strict review of New Zealand's humanitarian role in the reception and resettlement of refugees (Peters 2005; Venter 2004).

On the other side, proponents echo the concerns of the individual rights model. They emphasise that as a liberal democratic country New Zealand should respect international human rights conventions, and the rights which individuals exercise based on these conventions. The curtailment of individual rights in the name of security, it is asserted, is not consistent with New Zealand's obligations under the conventions, and is an unjustified state incursion on individual liberties (Locke 2001, 2003; Chisholm 2004). The need for compassion to be shown to 'some of the most vulnerable people on the planet' is also a theme of the pro-refugee argument (Campbell 2004). Similarly, advocates stress that New Zealand receives only a tiny proportion of the world's refugees, that refugees comprise only a small proportion of the immigrant population which enters the country each year, and that New Zealand should continue to demonstrate humanitarianism in its treatment of refugees (Hill 2002; Campbell 2004).

REFUGEE POLICY: INTO THE FUTURE

New Zealand's refugee policy has been underpinned by humanitarian principles, and a determination to take seriously the country's commitment to the Refugee Convention. Like other developed states, though, New Zealand has over the last four years instituted changes to border security and control aimed at deterring and containing unwanted migrants. This has had serious impacts for asylum-seekers. As Manning (2002) notes:

> Before 19 September 2001 only about 5 per cent of refugee claimants were detained. However, on 19 September 2001, the New Zealand Immigration Service (NZIS) issued an Operational Instruction to immigration officers concerning the detention of refugee

claimants under section 128(5) of the Act. Subsequent to that operational instruction approximately 94 per cent of border refugee claimants have been detained.

The new border detention policy was challenged in court[1] but upheld, and amendments to the Immigration Act in 2002 formalised the detention powers. The detention powers continue to be controversial, with some viewing them as 'a blow to New Zealand's credibility as a country that upheld individual rights' (Tunnah 2003).

Even more controversial has been the case of Ahmed Zaoui, an asylum-seeker who was imprisoned under the detention powers after arriving at Auckland Airport in 2002. The Zaoui case has raised important questions about the country's security services and their intelligence sources, security services' role in the refugee determination process, and the tension between national security and human rights. Although the Refugee Status Appeals Authority, after exhaustive investigation, declared that Zaoui met the criteria for refugee status, a national security certificate issued against him by the Security Intelligence Service kept him in jail for 736 days until the Supreme Court finally allowed him bail.

These events and recent changes mean that New Zealand in 2005 has become a more difficult place for asylum-seekers to find refuge, and the environment is one in which security interests are prevalent. What remains to be seen is whether a comprehensive review of the Immigration Act, announced in late 2004 (Immigration 2004; Swain 2005) and due to be completed by late 2006, will further tip the balance in favour of security over human rights.

The Labour–Progressive minority coalition government formed in October 2005 has been described as a centre-right administration (Clifton 2005). It also includes in the position of Minister of Foreign Affairs, Winston Peters, leader of the New Zealand First party. Peters has been the most outspoken and aggressive of all politicians about the need to curb refugee numbers. Although Peters will not be directly involved in refugee policy, he will have the opportunity to influence and persuade ministerial colleagues, and the ability still to cross the floor on issues outside the Foreign Affairs portfolio. As well, the confidence and supply agreement between the Labour and New Zealand First parties contains policy programme agreements, including one on immigration. The immigration agreement commits Labour to conduct

> a full review of immigration legislation and administrative practices within the immigration service, to ensure the system meets the needs of New Zealand in the 21st century and has appropriate mechanisms for ensuring the system is not susceptible to fraud or other abuse, and taking note of other items raised by New Zealand First (Confidence and Supply Agreement with New Zealand First 2005).

That commitment by Labour assures that the New Zealand First party will be both active and vociferous in the review process. From a refugee perspective, the coming parliamentary sessions may well evoke the Chinese curse, 'May you live in interesting times'.

DISCUSSION QUESTIONS

1 Outline the arguments for and against increasing the annual refugee quota.

2 What limits, if any, should there be to the humanitarian assistance that New Zealand offers in refugee crises?

3 How could the resettlement experiences of refugees in New Zealand be improved?

4 Who should have ultimate authority to decide the status of a refugee claimant, and why?

NOTE

1   Attorney-General v Refugee Council of New Zealand Inc. (CA 107/02 16 April 2003).

REFERENCES

Ager, A. (ed.) 1999, *Refugees: Perspectives on the Experience of Forced Migration*, Continuum, London and New York.

Altinkaya, J. & H. Omundsen 1999, ' "Birds in a Gilded Cage": Resettlement Prospects for Adult Refugees in New Zealand', *Social Policy Journal of New Zealand*, Issue 13, pp. 31–42.

Brooking, T. & R. Rabel 1995, 'Neither British Nor Polynesian: A Brief History of New Zealand's Other Immigrants', in S. Greif (ed.), *Immigration and National Identity in New Zealand: One people—Two people—Many peoples?*, Dunmore Press, Palmerston North.

Campbell, G. 2003, *The Intergenerational Settlement of Refugee Children in New Zealand: A Report on the Findings of a Survey Conducted for the New Zealand Refugee and Migrant Service*, New Zealand Science, Mathematics & Technology Teacher Fellowship Scheme.

Campbell, G. 2004, 'This Unfriendly Shore', *New Zealand Listener*, 193/3332, 20 March, available: www.listener.co.nz

Chisholm, D. 2004, 'Prisoner of Conscience', *Sunday Star Times*, 28 November 2004, available: io.knowledge-basket.co.nz

Clifton, J. 2005, 'Cross-Species Mating', *New Zealand Listener*, 201/3416, 29 October, available: www.listener.co.nz

Confidence and Supply Agreement with New Zealand First 2005, Available: www.labour.org.nz

Devere, H., K. McDermott & J. Verbitsky 2003, ' "Just a Refugee": Rights and Status of Refugees in New Zealand', in F. Crepeau, D. Nakache, M. Collyer et al. (eds) *Forced Migration and Global Processes: A View from Forced Migration Studies*, Lexington Books, Maryland.

Elliott, S. 1997, ' "Like Falling Out of the Sky": Communities in Collision', in C. Bell (ed.), *Community Issues in New Zealand*, Dunmore Press, Palmerston North.

Espiner, C. 2005, 'Peters Alleges Baathist in NZ', *The Press*, 29 April, available: io.knowledge-basket.co.nz

Goodwin-Gill, G. 2001, 'After the Cold War: Asylum and the Refugee Concept Move On', *Forced Migration Review*, No. 10, pp. 14–16.

Hill, D. 2002, 'Lessons of History Invite us to Welcome the Refugees', *New Zealand Herald*, 9 May, available: io.knowledge-basket.co.nz

Human Rights Watch 2001, 'Fifty Years On What Future for Rights Protection?', available: www.hrw.org/campaigns/refugees/text1.htm

Immigration Service 2004, 'Immigration Act Terms of Review', available: www.immigration.govt.nz/migrant/general/generalinformation/news

Jones, D. 2004, 'NZ No Place for Australian Rejects', 21 December, available: www.nzfirst.org.nz

Locke, K. 2001, 'Afghan Refugees Shouldn't Be Detained', 25 September, available: www.greens.org.nz/searchdocs/PR4670.html

Locke, K. 2003, 'Dalziel Wrong: Court Decision Doesn't Endorse Wholesale Detention of Refugees', 17 April, available: www.greens.org.nz/searchdocs/PR6229.html

Loescher, G. 1999, 'Refugees: A Global Human Rights and Security Crisis', T. Dunne & N. Wheeler (eds), *Human Rights in Global Politics*, Cambridge University Press, Cambridge.

Manning, D. 2002, 'The Detention of Refugee Claimants: Law Procedure and Practicalities', Auckland District Law Society Seminar, 25 November, available: www.refugee.org.nz/Reference/ADLS5.htm

McLoughlin, D. 2004, 'Refugee Warning from Terror Expert', *Dominion Post*, 26 November, available: io.knowledge-basket.co.nz

Nash, M. & A. Trlin 2004, Social Work with Immigrants, Refugees and Asylum Seekers in New Zealand, *New Settlers Programme Occasional Publication No. 8*, Massey University, Palmerston North.

New Zealand Federation of Business and Professional Women Inc. 2004, *Resettlement Issues for Refugee and Migrant Women: The Workshops Report from 39th Annual Conference of The New Zealand Federation of Business and Professional Women Inc. 2003*, Auckland.

New Zealand Herald 2005, 'Brash Adamant & NBSP: National Not Anti-immigration', 10 August, available: io.knowledge-basket.co.nz

New Zealand Herald 2005, 'Government Signals Migrant Rules to Get Tougher', 25 May, available: io.knowledge-basket.co.nz

New Zealand Immigration Service 2004, *Refugee Voices: A Journey Towards Resettlement*, Wellington.

New Zealand Immigration Service 2005, 'The New Zealand Settlement Strategy in Outline: A Future Together', Available: www.immigration.govt.nz

Newman, M. 2005, 'The Government's Politically Incorrect Immigration Agenda', 6 May, available: www.act.org.nz/item/aspx.26923

Peters, W. 2005, 'NZ First Immigration Policy—Orewa Speech', 27 May, available: www.nzfirst.org.nz

RefNZ Statistics 2005, 'New Zealand Refugee Statistics', available: www.refugee.org.nz/Stats/stats.htm

RMS Refugee Resettlement 2003, 'Refugees in the New Zealand Context', available: www.rms.org.nz

RMS Refugee Resettlement 2004, 'Annual Report 2003–2004', available: www.rms.org.nz

Ryall, T. 2005, 'Labour's Hypocrisy on Refugees', 10 August, available: www.national.org.nz

Social Report 2005, Ministry of Social Development, Wellington.

Swain, P. 2005, 'Terms of Reference for the Immigration Act Review Released', 24 May, available: www.beehive.govt.nz

The Press 2005, 'Rogues Unwelcome', 25 May, available: io.knowledge-basket.co.nz

The Press 2004, '90% of Refugees Rely on Benefit', 22 July, available: io.knowledge-basket.co.nz

Tunnah, H. 2003, 'Top Court Clears Refugee Detention', *New Zealand Herald*, 17 April, available: io.knowledge-basket.co.nz

UNHCR 1993, *The State of the World's Refugees 1993: The Challenge of Protection*, Oxford University Press, Oxford.

UNHCR 2005, 'UNHCR—Refugees by Numbers 2005', available: www.unhcr.ch/cgi-bin/texis/vtx/basics/opendoc.htm

Venter, N. 2004, 'National Calls for Cut in Refugees', *Dominion Post*, 26 August, available: io.knowledge-basket.co.nz

White, C., N. Watts & A. Trlin 2002, 'New Zealand as an English-language Learning Environment: Immigrant Experiences, Provider Perspectives and Social Policy Implications', *Social Policy Journal of New Zealand*, Issue 18, pp. 148–62.

FURTHER READING

Ager, A. (ed.) 1999, *Refugees: Perspectives on the Experience of Forced Migration*, Continuum, London & New York.

NZ Federation of Business and Professional Women Inc. 2004, *Resettlement Issues for Refugee and Migrant Women: The Workshops Report from 39th Annual Conference of The New Zealand Federation of Business and Professional Women Inc. 2003*, Auckland.

NZ Immigration Service 2004, *Refugee Voices: A Journey Towards Resettlement*, Wellington.

Regional Security

David Capie

This chapter examines New Zealand's evolving security policy in the Pacific in the light of changing approaches to security.[1] Over the past two decades there has been an important rethinking of how best to manage and respond to armed conflict. During the Cold War, understandings of security were dominated by a paradigm largely informed by the theory of realism (Waltz 1979). Realism assumes that the key focus of defence planning is the state. The referent object of security (the object needing to be made secure) is usually the territory or borders of the state, and threats are usually understood as the military challenge presented by other states. The best way to respond to these is through 'self-help'—the maintenance of defence forces—and military alliances. In addition, this traditional security paradigm stressed the importance of sovereignty and drew a clear line between what were deemed to be domestic issues and those regarded as international.

In the last fifteen years almost all the elements of this paradigm have been challenged. First, a wide range of non-military problems, such as infectious disease, natural disasters, and environmental degradation, have come to be described in the language of security. Second, contemporary security threats are increasingly seen as coming from non-state actors such as trans-national criminal networks and terrorist groups, as well as rival states. Finally, there has been a breakdown in the sharp distinction drawn between domestic and international issues. By far the majority of contemporary conflicts are civil wars and since the end of the Cold War there has been a much greater willingness on the part of the international community to intervene in these 'internal' conflicts (Human Security Report 2005). The erosion of an absolutist principle of state sovereignty has also led to a shift in security policy. The emphasis on military responses, while still important, has been augmented with strategies promoting nation-building and good governance (Duffield 2001).

This is the context for this chapter's discussion of New Zealand's approaches to security in the Pacific region. The first section provides an overview of contemporary threats in the region, including traditional and non-traditional challenges to peace and stability. The second section examines New Zealand's response to these challenges, focusing in particular on the growing emphasis on regional cooperation. It makes the argument that there has been an important shift in New Zealand's approach to regional security, with a much greater interest in internal issues and a growing convergence between development and security policy.

SECURITY AGENDA IN THE PACIFIC

In marked contrast to many parts of the world, the Pacific has remained largely free of inter-state rivalries and conflict since the end of the Cold War. The conflict on the island of Bougainville between 1988 and 1997 occasionally spilled over into 'hot pursuit' chases that took the Papua New Guinean Defence Force (PNGDF) into Solomon Islands territory. The border between Indonesian-controlled West Papua and PNG has also been the site for some tensions as Indonesian troops have crossed into PNG in pursuit of Free Papua Movement rebels. More recently, Fiji and Tonga have fired off verbal salvoes over the disputed ownership of an unpopulated reef. But despite occasional moments of friction, open inter-state warfare has never seemed likely. Instead, the closest there has been to a traditional struggle for influence in the region has come between two outside players: China and Taiwan. The Taiwanese government has long been interested in the Pacific as a source of diplomatic support.[2] Beijing's presence in the region is motivated in part by a desire to block Taipei's efforts, but it also sees the Pacific as important in 'its broader quest to become a major Asia–Pacific power' (Henderson & Reilly 2003, p. 94).

The rivalry has become increasingly desperate in recent years, with money changing hands and large development projects offered as part of a bidding war to secure loyalty. Aid money has often been granted without proper oversight and the role of Taiwanese 'dollar diplomacy' in financing corrupt payments in the Solomon Islands has been well documented (Fraenkel 2004, pp. 125–6). New Zealand has become increasingly concerned about the impact of this rivalry on the region. In December 2005, Pacific Islands Affairs Minister Phil Goff warned both Beijing and Taipei that their 'ongoing rivalry and chequebook diplomacy in the Pacific, wanting diplomatic recognition from these countries, is unhelpful for their developmental needs and the Pacific as a whole' (Gregory 2005).

Aside from the spill-over from the China–Taiwan rivalry, however, the Pacific's contemporary security dilemmas bear little resemblance to the traditional concerns of realist defence planners. While there is no single template that can be applied to a region as large and diverse as the Pacific, security concerns today generally fall into two categories: first, those presented by a range of increasingly sophisticated non-state actors, and second, a number of 'non-traditional' security concerns, including internal instability, environmental degradation and resource depletion.

TERRORISM

Concern about terrorism is not new to the Pacific. The 1992 Honiara Declaration on Law Enforcement Cooperation warned that terrorism was a threat to the 'political and economic security of the region.' But it was the 9/11 attacks in the USA in 2001 and the October 2002 Bali bombings that pushed the issue to the top of the Pacific's security agenda. According to one scholar, Bali was 'Oceania's 9/11' (Henderson 2005, p. 73) primarily because of the way it led policy-makers in Australia, and to a lesser extent New Zealand, to dramatically rethink the challenge presented by weak states and poor governance in their 'backyard'.

Prior to the Bali bombings, Canberra had shown little interest in intervening directly in the Pacific, preferring what one commentator has called a strategy of 'benign neglect' (Hughes 2004). After Bali, however, Australian defence planners began to identify the Pacific as a possible safe haven for terrorist groups. A report of the Australian Strategic Policy Institute (ASPI), *Our Failing Neighbour*, warned that the collapse of law and order in states like the Solomon Islands could create a 'Petri dish' for terrorism (Wainwright 2003). Australian Foreign Minister Alexander Downer declared that while 'we don't have evidence that the South Pacific has been a haven for terrorism … what I would say is that a failed state is a state that *could possibly* be exploited by terrorists' (Fraenkel 2004, p. 162). The 'failed state' argument was criticised by many as exaggerated and imprecise, but it proved extraordinarily influential in terms of policy. In July 2003, an Australian-led regional intervention force (RAMSI) made up of more than 2200 troops and police was deployed to restore order in the Solomons.

While New Zealand does not share all of Australia's concerns, it attaches a high priority to counter-terrorism. Prime Minister Helen Clark has said that 'while the risk of an attack in the Pacific is low, it is important that the region is not a weak link in the counter-terrorism chain'. In 2004, she told a gathering of regional security officials that 'the Pacific might present a tempting target, either for an attack like the one in Bali, or as a base from which terrorist cells might undertake the planning and groundwork for an attack somewhere else' (Clark 2005; Clark 2004).

Despite the rhetoric, there is little evidence of direct links between international terrorism and the Pacific. Most analysts believe that Pacific Island states' remote location, small populations and close-knit societies make them an unlikely haven for terrorists. For the most part, Pacific governments do not attach the same priority to terrorism as Australia and New Zealand. Former Cook Islands prime minister Geoffrey Henry has said that terrorism is of 'little relevance' to Pacific Islanders. The Secretary General of the Pacific Islands Forum, Greg Urwin, admits that 'combating terrorism has not been a top priority for Forum Island Countries' (Urwin 2004).

TRANS-NATIONAL CRIME

If there is disagreement over the threat presented by terrorism, there is consensus about the growing threat posed by trans-national crime. Globalisation has effectively shrunk the distance between the South Pacific and the rest of the world, creating new opportunities for legitimate commerce but also expanding openings for illicit activities. Sophisticated trans-national criminal networks have been quick to take advantage of weak law enforcement regimes to establish themselves in a number of areas, including drug trafficking, people smuggling, and financial crime. In 2000, a haul of 357kg of heroin was seized in Fiji and a large methamphetamine laboratory was also uncovered in June 2004. According to one report, Fiji is now a regional hub for trans-national crime involving narcotics, credit card and passport fraud (Atkinson 2005).

Mafia groups and organised crime syndicates have also used the Pacific to launder the profits from their illegal activities. In 2001, four Pacific states, Nauru, the Cook Islands, the Marshall Islands, and Niue were threatened with sanctions by the G7's powerful Financial Action Task Force (FATF) for failing to deal with their secretive banking systems—systems that appeared to facilitate money laundering. Financial crime has come to take on a much greater significance since 9/11 as allegations have been made about links to terrorism. According to one report, Nauru's banks reportedly laundered some $400 million annually, with about one-third of the money coming from the Middle East (Finin 2002). In October 2005, Nauru was the final Pacific state to be removed from the FATF's list of 'non-cooperative' countries after it abolished 400 shell banks, thus eliminating the major money-laundering risk.

Poor surveillance and corruption have also helped create a permissive environment for the illicit movement of people. Large numbers of illegal migrants have been smuggled into Pacific nations either to work or in transit to Australia, New Zealand, or the USA. US officials have alleged that there is a well-established trafficking route moving people from the Chinese province of Fujian to Guam and as many as 10,000 illegal Chinese migrants are reported to be working in Papua New Guinea (Payne 2004). PNG's border security was not helped when the department of foreign affairs' entire computer system and software for processing passports, along with a number of blank passports, were stolen in late 2003.

INTERNAL WEAKNESS

Predatory non-state actors like the ones described above are attracted to the Pacific in large part because of the inherent weakness of a number of states. In many countries, the police, immigration, and customs services lack the numbers, the resources, or the skills needed to be effective. Corruption and poor leadership also contribute to inefficiency, increased levels of poverty and failing social services. In addition to weak state capacity, grievances over land and inter-communal tensions have also combined to undermine peace in recent years. Ironically, the forces of law and order have often been at the heart of instability and violence. In the last decade there have been a number of incidents that have called into question the role and efficacy of the so-called 'disciplined forces' in several regional states. For example, in 1996 and 2002 the Vanuatu police were involved in armed mutinies and in 1997 Papua New Guinea's Defence Force surrounded the country's parliament after the prime minister hired a small army of mercenaries to fight rebels on Bougainville (O'Callaghan 1999). The three Fiji coups of 1987 (two) and 2000 (one) were orchestrated by elements of the military. Much of the fighting in the Solomon Islands between 1998 and 2003 involved members of that country's paramilitary police force.

Indiscipline among serving forces is not the only potential problem, however. Pacific security forces may present a new threat in the future as hundreds of former Fijian troops return from work as private security contractors in Iraq and other conflict zones. According to one report, Fijian veterans of Afghanistan and Iraq have already been involved in mercenary operations protecting a Bougainville criminal wanted for fraud (Field 2005a).

Armed conflicts like those in the Solomon Islands and on Bougainville are made possible through the provision of arms and ammunition. The illicit trade in small arms and light weapons has become an international issue in recent years and has attracted attention in the Pacific. While some authors have emphasised the danger caused by the trafficking of illicit small arms and light weapons across borders (Laki 2004), evidence suggests that most arms used in the Solomon Islands and Bougainville came from poorly guarded domestic police and military stockpiles (Capie 2003). The security of police and military arsenals across the region has come under scrutiny and there have been some efforts to forge a regional effort to improve the control of civilian and security force weapons.

SECURITISING OTHER THREATS

Beyond these concerns there have also been efforts by some regional governments to use the language of security to raise the profile and the resources devoted to other policy issues. For example, climate change and rising sea levels present a threat to the very existence of low-lying micro-states such as Kiribati and Tuvalu, and have been likened to a 'doomsday threat' by the president of the Federated States of Micronesia (Falcam 2001). The government of the Marshall Islands has developed an evacuation plan in case of submersion, and the Tuvalu government has approached both Australia and New Zealand seeking the right to resettle its population should the sea-level rise (Shibuya 2003, p. 148). Even states not at risk of being flooded face threats to their drinking water supplies, agriculture, and infrastructure.

While most Pacific Island states have a small landmass, they have some of the largest maritime Exclusive Economic Zones (EEZs) in the world. Concerns about poaching, overfishing, and the destructive practice of bottom-trawling have also been raised by several countries. On land, uncontrolled mining and illegal logging in Melanesia have caused extensive environmental damage and affected some traditional livelihoods. Some commentators have also pointed to these practices as responsible for exacerbating armed conflicts. In the Solomons, corrupt payments by Asian logging companies helped foster a climate of croneyism that ultimately led to the collapse of the government.

The spread of disease has also become a growing concern in the Pacific. Levels of HIV/AIDs have increased alarmingly in recent years, with some warning that the Pacific could suffer an HIV disaster similar to the one in Africa. According to one report, Papua New Guinea accounts for more than 7300 of the 8200 cases of HIV/AIDS in the region and cases are reportedly increasing at 15–30 per cent annually (von Strokirch 2005). The Pacific AIDS Foundation has warned that Tuvalu's high infection rate could lead to the collapse of the state. A meeting of Pacific leaders in Port Moresby in October 2005 also added avian flu to the growing list of disease threats.

NEW ZEALAND'S INTERESTS AND POLICY

How then has New Zealand responded to this diverse range of Pacific security issues? For much of its history, New Zealand took a narrow approach to regional security. Its primary concern was 'strategic denial'—keeping hostile powers out of the region. It did this with the support of first the Royal Navy and, after 1951, through its ANZUS defence relationship with the USA. According to Mary Boyd, outside of wartime the Pacific was generally regarded as 'strategically unimportant' (Boyd 1971, p. 61). When regional leaders did meet to discuss security issues, the internal affairs of sovereign states were off the agenda. Former prime minister David Lange recalled that the rule at Pacific Forum meetings was that: 'In no circumstances will anything be discussed, no matter how important, which involves the internal affairs of a member. We met in Apia in 1987, shortly after the Fiji coup, and pretended it hadn't happened' (Venter 2000).

Today, New Zealand has a much broader range of security interests in the Pacific. It maintains a responsibility for the defence of the Cook Islands, Niue, and Tokelau and has treaty obligations to Samoa under a 1962 Treaty of Friendship. It continues to have an interest in safeguarding the region from external aggressors, but recognises that the Pacific does not face 'an obvious external security threat' (Ministry of Defence 2000, p. 2). Instead, New Zealand's security policy is increasingly concerned with a diverse range of issues within Pacific states. The government's defence policy states that

New Zealand has 'special obligations' to Pacific neighbours, not just in maintaining the peace, but also 'preserving the environment, promoting good governance and helping achieve economic well being' (NZDF 2005, p. 13). According to the Ministry of Foreign Affairs and Trade (MFAT), 'Supporting good governance and increased regional cooperation are the new themes of New Zealand's modern Pacific diplomacy' (MFAT 2005).

This approach to regional security reflects changing norms regarding state sovereignty and a fundamental re-articulation of the relationship between development and security. A lack of economic opportunity and political stability is now understood as a factor contributing to contemporary armed conflict. Increasingly, underdevelopment is seen as dangerous and the source of new threats. For example, in its major policy statement, the New Zealand police force links underdevelopment and terrorism, claiming that 'terrorist group activity … is known to exist in our region and directly threatens the safety of New Zealanders. Failure or decay of state systems *and development prospects* in countries in the Pacific raises significant risks for New Zealand' (Police 2005, p. 27, emphasis added). New Zealand's aid agency, NZAID, similarly links development and security, arguing that 'security and stability are the most critical preconditions to poverty reduction and sustainable development' (NZAID 2004).

New Zealand seeks to respond to the challenges of development and security in the Pacific using a 'whole of government' model in which a diverse range of government actors—including Defence, MFAT, NZAID, the police, and customs—all contribute to security policy. The Secretary of Foreign Affairs has said the challenge for New Zealand is to forge 'a new model of inter-agency cooperation to prevent or manage security events' (Murdoch 2003). Within this framework, security policy in the Pacific has two components: first, building capacity within regional states to help them deal with their own security challenges; and second, working to strengthen regional cooperation.

BILATERAL COOPERATION

Historically, bilateral defence cooperation has been an important part of New Zealand's relationship with its Pacific neighbours. The New Zealand Defence Force (NZDF) conducts training and provides equipment to six Pacific states under its Military Assistance Programme (MAP).[3] New Zealand officials frequently stress that the high proportion of Māori and Polynesian personnel in the NZDF has been an advantage when working in post-conflict situations in the Pacific. In recent years, however, concern about the role played by militaries in instability in Fiji and Papua New Guinea has meant greater attention has been given to strengthening law enforcement. New Zealand police personnel were deployed to Bougainville and the Solomon Islands as part of peace settlements and according to former Foreign Minister Phil Goff, the police are better equipped to help 'with nation-building and the achievement of good governance, and dealing with issues relating to internal security such as terrorism and crime' (Goff 2005). New Zealand has also established a 'Pacific Security Fund' to help Island states comply with international obligations, and to reduce their vulnerability to terrorism and trans-national criminal groups.

New Zealand's official development assistance also contributes to foreign policy and security goals. NZAID describes itself as having a 'core but not exclusive focus' on the Pacific and spends almost half of its total budget in the region. Six of the eight aid programmes targeted for growth in the future are in the Pacific: Solomon Islands, Vanuatu, Papua New Guinea, Fiji, Tokelau, and Niue. Alongside poverty alleviation, the promotion of good governance is a key objective. NZAID currently spends almost one-third of its Pacific budget on governance-related programmes including the strengthening of the law and justice sectors. It also supports peace building and conflict resolution initiatives, funding disarmament, dialogue, and third party mediation (NZAID 2005).

REGIONAL RESPONSES

While bilateral ties remain important, New Zealand has increasingly given attention to strengthening security cooperation at the regional level. As one MFAT report notes, 'While this is a part of the world where what New Zealand does can have considerable impact, the scale of Pacific problems is far beyond our capacity to tackle on our own … Our contribution can be enhanced if we work in tandem with major donors … and regional organisations' like the Pacific Islands Forum (MFAT 2001, para 4).

At the regional level, the changing approach to security can be seen in several important initiatives strongly supported by New Zealand. The first was the signing of the Biketawa Declaration in Kiribati in October 2000. Meeting shortly after coups in Fiji and the Solomon Islands, regional leaders agreed that 'in time of crisis or in response to members' request for assistance', action could be taken by other regional states to address a threat to peace and security. Such actions could include what it called 'targeted measures', widely seen as a euphemism for sanctions or intervention.

The Biketawa Declaration marked a major change in regional attitudes towards state sovereignty. It stresses the need to address 'underlying causes of tensions and conflict (ethnicity, socio-economic disparities, and lack of good governance, land disputes and erosion of cultural values)' rather than simply waiting until violence has broken out. As Stewart Firth has argued, while a broad approach to security in the Pacific is not new, the Biketawa Declaration, 'reasserts multidimensionality in a new way by focusing on good governance as the foundation of regional security'. In other words, 'the new agenda for regional security … is developmental rather than military' (Firth 2003, 51).

RAMSI

The second key event came in July 2003 following several years of lawlessness and inter-communal violence in the Solomon Islands that had left more than a hundred people dead and seen tens of thousands forced from their homes. After initially refusing to get involved, Australia decided to lead a large intervention force (the Regional Assistance Mission to the Solomon Islands or RAMSI) to restore law and order. New Zealand committed 260 military personnel and thirty-five police officers to what became the largest military operation in the Pacific since the Second World War. RAMSI was initially charged with restoring law and order and disarming the militants and its presence had an immediate impact. More than 3,700 weapons were collected and destroyed, leading militants were arrested and a long-term process of rebuilding the police force was begun.

According to New Zealand officials, RAMSI was always conceived as a 'comprehensive operation'. This means that while the military and police elements of the mission have attracted the most attention, 'RAMSI also addresses the rebuilding of the machinery of government and the reconstruction of the economy' (Goff 2004a). In keeping with what MFAT calls an 'integrated' approach to conflict resolution, New Zealand seconded civilian staff into the Solomon Islands public service, contributing towards 'reform in the machinery of government and economic development' (MFAT n.d.). Addressing the threat to regional security requires more than simply bringing an end to violence; it also necessitates the rebuilding of the Solomon Islands state.

THE PACIFIC PLAN

The third sign of a new approach to regional security can be seen in New Zealand's efforts to forge a stronger model of cooperation through the Pacific Islands Forum and the Pacific Plan. Attempts at building a regional community in the Pacific are not new. The South Pacific Commission was established by the colonial powers in 1947 and the South Pacific Forum was created in 1971. However, these institutions remained limited by political constraints and insufficient resources. As one recent report concludes 'the Pacific has a mixed track record on regional cooperation and for a range of reasons, has not experienced the deepening of cooperation and integration that has been evident recently in other regions' (ADB 2005, ix).

At the New Zealand government's behest, the 2003 Forum Leaders Meeting agreed to develop a 'Pacific Plan' of actions designed to improve security and governance in the region. The Plan is based on the assumption that there should be 'stronger and deeper links between the sovereign countries of the region'. It explores cooperation in four areas: economic growth, sustainable development, good governance, and security.

After a lengthy period of consultation around the region, a road-map of initiatives was endorsed by regional leaders at the Port Moresby Forum in October 2005, with several marked for immediate implementation. Many of the actions in the area of security reflect Australian and New Zealand priorities. These include strengthened security measures at airports and ports and a new regional strategy for border control. The Plan also calls for regional action against trans-national crime through greater law enforcement training and a Regional Policing Initiative. As well as seeking to strengthen intelligence, police, customs, and exclusive economic zone (EEZ) patrol programmes, the Pacific Plan also talks about the need to address family, domestic, gender, and sexual violence; human rights; juvenile justice; and drug control. A wide range of public policy areas that would normally be considered domestic affairs have been linked to insecurity and identified as warranting coordinated regional action.

Despite receiving the stamp of approval of regional leaders, there have been grumblings about divergent priorities within the regional cooperation framework. A key part of the Pacific Plan's economic strategy is the progressive dismantling of trade barriers in the region under the Pacific Agreement on Closer Economic Relations (PACER). Calls for closer economic integration and the reduction of tariffs have been condemned by some critics as disproportionately benefiting Australia and New Zealand, and threatening Island economies (Kelsey 2004). At the same time, pleas by Pacific Island leaders for greater rights for temporary worker access to Australia and New Zealand have been turned down. How this issue is resolved remains to be seen, but continuing economic inequality within and between states in the Pacific carries with it the seeds of future conflict.

CONCLUSION

New Zealand has important security interests in the Pacific arising out of historical, constitutional and cultural ties. For much of its past, its primary concern was keeping the region free from hostile powers. In the last five years in particular, instability and violence in parts of the Pacific, together with the influence of the 'War on Terror', have led to a fundamental rethinking of security policy. The weakness and underdevelopment of some regional states have come to be seen as possible sources of threat and insecurity and the result has been an opening up of domestic issues to outside scrutiny. Security policy has become increasingly fused with development goals in seeking the strengthening of state capacity, good governance, sustainable economic growth, and improved law and order. New Zealand's support for the Biketawa Declaration, the Regional Assistance Mission to the Solomon Islands (RAMSI), and the Pacific Plan are evidence of a growing regional approach to building security within Island states.

Many of these initiatives have been welcomed by leaders and people in the Pacific and will go a long way towards making the region a more peaceful and prosperous place. However, as New Zealand's security interests in the region increasingly cross over into areas previously considered the preserve of sovereign states, there will be the possibility of tensions arising. As New Zealand officials recognise, Pacific Island states are 'as jealous of their national sovereignty as we are of New Zealand's' (MFAT 2001). Australia has already encountered resistance with its planned Enhanced Cooperation Programme (ECP) in Papua New Guinea. New Zealand's approach is less assertive and more consensual, but how well New Zealand and Pacific Island leaders are able to forge a shared sense of regionalism and build a genuine security community remains to be seen.

DISCUSSION QUESTIONS

1 What are New Zealand's national interests in the Pacific? What should our role be in promoting regional security?
2 What are the most serious threats in the Pacific? Do New Zealand and Pacific Island states have different security concerns?
3 How did the 9/11 and 2002 Bali terrorist attacks affect Pacific security? Is terrorism a threat to the Pacific region?
4 How has globalisation changed Pacific security issues?
5 Do New Zealand and Australia have a different approach to regional security? If so, how and why?
6 Does it make sense to describe global warming and disease as 'security' threats? Why? Are there reasons not to use the language of security?

NOTES

1   I am very grateful to Roderic Alley, Gerald McGhie, and Sally Hill for comments on an earlier draft of this chapter. The term 'Pacific' is used here to refer to the area also sometimes called Oceania. It includes Australia, New Zealand, and the fourteen other members of the Pacific Islands Forum (PIF). These are the Cook Islands, Federated States of Micronesia, Fiji, Kiribati, Nauru, Niue, Palau, Papua New Guinea, the Republic of the Marshall Islands, Samoa, Solomon Islands, Tonga, Tuvalu, and Vanuatu.
2   Of the approximately twenty-five states that recognise Taipei, five are in the Pacific: Tuvalu, the Marshall Islands, Kiribati, Palau, and the Solomon Islands.
3   In the Pacific, MAP participants are Tonga, Papua New Guinea, Samoa, Vanuatu, Solomon Islands, and Cook Islands. Niue is not a member, but occasionally receives assistance.

REFERENCES

Asian Development Bank (ADB) 2005, *Toward a New Pacific Regionalism*, Manila.

Atkinson, K. 2005, 'Triads Spinning Murderous Web', *New Zealand Herald*, 25 October.

Boyd, M. 1971, 'The South-West Pacific in the 1970s', in B. Brown (ed.) *Asia and the Pacific in 1970s*, Reed, Auckland.

Capie, D. 2003, *Under the Gun: The Small Arms Challenge in the Pacific*, Victoria University Press, Wellington.

Clark, H. 2004, 'Opening Address to Pacific Roundtable on Counter-Terrorism', 10 May. Available online at: www.beehive.govt.nz/ViewDocument.aspx? Document ID=19640.

Clark, H. 2005, 'Pacific Puts Counter-terrorism Preparations under the Spotlight', press release, 8 November. Available online at: www.beehive.govt.nz/ViewDocument. aspx?DocumentID=24323.

Duffield, M. 2001, *Global Governance and the New Wars: The Merging of Development and Security*, Zed Books, London.

Falcam, L. 2001, Speech to the Senior Policy Seminar, Asia–Pacific Center for Security Studies, Honolulu, August.

Field, M. 2004, 'It's Paradise, But This Tiny Atoll Nation is Sinking under the … King of Tides', *Daily Telegraph* (Sydney) 21 February 2004.

Field, M. 2005, 'The Enemy Within', *The Dominion*, 30 November 2005, B5.

Finin, G. 2002, 'Vulnerable in the South Pacific', *International Herald Tribune*, 29 January.

Firth, S. 2003, in E. Shibuya & J. Rolfe (eds) *Security in Oceania in the 21st Century*, Asia–Pacific Center for Security Studies, Honolulu.

Fraenkel, J. 2004, *The Manipulation of Custom: From Uprising to Intervention in the Solomon Islands*, Pandanus Books and Victoria University Press, Wellington.

Goff, P. 2004, 'Pacific Regionalism: Tradition, Continuity, Renewal', speech to the University of Otago Foreign Policy School, Dunedin, 30 June.

Goff, P. 2004a, Speech delivered for Launch of 'The Manipulation of Custom, From Uprising to Intervention in the Solomon Islands' by Jon Fraenkel, at the Pacific Cooperation Foundation, Boulcott St, Wellington, 1 December.

Goff, P. 2005, 'NZ's International Police Deployments', 13 October.

Gregory, A. 2005, 'Goff warns Pacific nations on chequebook diplomacy', *New Zealand Herald*, 10 December 2005.

Henderson, J. 2004, ' "New" Security in Oceania', in P. Cozens (ed.) *Engaging Oceania with Pacific Asia*, Centre for Strategic Studies, Wellington, pp. 31–41.

Henderson, J. 2005, 'Security in Oceania in the Post-9/11 and Bali Era', in R. Pettman (ed.) *New Zealand in a Globalising World*, Victoria University Press, Wellington, pp. 73–82.

Henderson, J. & Reilly, B. 2003, 'Dragon in Paradise: China's Rising Star in Oceania', *The National Interest*, vol. 72 (Summer 2003).

Hughes, H. 2004, 'Canberra is Finally Helping Papua New Guinea Come Back from the Brink', *The Australian*, 15 July.

Human Security Report 2005, Oxford University Press, New York.

Kelsey, J. 2004, *A People's Guide to PACER*, Pacific Network on Globalization, Suva.

Laki, J. 2004, 'Transnational Issues Linking Oceania and Asia', in P. Cozens (ed.) *Engaging Oceania with Pacific Asia*, Centre for Strategic Studies, Wellington, pp. 111–26.

Ministry of Foreign Affairs and Trade 2001, 'Review of Pacific Policy', available online at: www.mfat.govt.nz/foreign/regions/pacific/generalinfo/policy/policyreview.html

Ministry of Foreign Affairs and Trade 2005, *Statement of Intent 2005—2008 Incorporating the 2005–2006 Departmental Forecast Report*, Wellington.

Ministry of Foreign Affairs and Trade 2005a, 'Post-election Brief', available online at www.mfat.govt.nz/about/oppu/postelectionbrief/peb5.html#Counter-Terrorism_Policy (September).

Ministry of Foreign Affairs and Trade n.d., 'New Zealand's Contributions to Peace Support Operations', available online at: www.mfat.govt.nz/foreign/spd/peacekeeping/pkoinfo.html

Ministry of Defence 2000, *The Government's Defence Policy Framework*, Wellington.

Murdoch, S. 2003, 'Speech by Simon Murdoch, Secretary, Ministry of Foreign Affairs and Trade to the New Zealand Defence Force', Trentham, 11 June.

NZAID 2004, *What We Do: Annual Report 2003/04* available online at www.nzaid.govt.nz/library/docs/ar-what-do-we-do.pdf p. 15.

NZAID 2005, *Preventing Conflict and Building Peace*, Wellington, available online at www.nzaid.govt.nz/library/docs/nzaid-peace-policy.pdf.

New Zealand Defence Force 2005, *Statement of Intent of the New Zealand Defence Force for the period 1 July 2005 to 30 June 2008*, Wellington.

New Zealand Police 2005, *Statement of Intent of the New Zealand Police Force 2005/2006*, Wellington, available online at www.police.govt.nz/resources/2005/statement-of-intent/

O'Callaghan, M. 1999, *Enemies Within: Papua New Guinea, Australia and the Sandline Crisis: The Inside Story*, Random House, Glenfield.

Payne, R. J. 2003, 'Changing US Security Policy in the Pacific', in Shibuya E. & Rolfe J. (eds) *Security in Oceania in the 21st Century*, Asia–Pacific Center for Security Studies, Honolulu, pp. 53–68.

Shibuya E. & Rolfe J. (eds) 2003, *Security in Oceania in the 21st Century*, Asia–Pacific Center for Security Studies, Honolulu.

Urwin, G. 2004, 'Terrorism: The Risk to Pacific Island Economies', presentation to the Reserve Banks Economics Association, 19 May.

Venter, N. 2000, 'Pacific Forum goes on trial', *The Dominion*, 27 October.

Von Strokirch, K. 2005, 'The Region in Review: International Issues and Events', *The Contemporary Pacific*, vol. 17, no. 2 (Fall) pp. 416–33.

Wainwright E. et al. 2003, *Our Failing Neighbour: Australia and the Future of the Solomon Islands*, Australian Strategic Policy Institute, Canberra.

Waltz, K. 1979, *Theory of International Politics*, Addison-Wesley, Reading.

FURTHER READING

Fraenkel, J. 2004, *The Manipulation of Custom: From Uprising to Intervention in the Solomon Islands*, Pandanus Books and Victoria University Press, Wellington.

Henderson J. & G. Watson (eds) 2006, *Securing a Peaceful Pacific*, Canterbury University Press, Christchurch.

Shibuya E. & J. Rolfe (eds) 2003, *Security in Oceania in the 21st Century*, Asia-Pacific Center for Security Studies, Honolulu.

Logistic regressions: Not voting, competitiveness, and proportional representation, full model

	I: Base Model			II: PR and Competitiveness			III: Full model, 1990–		
	B	Prb#	S.E.	B	Prb#	S.E.	B	Prb#	S.E.
Reference Group: 1933 and earlier									
Born 1934–44	0.27	**0.04** *	0.10	0.26	**0.03** **	0.08	0.35	**0.03**	0.17
Born 1945–51	0.36	**0.05** **	0.12	0.33	**0.04** **	0.09	0.51	**0.05** *	0.22
Born 1952–64	0.77	**0.11** **	0.15	0.72	**0.10** **	0.10	0.72	**0.07** *	0.29
Born 1965–74	1.18	**0.19** **	0.19	1.13	**0.18** **	0.13	1.20	**0.15** **	0.37
Born 1975–	1.43	**0.26** **	0.22	1.40	**0.25** **	0.16	1.21	**0.16** **	0.44
Age (18–100)	-0.01	**-0.06**	0.00	-0.01	**-0.07** *	0.00	0.01	**0.08**	0.01
1999	-0.32	**-0.04** **	0.05				-0.39	**-0.04** **	0.08
1996	-0.58	**-0.06** **	0.06				-0.57	**-0.03** **	0.09
1993	-0.09	**-0.01**	0.08				-0.32	**-0.05** *	0.13
1990	-0.12	**-0.01**	0.08				-0.57	**-0.03** **	0.14
1987	-0.49	**-0.05** **	0.12						
1981	-0.41	**-0.04** **	0.12						
1975	0.12	**0.01**	0.12						
1963	-0.11	**-0.01**	0.15						

(Continued)

	I: Base Model			II: PR and Competitiveness			III: Full model, 1990–		
	B	Prb#	S.E.	B	Prb#	S.E.	B	Prb#	S.E.
Competitiveness				0.03	**0.07** **	0.00			
PR				-0.30	**-0.04** **	0.05			
Female							-0.11	**-0.01** *	0.06
House Income							0.00	**-0.01**	0.00
Married							-0.26	**-0.02** **	0.07
University							-0.37	**-0.03** **	0.09
Māori							0.69	**0.08** **	0.09
Born Elsewhere							0.34	**0.03** **	0.08
Party Identity							-0.31	**-0.03** **	0.06
Political Interest							-1.16	**-0.12** **	0.12
Civic Duty							-2.89	**-0.48** **	0.12
Constant	-1.75	**	0.31	-2.00		0.17	0.64		0.63
Cox and Snell R^2	0.05			0.05			0.12		
% concordant	83.0			83.0			86.4		

*   Significant at < .05.

**   Significant at < .01.

\#   Probability effects are those between the maximum and minimum values of each variable, setting the values of all other variables at their means. Most of the variable values are 0 or 1, or range from 0 to 1. Exceptions are age (measured between 18 and 100), income, measured in $000s, and competitiveness (0.2 to 20.4).

Per cent probabilities of not voting under proportional representation versus first past the post by generations

Generations	−1933	1934–44	1945–52	1953–64	1965–74	1975–
At Age						
			PR			
18		13	14	19	26	31
30	9.5				22	30
44	9	11	12	16	21	
50					20	
70	7	9	10	14		
			FPP			
18		17	18	24	28	39
30	13				28	37
44	11	14	15	21	26	
50					25	
70	10	12	13	18		

Source: Appendix A, model II

Index

'100% pure New Zealand'
  campaign   76

ACT party   11, 177, 193, 194, 309,
  332, 371, 384, 502, 598
advertising and election campaigns
  480–1
advisers *see* policy, advice
agenda-setting   315, 486, 574, 575
aging population   18–19
'agree to disagree' process   202, 204,
  226, 246, 251
agriculture, genetic engineered   75–6
America's Cup   78–9, 81, 503–4
Anderton, Jim   10–11, 199, 200, 208,
  220, 231, 247, 248, 308, 340, 341,
  345, 346, 496, 552
anti-corruption campaigns   383–4
anti-smoking groups and government
  529–30
Area Health Boards (AHBs)   617, 618,
  620
Association of Consumers and Taxpayers
  see ACT party
asylum-seekers   384, 653, 655, 656,
  657–8
  see also refugees
Australia/NZ relations   89–90, 93

Barber, David James   219, 220, 221–2

Bergman, T.   237–8, 239
biculturalism   30–2
Bill of Rights   106, 107, 108,
  109–10, 117–18, 120, 122–3, 124,
  125, 127, 135, 156, 170, 445
birth rates   16–18
Blackheart campaign   79–80
Blair, Tony   50, 93, 136, 488, 493, 494
Bolger, James   9, 109, 134, 136, 203,
  211–12, 218, 220, 227, 228, 229–30,
  231–2, 367, 377, 379
Brand New Zealand   74, 77
branding   74, 77, 75–6
  government   77–8
Brash, Don   10, 94, 110, 180, 218,
  219–20, 221, 228, 331, 338–9,
  341–3, 345–6, 347–8, 367, 371, 374,
  402, 405, 412, 483, 496, 539, 595,
  598, 609, 610–11, 612
broadcasting
  deregulation of   454–5, 456–8
  Māori   30, 457–8
  see also media; radio
Broadcasting Act 1989   303, 339, 445,
  447, 454–5, 456, 457
Broadcasting Commission   454–5
bureaucracy, models of   258–60
  public-choice model   259–60, 270
  Westminster model   106, 258, 259,
  268

678